Lecture Notes in Computer S

T0238107

Commenced Publication in 1973
Founding and Former Series Editors:
Gerhard Goos, Juris Hartmanis, and Jan van Leeuwen

Mauro Barni   Ingemar Cox
Ton Kalker   Hyoung Joong Kim (Eds.)

Digital
Watermarking

4th International Workshop, IWDW 2005
Siena, Italy, September 15-17, 2005
Proceedings

 Springer

Volume Editors

Mauro Barni
University of Siena, Department of Information Engineering
Via Roma 56, 53100 Siena, Italy
E-mail: barni@dii.unisi.it

Ingemar Cox
University College London, Torrington Place, UK
E-mail: i.cox@ee.ucl.ac.uk

Ton Kalker
Hewlett-Packard Labs
1501 Page Mill Road, Palo Alto, CA 94305, USA
E-mail: Ton.Kalker@hp.com

Hyoung Joong Kim
Kangwon National University, Chunchon, 200-701, Korea
E-mail: khj@kangwon.ac.kr

Library of Congress Control Number: 2005931932

CR Subject Classification (1998): K.4.1, K.6.5, H.5.1, D.4.6, E.3, E.4, F.2.2, H.3, I.4

ISSN   0302-9743
ISBN-10   3-540-28768-X Springer Berlin Heidelberg New York
ISBN-13   978-3-540-28768-1 Springer Berlin Heidelberg New York

Springer is a part of Springer Science+Business Media

springeronline.com

© Springer-Verlag Berlin Heidelberg 2005
Printed in Germany

Typesetting: Camera-ready by author, data conversion by Scientific Publishing Services, Chennai, India
Printed on acid-free paper   SPIN: 11551492   06/3142   5 4 3 2 1 0

Preface

We are delighted to welcome the attendees of the Fourth International Workshop on Digital Watermarking (IWDW). Watermarking continues to generate strong academic interest. Commercialization of the technology is proceeding at a steady pace. We have seen watermarking adopted for DVD audio. Fingerprinting technology was successfully used to determine the source of pirated video material. Furthermore, a number of companies are using watermarking as an enabling technology for broadcast monitoring services. Watermarking of digital cinema content is anticipated. Future applications may also come from areas unrelated to digital rights management. For example, the use of watermarking to enhance legacy broadcast and communication systems is now being considered. IWDW 2005 offers an opportunity to reflect upon the state of the art in digital watermarking as well as discuss directions for future research and applications.

This year we accepted 31 papers from 74 submissions. This 42% acceptance rate indicates our commitment to ensuring a very high quality conference. We thank the members of the Technical Program Committee for making this possible by their timely and insightful reviews. Thanks to their hard work this is the first IWDW at which the final proceedings are available to the participants at the time of the workshop as a Springer LNCS publication.

This year's program reflects all the major interests of the watermarking community. The accepted papers cover a full range of topics, including robust and fragile watermarking, steganography and steganalysis, security and attacks, and fingerprinting and benchmarking. These papers address the theoretical and practical issues that we felt to be of broad interest to our community. Moreover, this year we will also have a very relevant special session on foundational and practical aspects of watermarking security.

Finally, this year's workshop is special since it is the first installment of IWDW to be held outside of Korea. It is our aim that future IWDW workshops will rotate between locations in Asia, Europe and the Americas. We hope you will find the workshop useful and enjoyable, and we look forward to meeting you again in the context of IWDW.

Welcome to IWDW 2005 in Siena!

July 2005

Ingemar Cox
Ton Kalker
Hyoung Joong Kim
Mauro Barni

Organization

General Chairs

Mauro Barni (University of Siena, Italy)
Daeho Kim (NSRI, Korea)

Technical Program Chairs

Ingemar J. Cox (UCL, UK)
Ton Kalker (HP, USA)
Hyoung Joong Kim (Kangwon National University, Korea)

Finance Chair

Roberto Caldelli (University of Florence, Italy)

Publicity Chair

Vito Cappellini (University of Florence, Italy)

Electronic Media Chair

Alessia De Rosa (University of Florence, Italy)

Publications Chair

Enrico Magli (Politecnico di Torino, Italy)

Technical Program Committee

Roberto Caldelli (U. of Florence, Italy)
Patrizio Campisi (U. of Roma III, Italy)
Alessia De Rosa (U. of Florence, Italy)
Jana Dittman (U. Magdeburg, Germany)
Jean-Luc Dugelay (Eurecom, France)
Touradj Ebrahimi (EPFL, Switzerland)

Jessica Fridrich (SUNY Binghamton, USA)
Teddy Furon (IRISA, France)
Miroslav Goljan (SUNY Binghamton, USA)
Yo-Sung Ho (K-JIST, Korea)
Jinwoo Hong (ETRI, Korea)
Jiwu Huang (Zhongshan U., China)
Ebroul Izquierdo (Q. Mary Univ. London, UK)
Mohan Kankanhalli (NUS, Singapore)
Stefan Katzenbeisser (Technical Univ. Munich, Germany)
Inald Lagendijk (Delft U. of Tech., The Netherlands)
Heung-Kyu Lee (KAIST, Korea)
Benoit Macq (UCL, Belgium)
Enrico Magli (Politecnico di Torino, Italy)
Nasir Memon (Polytechnic U., USA)
Kivanc Mihcak (Microsoft, USA)
Matt Miller (NEC, USA)
Pierre Moulin (U. of Illinois, USA)
Hideki Noda (Kyushu Inst. Tech., Japan)
Fernando Pérez-González (U. of Vigo, Spain)
Ioannis Pitas (U. of Thessaloniki, Greece)
Alessandro Piva (U. of Florence, Italy)
William Puech (LIRMM, France)
Hayder Radha (Michigan State U., USA)
Yong-Man Ro (ICU, Korea)
David Saad (Aston University, UK)
Kouichi Sakurai (Kyushu U., Japan)
Farook Sattar (Nanyang Tech. U., Singapore)
Yun-Qing Shi (New Jersey Inst. of Tech., USA)
Shan Suthaharan (Tennesee St. U., USA)
Kiyoshi Tanaka (Shinshu University, Japan)
Sviatoslav Voloshynovsky (U. of Geneva, Switzerland)
Chee Sun Won (Dongguk University, Korea)
Min Wu (U. of Maryland, USA)

Table of Contents

Session IV: Attacks

Session V: Special Session on Watermarking Security

Session VI: Watermarking of Unconventional Media

Session VII: Channel Coding and Watermarking

Session VIII: Theory

Session IX: Watermarking II

Session X: Applications

A New Approach to Estimating Hidden Message Length in Stochastic Modulation Steganography

Junhui He[1], Jiwu Huang[1,*], and Guoping Qiu[2]

[1] School of Information Science and Technology,
Sun Yat-sen University, Guangzhou, China, 510275
isshjw@zsu.edu.cn

[2] School of Computer Science, University of Nottingham, NG8 1BB, UK

Abstract. Stochastic modulation steganography hides secret message within the cover image by adding a weak noise signal with a specified probabilistic distribution. The advantages of stochastic modulation steganography include high capacity and better security. Current steganalysis methods that are applicable to the detection of hidden message in traditional least significant bit (LSB) or additive noise model based steganography cannot reliably detect the existence of hidden message in stochastic modulation steganography. In this paper, we present a new steganalysis approach which can reliably detect the existence and accurately estimate the length of hidden message in stochastic modulation steganography. By analyzing the distributions of the horizontal pixel difference of the images before and after stochastic modulation embedding, it is shown that for non-adaptive steganography, the distribution of the stego-image's pixel difference can be modeled as the convolution of the distribution of the cover image's pixel difference and that of the quantized stego-noise difference, and that the estimation of the hidden message length in stochastic modulation can be achieved by estimating the variance of the stego-noise. To estimate the variance of the stego-noise, hence determining the existence and the length of hidden message, we first model the distribution of the cover image's pixel difference as a generalized Gaussian and estimate the parameters of the distribution using grid search and Chi-square goodness of fit test, and then exploit the relationship between the distribution variance of the cover image's pixel difference and that of the stego-noise difference. We present experimental results to demonstrate that our new approach is effective for steganalyzing stochastic modulation steganography. Our method provides a general theoretical framework and is applicable to other non-adaptive embedding algorithms where the distribution models of the stego-noise are known or can be estimated.

1 Introduction

Steganography [1] conceals the occurrence of communication by embedding message into the cover medium such as an image, an audio recording, or a video film

---

* Correspondence author.

M. Barni et al. (Eds.): IWDW 2005, LNCS 3710, pp. 1–14, 2005.
© Springer-Verlag Berlin Heidelberg 2005

and has received much attention in secret communication. Image is one of the most important cover media for steganography.

To be useful, a steganographic system should be able to provide a relatively high capacity of information hiding. At the same time, the embedded secret message should be undetectable. If the existence of secret message can be detected by an attacker with a probability higher than random guessing, the corresponding steganography technique is considered to be invalid. Similar to cryptography, steganography techniques may suffer from many active or passive attacks (referred as steganalysis [2]) such as detecting the existence of hidden message, searching the steganography key or estimating the secret message length.

The LSB-based steganography is one of the conventional techniques capable of hiding a long secret message in the cover image without introducing perceptible distortions. It works by replacing the LSBs of sequentially or randomly selected pixels in the cover image with the secret message bits. The ways in which pixels are selected are usually determined by a secret key. Without the knowledge of this key, it is difficult for an attacker to extract the embedded message.

Many steganography tools using LSB-based steganography techniques, including Steghide, S-Tools, Steganos, SteganoDos, Winstorms, etc., are available on the Internet[1]. In recent years, LSB-based steganography has been widely investigated and many steganalytic approaches, such as Chi-square statistical attack [3], generalized Chi-square statistical attack [4], Regular-Singular method [5], detection based on difference histogram [6] and Sample Pairs analysis [7], have been proposed. These steganalysis methods can detect hidden message with high reliability or accurately estimate the length of secret message embedded with LSB-based steganography.

However, there are some more advanced steganograhpy algorithms, examples including, Hide [8], the spread spectrum image steganography (SSIS) [9], and the stochastic modulation steganography [10], are robust against most of the steganalysis methods mentioned above. These techniques, referred to as additive noise steganography in this paper, hide secret message in the cover image by adding stego-noise with a specific probabilistic distribution and have better security.

With the advance of research in steganalysis, Hide and SSIS steganography have been successfully steganalyzed by neighbor colors histogram (NCH) analysis [11] and histogram characteristic function center of mass (HCF-COM) analysis [12], respectively. The NCH method counts the number of neighbors of each unique color in the image to reliably detect the existence of hidden message in Hide steganography. However, it is only applicable to the images that do not have a large number of unique colors. If the cover image is grayscale or high quality color image, this attack works less reliably and may have high false positives. The HCF-COM method shows that some additive noise embedding methods are equivalent to low pass filtering the cover image's histogram and builds a classifier which performs very well on SSIS. However, the method

---

[1] http://www.stegoarchive.com

needs proper choice of training images and it may be hard or impractical to find a universal threshold for a sufficiently wide class of images. According to the principles of these two steganalysis methods, it will be extremely difficult for them to accurately estimate the secret message length in stochastic modulation steganography. Although a steganalytic technique based on the analysis of translation coefficients between the pixel difference histograms and capable of estimating the secret message length in LSB steganography has been proposed in [6], it may not be directly applicable to the steganalysis of additive noise steganography.

In this paper, we propose a new steganalysis method for reliably detecting the existence and for accurately estimating the length of secret message embedded with stochastic modulation steganography. We model the distribution of the cover image's pixel difference as generalized Gaussian, and model the distribution of the stego-image's pixel difference as the convolution of the distribution of the cover image's pixel difference and that of the quantized stego-noise difference. We estimate the generalized Gaussian's parameters using grid search and Chi-square goodness of fit test, and estimate the variance of the stego-noise which in turn determines the length of hidden message by exploiting the relationship between the distribution variance of the cover image's pixel difference and that of the quantized stego-noise difference. We present experimental results which show that the proposed method is effective.

The rest of this paper is organized as follows. In Sect. 2, we first briefly review the stochastic modulation steganography, we then discuss the statistical models of the image's pixel difference before and after message embedding, and finally, we describe the estimation of the length of the hidden message in detail. Experimental results and analysis are given in Sect. 3. We conclude our work in Sect. 4.

2   Steganalysis of Stochastic Modulation

It is known that the pixel difference histogram of natural image can be modeled as a generalized Gaussian distribution (GGD) [13]. However, this may be not true for the distribution of the stego-image's pixel difference due to the stego-noise added by steganography. For the stochastic modulation steganography, we may assume that the stego-noise is independent from the cover image. Therefore, the distribution of stego-image's pixel difference is a convolution of the probabilistic distribution of the stego-noise difference and that of the cover image's pixel difference. Based on the independence assumption, we will derive an estimator to estimate the hidden message length through the following subsections.

Let $\{c_{i,j}\}$ and $\{s_{i,j}\}$ denote the cover image and the stego-image, respectively, where $c_{i,j} \in \{0, \cdots, 255\}$, $s_{i,j} \in \{0, \cdots, 255\}$, $i \in \{1, \cdots, M\}$ and $j \in \{1, \cdots, N\}$. The message m_k ($k = 1, \cdots, K$, where K denotes the absolute length of secret message in bits) consists of a binary random sequence and $m_k \in \{+1, -1\}$. Let $n_{i,j}$ denote the stego-noise, which will be rounded off to the quantized stego-noise $z_{i,j}$ during embedding. The random variables ξ_c, ξ_s, ξ_n

and ξ_z model the cover image's pixel $c_{i,j}$, the stego-image's pixel $s_{i,j}$, the stego-noise $n_{i,j}$ and the quantized stego-noise $z_{i,j}$. Similarly, the cover image's pixel difference $dc_{i,j}$, the stego-image's pixel difference $ds_{i,j}$, the stego-noise difference $dn_{i,j}$, and the quantized stego-noise difference $dz_{i,j}$ are modeled as samples of the random variables $d\xi_c$, $d\xi_s$, $d\xi_n$ and $d\xi_z$.

2.1 Stochastic Modulation Steganography

Stochastic modulation steganography [10] adds stego-noise with a specific probability distribution in the cover image to embed the secret message. A steganography capacity as high as 0.8 bpp (bits per pixel) may be achieved with the use of a special parametric parity function. The parametric parity function $p(c_{i,j}, z_{i,j})$ used in stochastic modulation steganography is required to satisfy the anti-symmetric property for $c_{i,j}$, i.e. $p(c_{i,j} + z_{i,j}, z_{i,j}) = -p(c_{i,j} - z_{i,j}, z_{i,j})$ $(z_{i,j} \neq 0)$. The definition of the parity function proposed in [10] is given as follows.

(a). If $c_{i,j} \in [1, 2z_{i,j}]$, $p(c_{i,j}, z_{i,j}) = \begin{cases} (-1)^{c_{i,j}+z_{i,j}} & \text{if } z_{i,j} > 0, \\ 0 & \text{if } z_{i,j} = 0. \end{cases}$

(b). If $c_{i,j} \notin [1, 2z_{i,j}]$, $p(c_{i,j}, z_{i,j})$ can be computed according to the anti-symmetric property and the above item (a).

The embedding procedure of stochastic modulation is described as below.

(1). Sequential or random visiting path and the stego-noise $n_{i,j}$ are generated using a secret key.

(2). For each pixel $c_{i,j}$ along the visiting path, one sample $n_{i,j}$ of the stego-noise ξ_n is rounded off to an integer $z_{i,j}$. If $z_{i,j} = 0$, the pixel $c_{i,j}$ is skipped and move to the next pixel in the visiting path, at the same time, the next stego-noise sample is input and rounded; If $z_{i.j} \neq 0$, the pixel $c_{i,j}$ will be modified according to the value of the parity function, i.e.

$$\text{if} \quad p(c_{i,j} + z_{i,j}, z_{i,j}) = m_k \qquad \text{then} \quad s_{i,j} = c_{i,j} + z_{i,j},$$
$$\text{elseif} \quad p(c_{i,j} + z_{i,j}, z_{i,j}) = -m_k \qquad \text{then} \quad s_{i,j} = c_{i,j} - z_{i,j}.$$

During the embedding process, those pixels which may fall out of the range $[0, 255]$ will be truncated to the nearest value in this range with the desired parity.

2.2 Statistical Model of Difference

In this article, the distributions of the horizontal difference of images and stego noise are studied. The definitions of horizontal difference are given by (1).

$$\begin{aligned} dc_{i,j} &= c_{i,j} - c_{i,j+1} \ , \\ ds_{i,j} &= s_{i,j} - s_{i,j+1} \ , \\ dn_{i,j} &= n_{i,j} - n_{i,j+1} \ , \\ dz_{i,j} &= z_{i,j} - z_{i,j+1} \ , \end{aligned} \qquad (1)$$

where $i = 1, \cdots, M$ and $j = 1, \cdots, N - 1$.

According to [13], the distribution of natural image's pixel difference fits very well with generalized Gaussian function. The probability density function (PDF) of $d\xi_c$ can thus be expressed as

$$f_{d\xi_c}(x; \alpha, \beta) = \frac{\beta}{2\alpha \Gamma(1/\beta)} \exp\left\{-\left(\frac{|x|}{\alpha}\right)^\beta\right\}, \qquad (2)$$

where $\Gamma(x) = \int_0^\infty t^{x-1} e^{-t} dt$ is the standard Euler Gamma function. This PDF is a two-sided symmetric density with two distributional parameters β and α that control the shape and standard deviation of the density, respectively. For example:

- With $\beta = 2$, $\alpha = \sqrt{2}$, it becomes a standard normal distribution;
- As $\beta \to \infty$, it approximates the uniform distribution;
- By setting $\beta = 1$, $\alpha = 1/\lambda$, the Laplacian distribution is obtained.

In this article, for the general case, we assume that the stego-noise used in the stochastic modulation steganography is Gaussian $N(0, \sigma_n^2)$, that is, the PDF of ξ_n is

$$f_{\xi_n}(x; \sigma_n) = \frac{1}{\sqrt{2\pi}\sigma_n} \exp\left\{-\frac{x^2}{2\sigma_n^2}\right\}. \qquad (3)$$

The quantized stego-noise $z_{i,j}$, instead of $n_{i,j}$, is superimposed on the cover image during embedding, and $z_{i,j}$ is defined by $z_{i,j} = \text{Round}(n_{i,j})$, where $\text{Round}(\cdot)$ is the nearest integer. Thus the probability mass function (PMF) of ξ_z may be defined as

$$f_{\xi_z}(z_{i,j}; \sigma_n) = P(\xi_z = z_{i,j}; \sigma_n) = \int_{z_{i,j}-0.5}^{z_{i,j}+0.5} f_{\xi_n}(x; \sigma_n)\, dx. \qquad (4)$$

In our work, we observe that the distributions of $dz_{i,j}$ and $\text{Round}(dn_{i,j})$ differ little from each other, as illustrated in Fig.1(a). It may be assumed that the stego-noise $n_{i,j}$ and $n_{i,j+1}$ are independent and have the identical distribution $N(0, \sigma_n^2)$. According to the probability theory, the distribution function of $dn_{i,j}$ is Gaussian $N(0, 2\sigma_n^2)$, which is demonstrated in Fig.1(b). The PDF of $d\xi_n$ is given by

$$f_{d\xi_n}(x; \sigma_n) = \frac{1}{\sqrt{2\pi(2\sigma_n^2)}} \exp\left\{-\frac{x^2}{2(2\sigma_n^2)}\right\}. \qquad (5)$$

Hence, the PMF of $d\xi_z$ yields

$$f_{d\xi_z}(dz_{i,j}; \sigma_n) = P(d\xi_z = dz_{i,j}; \sigma_n) = \int_{dz_{i,j}-0.5}^{dz_{i,j}+0.5} f_{d\xi_n}(x; \sigma_n)\, dx. \qquad (6)$$

In order not to introduce perceptible distortions in the cover image, the variance of stego-noise should not be too large. Thus $dz_{i,j}$ will take only limited number

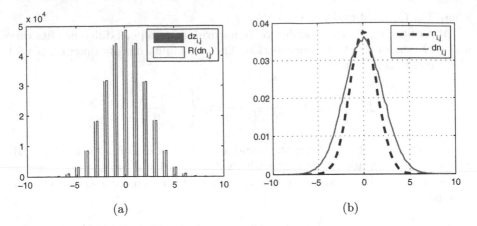

Fig. 1. The distributions of the quantized stego-noise difference $dz_{i,j}$ and the rounded stego-noise difference $\mathrm{Round}(dn_{i,j})$ (a); And the distributions of stego-noise $n_{i,j}$ and its difference $dn_{i,j}$ (b)

of values, which are denoted by dz_i, $i = 1, \cdots, U$. Then the distribution function of $d\xi_z$ can be rewritten as

$$f_{d\xi_z}(x; \sigma_n) = \sum_{i=1}^{U} P(d\xi_z = dz_i; \sigma_n)\delta(x - dz_i) \; , \tag{7}$$

where $\delta(\cdot)$ is the standard Delta function.

In practice, stochastic modulation steganography is equivalent to adding quantized stego-noise to the cover image. The embedding operation can be modeled as

$$s_{i,j} = c_{i,j} + z_{i,j} \; , \tag{8}$$

where $i = 1, \cdots, M$ and $j = 1, \cdots, N$. We substitute (8) in (1) and obtain

$$\begin{aligned}
ds_{i,j} &= s_{i,j} - s_{i,j+1} \\
&= (c_{i,j} + z_{i,j}) - (c_{i,j+1} + z_{i,j+1}) \\
&= (c_{i,j} - c_{i,j+1}) + (z_{i,j} - z_{i,j+1}) \\
&= dc_{i,j} + dz_{i,j} \; .
\end{aligned} \tag{9}$$

By replacing the sample values with their corresponding random variables, we can rewrite (8) and (9) as

$$\xi_s = \xi_c + \xi_z \; , \tag{10}$$

$$d\xi_s = d\xi_c + d\xi_z \; . \tag{11}$$

For stochastic modulation steganography, the quantized stego-noise and the cover image may be assumed to be independent and their horizontal differences are also independent. Clearly, referring to (11), the stego-image's pixel difference is the addition of the cover image's pixel difference and the quantized stego-noise difference, which are modeled by two independent random variables $d\xi_c$ and $d\xi_z$. According to probability theory, the addition of two independent random variables results in a convolution of their probability density functions. Thus, the PDF of $d\xi_s$ is obtained as follows.

$$f_{d\xi_s}(x; \alpha, \beta, \sigma_n) = f_{d\xi_c}(x; \alpha, \beta) * f_{d\xi_z}(x; \sigma_n) . \tag{12}$$

Equation (12) shows that the distribution of the stego-image's pixel difference can be computed, if the distributional parameters α, β of the cover image's pixel difference and the variance σ_n of the stego-noise are known.

2.3 Estimation of Hidden Message Length

A. Capacity of Stochastic Modulation Steganography

According to the embedding algorithm described in Sect. 2.1, the hiding capacity of the stochastic modulation steganography, denoted by p, is equal to the maximum bit rate of 1 bpp subtracting the probability of occurrence of '0' in the quantized stego-noise, that is,

$$\begin{aligned}
p &= 1 - f_{\xi_z}(0; \sigma_n) \\
&= 1 - \int_{-0.5}^{+0.5} f_{\xi_n}(x; \sigma_n) dx \\
&= 1 - \int_{-0.5}^{+0.5} \frac{1}{\sqrt{2\pi}\sigma_n} \exp\left(-\frac{x^2}{2\sigma_n^2}\right) dx \\
&\xLeftrightarrow{x/\sqrt{2}\sigma_n=t} 1 - \frac{2}{\sqrt{\pi}} \int_0^{\frac{1}{2\sqrt{2}\sigma_n}} e^{-t^2} dt \\
&= 1 - erf\left(\frac{1}{2\sqrt{2}\sigma_n}\right) ,
\end{aligned} \tag{13}$$

where $erf(\cdot)$ is the statistical error function defined by $erf(x) = \frac{2}{\sqrt{\pi}} \int_0^x e^{-t^2} dt$.

From (13), we know that the estimation of the secret message length can be achieved by estimating the variance σ_n^2 of the stego-noise. In the blind steganalysis case, only the stego-image and the steganographic algorithm are known to us. Therefore, we must find a way to estimate σ_n^2 from the stego-image. In the following subsections, after analyzing the relationship among α, β and σ_n^2, we present a method to estimate.

B. Relationship among α, β and σ_n^2

Referring to (2) and (5), the distributions of $d\xi_c$ and $d\xi_n$ are symmetrical about zero. Therefore the mean of $d\xi_c$ and $d\xi_z$ approximates zero. According to (11), we have

$$E(d\xi_s) = E(d\xi_c) + E(d\xi_z) \approx 0 . \tag{14}$$

As discussed in Sect. 2.2, $d\xi_s$ is the addition of two independent random variables $d\xi_c$ and $d\xi_z$. It is well known from probability theory that the variance of the sum of two independent random variables is equal to the sum of their variances. Thus we obtain

$$V(d\xi_s) = V(d\xi_c) + V(d\xi_z) \ , \tag{15}$$

where $V(\cdot)$ denotes the variance of a random variable. According to the definition of variance, the variance of the cover image's pixel difference is readily calculated as below using its PDF expressed in (2).

$$V_{d\xi_c}(\alpha, \beta) = \int x^2 f_{d\xi_c}(x; \alpha, \beta) dx = \frac{\alpha^2 \Gamma(3/\beta)}{\Gamma(1/\beta)} \ . \tag{16}$$

And we can estimate the variance of the stego-image's pixel difference using the following equation

$$V_{d\xi_s} = \frac{1}{M(N-1)} \sum_i^M \sum_j^{N-1} ds_{i,j}^2 \ . \tag{17}$$

Moreover, the variance of $d\xi_z$ can be computed by

$$V_{d\xi_z} = \int x^2 f_{d\xi_z}(x; \sigma_n) dx \ . \tag{18}$$

If α and β are known, then σ_n can be solved by inserting (16), (17), (18) into (15), however it is difficult to get a closed form solution. In order to simplify the computing procedure, we use the variance of the stego-noise difference to approximate the variance of the quantized stego-noise difference, i.e. $V_{d\xi_z} \approx V_{d\xi_n}$. As previously analyzed in Sect. 2.2, $d\xi_n$ has the distribution $N(0, 2\sigma_n^2)$ and its variance equals $2\sigma_n^2$. Thus, the variance of the stego-noise is estimated by

$$\sigma_n^2 = \frac{1}{2} \left(\frac{1}{M(N-1)} \sum_i^M \sum_j^{N-1} ds_{i,j}^2 - \frac{\alpha^2 \Gamma(3/\beta)}{\Gamma(1/\beta)} \right) \ . \tag{19}$$

C. Rough Estimation of α and β

Table 1 shows the values of α and β computed for several cover images from USC-SIPI image database[2] with various lengths of embedded message. It is seen that the values of α and β increase with the length of secret message embedded with stochastic modulation steganography. However, the changes of α and β are not so large which shows that it is possible for us to obtain rough estimates of α and β from the stego-image.

The coefficients α and β shown in Table 1 are computed by measuring the first and second moment of the GGD distribution. This method was introduced in [14].

$$m_1 = \int |x| f_{d\xi_c}(x; \alpha, \beta) dx = \frac{\alpha \Gamma(2/\beta)}{\Gamma(1/\beta)} \ . \tag{20}$$

---

[2] http://sipi.usc.edu/database

Table 1. Effect of stochastic modulation impacting on α and β

Image	α, β	Message Length (bpp)								
		0.0	0.1	0.2	0.3	0.4	0.5	0.6	0.7	0.8
Stream	α	6.6941	6.8450	6.9846	7.1050	7.2272	7.3493	7.5347	7.7766	8.3774
Bridge	β	0.7263	0.7322	0.7377	0.7424	0.7472	0.7517	0.7587	0.7677	0.7893
Fishing	α	2.0734	2.0899	2.1036	2.1232	2.1436	2.1768	2.2269	2.3605	2.7017
Boat	β	0.5377	0.5387	0.5395	0.5406	0.5418	0.5437	0.5465	0.5539	0.5720
Aerial	α	2.4861	2.5199	2.5570	2.5853	2.6224	2.6842	2.7820	3.0076	3.5582
	β	0.5527	0.5544	0.5564	0.5579	0.5598	0.5630	0.5680	0.5792	0.6051

$$m_2 = \int x^2 f_{d\xi_c}\left(x; \alpha, \beta\right) dx = \frac{\alpha^2 \Gamma\left(3/\beta\right)}{\Gamma\left(1/\beta\right)} . \tag{21}$$

From the above two equations, we can derive that

$$\frac{m_1^2}{m_2} = \frac{\Gamma^2\left(2/\beta\right)}{\Gamma\left(1/\beta\right)\Gamma\left(3/\beta\right)} . \tag{22}$$

Given the stego-image $s_{i,j}$, we estimate m_1 and m_2 using (23) and (24).

$$\hat{m}_1 = \frac{1}{M\left(N-1\right)} \sum_{i=1}^{M} \sum_{j=1}^{N-1} |ds_{i,j}| , \tag{23}$$

$$\hat{m}_2 = \frac{1}{M\left(N-1\right)} \sum_{i=1}^{M} \sum_{j=1}^{N-1} ds_{i,j}^2 . \tag{24}$$

where $\hat{m}_1$ and $\hat{m}_2$ are the estimates of m_1 and m_1. By substituting $\hat{m}_1$ and $\hat{m}_2$ into (22), we obtain a rough estimate of β represented by $\hat{\beta}$. And then the estimate of α, which is denoted by $\hat{\alpha}$, may be solved by inserting (23) to (20) or inserting (24) to (21).

D. Estimation of Hidden Message Length

Having obtained the rough estimates of α and β, we make use of grid search and Chi-square goodness of fit test to find the more accurate estimates of α and β.

Firstly, we let $\alpha \in [\hat{\alpha} - \alpha_e, \hat{\alpha} + \alpha_e]$ and $\beta \in [\hat{\beta} - \beta_e, \hat{\beta} + \beta_e]$, which may make up of a rectangle searching region. According to Table 1, the difference of α or β between the cover image and the stego-image with maximum message embedded varies from image to image, thus it is not so appropriate to choose α_e or β_e to be an constant for different images. In our experiments, α_e and β_e are chosen to be in proportion to $\hat{\alpha}$ and $\hat{\beta}$ respectively.

Then for each different combinations of coefficients α and β, an estimate of the distribution of the cover image's pixel difference may be computed by equation (2). And the corresponding theoretical distribution of the stego-image's pixel difference may be obtained by solving equation (19) and equation (12). Let the histogram of the stego-image's pixel difference be represented by O_i $(i = 1, \cdots, B)$, where B is the number of classes used in the Chi-square goodness of fit test. Then the Chi-square test statistic χ^2 is computed by (25).

$$\chi^2 = \sum_i^B \frac{(O_i - E_i)^2}{E_i} \; , \tag{25}$$

$$E_i = M(N-1) \int_{R_i} f_{d\xi_s}(x; \alpha, \beta, \sigma_n) \, dx \; . \tag{26}$$

where R_i is the bin interval of class i $(i = 1, \cdots, B)$.

After the optimal coefficients denoted by α_{opt} and β_{opt} among all the combinations of α and β are found by Chi-square goodness of fit test, the secret message length p is then estimated using the optimal coefficients according to (19) and (13).

3   Experimental Results and Analysis

200 images selected at random from the Greenspun image database[3] are used to demonstrate the performance of the proposed steganalytic method. All the original images were converted to grayscale with the size of 512×512. In the tests, random message with relative message length $p = 0.0, 0.1, 0.2, 0.3, 0.5, 0.6, 0.7$ and 0.8 (bpp) is hidden within each of the images using stochastic modulation steganography [10]. The estimates of secret message lengths in all the images are shown in Fig.2. The mean and the standard variance of these estimates are provided in Table 2.

Table 2. The mean and standard variance of estimates in 200 images

Actual length		0.0	0.1	0.2	0.3	0.4	0.5	0.6	0.7	0.8
Estimate	Mean	0.000	0.115	0.262	0.362	0.446	0.527	0.616	0.706	0.801
	Std.Var	0.001	0.018	0.018	0.015	0.011	0.009	0.006	0.004	0.002

We can see from Fig.2 that the estimations of the secret message lengths without any message embedded are very close to zero. If we choose a relatively small value as the classifying threshold to discriminate the cover images and the stego-images, high detection rates can be expected. At the same time, we

---

[3] http://philip.greenspun.com

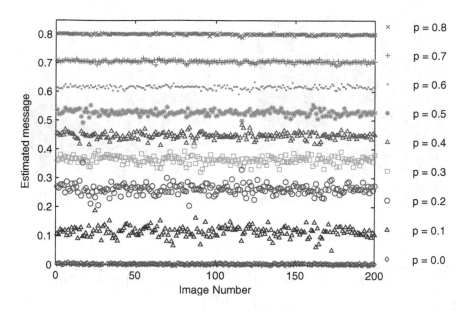

Fig. 2. The estimates of secret message length in 200 images

find that the standard deviation is very small (see Table 2). It implies that the estimated results for different images do not differ significantly. Therefore, the detection of the existence of hidden message should not introduce high false positives. As showed in Table 2, with the hidden message length increasing, the performance of our estimator improves dramatically and the variances of the estimates decrease. This is also reflected in Fig.2 , where it is seen that the distributions of the estimated hidden message lengths for different cover images become more and more centralized around the true secret message lengths as p varying from 0.1 bpp to 0.8 bpp.

From these results, it is clearly seen that our new method can indeed reliably detect the existence of hidden message. It is also seen that estimated lengths of the hidden message are quite accurate, especially when the true hidden message lengths are of high bpp.

The proposed method relies on two reasonable assumptions. One is that the cover image's pixel difference may be well modeled as generalized Gaussian distribution and the other is the independence between the cover image and the stego-noise. As described in Sect. 2.1, the embedding of stochastic modulation steganography is non-adaptive, so the assumption that the stego-noise and the cover image are independent should hold. In our experiments, however, we observed that the pixel difference histograms of different images follow the fitted generalized Gaussian distributions differently and two examples are shown in Fig.4. For some images, it is difficult to find good shape and variance parameters that will fit a generalized Gaussian into the difference histogram well. As a result, the mismatching between the difference histogram and the fitted gen-

Fig. 3. The left image is Girl-elaine and the right one is Fishing-boat

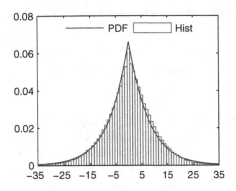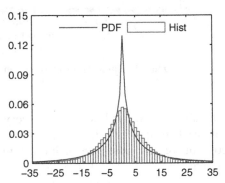

Fig. 4. The pixel difference histograms and the fitted PDFs of Girl-elaine image (left) and Fishing-boat image (right)

eralized Gaussian may affect the accuracy of the estimation results. Also, the use of Mallat's method and numerical rounding effects may also introduce errors in the estimation of the distributional parameters α and β. In Sect. 2.3, we use the variance of the stego-noise difference to estimate the variance of the quantized stego-noise difference. In practice, the variance of $d\xi_z$ may differ from the variance of $d\xi_n$, so the approximation may also affect the accuracy of our estimator.

Fig.3 shows the two sample images downloaded from USC-SIPI image database and Fig.4 illustrates their difference histograms and PDFs of fit.

4   Conclusions

Based on the analysis of the pixel difference distributions of images before and after secret message embedding, we have developed a new algorithm to estimate the length of secret message embedded with the stochastic modulation steganography. Experimental results show that our new approach may discriminate cover images and stego-images with low false positives and estimate the secret message length with high accuracy.

Under the assumption that the cover image and the stego-noise are independent, we establish a statistical model describing the relations of the distributions of the differences of the cover image, the stego-image and the stego-noise. This model is not only applicable to stochastic modulation steganography, but also can be applied to other additive noise steganography techniques. Moreover, the approach described in this paper provides a steganalysis framework and the idea may be suitable for other non-adaptive steganographic techniques, such as LSB-based steganography, $\pm k$ steganography, and stochastic modulation using noise of distributions other than Gaussian, provided that the distortions of embedding can be well modeled as some well-defined statistical distributions.

Acknowledgments

Authors appreciate the support received from NSFC (60325208, 60133020), NSF of Guangdong (04205407), and funding of China National Education Ministry.

References

1. R.J. Anderson and F.A.P. Petitcolas, On the Limits of Steganography, in *IEEE Journal of Selected Areas in Communications, Special Issue on Copyright and Privacy Protection*, vol.16(4), pp.474-481, 1998.
2. N.F. Johnson and S. Jajodia, Steganalysis of Images Created Using Current Steganography Software, in *Lecture Notes in Computer Science*, vol.1525, pp.273-289, Springer-Verlag, Berlin, 1998.
3. A. Westfeld and A. Pfitzmann, Attacks on Steganographic Systems, in *Proceedings of the Third International Workshop on Information Hiding*, pp.61-76, 1999.
4. N. Provos and P. Honeyman, Detecting Steganographic Content on the Internet, in *ISOC NDSS02*, San Diego, CA, February 2002.
5. J. Fridrich, M. Goljan and R. Du, Detecting LSB Steganography in Color and Gray-Scale Images, in *Magazine of IEEE Multimedia Special Issue on Security*, pp.22-28, October-November, 2001.
6. T. Zhang and X.J. Ping, Reliable Detection of Spatial LSB Steganography Based on Difference Histogram, in *The Journal of Software*, China, vol.15, no.1, pp.151-158, 2004.
7. S. Dumitrescu, X. Wu and Z. Wang, Detection of Lsb Steganography Via Sample Pair Analysis, in *IEEE Transactions On Signal Processing*, vol.51, no.7, pp.1995-2007, 2003.
8. T. Sharp, An Implementation of Key-Based Digital Signal Steganography, in: I. S. Moskowitz (eds.): *4th International Workshop on Information Hiding, LNCS 2137*, pp.13C26, Springer-Verlag, New York, 2001.
9. L.M. Marvel, C.G. Boncelet and C.T. Retter, Spread Spectrum Image Steganography, in *IEEE Transactions on Image Processing*, vol.8, no.8, pp.1075-1083, Aug, 1999.

10. J. Fridrich and M. Goljan, Digital Image Steganography Using Stochastic Modulation, in *Security and Watermarking of Multimedia Contents V*, vol.5020, pp.191-202, 2003.
11. A. Westfeld, Detecting Low Embedding rates, In: Petitcolas et al. (eds.): *Pre-proceedings 5th Information Hiding Workshop*. Noordwijkerhout, Netherlands, Oct.7.9, 2002.
12. J.J. Harmsen and W.A. Pearlman, Steganalysis of Additive Noise Modelable Information Hiding, in *Proc. SPIE Electronic Imaging*, Santa Clara, January 21-24, 2003.
13. J. Huang and D. Mumford , Statistics of Natural Images and Models, in *Proc. IEEE Conf. Computer Vision and Pattern Recognition*, pp.541-547, 1999.
14. S.G. Mallat, A Theory for Multiresolution Signal Decomposition: The wavelet Represention, in *IEEE Transations on Pattern Analysis and Machine Intelligence*, vol.11, No.7, pp.674-693, July, 1989.

Information Transmission and Steganography

Ingemar J. Cox[1], Ton Kalker[2], Georg Pakura[3], and Mathias Scheel[3]

[1] University College London, Torrington Place, London
[2] HP Labs, Palo Alto, CA
[3] University of Rostock, 18059 Rostock, Germany

Abstract. Recently there has been strong interest in developing models of steganography based on information theory. Previous work has considered under what conditions the security of the stegosystem can be guaranteed and the number of bits that can then be embedded in a cover Work. This work implicitly assumes that the hidden message is uncorrelated with the cover Work, the latter simply being used to conceal the hidden message. Here, we consider the case in which the cover Work is chosen such that it is correlated with the covert message. In this situation, the number of bits needed to encode the hidden message can be considerably reduced. We discuss the information that can then be transmitted and show that it is substantially greater than simply the number of embedded bits. We also note that the security of the system as defined by Cachin need not be compromised. However, the Shannon security may be compromised, but it remains unclear to what extent. Experimental results are presented that demonstrate the fundamental concepts.

1 Introduction

The history of steganography can be traced back thousands of years, examples of which are described in [3]. Steganography seeks to provide a covert communication channel between two parties. In [1] the problem is framed as one in which two prisoners, Alice and Bob, are permitted to communicate between one another, while under the surveillance of a Warden. The Warden will prevent communication between Alice and Bob if any communications between them is determined to contain a hidden message.

In steganography, we have a hidden message that Alice wishes to transmit to Bob. This message is hidden in a cover Work, which might be an image, video, audio or text message, for example. The combination of cover Work and hidden message is refered to as the stegowork, or more specifically, the stegotext, stegoimage, etc depending on the particular instance of the cover Work. It is assumed that Alice and Bob share a secret key and a public function that takes as input the key and the stegowork and outputs the secret message. Alice sends Bob a transmitted Work which may either be a cover Work, i.e. there is no hidden message, or a stegoWork, i.e. there is a hidden message. The Warden, Eve, is free to examine all transmitted Works between Alice and Bob and must decide whether such transmissions include a hidden message.

M. Barni et al. (Eds.): IWDW 2005, LNCS 3710, pp. 15–29, 2005.

Steganography differs from cryptography. Cryptography attempts to prevent a message between Alice and Bob being decoded by a third party who has intercepted the message. That is, in the latter case, it is known that Alice and Bob are conducting a private communication, but interception of the encrypted message hopefully does not allow the adversary to interpret the message. However, cryptography does not prevent the adversary from disrupting or destroying the communication channel between Alice and Bob, thereby preventing any further communication. Steganography attempts to hide the very fact that Alice and Bob are conducting a private communication. An adversary may know that the two parties are communicating, but this communication appears to the Warden to be a benign communication with no covert subtext.

Steganography differs from watermarking. In steganography, the cover Work is not considered to be of value to the two communicators, Alice and Bob. Thus, it is perfectly acceptable for example, for an image of a person in a grey suit to be altered to an image of a person in a blue suit, provided, of course, that such alteration does not raise the suspicion of the Warden. In contrast, in digital watermarking, the cover Work is considered to be valuable to at least one of the communicators and the fidelity of the cover Work must be preserved.

The adversary in a stegosystem can be assumed to be either active or passive. In the active case, the Warden is free to alter the Work transmitted by Alice, before delivering it to Bob. That is, the Warden is free to attempt to remove any possible hidden message from the stegowork before passing it on the Bob. In the passive case, the Warden is not permitted to alter the transmitted Work. Rather, the adversary must decide whether the transmitted Work contains a hidden message and if so, is then free to prevent receipt of the transmission to Bob. For the purposes of this paper, we assume a passive adversary.

Shannon [4] first considered secrecy systems from the viewpoint of information theory. Shannon identified three types of secret communication which he described as (i) "*concealment systems, including such methods as invisible ink, concealing a message in an innocent text, or in a fake covering cryptogram, or other methods in which the existence of the message is concealed from the enemy*", (ii) privacy sytems and (iii) cryptographic systems. On concealment systems, i.e. steganography, Shannon stated that such "*systems are primarily a psychological problem*" and did not consider them further.

Anderson and Petitcolas [5,3] revisited the question of steganography from an information theoretic viewpoint, suggesting that indeed information theory could also be used to describe such systems. They considered the ideal scenario of perfect source encoding, say for music. In this case, a source decoder would decompress any random bit string into an acceptable musically piece. Thus, Alice could take an encrypted hidden message and then pass this message through the ideal source *decoder* to produce a stegotext that would appear to the Warden, Eve, as an acceptable cover Work. Eve would not be able to determine that such a stegotext contained a hidden message. On receipt, Bob would input the stegotext into the source *encoder* to again produce the encrypted hidden message which is then decrypted. This thought experiment reveals that under certain circumstances steganography may be impossible to detect.

In fact, we do not even need perfect compression in order to ensure that steganography is undetectable. Very low bit rate steganography is indeed impossible to detect (at least from a statistical perspective). For example, if Alice and Bob share a secret key, then a public hash function can be used to map a string of bits plus the key into an n-bit hash. Then for $n < 20$, say, it is perfectly feasible for Alice to search through a collection of approximately 1 million images and identify the image which hashes to the desired n-bit string. Since the image has not been altered in any way, it is not possible for the Warden to determine that the communication of the image contains a covert message.

Unfortunately, for $n > 20$, the size of the database quickly becomes prohibitive. For example, for $n = 40$, we must search a database of approximately one trillion items. The continuing increase in storage and computational power does not significantly help - to send an extra 20 bits, e.g. $n = 60$, requires a million-fold increase in capacity. Thus, to send messages of greater length will require sending multiple partial messages. For example, for $n = 20$ and a message size of 100k bits, Alice must send over 5,000 stegoWorks to Bob. This may well raise the suspicion of the Warden. Ideally, Alice would like to hide as much information as possible in a coverWork while maintaining the security of the system. Thus, a key question in steganography is how many bits can be safely embedded in a cover Work without raising the risk of detection by the Warden above some small probability.

Cachin [6] examined this problem from an information theoretic view point. Cachin assumes a passive adversary whose decision is based on a statistical hypothesis test as to whether the stegowork is drawn from the distribution of allowable benign communications, i.e. coverWorks, or otherwise. Under these conditions, Cachin defines conditions for both a *perfectly secure* and an ϵ-*secure* stegosystem. Section 2 summarizes this contribution. Cachin defines the conditions under which the probability is either zero or negligible that an adversary will detect the existence of a covert communication. However, this work does not indicate how many bits can be embedded. Sallee [7] provided an answer to this question, the results of which are discussed in Section 2.1.

One might now conclude that the question of how much information can be transmitted between Alice and Bob is answered. And if it is assumed that the hidden message and the cover Work are statistically independent, then this is indeed the case. However, what if the covert message and the cover Work are correlated? That is, the mutual information between the hidden message and the cover Work is non-zero? Clearly, if the cover Work has non-zero mutual information with the message, then there is leakage of information to the Warden. However, we argue that in many circumstances, this leakage may not be sufficient for the Warden to learn anything significant. For example, consider the case where Alice wishes to transmit a covert image to Bob. Given the covert image, Alice selects a cover Work (image) from a database such that the mutual information between the cover Work and covert image is non-zero. Thus, the number of bits needed to encode the covert image will be (much) less than would otherwise be needed. The Warden may learn that the class of covert messages is an image. However, it may not be possible to determine what that message is. And more importantly, if the number of bits needed to encode the covert image is less than the upper bound provided by Sallee, then the Warden will not be able to determine that a covert message is even present. However, the amount of information received by Bob is much greater that the number of bits needed to encode the hidden message! This is because the cover Work provides more than a cover. Rather, it defines a probability distribution which permits a very efficient source coding of the hidden message.

In this paper, we consider the situation in which the hidden message and the cover Work are correlated. In this case, the number of bit needed to communicate the hidden message may be much less than for the case where the cover Work is statistically independent. Source coding of correlated information sources has been studied [8] and these results are discussed in Section 3.1.

Section 3 describes our proposed steganography system and provides an estimate of the information that can be communicated between the two communicating parties. It is different from Cachin's and Sallee's results in that the question we ask is not how many bits can safely be embedded in a cover Work, but rather, how much information can the receiving party learn. Section 4 then illustrates the steganographic principle with a demonstration of embedding a covert image within a cover image. Finally, Section 5 concludes with a summary and directions for future work.

2   An Information-Theoretic Model of Steganography

In order to discuss information theoretic models of steganography, we first provide a brief summary of some basic results in information theory.

Consider an ensemble $\mathcal{X} = (x, A_\mathcal{X}, P_\mathcal{X})$, where the outcome x is the value of a random variable. The values of x are drawn from an alphabet $A_\mathcal{X} = (a_1, a_2, \cdots a_l)$ with probabilities $P_\mathcal{X} = (P_1, P_2, \cdots P_l)$ such that

$$P(x = a_i) = P_i, P_i \geq 0 \text{ and } \sum_{a_i \in A_\mathcal{X}} P(x = a_i) = 1 \tag{1}$$

The Shannon information content of an outcome x is

$$h(x) = log_2 \frac{1}{P(x)} \tag{2}$$

and the entropy of the ensemble $\mathcal{X}$ is

$$H(\mathcal{X}) = \sum_{x \in A_\mathcal{X}} P(x) log_2 \frac{1}{P(x)} \tag{3}$$

The entropy provides a lower bound on the number of bits that are needed to encode x, for infintely long, independent, identically distributed (iid) sequences.

The entropy $H(\mathcal{X}) \geq 0$ and is only zero if $P(x_i) = 1$, i.e. the signal is entirely deterministic.

The joint entropy between $\mathcal{X}$ and $\mathcal{Y}$ is defined as

$$H(\mathcal{X}, \mathcal{Y}) = \sum_{x,y \in A_{\mathcal{X}} A_{\mathcal{Y}}} P(x,y) log \frac{1}{P(x,y)} \tag{4}$$

where $P(x,y)$ is the joint probability of the outcomes x and y occuring.

$$H(\mathcal{X}, \mathcal{Y}) = H(\mathcal{X}) + H(\mathcal{Y}) \text{ iff } P(x,y) = P(x)P(y) \tag{5}$$

i.e. x and y are independent of one another.

The conditional entropy of $\mathcal{X}$ given $y = b_k$, is the entropy of the probabilty distribution $P(x|y = b_k)$ and is given by

$$H(\mathcal{X}|y = b_k) = \sum_{x \in A_{\mathcal{X}}} P(x|y = b_k) log \frac{1}{P(x|y = b_k)} \tag{6}$$

The conditional entropy of $\mathcal{X}$ given $\mathcal{Y}$ is the average over y of the conditional entropy of $\mathcal{X}$ given y, i.e.

$$H(\mathcal{X}|\mathcal{Y}) = \sum_{x,y \in A_{\mathcal{X}}, A_{\mathcal{Y}}} P(x,y) log \frac{1}{P(x|y)} \tag{7}$$

The conditional entropy measures the uncertainty in x given knowledge of y. Thus, to code x, given y, we only need $H(\mathcal{X}|\mathcal{Y})$ bits rather than $H(\mathcal{X})$.

A related measure is the mutual information between $\mathcal{X}$ and $\mathcal{Y}$ and is given by

$$I(\mathcal{X}; \mathcal{Y}) = H(\mathcal{X}) + H(\mathcal{Y}) - H(\mathcal{X}|\mathcal{Y}) \tag{8}$$

The mutual information is always greater than or equal to zero and measures the average reduction in uncertainty of x given y.

The relative entropy or Kullback-Leibler divergence between two distributions $P(x)$ and $Q(x)$ that are defined over the same alphabet $A_{\mathcal{X}}$ is

$$D_{KL}(P \parallel Q) = \sum_x P(x) log \frac{P(x)}{Q(x)} \tag{9}$$

The relative entropy can be thought of as the difference between Huffman coding a source with pdf P using a table determined by P and an alternative Q (suboptimal choice of codeword lengths). Note that the relative entropy, $D_{KL}(P \parallel Q) \geq 0$ with equality iff $P = Q$.

2.1   Steganography, Steganalysis and Information Theory

In a stegosystem, Alice sends Bob an innocent looking message, the cover Work, inside of which may be hidden a secret message. Communication is over a public channel that allows the adversary, Eve, to inspect the message.

Alice may send either a cover Work with no hidden message or a cover Work with a hidden message. Eve must decide whether Alice and Bob are communicating covertly.

Let c denote the cover Work, which is drawn from a distribution, P_C, that is known to Eve. Let s denote the stegotext, and P_S its distribution. If Eve's decision is based on comparing the known distribution of the cover Works, P_C, with the suspected stegotext, then clearly if

$$D_{KL}(P_C \parallel P_S) = 0 \qquad (10)$$

then $P_C = P_S$ and Cachin defines this as *perfectly secure*, i.e. it is impossible for Eve to distinguish between cover Works that contain or do not contain a hidden message.

If $D_{KL}(P_C \parallel P_S) \leq \epsilon$, then the system is said to be ϵ-secure.

Cachin analysed Eve's detection performance using the theory of hypothesis testing [9]. Eve must decide between the two hypotheses, H_0, representing the hypothesis that the transmission does not contain a hidden message and H_1, representing the hypothesis that the transmission does contain a hidden message. Given the observation space, C, there are two probability distributions, P_0 and P_1, such that if H_0 is true then the observed message, C, was generated according to P_0. Conversely, if H_1 is true, then C was generated from the distribution P_1.

Eve can make two forms of error. First, accepting H_1 when H_0 was true, often referred to as a false positive, and second, accepting H_0 when H_1 is true, often referred to as a false negative. Let α and β denote the probabilities of type 1 and type 2 errors, respectively. The binary relative entropy, $d(\alpha, \beta)$, is given by

$$d(\alpha, \beta) = \alpha \log \frac{\alpha}{(1 - \beta)} + (1 - \alpha) \log \frac{(1 - \alpha)}{\beta} \qquad (11)$$

and

$$d(\alpha, \beta) \leq D(P_0 \parallel P_1) \qquad (12)$$

This inequality can be used to determine a lower bound on the probability of type 2 errors, β, given a desired upper bound on the probability of a type 1 error, α. In particular, Cachin shows that if the probability of a type 1 error is $\alpha = 0$, i.e. Eve is not permitted to accuse Alice of transmitting a covert message when in fact she has not, then the probability of a type 2 error, β, i.e. of missing a covert communication is

$$\beta \geq 2^{-\epsilon} \qquad (13)$$

That is, the probability of *not* detecting a covert communication is very high.

Sallee [7] extended the work of Cachin to ask what is the maximum message length that can be securely hidden.

Given an instance of cover text, c, drawn from a distribution, P_C, Sallee seperates it into two distinct parts, c_a, which remains unchanged after embedding, and c_b, which is replaced by c'_b, to encode the hidden message. For example, c_b, may be the least significant bit of each pixel and c_a the remaining higher order bits.

These two parts are assumed to be drawn from two distributions, $\mathcal{C}_a$ and $\mathcal{C}_b$. Given the distribution of P_C, or a model thereof, we can estimate the conditional distribution, $P_{\mathcal{C}_b | \mathcal{C}_a}(\mathcal{C}_b | \mathcal{C}_a = c_a)$. Then, if $\mathcal{C}_b'$ is chosen to obey this conditional distribution, then the resulting stegotext, $C' = (c_a, c_b')$ will have the same distribution, P_C, as the cover work.

Sallee suggested using an arithmetic entropy encode/decoder [10]to accomplish this. Arithmetic coding is a method for very efficient compression of strings given a model of their distribution. However, if a random bit string (read hidden message) is fed into an arithmetic *decoder*, the output bit sequence will have the same distribution as the model distribution. This is a practical means for generating the distributions required by Cachin to ensure perfect security. Note the similarity between this and the ideas of Anderson and Petitcolas [3] regarding ideal compresison that were described earlier.

Sallee's method has a capacity equal to the entropy of the conditional probability distribution, $P_{\mathcal{C}_b | \mathcal{C}_a}$

$$H(\mathcal{C}_b | \mathcal{C}_a = c_a) = -\sum_{c_b} P_{\mathcal{C}_b | \mathcal{C}_a}(c_b | c_a) log P_{\mathcal{C}_b | \mathcal{C}_a}(c_b | c_a) \qquad (14)$$

Essentially, $\mathcal{C}_b$ is an open communications channel without any restriction. Note that this capacity is independent of the distribution of the message to be hidden.

3   Information Transmission with Correlation Between Cover and Covert Works

Consider a message m drawn from a distribution, $P_\mathcal{M}$ and a cover Work c drawn from a distribution, P_C. If m is independent of c, then the minimum number of bits needed to encode the message is the message's entropy, $H(m)$. However, if m and c are correlated, then the number of bits needed to encode m given c is the conditional entropy, $H(m|c)$. The conditional entropy, $H(m|c)$, may be much less than the entropy of the message, $H(m)$.

What if $m = c$, or more usefully, m is a deterministic function of the cover Work, c? Then, the conditional entropy is zero and there is no need to embed a secret message. At first sight, this would not appear to offer any form of covert channel. However, if Alice and Bob share a secret key, then even if the deterministic function is known publicly, this offers a perfectly secure channel, since the distribution of c is unchanged. This form of steganography was discussed in the introduction using a one-way hash function, though any receiver function will suffice.

The key question then is how much information can Alice transmit to Bob without being detected by Eve. Assuming that we split the covertext into two parts, then from [7], we know that given a covertext, c, the maximum size of the hidden message is given by Equation 14. Thus, if the hidden message is uncorrelated with the cover Work, then the maximium information transmitted is simply this number of bits. However, the information transmitted to Bob includes both the message *and* the cover Work. Traditionally, the cover Work has been ignored. It is simply a means by which to conceal the hidden message. However, this need not be the case.

Given a message m and cover Work, c with conditional entropy, $H(m|c)$, then we only need to encode $H(m|c)$ bits of information in c in order to encode m. For explanatory purposes, let's assume that the encoding procedure splits the covertext into two parts. Then, the information received by Bob is

$$H(c, m) = H(c_a) + H(c_b) = H(c_a) + H(m|c) = H(c) \qquad (15)$$

which is potentially much greater than simply $H(m)$.

Thus, given a hidden message, we choose a cover Work from a set of cover Works, such that the correlation between the two permits a very efficient source coding of the hidden message.[1] We believe that the search for a correlated coverWork is significantly easier than finding a coverWork that hashes to a desired n-bit value. In the latter case, for large n, this is almost impossible. However, most images, for example, exhibit correlation with one another.

If the cover Work is highly correlated with the message, m, then the number of embedded bits needed will be very low. What does this imply regarding the secrecy of the covert channel?

First, Eve cannot distinguish between a cover text with no hidden message and a stegotext provided we ensure that the number of embedded bits is less than that given by Equation 14. Thus, provided this condition is met, then there is no reduction in security as defined by Chachin.

Shannon [4] defines *perfect security* as *"a system that after a cryptogram is intercepted by the enemy, the a posteriori probabilities of this cryptogram representing various messages be identically the same as the a priori probabilities of the same messages before the interception"*. Thus, a system that exploits the mutual information between the hidden message and the cover Work would not appear to be perfectly secure, as defined by Shannon.

From the sender's perspective, the cover Work defines a probability distribution that permits a very efficient source coding of the hidden message. Without this, Alice would need at least $H(m)$ bits to encode the message, m. With the cover Work, Alice only needs $H(m|c)$, bits. A judicious choice of the cover Work, c, will then permit a very significant reduction in the number of bits that need to be embedded. These bits can then be encrypted using the secret key shared by Alice and Bob. The encryption does not increase the number of bits, but prevents the Warden from decoding the message, assuming it is detected. This

---

[1] There is a similarity between this and digital watermarking, where, given a cover Work, it is common to choose a watermark from a set of watermarks such that the watermark is easy to embed. Such techniques are based on the modeling watermarking as communication with side information [11,12,13] and the watermarks are often referred to as dirty paper codes [14,15]. However, digital watermarking does not use the correlation between the message and the cover work to reduce the number of bits needed to encode the message. Rather, the purpose is to reduce or eliminate the "noise" due to the cover Work and thereby improve the robustness and/or fidelity.

pseudo-random encrypted bit sequence is then embedded into the cover Work. This can be accomplished using Sallee's method.

If Eve suspects that Alice is exploiting the conditional entropy between the cover Work and message, then what can Eve learn from examining the cover Work? Certainly, upon interception of the stegowork, the adversary, Eve, has learned something about the hidden message. For example, if the cover Work is an image, the adversary may confidently conclude that the hidden message is also an image. However, our earlier example demonstrated that even if the conditional entropy is zero, Eve may still not be able to learn anything about the message, since she does not have knowledge of the key shared between Alice and Bob. In fact, the cover Work informs the Warden of the probability distribution used by Alice to perform the source encoding. However, this is not sufficient to decode the message.

We do not claim that steganography based on coding that exploits the conditional entropy between the hidden message and the cover Work is perfectly secure in the Shannon sense. However, it can certainly be perfectly secure of ϵ-secure in the Chachin sense.

3.1   Encoding of Correlated Sources

The encoding of correlated sources has been well studied. Interestingly, Slepian and Wolf [8] showed that efficient noiseless coding of two correlated sources $\mathcal{X}$ and $\mathcal{Y}$ could be achieved even if the two source encoders do *not* have access to the other signal, provided both signals are available to the decoder.

More recently, Pradhan and Ramchandran [16,17] extended these results to provide a constructive procedure for distributed source coding based on syndrome codes.

Together with Chou, they also recognized the duality between distributed source coding and data hiding [12]. However, while this paper demonstrated how to embed a hidden message in a cover Work using syndrome coding, it did not consider exploiting the mutual information between the cover Work and the hidden message. Rather, it can be considered an efficient implementation of results due to Costa [18] in which it was shown that the channel capacity of system with two noise sources, the first of which is entirely known to the transmitter, but neither of which is known to the receiver, is equivalent to the channel capacity of a system in which the known first noise source is absent. From a data hiding perspective, the first noise source represents the cover Work while the second noise source represents the distortion in the stegoWork prior to its receipt. This forms the foundation for considerable work on modeling watermarking as communication with side information [11,12,13].

Chou *et al* [12] also observed the similarity between distributive source coding, digital watermarking and that of writing on defective memories [19]. More recently, Fridrich *et al* [20] have applied these ideas to steganography. Their "wet paper" codes assume a cover Work consisting of n samples, k of which are "dry" and can be modified while the remaining $(n - k)$ bits are "wet" and must not be altered. They show that it is possible to embed k-bits of information into a cover

Work without the decoder knowing which of the k samples have been modified. Once again, correlation between the hidden message and the cover Work is not considered and the capacity of the system is considered to be k-bits.

4 Experimental Results

To demonstrate the concepts discussed in the previous section, we modified a steganographic method due to Chan et al [21]. They describe a procedure for embedding a covert image within a cover image. While their paper does not discuss relative entropy, relative entropy is exploited in order to reduce the number of bits needed to encode the covert image. In this example, we did not search for a cover image with high correlation with the hidden image, but rather, relied on the correlation that is present between 8×8 blocks across all images. It should be noted that this example is for illustrative purposes only and does not represent the most efficient means to implement our proposal.

The embedding procedure consists of:

1. Partition the cover image and covert image into 8×8 blocks, denoted c_i and m_j respectively
2. For all i and j, compute the error-matrix, $EM_{i,j}$ and the normalized error-matrix, $NEM_{i,j}$ defined as:

$$EM_{i,j} = m_i - c_j \tag{16}$$

and

$$NEM_{i,j} = EM_{i,j} - min(EM_{i,j}) \tag{17}$$

3. The range of errors, is refered to as the distance degree (DD) and is defined as

$$DD_{i,j} = max(EM_{i,j}) - min(EM_{i,j}) \tag{18}$$

where the min and max operations are over the 8×8 elements of the blocks.
4. For each hidden image block m_j, find the cover image block c_i such that $DD_{i,j}$ is a minimum. The location of the cover image block is referred to as the reference-block-index $RBI(j) = i$.
5. Given $DD_{RBI(j),j}$, the quantization error matrix is selected according to Table 1
6. Quantize the $NEM_{RBI(j),j}$
7. Embed the extra information of (i) the referenced block number, (ii) the quantization error matrix and (iii) the minimum element in the error matrix.
8. Embed this extra information in the LSB of the DCT coefficients, according to the method of [7].

The extraction procedure follows:

1. Extract the RBI
2. extract the QEM
3. extract the minimum element
4. reconstruct the secret image as

$$S_j = H'_i + QEM + min(EM_{i,j}) \tag{19}$$

Table 1. Quantization error matrix

DD_{c_i,m_j}	QEM_{c_i,m_j}
(3 - 4)	2
(5 - 6)	3
(7 - 8)	4
(9 - 11)	5
(12)	6
(13),(26 - 27), (52 - 55), (104 - 111)	$\lfloor \frac{NEM}{7} \rfloor \times 7 + 3$
(14 - 15),(28 - 31), (56 - 63), (112 - 127)	$\lfloor \frac{NEM}{8} \rfloor \times 8 + 3$
(16 - 17),(32 - 35), (64 - 71), (128 - 143)	$\lfloor \frac{NEM}{9} \rfloor \times 9 + 4$
(18 - 19),(36 - 39), (72 - 79), (144 - 159)	$\lfloor \frac{NEM}{10} \rfloor \times 10 + 4$
(20 - 21),(40 - 43), (80 - 87), (160 - 175)	$\lfloor \frac{NEM}{11} \rfloor \times 11 + 5$
(22 - 23),(44 - 47), (88 - 95), (176 - 191)	$\lfloor \frac{NEM}{12} \rfloor \times 12 + 5$
(24 - 25),(48 - 51), (96 - 103), (192 - 207)	$\lfloor \frac{NEM}{13} \rfloor \times 13 + 6$
(208 - 223)	$\lfloor \frac{NEM}{14} \rfloor \times 14 + 6$
(224 - 239)	$\lfloor \frac{NEM}{15} \rfloor \times 15 + 7$
(240 - 255)	$\lfloor \frac{NEM}{16} \rfloor \times 16 + 7$

Figure 1 shows an image used as a cover image. Figure 2 shows the image that is to be hidden in Figure 1.

Using the method outlined above, the number of bits needed to encode the hidden image was 222144 or 0.8474 bits per pixel. This approach uses lossy compression and the relative entropy of image 1 given image 2, may be higher. Nevertheless, this example serves to illustrate the considerable reduction in the number of bits that must be embedded when the cover Work is correlated with the hidden message. Independent coding of the the hidden image would have required 8 bits per pixel.[2]

---

[2] For this example, a similar or smaller number of bits per pixel would be possible by simple lossy compression of the hidden image using say JPEG compression. However, this need not be the case and we emphasise that the experimental results described here are purely for illustrative purposes.

Fig. 1. Cover image

Fig. 2. Image to be hidden

The number of bits that can safely be inserted in the cover Work according Equation 14 is 223110 or 0.8511 bits per pixel. Thus, the hidden message cane be embedded without risk of detection from a Warden.

Note that the resulting stegoImage has a 50.57dB signal-to-noise ratio compared with the original cover Work. Similarly, the recovered hidden image has a 38.93 dB SNR compared with the original hidden image, prior to embedding.

5   Conclusion

Previous work on modeling steganography using information theory has assumed that the hidden message is uncorrelated with the cover Work. In this scenario, the cover Work serves only to hide the covert message. However, it may often be the case that the sender of a stegotext, Alice, may be able to chose a cover Work that is correlated with the hidden message. In this case, the cover Work not only serves to hide the covert message, but also defines a probability distribution which permits a very efficient source coding of the message.

It is well known that if a message, m has entropy $H(m)$, this entropy defines a lower bound on the number of bits needed to reliably code the message. However, given a coverWork, c, that is correlated with the message, then it is also well-known that the message m requires only $H(m|c)$ additional bits, where $H(m|c)$ is the conditional entropy between the message and coverWork. This may be very much less than $H(m)$.

The reduction in the number of bits needed to encode the message is very beneficial, especially in ensuring security, as defined by Cachin. However, more importantly, we point out that the information received by Bob is much more than simply the number of encoded bits. Rather, Bob receives information that it equivalent to the entropy of the coverWork. This is much higher than previously thought possible.

We discussed the security issues related to steganography using mutual information between cover work and covert message. It is clear that from the perspective of detectability, we can still ensure that the system is perfectly secure or ϵ-secure as defined by Cachin. In fact, given that we need far fewer bits to encode the secret message, it should be easier to ensure such security. However, from the perpsective of perfect secrecy as defined by Shannon, the adversary learns a probability distribution defined by the cover Work which the hidden message is correlated with. Nevertheless, it is unclear how useful this knowledge is to the Warden.

We provided experimental results that are intended to illustrate that basic concepts of the method. Specifically, we discussed hiding an image within another cover image. This example was purely illustrative and more sophisticated techniques based on the approach proposed here are the subject of future work. We also note that this approach is applicable to many different kinds of cover Works and covert messages, including text, audio, video, computer graphics, maps, and electronic schematics.

There is clearly a deep connection between coding of correlated sources, distributed source coding, digital watermarking and steganography. We (and others) have identified a number of these connections but a rigorous mathematical model needs to be developed further. The basic problem can be described as given a message m that we wish to hide, first find a covertext, c, that is correlated with the message. We than want to jointly encode m and c into a stegotext, s such that s has the same source model as c and m should be recoverable from s up to some distortion (given some secret shared between Alice and Bob). An optimum solution to this problem remains a goal of future work.

Acknowledgement

The author thanks Matt L. Miller of NEC and Nasir Memon of Polytechnic University for valuable discussions of this work. Also Professor L. M. Cheng of the City University of Hong Kong for assistance with the experiments. Ingemar Cox is currently BT Chair of Telecommunications and thanks British Telecom for their support. This research was sponsored by the Air Force Office of Scientific Research, Air Force Material Command, USAF, under grant number FA8655-03-1-3A46. The U.S. Government is authorized to reproduce and distribute reprints for Government purpose notwithstanding any copyright notation thereon. The views and conclusions contained herein are those of the authors and should not be interpreted as necessarily representing the official policies or endorsements, either expressed or implied, of the Air Force Office of Scientific Research or the U.S. Government.

References

1. G. J. Simmons, "The prisoner's problem and the subliminal channel," in *Proc. of CRYPTO'83*, 1984, pp. 51–67.
2. Herodotus, *The Histories*, Penguin Books, London, 1996, translated by Aubrey de Sélincourt.
3. R. J. Anderson and F. A. P. Petitcolas, "On the limits of steganography," *IEEE J. of Selected Areas in Communications*, vol. 16, no. 4, pp. 474–481, 1998.
4. C. E. Shannon, "communications theory of secrecy systems," *Bell System technical Journal*, vol. 28, pp. 656–715, 1954.
5. R. J. Anderson, "Stretching the limits of steganography," in *Proc. on the First Workshop on Information Hiding*, 1996, vol. 1174 of *Springer Lecture Notes in Computer Science*, pp. 39–48.
6. C. Cachin, "An information-theoretic model for steganography," in *Proc. on the Second Workshop on Information Hiding*, 1998, vol. 1525 of *Springer Lecture Notes in Computer Science*, pp. 306–318.
7. P. Sallee, "Model based steganography," in *Int. Workshop on Digital Watermarking*, T. Kalker, I. J. Cox, and Y. M. Ro, Eds., 2004, vol. 2939 of *Springer Lecture Notes in Computer Science*, pp. 154–167.
8. D. Slepian and J. K. Wolf, "Noiseless coding of correlated information sources," *IEEE Trans. on Information Theory*, vol. IT-19, no. 4, pp. 471–480, 1973.
9. R. E. Blahut, *Principles and Practice of Information theory*, Addison-Wesley, 1987.
10. D. J. C. MacKay, *Information Theory, Inference and Learning Algorithms*, Cambridge University Press, 2003.
11. I. J. Cox, M. L. Miller, and A. L. McKellips, "Watermarking as communications with side information," *Proc. IEEE*, vol. 87, pp. 1127–1141, July 1999.
12. J. Chou, S. S. Pradhan, and K. Ramchandran, "On the duality between distributed source coding and data hiding," in *Proc. Thirty-third Asilomar Conference on Signals, Systems, and Computers*, Pacific Grove, CA, USA, Oct. 1999, vol. 2, pp. 1503–1507.
13. B. Chen and G. W. Wornell, "An information-theoretic approach to the design of robust digital watermarking systems," in *Proc. IEEE Int. Conf. on Acoustics, Speech, and Signal Processing*, Phoenix, Arizona, USA, March 1999, vol. 4, pp. 2061–2064.
14. M. L. Miller, G. J. Doërr, and I. J. Cox, "Dirty-paper trellis codes for watermarking," in *Proc. IEEE Int. Conf. on Image Processing*, Rochester, New York, USA, Sept. 2002, vol. 2, pp. 129–132.

15. M. L. Miller, G. J. Doërr, and I. J. Cox, "Applying informed coding and embedding to design a robust high-capacity watermark," *IEEE Trans. Image Processing*, vol. 13, pp. 792–807, June 2004.
16. S. S. Pradhan and K. Ramchandran, "Distributed source coding using syndromes (DISCUS): Design and construction," in *Proc. of the 1999 IEEE Data Compression Conference*, 1999.
17. S. S. Pradhan and K. Ramchandran, "Distributed source coding using syndromes (DISCUS): Design and construction," 2003, vol. 49, pp. 626–643.
18. M. Costa, "Writing on dirty paper," *IEEE Trans. Inform. Theory*, vol. 29, pp. 439–441, May 1983.
19. C. Heegard and A. El Gamal, "On the capacity of a computer memory with defects," *IEEE Trans. on Information Theory*, vol. 29, 1983.
20. J. Fridrich, M. Goljan, and D. Soukal, "Perturbed quantization steganography with wet paper codes," in *ACM Multimedia Workshop*, 2004.
21. C-K Chan, L. M. Cheng, K-C Leung, and S-L Li, "Image hiding based on block difference," in *8th Int. Conf. on Control, Automation, Robotics and Vision*, 2004.

On the Existence of Perfect Stegosystems

Valery Korzhik[1], Guillermo Morales-Luna[2,*], and Moon Ho Lee[1,**]

[1] Department of Information and Communication at Chonbuk,
National University, Korea
moonho@chonbuk.ac.kr
[2] Computer Science, CINVESTAV-IPN, Mexico City, Mexico
gmorales@cs.cinvestav.mx

Abstract. There are several steganography techniques (e.g. linguistic or least significant bit embedding) that provide security but no robustness against an active adversary. On the other hand it is rather well known that the spread-spectrum based technique is robust against an active adversary but it seems to be insecure against a statistical detection of stegosignal. We prove in this paper that actually this is not the case and that there exists an stegosystem that is asymptotically both secure to statistical detection and robust against a jamming of stegosignal by an active adversary. We call such stegosystems *quasiperfect* whereas we call them *perfect* if in addition the data rate of secret information is asymptotically constant. We prove that perfect stegosystems do not exist for both blind and informed decoders. Some examples using the simplex and the Reed-Muller codes jointly with stegosystems are given.

Keywords: Stegosystem, Security, Robustness, Correlator, Error Probability, Relative Entropy, Error Correction Codes, Reed-Muller Codes.

1 Introduction

Steganography (SG) is the information hiding technique that embeds the hidden information into an innocent *cover message* (CM) under the conditions that the CM is not corrupted significantly and that it is not even detected the fact that the additional information is present into the CM. There are several examples of secure SG systems.

The general way to design them is the following: find some elements at the CM that do not affect its quality and that are uniformly distributed; then replace these elements by the ciphertext obtained after a perfect encryption of additional information [1].

In *linguistic steganography* it is possible to find some words in the meaningful text that have collocation-proven synonyms and then replace them by equivalent synonyms according to some key-dependent rule [2]. A common SG technique

---

* Dr. Morales-Luna acknowledges the support of Mexican Conacyt.
** Dr. Korzhik and Dr. Lee are supported by an University IT Research Center Project granted by the Korean Ministry of Information and Communication.

M. Barni et al. (Eds.): IWDW 2005, LNCS 3710, pp. 30–38, 2005.

is the so called *least significant bit embedding* (LSB), in which case the LSB's are replaced by ciphertext taking into account that the magnitude of CM noises is comparable to that of LSB and the embedding will not cause remarkable difference from CM. If the length of the embedded bit sequence is enough small, with respect to the length of the CM, then the detection of the SG signal presence is very hard [3]. However these SG systems have a common defect: they are not robust against an active adversary. In fact the additional secret information can be easily removed by a randomization of either the synonyms or the LSB without any additional corruption of the CM.

In order to prevent a removal of secret information by an active adversary it is possible to use the so called *spread-spectrum-based stegosystems* (SSS). Let us consider firstly uncoded SSS in which one bit of secret message is embedded into N samples of CM. It does not necessary mean that this message is embedded directly in "time" domain. This can be done after some "good transform" (for instance DCT) followed by the inverse of the "good transform" [4]. The sequence of samples of the stegosignal $\mathbf{C}_w = (C_w(n))_{n=1}^{N}$ can be thus presented as follows:

$$C_w(n) = C(n) + (-1)^b \sigma_w \pi_r(n), \quad n = 1, \ldots, N \tag{1}$$

where $\mathbf{C} = (C(n))_{n=1}^{N}$ is the CM, $b \in \{0,1\}$ is the bit acting as the hidden message, σ_w is the depth of the embedding, $\boldsymbol{\pi}_r = (\pi_r(n))_{n=1}^{N}$ is the reference sequence that should be kept in secret except to legal users and N is the length (base) of the spread-spectrum sequence. Indeed, $\boldsymbol{\pi}_r$ can be chosen as an i.i.d. zero mean Gaussian sequence with variance 1.

The quality of CM just after embedding can be estimated by the *signal-to-noise* ratio

$$\eta_w = \frac{\sigma_c^2}{\sigma_w^2} \tag{2}$$

where σ_c^2 is the variance of $\mathbf{C}$. We assume that an active attacker does only additive noise attack on SSS, e.g. the attacked by adversary SG signal is

$$C_w(n)' = C_w(n) + \varepsilon(n), \quad n = 1, \ldots, N \tag{3}$$

where $\boldsymbol{\varepsilon} = (\varepsilon(n))_{n=1}^{N}$ is any wide sense stationary zero mean additive noise. The quality of CM after both the embedding and the attack can be described by the corresponding signal-to-noise ratio

$$\eta_a = \frac{\sigma_c^2}{\sigma_w^2 + \sigma_\varepsilon^2} \tag{4}$$

where $\sigma_\varepsilon^2 = \mathrm{Var}\,(\boldsymbol{\varepsilon})$.

The method to estimate the security of SSS is considered in Section 2. Section 3 describes a robustness of SSS with blind decoder (including coded SSS) against additive noise attack. The notions of quasiperfect and perfect SG systems are introduced there and it is proved that there exist quasiperfect but no perfect SG systems. The results are then extended to SSS with informed decoder in Section 4. Section 5 contains some conclusion and poses resulting open problems.

2   An Estimation of SSS Security

Let us assume that the CM is a zero-mean wide-sense stationary i.i.d. Gaussian sequence with variance σ^2. We select the sequence $\boldsymbol{\pi}_r$ appearing in eq. (1) also as a zero-mean wide-sense stationary i.i.d. Gaussian sequence with variance 1. Then any adversary aiming to break the security of such SG system has to perform a hypothesis testing in order to decide which of the two hypothesis H_0 (absence of the SG message) or H_1 (presence of the SG message) is the true explanation for the observed measurements $\mathbf{C}_w = (C_w(n))_{n=1}^N$. Under the assumed conditions, both H_0 and H_1 correspond to Gaussian zero-mean sequences, but they have distinct variances, σ_c^2 and $\sigma_c^2 + \sigma_w^2$ respectively.

The efficiency of hypothesis testing can be characterized by two probabilities: the probability p_m of *missing* (when the SG signal has been embedded but the detector wrongly declares its absence) and the probability p_{fa} of *false alarm* (when the SG signal has not been embedded but the detector wrongly declares its presence). It is a very simple problem in statistics to distinguish two Gaussian zero-mean distributions with different variances. But for our purposes it is more convenient to use an information-theoretic measure of hypothesis testing, namely the *relative entropy*, $D\left(p_{H_0}||p_{H_1}\right)$, [1,5]. It follows from Information Theory [5] that, for any hypothesis testing rule, the following inequality holds:

$$p_{fa} \log\left(\frac{p_{fa}}{1-p_m}\right) + (1-p_{fa})\log\left(\frac{1-p_{fa}}{p_m}\right) \leq D\left(p_{H_0}||p_{H_1}\right) \qquad (5)$$

If we let $p_{fa} = 0$ then we get from relation (5)

$$p_m \geq 2^{-D\left(p_{H_0}||p_{H_1}\right)} \qquad (6)$$

We can see from (5) and (6) that the SG system will be *unconditional secure* if $D\left(p_{H_0}||p_{H_1}\right) = 0$ (this fact has been remarked in [1]).

In the case of continuous independent samples, the relative entropy can be presented as

$$D\left(p_{H_0}||p_{H_1}\right) = N \int_{-\infty}^{\infty} p_{H_0}(x) \log\left(\frac{p_{H_0}(x)}{p_{H_1}(x)}\right) dx \qquad (7)$$

where $p_{H_i} : x \mapsto p_{H_i}(x)$, $i = 0, 1$, are corresponding probability normal density functions $N(0, \sigma_c^2)$ and $N(0, \sigma_c^2 + \sigma_w^2)$. Substituting these probability distributions into (7) we get after simple transforms

$$D\left(p_{H_0}||p_{H_1}\right) = 0.77N\left[\ln\left(1 + \eta_w^{-1}\right) - (1 + \eta_w)^{-1}\right] \qquad (8)$$

where η_w is given by eq. (2). For large signal-to-noise ratios η_w we may approximate (8) as

$$D\left(p_{H_0}||p_{H_1}\right) \approx 0.77\frac{N}{2\eta_w^2} = 0.38N\eta_w^{-2} \qquad (9)$$

and consequently

$$\eta_w \approx 0.62 \sqrt{\frac{N}{D\left(p_{H_0} \| p_{H_1}\right)}} \tag{10}$$

We can see from (10) that the SG system can provide any desired value of asymptotic security $D\left(p_{H_0} \| p_{H_1}\right) > 0$ whenever $\eta_w \to \infty$ as $N \to \infty$ (this fact is consistent with our intention because the larger is N the more information has an attacker to test hypothesis and, in order to compensate its growth, it is necessary to increase η_w or, equivalently, to decrease the depth of embedding σ_w since the variance σ_c^2 of CM is kept fixed).

3   Robustness of SSS with Blind Decoder

3.1   Uncoded SSS

We consider the robustness of SSS against *additive noise attack* just because the analysis of any other attack is a rather intractable problem. This attack can be modeled by eq. (3) and we will estimate the quality of CM after both embedding and attack by the signal-to-noise ratio given in (4). Namely, the *correlation detector* will be used as a blind decoder. The reason to avoid other types of blind detectors is that the correlator is robust against any additive noise attack if SS signal is used and then an upper bound for the error probability can be taken for granted.

A decision $\tilde{b}$ about the embedded bit b is taken (by any legal user) as follows

$$\Lambda = \sum_{n=1}^{N} C_w(n)' \pi_r(n) \; \Rightarrow \; \tilde{b} = \begin{cases} 0 \text{ if } \Lambda \geq 0 \\ 1 \text{ otherwise} \end{cases} \tag{11}$$

In order to prove the formula for the probability of error $p_e = \text{Prob}\left(\tilde{b} \neq b\right)$ we apply the Central Limit Theorem to the sum in (11) assuming that π_r is an i.i.d. sequence. Then we get for $b = 0$ (without any loss of generality) the following equation for the probability of error

$$p_e = \text{Prob}\left(\tilde{b} \neq 0\right) = Q\left(\frac{E\left(\Lambda | b = 0\right)}{\sqrt{\text{Var}\left(\Lambda | b = 0\right)}}\right) \tag{12}$$

where $Q : x \mapsto Q(x) = \frac{1}{\sqrt{2\pi}} \int_x^{+\infty} e^{-\frac{t^2}{2}} \, dt$ is the well known [6] Q-function. After a simple but tedious work we get

$$E(\Lambda) = N\sigma_w \quad , \quad \text{Var}\left(\Lambda\right) = N\left(\sigma_c^2 + \sigma_\varepsilon^2 + 2\sigma_w^2\right) \tag{13}$$

By substituting (13) into (12) we obtain

$$p_e = Q\left(\frac{\sqrt{N}\sigma_w}{\sqrt{\sigma_c^2 + \sigma_\varepsilon^2 + 2\sigma_w^2}}\right) \tag{14}$$

Since the inequality $\sigma_\varepsilon^2 \gg \sigma_w^2$ holds as a rather general rule, even more in asymptotic terms, we get from (14)

$$p_e \approx Q\left(\frac{\sqrt{N}\sigma_w}{\sqrt{\sigma_c^2 + \sigma_\varepsilon^2}}\right) \tag{15}$$

In order to provide an appropriated quality of CM after attack, the value η_a given at (4) has to be lower bounded by some threshold $\tilde{\eta}_a$, e.g. it should be $\eta_a \geq \tilde{\eta}_a$. This, together with (4) and taking into account that $\eta_w \to \infty$ as $N \to \infty$, as it was shown in previous section, we get $\sigma_\varepsilon^2 \leq \frac{\sigma_c^2}{\tilde{\eta}_a}$. And substitution of this inequality into (15) gives

$$p_e \leq Q\left(\sqrt{\frac{N\tilde{\eta}_a}{\eta_w(1 + \tilde{\eta}_a)}}\right) \approx Q\left(\sqrt{\frac{N}{\eta_w}}\right) \tag{16}$$

the last approximation follows from the common condition $\tilde{\eta}_a \gg 1$. By substituting (10) into (16) one obtains $p_e \leq Q\left(1.27\left(N\,D\left(p_{H_0}\|p_{H_1}\right)\right)^{\frac{1}{4}}\right)$. From last equation it can be seen that for any given value $D\left(p_{H_0}\|p_{H_1}\right) > 0$ (which according to (5), (6) corresponds to a security level (p_m, p_{fa})) the probability of error tends to zero as N increases, $p_e \to 0$ as $N \to \infty$. This means that such SG system is *asymptotically both secure and robust*. We will say that it is a *quasiperfect* system in order to distinguish with the notion of *perfect* SG systems which should have in addition a *constant data rate* whereas our system has a data rate $R \to 0$ as $N \to \infty$.

Up to now, we have shown that a quasiperfect SG system exist under assumption of additive noise attack and a Gaussian wide sense stationary i.i.d. model of CM. (The key remark in support of this statement is the fact that relative entropy as given by (9) decreases *inversely proportionally to the square of the signal-to-noise ratio* η_w).

In order to check the existence of perfect SG systems, we must consider SG systems with coding (in the same way as in ordinary communication systems, where, due to Shannon's Theorem, one has $p_e \to 0$ as $N \to \infty$ for any constant R whenever $R < C$, being C the channel capacity.)

3.2   Coded SSS

In this case an embedding procedure can be presented as

$$C_w(n) = C(n) + (-1)^{b_{in}}\sigma_w\pi_r(n), \quad n = 1, \ldots, N$$

with the connotations given as in eq. (1), where now b_{in} denotes the n-th bit of the i-th codeword of length N. We will restrict our attention to binary linear systematic (N, K, d)-codes varying i in the interval $\{1, 2, \ldots, 2^K\}$. In this situation the blind correlation detector takes a decision about the embedding of the j-th codeword by making

$$j = \operatorname*{Arg\,Max}_{1 < i < 2^K} \sum_{n=1}^{N} C'_w(n)(-1)^{b_{in}} \sigma_w \pi_r(n)$$

where $\mathbf{C}'_w = \mathbf{C}_w + \varepsilon$ is the attacked signal.

Using the well known union bound for the probability of block error p_{be} [6] and the fact that $Q(\sqrt{x})$ is dominated as $Q(\sqrt{x}) \leq \exp(-x/2)$, from (10) and (16) there results

$$p_{be} = (2^K - 1)Q\left(\sqrt{\frac{d(N)}{\eta_w(N)}}\right) \leq \exp\left(-\frac{d(N)}{2\eta_w(N)} + RN\ln 2\right)$$
$$= \exp\left(-\frac{d(N)\sqrt{D}}{1.24\sqrt{N}} + RN\ln 2\right) \tag{17}$$

Substituting the lower Plotkin's bound for the minimum code distance [7],

$$d(N) \leq \frac{N(1-R)}{2}, \tag{18}$$

into (17) we get

$$p_{be} \leq \exp\left(-(1-R)\frac{\sqrt{ND}}{1.24} + RN\ln 2\right) \tag{19}$$

The relation (19) shows that in order to get an exponential decreasing of p_{be} to zero as $N \to \infty$, the code rate R has to be upper bounded as $R < \frac{\sqrt{D}}{1.24\ln 2\ \sqrt{N}} \approx 1.16\sqrt{D/N}$, and from this one can see that $R \to 0$ as $N \to \infty$, which disagrees with Shannon's theorem for ordinary (not secure) communication systems. Thus we can assert that *perfect SG systems* (i.e. secure and robust with constant data rate) *do not exist* at least for the embedding in a direct additive manner. Nevertheless we can use coded SG systems in order to send multi-bit secret messages. Let us consider some low rate families of error correcting codes that are applied more conveniently to the current situation.

3.3   Simplex Codes

The *simplex* (i.e. dual to Hamming) codes have the following parameters [7]:

$$N = 2^m - 1, \quad K = m, \quad d(N) = 2^{m-1}, \quad R = \frac{m}{N} \tag{20}$$

which, substituted into (17), give

$$p_{be} \leq \exp\left(-\frac{2^{\frac{m}{2}-1}}{1.24}\sqrt{D} + 0.69\,m\right) \tag{21}$$

Example. Let us fix $D = 0.1$ (then $p_m \geq 2^{-D} \approx 0.933$ if $p_{fa} = 0$ according to (6)). If we take $m < 14$ in (21), then it follows the trivial result $p_{be} \leq 1$. For $m = 14$ we obtain $p_{be} \leq 1.3 \times 10^{-3}$ and the code rate 8.5×10^{-4}.

3.4 Reed-Muller Codes

These codes have parameters [7]:

$$N = 2^m \ , \ K = \sum_{i=1}^{r} \binom{m}{i} \ , \ d(N) = 2^{m-r} \ , \ m \in \mathbb{N} \ , \ m \geq 3 \qquad (22)$$

which, substituted into (17), give

$$p_{be} \leq \exp\left(-\frac{2^{\frac{m}{2}-r}}{1.24} \sqrt{D} + \ln 2 \sum_{i=1}^{r} \binom{m}{i} \right) \qquad (23)$$

Example. If we take as before $D = 0.1$ and $m < 24$ we get the trivial bound $p_{be} \leq 1$. For $m = 24$ we obtain $K = 300$, $R = 1.8 \times 10^{-5}$ and, from (23), $p_{be} \leq 10^{-24}$. Although the data rate is very small, we may transmit both in a reliable and secure way 300 bits.

4 Robustness of SSS with Informed Decoder

4.1 Uncoded SSS

In this situation we have the same embedding model as (1), the same additive noise attack as in (3) but a decision $\tilde{b}$ about the embedded bit b is taken in a different manner than in (11) because the CM $\mathbf{C}$ is known at the decoder. Thus for an informed decoder we have the following decision rule:

$$\Lambda = \sum_{n=1}^{N} (C_w(n)' - C(n)) \, \pi_r(n) \ \Rightarrow \ \tilde{b} = \begin{cases} 0 \text{ if } \Lambda \geq 0 \\ 1 \text{ otherwise} \end{cases}$$

Proceeding in the same manner as when proving the relation (15), we get for an informed decoder the error probability $p_e \approx Q\left(\sqrt{N} \frac{\sigma_w}{\sigma_e} \right)$. Also using a lower bound $\tilde{\eta}_a$ to the signal-to-noise ratio after attack η_a as was done before, we can express last relation as $p_e \approx Q\left(\sqrt{N \frac{\tilde{\eta}_a}{\eta_w}} \right)$ and using (10) it results

$$p_e \approx Q\left(1.27 \, (N\,D)^{\frac{1}{4}} \, \tilde{\eta}_a^{\frac{1}{2}} \right) \qquad (24)$$

and from here it follows that $p_e \to 0$ as $N \to \infty$ in a similar way as for the case of a blind decoder and even faster convergence due to the coefficient $\tilde{\eta}_a \gg 1$.

4.2   Coded SSS

Using error correcting codes with parameters (N, K, d) and the union bounding we have

$$p_{be} \leq \exp\left(-\frac{d(N)\tilde{\eta}_a\sqrt{D}}{1.24\sqrt{N}} + RN\ln 2\right) \tag{25}$$

Substituting Plotkin's bound (18), we get $p_{be} \leq \exp\left(-\frac{\sqrt{ND}(1-R)\tilde{\eta}_a}{1.24} + RN\ln 2\right)$.
Then the condition of exponential decreasing of p_{be} to zero as $N \to \infty$ results in the following upper bound for data rate $R < 1.16\sqrt{\frac{D\tilde{\eta}_a}{N}}$ and this inequality claims that it is *impossible to design a SG system even with informed decoder that would be perfect*. But an implementation of finite length error correcting codes gives much better results than for the case of a blind decoder. In fact, for simplex codes we have from (20) and (25),

$$p_{be} \leq \exp\left(-\frac{2^{\frac{m}{2}-1}\sqrt{D\eta_a^2}}{1.24} + 0.69m\right) \tag{26}$$

For Reed-Muller codes we get from (22) and (25)

$$p_{be} \leq \exp\left(-\frac{2^{\frac{m}{2}-r}\sqrt{D\eta_a^2}}{1.24} + \ln 2 \sum_{i=1}^{r}\binom{m}{i}\right) \tag{27}$$

Example. If we take $D = 0.1$, $\tilde{\eta}_a = 20$ then we get for the simplex code with parameter $m = 4$, from (26), $p_{be} \leq 7.1 \times 10^{-4}$. For Reed-Muller code with parameters $m = 14$, $r = 3$, $K = 469$, $\tilde{\eta}_a = 85$ (that is more common in practice) we get, from (27), $p_{be} \leq 10^{-7}$.

5   Conclusions

The main contribution of our paper is the proof that it is possible to design both secure and robust SG systems against active adversary (we called such SG systems quasiperfect ones). Naturally, we restrict our consideration by some conditions. First of all, we model the CM as a wide-sense stationary i.i.d. Gaussian process. Real CM (such as images for instance) may be approximated by the proposed model in the frequency domain, except for a stationary property. We remark that this model can be very close to real situations whenever the SG systems based on noisy channels are considered, since then the Gaussian stegosignal is camouflaged by a Gaussian channel noise [8]. Besides, we considered only an additive noise attack and it is an open problem to develop this theory to other types of attacks. But we conjecture that the existence of quasiperfect SG systems can be also proved for other attacks. We have proved also that in contrast to Shannon's theory, there do not exist SG systems that are simultaneously secure, robust and with constant data rate (which we have called perfect SG systems).

Our statement is based on the upper union bound that seems to fail but it is known that this bound gives a good approximation of small probabilities of incorrect decoding in asymptotic case.

Evidently the formula for the relative entropy (9) may fail to hold for any arbitrary model of CM and an arbitrary embedding method but in any case it seems to be unlikely that relative entropy is constant as the number N of samples increases. If we agree that relative entropy has increased as N increases then it would require to increase $\eta_w(N)$ with N in order to provide asymptotic security to the SG system. On the other hand if we take an intermediate part of eq. (17) and substitute there Plotkin's bound it is obtained $p_{be} \leq \exp\left(-\frac{(1-R)N}{4\eta_w(N)} + RN\ln 2\right)$. From here, it follows that the code rate R should be upper bounded as $R < (2.77\eta_w(N) + 1)^{-1}$. This implies that for any function of increasing $\eta_w(N)$ with respect to N the code rate R decreases and hence the SG system cannot be asymptotically perfect.

We have also proved in the current paper that although an informed decoder does not allow to get perfect SG system, the use of this kind of decoder improves significantly the efficiency of coded SG systems. It would be very interesting to consider an informed coder based on the Improved Spread Spectrum technique (ISS) [4] because this system is closer to practice. However ISS does not give a Gaussian model of the watermarked signal even for both Gaussian CM and embedding. Therefore it is an interesting open problem to estimate the security of such SG systems.

References

1. Cachin, C.: An information-theoretic model for steganography. In: International Workshop on Information Hiding 1998, Springer LNCS (1998) 306–318
2. Bolshakov, S.: A method of linguistic steganography based on collocation-proven synonymy. In: International Workshop on Information Hiding 2004. Volume 3200., Dresden, Germany, Springer LNCS (2004) 13–23
3. Damitrescu, S., Wu, X., Wang, Z.: Detection of LSB steganography via sample pair analysis. In: International Workshop on Information Hiding 2002. Volume 2578., Springer LNCS (2002) 355–372
4. Malvar, H.S., Florencio, D.: Improved spread spectrum: A new modulation technique for robust watermarking. IEEE Transaction on Signal Processing **51** (2003) 898–905
5. Cover, T., Thomas, J.: Elements of Information Theory. John Wiley and Sons, Inc. (1991)
6. Proakis, J.: Digital Communications, Fourth Edition. Mc Graw Hill (2001)
7. MacWilliams, F., Sloan, N.: The Theory of Error Correcting Codes. Bell Labs. (1991)
8. Korjik, V., Morales-Luna, G.: Information hiding through noisy channels. In: International Workshop on Information Hiding 2004. Volume 2137., Springer LNCS (2001) 42–50

Towards Multi-class Blind Steganalyzer for JPEG Images

Tomáš Pevný[1] and Jessica Fridrich[2]

[1] Department of Computer Science
[2] Department of Electrical and Computer Engineering,
SUNY Binghamton, Binghamton, NY 13902–6000

Abstract. In this paper, we use the previously proposed calibrated DCT features [9] to construct a Support Vector Machine classifier for JPEG images capable of recognizing which steganographic algorithm was used for embedding. This work also constitutes a more detailed evaluation of the performance of DCT features as in [9] only a linear classifier was used. The DCT features transformed using Principal Component Analysis enable an interesting visualization of different stego programs in a three-dimensional space. This paper demonstrates that, at least under some simplifying assumptions in which the effects of double compression are ignored, it is possible to reliably classify stego images to their embedding techniques. The classifier is capable of generalizing to previously unseen techniques.

1 Introduction

The goal of steganography is to hide the very presence of communication by hiding messages in innocuous looking objects, such as digital media files. The original object, also called the cover object, is slightly modified to obtain the stego object that carries the secret message. In a symmetric communication scheme, the embedding process depends on a secret (stego key) shared between both communicating parties. The main requirement of steganalysis is undetectability of the hidden data by an unauthorized party who knows all details of the embedding mechanism and the source of cover objects but does not have the stego key (Kerckhoffs' principle). The concept of steganographic security (undetectability) was formalized, for example, in [2,5,25,14].

Methods for discovering the presence of hidden messages and determining their attributes belong to steganalysis. In practice, a steganographic scheme is considered secure if no existing steganalytic attack can be used to distinguish between cover and stego objects with success better than random guessing [6].

Steganalytic methods can be roughly divided into two categories. The first category is formed by methods targeted to a specific embedding technique, capitalizing on the assumption that we know the embedding algorithm [10]. The second category is formed by blind approaches in which the knowledge of the embedding algorithm is not assumed [9,8,3,4]. Instead, most blind approaches

M. Barni et al. (Eds.): IWDW 2005, LNCS 3710, pp. 39–53, 2005.

assume that one can somehow characterize all "natural images" using an appropriate set of features that should be as sensitive to steganographic modifications as possible. A classifier is then built to distinguish in the feature space between natural images and stego images.

As one can expect, targeted approaches should provide better reliability and accuracy than blind approaches. Targeted methods range from very specific simple ideas that pertain to a specific implementation to more general methods that address a general embedding paradigm, such as LSB embedding [10,7], and finally to methods that can be easily adjusted to address a very large spectrum of data hiding methods (e.g., detection of additive signals, such as ±1 embedding [22,16,15]). The disadvantage of targeted methods is that their design cannot be automatized and new techniques might have to be developed each time a new steganographic methodology appears. This problem of extensibility is removed by blind approaches.

From a certain point of view, however, there is no difference between targeted and blind approaches as they both benefit from progress in the other. In fact, in each targeted method one or more quantities (distinguishing statistics [10]) are calculated, some with a definite meaning, e.g., an estimate of the message length, and then thresholded to reach a decision about the presence of hidden message. It is certainly possible to add such distinguishing statistics to blind steganalyzers and further improve their performance. Because distinguishing statistics are designed to be sensitive to embedding changes of certain kind, they also provide guiding principles for constructing good features. This was the case with features designed for DCT coefficients of JPEG files [9]. The idea of calibration, which was originally invented for targeted attacks against F5 [10] and OutGuess [10], was adopted for construction of calibrated features that are sensitive to embedding modifications but exhibit less variation from image to image. Based on the results quoted in [9,17] and the results shown in Section 3, classifiers based on these features currently achieve the most reliable and accurate performance for blind steganalysis of JPEG images. This is why they were chosen for this study.

The goal of this paper is to construct a classifier for JPEG images capable of not only distinguishing cover images from stego images but also assigning stego images to known JPEG steganographic techniques. Such a tool is essential for steganalysis in the wide sense (forensic steganalysis) whose main goal is to recover the hidden data. Obviously, the first step is to identify the stego algorithm used to embed the data. In this paper, we use the calibrated DCT based features [9] calculated directly in the DCT domain to construct a Support Vector Machine (SVM) classifier. We focus on steganalysis of JPEG images because the JPEG format is by far the most common image format in use today. As our goal is to investigate the fundamental issues associated with building such classifier rather than constructing a ready-to-use application, we constrained ourselves to a database of test images with known processing history and origin. This gives us the possibility to better understand the influence of processing, analyze the outliers, and identify the limitations of the proposed approach. Also, in this study we chose to ignore the difficult issue of double compression by presenting the cover images compressed with the same quality factor as the one used for the stego images.

In the next section, first we briefly discuss previous art in blind steganalysis and the DCT-based features. In Section 3, we give the implementation details of SVMs used in this paper, we discuss various issues associated with training and testing procedures, and describe the image database. Section 4 starts with building two-class SVMs for individual steganographic techniques. We also include a comparison of the performance of DCT features with wavelet-based features [8] on the most popular JPEG stego programs. The section continues with an attempt to visualize the stego programs in the feature space transformed using the Principal Component Transformation. Then, we give experimental results obtained from a universal steganalyzer designed to distinguish between two classes of cover and stego images. Finally, at the end of Section 4 we present and analyze the results of experiments with the multi-class steganalyzer. The paper is concluded in Section 5.

2   Blind JPEG Steganalysis

The idea to use a trained classifier to detect data hiding was first introduced in a paper by Avcibas et al. [3]. In this paper, image quality metrics were proposed as features and the method was tested on several robust watermarking algorithms as well as LSB embedding. Avcibas et al. [4] later proposed a different set of features based on binary similarity measures between the LSB plane and the second LSB plane capitalizing on the fact that most steganographic schemes use the LSB of image elements as the information-carrying entity. Farid [8] constructed the features from higher-order moments of distribution of wavelet coefficients and their linear prediction errors from several high-frequency sub-bands. The same authors also showed that SVMs generally provide better performance as classifiers compared to linear classifiers. Other authors have investigated the problem of blind steganalysis using trained classifiers [23,11].

The steganalyzer described in this paper is based on features obtained from the DCT coefficients as described in [9]. Calculating the features directly in the JPEG domain provides certain attractive features. First, we expect the biggest sensitivity for features calculated in a domain in which the embedding changes are lumped — the DCT domain. Second, targeted analysis showed us the benefit of calibration, which is the process of estimating the macroscopic properties of the cover image from a slightly geometrically deformed decompressed stego image recompressed with the same quantization matrix.

The DCT features are constructed from 23 vector functionals f of three types — 17 first order functionals, 4 second order functionals, and 2 blockiness functionals. The first order functionals are histograms of 5 lowest-frequency AC DCT modes, the global DCT histogram, and 11 dual histograms (distribution of a certain value d among all 64 DCT modes for $d = \{-5, \ldots, 5\}$). The higher order functionals capture the inter-block dependency of DCT coefficients. They include the variation of coefficients (sum of absolute values of differences of DCT coefficients from neighboring blocks) and 3 quantities derived from co-occurrence matrices. The two blockiness functionals are the sum of discontinuities along 8×8 block boundaries and they are also the only functionals calculated in the spatial domain.

The values of the functionals $f_1, f_2, \ldots, f_{23}$ for the cover image are estimated from a slightly geometrically deformed (e.g., cropped by a few pixels) stego image recompressed using the same quantization table. Denoting the estimated functionals as $\hat{f}_1, \hat{f}_2, \ldots, \hat{f}_{23}$, the final features are calculated as the L1 norm $\|f_i - \hat{f}_i\|$ between the functional f calculated from the stego image and the same functional calculated from the cropped and recompressed stego image. The logic behind this choice for features is the following. The cropping and recompression produce a "calibrated" image with most macroscopic features similar to the original cover image. This is because the cropped stego image is perceptually similar to the cover image and thus its DCT coefficients should have approximately the same statistical properties as the cover image. The cropping is important because the 8×8 grid of recompression "does not see" the previous JPEG compression and thus the obtained DCT coefficients are not as influenced by previous quantization (and embedding) in the DCT domain. One can think of the cropped / recompressed image as an approximation to the cover image or as a side-information.

3   Constructing Classifiers

3.1   2-Class Support Vector Machines

Support Vector Machines are the tool of choice for steganography classifiers [8,17]. However, in most papers dealing with steganalysis, the authors rarely provide implementation details. We strongly believe that providing the details is necessary to enable fair independent verification of the reported results by peers. Thus, in this section, we describe all important elements of our realization of classifiers using SVMs.

Despite the advantages and simplicity of linear Support Vector Machines (SVM), in most applications, they are not sufficient, since we usually deal with noisy data in non linearly separable regions. SVMs with nonlinear kernels and the penalty parameter C can deal both with nonlinearity and outliers. The price of this extension is that before the training can start, we have to determine the penalty parameter C and the kernel and its parameters. There exist many different kernels that can even be combined together. In our preliminary experiments, we tried the linear, Gaussian, polynomial, and exponential kernels. As the Gaussian kernel ($\exp(-\gamma \|x - y\|^2)$) gave us the best overall results, we used it in all experiments described in this paper. The Gaussian kernel has one parameter γ controlling its width. The extended SVM capable of dealing with outliers has an additional penalty parameter C. These parameters affect the overall performance of the classifier and are highly data/problem dependent. Following the guide [12], the parameters were determined through a search on a multiplicative grid $(\gamma, C) \in \left\{ (2^i, 2^j) \mid i \in \{-5, \ldots, 3\}, j \in \{-2, 9\} \right\}$ with 5-fold cross-validation.

This means that for each pair (γ, C) the training set was divided into 5 subsets. Four of them were used for training and the remaining fifth subset was used to calculate the validation error. This was repeated five times for each subset. The validation errors from each subset were averaged, to obtain an estimate of the performance on unknown data. The final values of the parameters (C, γ) were determined by the least average validation error. After determining the parameters, we used the whole training set to train the SVM. We note that we have implemented the SVM ourselves and did not use any publicly available library.

Data preprocessing has a major influence on the performance of the SVM. We tested two different preprocessings — one consisting only of scaling and the second one of Principle Component Transformation (PCT) and subsequent scaling. Our experiments were inconclusive as to which preprocessing was better. Although the error on the training set was usually lower when the PCT was used, the error on the testing set was higher. Therefore, we chose scaling as the only preprocessing step in all experiments described in this paper. As shown in Section 4.2, the PCT is useful for visualizing the features.

By scaling, we understand that all elements of the feature vector were linearly scaled to the interval $[-1, +1]$. The scaling coefficients are always derived from the training set. When the n-fold cross-validation is employed, coefficients are computed on $n - 1$ subsets used for training to estimate the validation error of the remaining subset.

3.2 Multi-class Support Vector Machines

Support vector machines are naturally able to classify only 2 classes. There exist various extensions to enable the SVMs to handle more then two classes. They can be roughly divided into two groups − "all-together" methods and methods based on binary classifiers. A good survey with comparisons is the paper by Hsu [13] where the authors conclude that methods based on binary classifiers are better for practical applications. We tested the "Max Wins" and Directed Acyclic Graph (DAG) SVMs [19]. Both methods employ $\frac{n(n-1)}{2}$ binary classifiers for every pair of classes (n is the number of classes into which we wish to classify). Since both approaches had very similar performance in our tests, we only present the results from the "Max Wins" classifier.

In the Max Wins method, the sample that we want to classify is presented to all classifers and the histogram of their answers is created. The class corresponding to the highest peak is selected as the target class.

3.3 Database of Images

For our experiments, we created a database containing more than 35000 images obtained from 3436 different source images taken by various digital cameras all originally stored in the raw or lossless TIFF format (Nikon D100, Canon G2, Olympus Camedia 765, Kodak DC 290, Canon PowerShot S40, and images from Nikon D100 scaled by a factor of 2.9 and 3.76). For each image, we embedded a random binary stream of different lengths using five different algorithms —

Table 1. Training set for the 2-class SVMs. The leftmost column denotes the particular SVM, the remaining columns contain the number of randomly chosen images in the training set.

Machine	cover	OutGuess 100% /50% /25%	F5 100% / 50% / 25%	MB1 100% / 50% / 25%	MB2 30%
cover×F5	2700	—	900 / 900 / 900	—	—
cover×MB1	2700	—	—	900 / 900 / 900	—
cover×MB2	2700	—	—	—	2700
cover×OutGuess	2700	900 / 900 / 900	—	—	—
cover×stego	2700	225 / 225 / 225	225 / 225 / 225	225 / 225 / 225	675
MB1×F5	—	—	900 / 900 / 900	900 / 900 / 900	—
MB1×MB2	—	—	—	900 / 900 / 900	2700
MB1×OutGuess	—	900 / 900 / 900	—	900 / 900 / 900	—
MB2×F5	—	—	900 / 900 / 900	—	2700
MB2×OutGuess	—	900 / 900 / 900	—	—	2700
OutGuess×F5	—	900 / 900 / 900	900 / 900 / 900	—	—

OutGuess ver 0.2 [20], F5 [24], MB1, MB2 [21], and JP Hide&Seek [1]. For F5, MB1, and OutGuess we created three different versions of each image with different lengths of the embedded message — 100%, 50%, 25% of the maximal capacity for a given image and embedding algorithm. For MB2, we embedded only one message of length equivalent to 30% of the capacity of MB1 to minimize the cases when the deblocking algorithm fails. For JP Hide&Seek, in compliance with the directions provided by its author we inserted messages with length equal to 10% of the image size.

If we summarize our database, each raw image is present in 12 different forms — MB1 100%, MB1 50%, MB1 25%, MB2 30%, F5 100%, F5 50%, F5 25%, OutGuess 100%, OutGuess 50%, OutGuess 25%, JP Hide, and cover JPEG. All cover and stego images used the same quality factor of 75.

In the beginning of our experiments, we divided the images into two disjoint sets — the training and testing sets. The training subset contained 2900 images (referring to the unique source images). From this set we have randomly chosen the training sets (Table 1) used for determining the parameters of each SVM and for its training as described in Section 3.1. The testing subset consisted of the remaining 534 source images. By dividing the source images into two disjoint sets, we made sure that during training no images from the testing set were used in any of their forms.

In our experiments, we built various SVMs all of which were trained on randomly chosen images from the training set. Thus, it could happen that one image was present in the training set in several different forms (the same source image with different message lengths, embedded with different stego-algorithm, or of different sizes).

Table 1 summarizes the number of examples in the training sets used in our experiments.

4   Experimental Results

In this section, we present experimental results from our classifiers. Unless stated otherwise, all results were derived on samples from the testing set that were not used in any form during training.

4.1   Two-Class SVMs

We started our experiments by first constructing a set of two-class SVMs for distinguishing cover JPEG images from stego images embedded with a specific steganographic software. We construct such classifiers for both the DCT features and wavelet features [8] to obtain some performance comparison. The Matlab program for calculating the wavelet features was obtained from the authors' web site (http://www.cs.dartmouth.edu/~farid/research/steganography.html). Since the authors of [8] do not describe the configuration of their SVM, we determined the parameters ourselves as described in Section 3.1. The features were compared on four different tasks — distinguishing between cover images and one specific steganographic algorithm (F5, MB1, and OutGuess 0.2 embedded with 100%, 50%, and 25% messages, and MB2 embedded with 30% message of the MB1 capacity).

Although the wavelet features were originally proposed to be calculated from the luminance component only, it has later been shown that they benefit from considering the chrominance channels as well, which is especially true for detection of the F5 algorithm [24,18]. As we are interested in performance comparison also for grayscale images, which in general appears to be the worst case for steganalysis both in the DCT and spatial domains, in our experiments we calculated both feature sets only from the luminance part of JPEG images. Thus, there were

Table 2. Error on training and testing sets for wavelet and DCT features (default zero threshold for all machines). Each set includes an equal number of examples of cover and stego images. Due to the high computational load associated with training on the wavelet features, in this submission we only provide results for a smaller database cosisting of 800 training and 320 testing images. Results for the full database will appear in the final version.

Classifier	γ	C	Misclassification on train. set	Misclassification on test. set	False positives on train. set	False positives on test. set
DCT — cover×F5	0.5	64	1.29%	1.8%	0.59%	1.8%
DCT — cover×MB1	0.25	128	1.26%	1.6%	1.07%	1.4%
DCT — cover×MB2	0.5	64	1%	1.8%	1.3%	3.8%
DCT — cover×OutGuess	0.25	32	0.07%	1%	0.1%	0.2%
Wavelet — cover×F5	0.5	128	4.8%	24.6%	3.4%	17.2%
Wavelet — cover×MB1	0.0625	512	23.7%	34.2%	18.5%	22%
Wavelet — cover×MB2	0.03125	64	39.8%	40%	40%	42.4%
Wavelet — cover×OutGuess	0.25	256	3.26%	16.4%	1.7%	11.6%

total of 23 DCT features and 72 wavelet features. The composition of training examples for each particular SVM is given in Table 1.

The SVM parameters together with errors on the training and testing sets are shown in Table 2. We conclude that for grayscale JPEG images, the DCT features perform better than wavelet features. This is not surprising as the DCT features were built specifically for JPEG files while the wavelet features are more universal and can be used for steganographic methods that embed in any domain. The results are also compatible with the previously published evaluation of blind steganalyzers in [17] and the work [9]. Another conclusion we can draw is that the least detectable stego program among the tested algorithms is the MB2 algorithm (Model Based Steganography with deblocking). At 30% of capacity of MB1, the MB2 algorithm is detected in 98.2% cases with 3.8% false alarms. Comparing this with the results for MB2 reported for the same features with a linear classifier in [9], we see that the SVM classifier has markedly better performance. Another advantage of DCT features is that the training is faster because the features have lower dimension and better separability compared to the wavelet features.

4.2   Principal Component Analysis

We used the PCT to analyze the effective dimensionality of the DCT-based feature space. The features were computed from only 1073 images embedded with the maximal message length using OutGuess 0.2, F5, and MB1. Since there were only three eigenvalues with magnitude above 0.02, we could plot the features in a three-dimensional space and nicely visualize the clouds of feature points corresponding to different steganographic algorithms (Figure). This representation enables visual inspection and interpretation, which could be a useful forensic tool by itself.

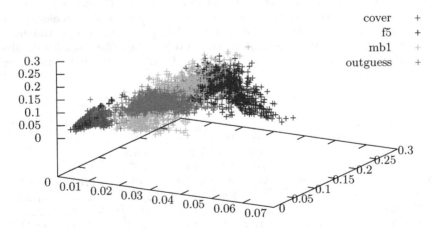

Fig. 1. First 3 coordinates with the highest variance after applying PCT to DCT features

4.3   Universal Machine

By universal, we mean a classifier able to classify images into two classes — cover and stego images. The training set for this machine is described in Table 1 in the row "cover×stego". The SVM was trained with parameters $\gamma = 0.25$, and $C = 512$ determined using the multiplicative grid search. The error on the training set was 1.44% (1.96% misclassification, 1.09% false positives). Table 3 covers the performance of the universal machine on all images from the testing set in our database. The number of images varies between algorithms because some algorithms fail on some images (e.g., blue sky images). The leftmost column contains the class (algorithm and relative size of the message) to which the examples belong. The remaining columns show the number and percentage of images recognized by the universal machine as cover and stego images for two choices of the threshold.

We see that the universal machine was able to generalize and detect images embedded with JP Hide as stego images even though it was not trained on such images. The second and the third columns of Table 3 show the performance of the universal machine with the default threshold 0. We can see very good detection (above 98%) for all methods for images with messages whose length is greater than 50% of the image capacity with the overall rate of false alarms at 3.5%. After adjusting the threshold from the default value 0 to 0.994593 in order to obtain less than 1% of overall false alarms (fourth and fifth columns), the overall false positive rate lowers to 1.3% and the detection accuracy of stego-images with message length greater than 50% remains at a very good level but the performance on stego images with small messages is worsened. This is especially true for F5, which we attribute to the effects of matrix embedding that improves

Table 3. Performance of the universal machine with the default threshold 0 (second and third columns) and with the adjusted threshold to obtain less than 1% of false alarms (fourth and fifth columns)

Embedding algorithm	Classified as		Classified as	
	cover	stego	cover	stego
F5 100%	2 (0.37%)	532 (99.6%)	5 (0.93%)	529 (99%)
MB1 100%	3 (0.56%)	530 (99.4%)	3 (0.56%)	530 (99.4%)
OutGuess 100%	3 (0.56%)	531 (99.4%)	5 (0.93%)	529 (99%)
F5 50%	2 (0.37%)	532 (99.6%)	7 (1.31%)	527 (98.6%)
MB1 50%	2 (0.37%)	531 (99.6%)	4 (0.75%)	529 (99.2%)
OutGuess 50%	3 (0.56%)	531 (99.4%)	4 (0.74%)	530 (99.25)
MB2 30%	27 (5.06%)	506 (94.9%)	73 (13.7%)	460 (86.3%)
F5 25%	54 (10.1%)	480 (89.8%)	149 (27.9%)	385 (72%)
MB1 25%	38 (7.12%)	495 (92.8%)	90 (16.8%)	443 (83.1%)
OutGuess 25%	5 (0.93%)	529 (99%)	10 (1.87%)	524 (98.1%)
JP Hide	6 (1.12%)	528 (98.8%)	10 (1.87%)	524 (98.1%)
cover	515 (96.4%)	19 (3.5%)	527 (98.8%)	7 (1.3%)

the embedding efficiency by a large margin for short messages. We also point out the high detection of OutGuess with 25% messages (98.1%). As the capacity of OutGuess is already small, we conclude that OutGuess 0.2 is highly detectable and quite unsafe for steganography.

Some authors report the performance of classifiers using detection accuracy ρ (the area between the ROC curve and the diagonal normalized to 1 for perfect detection) and the false positive rate at 50% detection of stego images. For our universal machine we obtained $\rho = 0.98$ and 0% false positives at 50% stego detection on a database of 480 cover images and the same number of stego images embedded as in Table 3.

4.4   Max Wins Multiclassifier

One of the main goals of this paper is to build a classification machine able to detect not only the presence of secret messages in images, but also recognize steganographic algorithms. For this task, we chose the "Max Wins" algorithm, briefly described in Section 3.2. It consisted of 10 two-class SVMs (all SVMs from Table 1 except for cover×stego) classifying between every pair out of five classes (cover, F5, MB1, MB2, and OutGuess 0.2 classes). The parameters of the binary SVMs are summarized in Table 4. The confusion matrix in Table 5 is used to evaluate the performance.

Similar to the universal machine, the performance significantly improves as the size of messages exceeds 50% of the image capacity. In this case, the "Max Wins" machine is able to correctly identify the algorithm used for embedding with a very good accuracy (over 97%). Comparing its ability to separate cover and stego images with the universal machine, we see that the "Max Wins" has a better performance on images with a low embedding rate. The difference in performance is especially noticeable on images 25% embedded with F5 when the universal machine has a detection rate of 89.9% vs. 96.8% for the "Max Wins" multi-classifier. The universal machine has a lower overall false positive rate of 3.5% vs. 4.5% for the "Max Wins" classifier. The better performance of the "Max Wins" classifier on images with a lower embedding rate is probably due to the higher total number of examples used during training.

Since a high false positive rate is not desirable, we adjusted the decision threshold for each SVM detecting cover images. For this purpose, we created

Table 4. Parameters (C, γ) of SVMs with the Gaussian kernel used in the "Max Wins" multi-classifier

SVM	cover×F5	cover×MB1	cover×MB2	cover×OutGuess	MB1×F5
C	64	128	64	32	8
γ	0.5	0.2564	0.5	0.25	1
SVM	MB1×MB2	MB1×OutGuess	MB2×F5	MB2×OutGuess	OutGuess×F5
C	16	64	64	32	64
γ	0.5	0.25	0.5	0.25	0.125

Table 5. Confusion matrix for the "Max Wins" multi-classifier with default thresholds. Images are from the testing set only. The left most column contains the algorithm and the embedded message length. The remaining columns show the results of classification.

Embedding algorithm	cover	Classified as F5	MB1	MB2	OutGuess
F5 100%	2 (0.37%)	531 (99.4%)	1 (0.18%)	0 (0%)	0 (0%)
MB1 100%	3 (0.56%)	0 (0%)	526 (98.6%)	1 (0.19%)	3 (0.56%)
OutGuess 100%	2 (0.37%)	0 (0%)	0 (0%)	0 (0%)	532 (99.6%)
F5 50%	4 (0.74%)	522 (97.7%)	7 (1.3%)	1 (0.18)	0 (0%)
MB1 50%	3 (0.56%)	7 (1.3%)	506 (94.9%)	12 (2.26%)	5 (0.93%)
OutGuess 50%	3 (0.56%)	1 (0.18%)	3 (0.56%)	0 (0%)	527 (98.6%)
MB2 30%	8 (1.5%)	14 (2.6%)	17 (3.2%)	492 (92.3%)	2 (0.38%)
F5 25%	17 (3.2%)	463 (86.7%)	27 (5.1%)	26 (5.9%)	1 (0.19%)
MB1 25%	16 (3%)	26 (4.9%)	411 (77.1)	75 (14.1%)	5 (0.93%)
OutGuess 25%	4 (0.75%)	7 (1.31%)	16 (3%)	23 (4.3%)	484 (90.6%)
JP Hide	9 (1.7%)	334 (62.5%)	158 (29.6%)	27 (5.1%)	6 (1.1%)
cover	510 (95.5%)	5 (0.93%)	4 (0.75%)	15 (2.8%)	0 (0%)

Table 6. New thresholds of two-class SVMs used in "Max Wins" classifier

	cover×F5	cover×MB1	cover×MB2	cover×OutGuess
Threshold	0.748756	1.26615	0.653331	-0.699928
False positives	0.8%	0.8%	0.8%	0.8%
Detection rate	95.6%	89.7%	95.4%	99.3%

special training sets intended only for the purpose of adjusting the thresholds. These sets contained the same number of cover and stego images for each embedding algorithm. For example, to adjust the threshold for cover×F5, we prepared a set consisting of 480 cover images, 160 images with 100% message, 160 images with 50% messages, and 160 images with 25% messages. Then we adjusted the threshold to obtain a false positive rate less than 1%.

Table 6 shows the false positive rate and the detection rate for a given machine and threshold. The thresholds were chosen as the smallest values producing the false positive rate below 1%. The thresholds of all remaining SVMs used in the "Max Wins" classifier were set to the default value of 0.

Table 7 shows the performance of the multi-classifier with thresholds adjusted to lower the false positives. We see that the false positive rate was decreased to 1.69%, while the machine kept its good classification performance on images with larger messages. In comparison with the universal classifier, the false positive rate is now similar (universal — 1.3%×"Max Wins" — 1.7%) but the detection performance of the "Max Wins" classifier images with short messages still outperforms the universal classifier. We note that the training of the "Max Wins" classifier is significantly more time consuming, since it is necessary to train $\frac{n(n-1)}{2}$ more SVMs, while the size of the training set remains the same.

Table 7. Confusion matrix for the "Max Wins" classifier with adjusted thresholds

Embedding algorithm	cover	F5	Classified as MB1	MB2	OutGuess
F5 100%	4 (0.75%)	529 (99.1)	1 (0.19%)	0 (0%)	0 (0%)
MB1 100%	5 (0.94%)	0 (0%)	524 (98.3%)	1 (0.19%)	3 (0.56%)
OutGuess 100%	2 (0.37%)	0 (0%)	0 (0%)	0 (0%)	532 (99.63%)
F5 50%	4 (0.75)	521 (97.6%)	7 (1.31%)	1 (0.19%)	1 (0.19%)
MB1 50%	3 (0.56%)	7 (1.31%)	506 (94.9%)	12 (2.6%)	5 (0.94%)
OutGuess 50%	3 (0.56%)	1 (0.19%)	3 (0.56%)	0 (0%)	527 (98.7%)
MB2 30%	29 (5.4%)	11 (2.1%)	14 (2.6%)	477 (89.5%)	2 (0.38%)
F5 25%	64 (12%)	426 (79.8%)	20 (3.8%)	22 (4.1%)	2 (0.37%)
MB1 25%	85 (15.6%)	20 (3.8%)	358 (67.2%)	65 (12.2%)	5 (0.93%)
OutGuess 25%	5 (0.94%)	6 (1.1%)	16 (3%)	22 (4.1%)	485 (90.8%)
JP Hide	10 (1.9%)	332 (62.2%)	159 (29.8%)	27 (5.1%)	6 (1.1%)
cover	525 (98.3%)	1 (0.19%)	3 (0.56%)	5 (0.94%)	0 (0%)

Note that images embedded with the JP Hide algorithm are again correctly identified as stego images and the classifier identifies them mostly as F5 (62%) and MB1 (30%). This suggests a potential similarity between the embedding mechanisms. Obviously, it is possible that different stego programs use the same or very similar embedding mechanisms in which case, their separation by a blind classifier may become impossible. In our future work, we intend to further expand the proposed approach to allow the multiclassifier to recognize a new class (a new embedding mechanism).

Next, we examined the images that were misclassified by the multi-classifier with the intention to learn more about its performance. In particular, we inspected all misclassified cover images and stego images containing a message larger than 50% of the image capacity. Most of the misclassified images were taken by Nikon D100 camera or they were scaled versions of an image taken by this camera. This is surprising, because images taken by Nikon D100 were large (3008×2000) to provide sufficient statistics. We noticed that some of these images were very noisy (images taken at night using 30 second exposures), while others did not give us any visual clues as to why they were misclassified. We note, though, that the capacity of these images was usually below the average capacity of images with the same size.

As the calibration used in calculating the DCT features subjects an image to compression twice, the calibrated image has a lower noise content than the original JPEG image. Thus, we hypothesize that very noisy images might produce outliers. To test this hypothesis, we had blurred the misclassified Nikon D100 cover images (false positives) using a blurring filter with Gaussian kernel with diameter 1 and reclassified them. After this slight blurring, all of them were properly classified as cover images thus confirming our hypothesis.

Most of the misclassified images from the remaining cameras (Canon G2, Olympus Camedia 765, Kodak DC 290, and Canon PowerShot S40) were "flat" images, such as blue sky shots or completely dark images taken with a covered lens (these images were test images used by other members of our research group). The flat images do not provide sufficient statistics for steganalysis. As these images have a very low capacity (in tens of bytes) for most stego schemes, they are not suitable for steganography anyway.

5 Conclusions

In this paper, we build a multi-class steganalytic classifier capable of not only detecting stego images but also classifying them to appropriate stego algorithms. The classifier is a support vector machine with a Gaussian kernel trained on calibrated features calculated directly in the DCT domain [9]. We have trained the classifier on over 35000 images obtained by embedding messages of different sizes using different stego programs in almost 3436 unique source images from several digital cameras.

First, two class machines are built that distinguish between all pairs of image classes (cover, F5, MB1, MB2, OutGuess 0.2). These machines are used to compare the performance with the previously proposed classifier that uses wavelet-based features [8]. The two-class machines are then used to build a multi-class machine using the "Max Wins" approach . The performance is evaluated via confusion matrices. We conclude that it is, indeed, possible to reliably classify stego images to their appropriate stego methods, at least for sufficiently long messages. The multi-class machine is also capable to generalize to previously unseen stego methods (JP Hide&Seek). By analyzing the misclassified images, we conclude that images with a high level of noise are more likely to be misclassified, indicating a possible limitation of the calibration process for calculating features. Including non-calibrated version of the DCT features might help resolve this issue.

In our future work, we plan to extend this multi-classifier to other JPEG steganographic techniques available on the Internet and extend its scope to deal with double compressed images. Also, it is desirable that the classifier can automatically recognize a new embedding algorithm and automatically create a new class of stego images. This is, however, not an easy task to do with support vector machines. Further investigation of this topic is part of our future effort, as well.

Acknowledgements

The work on this paper was supported by Air Force Research Laboratory, Air Force Material Command, USAF, under the research grants number FA8750–04–1–0112 and F30602–02–2–0093. The U.S. Government is authorized to reproduce and distribute reprints for Governmental purposes notwithstanding any copyright notation there on. The views and conclusions contained herein are those of the authors and should not be interpreted as necessarily representing the official policies, either expressed or implied, of Air Force Research Laboratory, or the U. S. Government. Special thanks belong to Walker Land for help with multiclass support vector machines and to Jozef Sofka for providing us with his collection of images.

References

1. JP Hide&Seek. http://linux01.gwdg.de/~alatham/stego.html.
2. R.J. Anderson and F.A.P. Petitcolas. On the limits of steganography. *IEEE Journal of Selected Areas in Communications, Special Issue on Copyright and Privacy Protection*, 16(4):474–481, 1998.
3. I. Avcibas, N. Memon, and B. Sankur. Steganalysis using image quality metrics. In *Proceeedings of SPIE Electronic Imaging, Security and Watermarking of Multimedia Contents*, volume 4314, pages 523–531, San Jose, CA, 2001.
4. I. Avcibas, B. Sankur, and N. Memon. Image steganalysis with binary similarity measures. In *Proceedings of International Conference on Image Processing*, volume 3, pages 645–648, 2002.
5. C. Cachin. An information-theoretic model for steganography. In D. Aucsmith, editor, *Information Hiding. 2nd International Workshop*, volume 1525 of *Lecture Notes in Computer Science*, pages 306–318. Springer-Verlag, 1998.
6. R. Chandramouli, M. Kharrazi, and N. Memon. Image steganography and steganalysis. In T. Kalker, I. Cox, and Yong Man Ro, editors, *International Workshop on Digital Watermarking*, volume 2939 of *Lecture Notes in Computer Science*, pages 25–49, 2002.
7. S. Dumitrescu, Wu Xiaolin, and Zhe Wang. Detection of LSB steganography via sample pair analysis. In F.A.P. Petitcolas, editor, *Information Hiding. 5th International Workshop*, volume 2578 of *Lecture Notes in Computer Science*, pages 355–374. Springer-Verlag, 2003.
8. H. Farid and L. Siwei. Detecting hidden messages using higher-order statistics and support vector machines. In F.A.P. Petitcolas, editor, *Information Hiding. 5th International Workshop*, volume 2578 of *Lecture Notes in Computer Science*, pages 340–354. Springer-Verlag, 2003.
9. J. Fridrich. Feature-based steganalysis for JPEG images and its implications for future design of steganographic schemes. In J. Fridrich, editor, *Information Hiding, 6th International Workshop*, volume 3200 of *Lecture Notes in Computer Science*, pages 67–81. Springer-Verlag, 2005.
10. J. Fridrich, M. Goljan, D. Hogea, and D. Soukal. Quantitative steganalysis: Estimating secret message length. *ACM Multimedia Systems Journal. Special issue on Multimedia Security*, 9(3):288–302, 2003.
11. J.J. Harmsen and W.A. Pearlman. Steganalysis of additive noise modelable information hiding. In *Proceedings of SPIE Electronic Imaging, Security, Steganography, and Watermarking of Multimedia Contents V*, pages 131–142, Santa Clara, CA, 2003.
12. C. Hsu, C. Chang, and C. Lin. *A practical guide to support vector classification*. Department of Computer Science and Information Engineering, National Taiwan University, Taiwan. http://www.csie.ntu.edu.tw/~cjlin/papers/guide/guide.pdf.
13. C. Hsu and C. Lin. A comparison of methods for multi-class support vector machines. Technical report, Department of Computer Science and Information Engineering, National Taiwan University, Taipei, Taiwan, 2001. http://citeseer.ist.psu.edu/hsu01comparison.html.
14. S. Katzenbeisser and F.A.P. Petitcolas. Security in steganographic systems. In *Proceedings of SPIE Electronic Imaging, Security and Watermarking of Multimedia Contents IV*, volume 4675, pages 50–56, San Jose, CA, 2002.
15. A. Ker. Resampling and the detection of LSB matching in colour bitmaps. In *Proceedings of SPIE Electronic Imaging, Security, Steganography and Watermarking of Multimedia Contents VII*, San Jose, CA, 2005. To appear.

16. A. Ker. Steganalysis of LSB matching in grayscale images. *IEEE Sig. Proc. Letters*, 2005. To appear.

17. M. Kharrazi, H. T. Sencar, and N. Memon. Benchmarking steganographic and steganalytic techniques. In *Proceedings of SPIE Electronic Imaging, Security, Steganography and Watermarking of Multimedia Contents VII*, San Jose, CA, 2005. To appear.

18. S. Lyu and H. Farid. Steganalysis using color wavelet statistics and one-class support vector machines. In *Proceedings of SPIE Electronic Imaging, Security, Steganography, and Watermarking of Multimedia Contents*, pages 35–45, San Jose, CA, 2004.

19. J. Platt, N. Cristianini, and J. Shawe-Taylor. Large margin DAGs for multiclass classification. In S.A. Solla, T.K. Leen, and K.-R. Mueller, editors, *Advances in Neural Information Processing Systems 12*, pages 547–553, 2000.

20. N. Provos. Defending against statistical steganalysis. In *10th USENIX Security Symposium*, Washington DC, 2001.

21. P. Sallee. Model based steganography. In Kalker, I.J. Cox, and Yong Man Ro, editors, *Digital Watermarking. 2nd International Workshop*, volume 2939 of *Lecture Notes in Computer Science*, pages 154–167. Springer-Verlag, 2004.

22. D. Soukal, J. Fridrich, and M. Goljan. Maximum likelihood estimation of secret message length embedded using PMK steganography in spatial domain. In *Proceedings of SPIE Electronic Imaging, Security, Steganography and Watermarking of Multimedia Contents VII*, San Jose, CA, 2005. To appear.

23. R. Tzschoppe, R. Bäuml, J.B. Huber, and A. Kaup. Steganographic system based on higher-order statistics. In *Proceedings of SPIE Electronic Imaging, Security, Steganography, and Watermarking of Multimedia Contents V*, pages 156–166, Santa Clara, CA, 2003.

24. A. Westfeld. High capacity despite better steganalysis (F5 a steganographic algorithm). In I.S. Moskowitz, editor, *Information Hiding. 4th International Workshop*, volume 2137 of *Lecture Notes in Computer Science*, pages 289–302. Springer-Verlag, 2001.

25. J. Zöllner, H. Federrath, H. Klimant, A. Pfitzmann, R. Piotraschke, A. Westfeld, G. Wicke, and G. Wolf. Modeling the security of steganographic systems. In D. Aucsmith, editor, *Information Hiding. 2nd International Workshop*, volume 1525 of *Lecture Notes in Computer Science*, pages 344–354. Springer-Verlag, 1998.

An Efficient Fingerprinting Scheme with Symmetric and Commutative Encryption*

Seunglim Yong and Sang-Ho Lee

Department of Computer Science and Engineering, Ewha Womans University,
11-1 Daehyun-dong, Seodaemun-gu, Seoul, Korea
dragon@ewhain.net, shlee@ewha.ac.kr

Abstract. The illegal copying and redistribution of digital content is a crucial problem to distributors who electronically sell digital content. Fingerprinting scheme is a technique which supports the copyright protection to track redistributors of digital content using cryptographic techniques. Anonymous fingerprinting scheme prevents the content provider from framing the buyer by making the fingerprinted version known to the buyer only. In designing a fingerprinting scheme, it is important to make it more practical and efficient.

In this paper, we proposed a fingerprinting protocol to address the problem using cryptographic technologies and watermarking scheme. The digital content is encrypted using symmetric encryption. And keys, which are used to decrypt encrypted digital content, are double locked by two encryption keys kept separately by the buyer and the content provider. In the protocol, the buyer only gets a few of keys and can decrypt a few of fingerprinted digital contents in a transaction and the content provider has no idea how the fingerprint is formed. This facilitates the authority to determine the unethical party in case of illegal distributions of digital contents.

1 Introduction

Today's progress of computer networks along with the development of internet facilitates the illegal distribution of digital contents without any quality degradation. Accordingly, the protection of digital intellectual property has become a crucial issue. Preventing illegal copying requires either some hardware enforcement or some cryptographic software routines, but these techniques are usually broken into by hackers in a relatively short time. Thus, copy detection techniques appear as the main solution for protecting the copyright of content in electronic format. The idea here is to track who made illegal copies rather than preventing them. A lot of research has been invested in designing methods that technically support the copyright protection of digital contents. One type of such methods is a technique called fingerprinting schemes.

Fingerprinting scheme is a cryptographic technique that supports the copyright protection of digital content[15]. Buyers who redistribute copies disregarding the copyright conditions are called traitors. Fingerprinting schemes support

---

* This work was partially supported by Brain Korea 21 project.

M. Barni et al. (Eds.): IWDW 2005, LNCS 3710, pp. 54–66, 2005.

the copyright protection by enabling the original content provider to identify a traitor who originally purchased the data item. Fingerprinting schemes can be classified into the following three classes: Symmetric, asymmetric and anonymous asymmetric. In symmetric schemes, the content provider fingerprints digital contents, slightly differently from the original data item and unique to the buyer, and distributes the digital data. Thus the malicious content provider himself could spread the version sold to some buyer and then accuse that buyer of his own actions [2,3,18,19]. In asymmetric schemes, the buyer and the content provider perform interactive protocol where the buyer embeds his own secret to fingerprint the copy. At the end of the protocol only the buyer knows the fingerprinted copy. The advantage of this solution is that the content provider can obtain proof against the buyer that can convince any honest third party. But the drawback is that the content provider knows the buyer's identity even when the buyer is innocent[16]. In anonymous asymmetric fingerprinting, the buyer can purchase a fingerprinted copy without revealing his identity to the content provider. The buyer no longer has to identify himself when purchasing the copy and remains anonymous as long as he keeps the purchased good secret, i.e., does not distribute it. More precisely, the content provider can learn the buyer's identity only if he obtains the purchased copy. Upon finding a fingerprinted copy, the content provider needs the help of a registration authority to identify a traitor[11,12,15,17]. To insert the fingerprint anonymously, previous schemes used secure two-party computation or bit commitment [17,11,15]. However, these schemes are inefficient and impractical because they are based on secure two-party computations[6] with high complexity or they use [3] scheme as the building block for collusion resistance.

In this paper, we concentrate on practical anonymous fingerprinting protocols in the sense that buyers can buy goods anonymously, but can still be identified if they redistribute the goods illegally. Our protocol employs a symmetric key encryption to encrypt contents and a commutative encryption to encrypt keys. The content provider generates two versions of fingerprinted contents and encrypts them using symmetric key encryption with different key vectors. Two key vectors are double locked by two encryption keys kept separately by the buyer and the buyer selects one key vector of the two but the content provider cannot know which key vector the buyer selects. This scheme is very efficient and practical in computation complexity and storage requirement. In section 2, we briefly describe preliminary concepts used in our protocol and previous schemes. In section 3 we present the security of the proposed scheme. In section 4 we present our protocol details. We then discuss the security of the proposed method in section 5. Finally, we conclude in section 6.

2   Preliminaries and Related Works

In this section, we briefly review the preliminary concepts and related works.

2.1   Preliminaries

Commutative Encryption Scheme. We employ in the proposed protocol a special class of encryption algorithm that has the property of being commutative.

One instance of such encryption algorithm is proposed in [1]. An encryption algorithm CE is commutative if it satisfies the following property: for any two keys k_1 and k_2 and any message m:

$$CE(k_1(CE(k_2,m)) = CE(k_2(CE(k_1,m))$$

The decryption of a cipher message $c = CE(k,m)$ is denoted $m = CE^{-1}(k,c)$. It should be noted that if a message is encrypted by two different keys k_1 and k_2, then it can be recovered by decrypting the cipher message using k_1, followed by decrypting using k_2. The original message can also be recovered by decrypting the cipher message using k_2, followed by decrypting using k_1.

Watermarking Schemes. The so-called fingerprinting techniques use a watermarking system in order to embed a mark that identifies the buyer who has bought a certain copy of the content.

Watermarking schemes refer to the use of signal processing techniques to process watermarking signals in a few of digital contents[10]. Existing watermarking schemes generally involve two stages: watermark insertion and watermark detection. Suppose we have a digital content $X = \{x_1, x_2, ..., x_n\}$ and a watermark $W = \{w_1, w_2, ..., w_m\}$ with $n \geq m$. A watermarked content X' can be generated where $X' = I(X, W)$. The insertion algorithm I is given by:

$$X \oplus W = \{x_1 \oplus w_1, \ x_2 \oplus w_2, ..., \ x_m \oplus w_m, \ x_{m+1}, ..., \ x_n\}$$

Corresponding to the watermark insertion function I, there is a watermark detection function D, which returns a confidence measure of the existence of a watermark W in a few of contents X'.

2.2   Related Works

Pfitzman and Waidner[17] are known to be the first to propose the concept of anonymous fingerprinting, corresponding to the needs to achieve personal privacy in the overall context of e-commerce. However, their proposed scheme, based on secure two-party computation, is impractical since the underlying blocks are too complex to be efficient. Afterwards, many researchers suggested methods without relying on two-party computations[15,14,4], but some of them are not practical because the building block[3] uses long codes for embedding and some of them do not provide any anonymity.

Recently, for practical copyright protection, a commutative encryption based fingerprinting scheme has been proposed. The first-known commutative encryption based scheme is proposed by Bao et.al[1]. Bao et.al proposed a watermarking protocol to protect the privacy of watermarks using a commutative encryption algorithm. The drawback of this scheme is that it requires a public directory. Other schemes are attributed to Chang and Chung[4] and Choi et. al[8,9]. But these schemes are not practical because the computation of commutative encryption can be expensive in case of a transactions involving large amounts of digital content. Cheung et. al[7] proposed a more practical fingerprinting protocol in computation complexity and storage requirements by dividing the watermarked content into frames. But this scheme did not provide the buyer's anonymity. We introduce the Cheung's scheme briefly which is the basis of our protocol.

A Commutative Encrypted Protocol Due to Cheung et. al. The buyer and the content provider assume that each buyer has two different watermarks. The content provider generates two identical copies of digital contents M_1 and M_2 and splits each copy into ζ frames. The content provider then embeds watermarks into each ζ frame of two copies of digital content, respectively. The content provider selects a random secret key S and the buyer randomly chooses a secret key R. And then they perform as the following.

1) The content provider sends $c_{1,i}$ and $c_{2,i}$ to the buyer:
$$c_{1,i} = CE(S, M_{1,i})$$
$$c_{2,i} = CE(S, M_{2,i}) \text{ ,where } i = \{1, 2, ..\zeta\}$$

2) The buyer arbitrarily chooses c_i' from either $c_{1,i}$ or $c_{2,i}$ and sends them to the content provider :
$$d_i = CE(R, c_i')$$

3) The content provider decrypts d_i and sends them to the buyer:
$$u_i = CE^{-1}(S, d_i)$$
$$= CE^{-1}(S, CE(R, c_i')) \text{ ,where } i = \{1, 2, ..\zeta\}$$

4) The buyer decrypts and gets digital contents:
$$M_i' = CE^{-1}(R, u_i)$$
$$= CE^{-1}(R, CE^{-1}(S, d_i))$$
$$= CE^{-1}(R, CE(R, M'))$$

Here, $CE(.), CE^{-1}(.)$ are the commutative encryption and decryption algorithm, respectively[1]. The buyer obtains all ζ frames of watermarked contents by decrypting each u_i with the key R in step 4. Finally, the buyer gets a complete watermarked content by assembling these frames in sequence.

3   Overview of Our Scheme

The involved parties in our protocol are the buyer $\mathcal{B}$, the content provider $\mathcal{CP}$, the registration center $\mathcal{RC}$, and the judge $\mathcal{J}$. We assume that $\mathcal{J}$ is a trusted third party. For the purpose of fingerprinting, it is required in this model that buyers register themselves to $\mathcal{RC}$. There is no special restriction on $\mathcal{J}$. The main subprotocols of the construction are registration, fingerprinting, and identification.

There are two steps where fingerprinting techniques are used for rightful ownerships. We assume that each buyer owns at least two legitimate fingerprints identifying the buyer. In the first step, the content provider inserts two fingerprints into the digital content and encrypts it with symmetric key cryptosystem. The content provider generates two identical copies of *item* and splits each copy into t frames. The content provider generates different fingerprinted digital contents $item^0$ and $item^1$ by embedding two fingerprints into each t frame. And he randomly generates two secret key vectors K_0 and K_1. Then the content provider encrypts $item^0$ with key vector K_0 and $item^1$ with key vector K_1 using symmetric key cryptosystem. Each key vector consists of t different keys and each frame of $item^i$ is encrypted by each key of key vector K_i.

In the second step, the content provider encrypts two secret key vectors using commutative encryption algorithm. The buyer obtains t keys, which enables him to decrypt the encrypted contents, by choosing, at his own will, the first key of the key vector from either K_0 or K_1, the second key of the key vector from either K_0 or K_1, and so on. After obtaining t keys, the buyer can decrypt the encrypted digital contents with the selected keys.

In our protocol, commutative encryption algorithm is employed to ensure that the buyer can only obtain one complete digital content. The digital content is embedded with the buyer's two fingerprints in a particular fingerprint pattern, and that pattern is not revealed to the content provider. In other words, after a transaction, the content provider has no idea what the fingerprint pattern of the content is. Thus, the anonymity of the buyer is guaranteed. A detailed description of the protocol will be given in section 4.

Now, we can state the main security properties of our protocol as the following.

- Security for the content provider: An honest content provider must be able to identify a traitor and win the corresponding trial for every illegally redistributed copy of the data item he finds, as long as the collusion does not exceed a certain size.
- Security for the buyer and registration center: No honest buyer or honest registration center should be guilty by an honest judge; at least no honest judge will believe it.
- Anonymity: Without obtaining an illegally redistributed copy, the content provider cannot identify the buyer. Also, the purchases of honest buyers should not be linkable even by a collusion of all content provider, registration center and other buyers.

4   Proposed Scheme

In this section, we propose an efficient anonymous fingerprinting scheme.

Algebraic structure. All arithmetic operations are performed in a group G_q of order q. Any group G_q satisfying these requirements and in which the computation of discrete logarithms is infeasible and can be a candidate. For concrete constructions one can assume that G_q is the unique subgroup of prime order q of the multiplicative group Z_p^* where p is prime such that $q = (p-1)/2$ is also prime and $q|(p-1)$. Let g be a generator of G such that computing discrete logarithms to the base g is difficult.

Notation. Let $item$ denote some digital content that is fingerprintable. The fingerprinted copy, some of its bits can be altered, remains "close" to $item$. But without knowing which particular bits were changed, the altering of these bits is impossible without rendering the content useless. We refer to the formal definition of "marking assumption" [3]. We establish some notation as the following.

- $item$: Original digital content that is fingerprintable
- $\oplus$: Fingerprint embedding operation
- SE/SE^{-1}: Symmetric encryption / decryption algorithm
- CE/CE^{-1}: Commutative encryption / decryption algorithm
- E: Public key encryption algorithm
- H: Collision-free one-way hash function

4.1   Registration

Assume that both the buyer and the registration center have public and secret key pairs. The buyer's secret key is x_B and his public key is $y_B = g^{x_B}$. The registration center uses its secret key to issue certificates which can be verified using the registration center's public key. The public keys of the registration center and all buyers are assumed to be known and certified.

1) $\mathcal{B}$ randomly chooses two secret values $x_1, x_2 \in Z_p$ such that $x_1 + x_2 = x_B \in Z_p$. $\mathcal{B}$ sends $y_B, y_1(y_1 = g^{x_1})$ and $E_{\mathcal{RC}}(x_2)$. The buyer convinces the registration center of zero-knowledge of possession of x_1. The proof given in [5] for showing possession of discrete logarithms may be used here.
2) $\mathcal{RC}$ decrypts $E_{\mathcal{RC}}(x_2)$ and computes $y_2 = g^{x_2}$ and checks that $y_1 y_2 = y_B$. If it is verified, it returns to $\mathcal{B}$ a certificate $Cert(y_1)$. The certificate states the correctness of y_1 and registration of $\mathcal{B}$.

By going through the registration procedure above several times, the buyer can obtain several different keys y_1.

4.2   Fingerprinting

$\mathcal{B}$ sends y_1 and $Cert(y_1)$ to $\mathcal{CP}$ and requests the digital content $item$. On receiving the request and the due payment from $\mathcal{B}$, $\mathcal{CP}$ verifies $Cert(y_1)$ and generates $\mathcal{B}$'s two fingerprints(watermarks) F_B^0 and F_B^1. Each fingerprint F_i of our protocol and W of Cox scheme[1] has the same property. Next, $\mathcal{CP}$ and $\mathcal{B}$ execute the fingerprinting protocol as the following.

Step.1 Encrypt fingerprinted contents

1) $\mathcal{CP}$ generates two identical copies of $item$(denotes as $item^0$ and $item^1$), and splits each copy into t frames, i.e

---

[1] Cox et al., embed a set of independent real numbers $W = \{w_1, ..., w_n\}$ drawn from a zero mean, variance 1, Gaussian distribution into the m largest DCTAC coefficients of an image. Results reported using the largest 1000AC coefficients show the technique to be remarkably robust against various image processing operations and after printing and rescanning and multiple-document (collusion) attack.

$$item^i = \{item^{i,1}, item^{i,2}, ..., item^{i,t}\}, \quad i = \{0, 1\}$$

CP then embeds F_B^0 into each of the t frames of $item^0$ and F_B^1 into each of the t frames of $item^1$. That is:

$$item_B^i = \{item_B^{i,1}, item_B^{i,2}, ..., item_B^{i,t}\}, \ where$$
$$item_B^{i,j} = item^{i,j} \oplus F_B^i, \ i = \{0, 1\}, j = \{1, 2, ..., t\}$$

Remark 1: We use a specific construction which introduced a spread-spectrum watermarking techniques proposed by Cox et al[10] for collusion-tolerance.

2) CP generates two secret key vectors K_0 and K_1. Each key vector consists of t keys which are arbitrarily selected.

$$K_0 = \{k_{0,1}, k_{0,2}, ..., k_{0,t}\}$$
$$K_1 = \{k_{1,1}, k_{1,2}, ..., k_{1,t}\}$$

3) Then CP encrypts the $2t$ frames of $item_B^i$ using $2t$ keys selected above. They are encrypted using symmetric key encryption(deterministic encryption algorithm, say, DES or AES). CP generates two encrypted digital content vectors X_B^0, X_B^1, and sends them to B. The key vector K_i is used for encrypting $item_B^i$. That is :

$$X_B^0 = SE(K_0, item_B^0)$$
$$= SE(k_{0,j}, item_B^{0,j}), \ where \ j = \{1, 2, ..., t\}$$
$$X_B^1 = SE(K_1, item_B^1)$$
$$= SE(k_{1,j}, item_B^{1,j}), \ where \ j = \{1, 2, ..., t\}$$

Encryption of the fingerprinted contents is shown in Figure 1.

Step.2 Encrypt key vector and decrypt encrypted contents

4) CP selects a secret key S and uses commutative encryption algorithm CE to encrypt the two key vectors K_i and generates two encrypted key vectors C_0 and C_1 as shown in the following. Then CP sends C_0 and C_1 to B.

$$C_0 = \{c_{0,1}, c_{0,2}, ..., c_{0,t}\}, \ where \ c_{0,j} = CE(S, k_{0,j})$$
$$C_1 = \{c_{1,1}, c_{1,2}, ..., c_{1,t}\}, \ where \ c_{1,j} = CE(S, k_{1,j})$$

5) When B receives C_0 and C_1, he constructs a new encrypted vector $C' = (c'_1, c'_2, ..., c'_t)$ by randomly choosing c'_j from either $c_{0,j}$ or $c_{1,j}$. B generates a t-bit integer L_B, which is denoted as a bit pattern $\{l_1, l_2, ..., l_t\}$ where $l_j = \{0, 1\}$. If B chooses $c'_j = c_{0,j}$ then the bit $l_j = 0$ and if $c'_j = c_{1,j}$, then the bit $l_j = 1$. The bit pattern $\{l_1, l_2, ..., l_t\}$ should not be $\{0, 0, ..., 0\}$ or $\{1, 1, ..., 1\}$.

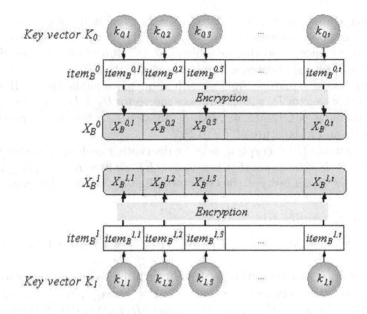

Fig. 1. Encrypt fingerprinted contents

6) After generating C', $\mathcal{B}$ randomly chooses a secret key R and uses CE to encrypt C' to get two encrypted vectors $D_1 = \{d_1, d_2, ..., d_{t/2}\}$, $D_2 = \{d_{(t+1)/2}, ..., d_t\}$, where

$$d_i = CE(R, c_i') = CE(R, CE(S, k_{l_j,j})) = CE(S, CE(R, k_{l_j,j}))$$

Then $\mathcal{B}$ sends the encrypted vector D_1 to $\mathcal{CP}$.

7) $\mathcal{CP}$ decrypts vector D_1 with S and gets the vector $U_1 = \{u_1, u_2, ..., u_{t/2}\}$, where $u_i = CE^{-1}(S, d_i)$. After the decryption, $\mathcal{CP}$ sends U_1 to $\mathcal{B}$.

$$
\begin{aligned}
u_i &= CE^{-1}(S, d_i) \\
&= CE^{-1}(S, CE(R, c_i')) \\
&= CE^{-1}(S, CE(R, CE(S, k_{l_j,j}))) \\
&= CE^{-1}(S, CE(S, CE(R, k_{l_j,j}))) \\
&= CE(R, k_{l_i,j})
\end{aligned}
$$

8) $\mathcal{B}$ now obtains $t/2$ decrypting keys by decrypting each u_i in vector U_1 with the key R, i.e., $k_{l_j,j} = CE^{-1}(R, u_i) = CE^{-1}(R, CE(R, k_{l_j,j}))$. $\mathcal{B}$ gets a key vector K_{B_1}, where $K_{B_1} = \{k_{l_j,1}, k_{l_j,2}, ..., k_{l_j,t/2}\}$. Now $\mathcal{B}$ can decrypt the encrypted digital content using K_{B_1}. Each frame of encrypted digital content is decrypted by the corresponding key as the following.

$$
\begin{aligned}
item_B^{l_j,j} &= SE^{-1}(k_{l_j,j}, X_B^{l_j,j}) \\
&= SE^{-1}(k_{l_j,j}, SE(k_{l_j,j}, item_B^{l_j,j})), \ where \ j = \{1, 2, ..., t/2\}
\end{aligned}
$$

9) $\mathcal{B}$ generates an encapsulated data $T_B = E_{\mathcal{J}}(L_B)$ and a signature $Sig(T_B)$ on T_B using an anonymous public key y_1. The value T_B and $Sig(T_B)$ are used as evidence for solving possible piracy disputes in the future. $\mathcal{B}$ should send T_B, $Sig(T_B)$ and D_2, generated in step 6, to $\mathcal{CP}$.

10) $\mathcal{CP}$ verifies the signature $Sig(T_B)$ with anonymous public key y_1. If it is OK, $\mathcal{CP}$ decrypts vector D_2 with S and gets the vector $U_2 = \{u_{(t+1)/2}, u_{(t+2)/2}, ...,$ $u_t\}$, where $u_i = CE^{-1}(S, d_i)$, like U_1 in step 7. After the decryption, $\mathcal{CP}$ sends U_2 and a signature of T_B to $\mathcal{B}$.

11) $\mathcal{B}$ now obtains $t/2$ decrypting keys by decrypting each u_i in vector U_2 with the key R. $\mathcal{B}$ gets an another key vector K_{B_2}, where $K_{B_2} = \{k_{l_j, (t+1)/2}, ...,$ $k_{l_j, t}\}$. Now $\mathcal{B}$ can decrypt the encrypted digital content using K_{B_2}.

$$item_B^{l_j, j} = SE^{-1}(k_{l_j, j}, X_B^{l_j, j})$$
$$= SE^{-1}(k_{l_j, j}, SE(k_{l_j, j}, item_B^{l_j, j})), \; where \; j = \{(t+1)/2, ..., t\}$$

As a result, $\mathcal{B}$ gets a complete piece of fingerprinted content $item_B$ by assembling these frames in sequence, i.e. $item_B = \{item_B^{l_j, 1}, item_B^{l_j, 2}, ..., item_B^{l_j, t}\}$.

12) $\mathcal{B}$ sends $TN_B = E_{\mathcal{J}}(H(item_B), H(item_B) \oplus H(L_B))$ to $\mathcal{CP}$. $\mathcal{CP}$ keeps records Rec_B of all transactions in his database, where each transaction is summarized as a seven-order tuple $< y_1, Cert(y_1), F_B^0, F_B^1, T_B, Sig(T_B), TN_B >$.

4.3   Identification

After finding an illegally redistributed digital content, $\mathcal{CP}$ extracts the fingerprint pattern in it. For robust embedding algorithm, by computing correlations of extracted fingerprint and every fingerprint stored in records Rec_B, $\mathcal{CP}$ finds with the highest correlation and should reconstructs $item_B^0$ and $item_B^1$ with fingerprints F_B^0 and F_B^1. $\mathcal{CP}$ then submits $item_B^0$ and $item_B^1$ with the transaction record to $\mathcal{J}$, who will determine who is guilty by decrypting and checking the data T_B and TN_B. $\mathcal{J}$ verifies the presence of F_B^0 and F_B^1 in the $item_B$ and checks the bit pattern whether L_B corresponds to the fingerprint pattern. And then $\mathcal{J}$ verifies the signature $Sig(T_B)$ with anonymous public key y_1 whether $\mathcal{B}$ generates T_B or not. If it is checked, he decrypts TN_B and checks the hash value of $item_B$ and $(H(item_B) \oplus H(L_B))$, generated using L_B obtained above, corresponds to decrypted TN_B. If the value is verified, $\mathcal{J}$ sends y_1 and asks for the identity of the traitor to $\mathcal{RC}$. Thus $\mathcal{CP}$ can identify the traitor.

5   Security Analysis

In this section we present the proof sketch in detail for the security of our protocol. We assume that all underlying primitives are secure, and the security of our scheme relies on that of the underlying watermarking algorithm and cryptosystem.

5.1   Security for the Content Provider

$\mathcal{B}$ wants to obtain two or more valid $item_B$ so that he can make unauthorized distributions of $item'_B$ without being accused. However, $\mathcal{B}$ can only obtain one piece of valid fingerprinted content $item_B$ in the implementation of the protocol once. In our protocol, the digital contents are divided into t frames and each frame is encrypted by different keys. To acquire two or more valid $item_B$, $\mathcal{B}$ should obtain more than t keys in order to decrypt more than t frames of contents. But $\mathcal{B}$ can only obtain t keys. It is unlikely for $\mathcal{CP}$ to perform the decryption operation on more than one vector D sent by $\mathcal{B}$. Therefore, $\mathcal{B}$ cannot get two different key vectors by sending two D to $\mathcal{CP}$ and he can decrypt only t frames of encrypted digital content.

For redistributing the digital content without being accused, $\mathcal{B}$ is willing to make a false T_B by encapsulating a false L_B in the T_B sent to $\mathcal{CP}$. In fingerprinting, $\mathcal{B}$ randomly generates a t-bit integer L_B for choosing keys from vector C_0 and C_1, and finally obtains a corresponding fingerprinted content $item_B$. Suppose $\mathcal{B}$ puts a false L'_B, instead of L_B, to generate $T'_B = E_{\mathcal{J}}(L'_B)$, which is sent to $\mathcal{CP}$ to record. Although $\mathcal{CP}$ cannot notice $\mathcal{B}$'s trick, such cheating of $\mathcal{B}$ will be detected by $\mathcal{CP}$. That is, when receiving an accusation request from $\mathcal{CP}$, $\mathcal{J}$ verifies the signature $Sig(T_B)$. If it is verified, the fact is guaranteed that $\mathcal{B}$ generated the value T_B. $\mathcal{J}$ decrypts the T_B for checking. From the L'_B, $\mathcal{J}$ can recover a fingerprinted content, denoted by $item'_B$. Clearly, the $item'_B$ is not equal to $item_B$ since $L'_B \neq L_B$. Also, $\mathcal{B}$ is judged to be guilty because the hash value of the recovered $item'_B$ does not equal $H(item_B)$ and $(H(item'_B) \oplus H(L_B))$ does not equal $(H(item_B) \oplus H(L_B))$, which is extracted from TN_B. Moreover, the signature $Sig(T_B)$ on T_B is used as non-repudiation evidence, so $\mathcal{B}$ cannot deny the fact that he has generated T_B.

So, we show that our protocol is secure against malicious buyer as well, which means that the buyer making unauthorized distribution will always be successfully identified.

5.2   Security for the Buyer

We assume that $\mathcal{RC}$ does not reveal the buyer's ID if the buyer is honest. An honest buyer is secure if the attackers cannot convince the judge, even if the other parties collude and obtain other digital content that he bought.

It is impossible for $\mathcal{CP}$ to figure out which information $\mathcal{B}$ selects, even if he is trying to make an incorrect performance. In fingerprinting, we can see that the only available information for $\mathcal{CP}$ from $\mathcal{B}$ is $D_1 = \{d_1, d_2, ..., d_{t/2}\}$ and $D_2 = \{d_{t+1/2}, ..., d_t\}$, where $d_i = CE(R, c'_i)$. To trace the origin of c'_i, in other words, to find out whether c'_i is c_0 or c_1, $\mathcal{CP}$ has to calculate c'_i from d_i without knowing R, which is the secret key held privately by $\mathcal{B}$. Such computation, however, is as hard to break as the encryption algorithm CE, which is generally agreed to be computationally intractable. Besides, the probability of $\mathcal{CP}$ knowing $\mathcal{B}$ chose whether c'_i is c_0 or c_1 on the total t frames would be equal to $1/2^t$. Note that the value of R is randomly chosen by $\mathcal{B}$ in each transaction. There is no relation between the values of R and each of transaction.

Another possible attack from CP is to generate two pieces of identical finger-printed contents instead of two different ones so that he can easily trace them. Such cheating of CP, however, will be detected by J in our protocol. To cheat, CP generates the two identical copies of $item_B^i$ with the same fingerprint. For example, CP generates two identical fingerprinted contents with the fingerprint pattern as $\{0, 1, 1, 0, ..1\}$ and sends the encrypted forms to B. In such case, B is not conscious of the cheating behavior of CP, since X_B^0 and X_B^1 are not the same because each frame of $item_B^i$ is encrypted with different keys. But in fingerprint-ing, B arbitrarily chooses the bit pattern as $\{1, 0, 1, 1, ..., 0\}$; the bit pattern is different from the fingerprint pattern. That is, in identification protocol, since the bit pattern, which is generated by B, and the fingerprint pattern are not in accord, J notices the cheating behavior of CP.

An honest B cannot accused of reselling an unauthorized copy by malicious CP or other malicious third party. Although CP knows B's two watermarked contents, the watermarked contents are split into t frames respectively, he has no idea which frames are chosen by B eventually to construct the $item_B$. It is easy to calculate that there are totally 2^t possible assembling combinations from those frames to generate full watermarked contents. And a malicious CP makes an L_B'' and just reveal a watermarked item $item_B''$ himself and accuse the buyer. In this case, CP must make a valid signature $Sig(T_B'')$ on $T_B'' = E_J(L_B'')$ and the value $H(L_B'') \oplus H(item_B'')$. But he does not know the B's secret key for the signature, he cannot forge a valid signature $Sig(T_B'')$ and cannot make a valid TN_B''.

5.3   Buyer's Anonymity

An honest buyer who follows fingerprinting protocol will not be identified. We assume that RC does not reveal the buyer's ID and does not collude with CP if the buyer is honest. In fingerprinting protocol, CP knows y_1. Finding y_B requires knowledge of x_2. However, if the encryption algorithm is secure, he cannot find x_2. Besides, the digital content is embedded with the buyer's two fingerprints in a particular fingerprint pattern. Although CP knows the buyer's two fingerprints, CP has no idea what the fingerprint pattern is after the transaction. Thus, the buyer's anonymity is guaranteed.

5.4   Efficiency

The proposed scheme is very efficient in storage and computation. In general, the computation of commutative encryption can be expensive in case of a transaction involving large amounts of digital content. But the symmetric encryption scheme is suitable for such case. By employing symmetric encryption to encrypt the digital content and commutative encryption to encrypt the keys, we can improve the efficiency compared to previous schemes[7,8,9].

Our scheme provides the buyer's anonymity and efficiency by employing sym-metric encryption to encrypt the digital content in comparison to [7]. Since the commutative encryption is applied to encrypt the keys instead of watermarks, our scheme is more efficient than [8]. Let us assume that the key size is 56 bits and the length of digital watermark is 1024 bits and a piece of digital content partitioned into $t(t = 32$ here) frames. In our protocol, the 3584 bits are encrypted using commutative encryption. On the other hand, in [8], $n * 1024 * \alpha (\alpha$ is larger than 1 because the length of ciphertext which is resulted on homomorphic encryption is longer than the length of plaintext) bits are encrypted for encrypting n watermarks.

Moreover, our scheme does not need any public directories like [1] and a large storage for recorded list of transaction. In fingerprinting, $\mathcal{CP}$ should maintain a database for all transactions. If a recorded list of transactions is too large for storage, then the protocol is not practical. In our protocol, a recorded list Rec_B only includes seven-tuple $< y_1, Cert(y_1), F_B^0, F_B^1, T_B, Sig(T_B), TN_B >$. Since the probability of $\mathcal{CP}$ knowing which fingerprinted contents a buyer chose on the total t frames would be equal to $1/2^t$, if the digital contents is divided into frames more than two, our scheme is more efficient compared to [9].

6   Conclusion

In this paper, we have proposed an efficient protocol where all protocols are explicit and fairly efficient. The proposed scheme is efficient with lower computation complexity. For this, we applied symmetric encryption algorithm for encrypting large amounts of digital content and commutative encryption to encrypt keys. Through a security analysis, we have shown that our protocol is secure from both the content provider and the buyer. Since non-repudiation is also provided by the digital signature scheme, the buyer and the content provider cannot deny their actions. Besides the security feature, our protocol is economic with respect to storage requirements. But the drawback of our scheme is that we have to generate $2t$ different symmetric key though we improved the computation complexity and storage requirements. A further direction of this study will be to reduce key generation overhead.

References

1. F. Bao, R. H. Deng and P. Feng, "An efficient and practical scheme for privacy protection in the E-commerce of digital goods," ICICS'00, LNCS2836, pp. 162-170, 2001.
2. G. Blakley, C. Meadow and G. B. Purdy, "Fingerprinting long forgiving messages," Advances in Cryptology - CRYPTO'85, LNCS 218, pp. 180-189, 1986.
3. D. Boneh and J. Shaw, "Collusion-secure fingerprinting for digital data," Advances in Cryptology - CRYPTO'95, LNCS 963, pp. 452-465, 1995.
4. C. C. Chang and C. Y. Chung, "An enhanced buyer-seller watermarking protocol," Proc. ICCT2003, pp. 1779-1783, 2003.
5. D. Chaum, "An impoved protocol for demonstrating possession of discrete logarithms and some generalizations," EUROCRYPT'87, LNCS 304, pp. 127-141, 1987.
6. D. Chaum, I. B. Damagaard and J. vad de Graaf, "Multiparty computations ensuring privacy of each party's input and correctness of the result," Advances in Cryptology - CRYPTO'87, LNCS 293, pp. 87-119, 1988.

7. S. Cheung, H. Leung and C. Wang, "A commutative encrypted protocol for the privacy protection of watermarks in digital contents," HICSS'04, pp. 40094a, 2004
8. J. G. Choi, K. Sakurai, J. H. Park, "Does it need trusted third party? Design of buyer-seller watermarking protocol without trusted third party," ACNS'03, LNCS 2846, pp. 265-279, 2003.
9. J. G. Choi, J. H. Park and K. R. Kwon, "Analysis of COT-based fingerprinting schemes: new approach to design practical and secure fingerprinting scheme," IHW'04, LNCS 3200, pp. 253-265, 2004.
10. I. J. Cox, J. Kilian, T. Leighton, and T. Shamnon, "Secure spread spectrum watermarking for image, audio and video", IEEE Transactions on Image Processing, 6(12), pp. 1673-1678, 1997.
11. J. Domingo-Ferrer, "Anonymous fingerprinting based on committed oblivious transfer," PKC 1999, LNCS 1560, pp. 43-52, 1999.
12. J. Domingo-Ferrer, "Anonymous fingerprinting of electronic information with automatic identification redistributors," IEE Electronic Letters, 43(13), pp. 1303-1304, 1998.
13. M. Kuribayashi and H. Tanaka, "A new anonymous fingerprinting scheme with high enciphering rate," INDOCRYPT'01, LNCS 22247, pp. 30-39, 2001.
14. N. Memon and P. W. Wong, "A buyer-seller watermarking protocol," IEEE Transactions on Image Processing, 10(4), pp. 643-649, 2001.
15. B. Pfitzmann and A. R. Sadeghi, "Coin-based anonymous fingerprinting," Advances in Cryptology - EUROCRYPT'99, LNCS 1592, pp. 150-164, 1999.
16. B. Pfitzmann and M. Schunter, "Asymmetric fingerprinting," Advances in Cryptology - EYROCRYPT'96, LNCS 1070, pp. 84-95, 1996.
17. B. Pfitzmann and M. Waidner, "Anonymous fingerprinting," Advances in Cryptology - EUROCRYPT'97, LNCS 1233, pp. 88-102, 1997.
18. W. Trappe, M. Wu and K. Liu, "Collusion-resistant fingerprinting for multimedia," IEEE International Conference on Acoustics, Speech, and Signal Processing, 4, pp. 3309-3312, 2002.
19. N. R. Wanger, "Fingerprinting," IEEE Symposium on Security and Privacy, pp. 18-22, 1983.

Collusion Secure Convolutional Spread Spectrum Fingerprinting

Yan Zhu[1,2], Dengguo Feng[2], and Wei Zou[1]

[1] Institute of Computer Science and Technology,
Peking University, Beijing 100871, China
[2] State Key Laboratory of Information Security,
The Chinese Academy of Sciences, Beijing 100049, China
martinzhu@msn.com

Abstract. Digital Fingerprinting is a technique for the merchant who can embed unique buyer identity marks into digital media copy and also makes it possible to identify 'traitors' who redistribute their illegal copies. This paper first discusses the collusion-resistant properties of spread-spectrum sequence against malicious attacks such as collusion combination, collusion average and additive noise. A novel two-layers secure fingerprinting scheme is then presented by concatenating the spread-spectrum code with a convolutional code. Moreover, Viterbi algorithm is improved by using Optional Code Set. The code length, collusion security and performance are proved and analyzed. As the results, the proposed scheme for perceptual media has shorter fingerprinting length and achieves optimal traitor searching.

Keywords: Digital fingerprinting; Collusion secure; Spread spectrum; Convolutional code.

1 Introduction

Digital fingerprinting is a technique for the merchant who can embed unique buyer identity marks into digital media copy, and also makes it possible to identify 'traitors' who redistribute their illegal copies by obtaining the sellers' information from the redistributed contents. Such unique marks of the buyer are called fingerprint. Initially, digital fingerprinting is considered as a coding technique. Chor, Fiat and Naor first address 'tracing traitor' problem by using $O(k^4 log(k))$-bits information to protect k different copies from collusion attacks. After this, Boneh and Shaw present the relatively perfect concept and scheme of digital fingerprinting (called BS model)[1]. The presented scheme adapts to expression medium, such as text, broadcast, programme language, but it is not suitable for perceptual medium, such as image, audio, video. Especially when such fingerprint code is regarded as watermark marks embedded into a copy of digital content, the constructed copy with fingerprint can not denoted by BS model since the watermark marks overlap each other in the digital content. Moreover, it cannot obtain the properties of imperceptibility and robustness,

M. Barni et al. (Eds.): IWDW 2005, LNCS 3710, pp. 67–83, 2005.

and then the fingerprint code length is too long for perceptual medium to be implemented in practice.

Direct Sequence Spread Spectrum (DSSS) is a efficient watermarking technique that is robust to extremely severe distortions, such as compressing, cropping and rotating. For collusion attacks of fingerprinting, Cox *et al* first indicated that Spread Spectrum (SS) sequence has the properties of collusion-resistance[2]. After this, Frgun and Kilian build a model using Euclidean metric as criterion to distinguish different copies. This model shows that at most $O(\sqrt{n/\ln n})$ adversaries can defeat any watermarking scheme if the effective document length is n. [3] shows that $\Omega(\sqrt{n/\ln m})$ copies are required to successfully erase any mark with non-negligible probability if the sequences have a component-wise normal distribution, where m is the number of different copies distributed. Although these researches provide the bound of collusion security, they are builded on the abstract model but not on a certain scheme. In the aspect of fingerprint coding, [1] firstly presented the coding problem about c-secure fingerprint and proved that there are no totally c-secure code under Marking Assumption. Hence they constructed a c-frameproof code with ε-error by employing Error Correcting Codes. However, tracing algorithm in model is NP-hard problem. To resolve this problem, In [4] Barg *et al* construct a code with Identifiable Parent Property (IPP) based on algebraic codes. But the codes is only suitable for the case of size 2 coalitions, either one of the traitors is identified with probability 1 or both traitors are identified with probability $1 - \exp(\Omega(n))$. In conclusion, the present fingerprinting schemes still have many practical problems required to solve.

On the basis of the analysis of collusion attacks, include in collusion combination attack, collusion average attack and additional noise attack, this paper shows that spread-spectrum code has strong security and robustness properties, and then illustrates the collusion-resistent properties of spread-spectrum fingerprint code and the interrelation among the code length, collusion size and error probability. Furthermore, we propose a fingerprinting scheme on two-levels structure by concatenating the spread-spectrum codes with convolutional code[5, 6]. Due to the spread-spectrum codes have the capacity to trace many codewords of coalition, Viterbi algorithm is improved by optional code sets. And then its code length, collusion security and efficiency are proved and analyzed. As the results, this coding scheme is easy to implement and has lower complexity. Moreover, it achieves a shorter fingerprinting length and more optimal traitor searching.

The remainder of this paper is organized as follows. Section 2 gives a brief description on digital fingerprinting for perceptual media. Section 3 analyzes the collusion-resistance properties of spread-spectrum code. Section 4 describes our fingerprinting scheme as well as its encoding and decoding algorithms. The Performances are analyzed in section 5. Finally, section 6 gives conclusion.

2   Digital Fingerprinting for Perceptual Medium

Without loss of generality, a digital watermarking scheme is composed of algorithm pair (E_w, D_w) and a symbol set in $\Sigma = \{1, 2, \cdots, q\}$. The embedding algorithm E_w generates copy O^i with fingerprint i in terms of the input of a digital object O, a symbol i and a secret key k, i.e. $O^i = E_w(O, i, k)$. detection algorithm D_w can one or more symbols in $\Sigma' = \Sigma \cup \{?\}$, i.e. $i' = D_w(O', k)$. Where, we denote the algorithm output in an invalid state by symbol '?'.

Digital fingerprinting scheme based on perceptual media construct fingerprint coding and embedding system. Fingerprint coding is composed of a fingerprint sequence set and a algorithm pair (E_f, T_f), where E_f is fingerprint generating algorithm and T_f is tracing algorithm. Fingerprint embedding system is similar to the watermarking scheme. In order to embed fingerprint of user u_i to original object O, at first, we apply E_f to generate a fingerprint $I_{u_i} = (i_1.i_2, \cdots, i_L)$, i.e. $I_i = E_f(u_i)$, where $i_j \in \Sigma$ $(1 \leq j \leq L)$. Secondly, the object O is divided into blocks and randomly choose L blocks into sequence $O = (o_1, o_2, \cdots, o_L)$. Next, embedding algorithm E_w creates a copy $O^{(u_i)}$ by embedding i_j into o_j. When a pirated copy is found, the detection algorithm D_w extracts the marks from every block and outputs all the fingerprint $I' = (i'_1, i'_1, \cdots, i'_L)$. Finally, the tracing algorithm T_f identifies the coalition $C = \{u_1, u_2, \cdots, u_c\}$ according to the record M, i.e. $C = T_f(I', M)$.

Fingerprinting progression generally involves four steps: information coding, mark embedding, mark detection and tracing traitor. Here, the embedding of one symbol of the fingerprint is called a mark. It is inevitable for fingerprinting to make the same content contain different marks. Let $C = \{u_1, u_2, \cdots, u_c\}$ is a coalition of c users who hold many copies with fingerprint. It is a feasible attack policy for a coalition of users to detect specific marks if they differs between their copies, and then the colluders construct a illegal copy by selecting different blocks of marks from among their content and piecing the new blocks together. Another kind of cost-effective attack is a process in which several differently marked copies of the same content are averaged to disrupt the underlying watermarks. These attacks by a coalition of users with the same content containing different marks are called 'Collusion Attack'. Fingerprinting scheme can provide support for copyright protection on the basis of collusion resistance. Digital fingerprinting scheme is defined as follow:

Definition 1. *(Digital Fingerprinting)* (L, N)-*fingerprinting scheme is a function* $\Phi(m^u)$ *which maps a user information* m^u $(1 \leq u \leq N)$ *to a codeword in* Σ^L, *where* Σ *is an alphabet. When a coalition of at most* c *users,* $C = \{u^1, u^2, \cdots, u^c\}$, *employs* $C' = (\Phi(m^{u_1}), \Phi(m^{u_2}), \cdots, \Phi(m^{u_c}))$ *to create a word* $z \in \Sigma^L$, Φ *is called* c-*secure with* ε-*error if there exists a tracing algorithm* A *that finds some* $\Phi(m^{u_i})$ *with probability of at least* $1 - \varepsilon$, *where probability is taken over the random choice of* Φ *and coalition* C.

3   Spread Spectrum Coding for Collusion Security

According the property of spread spectrum coding, Assuming Σ denotes real space with normal distribution and set $\Gamma = \{W^{(1)}, W^{(2)}, \ldots, W^{(n)}\} \subseteq \Sigma^l$ is known as a (l, n)-spread spectrum code (SS code), if each codeword $W^{(k)} = (w_1^k, w_2^k, \ldots, w_l^k)$ $(k = 1, 2, \ldots, n)$ in Γ is an orthonormal pseudo-random sequence, where w_i^k $(i = 1, 2, \ldots, l)$ independently chooses according normal distribution $N(0, \sigma_w^2)$ and $E(\frac{1}{l} \sum_{i=0}^{l} w_i^{k_j} w_i^{k_r}) = 0$ denotes orthogonality, $j \neq r$. We refer to the set of words in Γ as the codebook. Let $X = (x_1, x_2, \ldots, x_l)$ denotes the original content and g_i is a weight factor for x_i in terms of the perceptual masking model. The SS sequence $W^{(k)}$ is embedded into X by

$$x_i^k = x_i + g_i w_i^k, (i = 1, 2, \cdots, l), \tag{1}$$

where $X^{(k)} = (x_1^k, x_2^k, \ldots, x_l^k)$ is a corresponding copy with fingerprint.

When a illegal copies X' is obtained, a correlation coefficient is calculated by correlation detection to verify verify whether there exists the SS sequence. In contrast with watermarking detection, which generally employs blind detection without any knowledge of the original content, fingerprinting detection is not used to blind detection because the verifier is the merchant who has the original content(blind fingerprinting detection see[8]). The correlation coefficient of fingerprint $W^{(k)}$ can be summarized in the following formula:

$$r^k = \frac{1}{l} \sum_{i=1}^{l} (x_i' - x_i) w_i^k. \tag{2}$$

For a pre-specified threshold t, the fingerprint codeword W^k is determined if $r^k > t$, otherwise the codeword does not exist. In order to conveniently compute, suppose that watermarking weight factor $g_i \equiv 1$. Without adversary attacks, the mean value of the correlation coefficient r^k is given by

$$E(r^k) = \frac{1}{l} \sum_{i=1}^{l} E\left((x_i' - x_i) w_i^k\right) = \frac{1}{l} \left(\sum_{i=1}^{l} E\left(w_i^k\right)^2 \right) = \sigma_w^2. \tag{3}$$

Under the assumption that w_i^k is a normal distribution with variance σ_w^2, we can calculate $var(w_w^k)^2 = 2\sigma_w^4$, the variance of r^k is given by

$$var(r^k) = \frac{1}{l^2} \left(var \left(\sum_{i=1}^{l} (w_i^k)^2 \right) \right) = \frac{2\sigma_w^4}{l}. \tag{4}$$

Hence, the distribution of r^k tends to be close to normal, that is $r^k \sim N(\sigma_w^2, 2\sigma_w^4/l)$. fingerprint codeword length l is larger, the variance is smaller. To validate the distributing of correlation detection, the experiments employs pseudo-random generation of normal distribution to produce sequence $w_i^{(k)} \sim N(0, 1)$ with code length $l = 1024$.

Fig.1(a) shows the distribution histogram of SS sequences and the Gaussian fit (solid curve) that indicates that sequence is approximate Gaussian distribution with zero mean. Fig.1(b) shows the distribution histogram from its correlation detection coefficients and the Gaussian fit (solid curve) that indicates the mean is 1 and the variance is 0.00018. according to (4), the variance can be computed by $var(r) = 2\sigma_w^4/l = 2/1024 = 0.00195$. This is approximate to the experiment result.

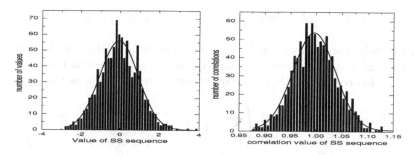

Fig. 1. The distribution histogram of (a) Spread spectrum sequences and (b) its correlation detection coefficients

In digital fingerprinting each copy includes an unique fingerprint sequence. Unlike watermarking, in which all copies of a content have the same or similar marks (copyright information), collusion attacks are feasible for fingerprinting. Moreover, for perceptual medium, collusion attacks are more complex than 'Marking Assumption' in BS model. The attacks involve collusion combination attack, collusion average attack and addition noise attack. These attacks are analyzed respectively as follows.

3.1   Collusion Combination Attack

Similarly to Marking Assumption in BS model, collusion combination attack is that several buyers can pool and piece together their copies so as to remove or generate a copy with a new fingerprint that is different from those they were assigned. Not considering erasuring marks, this attack is defined as follow:

Definition 2. *Let $\Gamma = \{W^{(1)}, W^{(2)}, \cdots, W^{(n)}\}$ is an (l, n)-code and $C = \{u_1, u_2, \cdots, u_c\}$ is a coalition of c-traitors. Let we say that position i is undetectable for C if the words assigned to users in C match in i'th position, that is $w_i^{(u_1)} = \cdots = w_i^{(u_c)}$. For detectable position, we define the feasible set Γ of C as*

$$\Gamma(C) = \{x = (x_1, \cdots, x_l) \in \Sigma^l | x_j \in \{w_j^{(u_i)} | 1 \le i \le c\}, 1 \le j \le l\} \qquad (5)$$

According to DSSS, SS code is a random, uniform and orthonormal sequence. Here the random of sequence provides unconditional security, that is an adversary cannot statistically distinguish between arbitrary sequences. Consequently, adversary cannot distinguish and guess fingerprint marks when several adversaries contrast the copies of each other. Assuming that a coalition of c-adversary is $C = \{u_{k_1}, u_{k_2}, \cdots, u_{k_c}\}$, a feasible strategy is to uniformly piece together the copies, include in $\min_i \{w_j^{(u_i)}\}$, $\max_i \{w_j^{(u_i)}\}$ and $\text{median}_i \{w_j^{(u_i)}\}$. Every adversary chooses averagely l/c elements to combine a new copy, here we assume the combined sequence as

$$W' = (w_1^{k_1}, \cdots, w_{l/c}^{k_1}, w_{l/c+1}^{k_2}, \cdots, w_{2l/c}^{k_2}, \cdots, w_{l(c-1)/c+1}^{k_c}, \cdots, w_l^{k_c}). \qquad (6)$$

Apparently, the sequence still subjects to normal distribution $N(0, \sigma_w^2)$ but the statistical property of orthonormal sequence becomes worse. For a user u_{k_1}, the correlation coefficient r^{k_1} is (the other users are the same as the user u_{k_1})

$$r^{k_1} = \frac{1}{l}\sum_{i=1}^{l}(x_i' - x_i)w_i^{k_1} = \frac{1}{l}\left(\sum_{i=1}^{l/c}g_i\left(w_i^{k_1}\right)^2 + \sum_{i=l/c+1, j\neq 1}^{l}g_i w_i^{k_j} w_i^{k_1}\right). \qquad (7)$$

Suppose $g_i \equiv 1$, the mean of correlation coefficient is

$$E(r^{k_1}) = \frac{1}{l}\sum_{i=1}^{l}E\left((x_i' - x_i)w_i^{k_1}\right)$$

$$= \frac{1}{l}\left(\sum_{i=1}^{l/c}E\left(w_i^{k_1}\right)^2 + \sum_{i=l/c+1, j\neq 1}^{l}E(w_i^{k_j}w_i^{k_1})\right) = \frac{\sigma_w^2}{c}. \qquad (8)$$

The variance of r^{k_1} is

$$var(r^{k_1}) = \frac{1}{l^2}\left(var\left(\sum_{i=1}^{l/c}\left(w_i^{k_1}\right)^2\right) + var\left(\sum_{i=l/c+1, j\neq 1}^{l}w_i^{k_j}w_i^{k_1}\right)\right)$$

$$= \frac{1}{l^2}\left(\frac{2l\sigma_w^4}{c} + \sum_{i=l/c+1, j\neq 1}^{l}E(w_i^{k_j}w_i^{k_1})^2\right)$$

$$= \frac{1}{l^2}\left(\frac{2l\sigma_w^4}{c} + \frac{(c-1)l\sigma_w^4}{c}\right) = \frac{\sigma_w^4(c+1)}{lc}. \qquad (9)$$

This shows that the mean of r^{k_1} reduces c-times and the variance gradually decreases to σ_w^4/l after attacks. Fig.2(a) shows the distribution histogram of SS sequences with code length $l = 1024$ under 8-user collusion combination attack. The result of the Gaussian fit indicates that sequence subjects to an approximate

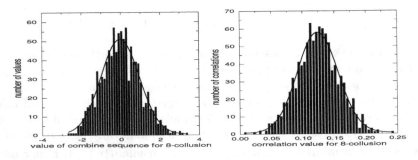

Fig. 2. The distribution histogram of (a) SS sequences and (b) its correlation detection coefficients for 8-collusions combination attack

Gaussian distribution $N(0, 0.98)$, which is consistent with the analysis. Fig.2(b) shows the histogram of correlation coefficient of arbitrary sequence in Fig.2(a). The result of the Gaussian fit indicates that the mean is 0.124 and the variance is 0.0011, According (8) and (9), the mean in theory is $E(r) = \sigma_w^2/c = 1/8$ and the variance is $var(r) = (c+1)\sigma_w^4/(c \cdot l) = 9/(8 \cdot 1024) = 0.0011$, which is approximate to the experiments.

3.2   Collusion Average Attack

A coalition of $C = \{u_{k_1}, u_{k_2}, \cdots, u_{k_c}\}$ averages their copies to generate a new copy, which is called as collusion average attack. This attack applies to the perceptual medium but not exist in BS model. This attack can be denoted by

$$\bar{X} = \frac{1}{c}\sum_{i=1}^{c} X^{(k_i)} = \frac{1}{c}\sum_{i=1}^{c}\left(X + W^{(k_i)}\right) = X + \frac{1}{c}\sum_{i=1}^{c} W^{(k_i)}. \quad (10)$$

According the property of Gaussian distribution, $var\left(\frac{1}{c}\sum_{i=1}^{c} W^{k_i}\right) = \sigma_w^2/c$, that is $\bar{X} \sim N(0, \sigma_w^2/c)$. The the correlation coefficient r^{k_1} of the user u_{k_1} is

$$r^{k_1} = \frac{1}{l}\sum_{i=1}^{l}(\bar{x}_i - x_i)w_i^{k_1} = \frac{1}{cl}\sum_{i=1}^{l}(\sum_{j=1}^{c} w_i^{k_j})w_i^{k_1} = \frac{1}{cl}\sum_{i=1}^{l}\left(\sum_{j=1}^{c} w_i^{k_j} w_i^{k_1}\right), \quad (11)$$

where $\bar{x}_i = x_i + \frac{1}{c}\sum_{j=1}^{c} w^{(k_j)}$. Suppose $g_i \equiv 1$, the mean of r^{k_1} is

$$\begin{aligned}
E(r^{k_1}) &= \frac{1}{l}\sum_{i=1}^{l} E\left((\bar{x}_i - x_i)w_i^{k_1}\right) = \frac{1}{cl}\sum_{i=1}^{l} E\left(\sum_{j=1}^{c} w_i^{k_j} w_i^{k_1}\right) \\
&= \frac{1}{cl}\sum_{i=1}^{l}\left(\sum_{j=1}^{c} E\left(w_i^{k_j} w_i^{k_1}\right)\right) = \frac{1}{cl}\sum_{i=1}^{l}\left(E\left(w_i^{k_1}\right)^2\right) \\
&= \frac{1}{cl}\sum_{i=1}^{l}\sigma_w^2 = \frac{\sigma_w^2}{c}. \quad (12)
\end{aligned}$$

The variance of r^{k_1} is

$$\begin{aligned}
var(r^{k_1}) &= \frac{1}{l^2}\sum_{i=1}^{l} var\left((\bar{x}_i - x_i)w_i^{k_1}\right) = \frac{1}{c^2 l^2}\sum_{i=1}^{l} var\left(\sum_{j=1}^{c} w_i^{k_j} w_i^{k_1}\right) \\
&= \frac{1}{c^2 l^2}\sum_{i=1}^{l}\left(var(w_i^{k_1})^2 + \sum_{j=2}^{c} var\left(w_i^{k_j} w_i^{k_1}\right)\right) \\
&= \frac{1}{c^2 l^2}\sum_{i=1}^{l}(2\sigma_w^4 + (c-1)\sigma_w^4) = \frac{c+1}{c^2 l}\sigma_w^4. \quad (13)
\end{aligned}$$

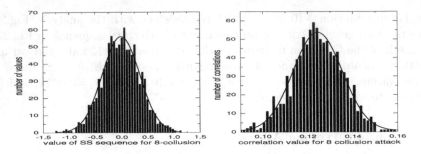

Fig. 3. The distribution histogram of (a) SS sequences and (b) its correlation detection coefficients for 8-collusions average attack

This shows that the mean of r^{k_1} reduces c-times and the variance gradually decreases to $\sigma_w^4/(cl)$ after attacks, i.e. r^{k_1} subjects to approximate Gaussian distribution $r^{k_i} \sim N(\sigma_w^2/c, \sigma_w^4/cl)$, which indicates the distortion is decreased. Fig3.(a) shows the distribution histogram of SS sequences with code length $l = 1024$ under 8-user collusion average attack. The result of the Gaussian fit indicates that sequence subjects to an approximate Gaussian distribution $N(0, 0.125)$, which is consistent with $\sigma_w^2/c = 1/8$ in theory. Fig.2(b) shows the histogram of correlation coefficient of arbitrary sequence in Fig.2(a). The result of the Gaussian fit indicates that the mean is 0.124 and the variance is 0.00013, According (12) and (13), the mean in theory is $E(r) = \sigma_w^2/c = 1/8$ and the variance is $var(r) = (c+1)\sigma_w^4/(c^2 \cdot l) = 9/(8^2 \cdot 1024) = 0.000137$, which is approximate to the experiments.

3.3   Additional Noise Attack

The influence of addition noise does not take into account in BS model, but the perceptual medium is usually prone to noise attack. Although this attack does not belong to collusion attack, in experiment we find it is a good attack method. Suppose fingerprint suffers from noise attack $x_i' = x_i + n_i$ where $n_i \sim N(0, \sigma_n^2)$, In (2) the correlation coefficient r^k can be denoted by

$$r^k = \frac{1}{l}\sum_{i=1}^{l}(x_i' - x_i)w_i^k = \frac{1}{l}\sum_{i=1}^{l}(n_i + g_iw_i^k)w_i^k. \tag{14}$$

Moreover, the expectation of r^k can be calculated by

$$E(r^k) = \frac{1}{l}\sum_{i=1}^{l}E\left((x_i' - x_i)w_i^k\right) = \frac{1}{l}\sum_{i=1}^{l}E\left((n_i + g_iw_i^k)w_i^k\right)$$

$$= \frac{1}{l}\sum_{i=1}^{l}\left[E(n_iw_i^k) + E\left(g_i(w_i^k)^2\right)\right] = \frac{\sigma_w^2}{l}\sum_{i=1}^{l}g_i. \tag{15}$$

The variance of r^k is

$$var(r^k) = \frac{1}{l^2} \sum_{i=1}^{l} var\left((x_i' - x_i)w_i^k\right) = \frac{1}{l^2} \sum_{i=1}^{l} var\left((n_i + g_i w_i^k)w_i^k\right)$$

$$= \frac{1}{l^2} \sum_{i=1}^{l} \left[var(n_i w_i^k) + var\left(g_i(w_i^k)^2\right)\right] = \frac{\sigma_w^2}{l^2} \sum_{i=1}^{l} (\sigma_n^2 + 2g_i^2\sigma_w^2). \quad (16)$$

Let $g_i \equiv 1$, the distribution approximates $r^k \sim N(\sigma_w^2, (\sigma_n^2 + 2\sigma_w^2)\sigma_w^2/l)$ after noise attack. Addition noise has not influence of the expectation but increases the variance. Hence the detection error probability is increased. In the allowable instance of content quality, noise attack and collusion attack can be combined to reach the better effect.

3.4   Collusion Security of Spread Spectrum Code

The foregoing analysis of collusion attack indicates that collusion combination attack is better than collusion average attack. Hence we can use collusion combination attack as an example to illustrate the security property of SS code and the relation of collusion size and code length as follows:

Theorem 1. *Consider the Spread-Spectrum code $\Gamma(l,n)$ where $l = O(-c^2 \log (\sqrt{c}\varepsilon))$. Let U be the set of users which the correlation detection algorithm pronounces as guilty by word for word on input illegal copy X' with c-collusion. Then with probability at least $1 - \varepsilon$, the set U is a subset of the coalition C that produced X'.*

Proof. In the Spread-Spectrum code Γ, suppose the correlation coefficient approximately subjects to Gaussian distribution. in general, the problem of fingerprint detection can be considered as the hypothesis testing problem under two hypothesis H_0 and H_1. For the arbitrary codeword $W^{(k)}$ in Γ, H_0 denotes that the illegal copy includes $W^{(k)}$ and H_1 denotes that the copy does not include $W^{(k)}$. Two hypothesis can be illustrated as follow:

$$\begin{cases} H_0 : X'(n) = Y(n) \\ H_1 : X'(n) = Y(n) + W^{(k)}(n) \end{cases} \quad (17)$$

where, Y includes the other codeword except X. under the H_0 hypothesis, the correlation coefficient approximates $r \sim N(0, \sigma_w^4/l)$. Under the H_1 hypothesis, the correlation coefficient approximates $r \sim N(\sigma_w^2/c, \sigma_w^4(c+1)/(lc))$. When the collusion size is larger $(c \gg 1)$, $r \sim N(\sigma_w^2/c, \sigma_w^4/l)$. For a given threshold t, the detection error probability P_{errer} can be calculated by

$$P_{errer} = P(r < t|H_1)P(H_1) + P(r > t|H_0)P(H_0)$$

$$= \frac{1}{2} \frac{\sqrt{l}}{\sqrt{2\pi}\sigma_w^2} \int_{-\infty}^{t} \exp\left(-\frac{r^2 l}{2\sigma_w^4}\right) dr$$

$$+ \frac{1}{2} \frac{\sqrt{l}}{\sqrt{2\pi}\sigma_w^2} \int_{t}^{\infty} \exp\left(-\frac{(r - \sigma_w^2/c)^2 l}{2\sigma_w^4}\right) dr. \quad (18)$$

Suppose that false alarm and missed detection have equal probability, then let $t = \sigma_w^2/2c$. This leads to

$$
\begin{aligned}
P_{error} &= 2 \left(\frac{1}{2} \frac{\sqrt{l}}{\sqrt{2\pi\sigma_w^2}} \int_{-\infty}^{t} \exp\left(-\frac{r^2 l}{2\sigma_w^4} \right) dr \right) \\
&= Q \left(\frac{\sigma_w^2/2c}{\sqrt{\sigma_w^4/l}} \right) = Q \left(\frac{\sqrt{l}}{2c} \right),
\end{aligned} \tag{19}
$$

where, $Q(t) = \frac{1}{\sqrt{2\pi}} \int_{t}^{\infty} \exp\left(-\frac{r^2}{2} \right) dr$. It is obvious that error probability is in inverse proportion to codeword length l and is in direct proportion to collusion size c. $Q(x)$ can approximately denoted by $Q(x) \approx \frac{1}{\sqrt{2\pi x}} \exp(-\frac{x^2}{2})$, this means that

$$
P_{error} = Q \left(\frac{\sqrt{l}}{2c} \right) \approx \frac{2c}{\sqrt{2\pi l}} \exp\left(-\frac{l}{8c^2} \right) > \frac{1}{k\sqrt{c}} \exp\left(-\frac{l}{8c^2} \right), \tag{20}
$$

where, according to codeword length bound $l < Kc^3$ in [7], the inequality can be calculated by $\sqrt{l} < kc\sqrt{c}$, where K and k are constant. Hence we have that

$$
l > -8c^2 \ln\left(k\sqrt{c}P_{error} \right). \tag{21}
$$

In digital fingerprinting, in usually ε denotes the error probability P_{error} and $\sqrt{c}\varepsilon < 1$. Hence the codeword length is $l = O(-c^2 \log(\sqrt{c}\varepsilon))$.   □

In BS model [1] the codeword length of $\Gamma_0(n, d)$ code with n-secure ε-error is $l = (n - 1)d$ and $d = 2n^2 \log(2n/\varepsilon)$. In contrast with Theorem (1), the SS code length much reduces Because $1/(\varepsilon\sqrt{c}) < c/\varepsilon$. Here we can select the codeword length by

$$
l = 8c^2 \log(c/\varepsilon). \tag{22}
$$

This ensures that the detection error probability P_{error} is at most ε.

4   Convolutional Spread-Spectrum Fingerprinting Scheme

The target of this paper is that constructs a ε-error and c-secure fingerprinting scheme for N-users to improve runtime and reduce storage. For this purpose, this section presents a convolutional spread-spectrum fingerprinting scheme for perceptual medium. In this scheme, the construction of fingerprint codes uses the structure provided by algebraic codes. We replace the general Error Correcting Codes in BS model with convolutional codes. The scheme employs two-layer structure by composing an inner SS code with an outer convolutional code. The major differences between the presented scheme and classical BS model are:

1. The inner codes are constructed by SS codes in order to achieve collusion-resistent, robustness and imperception.
2. The outer codes are constructed by convolutional codes to reduce codeword length, and the decoding efficiency is improved by Maximum Likelihood Decoding algorithm. It is realized that the fingerprinting information length is irrelative to user size and inner codeword length.

The scheme is illustrated from the encoding and decoding process as follows.

4.1 Convolutional SS Fingerprinting Encoding

Convolutional error correcting codes were first introduced by Elias and are widely applied today in telecommunication systems, e.g., radio, satellite links, mobile communication [9]. Convolutional codes differ from the block codes in that each encoding operation depends on current and a number of previous information groups. Convolutional code has some advantage to build self-orthogonal code and punctured code. Therefore, convolutional decoding can be performed using a Viterbi algorithm which is the more convenient to obtain the optimum decoding than block codes. Hence, this paper constructs the Convolutional Spread-Spectrum Fingerprint (CSSF) code based on the convolutional code.

The presented $\Phi(L, N, l, n)$-fingerprint code has two-layer concatenate structure: the upper layer is $\Im(n_0, k_0, m_0)$-convolutional code called Convolutional Error-Correcting Layer and the lower layer is $\Gamma(l, n)$-SS code called Spread-Spectrum Fingerprint Layer, where N is the user number and L is convolutional code length. A convolutional code group is called as a fingerprint word. Let c is the maximum collusion number, $m^{(u_i)}$ denotes the identification symbol string of user u_i $(1 \leq i \leq N)$. The $m^{(u_i)}$ is assigned randomly with uniform distribution and assures unique to each user. Let an (n_0, k_0, m_0) convolutional encoder over the Galois field $GF(2^q)$, where q is the number of bits in a group, is a k_0-input, n_0-output finite-state machine of encoder memory order m_0 [10]. Thus, the set of k_0 data groups, each of a fixed length q, is input into an (n_0, k_0, m_0) convolutional encoder, and $(n_0 - k_0)$ redundant packets are generated based on a generator matrix. Parameter m_0 refers to the memory of the encoder, and indicates how many previous code groups influence the redundant packet.

In the process of encoding, information $m^{(u_i)}$ is firstly partitioned into the blocks that is introduced into the convolutional encoder to obtain the fingerprint codewords. And then these codewords are encoded by SS encoder to the fingerprint sequences. Finally, these fingerprint sequences are concatenated into a fingerprint code. The $\Phi(L, N, l, n)$-code defined as follow: Suppose that a codeword $v = (v_1, v_2, \cdots v_L) \in \Im$ is an output of the convolutional encoder for information $m^{(u_i)}$, Let

$$W_v = (W^{(v_1)} \parallel W^{(v_2)} \parallel \cdots \parallel W^{(v_L)}), \qquad (23)$$

where $\parallel$ means concatenation of strings. The code Φ is the set of all words W_v, i.e. $\Phi = \{W_v \mid v \in \Im\}$.

SS Fingerprint Layer Encoding. The aim is to resist collusion attacks at finite codebook and verify traitor codewords in spread-spectrum fingerprint layer. Let Σ denotes the real space with normal distribution. Given a set $\Gamma = \{W^{(1)}, W^{(2)}, \cdots, W^{(n)}\} \subseteq \Sigma^l$ and $I = \{i_1, i_2, \cdots, i_n\}$. If each codeword $W^{(k)} = (w_1^k, w_2^k, \cdots, w_l^k)$ is orthonormal pseudo-random sequence $(k = 1, 2, \cdots, n)$, Γ is called an (l, n)-spread spectrum fingerprint code. Each codeword $W^{(k)}$ is assigned to a element i_k in I. Suppose $X = (x_1, x_2, \cdots, x_l)$ denotes the original content and g_i is the perceptual weight of signal x_i, for $W^{(k)}$ the embedding formula are:

$$x_i^k = x_i + g_i w_i^k, (i = 1, 2, \cdots, l) \tag{24}$$

where $X^{(k)} = (x_1^k, x_2^k, \ldots, x_l^k)$ is a copy with corresponding fingerprint. SS fingerprint layer encoding algorithm is described as follow:

Algorithm 1 (Spread-spectrum fingerprint encoding algorithm)

```
SS_Encoding (original document X, number k)
    Draw pseudorandom sequence W^(k)
    Compute G from X according to perceptual masking model
    Return marked copy X^(k) = X + G·W^(k)
End
```

Convolutional Error-Correcting Layer Encoding. In $\Im(n_0, k_0, m_0)$, a user identification $m^{(u_i)}$ are divided into L groups with k_0 bits in each group, which involves m_0 groups to guarantee return to the initial state. $m^{(u_i)}$ is convolutional encoded as $v = (v_1, v_2, \cdots v_L)$ which is a binary sequence of length $n_0 L$. Here, $\Im$ is prone to choose the convolutional code with more free distance between codewords. We know that each v_i has $2^{k_0 m_0}$ states in state transition diagram. For the purpose of concatenating SS code, let $n \geq 2^{k_0 m_0}$ and each v_i is assigned to a codeword $W^{(v_i)}$ in Γ. Hence we can obtain L codes $(W^{(v_1)}, W^{(v_2)}, \cdots, W^{(v_L)})$ and concatenate those into a string. Finally, the string are randomly permuted by π to generate a CSSF code. the permutation π prevents the coalition from distinguishing the codeword $W^{(v_i)}$. Consequently, the distance restrict between codewords is eliminated in BS model. The security of fingerprinting depends only on the secret permutation π chosen randomly by merchant and the randomicity of spread-spectrum sequence.

The encoding process is described as follows: Suppose $X = (X_1, X_2, \cdots, X_L)$ is cover data from the original content S, where X_i is the sequence of length l, i.e. $X_i = (x_{i,1}, x_{i,2}, \cdots, x_{i,l})$ $(i = 1, 2, \cdots, n)$. For user u_i, we can encode $m^{(u_i)}$ and number i as $v = (v_1, v_2, \cdots, v_L)$ by using convolutional encoder. And then each v_j is encoded $W^{(v_j)} = (w_1^{(v_j)}, w_2^{(v_j)}, \cdots, w_l^{(v_j)})$ in SS fingerprint laryer. Furthermore, these codes are concatenated and randomly permuted by π to generate fingerprint code $W^{(v_j)}$, that is $W^{(v)} = \pi \left(W^{(v_1)} \parallel W^{(v_2)} \parallel \cdots \parallel W^{(v_L)} \right)$, where $\parallel$ can be realized in transform domain. Finally, similarly to algorithm (1), fingerprint $W^{(v)}$ is embedded into X to obtain the copy $X^{(u_i)}$ of user u_i. The CSSF encoding algorithm is described as follow:

Algorithm 2 (Convolutional fingerprint encoding algorithm)

```
Fingerprinting_Encoding (original document X, message m^(u_i),
    permutation π)
    Let v = Convolutional_Encoding(m^(u_i), i)
    For each 1≤j≤L
        Draw pseudorandom sequence W^(k)
    Let W^(v) = π(W^(v_1) || W^(v_2) || ··· || W^(v_L))
    Compute G from X according to perceptual masking model
    Return marked copy X^(u_i) = X + G·W^(v)
End
```

4.2 Convolutional SS Fingerprinting Decoding

The fingerprint decoding is a tracing algorithm that can identify traitors as many as possible by efficient means. It is requested that the tracing algorithm never accuses an innocent user and the probability that tracing fails can be made arbitrarily small. The identification algorithm of BS model involves the decoding of a random code, that is known to be a NP-hard problem. To resolve this problem, we present an optimal probability decoding algorithm by improving spread spectrum tracing algorithm and convolutional Viterbi algorithm.

SS Fingerprint Layer Decoding. After the fingerprint is attacked by coalition, $\Gamma_0(l, d)$-decoder in BS model does not find out many illegal codewords but arbitrarily choose one of those codewords as a result of the limit of $(L, N, D)_p$-ECC codes. Moreover, the ultimate result of fingerprint decoding can only find at most a member of the guilty coalition. In contrast with BS model, we present a decoding algorithm of $\Gamma(l, n)$-SS code that can output a codeword set of coalition. Such a codeword set is called an Optional Code Set (OCS). In SS fingerprint decoding, the decoder adopts the correlation detection similar to Formula(2). For each $W^{(k)}$ in $\Gamma(l, n)$ $(k = 1, 2, \cdots, n)$, we verify one by one whether the correlation is greater than a given threshold t, that is $S(W, W^{(k)}) > t$, where $S(W, W')$ computes the correlation coefficient between two sequences. The algorithm will finally output all suspicious codewords that is greater than t.

Algorithm 3 (spread-spectrum fingerprint decoding algorithm)

```
SS_Decoding(suspect document Y, original document X)
    Let U = {}, W = Y - X
    For each 1≤k≤n
        If S(W, W^(k)) > t Then U = U ∪{k}
    Return U
End
```

---

convolutional Error-Correcting Layer Decoding. Maximum-likelihood (ML) decoding of convolutional codes is often implemented by means of the

Viterbi algorithm. However, The Viterbi algorithm must be improved to perform optimal probability decoding because the codeword space of convolutional is extended by the optical code sets of SS fingerprint codes. The Viterbi decoding is a minimum-distance probability decoding algorithm for convolutional codes. In trellis, assumption that the received symbol sequences is $R = (r_1, r_2, \cdots, r_L)$, where each optional code set r_i is composed by some suspicious codewords, i.e. $r_I = \{r_{i,1}, r_{i,2}, \cdots, r_{i,t}\}$ and $t \in N$. The optimal decoding tries to find out a shortest path that the encoder goes across in trellis, which is equivalent to compute a maximum-likelihood path among $2^{k_0 L}$ paths of length L, i.e. $\max_i(\log(\Pr(R|H_i)))$ $(1 \le i \le 2^{k_0 L})$, where $\Pr(R|H_i)$ is likelihood function between R and H_i. Let R_i be the set of all paths before stage i among the received sequence R, i.e. $R_i = (r_1, r_2, \cdots, r_i)$; C_i be all arrived branches at stage i; $C_{i,j}$ be the branches to arrive state S_j at stage i; $e_{i,j}$ be a branch from state S_i to S_j; function $D(X|Y)$ be the path metric between path X and Y. In stage i, there exist many paths $C_{i,j}$ to reach state S_j, but only the maximum-likelihood path among $C_{i,j}$ are called survivor path $sp_{i,j} = (e_{1,i_1}, e_{2,i_2}, \cdots, e_{i,i_i})$. the path metric between $sp_{i,j}$ and R_i is called part metric. Since maximum likelihood decoding and minimum distance decoding are the same for a Binary Symmetric Channel (BSC), the part metric has minimum hamming distance, i.e. $d_{i,j} = D(sp_{i,j}) = \min D(R_i|C_{i,j})$. Hence, this section employs minimum distance to illustrate algorithms.

The proposed Viterbi algorithm can implement the maximum-likelihood decoding based on the optical code sets. The algorithm performs step-by-step as follows:

1. Initialization (at stage 0): Set the part metric of the original state S_1 of the trellis at 0 and others at ∞, the survivor path of each state is *null*.
2. Computation next stage: We suppose that at the previous stage k we have identified all survivor paths and stored each state's survivor path and part metric. For each state $S_j(1 \le j \le n)$ at stage $k + 1$, the candidate path $sq_{i,j}$ is computed as the addition of all incoming branches $e_{i,j}$ and the survivor path $sp_{k,i}$ in connection with this branch, i.e. $sq_{i,j} = (sp_{k,i}, e_{i,j})$. In order to compute the minimum path metric $d_{k+1,j}$ between the candidate path $sq_{k+1,j}$ and the received path R_{k+1} before stage $k + 1$ among R, for each incoming branch $e_{i,j}$, we compute the minimum metric $\min D(r_{k+1}|e_{i,j})$ between $e_{i,j}$ and optional code set r_{k+1}, and then the part metric $d_{k+1,j}$ of state S_j is computed as the minimum value of the addition of it and the part metric $d_{k,i}$ of state S_i, i.e.

$$d_{k+1,j} = \min D(R_{k+1}|sq_{i,j}) = \min_i(d_{k,i} + \min D(r_{k+1}|e_{i,j})), \qquad (25)$$

where, the minimum metric between the optional code set $r_{k+1} = \{r_{k+1,1}, r_{k+1,2}, \cdots, r_{k+1,t}\}$ and the branch $e_{i,j}$ is computed by $\min D(r_{k+1}|e_{i,j}) = \min_{1 \le l \le m} D(r_{k+1,l}|e_{i,j})$. The path corresponding to $d_{k+1,j}$ is survivor path $sp_{k+1,j}$. Finally, we store each state's survivor path $sp_{k+1,j}$ and part metric $d_{k+1,j}$ and delete the candidate paths.

3. Final stage: If $k \leq L$, then repeat step (2). Otherwise, we continue the computation until the algorithm reaches the termination symbol, at which time it makes a decision on the maximum-likelihood path that is equation to the survivor path corresponding to the minimum part metric $\min_{1 \leq j \leq n}(d_{L,j})$.

Finally, the decoding algorithm outputs the sequence of bits corresponding to this optimum path's branches. Convolutional fingerprint decoding algorithm is described at details as follow:

Algorithm 4 (Convolutional fingerprint decoding algorithm)

```
Convolutional-Decoding (suspect documentY, original documentX)
    Let d₀,ᵢ = ∞ , sp₀,ᵢ = {} for (1≤i≤n) except d₀,₁ = 0
        For each 1 ≤ k ≤ L
            Let rₖ = SS-Decoding(Yₖ ,Xₖ )
            For each state sⱼ
                For each the incoming branch eᵢ,ⱼ
                    For each the element rₖ,ₗ∈rₖ (1≤l≤m)
                        cₖ,ₗ = D(rₖ,ₗ | eᵢ,ⱼ )
                        Let sqᵢ,ⱼ = (spₖ,ᵢ,eᵢ,ⱼ), tᵢ,ⱼ = dₖ₋₁,ᵢ + min₁≤l≤m cₖ,ₗ
                    Let dₖ,ⱼ = minᵢ(tᵢ,ⱼ ) for exist eᵢ,ⱼ
                    Let spₖ,ⱼ = sqₗ,ⱼ for all dₖ,ⱼ == tₗ,ⱼ
        Let d_{L,l} = min₁≤j≤n(d_{L,j} )
        Return M(sp_{L,l} )
End
```

---

5   performance Analysis

Theorem 2. *The survivor path is maximum likelihood path in the improved Viterbi decoding algorithm (4) , namely, there exist survivor path sp for all candidate paths $sq \neq sp$, $D(R|sp) \geq D(R|sq)$.(For proof see [11])*

For the purpose of protecting innocent user from needless accusation, according to the properties of spread-spectrum code and convolutional code , we prove that the presented algorithm can find a member of the coalition with probability at least $1 - \varepsilon$.

Theorem 3. *Given integers N, c and $\varepsilon > 0$, set $l = 8c^2(\log(4c) + r)$, $r = (2/d_f)\log(A_{d_f}/P_e)$, where d_f is free distance of the code, A_{d_f} is the number of the code with weight d_f. Then spread-spectrum convolutional code $\Phi(L, N, l, n)$ is a code which is c-secure with ε-error. The code contains N codewords. Let x be a word which was produced by a coalition C of at most c users. Then Algorithm 3 will output a codeword of C with probability at least $1 - \varepsilon$.*

Proof. According to the properties of convolutional codes, in BSC channel, the error probability P_e of Viterbi decoder is

$$P_e \approx A_{d_f} 2^{d_f} p^{d_f/2}, \tag{26}$$

where, d_f is free distance of the code, A_{d_f} is the number of the code with weight d_f and p is channel transfer probability. Let the decoding error probability of SS code $\Gamma(l, n)$ is ε', the channel transfer probability is equation to the error probability of fingerprint codes Γ, i.e. $p = \varepsilon' = \frac{1}{4}(P_e/A_{d_f})^{2/d_f}$. On the basis of collusion-resistant properties of the fingerprint code Γ in Theorem (1), the codeword length is $l = 8c^2 \log(c/\varepsilon')$. Then, the codeword length of Φ is

$$l = 8c^2(\log(4c) + (2/d_f) \log(A_{d_f}/P_e)). \tag{27}$$

Notice that the properties of convolutional codes decides that the codeword length be independent of the error probability. Since $P_e = \varepsilon$ in Φ, the code Φ may occur the decoding error with probability at most ε when x be a fingerprint word which was produced by a coalition C of at most c users. Moreover, Theorem (2) denotes that the improved decoding algorithm can perform effectively the maximum likelihood search. As a result, algorithm (4) will output a codeword of C with probability at least $1 - \varepsilon$. □

Here, we don't intent to discuss the performance of encoding algorithm because it is obvious that the algorithm is lower complexity than previous algorithms. we focus our attention on the decoding algorithm from the following aspects:

Encoding length. The code length of fingerprinting encoder is Ll. In contrast with the code length $Ld(n - 1)$ in BS model, the code length is greatly reduced because $d(n - 1) > l$. At the same time, in BS model each $\Gamma_0(l, d)$-code bears with the error probability of $\varepsilon/2L$ and L depend on N and ε. Hence block length d is augmented along with increases of L. But in the proposed scheme l increase fix $8rc^2$ bits in terms of Theorem (3) since the current group depends only on m_0 previous groups according to the property of convolutional codes. As a result, L is independent of l, the code length is shorter than the other FP codes and then the parameters of CSSF code can be predefined.

Decoding complexity. The decoding complexity of spread-spectrum codes is in direct ratio to $O(nLl)$ and (n_0, k_0, m_0) convolutional codes is $O(nL)$ by processing L steps and searching n states at each step. The whole decoding complexity is still $O(nLl)$.

Storage performance. In respect of storage, general convolutional decoder must retain $n = 2^{k_0 m_0}$ states and only the survivor path and its metric must be stored for each state at the current trellis stage, as the decoding algorithm progresses. Hence it is obvious that the storage complexity of the whole decoder is $O(nL)$, where $n = 2^{k_0 m_0}$ and $n \geq c$. Usually $m_0 \leq 10$ and the length of the user information $m^{(u)}$ requests $|m| = k_0 L$. However, for finite length of the original medium, CSSF code allows us to shorten L by adjusting k_0 and m_0. It isn't difficult to choose the better convolution code even if the coalition size c is larger.

6 Conclusion

This paper provides a new approach for encoding and decoding fingerprinting to perceptual media based on spread-spectrum and convolutional code. This coding system is easy to implement and has acceptably low complexity. Furthermore, It also has significant reference value and guidance meaning for Intellectual Property Protection and relative field in theory and practice.

References

[1] D. Boneh and J. Shaw. Collusion-Secure Fingerprinting for Digital Data. In Proc. Advances in Cryptology - CRYPTO '95, Lecture Notes in Computer Science **963**, Berlin: Springer-Verlag (1995) 452–465

[2] I.J.Cox, J.Kilian, T. Shamoon, T. Leighton. Secure Spread Spectrum Watermarking for Multimedia, in IEEE Trans. on Image Processing. **6**(12) (1997) 1673–1687

[3] F. Ergun, J. Kilian, and R. Kumar, A note on the limits of collusion-resistant watermarks, in Eurocrypt '99, Lecture Notes in Computer Science **1592**, Berlin: Springer-Verlag (1999) 140–149

[4] A.Barg, G.R. Blakly, and G. Kabatiansky. Digital Fingerprinting Codes: Problem Statements, Constructions, Identification of Traitors, Technical report, DIMACS2001-52, (2001)

[5] A. Silverberg, J. Staddon, and J. Walker, Efficient Traitor Tracing Algorithms Using List Decoding. in Proc. Advances Cryptology - ASIACRYPT '01, Lecture Notes in Computer Science **2248**, Berlin: Springer-Verlag (2001) 175–192

[6] M. Fernandez and M. Soriano. Identification of Traitors in Algebraic-Geometric Traceability Codes. in IEEE Trans. on Signal Processing. Supplement on Secure Media , **52**(10) (2004) 3073–3077

[7] J. Kilian, F. T. Leighton, L. R. Matheson, T. G. Shamoon, R. E. Tarjan, and F. Zane. Resistance of Digital Watermarks to Collusive Attacks. Technical Report TR-585-98, Princeton University, Computer Science Department, July (1998). http://citeseer.ist.psu.edu/ kilian98 resistance.html

[8] Y. Zhu, Z.W. Sun, D.G. Feng and Y.T. Yang, Performance Analysis of Spread Spectrum CDMA Watermarking and Applied Reasearch in Multiwavelet Domain, Chinese Journal of Computers, (2005) (in print)

[9] F. Chan and D. Haccoun. Adaptive Viterbi Decoding of Convolutional Codes over Memoryless Channels. IEEE Transactions on Communications, **45**(11) (1997) 1389–1400

[10] Forney, G. D., Jr., Convolutional Codes I: Algebraic Structure, IEEE Trans. on Information Theory, **IT-16**(6), November (1970) 720–738

[11] Y. Zhu, D.G. Feng, Y.T. Yang. Convolutional Fingerprinting Information Codes for Collusion Security. in Proceedings of the SPIE conference on Mathematics of Data/Image Coding, Compression, and Encryption VIII with Applications, San Diego, August (2005) (to appear)

Performance Study on Multimedia Fingerprinting Employing Traceability Codes *

Shan He and Min Wu

University of Maryland, College Park, U.S.A
{shanhe, minwu}@eng.umd.edu.

Abstract. Digital fingerprinting is a tool to protect multimedia content from illegal redistribution by uniquely marking copies of the content distributed to each user. Collusion attack is a powerful attack whereby several differently-fingerprinted copies of the same content are combined together to attenuate or even remove the fingerprint. Coded fingerprinting is one major category of fingerprinting techniques against collusion. Many fingerprinting codes are proposed with tracing capability and collusion resistance, such as Traceability (TA) codes and Identifiable Parent Property (IPP) codes. Most of these works treat the important embedding issue in terms of a set of simplified and abstract assumptions, and they do not examine the end-to-end performance of the coded multimedia fingerprinting. In this paper we jointly consider the coding and embedding issues and examine the collusion resistance of coded fingerprinting systems with various code parameters. Our results show that TA codes generally offer better collusion resistance than IPP codes, and a TA code with a larger alphabet size and a longer code length is preferred.

1   Introduction

Technology advancement has made multimedia content widely available and easy to process. These benefits also bring ease to unauthorized users who can duplicate and manipulate multimedia content, and re-distribute it to a large audience. The protection of multimedia content becomes increasingly important. Digital fingerprinting is an emerging technology to protect multimedia content from unauthorized dissemination, whereby each user's copy is identified by a unique ID embedded in his/her copy and the ID, which we call *fingerprint*, can be extracted to help identify culprits when a suspicious copy is found. A powerful, cost-effective attack from a group of users is collusion attack, where the users combine their copies of the same content to generate a new version. If designed improperly, the fingerprints can be weakened or removed by the collusion attacks.

A growing number of techniques have been proposed in the literature to provide collusion resistance in multimedia fingerprinting systems. Many of them fall

---

* This work was supported in part by the U.S. Office of Naval Research under Young Investigator Award N000140510634 and the U.S. National Science Foundation under CAREER Award CCR-0133704.

M. Barni et al. (Eds.): IWDW 2005, LNCS 3710, pp. 84–96, 2005.

in one of the two categories, namely, the non-coded fingerprinting and the coded fingerprinting. The orthogonal fingerprinting is a typical example of non-coded fingerprinting. It assigns each user a spread spectrum sequence as the fingerprint and the sequences among users are mutually orthogonal. The collusion resistance of orthogonal fingerprinting has been well studied by Wang et al. [1] and Ergun et al. [2]. Coded fingerprinting employs an explicit coding step to build the fingerprint sequences. One of the earliest works is by Boneh and Shaw [3], where a two-level code construction known as a c-secure code was proposed to resist up to c colluders with a high probability. This binary code was later used to modulate a direct spread spectrum sequence to embed the fingerprints in multimedia signals [4]. Following Boneh and Shaw's framework, many recent works consider the construction of fingerprinting codes for generic data that have tracing capability and are able to resist collusion. We collectively call these codes traceability codes, which include Identifiable Parent Property (IPP) codes and Traceability (TA) codes[1] [5]- [9]. In [10] and [11], TA codes are applied to multimedia fingerprinting and extended to deal with symbol erasures contributed by noise or cropping in multimedia signal domain. Fernandez and Soriano [12] employ TA codes constructed through algebraic-geometry codes for fingerprinting multimedia content. They define identifiable colluders and propose to employ the Guruswami-Sudan soft-decision list decoding algorithm for algebraic-geometry codes to find such users. Existing coded fingerprinting mainly focuses on the code layer and treat the embedding issues through an abstract model known as the *marking assumption* [3] [10]. It typically assumes that colluders can only change fingerprint symbols where they have different values, and the colluders assemble pieces of their codes to generate a colluded version. Although the marking assumption may work well with generic data, it alone is not always appropriate to model multimedia fingerprinting. Both coding and embedding issues need to be considered in multimedia fingerprinting. A recent work by Trappe et al. [13] has shown very promising results by this joint consideration. In their work, a code based on combinatorial design was proposed, and each code bit is embedded in an overlapped fashion by modulating a spreading sequence that covers the entire multimedia signal. The overlap spreading confines the types of manipulation from colluders, and colluders can be identified through the code bits shared by them.

In our recent work on coded fingerprinting [14] [15] [16], we jointly consider coding and embedding and have found that coded fingerprinting allows for a much more efficient detection than non-coded orthogonal fingerprinting [1], but it has rather limited collusion resistance. Based on this joint consideration, we propose a *Permuted Subsegment Embedding (PSE)* technique [16] which substantially improves the collusion resistance of coded fingerprinting. With this improvement, coded fingerprinting has a better trade-off between collusion

---

[1] The term "traceability codes", in a broad sense, refers to the collection of fingerprinting codes with tracing capability, and in a narrow sense, refers to a specific type of traceability codes that will be discussed later. To avoid confusion, in this paper, we will use "TA codes" to represent the narrow-sense traceability codes.

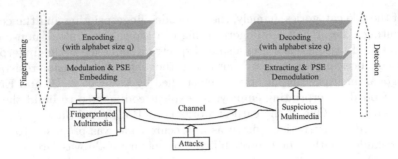

Fig. 1. Framework of traceability code based fingerprinting scheme

resistance and detection efficiency than the non-coded fingerprinting. One question that remains to be answered is the effect of the code parameters on the performance of the fingerprinting systems.

In this paper, building upon a cross-layer framework and employing our previously proposed PSE technique, we examine the effect of different codes on the collusion resistance of coded multimedia fingerprinting. The paper is organized as follows. Section 2 provides a general background on coded fingerprinting and reviews fingerprinting codes with emphasis on IPP code and TA code. We examine the collusion resistance of multimedia fingerprinting based on IPP codes and TA codes through analysis and simulations in Section 3. Finally the conclusions are drawn in Section 4.

2   Background on Coded Fingerprinting for Multimedia

2.1   System Framework

A typical framework for coded multimedia fingerprinting includes a code layer and a spread spectrum based embedding layer [14]. For anti-collusion purposes, the fingerprint code is constructed such that a colluded codeword by a coalition of c colluders can be traced back to one of the colluders. Each codeword is then assigned to one user as the fingerprint. To embed a codeword, we first partition the host signal into L non-overlapped segments with one segment corresponding to one symbol. Then we build q mutually orthogonal spread spectrum sequences $\{\mathbf{w}_j, j = 1, 2, ..., q\}$ with identical energy $||\mathbf{w}||^2$ to represent the q possible symbol values in the alphabet. Each user's fingerprint sequence is constructed by concatenating the spreading sequences corresponding to the symbols in his/her codeword. Before the embedding of the spreading sequence, we employ the *Permuted Subsegment Embedding (PSE)* technique proposed in our recent work [16] to get better collusion resistance. In PSE, each segment of the fingerprint sequence is partitioned into β subsegments and these subsegments are then randomly permuted according to a secret key. The permuted fingerprint sequence is added to the host signal with perceptual scaling to form the final fingerprinted signal.

After the distribution of the fingerprinted copies, users may collaborate and mount cost-effective collusion attacks. The existing works on coded fingerprinting have primarily targeted code-level collusion resistance. The widely considered collusion model is the *interleaving collusion*, whereby each colluder contributes a non-overlapped set of segments (corresponding to symbols) and these segments are assembled to form a colluded copy. Additional distortion may be added to the multimedia signal during the collusion, which we model as additive noise. Since few colluders would be willing to take higher risk than others, they generally would make contributions of an approximately equal amount in the collusion. Another major type of collusion is done in the signal domain. A typical example is the *averaging collusion* [1], whereby colluders average the corresponding components in their copies to generate a colluded version. The averaging collusion can be modelled as follows:

$$\mathbf{z} = \frac{1}{c} \sum_{j \in S_c} \mathbf{s_j} + \mathbf{x} + \mathbf{d}, \tag{1}$$

where $\mathbf{z}$ is the colluded signal, $\mathbf{x}$ is the host signal, $\mathbf{d}$ is the noise term, $\mathbf{s}_j$ represents the fingerprint sequence for user j, S_c is the colluder set, and c is the number of colluders. For simplicity in analysis, we assume that the additional noise under both collusions follows *i.i.d.* Gaussian distribution.

At the detector side, our goal is to catch one colluder with a high probability. We first extract the fingerprint sequence and inversely permute it according to the secret key used in the PSE. We then determine the symbol that is most likely to be present in each multimedia segment using a correlation detector commonly used for spread spectrum embedding [17]. We search the codebook and identify the colluder to be the one whose codeword has the smallest Hamming distance to the extracted codeword. Alternatively, after the inverse permutation of the fingerprint sequence, we can employ a correlation detector to correlate the entire test signal directly with every user's fingerprint signal $\mathbf{s}_j$. In this case, the decision is based on the overall correlation and no intermediate hard decision needs to be made at the symbol level. The user whose fingerprint has the highest correlation with the test signal is identified as the colluder, i.e. $\hat{j} = arg\,\max_{j=1,2,...,N_u} T_N(j)$. Here, the detection statistic $T_N(j)$ is defined as:

$$T_N(j) = \frac{(\mathbf{z} - \mathbf{x})^T \mathbf{s}_j}{\sqrt{\|\mathbf{s}\|^2}} \quad j = 1, 2, ..., N_u, \tag{2}$$

where $\mathbf{z}$ is the colluded signal, $\mathbf{x}$ is the original signal which is often available in fingerprinting applications, and $\|\mathbf{s}\| = \|\mathbf{s}_j\|$ for all j based on the equal energy construction. Compared with the former 2-step hard-decision scheme, the latter scheme takes advantage of the soft information on the symbol level and provides a better performance.

2.2   Fingerprinting Codes

At the code layer, a code with tracing capability is employed for the purpose of collusion resistance. In the literatures of fingerprint code design, codes such as

Identifiable Parent Property(IPP) codes and Traceability(TA) codes are widely studied [5]- [9]. We briefly review these two kinds of codes in the following.

c-TA Code. A c-TA code satisfies the condition that any colluded codeword by any c (or fewer) colluders has a smaller distance to at least one of these colluders' codewords than to the innocent users' [5]. We can construct a c-TA code using an established Error Correcting Code (ECC), provided that the minimum distance D is large enough and satisfies [5]

$$D > \left(1 - \frac{1}{c^2}\right) L. \tag{3}$$

Here L is the code length and c is the number of colluders that the code is intended to resist. With the minimum distance achieving the Singleton bound, a Reed-Solomon code is a natural choice for constructing a c-TA code. Then, the number of c-TA codewords over an alphabet of size q constructed through a Reed-Solomon code is $N_u = q^k$, where $k = \lceil L/c^2 \rceil$.

c-IPP Code. A c-IPP code satisfies the condition that any colluded codeword by a coalition of size at most c can be traced back to at least one member of the coalition [5]. A c-TA code is a c-IPP code, but a c-IPP code is not necessarily a c-TA code. Therefore, the set of c-TA codes is a subset of c-IPP codes. In terms of the traceability, the c-TA codes are stronger than those c-IPP codes that are not c-TA codes, which we call proper c-IPP codes. Van Trung et al. propose a method that can be used to construct a proper c-IPP code as follows [9]:

> Let A be an (L_2, N_2, q_2) c-IPP code with code length L_2, codeword number N_2 and alphabet size q_2. Let B be an (L_1, q_2, q_1) c-IPP code with code length L_1, codeword number q_2 and alphabet size q_1. Then the concatenated code C of A and B is an $(L_1 L_2, N_2, q_1)$ c-IPP code with code length $L_1 L_2$, codeword number N_2 and alphabet size q_1.

The concatenation of code A and code B is done by replacing each symbol in the alphabet of code A by a codeword in code B. Since a c-TA code is also a c-IPP code, the construction of a proper c-IPP code can be done by concatenating two c-TA codes.

In this paper, we are interested in the comparison of c-TA codes with proper c-IPP codes. From this point on, for the sake of brevity we use the term c-IPP codes to refer to proper c-IPP codes.

3 Performance Evaluation

In this section, we compare the collusion resistance of fingerprinting systems employing different codes. We try to answer the questions: what kind of code is better for collusion resistance and what parameter settings of the codes are favorable for building the fingerprint sequences? We provide analysis on the relationship between collusion resistance and code parameters. Simulations are then used to validate the analysis and conjectures.

3.1   Analysis of Collusion Resistance

We measure the collusion resistance of a fingerprinting system in terms of the probability of catching one colluder, denoted as P_d. To get the analytic approximation, first consider an ideal fingerprinting system whose fingerprint sequences have a constant pairwise correlation denoted as ρ. Without loss of generality, we assume that the first c users perform averaging collusion. (Notice that with the PSE technique, the interleaving collusion has similar effect to the averaging collusion. [16]) The vector of detection statistics T_N's defined in (2) follows a N_u-dimensional Gaussian distribution:

$$\mathbf{T} = [T_N(1), ..., T_N(N_u)]^T \sim N([\mathbf{m}_1, \mathbf{m}_2]^T, \sigma_d^2 \Sigma) \tag{4}$$

$$\text{with} \quad \mathbf{m}_1 = \|\mathbf{s}\| \left(\frac{1}{c} + \left(1 - \frac{1}{c} \right) \rho \right) \mathbf{1}_c, \quad \mathbf{m}_2 = \|\mathbf{s}\| \rho \mathbf{1}_{n-c},$$

where $\mathbf{1}_k$ is an all one vector with dimension k-by-1, and Σ is an n-by-n matrix whose diagonal elements are 1's and off-diagonal elements are ρ's, σ_d^2 is the variance of the noise, $\mathbf{m}_1$ is the mean vector for colluders, and $\mathbf{m}_2$ is the mean vector for innocent users. Given the same colluder number c and fingerprint strength $\|\mathbf{s}\|$, the mean correlation values with colluders and with innocents are separated more widely for a smaller ρ. This suggests that in the absence of any prior knowledge on collusion patterns, a smaller ρ leads to a higher colluder detection probability P_d. Therefore, we prefer fingerprint sequences with a small pairwise correlation ρ in the system design.

For the coded fingerprinting, the pairwise correlation can be calculated by examining the code construction. Codes with a larger minimum distance have a smaller upper bound on the correlation and thus are preferable. This is consistent with the principle indicated in (3) to employ codes with large minimum distance. Under the code construction with large minimum distance, the largest pairwise correlation between the fingerprinting sequences ρ_0 will be close to 0 and we can use the above equal pairwise correlation model with $\rho = \rho_0$ to approximate the performance of the coded fingerprinting under averaging collusion.

Taking a Reed-Solomon code based fingerprinting as an example, we calculate its pairwise correlation. We denote the alphabet size as q, dimension k, and code length L. The total number of codewords is $N_u = q^k$ and the minimum distance is $D = L - k + 1$. We use $\mathbf{s}_i$ and $\mathbf{s}_j$ to represent the fingerprint sequences for user i and user j, respectively, and $\mathbf{w}_{im}$ as the orthogonal sequence representing the symbol in user i's codeword at position m with $\|\mathbf{w}_{im}\| = \|\mathbf{w}\|$. The normalized correlation between $\mathbf{s}_i$ and $\mathbf{s}_j$ is

$$\frac{< \mathbf{s}_i, \mathbf{s}_j >}{\|\mathbf{s}\|^2} = \frac{< [\mathbf{w}_{i1} \mathbf{w}_{i2} \cdots \mathbf{w}_{iL}], [\mathbf{w}_{j1} \mathbf{w}_{j2} \cdots \mathbf{w}_{jL}] >}{L \|\mathbf{w}\|^2}$$

$$= \frac{\sum_{m=1}^{L} \mathbf{w}_{im} \mathbf{w}_{jm}^T}{L \|\mathbf{w}\|^2} \leq \frac{L - D}{L} = \frac{k - 1}{L} \triangleq \rho_0. \tag{5}$$

We can choose k and L to make ρ_0 close to 0 to achieve better collusion resistance.

3.2   Comparisons on Collusion Resistance

c-IPP Codes versus c-TA Codes. Inequality (3) shows the sufficient condition for a code to be a c-TA code, and it does not hold for a c-IPP code. Rewriting inequality (3) as

$$\frac{L-D}{L} < \frac{1}{c^2},$$

and combining it with Eqn.(5), we can see that a c-TA code has pairwise correlation $\rho_0 < 1/c^2$, while c-IPP code has pairwise correlation $\rho_0 > 1/c^2$. According to the analysis in Section 3.1, the fingerprinting system constructed on c-TA code should have better performance than the fingerprinting system employing c-IPP code.

To validate the analysis, we examine the performance of a c-IPP code based fingerprinting system and a c-TA code based fingerprinting system through simulation. For a host signal with length $N = 40,000$, we design two systems that are capable of holding $N_u = 256$ users as follows:

- System 1 is built upon a 2-IPP code (40,256,4) with code length L=40, codeword number $N_u = 256$ and alphabet size q=4. This 2-IPP code is constructed through the concatenation of two 2-TA Reed-Solomon codes (8,256,16) and (5,16,4) following the method proposed in [9]. The pairwise correlation of the fingerprint sequences ρ_0 is 0.3 according to Eqn. (5).
- System 2 is built upon a 2-TA Reed-Solomon code (8,256,16) with code length L=8, codeword number $N_u = 256$ and alphabet size q=16. The pairwise correlation ρ_0 is 0.14.

In both systems, we employ our previously proposed PSE technique and choose the same subsegment size 200 for permutation. We examine the probability of catching one colluder P_d of both systems against interleaving collusion and averaging collusion with colluder number c ranging from 2 to 30 and Watermark-to-Noise-Ratio(WNR) ranging from -20dB to 0dB. The simulation results are shown in Fig. 2. For ease of comparison, we show the case of WNR$=-12$dB in Fig. 2(e) and (f). From the results, we can see that under averaging collusion (Fig. 2(b), (d) and (f)) 2-TA code based System 1 has 8% gain in the probability of detection P_d. Under interleaving collusion (Fig. 2(a), (c) and (e)), the performance gain can be up to 30%. The results are consistent with our analysis that due to the low pairwise correlation among the fingerprint sequences, 2-TA code based system outperforms 2-IPP code based system in all the cases we examined.

c-TA Codes with Different Parameters. From the above comparison results, we can see that the fingerprint sequences constructed based on a c-TA code have lower correlation than the sequences constructed based on a c-IPP code. This low correlation helps defending against collusion attacks. A TA code is thus preferred in designing the fingerprint sequences. A natural question is, that given a host signal and the number of users the system needs to hold, how should we choose the parameters of TA codes to achieve good collusion resistance.

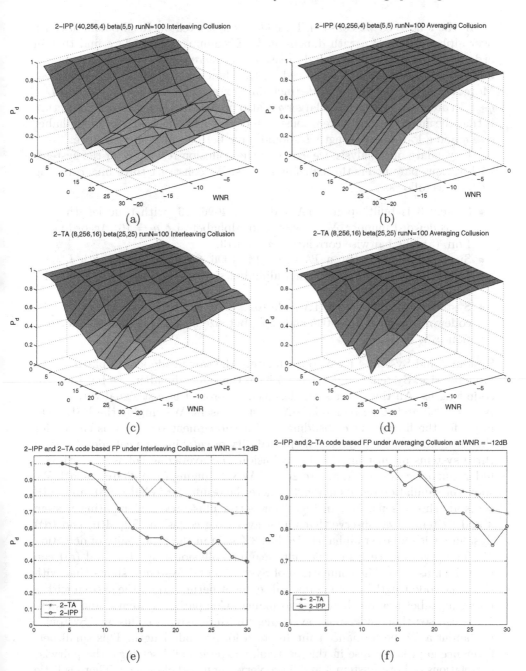

Fig. 2. Simulation results for IPP codes and TA codes based fingerprinting systems: the performance of 2-IPP code based system under (a) interleaving collusion and (b) averaging collusion; the performance of 2-TA code based system under (c) interleaving collusion and (d) averaging collusion. The performance of both systems under (e) interleaving collusion and (f) averaging collusion with WNR=−12dB.

In the following, we consider TA codes constructed on Reed-Solomon codes over alphabet size of q with dimension k. Examining Eqn. (5) we find that in order to get a small ρ_0, we can decrease k and increase L. In order to meet the desired number of users N_u and reduce the dimension k, larger q is preferred. Moreover, for Reed-Solomon code (including extended Reed-Solomon code), $L \leq q+1$. In order to get larger L, a larger q is also preferred. Therefore, our conjecture is that the fingerprinting system constructed on a TA code with a larger alphabet size q and a longer code length L should have better collusion resistance.

To validate our analysis, we examine the collusion resistance of the systems with various parameters through simulations. We construct three fingerprinting systems as follows:

- System 3 is built upon a TA code (15, 4096, 16) with code length $L = 15$, codeword number $N_u = 4096$ and alphabet size $q = 16$. According to Eqn. (5), the pairwise correlation ρ_0 is 0.13.
- System 4 is built upon a TA code (14, 4096, 64) with code length $L = 14$, codeword number $N_u = 4096$ and alphabet size $q = 64$. The pairwise correlation ρ_0 is 0.07.
- System 5 is built upon a TA code (62, 4096, 64) with code length $L = 62$, codeword number $N_u = 4096$ and alphabet size $q = 64$. The pairwise correlation ρ_0 is 0.016.

System 3 and System 4 have approximately the same code length but different alphabet size. System 4 and System 5 have the same alphabet size but different code lengths. All the systems are designed to protect a host signal with length $N = 15,000$ and to accommodate $N_u = 4096$ users. We employ the PSE technique for the fingerprint embedding, and a subsegment size of 50 is chosen for the permutation. We examine the probability of catching one colluder P_d of all three systems against interleaving collusion and averaging collusion, with colluder number c ranging from 2 to 20 and WNR ranging from -20dB to 0dB. We show the simulation results in Fig. 3, where the results for WNR = 0dB and -8dB cases are shown separately in Fig. 4 for better illustration. Comparing System 3 and System 4, we observe that under averaging collusion (Fig. 4(b) and (d)) System 4 with a larger alphabet size has 8% gain in the probability of detection P_d. The performance gain under interleaving collusion (Fig. 4(a) and (c)) can be as high as 40%. The comparison of System 3 and System 4 shows that with the same code length and the same subsegment permutation, the system with a larger alphabet size has better performance. Comparing System 4 and System 5, we can see that under both averaging and interleaving collusions, System 5 has about a 5% performance gain due to a longer code length. This small performance gain is because in this particular experimental settings, the pairwise correlations of both System 4 and 5 are very small and close to 0. There is little room for the improvement brought about by the smaller pairwise correlation of System 5. The simulation results of all three systems are consistent with our analysis in Section 3.1 in that TA codes with larger alphabet size q and longer code length L result in fingerprint sequences with smaller pairwise correlation, and thus better collusion resistance.

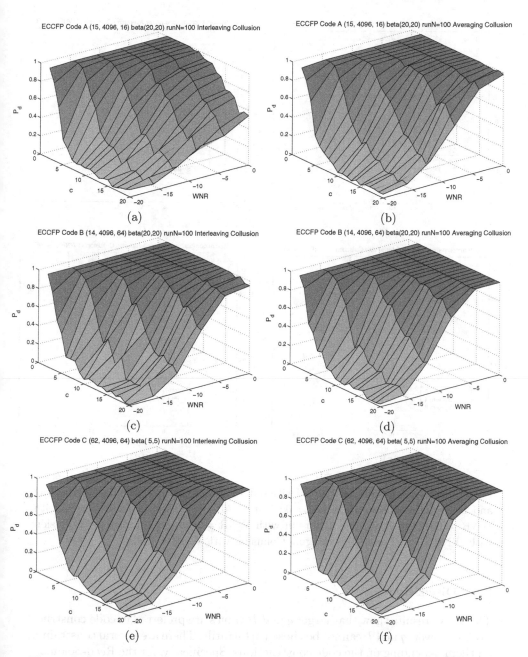

Fig. 3. Simulation results for systems with different code parameters under collusion attacks: System 3 under (a) Interleaving Collusion and (b) Averaging Collusion; System 4 under (c) Interleaving Collusion and (d) Averaging Collusion; System 5 under (e) Interleaving Collusion and (f) Averaging Collusion.

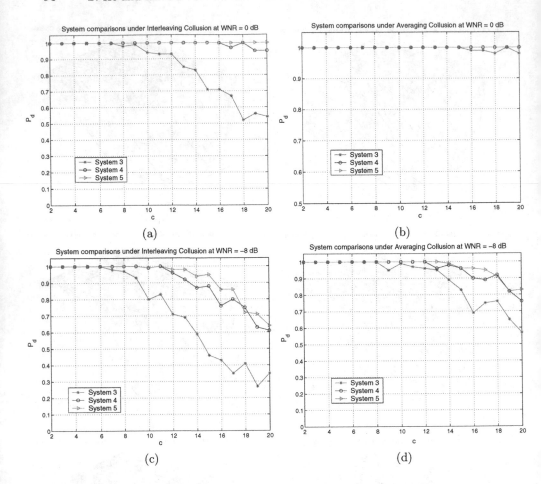

Fig. 4. Simulation results for systems with different code parameters under interleaving and averaging collusion at WNR = 0dB and -8dB. (a) Interleaving Collusion with WNR = 0dB; (b) Averaging Collusion with WNR = 0dB; (c) Interleaving Collusion with WNR = -8dB and (d) Averaging Collusion with WNR = -8dB.

3.3   Discussions

The above results show that larger q and L values are preferred in code construction. However, q and L cannot be chosen arbitrarily. There are several constraints on them depending on the code constructions. Specifically, for the Reed-Solomon code construction, we have following constraints:

$$\text{System requirement on the total user number:} \quad q = \sqrt[k]{N_u}; \quad (6)$$

$$\text{Reed-Solomon code construction constraint:} \quad L \leq q + 1; \quad (7)$$

$$\text{Orthogonality of the FP sequences for each segment:} \quad q \leq \frac{N}{L}. \quad (8)$$

where N is the host signal length, N_u is the total number of users, q is the alphabet size and L is the code length. Taking L as the maximum value $q + 1$, we get from (8) that

$$q(q + 1) \leq N; \tag{9}$$

which means the upper bound of q value is roughly on the order of $\sqrt{N}$. Usually, in multimedia fingerprinting the host signal length $N >> N_u$ and $k \geq 2$ for Reed-Solomon codes. Therefore, Eqn. (6) is a more stringent requirement on q. In Eqn. (6), the dimension k can be used to achieve the desired trade-off between the collusion resistance and the computational complexity in detection which is $O(qN)$ according to our previous study [16]. Notice that the extreme case of $k = 1$ reduces to orthogonal fingerprinting which has better collusion resistance but high computational complexity in detection [16].

Other c-TA code constructions can be analyzed in a similar way. It is worth mentioning that the TA code proposed in [8] can be regarded as a TA code with dimension k lying between 1 and 2, which offers a fine adjustment on the trade-off between the collusion resistance and detection efficiency.

4   Conclusions

In this paper, we examine the collusion resistance of the coded fingerprinting through jointly considering fingerprint encoding, embedding, and detection. The results show that for a given host signal the pairwise correlation among fingerprint sequences is a key indicator of the collusion resistance, the lower the correlation the higher the collusion resistance. According to this principle, c-TA codes can be used to introduce a lower correlation among fingerprint sequences and thus is preferred over c-IPP codes in fingerprint design. Furthermore, a TA code with a larger alphabet size and a longer code length can provide better collusion resistance. The fingerprinting code construction provides a systematic way to introduce the correlation and to achieve a desired trade-off between the collusion resistance and detection efficiency.

References

1. Z.J. Wang, M. Wu, H. Zhao, W. Trappe, and K.J.R. Liu, "Resistance of Orthogonal Gaussian Fingerprints to Collusion Attacks," *Proc. of ICASSP*, pp. 724-727, Apr. 2003.
2. F.Ergun, J.Kilian and R.Kumar, "A Note on the limits of Collusion-Resistant Watermarks", *Eurocrypt '99*, 1999.
3. D. Boneh and J. Shaw, "Collusion-secure Fingerprinting for Digital Data," *IEEE Tran. on Info. Theory*, 44(5), pp. 1897-1905, 1998.
4. Y. Yacobi, "Improved Boneh-Shaw Content Fingerprinting", *CT-RSA 2001, LNCS 2020*, pp. 378-391, 2001.
5. J.N. Staddon, D. R. Stinson, and R. Wei, "Combinatorial Properties of Frameproof and Traceability Codes", *IEEE Trans. on Information Theory*, vol. 47, no. 3, pp 1042-1049, March 2001.

6. D. To, R. Safavi-Naini and Y. Wang, "A 2-secure code with efficient tracing algorithm", *Progress in Cryptology - INDOCRYPT'02, Lecture Notes in Computer Science*, Vol. 2551, Springer-Verlag, pp. 149-162, 2002.

7. A. Barg, G.R. Blakley and G. Kabatiansky "Digital fingerprinting codes: Problem statements, constructions, identification of traitors" *IEEE Trans. Information Theory*, 49(4), pp. 852-865, April 2003.

8. T. van Trung and S. Martirosyan, "On a Class of Traceability Codes", *Designs, Codes and Cryptography*, 2004.

9. T. van Trung and S. Martirosyan, "New Constructions for IPP Codes", *IEEE International Symposium on Information Theory*, 2003.

10. R. Safavi-Naini and Y. Wang, "Collusion Secure q-ary Fingerprinting for Perceptual Content," *Security and Privacy in Digital Rights Management (SPDRM'01)*, pp. 57-75, 2002.

11. R. Safavi-Naini and Y. Wang, "Traitor Tracing for Shortened and Corrupted Fingerprints" *Proc. of Digital Right Management (DRM'02)*, pp. 81-100, 2003.

12. M. Fernandez, and M. Soriano, "Soft-Decision Tracing in Fingerprinted Multimedia Content", *IEEE Multimedia*, Vol.11 No.2, pp38-46, April-June 2004.

13. W. Trappe, M. Wu, Z.J. Wang, and K.J.R. Liu, "Anti-collusion Fingerprinting for Multimedia", *IEEE Trans. on Sig. Proc.*, 51(4), pp. 1069-1087, 2003.

14. S. He and M. Wu, "Performance Study of ECC-based Collusion-resistant Multimedia Fingerprinting," in *Proceedings of the 38th CISS*, pp. 827-832, March 2004.

15. S. He and M. Wu, "Group-Oriented Joint Coding and Embedding Technique for Multimedia Fingerprinting," SPIE Conference on Security, Watermarking and Stegonography, pp.96-105, January 2005.

16. S. He and M. Wu, "Improving Collusion Resistance of Error Correcting Code Based Multimedia Fingerprinting," in *Proceedings of ICASSP 2005*, pp. 1029-1032, March 2005.

17. I. Cox, J. Kilian, F. Leighton, and T. Shamoon, "Secure Spread Spectrum Watermarking for Multimedia", *IEEE Trans. on Image Processing*, 6(12), pp.1673-1687, 1997.

Regular Simplex Fingerprints and Their Optimality Properties*

Negar Kiyavash[1] and Pierre Moulin[2]

[1] Coordinated Science Laboratory, Dept. of Electrical and Computer Engineering,
University of Illinois at Urbana-Champaign
kiyavash@uiuc.edu
[2] Beckman Institute, Dept. of Electrical and Computer Engineering,
University of Illinois at Urbana-Champaign
moulin@ifp.uiuc.edu

Abstract. This paper addresses the design of additive fingerprints that are maximally resilient against Gaussian averaging collusion attacks. The detector performs a binary hypothesis test in order to decide whether a user of interest is among the colluders. The encoder (fingerprint designer) is to imbed additive fingerprints that minimize the probability of error of the test. Both the encoder and the attackers are subject to squared-error distortion constraints. We show that n-simplex fingerprints are optimal in sense of maximizing a geometric figure of merit for the detection test; these fingerprints outperform orthogonal fingerprints. They are also optimal in terms of maximizing the error exponent of the detection test, and maximizing the deflection criteria at the detector when the attacker's noise is non-Gaussian. Reliable detection is guaranteed provided that the number of colluders $K \ll \sqrt{N}$, where N is the length of the host vector.

Keywords: Fingerprinting, Simplex codes, Error exponents.

1 Introduction

Protection of digital property is an emerging need in light of growth of digital media and communication systems. Digital fingerprinting schemes are an important class of techniques devised for traitor tracing. In our view of digital fingerprinting, copyright protection is implicitly achieved through deterring users from illegally redistributing the digital content. Unlike watermarking where only one copy of the marked signal is circulated, in digital fingerprinting each user is provided with his own individually marked copy of the content. Although this makes it possible to trace an illegal copy to a traitor, it also allows for users to collude and form a stronger attack. One form of such attacks is averaging their copies and adding white Gaussian noise to create a *forgery*. The averaging reduces the power of each fingerprint and makes the detector's task harder.

Collusion-resistant fingerprints have been developed for various types of data, including binary sequences [1] and vectors in N-dimensional Euclidean

---

* This work was supported by NSF grant CCR03-25924.

M. Barni et al. (Eds.): IWDW 2005, LNCS 3710, pp. 97–109, 2005.

spaces [2,3]. According to Kilian *et al* [2], randomly generated Gaussian finger-prints can survive collusion of up to $O(\sqrt{N/\ln L})$ users, where L is the total number of fingerprints. The paper by Ergun *et al* [3] shows (under some as-sumptions) that any fingerprinting system can be defeated under collusion of $O(\sqrt{N/\ln N})$ users. In the aforementioned papers, the detector returns the in-dex of one guilty user. Of course, the kind of decision to be made by the detector impacts the collusion resistance. A very hard problem for the detector, for in-stance, is to return a reliable list of all guilty users.

Other work on Gaussian fingerprints includes [4], which presents a game-theoretic analysis of the problem; the host signal, fingerprints and attack channel are all assumed to be Gaussian, and *all users* are assumed to collude. It is shown that the error exponent of the detector decreases as $1/L$. The performance of orthogonal fingerprints is analyzed in [5], where upper and lower bound on the number of colluders that takes the detector to fail, are derived. One may ask whether either orthogonal or Gaussian fingerprints have any optimality property; this question has not yet been answered in the literature, so it is conceivable that some fingerprints constellations might be superior to orthogonal and random constellations.

In our problem setup, the detector has access to the host signal (non-blind de-tection) and performs a *binary hypothesis test* to verify whether a user of interest is colluding. The main contribution of this paper is a proof that regular simplex fingerprints are optimal in a certain minimum distance sense for the class of attacks considered. We also quantify the probability of error performance of our detector. In particular, they outperform orthogonal and Gaussian fingerprints; however the performance gap vanishes for large L.

The organization of the paper is as follows. In Section 2 we describe the attack channel and the notion of *focused* detector. In Section 3, we compute an upper bound on the performance of a given constellation of fingerprints. The main result of the paper is Theorem 2 of Section 4. In Section 5 we study the performance of a constellation against a size-K coalition, where the maximum number of colluders K is less than the number of available prints L. We shall consider the joint fingerprinting and watermarking of a host signal in Section 6. Finally we analyze the probability of error performance of our detector for size-K coalitions in Section 7.

2   Fingerprint and Detection Models

In this section we describe the mathematical setup of the problem, see Figure 1 for a black-box representation of the model. The host signal is a sequence $\mathbf{S} = (S(1), \ldots, S(N))$ in $\mathbb{R}^N$. Then L fingerprints, each of length N, are added to the host signal $\mathbf{S}$, where $L \leq N$ is the number of the users. In fact, typically we have $L \ll N$. User j is assigned a printed copy

$$\mathbf{X}_j = \mathbf{S} + \mathbf{Q}_j, \qquad j \in \{1, \ldots, L\}$$

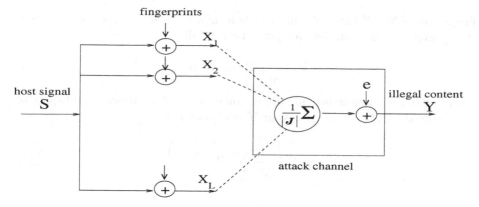

Fig. 1. Additive fingerprints and the averaging-plus-noise attack channel

where $\mathbf{Q}_j$ denotes the fingerprint assigned to user j. Moreover there is a power constraint on the fingerprints, $\|\mathbf{Q}_j\|^2 \leq N$. The power constraint imposes a unit per-sample squared-error distortion,

$$\|\mathbf{X}_j - \mathbf{S}\|^2 \leq N. \tag{1}$$

To simplify the analysis, we restrict the attack channel to collusion between a subset of users in the form of averaging their marked signals and subsequently contaminating the average with i.i.d Gaussian noise. The resulting illegal copy is of the form

$$\mathbf{Y} = \mathbf{S} + \frac{1}{|\mathcal{J}|} \sum_{j \in \mathcal{J}} \mathbf{Q}_j + \mathbf{e}$$

where $\mathcal{J}$, the *coalition*, is the index set of the colluding users, and $\mathbf{e}$ is an i.i.d. $\mathcal{N}(0, \sigma_e^2)$ Gaussian noise vector. We denote by $|\mathcal{J}|$ the cardinality of the set $\mathcal{J}$. Clearly $|\mathcal{J}| \leq L$. The host signal $\mathbf{S}$ is available at the detector and can be subtracted from $\mathbf{Y}$. Thus

$$\mathbf{Y} - \mathbf{S} \sim \mathcal{N}\left(\frac{1}{|\mathcal{J}|} \sum_{j \in \mathcal{J}} \mathbf{Q}_j, \sigma_e^2\right). \tag{2}$$

The detector performs a binary hypothesis test determining whether a certain user's mark is present in $\mathbf{Y}$. We shall denote the null or innocent hypothesis by H_0 while H_1 denotes the guilty hypothesis. We shall call this detector *focused*, because it decides whether a particular user of interest is a colluder. It does not aim at identifying all colluders. The *focused* detector above does not even need to know $|\mathcal{J}|$, the number of the colluders.

Since the total number of fingerprints is L, the detector can project the vector $(\mathbf{Y} - \mathbf{S}) \in \mathbb{R}^N$ onto the L-dimensional subspace spanned by $\{\mathbf{Q}_j\}_{j=1}^{L}$[1]. The

---

[1] If the dimension of span $\{\mathbf{Q}_j\}_{j=1}^{L}$ is less than L, then we can choose an arbitrary L dimensional embedding of subspace containing $\{\mathbf{Q}_j\}_{j=1}^{L}$.

projection of $\mathbf{Y} - \mathbf{S}$ onto this subspace is a sufficient statistic for the detection. It is convenient to normalize this projection as follows:

$$\mathbf{V} \triangleq \frac{1}{\sqrt{N}} \text{Proj}[\mathbf{Y} - \mathbf{S}] \qquad (3)$$

where Proj[.] denotes orthogonal projection onto the L-dimensional subspace of $\mathbb{R}^N$ spanned by $\{\mathbf{Q}_j\}_{j=1}^L$. The vector $\mathbf{V}$ is Gaussian with

$$\mathbf{V} \sim \mathcal{N}\left(\frac{1}{|\mathcal{J}|}\sum_{j \in \mathcal{J}} \mathbf{P}_j, \frac{1}{N}\sigma_e^2\right) \qquad (4)$$

where

$$\mathbf{P}_j \triangleq \frac{1}{\sqrt{N}} \text{Proj}[\mathbf{Q}_j] \in \mathbb{R}^L$$

and $\|\mathbf{P}_j\|^2 = 1$. We refer to $\pi = \{\mathbf{P}_j\}_{j=1}^L$ as the constellation of fingerprints on the L-dimensional unit sphere.

In the rest of the paper we will work with fingerprints $\{\mathbf{P}_j\}_{j=1}^L$. To illustrate the binary hypothesis testing at the detector, we present an example of a decision problem with three printed copies.

Example 1. Assume three fingerprinted copies $\mathbf{X}_j = \mathbf{S} + \mathbf{Q}_j$, $j = 1, 2, 3$. In light of (3), the detector forms the sufficient statistic $\mathbf{V}$. Without loss of generality, assume the detector wants to decide whether user 1 is guilty. Any combination of fingerprints in which $\mathbf{P}_1$ is present implies that user 1 was one of the colluders. In light of (4), this corresponds to the case that the mean of $\mathbf{V}$ is any of the entries of the left column in Table 1. On the other hand, if user 1 is not colluding, the mean of $\mathbf{V}$ must be one of the entries of the right column.

The entries of the table are vectors in $\mathbb{R}^L$. The vectors in the left column form a set $\mathcal{G}_1$ corresponding to the guilty hypothesis. The vectors that correspond to a not-guilty assumption form the set $\neg\mathcal{G}_1$. For a fixed user j, let

$$d_j \triangleq dist(\mathcal{G}_j, \neg\mathcal{G}_j) = \min_{(g,g') \in \mathcal{G}_j \times \neg\mathcal{G}_j} \|g - g'\| \qquad (5)$$

be the smallest distance between the sets $\mathcal{G}_j$ and $\neg\mathcal{G}_j$, e.g. d_1 is the smallest distance among the 12 possible distances between the entries of Table 1. Figure 2 depicts a constellation of three prints.

Table 1. Detector's binary decision sets $\mathcal{G}_1$ and $\neg\mathcal{G}_1$ for three colluders: $\mathcal{J} = \{1, 2, 3\}$

User 1 Guilty	User 1 Not Guilty
$\mathbf{P}_1$	
$\frac{1}{2}(\mathbf{P}_1 + \mathbf{P}_2)$	$\mathbf{P}_2$
$\frac{1}{2}(\mathbf{P}_1 + \mathbf{P}_3)$	$\mathbf{P}_3$
$\frac{1}{3}(\mathbf{P}_1 + \mathbf{P}_2 + \mathbf{P}_3)$	$\frac{1}{2}(\mathbf{P}_2 + \mathbf{P}_3)$

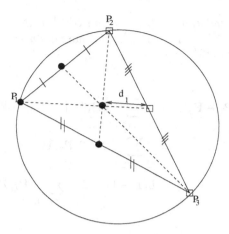

Fig. 2. A constellation of fingerprints for three users. The four bullets correspond to the elements of $\mathcal{G}_1$, while the three elements of set $\neg\mathcal{G}_1$ are represented by squares.

The exact calculation of probability of error for signal constellations for all signal to noise ratios is not easy when the vectors $\mathbf{P}_j$ are not orthogonal [6]. In channel coding problems, it is common to judge a constellation by its minimum distance [7], [8]. Here the appropriate figure of merit for a detector focused on user j is d_j.

However a good constellation must perform well regardless of which user is the person of the interest to detector. Hence we would like to choose a constellation that has the overall largest minimum distance. More precisely, we call

$$d_\pi = \min_{1 \le j \le L} d_j \tag{6}$$

the minimum distance of the constellation π. We wish to choose π that maximizes d_π. For Example 1, $d_\pi = \min(d_1, d_2, d_3)$. Note here that we assume all users are potential colluders, i.e., we may have $\mathcal{J} = \{1, \ldots, L\}$.

Definition 1. *Let* π^* *be a maximizer of* d_π. *The fingerprints obtained from* π^* *are called Optimal Focused Fingerprints (OFF).*

Next we will show that OFF constellations can be found for any number $L \le N$ of users.

3   Optimal Focused Fingerprints

In this section we derive an achievable upper bound for d_π. Let

$$\mathcal{S}^{L-1} = \{\mathbf{P} \in \mathbb{R}^L : \|\mathbf{P}\| = 1\}$$

denote the unit sphere in $\mathbb{R}^{L-1}$. Moreover the centroid of a constellation $\{\mathbf{P}_j\}_{j=1}^L$ is defined as $\frac{1}{L}\sum_{j=1}^L \mathbf{P}_j$. We derive necessary and sufficient conditions for L points on the sphere to maximize the sum of their mutual squared distances.

Lemma 1. *Any constellation of L points on $\mathcal{S}^{L-1}$ with its centroid at origin, maximizes the sum* $\sum\limits_{1 \leq i < j \leq L} \|\mathbf{P}_i - \mathbf{P}_j\|^2$. *The maximum is equal to L^2.*

Proof. We have

$$\sum_{1 \leq i < j \leq L} \|\mathbf{P}_i - \mathbf{P}_j\|^2 = \sum_{1 \leq i < j \leq L} \|\mathbf{P}_i\|^2 + \|\mathbf{P}_j\|^2 - 2\langle \mathbf{P}_i, \mathbf{P}_j \rangle$$

$$= \sum_{1 \leq i < j \leq L} 2 - 2\langle \mathbf{P}_i, \mathbf{P}_j \rangle$$

$$= L(L-1) - 2 \sum_{1 \leq i < j \leq L} \langle \mathbf{P}_i, \mathbf{P}_j \rangle. \tag{7}$$

Also

$$\left\| \sum_{i=1}^{L} \mathbf{P}_i \right\|^2 = \sum_{i=1}^{L} \|\mathbf{P}_i\|^2 + 2 \sum_{i<j} \langle \mathbf{P}_i, \mathbf{P}_j \rangle$$

$$= L + 2 \sum_{i<j} \langle \mathbf{P}_i, \mathbf{P}_j \rangle. \tag{8}$$

Combining (7) and (8), we obtain the upper bound

$$\sum_{1 \leq i < j \leq L} \|\mathbf{P}_i - \mathbf{P}_j\|^2 = L^2 - \left\| \sum_{i=1}^{L} \mathbf{P}_i \right\|^2 \leq L^2.$$

The upper bound is achieved when the centroid is at the origin.   □

Theorem 1. *For any constellation π of L fingerprints on $\mathcal{S}^{L-1}$, we have*

$$d_\pi \leq \frac{1}{L-1}.$$

Moreover any constellation π with its centroid at the origin achieves the upper bound, and therefore is OFF.

Proof. Again let d_j denote the smallest distance between the points of $\mathcal{G}_j$ and $\neg \mathcal{G}_j$. Since by definition $d_\pi \leq \min\limits_j d_j$, we obtain

$$d_\pi^2 \leq \frac{1}{L} \sum_{j=1}^{L} d_j^2. \tag{9}$$

Furthermore it can be shown that (details are lengthy and therefore are omitted) d_j, the smallest distance between the sets $\mathcal{G}_j$ and $\neg \mathcal{G}_j$, is achieved by the pair $\left(\frac{1}{L} \sum\limits_{i=1}^{L} \mathbf{P}_i, \frac{1}{L-1} \sum\limits_{i \neq j} \mathbf{P}_i \right)$, thus we have

$$d_j = \left\| \frac{1}{L(L-1)} \left[(L-1)\mathbf{P}_j - \sum_{i \neq j} \mathbf{P}_i \right] \right\| = \frac{1}{L(L-1)} \left\| \sum_{i \neq j} (\mathbf{P}_i - \mathbf{P}_j) \right\|. \quad (10)$$

Substituting d_j from (10) into (9) we have,

$$d_\pi^2 \leq \frac{1}{L} \sum_{j=1}^{L} \frac{1}{L^2(L-1)^2} \left\| \sum_{i \neq j} (\mathbf{P}_i - \mathbf{P}_j) \right\|^2$$

$$= \frac{1}{L^3(L-1)^2} \left[\sum_{i \neq 1} \|\mathbf{P}_i - \mathbf{P}_1\|^2 + 2\sum_{i<j} \langle \mathbf{P}_i - \mathbf{P}_1, \mathbf{P}_j - \mathbf{P}_1 \rangle + \dots \right.$$

$$\left. + \sum_{i \neq L} \|\mathbf{P}_i - \mathbf{P}_L\|^2 + 2\sum_{i<j} \langle \mathbf{P}_i - \mathbf{P}_L, \mathbf{P}_j - \mathbf{P}_L \rangle \right].$$

Regrouping terms we have,

$$d_\pi^2 \leq \frac{1}{L^3(L-1)^2} \left[2\sum_{i<j} \|\mathbf{P}_i - \mathbf{P}_j\|^2 + 2\sum_{k=1}^{L} \sum_{i<j} \langle \mathbf{P}_i - \mathbf{P}_k, \mathbf{P}_j - \mathbf{P}_k \rangle \right]. \quad (11)$$

For any fixed triple (k,i,j), there is a term of the form $\langle \mathbf{P}_i - \mathbf{P}_k, \mathbf{P}_j - \mathbf{P}_k \rangle$ in the sum, now depending on whether $k < j$ or $k > j$ either $\langle \mathbf{P}_k - \mathbf{P}_i, \mathbf{P}_j - \mathbf{P}_i \rangle$ or its equivalent $\langle \mathbf{P}_j - \mathbf{P}_i, \mathbf{P}_k - \mathbf{P}_i \rangle$ belongs to the sum as well. But $\langle \mathbf{P}_i - \mathbf{P}_k, \mathbf{P}_j - \mathbf{P}_k \rangle + \langle \mathbf{P}_k - \mathbf{P}_i, \mathbf{P}_j - \mathbf{P}_i \rangle = \langle \mathbf{P}_i - \mathbf{P}_k, \mathbf{P}_j - \mathbf{P}_k + (\mathbf{P}_i - \mathbf{P}_j) \rangle$ which in turn equals $\|\mathbf{P}_i - \mathbf{P}_k\|^2$.

For each user k, $\mathbf{P}_k$ is fixed and there are $\frac{1}{2}(L-1)(L-2)$ terms in $\sum_{i<j} \langle \mathbf{P}_i - \mathbf{P}_k, \mathbf{P}_i - \mathbf{P}_k \rangle$. But then summing this again over k results in $\frac{1}{2}L(L-1)(L-2)$ terms of the form $\|\mathbf{P}_i - \mathbf{P}_k\|^2$. Now grouping this with the other terms of the form $\sum_{i<j} \|\mathbf{P}_i - \mathbf{P}_j\|^2$, will have a contribution of $\frac{\frac{1}{2}L(L-1)(L-2)}{\frac{1}{2}L(L-1)} = L-2$ new terms. Substituting this into (11) we have

$$d_\pi^2 \leq \frac{1}{L^3(L-1)^2} \left[2\sum_{i<j} \|\mathbf{P}_i - \mathbf{P}_j\|^2 + (L-2)\sum_{i<j} \|\mathbf{P}_i - \mathbf{P}_j\|^2 \right]$$

$$= \frac{1}{L^2(L-1)^2} \sum_{i<j} \|\mathbf{P}_i - \mathbf{P}_j\|^2.$$

or

$$d_\pi \leq \frac{1}{L(L-1)} \sqrt{\sum_{i<j} \|\mathbf{P}_i - \mathbf{P}_j\|^2}. \quad (12)$$

From Lemma 1, $\sum_{i<j} \|\mathbf{P}_i - \mathbf{P}_j\|^2$ is maximized when the fingerprints form a constellation with its centroid at the origin. Combining this result with (12), we obtain $d_\pi \le \frac{1}{L-1}$.   □

Theorem 1 states that the bound is achievable by any constellation with centroid at the origin.

4 n-Simplex Fingerprints

In this section we formally define n-Simplex Fingerprints. These fingerprints have their centroid at the origin and therefore are OFF.

Definition 2. *[9] A simplex, sometimes called a hypertetrahedron, is the generalization of a tetrahedral region of space to n dimensions. If all the 1-faces (polytope edges) in the simplex are equal, it is regular.*

In one dimension, the regular simplex is the line segment $[-1, +1]$. In two dimensions, the regular simplex is the equilateral triangle. In three dimensions, the regular simplex is the regular tetrahedron. The regular simplex in four dimensions (the pentatope) ABCDE is obtained from the regular tetrahedron $ABCD$ by choosing a point E along the fourth dimension through the center of $ABCD$ so that $EA = EB = EC = ED = AB$. Similarly one can recursively construct a regular n-simplex from a regular $n-1$-simplex, by choosing a new vertex along the nth dimension through the centroid of the existing $n-1$-simplex, such that the new vertex is at equal distance form all the vertices of the $n-1$-simplex.

It is convenient to describe a simplex in barycentric coordinates. The vertices of the simplex in barycentric coordinates can be expressed as

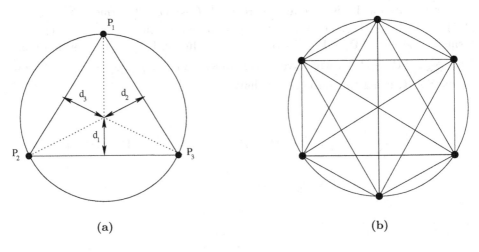

(a)   (b)

Fig. 3. (a) Planar graph representation for 2-simplex. (b) Planar graph representation for 5-simplex.

$(1, 0, 0, \ldots, 0), (0, 1, 0, \ldots, 0), \ldots, (0, 0, 0, \ldots, 1)$. There exists a planar graph representation for n-simplices. Figure 3 depicts the complete graph corresponding to 2 and 5-simplices.

Regular n-polytopes and thus the regular n-simplex may be inscribed in centered n-spheres; the smallest such sphere is called the circumsphere. In fact, there is an n-sphere touching the centers of all the elements bounding the n-polytope: vertices, edges, faces and polyhedra.

This property is essential for us. By the power constraint $\|\mathbf{P}_j\|^2 = 1$, our fingerprints are to lie on an L-dimensional sphere. In light of Theorem 1 the following theorem is immediate.

Theorem 2. *Under the Gaussian averaging attack of section 2, the L vertices of the $(L-1)$-simplex inscribed inside the unit sphere $\mathcal{S}^{L-1}$ form an OFF constellation for L users. Moreover, all the distances d_j, $1 \leq j \leq L$, are equal to $\frac{1}{L-1}$. The property $d_j \equiv d_\pi$ follows from the symmetry of the regular simplex.*

Proof. Because the centroid of the regular simplex is at the origin, the $(L-1)$-simplex achieves the upper bound of Theorem 1 on d_π and thus its L vertices form an OFF constellation. □

5   Size-K Coalitions

Although minimum distance d_π of Equation (6) is our basic figure of merit for constellation design, it is often necessary to study the performance of a scheme when at most K out of L potential colluders form the attack: $|\mathcal{J}| \leq K$. Table 2 shows the the modification of the sets $\mathcal{G}_j$ and $\neg \mathcal{G}_j$ of Example 1 for a coalition of size at most $K = 2$.

Table 2. Detector's binary decision sets $\mathcal{G}_1$ and $\neg \mathcal{G}_1$ when there are at most $K = 2$ colluders

User 1 **Guilty**	User 1 **Not Guilty**
$\mathbf{P}_1$	$\mathbf{P}_2$
$\frac{1}{2}(\mathbf{P}_1 + \mathbf{P}_2)$	$\mathbf{P}_3$
$\frac{1}{2}(\mathbf{P}_1 + \mathbf{P}_3)$	$\frac{1}{2}(\mathbf{P}_2 + \mathbf{P}_3)$

Let's assume the the user of interest is $\mathbf{P}_j$ and the attackers have formed a size-K coalition, i.e. $|\mathcal{J}| = K$. Similarly to Equation (5), the minimum distance between the two sets $\mathcal{G}_j$ and $\neg \mathcal{G}_j$ is

$$dist(\mathcal{G}_j, \neg \mathcal{G}_j) = \min_{(g, g') \in \mathcal{G}_j \times \neg \mathcal{G}_j} \|g - g'\|. \qquad (13)$$

Assuming $K < L$, this distance is achieved by the pair of forgeries $(\mathbf{F}_1, \mathbf{F}'_1)$, where

$$\mathbf{F}_1 = \frac{1}{K} \sum_{i \in \mathcal{J}} \mathbf{P}_i, \quad \mathbf{F}'_1 = \frac{1}{K} \left(\sum_{i \in \mathcal{J} \setminus \{j\}} \mathbf{P}_i + \mathbf{P}_k \right), \tag{14}$$

where k is any index that is not present in the coalition $\mathcal{J}$.

6 Fingerprinting Watermarked Data

Digital fingerprinting schemes are devised for traitor tracing. However it might be necessary to insert a watermark to protect the rights to the ownership of the original content. One way of achieving this joint watermarking and fingerprinting scheme is to first add watermark $\mathbf{W}$ to the content and then add the fingerprints,

$$\mathbf{X}_j = \mathbf{S} + \mathbf{W} + \mathbf{Q}_j, \quad j \in \{1, \ldots, L\}.$$

A natural choice for the watermark signal is to be perpendicular to the the span of the fingerprints: $\mathbf{W} \perp Span\{Q_j\}$. This choice implies that averaging the copies $\mathbf{X}_j$ cannot degrade the watermark $\mathbf{W}$.

For the *focused* detector of Section 2, Figure 4 depicts the signal constellation for joint fingerprints and the watermark. Observe that the distortion constraint of Equation (1) implies that there is less power available for the fingerprints $\mathbf{Q}_j$:

$$\|\mathbf{W}\|^2 + \|\mathbf{Q}_j\|^2 \leq N \quad j \in \{1, \ldots, L\}.$$

Thus, there is a tradeoff between the power allocated to the watermark $\mathbf{W}$ and the power of the prints $\mathbf{Q}_j$. The fingerprints still are chosen to be the vertices of an $L-1$-simplex , where L is the number of the fingerprints, but they are circumscribed in a smaller sphere. As an special case, in the L-dimensional

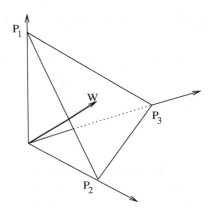

Fig. 4. Additive joint fingerprint and watermark constellation

space one can allocate the power between $\mathbf{W}$ and the fingerprints $\mathbf{Q}_j$ such that the resulting fingerprints are orthogonal. Note that $\|\mathbf{W}\|^2 \to 0$ as $L \to \infty$ in this case.

7   Probability of Error

The performance metric d_π in this paper is a geometric figure of merit for fingerprint constellations. From a detection standpoint however, the most natural performance criterion is $P_e(\pi)$, the *maximal probability of error of the focused detector* over all size K coalitions. Assume that the detector is focused on user j. Our detector forms the following correlation statistic:

$$T(\mathbf{Y}) = \mathbf{P}_j^T(\mathbf{Y} - \mathbf{S}) \underset{H_0}{\overset{H_1}{\gtrless}} \tau. \tag{15}$$

The decision boundary for this test is a hyperplane normal to the vector $\mathbf{P}_j$:

$$\Omega = \{\mathbf{Y} \ : \ \mathbf{P}_j^T(\mathbf{Y} - \mathbf{S}) = \tau\}.$$

Assume without loss of generality that the detector is focused on user 1 ($j = 1$), and that $\mathcal{J} = \{1, 2, \cdots, K\}$. For the forgery $\mathbf{F}_1$ defined in (14), we have

$$\begin{aligned}
T(\mathbf{Y}) &= \mathbf{P}_1^T \mathbf{F}_1 \\
&= \frac{1}{K} \sum_{i=1}^{K} \mathbf{P}_1^T \mathbf{P}_i \\
&= \frac{1}{K} \left(1 - \frac{K-1}{L-1}\right) \\
&= \frac{L-K}{K(L-1)} \triangleq \tau_{\max}.
\end{aligned} \tag{16}$$

Similarly, for the forgery $\mathbf{F}_1'$, we have

$$\begin{aligned}
T(\mathbf{Y}) &= \mathbf{P}_1^T \mathbf{F}_1' \\
&= \frac{1}{K} \sum_{i=2}^{K+1} \mathbf{P}_1^T \mathbf{P}_i \\
&= -\frac{1}{L-1} \triangleq \tau_{\min}.
\end{aligned} \tag{17}$$

If $\tau \geq \tau_{\max}$, the focused detector incorrectly decides H_0 upon seeing forgery $\mathbf{F}_1$. The worst-case probability of miss P_M is equal to 1. Likewise, if $\tau \leq \tau_{\min}$, the focused detector incorrectly decides H_1 upon seeing forgery $\mathbf{F}_1'$. The worst-case probability of false alarm P_F is equal to 1.

The threshold τ trades off P_F and P_M. To minimize probability of error, τ should be chosen as

$$\tau = \frac{\tau_{\min} + \tau_{\max}}{2} = \frac{L - 2K}{2K(L-1)}.$$

The relevant figure of merit for this test is

$$d_\pi(K) \triangleq \tau_{\max} - \tau_{\min} = \frac{L}{K(L-1)}. \tag{18}$$

Note that $d_\pi(K) \downarrow \frac{1}{K}$ as $L \to \infty$, and $\tau \uparrow \frac{1}{2K}$ as $\frac{L}{K} \to \infty$.

The significance of $d_\pi(K)$ in this context is as follows:

- For any constellation π, we have

$$P_e(\pi) = Q\left(\frac{\sqrt{N}d_\pi(K)}{2\sigma}\right),$$

  where $Q(t) \triangleq \int_t^\infty \frac{1}{\sqrt{2\pi}} e^{-\frac{x^2}{2}} dx$ is the Q function. Recall that for positive t, the Q function is bounded by $\frac{1}{t\sqrt{2\pi}} e^{-\frac{t^2}{2}} \le Q(t) \le e^{-\frac{t^2}{2}}$. Moreover $\ln Q(t) \sim -\frac{t^2}{2}$ as $t \to \infty$.
- The error exponent of the detection test, *for any fixed K*, is

$$e(\pi) \triangleq -\lim_{N \to \infty} \frac{1}{N} \ln P_e(\pi) = -\lim_{N \to \infty} \frac{1}{N} \ln Q\left(\frac{\sqrt{N}d_\pi(K)}{2\sigma}\right) = \frac{d_\pi^2(K)}{8\sigma^2}.$$

- If the noise $\mathbf{e}$ is non-Gaussian, $d_\pi(K)$ represents the *deflection criterion*, or generalized SNR [10], of the test.

It is noteworthy that as the number of colluders $K \to \infty$, the quantity

$$\frac{d_\pi^2(K)}{8\sigma^2} = \frac{(\frac{L}{L-1})^2}{8\sigma^2 K^2} \sim \frac{1}{4\sigma^2 K^2}$$

tends to zero. Hence the error exponent $e(\pi)$ is zero. Still, provided $K \ll \sqrt{N}$, the probability of error goes to zero:

$$P_e(\pi) = Q\left(\frac{\sqrt{N}d_\pi(K)}{2\sigma}\right) = Q\left(\frac{\sqrt{N}\frac{L}{L-1}}{2\sigma K}\right).$$

thus,

$$\left(\sqrt{2\pi}\frac{\sqrt{N}\frac{L}{L-1}}{2\sigma K}\right)^{-1} \exp\left(-\frac{NL^2}{8\sigma^2 K^2(L-1)^2}\right)$$

$$\le P_e(\pi) \le \exp\left(-\frac{NL^2}{8\sigma^2 K^2(L-1)^2}\right)$$

which implies $P_e(\pi) \to 0$.

However, when K is of the order of $\sqrt{N}$, $P_e(\pi)$ does not vanish as $N \to \infty$; and if $K \gg N$, $P_e(\pi)$ tends to $\frac{1}{2}$.

For large N, our optimal $d_\pi = \frac{1}{L-1}$ converges to $d_\pi = \frac{1}{L}$ that was derived in [4] under different assumptions: random design of the fingerprints (statistically orthogonal), and all users colluding. Moreover as shown in [5], geometrically orthogonal fingerprint designs achieve the same $d_\pi = \frac{1}{L}$.

Acknowledgements

The authors wish to thank Professor Peter Dragnev and Professor Richard E. Blahut for helpful comments.

References

1. D. Boneh and J. Shaw. Collusion-secure fingerprinting for digital data. In Don Coppersmith, editor, *Proc. Crypto '95*, pages 452–465. Springer, 1995. Lecture Notes in Computer Science No. 963.
2. J. Kilian, F.T. Leighton, L.R. Matheson, T.G. Shamoon, R.E. Tarjan, and F. Zane. Resistance of digital watermarks to collusive attacks. In *IEEE International Symposium on Information Theory*, page 271, 1998.
3. F. Ergun, J. Kilian, and R. Kumar. A note on the bounds of collusion resistant watermarks. In *EUROCRYPT'99*, pages 140–149, 1999.
4. P. Moulin and A. Briassouli. The Gaussian fingerprinting game. *Conference on Information Sciences and Systems, CISS'02*, March 2002.
5. Z. Wang, M. Wu, H. Zhao, W. Trappe, , and K.J.R. Liu. Collusion resistance of multimedia fingerprinting using orthogonal modulation. *IEEE Trans. on Image Proc.*, 14(6):804–821, 2005.
6. H.V. Poor. *An Introduction to Signal Detection and Estimation.* Springer-Verlang, 2nd edition, 1994.
7. R. Blahut. *An Introduction to Telecommunications.* Cambridge University Press, Cambridge. Preprint.
8. Jr. Forney, G.D. and L.-F. Wei. Multidimensional constellations. I. introduction, figures of merit, and generalized cross constellations. *IEEE Journal on Selected Areas in Communications*, 7(6):877 – 892, 1989.
9. J. R. Munkres. *Elements of Algebraic Topology.* Perseus Press, 1993.
10. R. J. Barton and H. V. Poor. On generalized signal-to-noise ratios in signal detection. *Mathematics of Control, Signals and Systems*, 5(1):81 – 91, 1992.

A Robust Multi-bit Image Watermarking Algorithm Based on HMM in Wavelet Domain

Jiangqun Ni[*], Rongyue Zhang, Jiwu Huang, and Chuntao Wang

Department of Electronic and Communication Engineering,
Sun Yat-Sen University, Guangzhou 510275, P. R. China
issjqni@mail.edu.cn

Abstract. Robustness is the key issue in the development of multi-bit watermarking algorithm. A new algorithm for robust multi-bit image watermarking based on Hidden Markov Model (HMM) in wavelet domain is proposed in this paper. The algorithm is characterized as follows: (1) the proposed blind detector based on vector HMM, which describes the statistics of wavelet coefficients, achieves significant improvement in performance compared to the conventional correlation detector; (2) adaptive watermark embedding scheme is applied to achieve the low distortion according to the Human Visual System (HVS); (3) optimal multi-bit watermark embedding strategy and maximum-likelihood detection for tree structure of vector HMM is proposed through system robustness analysis. Simulation results show that relatively high capacity for watermark embedding in low frequency subbands of wavelet domain is achieved with the proposed algorithm, and high robust results are observed against StirMark attacks, such as JPEG compression, additive noise, median cut and filter.

1 Introduction

With the popularity of Internet, the copyright protection of digital media is becoming increasingly important. And thus digital watermarking, especially for image and video, has become the domain of extensive research. According to Cox [2], watermark in transform domain should be embedded into low-frequency areas, which have more visual capacity. In [3-4], Huang embeds watermark signal directly into DC coefficients in DCT domain or LL subband in wavelet domain in order to increase the robustness. However, as there is relatively low capacity for watermarking in LL subband of wavelet domain, it's necessary to explore the possibility of robust watermarking scheme in low and middle frequency subbands for higher embedding capacity.

From the perspective of digital communication, the digital watermarking can be described as a process of transmission narrow-band spread spectrum signal over wide-band channel [5-7] and blind watermark detection is equivalent to the detection of weak signal from strong noise background. Consequently the performance of detector is heavily depended on the model of the "channel", i.e., the accuracy of the statistical model for the wavelet coefficients is vital for performance improvement of the detector.

---

[*] Corresponding author.

M. Barni et al. (Eds.): IWDW 2005, LNCS 3710, pp. 110–123, 2005.

Most of the existing model-based wavelet watermarking algorithms are based on the following two assumptions for wavelet coefficients distribution: (1) Gaussian Distribution (the correlation detector used in current wavelet based watermarking algorithm implies the Gaussian distribution [16-17]); (2) Generalized Gaussian Distribution, but independent among wavelet coefficients [8-9]. Unfortunately, the first assumption deviates from the true distribution of wavelet coefficients, while the second one ignores the dependence among wavelet coefficients. In this paper we propose a robust multi-bit image watermarking algorithm based on the vector Hidden Markov Model in wavelet domain (WD-VHMM), which takes into account both the energy correlation across the scale and the different subbands at the same scale of the wavelet pyramid. By incorporating other key technologies such as HVS, optimal coding/embedding and maximum likelihood detection for vector tree structure, channel coding and spread spectrum technology, the proposed algorithm shows high robustness against StirMark attacks, such as JPEG compression, additive noise, median cut and filter.

The remainder of this paper is organized as follows. Section 2 and 3 introduce briefly the Hidden Markov Model in wavelet domain and the HVS based adaptive watermark embedding scheme, respectively. Section 4 gives the optimal coding/embedding scheme and maximum likelihood detection for the vector tree structure. Simulation results and analysis are included in section 5. Finally, we draw the conclusion in section 6.

2 HMM in Wavelet Domain

Crouse et al. [10] points out that, besides its primary properties such as locality, multi-resolution and energy compaction, the wavelet transform has following two attractive secondary properties:

1. Non-Gaussianity: The wavelet coefficients have peaky, heavy-tailed marginal distributions;
2. Persistency: Large/small values of wavelet coefficients tend to propagate through the scales of the quad-trees.

Taking full advantages of above properties of wavelet transform, Crouse [10] proposes the Hidden Markov Model in wavelet domain, which can well describe the distribution of wavelet coefficients.

2.1 WD-HMM Model

In HMM model, each wavelet coefficient $w_{j,k}$ ($1 \le j \le J$, $j = 1$ represents the coarsest scale) has its hidden state $s_{j,k}$. If there is M hidden states, then $P(S_{j,k} = m) = p_{j,k}^{(m)}; m = 1, ..., M$. Given $S_{j,k} = m$, $w_{j,k}$ is modeled with a zero-mean Gaussian $g(0, \sigma_{j,k}^{(m)})$. Without loss of generality, we assume $M = 2$ in this paper, and the Probability Density Function (PDF) of $w_{j,k}$ is given by the two-state zero-mean Gaussian mixture model as follows:

$$f_j(w) = p_j^{(1)} g(w; \sigma_j^{(1)}) + p_j^{(2)} g(w; \sigma_j^{(2)}), \tag{1}$$

where $p_j^{(1)} + p_j^{(2)} = 1$ and $g(w; \sigma) = \dfrac{1}{\sqrt{2\pi\sigma^2}} \exp(-\dfrac{w^2}{2\sigma^2})$. $p_j^{(1)}, p_j^{(2)}$ in (1) represent the probability that $w_{j,k}$ is small or large (in statistical sense), respectively.

WD-HMM captures the energy dependency across scale by using Markov chain to describe the probability of hidden state transition from the parent node to its four child nodes, i.e.,

$$A_j = \begin{pmatrix} p_j^{1\to1} & p_j^{1\to2} \\ p_j^{2\to1} & p_j^{2\to2} \end{pmatrix}, \quad j = 2, 3, \cdots, J, \tag{2}$$

where $p_j^{m'\to m}$ represents the probability that child node is in state m given that its parent node is in state m'. The state probability of child node can be determined by that of its parent node and the transition matrix, i.e.,

$$p_j^{(m)} = \sum_{m'} p_{j-1}^{(m')} p_j^{m'\to m}, \quad j = 2, 3, \cdots, J. \tag{3}$$

Let $p_j = (p_j^1 p_j^2)$ and $p_j = p_{j-1} A_j$, then

$$p_j = p_1 A_2 A_3 \ldots A_j, \quad j = 2, 3, \cdots, J. \tag{4}$$

Therefore, the WD-HMM for a tree of wavelet coefficients is completely defined by a set of parameters:

$$\theta = \{p_1, A_2, \ldots, A_J; \sigma_j^{(m)}, (j = 1, \ldots, J, m = 1, 2)\}. \tag{5}$$

The WD-HMM model can efficiently describe the none-Gaussian behavior of wavelet coefficients and captures the statistical dependency of wavelet coefficients across scale. Moreover, there exists efficient EM algorithm [10] for fitting a WD-HMM to observed signal using the ML criterion.

The above WD-HMM model is based on the assumption that wavelet coefficients at different orientations are independent, which ignores the existing cross-correlation among sub-band coefficients from different orientations at the same scale. To enhance the capacity of WD-HMM in capturing cross-orientation dependency of wavelet coefficient, the vector WD-HMM is adopted in this paper, in which the coefficients at the same location and scale are grouped into a vector (see Fig.1(b)). Denote the wavelet coefficients at orientation d ($d = 1, 2, 3$ for H, V and D, respectively), scale j and location k as $w_{j,k}^d$, the grouping operation produces vectors of coefficients: $w_{j,k} = (w_{j,k}^{(1)} w_{j,k}^{(2)} w_{j,k}^{(3)})^T$. For vector WD-HMM model, we have

$$f_j(w) = p_j^{(1)} g(w; C_j^{(1)}) + p_j^{(2)} g(w; C_j^{(2)}), \tag{6}$$

where $g(w;C)$ denotes the zero-mean multivariate Gaussian density with covariance matrix C, i.e.,

$$g(w;C) = \frac{1}{\sqrt{(2\pi)^n |\det(C)|}} \exp(-w^T C^{-1} w).$$ (7)

n in (7) is the numbers of orientations (in this case $n=3$).

The wavelet coefficient vectors in vector WD-HMM have the similar quad-tree structure as that in scalar WD-HMM. Thus an image is modeled by one vector WD-HMM with a set of parameters:

$$\theta = \{p_1, A_2, ..., A_J; C_j^{(m)}, (j=1,...,J, m=1,2)\}.$$ (8)

As the proposed vector WD-HMM model captures both the statistical dependencies of wavelet coefficients across the scale and cross-correlation among sub-band coefficients at the same scale, it can be expected that the vector model can more accurately describe the statistical behavior of wavelet coefficients.

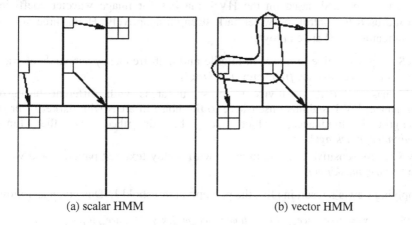

(a) scalar HMM   (b) vector HMM

Fig. 1. Hidden Markov Model (2 levels)

2.2 Parameters Estimation for WD-HMM

The parameter set θ for a general M-state WD-HMM includes (1) $p_{S_1}(m)$: the Probability Mass Function (PMF) for root node S_1; (2) $\varepsilon_{i,\rho(i)}^{mr}$: the conditional probability that S_i in state m given $S_{\rho(i)}$ in state r; and (3) $\mu_{i,m}$ and $\sigma_{i,m}^2$: the mean and variance, respectively, of the wavelet coefficient W_i given S_i in state m. The parameter vector θ can be estimated by EM algorithm, and the iterative structure is as follows:

1. Initialization: Select an initial model estimate $\theta = \theta^0$, and set iteration counter $l=0$.
2. E step: Calculate p(S|w, θ^l), which is the joint PMF for hidden state variables;

3. M step: Set $\theta^{l+1} = \arg \max \theta \, E[\ln f(\mathbf{w}, S|\theta)|\mathbf{w}, \theta^l]$;

4. Set $l=l+1$. If converged, then stop; else, return to E step.

For the proposed vector WD-HMM model, the only difference is that we use covariance matrix instead of covariance.

3 Human Visual System

HVS plays an important role in digital image processing. It is reported that [12] there are three key masking effects in HVS, i.e., frequency masking, luminance masking and texture masking. The invisible watermarking asks for two contradictory objectives, i.e., robustness and invisibility. Increasing the strength of watermark signal helps to improve the robustness performance, which in turn would decrease the objective of invisibility.

Following Watson's spirit [12], we propose an adaptive watermark embedding strategy incorporating the HVS property. The visual masking weights in wavelet domain are generated based on the HVS analysis for image wavelet coefficients, which are used to control the watermark strength adaptively. Here, three key HVS masking features [13] are employed:

1. HVS is less sensitive to noises in middle and high frequency subbands of wavelet pyramid, so we have the *frequency_masking()* ;
2. HVS has different sensitivity to noise in areas with different background luminance. HVS is almost insensitive to the noise in areas with darker or brighter background luminance, which can be described by the function *luminance_masking()*;
3. HVS is less sensitive to noise in areas with highly textured patterns, and we have the *texture_masking()*.

Applying Lewis's result in [13], the perceptual threshold JND is given as follows:

$$JND(j,o,x,y) = frequence\_m(j,o) * luminance\_m(j,x,y) * texture\_m(j,x,y)^{0.034}, \tag{9}$$

where

$$frequence\_m(j,o) = \begin{cases} \sqrt{2}, & if \ o = HH \\ 1, & if \ o = other \end{cases} * \begin{cases} 0.10, & if \ j = 1 \\ 0.16, & if \ j = 2 \\ 0.32, & if \ j = 3 \\ 1.00, & if \ j = 4 \end{cases}, \tag{10}$$

$$luminance\_m(j,x,y) = 3 + \frac{1}{256} \sum_{u=0}^{1} \sum_{v=0}^{1} I^{4,LL}(u+1+\frac{x}{2^{j-1}}, v+1+\frac{y}{2^{j-1}}), \tag{11}$$

$$texture\_m(j,x,y) = \sum_{k=1}^{j-1} 16^{-k} \sum_{o}^{HH,HL,LH} \sum_{u=o}^{1} \sum_{v=0}^{1} (I^{j-k,o}(u+\frac{x}{2^k}, v+\frac{y}{2^k}))^2$$
$$+ 16^{j-1} var(I^{4,LL}(\{1,2\}+\frac{x}{2^{j-1}}, \{1,2\}+\frac{y}{2^{j-1}})). \tag{12}$$

4 Watermark Embedding and Detection

4.1 Multi-bit Watermark Embedding Based on WD-HMM

Under the framework of vector WD-HMM, the carrier for watermark signal is the vector tree shown in Fig.1(b). In the interest of resisting against JPEG attack, the watermark is embedded only to the coarsest 2 wavelet scales. Therefore, the resulting vector tree includes only 15 nodes, which are used to embed the M-bit watermark. Fig.2 gives the diagram of the proposed HMM based watermark embedding scheme, which is made up of three major steps, i.e.,

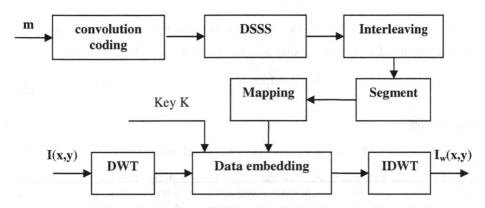

Fig. 2. HMM-based watermark embedding process

1. Watermark Coding: The watermark information **m** is coded with 1/3 convolution code, DSSS (Direct Sequence Spread Spectrum) and interleaving to generate a set of bit sequence, which is then grouped into M-bit ($M \leq 15$) segments. If the M-bit information is denoted as $\mathbf{b}_l = \{b_0, b_1, \ldots, b_{M-1}\}$, then there are totally $L=2^M$ code words i.e. $\mathbf{b} = \{b_l; l=0,1,\ldots k, \ldots 2^M-1\}$.

2. Pattern Mapping: For each 15-node vector tree, there are 2^{15} ways to modify the nodes, which thus can be considered as a 15-bit pattern denoted as $\mathbf{d} = \{d_i; d_i \in \{1,-1\}, i=0,1,\ldots,14\}$. Hence, in order to embed each M-bit segment into a 15-node vector tree, one should map the segment $\mathbf{b}_l$ into the 15-bit pattern $\mathbf{d}_l$. The optimal mapping strategy will be given in section 4.3.

3. Watermark Embedding: The 15-bit pattern $\mathbf{d}_l$ mapped from $\mathbf{b}_l$ with the mapping strategy K is then embedded into the 15-node vector tree with the following formula:

$$X(t,i) = X(t,i) + d_i \cdot \beta \cdot a(t,i), \qquad (13)$$

where $X(t,i)$ is the ith node in the tth vector tree, $a(t,i)$ is its corresponding HVS masking weight and β is the global adjustment factor for embedding strength.

After all M-bit segments are embedded into the 15-node vector trees selected with a secret key, inverse DWT is performed to obtain the watermarked image $I_w(x,y)$.

4.2 Maximum-Likelihood Watermark Detection

As described above, the M-bit segment $\mathbf{b}_l$ is mapped to a 15-bit pattern $\mathbf{d}_l$, which is then embedded into the tth vector tree $\mathbf{T}_x^t$. Assuming that the parameter set θ of the vector HMM model is given, the likelihood function for $\mathbf{T}_x^t$ can be defined as $f_x(\mathbf{T}_x^t \mid \theta)$. Hence, the multi-bits watermark detection can be formulated as the following maximum-likelihood detector in (14), which means that detected information $\mathbf{b}_l$ from $\mathbf{b}=\{b_l; l=0,1,\ldots,2^M-1\}$ is the one satisfying

$$\ln \frac{f_z(\mathbf{T}_z^t \mid \mathbf{b}_l)}{f_z(\mathbf{T}_z^t \mid \mathbf{b}_m)} > 0, \forall m \neq l, \tag{14}$$

where $f_Z(\mathbf{T}_z^t \mid \theta)$ stands for the likelihood function for vector tree $\mathbf{T}_z^t$. Considering the mapping $\mathbf{b}_l\text{->}\mathbf{d}_l$ and HVS masking $\mathbf{a}' = \{\beta \cdot \alpha(t,i); i = 0,1,\ldots14\}$, we have

$$\ln \frac{f_x(\mathbf{T}_z^t - \mathbf{a}'.*\mathbf{d}_l \mid \theta)}{f_x(\mathbf{T}_z^t - \mathbf{a}'.*\mathbf{d}_m \mid \theta)} > 0, \forall m \neq l. \tag{15}$$

Further more,

$$\ln f_x(\mathbf{T}_z^t - \mathbf{a}'.*\mathbf{d}_l \mid \theta) > \ln f_x(\mathbf{T}_z^t - \mathbf{a}'.*\mathbf{d}_m \mid \theta), \forall m \neq l. \tag{16}$$

The expression (16) indicates that the output pattern $\mathbf{d}_l$ for the vector HMM based detector is the one with the biggest logarithmic likelihood value. And the M-bit segment $\mathbf{b}_l$ is obtained through the inverse mapping of $\mathbf{d}_l$. All these M-bit segments $\mathbf{b}_l$ are then preceded with re-segment, de-interleaving, de-DSSS and Viterbi decoding to obtain the decoded watermark $\hat{\mathbf{m}}$.

4.3 Robustness Analysis

One of the key issues involved in the proposed HMM-based watermarking algorithm is the mapping K which is required for embedding the M-bit segment $\mathbf{b}_l$ into the 15-node vector tree. In this section, several design rules for the mapping are given according to the robustness analysis.

To simplify the analysis and without loss of generality, we first assume $M = 1$, which means that after mapping there are only 2 patterns, denoted as $\mathbf{g}$ and $\mathbf{h}$, to be embedded into the vector tree. Following the maximum-likelihood detection rule, if $\ln f_x(\mathbf{T}_z^t - \mathbf{a}'.*\mathbf{g} \mid \theta) > \ln f_x(\mathbf{T}_z^t - \mathbf{a}'.*h \mid \theta)$, then the output of the detector is $\mathbf{g}$. Obviously, given that pattern $\mathbf{g}$ is embedded into the tth tree, the larger the probability P_g for $\mathbf{g}$ is, the more robust the watermarking system would be. Here

$$P_g = P\{\ln f_x(\mathbf{T}_z^t - \mathbf{a}'.*g \mid \theta) > \ln f_x(\mathbf{T}_z^t - \mathbf{a}'.*h \mid \theta)\}. \tag{17}$$

If the watermarked image is not attacked, we then have:

$$\mathbf{T}_z^t = \mathbf{T}_x^t + \mathbf{a}'.*g. \tag{18}$$

To substitute (**18**) into (**17**), we have

$$p_g = P\{\ln f_x(\mathbf{T}_x^t \mid \theta) > \ln f_x(\mathbf{T}_x^t + \mathbf{a}^t.*(g-h) \mid \theta)\}. \tag{19}$$

In (**19**), the greater the difference between **g** and **h** is, the smaller the likelihood value $f_x(\mathbf{T}_x^t + \mathbf{a}^t.*(g-h) \mid \theta)$ will be. Thus a greater difference between **g** and **h** would help to improve the robustness of the detection. Here, the difference between **g** and **h** can be measured with the code distance, which would reach the maximum when each bit of **g** and **h** is different. However, even if the maximum code distance between **g** and **h** is achieved, the different pairs of **g** and **h** would have different contribution to the detection performance. For example, we consider the following two cases: (1) each bit of the pattern **g** is '1' while that of **h** is '-1'; (2) some bits of the pattern **g** are '1' and the other are '-1', while the pattern **h** is the reversed version of **g**. Although, the maximum code distance between **g** and **h** is achieved for both case (1) and (2), but their contributions to the change of $\hat{\mathbf{T}}_x^t = \mathbf{T}_x^t + \mathbf{a}^t.*(g-h)$ are different. For case (1), since all the nodes in the vector tree are added with a fixed value, $\hat{\mathbf{T}}_x^t$ is very similar to $\mathbf{T}_x^t$; while for case (2), each node of the vector tree is modified differently, and thus $\hat{\mathbf{T}}_x^t$ is less similar to $\mathbf{T}_x^t$. In short, the likelihood value $f_x(\mathbf{T}_x^t + \mathbf{a}^t.*(g-h) \mid \theta)$ in the case (2) is smaller than that in the case (1), which leads to the conclusion that the pattern design for **g** and **h** in case (2) is more robust than that in the case (1). In a word, the pattern pair **g** and **h** should be designed to change the vector tree node randomly while their distance is kept as large as possible, which gives rise to the first rule for optimal mapping design.

In addition, the modification on the parent node in a vector tree would have more contribution to the system robustness than that on its children. This is because that the modification of parent nodes would affect, within the framework of the vector WD-HMM, not only the statistical distribution of its own, but also that of its four children nodes by probability transition matrix. Therefore, this property can be used as the second rule for optimal mapping design, i.e., parent node should be preferably selected to embed data. Although the above two rules for optimal mapping design are obtained based on the robustness analysis for $M=1$, they can be generalized to $M > 1$ case.

4.4   Optimal Watermark Embedding Strategy

Incorporating the watermark embedding scheme in section 4.1 and the optimal mapping rules in the section 4.3, the proposed vector HMM based multi-bit watermark embedding algorithm is described as follows.

4.4.1   Watermark Coding

1. Convolution coding for watermark **m**: Let $\mathbf{m} = \{m_i; i = 1, 2, ..., L, m_i \in [0,1]\}$ be the watermark message, where L is the length of the message. Then **m** is coded with the 1/3 convolution code to generate a sequence $\mathbf{m}_c$ with the length of L_c. Here, the generating matrix G for convolution code is

$$G = \begin{bmatrix} 1 & 1 & 1 & 1 & 0 & 1 & 1 & 1 \\ 1 & 1 & 0 & 1 & 1 & 0 & 0 & 1 \\ 1 & 0 & 0 & 1 & 0 & 1 & 0 & 1 \end{bmatrix}.$$

2. DSSS for m_c: The coded message m_c is DSSS spreaded with PN sequence $p=\{p_i; i=1,2,\dots,N_p\}$ of length N_p, which is generated with a secret key. Thus we create a sequence $w=\{w_i; w_i \in \{-1,+1\}, i=1,2,\dots, L_c * N_p\}$.

3. Interleaving for w: a random sequence with the length of $L_c * N_p$ is generated and then sorted to create a new sequence s. w is then interleaved with the formula $w[i] = w[s]$ and thus the interleaved sequence w_l is create.

4. Grouping w_l: assuming M bits to be embedded into every vector tree, we can group w_l by every M bits and get $N_s = \lfloor (N_p * L_c + M - 1)/M \rfloor$ segments, where $\lfloor x \rfloor$ stands for a maximal integer not larger than x.

4.4.2 Optimal Mapping Strategy

As described in the section 4.1, each M-bit segment ($M \le 15$) needs to be embedded into a 15-node vector tree. In general, the larger the value M is set, the higher the information embedding capacity can be, but also more computation load will be required for watermark detection. Compromising to this contradiction, we set $M=5$ in this paper. Therefore, an optimal mapping K from 5-bit b_l to 15-bit patter d_l is developed based on the rules in the section 4.3. In our work, we design the optimal mapping as shown in Fig. 3, where the triangle and circle represent the repeated version of each 5-bit segment while the rectangle stands for the inversed version. Note that all these 15 bits are from the set of $\{+1, -1\}$.

The proposed mapping strategy in Fig.3 makes full use of the design rules given in section 4.3. The mapped pattern d_l of 15-bit is made up of 3 different versions of its corresponding message b_l of 5-bit, among which one version is the inversed one of the other two. The 3 different versions of b_l are spread into the 3 different branch of the vector tree, which keeps the "distance" between the pattern d_l and vector HMM model large and therefore increases the robustness of detection. In addition, the 3 root nodes are used to embed 3 different bits from the same version, which would also affect their children to some extent.

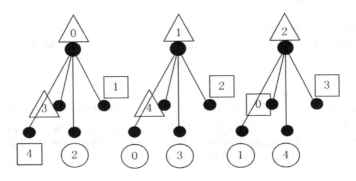

Fig. 3. Optimal mapping for $M=5$

4.4.3 Watermark Embedding

The original image $I(x,y)$ is decomposed with the 9/7 biorthogonal wavelet into 4-level pyramids and then the coarsest two levels (scale=3 and 4) are chosen to build the 2-level vector trees for watermark embedding. The encoded watermark sequence $\mathbf{w}_I$ is grouped into N_s segments of length M, and embedded into N_s vector trees randomly selected from totally T vector trees with a secret key.

Each M-bit segment $\mathbf{b}_l$ is optimally mapped to $\mathbf{d}_l$ as shown in Fig.3, which is then embedded bit by bit into a vector tree with the formula (13).

After all M-bit segments are mapped and embedded, the inverse DWT is performed to generate the watermarked image $I_w(x,y)$.

5 Simulation Results and Analysis

In our simulation, we test four 512*512*8b standard images with different texture. A 60-bit message is embedded into $\mathrm{HH}_i, \mathrm{HL}_i, \mathrm{LH}_i (i = 3,4)$ subbands with the related parameters set for $L=60$, $L_c=201$, $N_p=13$ and $\beta=1.05$. Fig.4 shows the watermarked images.

(a) (b)

(c) (d)

Fig. 4. Watermarked Images. (a) lena (PSNR=42.56dB) (b) baboon (PSNR=42.98dB) (c) peppers (PSNR=42.23dB) (d) fishingboat (PSNR=42.43dB).

To demonstrate the effectiveness of the proposed watermarking algorithm, we compare the performance of our HMM based detector versus the conventional correlation detector under StirMark attacks. Out of impartiality, the same vector tree structure and optimal mapping strategy are used for both detectors and the same 60-bit watermark is embedded. The correction detector used can be described as follows:

$$\text{Correlate}(\mathbf{T}_z^t | \mathbf{b}_l) > \text{Correlate}(\mathbf{T}_z^t | \mathbf{b}_m), \quad \forall m \neq l. \tag{20}$$

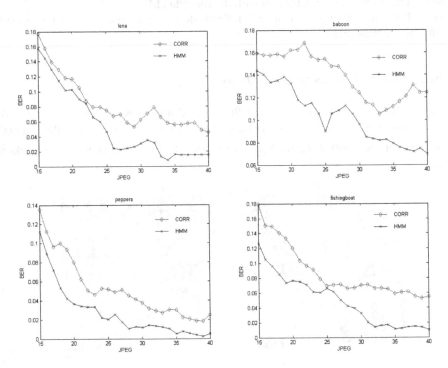

Fig. 5. BER performance comparison for Vector HMM-based Detector and correlation detector

Table 1. Performance of vector HMM based detector

Images \ Attacks	lena	baboon	f16	fishingboat	peppers
PSNR(db)	42.56	42.98	42.52	42.43	42.23
JPEG	13~100	11~100	11~100	12~100	11~100
Additive noise	1~3	1~3	1~5	1~3	1~5
MedianCut	7×7	7×7	9×9	7×7	7×7
Gaussian	Ok	Ok	Ok	Ok	Ok
Sharpening	Ok	Ok	Ok	Ok	Ok

Table 2. Performance of correlation detector

Images Attacks	lena	baboon	f16	fishingboat	peppers
PSNR(db)	42.56	42.98	42.52	42.43	42.23
JPEG	18~100	23~100	17~100	16~100	18~100
Additive noise	1~3	1	1~5	1~2	1~5
MedianCut	5×5	3×3	5×5	5×5	5×5
Gaussian	Ok	Ok	Ok	Ok	Ok
Sharpening	Ok	Ok	Ok	Ok	Ok

If the expression (**20**) is satisfied, then the embedded M-bit data $\mathbf{b}_l$ can be detected from the tth tree. Considering that the nodes in $\mathbf{T}_x^t$ are modified by $\mathbf{a}^t.*\mathbf{d}_l$ when $\mathbf{b}_l$ is embedded, we further have

$$\mathbf{T}_z^t * (\mathbf{a}^t.*\mathbf{d}_l)' > \mathbf{T}_z^t * (\mathbf{a}^t.*\mathbf{d}_m)', \quad \forall m \neq l. \tag{21}$$

Fig.5 shows the BER performance of the two detectors for the test images under JPEG attack. Compared with the correlation detector, it is observed that there is a significant improvement in BER performance with the proposed HMM-based detector.

The simulation results for the two detectors under StirMark attack are included in Table 1 and 2, which indicates that the proposed vector HMM-based watermarking algorithm is more robust against StirMark attack, such as JPEG compression, additive noise, median cut and filter.

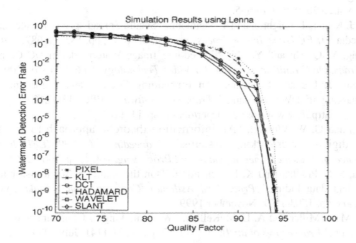

Fig. 6. Performance against JPEG compression in [17]

As a comparison, Fig.6 [17] gives the BER performance of different transform domain watermarking algorithm against JPEG compression, where the test image is "lena" and only 1-bit watermark is embedded. It is observed that the BER is more than 30% for almost all the watermarking algorithms in Fig.6 under JPEG_70 attack. Mayer [18] presents a multi-bit watermarking algorithm based on informed coding, which can survive JPEG_50 attack for "lena" image when embedded with 70 bits of watermark. Compared with Mayer's results, our vector HMM-based watermarking algorithm can resist JPEG_13 attack for the same image with 60-bit watermark embedded.

6 Conclusion

In this paper, we present a robust multi-bit watermarking algorithm based on the vector HMM in wavelet domain. The proposed algorithm employs a vector WD-HMM model, which takes into account both the energy correlation across the scale and the different subbands at the same scale of the wavelet pyramid. The optimal mapping strategy for M-bit segment message to vector tree is also given based on the robustness analysis.

By incorporating other key technologies such as HVS, optimal coding/embedding and maximum likelihood detection for vector tree structure, channel coding and spread spectrum, the proposed algorithm can provide robust embedding of relatively high watermark capacity. Simulation results show that, compared with conventional correlation detector, our vector HMM-based watermarking algorithm has significant improvement in performance against StirMark attacks, such as JPEG compression, additive noise, median cut and filter.

References

1. J. Huang and T. Tan, "A Review of Invisible Image Watermarking, " *ACTA Automatica Sinica*, vol.26 2000, pp.646-655.
2. J. Cox, J. Kilian, T. Leighton and T. Shamoon, "Secure Spread spectrum watermarking for multimedia," *IEEE Trans. Image Processing*, vol. 6, no. 12, pp. 1837-p1687, 1997.
3. J. Huang, Y. Q. Shi and Y. Shi, "Embedding Image Watermarks in DC Components," *IEEE Trans. On Circuits and Systems for Video Technology*, 10(6):974-979, 2000.
4. D. Huang, J. Liu and J. Huang, "An Embedding Strategy and Algorithm for Image Watermarking in DWT Domain, " *Trans. on Software, PRC,* 13(7):1290-1297, 2002. [online]. http://www.jos.org.cn/paper/detail.asp?id=1181
5. B. Chen and G. W. Wornell, "An information-theoretic approach to the design of robust digital watermarking systems," *Proceeding of 1999 IEEE International Conference on Acoustics, Speech, and Signal Processing*, vol. 4, pp. 2061-2064.
6. J. Chou, S. S. Pradhan and K. Ramchandran, "On the duality between distributed source coding and data hiding," *Proc. 33rd Asilomar Conference on Signals, Systems and Computers*, pp. 1503-1507, November 1999.
7. J. Cox, M. L. Miller and A. L. McKellips, "Watermarking as Communications with Side Information," *Proceedings of the IEEE* , vol. 87, pp. 1127-1141, July 1999.

8. Q. Cheng and T. S. Huang, "Blind Digital Watermarking for Images and Videos and Performance Analysis," *Proc. Int. Conf. Multimedia Expos., New York*, Aug. 2000.
9. Q. Cheng and T. S. Huang, "An Additive Approach to Transform-Domain Information Hiding and Optimum Detection Structure," *IEEE Trans. on Multimedia*, vol. 3, pp. 273–284, Sept. 2001.
10. M. S. Crouse, R. D. Nowak and R. G. Baraniuk, "Wavelet-Based Statistical Signal Processing Using Hidden Markov Models," *IEEE Trans. on Signal Processing*, vol.46, no.4, April 1998.
11. M. N. Do and M. Vetterli, "Rotation Invariant Texture Characterization and Retrieval using Steerable Wavelet-domain Hidden Markov Models," *IEEE Transactions on Multimedia*, vol. 4, Issue: 4, pp. 517-527, Dec. 2002.
12. B. Watson, G. Y. Yang, at el., "Visibility of wavelet quantization noise," *IEEE Trans. On Image Processing*, 1997, 1164 - 1175.
13. S. Lewis and G. Knowles, "Image compression using the 2-D wavelet transform," *IEEE Transactions on Image Processing*, vol. 1, Issue: 2, pp. 244 -250, Apr. 1992.
14. M. Barni, F. Bartolini, A. D. Rosa, and A. Piva, "Capacity of the watermark channel: How many bits can be hidden within a digital image?" in *Proceedings of SPIE, 1999*, pp. 437-448.
15. L. Harry and V. Trees, "Detection, Estimation and Modulation Theory," *New York: Wiley*, 1968, pt. I.
16. J. R. Hernandez, "DCT-Domain Watermarking Technique for Still Image: Detector Performance Analysis and a New structure," *IEEE Trans. on Image Processing*, vol. 9, no. 1, pp. 55-68, Jan. 2000.
17. C. Fei, D. Kundur and R. H. Kwong, "Analysis and Design of Watermarking Algorithms for Improved Resistance to Compression," *IEEE Trans. on Image Processing*, vol. 13, no. 2, pp. 126-144, Feb. 2004.
18. J. Mayer and R. A Silva, "Efficient informed embedding of multi-bit watermark," *IEEE International Conference on Acoustics, Speech, and Signal Processing, 2004, Proceedings (ICASSP '04)*, vol. 3, pp. III-389-392, May 2004.
19. StirMark, [Online], Available: http://www.cl.cam.ac.uk/~fapp2/watermarking /stirmark/.

Robust Detection of Transform Domain Additive Watermarks[*]

Xingliang Huang and Bo Zhang

Department of Computer Science & Technology, Tsinghua University,
Beijing 100084, P.R. China
hxliang98@mails.tsinghua.edu.cn
dcszb@mail.tsinghua.edu.cn

Abstract. Deviations of the actual coefficient distributions from the idealized theoretical models due to inherent modeling errors and possible attacks are big challenges for watermark detection. These uncertain deviations may degrade or even upset the performance of existing optimum detectors that are optimized at idealized models. In this paper, we present a new detection structure for transform domain additive watermarks based on Huber's robust hypothesis testing theory. The statistical behaviors of the image subband coefficients are modeled by a contaminated generalized Gaussian distribution (GGD), which tries to capture small deviations of the actual situation from the idealized GGD. The robust detector is a min-max solution of the contamination model and turns out to be a censored version of the optimum probability ratio test. Experimental results on real images confirm the superiority of the proposed detector with respect to the classical optimum detector.

1 Introduction

Digital watermarking is a technique that embeds secondary information into host multimedia signals in an imperceptible way, and it has been proposed as a promising solution for the increasingly urgent issues of intellectual property rights protection and data security. According to different application purposes, existing watermarking schemes can be classified into two categories [6], which correspond to two kinds of fundamental problems, i.e., watermark en/decoding and watermark detection, respectively. For watermark en/decoding, full decoding to extract the embedded message is necessary. While for watermark detection, deciding whether or not a particular message has been inserted usually suffices. The present paper will mainly discuss the problem of watermark detection.

Additive and multiplicative embedding rules are often adopted in the reported techniques [4]-[13]. In either case, the majority of early watermarking schemes use the heuristic correlation detector [4], which has been proved to be suboptimal in most cases [5],[7],[9]. In order to obtain optimum detection structures and theoretical analysis of the detector performance, watermark detection has been considered as the

---

[*] This work is supported by National Nature Science Foundation of China (60135010, 60321002) and Chinese National Key Foundation R & D Plan (2004CB318108).

M. Barni et al. (Eds.): IWDW 2005, LNCS 3710, pp. 124–138, 2005.

problem of classical hypothesis testing [3], and some probability models that can well characterize the image coefficient distributions are assumed. In [8], [9], optimal detector for discrete cosine transform (DCT) domain additive watermarking is derived, where the GGD is used to model the statistical behavior of the DCT coefficients, and the Laplacian and Gaussian distributions, as special cases of the GGD, are also discussed. In [10], [11], the Weibull distribution is adopted to describe the magnitudes of discrete Fourier transform (DFT) coefficients, and optimum detection of DFT based multiplicative watermarks is studied. In [7], the GGD is used, and asymptotically optimal detectors for additive watermarking in the DCT and discrete wavelet transform (DWT) domains are presented. Optimum and locally optimum (LO) detection of transform domain additive and multiplicative watermarks incorporating the GGD model are discussed in detail in [5], [6]. The problem of detecting DCT domain additive watermarks using LO nonlinearities is addressed in [12], where the Gaussian, Cauchy and Gaussian-tailed zero memory LO nonlinearities are compared.

All these work implies the general implicit assumption that the image coefficients which may carry watermarks can be perfectly modeled by certain model distributions, such as the GGD and the Weibull distribution. Furthermore, few of them take the impact of potential attacks which is crucial to watermarking systems into account. Due to modeling errors, there are always (small) deviations of the actual statistical behaviors of the image coefficients from the idealized model distributions. In addition, viewing from the detector side, intentional or unintentional attacks on watermarking systems can further add to the deviations. Moreover, it is hard to model the possible attacks because there are too many uncertainties that can be brought in by malicious attackers and general image processing operations. Although the attacking strength expects to be small in order to preserve the image quality, it is still possible for attackers to blind the watermark detector by exerting the deviations. Thus, it is more reasonable to assume that the true underlying distribution of the image coefficients lies in some neighborhood of the idealized model distribution, which is like the case that has been addressed by Huber [1]. As pointed out in [1], although small, the deviations may lead to the presence of "bad" observations, which can upset the performance of detectors that have been designed according to optimum criteria and under assumptions of idealized theoretical models. So what we need is a watermark detector that is insensitive to small deviations from the idealized assumptions. Specifically, the robust watermark detector should perform almost as well as the optimum detector when the image coefficients are perfectly characterized by the idealized model and should perform better than the optimum detector for a broad family of distributions that are in some sense near the idealized distribution. Unlike some other proposed watermarking schemes that are elaborately designed to withstand predefined attacks [13], the robust watermark detector does not assume any specific attack models. Instead, it tries to maintain fairly good, but not necessarily optimal, performance over a wide range of situations.

In this paper we shall focus on robust detection of transform domain additive watermarks, but the rationale is also applicable to the multiplicative case and other coefficient models. Image transforms that are favorable for additive watermarking mainly include the DCT, DWT and the pyramid transform, and the GGD has been proposed to capture the statistical properties of these subband coefficients. In order to formalize the small deviations from the idealized GGD model, we take the coefficient distribution function $F(\cdot)$ to be of the form

$$F(x) = (1-\varepsilon)G(x) + \varepsilon H(x), \quad 0 \le \varepsilon < 1, \tag{1}$$

where ε is a small fixed number, $G(\cdot)$ is the cumulative distribution function (cdf) of the GGD, and $H(\cdot)$ denotes an arbitrary distribution. According to this mixture model, $F(\cdot)$ is allowed to vary from the GGD within the neighborhood specified in terms of ε-contamination. Then, the robust watermark detector can be derived as the solution to a well-defined min-max testing problem based on the model of (1).

The rest of this paper is organized as follows. In Section 2, the general formalizations and techniques for robust detection problem are introduced. The robust detection structure for the contaminated GGD model is derived in Section 3. Experimental results are given in Section 4 to show the effectiveness of the robust watermark detector, and conclusions are found in Section 5.

2 Preliminaries

We are interested in the problem of robust hypothesis testing with a sequence of independent observations as

$$H_0: \quad P_0 = \prod_{i=1}^{N} P_{0i}$$

$$\tag{2}$$

$$H_1: \quad P_1 = \prod_{i=1}^{N} P_{1i},$$

where N denotes the number of samples, and P_{ji}, $j = 0,1$, are distributions of individual observations. Huber [1] has first derived a min-max solution that can be directly applied to problem (2) when the observations are independent and identically distributed (i.i.d.). Martin and Schwartz [2] then extend the results to cover the time-varying case. The formalizations are as follows.

Let (R,B) be a measurable space, and let P_{0i} and P_{1i}, $i = 1,2,\cdots,N$, be distinct probability measures on it, having densities p_{0i} and p_{1i} with respect to the measure $\mu_i = P_{0i} + P_{1i}$. The sets of measures $\{P_{0i}\} = \{P_{0i}\}_{i=1}^{N}$ and $\{P_{1i}\} = \{P_{1i}\}_{i=1}^{N}$ correspond to the simple hypothesis H_0 and the simple alternative H_1, respectively. In order to formalize the uncertainties in these measures, the simple hypotheses are replaced with the following composite ones

$$\mathsf{P}_j = \left\{ \{Q_{ji}\} = \{Q_{ji}\}_{i=1}^{N} \,\middle|\, Q_{ji} = (1-\varepsilon)P_{ji} + \varepsilon H_{ji}, H_{ji} \in \mathsf{H} \right\}, \quad j = 0,1, \tag{3}$$

where $0 \le \varepsilon < 1$ is a fixed number and H represents the class of all possibility measures on (R,B). As stated in [1], [2], we shall always assume that P_0 and P_1 do not overlap, otherwise the overlapping measures of the two hypotheses will thoroughly blind the detector and thus upset the problem. (The conditions that satisfy this assumption will be made more specific with the measures $\{P_{ji}\}$ being GGDs for watermark detection problem in Section 3.)

Let ϕ be any test between P_0 and P_1, and $R(\{Q_{ji}\}, \phi) = E_{\{Q_{ji}\}}(\phi)$ denote the expected loss, or risk associated with the pair $(\{Q_{ji}\}, \phi)$. Then the min-max testing problem we are concern with is

$$\phi' = \min_{\phi} \max_{\{Q_{1i}\}} R(\{Q_{1i}\}, \phi)$$

subject to

(4)

$$\sup_{\{Q_{0i}\}} R(\{Q_{0i}\}, \phi') \leq \alpha, \quad 0 \leq \alpha \leq 1.$$

We say that a pair $(\{Q'_{0i}\}, \{Q'_{1i}\})$, $\{Q'_{ji}\} \in P_j$, is least favorable for problem (4), if for any test ϕ and any pair $(\{Q_{0i}\}, \{Q_{1i}\})$, $\{Q_{ji}\} \in P_j$,

$$R(\{Q_{ji}\}, \phi) \leq R(\{Q'_{ji}\}, \phi), \quad j = 0, 1.$$

(5)

Then it follows from [2] that the probability ratio test ϕ' on the least favorable pair $(\{Q'_{0i}\}, \{Q'_{1i}\})$ is exactly the solution to the robust testing problem of (4). And $(\{Q'_{0i}\}, \{Q'_{1i}\})$ can be given in terms of their densities by

$$q'_{0i} = \begin{cases} (1-\varepsilon) p_{0i} & p_{1i}/p_{0i} < c''_i \\ (1/c''_i)(1-\varepsilon) p_{1i} & p_{1i}/p_{0i} \geq c''_i, \end{cases}$$

$$q'_{1i} = \begin{cases} (1-\varepsilon) p_{1i} & p_{1i}/p_{0i} > c'_i \\ c'_i(1-\varepsilon) p_{0i} & p_{1i}/p_{0i} \leq c'_i, \end{cases}$$

(6)

where the numbers $0 \leq c'_i < c''_i \leq \infty$ have to be determined such that q'_{0i} and q'_{1i} are probability densities, i.e.,

$$(1-\varepsilon)\{P_{0i}[p_{1i}/p_{0i} < c''_i] + (1/c''_i)P_{1i}[p_{1i}/p_{0i} \geq c''_i]\} = 1,$$
$$(1-\varepsilon)\{P_{1i}[p_{1i}/p_{0i} > c'_i] + c'_i P_{0i}[p_{1i}/p_{0i} \leq c'_i]\} = 1.$$

(7)

It follows from (6) and the i.i.d. assumption of the observations, Y, that the likelihood ratio of the least favorable pair is

$$l'(Y) = \prod_{i=1}^{N} q'_{1i}/q'_{0i}$$

(8)

with

$$q'_{1i}/q'_{0i} = \begin{cases} c''_i & p_{1i}/p_{0i} \geq c''_i \\ p_{1i}/p_{0i} & c'_i < p_{1i}/p_{0i} < c''_i \\ c'_i & p_{1i}/p_{0i} \leq c'_i. \end{cases}$$

(9)

Note that the robust nonlinearity q'_{1i}/q'_{0i} is a censored version of p_{1i}/p_{0i}. Accordingly, the desired robust probability ratio test is

$$\phi'(Y) = \begin{cases} 1 & l'(Y) > T \\ \alpha & l'(Y) = T \\ 0 & l'(Y) < T, \end{cases} \tag{10}$$

where the threshold T is set to satisfy $\alpha = R(\{Q_{0i}\}, \phi')$. The resulting ϕ' solves the min-max problem (4) in the Neyman-Pearson sense that the false alarm probability is no greater than α and the probability of detection is no less than $R(\{Q_{1i}\}, \phi')$ for the board class of nominal densities given by (3).

3   Robust Watermark Detection

Considering uncertain deviations due to inherent modeling errors and possible attacks, it is more reasonable to view watermark detection as a typical scenario of robust detection of signals. In this section, the robust hypothesis testing theory is applied to derive a new watermark detection structure. Although there are always uncertainties that are very likely to degrade the performance of the watermark detector, we may feel confident in using the new detector since it is designed to be robust over a broad class of image coefficient distributions.

3.1   Additive Embedding Rule and Robust Detection Structure

The commonly used additive embedding rule for transform domain watermarking is

$$y_i = x_i + \theta_i s_i, \quad i = 1, 2, \cdots, N, \tag{11}$$

where x_i and y_i are coefficients from the original and the watermarked transformed images, respectively, s_i is the watermark signal assumed to be known, and θ_i is the amplitude parameter controlling the watermark strength. In the literature, the subband coefficients are often modeled by i.i.d. GGD with the pdf

$$g(x) = A e^{-|\beta(x-m)|^d} \tag{12}$$

where

$$\beta = \frac{1}{\sigma} \left(\frac{\Gamma(3/d)}{\Gamma(1/d)} \right)^{1/2}, \quad A = \frac{\beta d}{2\Gamma(1/d)},$$

and d, m and σ are the shape parameter, mean and standard deviation, respectively, and $\Gamma(\cdot)$ is the Gamma function. Due to the orthogonality of many image transforms, the mean value of AC subband coefficients is usually close to zero, i.e. $m=0$. Thus the model of (12) can be simplified to

$$g(x) = A e^{-|\beta x|^d}. \tag{13}$$

Here we should consider deviations of the actual coefficient distribution from the perfect GGD. Recall that $G(x)$ denotes the corresponding cdf of $g(x)$. According to (3), these uncertainties can be formalized by the following composite hypothesis testing problem with the hypothesis H_0 being that the watermark is not present and the alterative H_1 being that it is present:

$$H_0: \quad P_0 = \left\{ Q_0 \middle| Q_0 = \prod_{i=1}^{N} \left((1-\varepsilon)G(y_i) + \varepsilon H_{0i} \right) \right\}$$

$$H_1: \quad P_1 = \left\{ Q_1 \middle| Q_1 = \prod_{i=1}^{N} \left((1-\varepsilon)G(y_i - \theta_i s_i) + \varepsilon H_{1i} \right) \right\},$$

(14)

where y_i is the observation, $0 \le \varepsilon < 1$ represents the deviation level, and H_{ji}, $j=0,1$, are arbitrary distributions. In problem (14), instead of the idealized GGD, the image coefficients are modeled by an ε-contaminated, or a nominal, version of it, which allows a rather broad range of deviations and attempts to set up the base for robust watermarking systems. We shall assume that the parameters, including d, σ, θ_i and ε, are known or can be reliably estimated from the observations at the detector side. (Detailed setup of these parameters will be discussed in Section 3.2.)

The key to the min-max solution for the composite hypothesis testing problem of (14) is to figure out c_i' and c_i''. Define the light-limiter function $r(x; y_1, y_2)$ as

$$r(x; y_1, y_2) = \begin{cases} y_2 & x \ge y_2 \\ x & y_1 < x < y_2 \\ y_1 & x \le y_1. \end{cases}$$

(15)

Then, if c_i' and c_i'' are obtained, the robust log-likelihood ratio test will be given by

$$l'(Y) = \sum_{i=1}^{N} \log \frac{q_{1i}'(y_i)}{q_{0i}'(y_i)} = \sum_{i=1}^{N} r\left(\log \frac{p_{1i}'(y_i)}{p_{0i}'(y_i)}; \log c_i', \log c_i'' \right)$$

$$= \sum_{i=1}^{N} r\left(\beta^d (| y_i |^d - | y_i - \theta_i s_i |^d); \log c_i', \log c_i'' \right),$$

(16)

where q_{0i}' and q_{1i}' represent the least favorable distribution pair. For the problem under consideration, a simple development based on (7) reveals that

$$1/c_i' = c_i''.$$

(17)

So it suffices to determine $c_i' < 1$ by the second equation of (7).

Let $c_0 = \operatorname{essinf} p_1(y)/p_0(y)$ and $l(\cdot, \cdot)$ denote the log-likelihood ratio of an individual observation, i.e.,

$$l(y, \theta s) = \log \frac{p_1(y)}{p_0(y)} = \beta^d (| y |^d - | y - \theta s |^d).$$

(18)

We are interested in the solutions of the following equation with a particular c satisfying $c_0 < c < 1$:

$$l(y, \theta \mid s \mid) = \beta^d \left(|y|^d - |y - \theta \mid s \parallel^d \right) = \log c.$$ (19)

Typical solution(s) of (19) for different d are shown in Fig. 1.

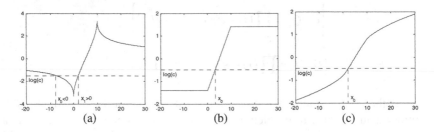

Fig. 1. Typical solution(s) of equation (19) for the cases of (a) $0<d<1$, (b) $d=1$, and (c) $d>1$

We can see that there is a unique solution x_0 for $d \geq 1$, and that there are two solutions when $0<d<1$, which we denote as x_0 and x_1, respectively. Let

$$f(c) = P_1[p_1/p_0 > c] + cP_0[p_1/p_0 \leq c]$$

$$= 1 + \int_{\{p_1/p_0 \leq c\}} (cp_0 - p_1) d\mu.$$ (20)

Combining (7), (20) and the results and notations in Fig. 1, we have c given implicitly by

$$\begin{cases} 1 + cG(x_0) - G(x_0 - \theta \mid s \mid) = 1/(1-\varepsilon) & d \geq 1 \\ 1 + c(G(x_1) - G(x_0)) + G(x_0 - \theta \mid s \mid) - G(x_1 - \theta \mid s \mid) = 1/(1-\varepsilon) & 0 < d < 1. \end{cases}$$ (21)

Huber has proved that f is continuous, $f(c) = 1$ for $0 \leq c \leq c_0$, and $f(c)$, which exactly equals the left side of (21), is strictly increasing for $c > c_0$. Thus, c, the solution of (21), can be easily obtained by numerical methods. After c_i' is obtained through (21) and c_i'' is subsequently given by (17), the robust probability ratio test $l'(Y)$ of the form (16) is determined. And finally, the robust detection structure is obtained by following (10).

As stated in Section 2, it is assumed that P_0 and P_1 in (14) do not overlap, i.e., the hypothesis and alternative measures for all i are disjoint, which will ensure that $c_i' < c_i''$. Because of the structure of the watermark detection problem, the disjointness requirement is equivalent to the condition that $|\theta_i s_i|$ is sufficiently large for a given $\varepsilon > 0$. For the GGD, it is easy to verify that the equivalent condition is

$$|\theta_i s_i| > \lambda > 0$$ (22)

where λ satisfies $\max_x \left(G(x) - G(x - \lambda) \right) = \varepsilon/(1-\varepsilon)$, i.e.,

$$G(\lambda/2) = \frac{1}{2(1-\varepsilon)}.$$
(23)

Typical values of λ are listed in Table 1.

Table 1. Typical values of λ.

		$\sigma=5$	$\sigma=10$	$\sigma=50$
$\varepsilon=0.01$	$d=0.5$	0.020	0.041	0.204
	$d=1.0$	0.072	0.144	0.718
	$d=2.0$	0.127	0.253	1.267
$\varepsilon=0.05$	$d=0.5$	0.122	0.244	1.222
	$d=1.0$	0.382	0.765	3.823
	$d=2.0$	0.660	1.320	6.601
$\varepsilon=0.10$	$d=0.5$	0.293	0.587	2.933
	$d=1.0$	0.833	1.666	8.329
	$d=2.0$	1.397	2.794	13.971

For watermarking problem, it is generally easy to satisfy the condition of (22). For the infrequent case that $|\theta_i s_i| \le \lambda$ for some i, we can leave the corresponding likelihood ratio of the individual term, $p_1(y_i)/p_0(y_i)$, as it is, which will hardly affect the overall performance of the robust detection structure.

The receiver operating characteristics (ROCs) of the robust and the optimal detectors for coefficient models of the idealized GGD, the least favorable distribution pair, and a generic nominal GGD are plotted in Fig. 2.

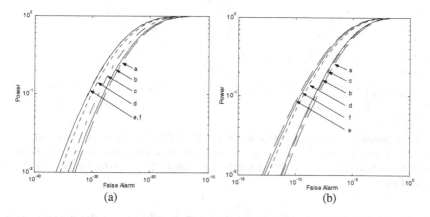

Fig. 2. Power and false alarm for robust detector and optimum detector: a–optimum detector minimum power; b–robust detector minimum power; c–optimum detector for nominal GGD; d–robust detector for nominal GGD; e–optimum detector for GGD; f–robust detector for GGD. The parameters are (a) $d=0.5$ and (b) $d=2.0$, and $\sigma=1$, $|\theta s|=0.5$, $\varepsilon=0.01$, and $N=100$. The generic nominal GGD is $f(x)=(1-\varepsilon)g(x)+\varepsilon g_{\sigma,m}(x)$, where $\sigma=0.0001$, $m=0.5$ for (a) and $\sigma=5$, $m=0$ for (b).

We can see that performance of the two detectors is very close for the idealized model, and that, as indicated by the minimum power, the robust detector performs better than the optimum detector when the contamination model with the least favorable pair is assumed. Moreover, in contrast to the optimum detector, the robust detector maintains fairly good performance under generic nominal GGD models.

3.2 Parameter Setup

Because of the imperceptibility requirement, the amplitudes of watermark signals have to be limited under a comparatively low level, and, in order to preserve the image quality, the attacking strength should not be large either. Thus, reliable estimations of the GGD parameters, d and σ, can be obtained from the possibly watermarked and attacked image instead of the original one [5]-[7], [12]. Specifically, σ can be estimated using the sample variance [7], and the shape parameter d can be estimated using the minimum relative entropy method [5]. The relative entropy, also called the Kullback-Leibler divergence, is often exploited to measure the distance between two distributions. The GGD is used to fit the empirical pdf from the histogram of subband coefficients, and the relative entropy between them is minimized to obtain a nice fit. Some fitting results are shown in Fig. 3. We can see that the agreement between the empirical and the fitted pdfs is quite good, as indicated by small relative entropies between them.

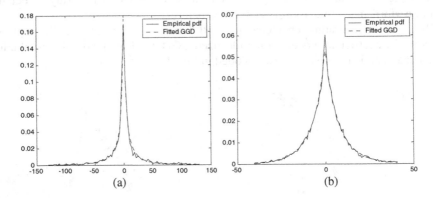

Fig. 3. Empirical pdfs and fitted GGDs for (a) LH2 DWT subband of Lena and (b) LH1 subband of Baboon, where low and high are in the order horizontal-vertical, and the number denotes the subband level. The fitted results are d=0.457, Δh=0.036 for (a) and d=0.887, Δh=0.004 for (b).

As for the watermark amplitude θ_i, it is certainly known at the detector when it equals a predefined global embedding strength [4] or some fixed domain-specific perceptual weight, such as the quantization matrix for DWT coefficients [15] which has been applied in [5], [15]. If it is the output of image-dependent perceptual models, it can also be estimated by reproducing the perceptual mask on the observed image. Since the embedded signals and attacking strength are weak, the estimation error will not be significant [12]. Actually, the robust detector may cover these small errors caused by estimations of d, σ and θ_i.

The mixing parameter ε in the contamination model of (3) denotes the uncertainty level with respect to idealized model distribution. In the watermark detection problem, it is designed to account for the deviations mainly caused by inherent modeling errors and possible attacks. In our scheme, the modeling errors can partly be represented by the relative entropy Δh between the empirical and the fitted pdfs of subband coefficients. Further considering potential attacks, we can let

$$\varepsilon = \gamma \Delta h \tag{24}$$

where the gain factor satisfies $\gamma \geq 1$ and should not be too large because an effective attack should subject to the requirement of image quality preserving. Of course, if other methods are applied to estimate d, Δh in (24) can be replaced accordingly.

3.3 Robust Detectors for GGDs with d=0.5, 1 (Laplacian), and 2 (Gaussian)

We shall further give specific expressions for calculating c and show the robust detection structures in these three typical scenarios.

Usually, the shape parameter d of the GGD for DWT coefficients in AC subbands is in the range [0.4,1], and most images have d around 0.5. For d=0.5, the two solutions of (19) are

$$x_0 = -\frac{1}{4}\left(t - \frac{w}{t}\right), \quad x_1 = \frac{1}{2}\left(w + t\sqrt{2w - t^2}\right), \tag{25}$$

where $t = \beta^{-1/2} \log c$ and $w = \theta \mid s \mid$. Then, c is determined implicitly by

$$c\left(2 - b(x_0) - b(x_1)\right) - b(x_0 - w) + b(x_1 - w) = \frac{2\varepsilon}{1 - \varepsilon} \tag{26}$$

where $b(x) = \left(1 + \mid \beta x \mid^{1/2}\right)\exp\left(-\mid \beta x \mid^{1/2}\right)$.

The AC coefficients of the DCT can be reasonably approximated using the Laplacian density, which is a special case of the GGD with d=1. Under this condition, the solution for (19) is

$$x_0 = \frac{1}{2}\left(\beta^{-1} \log c + \theta \mid s \mid\right), \tag{27}$$

and c is given explicitly by

$$c = \left(\frac{e^{-\beta \theta \mid s \mid / 2} + \sqrt{e^{-\beta \theta \mid s \mid} + 4\varepsilon /(1 - \varepsilon)}}{2}\right)^2. \tag{28}$$

The GGD with d=2 is exactly the Gaussian model, which is commonly used in the literature. The problem of robust detection in additive nearly normal noise has been addressed in [2], and, for generic Gaussian models, we can obtain c implicitly by

$$c\Phi\left(\frac{\sigma \log c}{\theta |s|} + \frac{\theta |s|}{2\sigma}\right) - \Phi\left(\frac{\sigma \log c}{\theta |s|} - \frac{\theta |s|}{2\sigma}\right) = \frac{\varepsilon}{1-\varepsilon} \qquad (29)$$

where Φ is the standard normal cdf.

Typical values of c are listed in Table 2, and the log-likelihood ratio of a single observation for the optimum detector and the corresponding robust nonlinearities are shown in Fig. 4.

Table 2. Typical values of c ($\theta |s|=10$)

		$\sigma=5$	$\sigma=10$	$\sigma=20$
$\varepsilon=0.01$	$d=0.5$	0.045	0.106	0.211
	$d=1.0$	0.078	0.263	0.513
	$d=2.0$	0.053	0.206	0.475
$\varepsilon=0.05$	$d=0.5$	0.111	0.199	0.342
	$d=1.0$	0.145	0.340	0.594
	$d=2.0$	0.150	0.387	0.685
$\varepsilon=0.10$	$d=0.5$	0.184	0.291	0.456
	$d=1.0$	0.227	0.437	0.697
	$d=2.0$	0.252	0.536	0.838

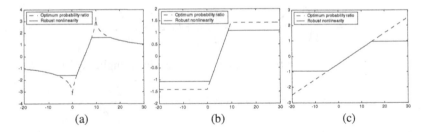

Fig. 4. Optimum probability ratios and robust nonlinearities for (a) $d=0.5$, (b) $d=1$, and (c) $d=2$

For the case of $d=2$, the robust nonlinearity results in the limiter-correlator detector for nearly Gaussian noise as in [2]. For the Laplacian case, i.e., $d=1$, the robust nonlinearity is generally a narrower version of the optimum nonlinearity. And for $d=0.5$, due to its heavy-tailed property, the censoring occurs over only finite intervals for both positive and negative inputs.

4 Experimental Results

Typical additive embedding approaches, as proposed in [5], [7], are adopted for tests. The watermark signal consists of a pseudorandom binary sequence $s_i \in \{+1, -1\}$ and is embedded in either the 8×8 block DCT or the DWT coefficients according to the additive rule (11). For robust watermarking, the image coefficients for carrying watermarks should be selected from low or mid-low frequency subbands of the DCT or high level subbands of the DWT. For example, the regions of $\Omega_{\text{DCT}} = \{(m, n) \mid 5 \leq m + n \leq 6\}$ alone the zig-zag scan line of the 8×8 DCT block or the DWT subbands $\Omega_{\text{DCT}} = \{(u, v) \mid u \geq 2, v = 2, 3, 4\}$, where u denotes the resolution level and v indexes the frequency orientation as $\{1,2,3,4\}=\{LL,HL,LH,HH\}$, can be selected to embed watermarks. In order to achieve better robustness while preserving imperceptibility, the watermark amplitudes are usually determined by certain perceptual models. Taking the analogous approaches of [5], we can set $\theta_i = Q_{\text{DCT}}(m, n)/2$ or $\theta_i = Q_{\text{DWT}}(u, v)/2$, where Q_{DCT} and Q_{DWT} are quantization matrices, which are obtain through psychovisual quantization experiments, for DCT-[14] and DWT-based [15] lossy image compression, respectively. The pdf parameters are considered here to be the same for all the selected coefficients [7], and the gain factor in (24) is simply set to $\gamma=1$.

We have conducted a number of experiments on several real images with size of 256×256, including Lena, Baboon, Fishing Boat, Peppers, and Bridge. The detector performance is evaluated under no attacks as well as under Gaussian/uniform noise adding and JPEG/JPEG2000 lossy compression. We vary the watermark signals and detection thresholds to obtain ROCs of both the robust and the optimum detectors. The shape of the ROC is not only determined by the pdf parameters, but also depends on the length of the watermark sequence, i.e., N. Without loss of generality, we shall adjust N in order to obtain ROCs in proper range for easy visualization and comparisons. When doing this, we will randomly pick up the N coefficients to be watermarked from the pool of all the selected subband coefficients for watermark embedding.

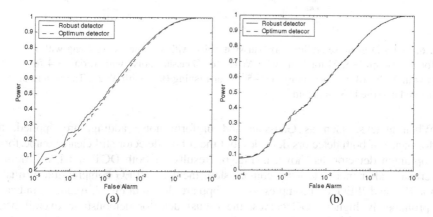

Fig. 5. ROCs when no attack is imposed for (a) Lena with d=0.456, Δh=0.047, N=10, and (b) Baboon with d=0.873, Δh=0.007, N=50. The watermarks are embedded into the DWT domain.

Results when no attack is imposed are shown in Fig. 5. The robust detector performs almost as well as the optimum detector for Baboon (with small relative entropy) and performs slightly better than the optimum detector for Lena (with larger relative entropy that indicates imperfect fitting of the GGD to the empirical pdf), which preliminarily shows the robustness of the proposed detector.

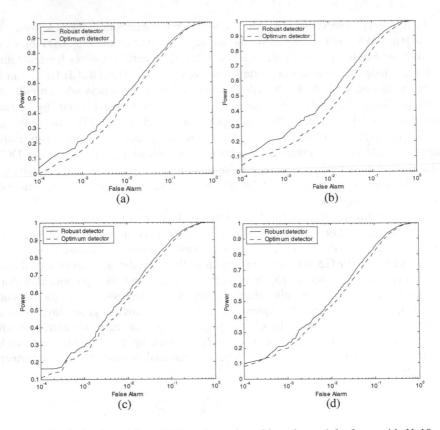

Fig. 6. ROCs after noise adding: (a) Gaussian noise with variance 4 for Lena with $N=10$; (b) uniform noise on $[-5, 5]$ for Lena with $N=10$; (c) Gaussian noise with variance 4 for Fishing Boat with $N=20$; (d) uniform noise on $[-5, 5]$ for Fishing Boat with $N=20$. The watermarks are embedded into the DWT domain.

When attacks, such as Gaussian and uniform noise adding, are applied, the performance of both detectors degrades, but the robust detector still clearly outperforms the optimum detector, as shown in Fig. 6. Results for both DCT and DWT domain watermarks after moderate lossy compression, including JPEG compression of quality factor 75% and JPEG2000 compression of 1bpp are shown in Fig. 7. Again, as indicated by prominently higher ROC curves, the robust detector demonstrate overall better performance than the classical optimum detector.

5 Conclusions

A robust detection structure for additive watermarking in transform domains is proposed. In our schemes, the statistical behavior of image coefficients is modeled by the ε-contaminated GGD. The mixture model allows small deviations from the idealized model distribution, which resembles the circumstance in watermarking

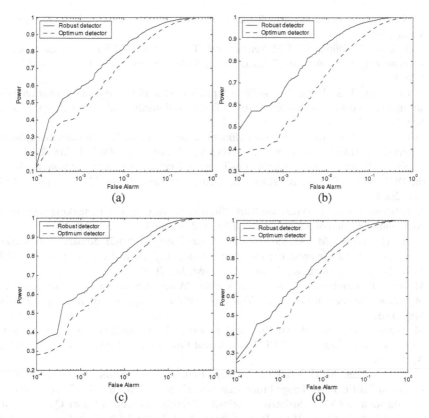

Fig. 7. ROCs after lossy compression: (a) JPEG compression (70%) for Lena with N=100; (b) JPEG2000 compression (1bpp) for Lena with N=100; (c) JPEG compression (70%) for Peppers with N=30; (d) JPEG2000 compression (1bpp) for Peppers with N=100. The watermarks are embedded into the DWT domain for Lena and into the DCT domain for Peppers.

systems where inherent modeling errors and attacks are very likely to occur in practice. The robust detector is determined by a least favorable distribution pair and turns out to be a censored version of the optimum probability ratio test. In experiments with real images, the proposed detector demonstrates more stable performance than the optimum detector under various situations. The rationale of robust detection is also applicable to other types of watermark detection schemes and is left as a future line of research.

References

1. P. J. Huber. "A robust version of the probability ratio test," Ann. Math. Stat., vol. 36, pp. 1753-1758, Dec. 1965.
2. R. D. Martin and S. C. Schwartz, "Robust detection of a known signal in nearly Gaussian noise," IEEE Trans. Inform. Theory, vol. IT-17, no. 1, pp. 50-56, Jan. 1971.

3. H. V. Poor, An Introduction to Signal Detection and Estimation, New York: Springer-Verlag, 1994.
4. I. J. Cox, J. Kilian, F. T. Leighton and T. Shammoon, "Secure spread spectrum watermarking for multimedia," IEEE Trans. Image Processing, vol. 6, pp. 1673–1687, Dec. 1997.
5. Q. Cheng and T. S. Huang, "An additive approach to transform-domain information hiding and optimum detection structure," IEEE Trans. Multimedia, vol. 3, no. 3, pp. 273-284, Sep. 2001.
6. Q. Cheng and T. S. Huang, "Robust optimum detection of transform domain multiplicative watermarks," IEEE Trans. Signal Processing, vol. 51, no. 4, pp. 906-924, Apr. 2003.
7. A. Nikolaidis and I. Pitas, "Asymptotically optimal detection for additive watermarking in the DCT and DWT domains," IEEE Trans. Image Processing, vol. 12, no. 5, pp. 563-571, May 2003.
8. J. R. Hernandez and F. Perez-Gonzalez, "Statistical analysis of watermarking schemes for copyright protection of images," Proc. IEEE, vol. 87, pp. 1142–1166, Jul. 1999.
9. J. R. Hernandez, M. Amado and F. Perez-Gonzalez, "DCT-domain watermarking techniques for still images: detector performance analysis and a new structure," IEEE Trans. Image Processing, vol. 9, no. 1, pp. 55-68, Jan. 2000.
10. M. Barni, F. Bartolini, A. De Rosa and A. Piva, "A new decoder for the optimum recovery of nonadditive watermarks," IEEE Trans. Image Processing, vol. 10, no. 5, pp. 755-766, May 2001.
11. M. Barni, F. Bartolini, A. De Rosa and A. Piva, "Optimum decoding and detection of multiplicative watermarks," IEEE Trans. Signal Processing, vol. 51, no. 4, pp. 1118-1123, Apr. 2003.
12. A. Briassouli and M. G. Strintzis, "Locally Optimum Nonlinearities for DCT Watermark Detection," IEEE Trans. Image Processing, vol. 13, no. 12, pp. 1604-1617, Dec. 2004.
13. A. Briassouli and M. G. Strintzis, "Optimal Watermark Detection Under Quantization in the Transform Domain," IEEE Trans. Circuits Syst. Video Technol., vol. 14, no. 12, pp. 1308-1319, Dec. 2004.
14. H. A. Peterson, A. J. Ahumada, Jr., and A. B. Watson, "Improved detection model for DCT coefficient quantization," in Proc. SPIE Conf. Human Vision, Visual Processing, and Digital Display IV, vol. 1913, pp. 191–201, Feb. 1993.
15. A. B. Watson, G. Y. Yang, J. A. Solomon, and J. Villasenor, "Visibility of wavelet quantization noise," IEEE Trans. Image Processing, vol. 6, no. 8, pp. 1164–1175, Aug. 1997.
16. I. Podilchuk and W. Zeng, "Image-adaptive watermarking using visual models," IEEE J. Select. Areas Commun., vol. 16, pp. 525–539, Apr. 1998.

Multi-band Wavelet Based Digital Watermarking Using Principal Component Analysis

Xiangui Kang[1,2], Yun Q. Shi[2], Jiwu Huang[1], and Wenjun Zeng[3]

[1] Dept. of Electronics and Communication Engineering,
Sun Yat-Sen (Zhongshan) University, Guangzhou 510275. China
{isskxg, isshjw}@zsu.edu.cn
[2] Dept. of ECE, New Jersey Institute of Technology, NJ 07102, USA
shi@njit.edu
[3] Dept. of CS, University of Missouri-Columbia, MO 65211, USA
zengw@missouri.edu

Abstract. This paper presents a novel watermarking scheme based on multi-band wavelet. Different from many other watermarking schemes, in which the watermark detection threshold is chosen empirically, the false positive rate of the proposed watermarking scheme can be calculated analytically so that watermark detection threshold can be chosen based solely on the targeted false positive. Compared with conventional watermarking schemes implemented in two-band wavelet domain, by incorporating the principal component analysis (PCA) technique the proposed blind watermarking in the multi-band wavelet domain can achieve higher perceptual transparency and stronger robustness. Specifically, the developed watermarking scheme can successfully resist common signal processing such as JPEG compression with quality factor as low as 15, and some geometric distortions such as cropping (cropped by 50%). In addition, the proposed multi-band wavelet based watermarking scheme can be parameterized, thus resulting in more security. That is, an attacker may not be able to detect the embedded watermark if the attacker does not know the parameter.

1 Introduction

Multimedia security and digital rights management (DRM) is becoming an increasingly important issue in multimedia applications and services [1]. One of the enabling technologies for DRM is digital watermarking. One significant advantage of the digital watermarking approach is that the protection is robustly integrated with the raw media data, independent of the specific representation format, which provides great flexibility that allows the protected content to be adapted or modified in the course of delivery without having to access the watermarking key for un-protection, adaptation, and re-protection. This network-friendly feature generally results in reduced processing overhead, lower cost, good error resiliency, and better end-to-end security.

Robustness and perceptual transparency are two fundamental issues in digital watermarking [2, 3]. Many existing watermarking techniques embed watermarks in the discrete dyadic wavelet transform (DWT) domain to take advantage of its unique characteristics. In terms of embedding strategy, most works propose that watermarks

M. Barni et al. (Eds.): IWDW 2005, LNCS 3710, pp. 139–146, 2005.

should be embedded in one or several selected detail frequency band coefficients because of the small impact on perceptual distortion [4]. Principle component analysis (PCA) has also been applied to *non-overlapping* spatial image blocks to achieve more robust watermark embedding [5], which nevertheless suffers from the common limitations of a *rigid* block based approach. This paper proposes a new approach that incorporates parameterized multi-band (M-band) wavelet transformation and PCA. By taking advantage of the strength of both multi-band wavelet transform (MWT) and PCA, the watermark energy is distributed to wavelet coefficients of every detail subband efficiently to achieve better robustness and perceptual transparency, and good localization.

2   Multi-band Wavelet Transformation

Different from conventional two-band wavelet ($M=2$), there are a scaling function $\phi(x) \in L^2(R)$ and M-1 wavelet functions $\{\psi_l(x) | 1 \leq l \leq M\text{-}1, M>2 \}$ in the newly developed multi-band wavelets [6, 7]. These functions satisfy the following equation respectively:

$$\phi(x) = \sum_{k \in Z} h_0(k)\phi(Mx - k) \tag{1}$$

$$\psi_l(x) = \sum_{k \in Z} h_l(k)\phi(Mx - k), \quad 1 \leq l \leq M - 1 \tag{2}$$

where Z is the integer set and sequence $\{h_l(k), \ 0 \leq l \leq M - 1\}$ has finite length. The one dimensional Mallat decomposition and reconstruction formulae of orthogonal multi-band wavelet are expressed in Equation (3) and (4), respectively [6]:

$$c_{j+1}(k) = M^{1/2} \sum_{k' \in Z} c_j(k') h_0(k' - Mk)$$
$$d_{j+1,l}(k) = M^{1/2} \sum_{k' \in Z} d_j(k') h_l(k' - Mk), \quad 1 \leq l \leq M - 1 \tag{3}$$

$$c_j(k) = M^{-1/2} \sum_{k' \in Z} c_{j+1}(k') h_0(k' - Mk) + M^{-1/2} \sum_{l=1}^{M-1} \sum_{k' \in Z} d_{j+1}(k') h_l(k' - Mk), \quad 1 \leq l \leq M - 1 \tag{4}$$

where $\{c_{j+1}(k), \ j = 0,1,2 \cdots\}$ is the approximation coefficients of the j+1 level M-band wavelet decomposition of one dimensional signal $\{c_0(k)\}$, and $\{d_{j+1}(k), \ j = 0,1,2 \cdots\}$ is the detail coefficients of the j+1 level M-band wavelet decomposition. For image signal, the above one-dimensional multi-band discrete wavelet transformation is easy to extend to two-dimensional multi-band discrete wavelet transformation (MWT) by applying one-dimensional multi-band wavelet transformation along the image rows then columns separately [6].

Fig. 1 shows an example of two-dimensional multi-band discrete wavelet transformation (MWT) [7] and two-band discrete wavelet transform (DWT). In multi-band discrete wavelet transformation, we only use the one-level image decomposition,

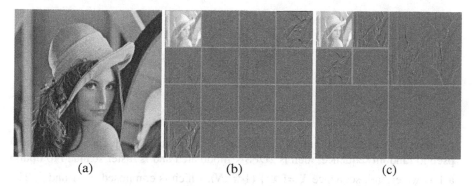

Fig. 1. (a) Original image; (b) one-level decomposition with 4-band wavelet; (c) two-level decomposition with 2-band DWT

every wavelet coefficient is a band-pass filtering result of a local region of the original image at the same scale. Every wavelet subband of MWT has the same number of coefficients (Fig. 1b). This is different from the two-level DWT (Fig. 1c), where the coefficients might belong to different scales.

The multi-band wavelet $\psi_l(x)$ used in this paper is symmetric, parameterized by a parameter $\lambda \in R$. Modulo value $t = mod\,(\lambda, 2\pi)$ assumes a real value between 0 and 2π [7]. Here *mod* denotes the signed remainder after division. Different values of t lead to different multi-band wavelets.

3 Watermark Embedding

An encrypted *logo* (Fig. 2) (watermark) is embedded in the principle component of the multi-band wavelet domain of the host image. The motivation of encryption is to enhance the security of the watermark, and make the watermark pseudo-random so that a reasonable watermark detection threshold is deducible. The motivations of incorporating multi-band wavelet and PCA are as follows: parameterized M-band wavelet provides a secure embedding domain and excellent space-frequency localization; while PCA further concentrates the energy of the wavelet coefficient vectors and distributes the watermark energy over all detail subbands, resulting in enhanced watermark invisibility and/or robustness. It is well known that even after the orthogonal wavelet decomposition, typically there still exists some correlation between the wavelet coefficients, especially those corresponding to the same spatially local region at the same scale. This correlation between the coefficients corresponding to different frequencies but the same spatial location could be removed based on the PCA technique and the energy of the image could be further concentrated, leading to an embedding domain that permits the embedding of larger watermark energy, which in turn lead to better perceptual transparency, or translates into improved robustness. This approach makes the watermark less visible or more robust to lossy compression than embedding watermarks in only one or several selected wavelet subbands.

The watermark embedding process (Fig. 3) is divided into the following steps.

1. Encrypt the embedding *logo* (Fig. 2) using a 2D pseudo-random sequence with the same size of the *logo*. The 2D pseudo-random binary (0 and 1) sequence is

Fig. 2. The embedding logo

generated by a key. The binary image *logo* (Fig. 2) is XOR operated with the 2D pseudo-random sequence, then is 2DPSK modulated and is raster scanned to obtain a 1-D watermark sequence $X = \{ x_i \}$ (1<i<N), which is composed of -1 and 1. The occurrence probability of -1 or 1 in X is close to 0.5 because the above encrypting binary sequence is a pseudo-random sequence (PN).

2. The multi-band discrete wavelet transformation (MWT) [6] is applied to the cover image $f(x, y)$ first. We obtain one approximate subband and fifteen detail subbands. (Fig. 1b).

3. Then the coefficients corresponding to the same spatial location in all detail subbands form a one-dimensional data array (e.g., a vector of a total of fifteen coefficients, one per subband, for the case of Fig. 1b).

4. The principle component analysis (PCA) [5] is then applied to the obtained one-dimensional arrays respectively. All the obtained first principle components form a 1-D array C in the same raster scanning fashion. Finally, watermark X is embedded in the principle components C using quantization-based method (Equation 5) to obtain C' [2, 8, 9], where $C(i)$ and $C'(i)$ denote the ith element in C and C', respectively. The quantizer $q(.)$ is a uniform, scalar quantization function of step size S, and $q(x) = kS + 0.5S$, $k = \left\lfloor \dfrac{x}{S} \right\rfloor$ ($k \in Z$), where $\lfloor . \rfloor$ denotes the *floor* operation.

The embedding strength S can be chosen so as to achieve a good compromise between the contending requirements of imperceptibility and robustness. Note that the difference between $C(i)$ and $C'(i)$ is between $-0.5S$ and $+0.5S$. If $x_i = -1$, $C'(i)$ *mod* S =0.25S. If $x_i = +1$, $C'(i)$ *mod* S =0.75S. Here *mod* denotes the signed remainder after division. By performing inverse PCA (IPCA in Fig. 3) [5] and inverse MWT (IMWT in Fig. 3) [6] on the modified image, we obtain a watermarked image $f'(x, y)$.

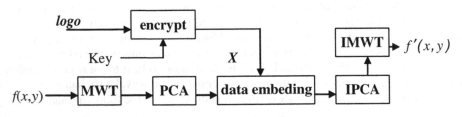

Fig. 3. The watermark embedding process

$$\begin{cases} C'(i) = q(C(i) - \dfrac{1}{4}S) + \dfrac{1}{4}S, \text{ if } x_i = 1 \\ \\ C'(i) = q(C(i) + \dfrac{1}{4}S) - \dfrac{1}{4}S, \text{ if } x_i = -1 \end{cases} \tag{5}$$

$$x_i^* = \begin{cases} +1, & r = C^*(i) \bmod S > \dfrac{S}{2} \\ \\ -1, & otherwise \end{cases} \tag{6}$$

4 Watermark Detection

The watermark extraction is the inverse process of watermark embedding. The test image is MWT decomposed, then PCA is applied, and the first principle components are obtained to form a 1-D array $C^*\{C^*(i), (1<i<N)\}$. $C^*(i)$ is the extracted principle component. According to Equation (6), we could extract the hidden binary data $X^*\{x^*(i), (1<i<N)\}$. Equation (6) indicates that if r ($r = C^*(i) \bmod S$) is in the interval $(0, 0.5S)$, then the decision is made in favor of "$x_i^* = -1$". Otherwise, "$x_i^* = 1$". Then the following correlation coefficient is used to decide if the watermark exists in the test image.

$$\rho_{X,X^*} = \frac{\mathbf{X} \cdot \mathbf{X}^*}{\|\mathbf{X}\|} \tag{7}$$

where $\|\mathbf{X}\|$ is the size of the watermark X (that is, N, in this paper), and $\mathbf{X} \cdot \mathbf{X}^*$ is the inner product of X and the extracted sequence X^*. If the correlation coefficient between the embedded sequence X and the extracted sequence X^* from a test image is larger than a threshold, i.e., $\rho_{X,X^*} \geq thresh$, we determine that watermark exits. Here we can calculate the corresponding probability of false positive as $H_{fp} = (0.5)^N \cdot \sum_{k=N-e}^{N} \binom{N}{k}$, where $e = round(\dfrac{N}{2}(1 - thresh))$, and $round(\cdot)$ means taking the nearest integer. In our work, we choose $N = 63 \times 63 = 3969$. When the threshold is set to 0.10, we have $H_{fp} = 1.27 \times 10^{-10}$, which may be sufficiently low for many applications. It should be noted that this is different from many other watermarking schemes, where the watermark detection threshold is chosen empirically [10]. In the above, we assume the embedded sequence X is a PN sequence.

5 Simulation Results

We have tested the proposed MWT algorithm on many images with StirMark 3.1 functions. The results on 256×256×8 image Lena, Baboon, Peppers are reported here.

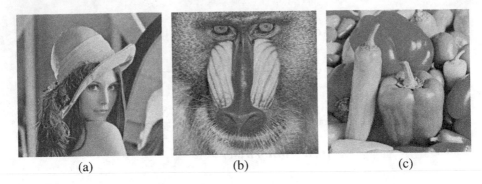

(a)   (b)   (c)

Fig. 4. The marked image with 4-band wavelet. (a) Lena (PSNR=40.1dB); (b) Baboon (PSNR = 40.1dB); (c) Peppers. (PSNR = 40.0dB).

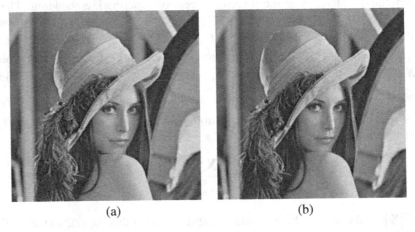

(a)   (b)

Fig. 5. (a) The marked image with DWT (PSNR=40.1dB); (b) The marked image with MWT

Table 1. Experimental results with Stirmark 3.1

StirMark functions	Lena	Baboon	Peppers
JPEG 15~100	1	1	1
Gaussian filtering	1	1	1
3x3median_filter	1	1	1
Cropping_25	1	1	1

In our work, we choose $S=36$, $N=63\times63$, *thresh*=0.10. Table 1 shows some test results with our proposed algorithms by using StirMark 3.1. In Table 1, "1" represents the presence of watermark, that is, the correlation coefficient ρ_{X,X^*} between the embedded sequence X and the extracted sequence X^* obtained from a test image is larger than *thresh*, while "0" means the absence of watermark. The watermark is robust to JPEG compression with quality factor as low as 15% (JPEG_15, Table 1) and is also robust to common image processing such as median filtering, Gaussian filtering etc. The watermark could be detected when the marked image has been cropped by 50%.

Table 2. Comparison of waterking in MWT and DWT domain

StirMark functions	MWT	DWT
JPEG 20~100	1	1
JPEG 15	1	0
Gauss filtering	1	1
3x3median_filter	1	1

We compare the proposed MWT watermarking with DWT watermarking on Lena image. For fair comparison, in DWT watermarking with Daubechies 9/7 filter, HL_2 subband is chosen to embed same watermark X with the same embedding Equation (5) and same embedding strength $S=36$, as is done with the above watermarking in MWT domain. The obtained marked images are shown in Fig. 5. The obtained PSNR value with DWT and MWT is the same, 40.1dB. But the marked image in DWT domain has obvious horizontal artifacts, while the marked image in MWT domain has excellent perceptual quality without any artifacts. The test results are shown in Table 2. It is noted that the scheme in MWT domain performs better in resisting JPEG compression. The watermark in MWT is robust to JPEG_15, while the watermark in DWT domain fails this test. Taking account of the improvement in the watermark invisibility, we can embed larger intensity watermark in MWT domain than in DWT domain to achieve more robustness, so the proposed MWT watermarking is more robust than the watermarking in DWT domain.

The parameterized M-band wavelet, which is parameterized by a parameter $\lambda \in R$, leads a secure watermark embedding domain. The parameter λ used in embedding needs to be known in watermark extraction, otherwise the watermark cannot be detected. For example, if $\lambda = 0.5$ is chosen in watermark embedding and $\lambda = 1.6$ is used in watermark extraction, the correlation coefficient $\rho_{X,X*}$ is less than threshold *thresh* even if the embedding strength S and original watermark X are known in extraction. If without usage of parameterized wavelet transform, only is the very same wavelet filter bank used. If the watermarking scheme is known to the public, the scheme is easy to be attacked [11]. So the parameterized M-band wavelet makes attacks more difficult.

6 Conclusions

The proposed watermarking scheme based on M-band wavelet and PCA technique has the following advantages.

1. We embed watermark in the principle components of the multi-band discrete wavelet coefficients. Specifically, watermark signal is embedded into the principle components of the multi-band wavelet coefficients corresponding to the same spatial location at the same scale. With such a well-chosen embedding domain, the watermark is robustly and efficiently distributed to every detail frequency subband. Our experimental results have shown that the watermark thus embedded has better invisibility and is more robust against JPEG compression than watermarks embedded in the DWT domain.
2. Parameterized multi-band wavelet leads to a more secure watermark embedding domain, which makes the attack more difficult.
3. Different from many other watermarking schemes, in which watermark detection threshold is chosen empirically, the detection threshold of the proposed watermarking scheme can be calculated according to the targeted false positive.

Acknowledgements

This work is supported by NSFC (60403045, 60325208, 60133020), NSF of Guangdong (04205407, 04009742), New Jersey Commission of Science and Technology via New Jersey Center of Wireless Networking and Internet Security (NJWINS). The first author thanks Dr. Ning Bi for helpful discussions in multi-band wavelets with him.

References

1. W. Zeng, J. Lan, and X. Zhuang: Network friendly media security: rationales, solutions, and open issues. Proc. IEEE Inter. Conf. Image Proc., Singapore, Oct. 2004.
2. M. Wu, B. Liu: Data hiding in images and video: Part I: Fundamental Issues and Solutions. IEEE Trans. on Image Processing, vol. 12, no. 6, (June 2003) 685-695.
3. Fabien A. P. Petitcolas: Watermarking schemes evaluation. IEEE Signal Processing, vol. 17, no. 5, (Sept. 2000) 58–64.
4. M. J. Tsai, K. Y. Yu, and Y. Z. Chen: Joint Wavelet and Spatial Transformation for Digital Watermarking. IEEE Trans. on Consumer Electronics, vol. 46, no. 1 (2000) 241~245.
5. T. D. Hien, Y. - W. Chen, and Z. Nakao: Robust Digital Watermarking Based on Principle Component Analysis. International Journal of Computational Intelligence and Applications, vol. 4, no. 2 (2004) 183-192.
6. Q. Sun, N. Bi, and D. Huang: An Introduction to Multi-band Wavelets, Zhejiang University Press (2001).
7. N. Bi, and D. Huang, Q. Dai, F. Li: A class of orthogonal and symmetric 4-band wavelets with one-parameter. Mathematica Numerica Sinica, vol. 27, no. 2, (May 2005) 1-10.
8. B. Chen, and G., W. Wornell: Quantization index modulation: A class of provably good methods for digital watermarking and information embedding. IEEE Trans. on Information Theory, vol. 47, no. 4, (May 2001) 1423- 1443.
9. X. Kang, J. Huang, and Y. Q. Shi, Y. Lin: A DWT-DFT composite watermarking scheme robust to both affine transform and JPEG compression. IEEE Trans. on Circuits and Systems for Video Technology, vol.13, no. 8 (Aug. 2003) 776-786.
10. Cox I, Kilian J, Leighton T, and Shamoon T: Secure spread spectrum watermarking for multimedia. IEEE Trans. on Image Processing, vol. 6, no. 12 (1997) 1673~1687.
11. J. Huang, J. Hu, D. Huang, Y. Q. Shi: Improve security of fragile watermarking via parameterized wavelet. In: Proc. IEEE Inter. Conf. Image Proc., Singapore (Oct. 2004).

A New Inter-frame Collusion Attack and a Countermeasure

P. Vinod and P.K. Bora

Department of Electronics & Communication Engineering,
Indian Institute of Technology Guwahati, Assam 781 039, India

Abstract. One of the challenging issues in video watermarking is its robustness to inter-frame collusion attacks. The Inter-frame collusion attacks exploit the inherent redundancy in the video frames or in the watermark to produce an unwatermarked copy of the video. A basic inter-frame collusion attack is the frame temporal filtering(FTF) attack, where temporal low-pass filtering is applied to the watermarked frames in order to remove *temporally uncorrelated* watermarks. If the video frames contain moving objects or camera motion, temporal low-pass filtering introduces visually annoying ghosting artifacts in the attacked video. Thus the applicability of the FTF attack is limited only to static scenes. We propose an extended FTF attack which overcomes this limitation by exploiting the motion within the video frames. Experimental results presented in this paper confirm the effectiveness of the proposed attack over the FTF attack. A countermeasure to this extended FTF attack is also presented.

1 Introduction

With the rapid spread of computer networks and the further progress of multimedia technologies, security issues such as copy protection and copyright protection of the digital multimedia data has become more and more important. Digital watermarking is a concept that emerged as a solution to this challenging problem of digital multimedia security. The basic idea of digital watermarking is to embed some information within the digital multimedia data in an insensible form for the human audio-visual system. Furthermore, the watermark has to be robust, which means that the subsequent processing of the watermarked data should not impair the detection of the embedded information. Since its inception in early 1990s, the watermarking research has been mainly devoted to still images [1].

Due to large amount of data and the inherent redundancy between frames, video watermarking introduces some unique issues [2]. Video signals are highly susceptible to pirates attacks, including frame dropping, frame swapping, collusion, statistical analysis, etc. Collusion attack generally refers to a set of malicious users merging their knowledge, eg. the watermarked data to produce an unwatermarked content. In the case of video, two types of collusion attacks are possible: inter-video collusion and inter-frame collusion. In inter-video collusion, different watermarked versions of the same video are combined to produce

M. Barni et al. (Eds.): IWDW 2005, LNCS 3710, pp. 147–157, 2005.

an unwatermarked copy of the video. Inter-frame collusion attacks exploit the inherent redundancy in the video frames or in the watermark to produce an unwatermarked copy of the video. In this work, we consider the inter-frame collusion issues. We propose a new inter-frame collusion attack. In this attack, the watermarked frames are temporally filtered along the motion trajectory using Motion Compensated Temporal Wavelet Transform (MC-TWT). The rest of the paper is organized as follows. In Sect. 2, we present the basic inter-frame collusion attacks in detail. Section 3 describes a more advanced inter-frame collusion attack. A brief description of motion compensated temporal wavelet transform (MC-TWT)is given in Sect. 4. The proposed collusion attack is presented along with the experimental results in Sect. 5. A possible countermeasure to the proposed collusion attack is presented in Sect. 6, and Sect. 7 concludes the paper.

2   Inter-frame Collusion Attacks

The basic idea behind inter-frame collusion attack is the exploitation of the redundancy, either in the host video frames or in the embedded watermark, to estimate the redundant component [3]. Depending on the redundancy, two types of inter-frame collusion attacks are possible.

Type I collusion attack: This type of collusion attack exploits the redundancy in the embedded watermark. Due to the imperceptibility constraint, the watermark is usually embedded in the spatial high-frequency components of the host frames. The difference between a watermarked frame and spatial low-pass filtered version of it gives an estimate of the watermark. A refined estimate of the watermark can be obtained by combining the individual estimates obtained from different frames. The estimated watermark is then subtracted from each watermarked frames to get an estimate of the host frames. This attack is known as Watermark Estimation Remodulation (WER) and is effective in visually dissimilar frames embedded with highly correlated watermarks.

Type II collusion attack: This type of collusion attack is possible when visually similar frames are marked with uncorrelated watermarks. Since such watermarks are in the temporal high-frequency band, it can be removed by temporal low-pass filtering of the watermarked frames. This attack is generally known as Frame Temporal Filtering (FTF) attack. This can be expressed as:

$$\hat{Y}_k = F(E_k), \qquad E_k = \{Y_i, 0 \le |\, i - k \,| \le L/2\} \ . \tag{1}$$

where Y_i is the ith watermarked frame, L is the length of the temporal window, $F(\cdot)$ is a temporal low-pass filter and $\hat{Y}_k$ is the kth attacked frame. In the case of simple frame averaging attack,

$$\hat{Y}_k = \frac{1}{L}\sum_i Y_i, \qquad 0 \le |\, i - k \,| \le L/2 \ . \tag{2}$$

Let the embedded watermark is a simple frame by frame additive spread spectrum watermark given by,

$$Y_k = X_k + \alpha W_k, \qquad k = 1, \cdots, N_f \ . \tag{3}$$

where X_k is the host video frames, W_k is the normally distributed zero mean unit variance watermark for the kth frame, α is constant and N_f is the number of frames in the video scene. If the watermark embedded in each frame are uncorrelated, then (2) can be written as,

$$\hat{Y}_k = \frac{1}{L}\sum_i X_i + \alpha\frac{1}{L}\sum_i W_i \approx \frac{1}{L}\sum_i X_i \ . \tag{4}$$

where $\sum_i W_i$ decreases to 0 because the watermarks are uncorrelated. This type of attack effective in static scenes where uncorrelated watermarks are embedded. The size of the temporal window used in filtering is limited by the content of the video frames. In static scenes, large window lengths can be used without degrading the visual quality of the attacked video and hence the attack will be more effective. But if the video frames contain moving objects severe blurring will occur and hence a lower window length should be used to preserve the visual quality of the attacked video.

3   Frame Temporal Filtering After Registration (FTFR)

It is clear from the previous discussion of the FTF attack that, (a) when the video frames contain moving objects, the FTF attack will not succeed without severe degradation in the quality of the attacked video (b) FTF attack will not be successful if the watermark embedded in the frames are highly correlated(eg. fixed watermark in all the video frames). A video frame and a shifted version of it will have very low correlation score. In such a case, a more effective FTF attack is possible by exploiting the motion in the video frames. Such an attack, Frame Temporal Filtering After Registration (FTFR), has been proposed by G. Doerr et al. [5]. The basic idea behind this attack is to compensate the camera motion before the temporal filtering. Each watermarked frame is registered with a reference frame before the temporal filtering. This can be written as,

$$\hat{Y}_k = F(E_k), \qquad E_k = \{Y_i^{(k)}, 0 \leq |\ i - k\ | \leq L/2\}\ . \tag{5}$$

where $Y_i^{(k)}$ are the original video frames after registration with the kth frame. The experimental results show that embedding neither a fixed watermark nor an uncorrelated watermark in each frame will not survive the FTFR attack.

Typically, camera motion is a combination of travelling displacements (horizontal, vertical, forward and backward translations), rotations (pan, roll and tilt), and zooming effects. In addition to that, the motion of the objects will also be considered for registration. Using such a complex motion model, Doerr et al. [6] extended their previous work , to a more effective collusion attack. In this attack, the background of a given frame is replaced with the estimated background from the neighboring frames. First, the moving objects in the given frame and the neighboring frames are separated from its background using video object segmentation techniques. The resulting background frames are registered with a reference frame and averaged to get an estimate of the background of the target frame. For the registration of the background frames, a first order polynomial motion model is used. Finally the objects in the target frame are inserted back into the estimated background to get the attacked frame. To counter this FTFR attack, they have proposed a background watermarking scheme in which the camera motion is compensated before the watermark embedding.

4   Motion-Compensated Temporal Wavelet Transform

Thee-dimensional sub-band wavelet coding of the video has been an active area of research in the video coding community as an alternative to the conventional hybrid coding techniques. In this approach, transform coding is extended to the temporal direction by applying discrete wavelet transform (DWT) along the temporal axis. In 3D-DWT scalable video coding techniques, the low-pass temporal wavelet frames are used to represent reduced frame-rate video. If the video scene contains moving objects, it will introduce ghosting artifacts into the temporal low-pass frames and substantial energy coefficients into the high-pass frames. This results in the reduction of the coding efficiency and the visual quality of the quality of the reduced frame-rate video. This is because of the fact that motion in the video frames are not considered during the temporal filtering. The aforementioned drawbacks can be eliminated if the temporal wavelet transform is performed along the motion trajectories [7]. This method is known as Motion-compensated temporal wavelet transform (MC-TWT).

MC-TWT can be implemented using *Transversal* or *Lifting-based* approach. In addition to the low-computational complexity, the lifting based approach can incorporate any motion model (local or global) with sub-pixel accuracy motion [7]. One level motion-compensated temporal Haar wavelet decomposition of a video sequence can be implemented using two lifting steps ,

$$h_k[\mathbf{n}] = x_{2k+1}[\mathbf{n}] - W_{2k \to 2k+1}(x_{2k})[\mathbf{n}] \qquad : \text{Prediction step}$$

$$l_k[\mathbf{n}] = x_{2k}[\mathbf{n}] + \frac{1}{2} W_{2k+1 \to 2k}(h_k)[\mathbf{n}] \qquad : \text{Update step}$$

where $x_k[\mathbf{n}] \equiv x_k[n_1, n_2]$ denotes the samples of kth video frame, $h_k[\mathbf{n}]$ and $l_k[\mathbf{n}]$ denote the high-pass and low-pass temporal frames, and $W_{k_1 \to k_2}$ denotes a motion compensated mapping of frame k_1 onto the coordinate system of frame k_2. The prediction and update lifting steps of motion-compensated 5/3 bi-orthogonal wavelet are given by,

$$h_k[\mathbf{n}] = x_{2k+1}[\mathbf{n}] - \frac{1}{2}[W_{2k \to 2k+1}(x_{2k})[\mathbf{n}] + W_{2k+2 \to 2k+1}(x_{2k+2})[\mathbf{n}]]$$

$$l_k[\mathbf{n}] = x_{2k}[\mathbf{n}] + \frac{1}{4}[W_{2k-1 \to 2k}(h_{k-1})[\mathbf{n}] + W_{2k+1 \to 2k}(h_k)[\mathbf{n}]]$$

The motion compensated Haar wavelet uses unidirectional motion compensation, where as the 5/3 bi-orthogonal wavelet uses bidirectional motion compensation. Thus the visual quality of the temporal low-pass frames given by motion compensated 5/3 bi-orthogonal filtering is better than that with motion compensated Haar filtering.

If the MC-TWT is applied along the true motion trajectory, the low-pass temporal frame will have high visual quality. But there are places like scene changes, occluded/uncovered regions where any motion model must necessarily fail. When the motion model fails to follow the true motion trajectory, the energy in the temporal high-pass frames increases and the subsequent update step adds this high energy coefficients back into the temporal low-pass frames. This causes ghosting artifacts in the low-pass temporal frames. Thus, there exists a direct relationship between the ghosting artifacts and the energy in the temporal high-pass frames. A method for reducing the ghosting artifacts from the temporal low-pass frames has been proposed in [8]. In this method, the update lifting steps are weighted according to the energy in the temporal high-pass frames. The normalized energy in the temporal high-pass frames are mapped to an update weight with a decreasing function.

5 Proposed Motion-Compensated Frame Temporal Filtering (MC-FTF) Attack

Motion in the video sequences are due to the camera motion and the motion of the objects. In the FTFR attack, only the camera motion is exploited. The portion of the watermark embedded in the moving objects will not be affected by the attack. So, the FTFR attack is less effective when moving objects occupy a considerable part of the video scene. Another drawback is its high computational complexity particularly when the video scene contains complex motion or multiple objects. We propose a more effective FTF attack: Motion-Compensated Frame Temporal Filtering (MC-FTF) attack, which exploits both the camera motion and the object motion.

The properties of the lifting based MC-TWT, namely: high visual quality low-pass temporal frames without ghosting artifacts and flexibility of incorporating any motion model motivate us to develop an improved FTF attack using lifting based MC-TWT. In the proposed MC-FTF attack, the video frames are temporally filtered using lifting based MC-TWT . Both the camera motion and the object motion are exploited by incorporating local motion estimation techniques (eg. block based or mesh based). First, the watermarked video frames are segmented into scenes. Lifting based MC-TWT is applied to the frames in each scene. The temporal decomposition is done without temporal sub-sampling. The low-pass temporal frames from all the scenes give the attacked video, having the same length as the watermarked video.

5.1 Experimental Results

The performance of the proposed MC-FTF attack is tested with 64 frames each from two standard test video sequences, "Mobile" and "Forman". The video sequences are watermarked with a frame-by-frame additive spread spectrum watermark as given in (3). All the frames are marked with the same watermark .

ie, ie. $W_k = W, \forall k$. The embedding strength α_k is chosen such a way that the average peak signal-to-noise ratio(PSNR) of the watermarked video is around 38 dB. All the experiments are performed with 20 different randomly selected watermarks and the average results are presented. The normalized correlation (NC) between the extracted watermark and the original watermark is used as the detection measure [2]. The normalized correlation(NC) is computed as,

$$ \text{NC} = \frac{<\hat{Y}_k - X_k, W_k>}{W_k \cdot W_k} . \tag{6} $$

where, $\hat{Y}_k$ are the attacked video frames. The watermarked video frames were subjected to MC-FTF attack with lifting based motion-compensated 5/3 bi-orthogonal wavelet. The watermarked frames were temporally filtered using three levels of MC-TWT without temporal sub-sampling. Motion is modelled using hierarchical variable size block matching (HVSBM), with 64×64 macro-blocks and block sizes down to 4×4, as in H.264. Integer-pixel and half-pixel accuracy motion-compensation were used in the experiments. For finding half-pixel accuracy motion vectors, cubic spline interpolation was used. Motion vectors were estimated for the prediction step and for the update step, the motion vectors are obtained by nearest-neighbor inversion of these estimated motion vectors [9]. The MC-FTF attack was also tested using MC-TWT with adaptive update step proposed in [8].

The results are plotted in Figs. 1-4. The PSNR values given are the PSNR of the attacked video frames with respect to the watermarked video frames. The PSNR plots show that the visual quality of the attacked video increases with the increase in accuracy of the motion estimation. But, the attack performance

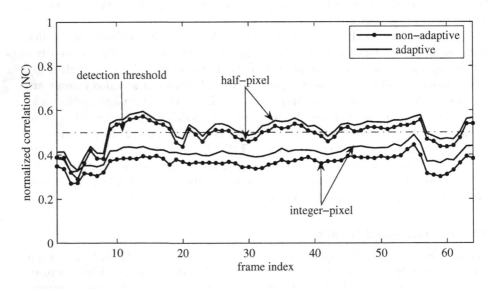

Fig. 1. Detector performance after MC-FTF attack ("Mobile")

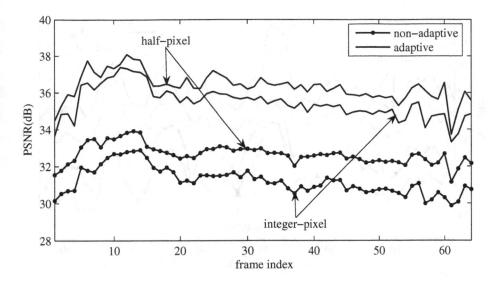

Fig. 2. PSNR performance after MC-FTF attack ("Mobile")

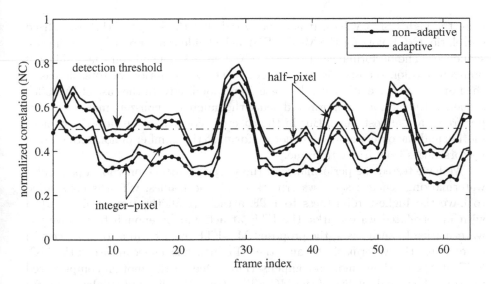

Fig. 3. Detector performance after MC-FTF attack ("Forman")

decreases (high NC values) with half-pixel accuracy motion estimation compared to integer-pixel motion estimation. This is due to the interpolation and motion inversion error in the update step [9]. As expected, the visual quality of the attacked video is better in the case of MC-FTF attack with adaptive update step.

The results show that the proposed MC-FTF attack is successful in reducing the normalized correlation values below the detection threshold which is usually kept at 0.5. The good visual quality of the MC-FTF attacked video is evident

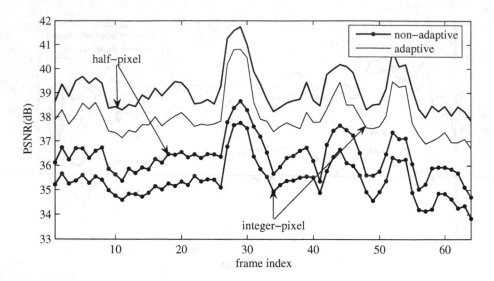

Fig. 4. PSNR performance after FTF and MC-FTF attack ("Forman")

from the high PSNR values. It is to be noted that the shape of the normalized correlation(NC) plots for the MC-FTF attacked videos are not same for the two sequences. The performance of the MC-TWT attack depends on the number of non-zero motion vectors. As the number of non-zero motion vectors increases, the normalized correlation will decrease correspondingly. In the case of "Mobile" sequence, the motion is uniform and hence the number of non-zero motion vectors per frame are almost same. But in the case of "Forman" sequence, the camera motion and the object motion are not uniform, so the number of non-zero motion vectors varies from frame to frame.

We have tested the performance of the proposed attack only for a particular watermarking scheme: same watermark in all the frames, which is considered to have the highest robustness to FTF attack. If all the frames are marked with uncorrelated watermarks, the FTF attack will be enough to remove the watermarks. In such cases, the proposed MC-FTF attack will also be successful in removing the watermarks because the FTF attack is a special case of the MC-FTF attack (without motion-compensation). Due to the motion-compensated filtering, the visual quality of the MC-FTF attacked video will be always better than that of FTF-attacked video.

6   Watermarking in the MC-TWT Domain

The success of MC-FTF attack lies in exploiting the motion in the video frames which is not considered during the watermark embedding. The motion-compensation step in the MC-FTF attack align similar regions in the video frames before averaging. If the similar regions contain uncorrelated watermark,

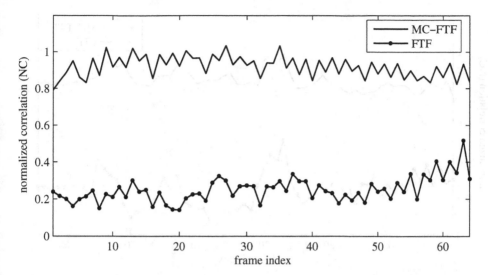

Fig. 5. Detector performance after FTF and MC-FTF attacks("Mobile")

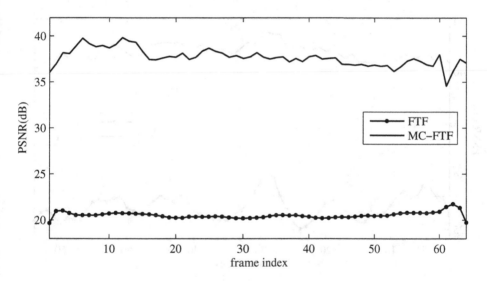

Fig. 6. PSNR performance after FTF and MC-FTF attacks("Mobile")

the subsequent temporal filtering will reduce the watermark energy. So, a possible way to counter the MC-FTF attack is to make the watermark coherent with the motion.

We have evaluated how compensating the motion before the watermark embedding will improve the robustness to MC-FTF attack. First, the video frames X_k were decomposed with MC-TWT, resulting in temporal low-pass and high-pass frames. The motion model used for MC-TWT decomposition is the same as the one used for MC-FTF attack in the previous section. Watermark was added

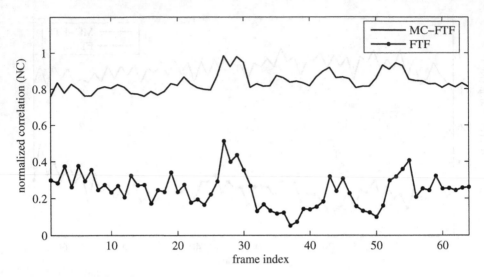

Fig. 7. Detector performance after FTF and MC-FTF attacks("Forman")

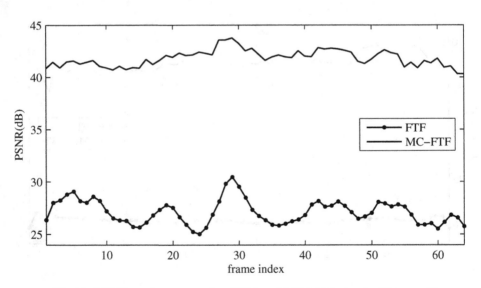

Fig. 8. PSNR performance after FTF and MC-FTF attacks("Forman")

to the temporal low-pass frames using (3). The watermarked frames Y_k were obtained by applying inverse MC-TWT. The normalized correlation as given in (6) was used as the detection measure, where $W_k = Y_k - X_k$.

The watermarked videos were attacked with FTF attack (averaging with temporal window of length 8) and the MC-FTF attack (integer-pixel accuracy motion compensation and adaptive update step). The results are given in Figs. 5-8. The PSNR value is the average PSNR between the watermarked and attacked video frames. The experimental results show that watermarking in the MC-TWT domain considerably increases the robustness to MC-FTF attack. It is also to be noted that the MC-TWT domain watermarking is not robust to FTF attack. It is acceptable since the visual quality of the FTF attacked video is less compared to that of MC-FTF attacked video.

7 Conclusions

We have proposed an improved Frame Temporal filtering (FTF) attack using Motion-compensated Temporal Wavelet Transform (MC-TWT). The experimental results confirm the improvement of the proposed attack over the FTF attack. We have considered only the block-based motion models for the MC-FTF attack. Using more advanced motion models like deformable mesh model [7], it may be possible to improve the visual quality of the attacked video. We have also proposed MC-TWT domain watermarking to counter the MC-FTF attack. In our experiments to evaluate the performance of the MC-TWT domain watermarking, it is assumed that the same motion model is used for watermarking and MC-FTF attack. But this cannot be guaranteed as the attacker is free to use any motion model. Our future work will study the robustness of MC-TWT domain watermarking to MC-FTF attack with different motion models other than the one used for watermarking.

References

1. G. Doerr and J.-L. Dugelay.: A guide tour of video watermarking; Signal Processing:Image Communication,18, (2003) 263–283
2. M. D. Swanson, B. Zhu and A. H. Tewfik.: Multiresolution scene-based video watermarking using perceptual models; IEEE Journal of Selected Areas in Communications, (May 1998) 540–550
3. K. Su, D. Kundur and D. Hatzinakos.: Statistical invisibility for collusion-resistant digital video watermarking; IEEE Transactions on Multimedia, (Feb. 2005) 43–51
4. K. Su, D. Kundur, and D. Hatzinakos.: A novel approach to collusion-resistant video watermarking; Security and Watermarking of Multimedia Contents IV, **4675**, (2002)
5. G. Doerr and J.-L. Dugelay.: New intra-video collusion attack using mosaicing; Proceedings of the IEEE International Conference on Multimedia and Expo. vol. **II**, (2003) 505–508
6. G. Doerr and J.-L. Dugelay.: Secure background watermarking based on video mosaicing; Security, Steganography and Watermarking of Multimedia Contents IV **5306**,(2004) 304–314
7. A. Secker and D. Taubman.: Lifting-based invertible motion adaptive transform (LIMAT) framework for highly scalable video compression; IEEE Transactions on image processing, (Dec. 2003) 1530–1542
8. Mehrseresht, N. and Taubman, D.: Adaptively weighted update steps in motion compensated lifting based scalable video compression; IEEE International Conference on Image Processing (ICIP2003), 771–774
9. Konrad, J. and Bozinovic, N.: Importance of motion in motion-compensated temporal discrete wavelet transforms; IST/SPIE Symposium on Electronic Imaging, Image and Video Communications and Proc.,2005.
http://vip.bu.edu/jkonrad/Publications/ local/cpapers/Bozi05icassp.pdf

Effectiveness of ST-DM Watermarking Against Intra-video Collusion

Roberto Caldelli[1], Alessandro Piva[1], Mauro Barni[2], and Andrea Carboni[1]

[1] Dept. of Electronics and Telecommunications, University of Florence, Italy
{caldelli, piva, carboni}@lci.det.unifi.it
[2] Dept.of Information Engineering, University of Siena, Italy
barni@dii.unisi.it

Abstract. The impact of intra-video collusion on ST-DM watermarking is considered by analyzing the robustness of a constant watermark with respect to Temporal Frame Averaging (TFA). We theoretically show that, as opposed to spread spectrum watermarking, in the ST-DM case it is not sufficient that the same watermark message is inserted within each video frame to ensure resistance against TFA. However robustness can still be achieved by increasing the spreading factor r. Moreover the higher the correlation between video frames the better the performance of ST-DM. We also evaluate the impact of the dithering factor d upon watermark robustness. As a last contribution, we evaluate the impact of TFA on the quality of the attacked video, demonstrating that, unless motion compensated averaging is used, only a few frames can be averaged without introducing annoying artifacts.

1 Introduction

Collusion attacks are among the most effective attacks that a pool of pirates may bring to any watermarking system. In general, we speak of collusion attacks when two or more pirates, called colluders, team together to fool the watermarking system. More practically, we can distinguish among two classes of collusion attacks. In a first scenario, each colluder is in possession of a different version of the same multimedia content, say a still image or a video sequence, containing a different watermark. The colluders can average all the images they have, so to weaken the strength of each particular watermark, without introducing any significant degradation between the averaged document and the original watermarked documents. If the number of different versions of the multimedia content the colluders have access to, is large enough, this kind of attack is a very effective mean to produce a document from which it is impossible to read any watermark.

The second type of collusion can be seen as the dual of the first type. In this case, the colluders are able to put together a number of different contents containing the same watermark. By assuming that the contents are independent of each other, a good estimate of the watermark can be obtained by averaging a sufficiently large number of documents (this approach only works if the watermark inserted within the host data does not depend on the data itself).

M. Barni et al. (Eds.): IWDW 2005, LNCS 3710, pp. 158–170, 2005.

Colluders can exploit the knowledge of the watermark either to remove it from the host document or to falsely insert it into other documents.

In the case of video watermarking, the implementation of collusion attacks does not require that several colluders team together each bringing a different version of the marked document [1,2,3]. As a matter of fact, in this case the pirate may exploit the availability of several watermarked frames. For example, the pirate may average several consecutive frames within a sliding window so to produce a video sequence from which it is no more possible to extract the watermark. This kind of attack, commonly named Temporal Frame Averaging (TFA) is clearly effective if consecutive frames contain a different watermark. More precisely, it is needed that consecutive frames contain the same watermarking signal[1], regardless of the embedded message.

At the other extreme, if the pirate relies on video frames belonging to different scenes, he may apply for the second kind of attack, i.e. try to estimate the watermark (or the watermark secret parameters) and then remove it (exploit such a knowledge to remove it) from the host signal. In this case we speak about Watermark Estimation and Remodulation attack (WER).

Robustness (or to better say security) against collusion attacks has been studied in [1,2,3], giving very important results for a large class of watermarking algorithms, namely spread spectrum, non-informed algorithms. In particular it has been shown that robustness against TFA requires that a constant watermark is used, i.e. the same watermarking signal is embedded in consecutive frames. On the contrary, in order to cope with WER it is preferable that a different watermark is used in different frames.

No similar analysis has ever been made for the case of QIM watermarking [4]. Yet this is an interesting problem, given the differences between spread spectrum systems, where the signal effectively embedded within the host data does not depend on the data themselves, and informed schemes, where the embedded signal always depends on the host data. In this paper we move a first step into this direction. More specifically, we analyze the impact of TFA on ST-DM watermarking [4,5], by assuming that the same message is embedded in contiguous frames. As it will be evident, as opposed to spread spectrum systems, in the ST-DM case it is not sufficient that the spreading direction is used in consecutive frames in order to ensure robustness against TFA.

Our analysis is carried out at two different levels: evaluation of the theoretical bit error probability in the presence of TFA for the case of a Gaussian (possibly correlated) signal, and evaluation of such a probability in the case of real videos. The impact of frame averaging on video quality will be investigated as well so to understand the real potentialities of the TFA attack.

As to the case of video, in this summary only some preliminary results are shown, the output of more extensive testing will be included in the final version of the paper.

---

[1] By watermarking signal the difference between the marked and the original signals is meant.

This paper is organized as follows. In section 2 we formalize the problem addressed in the paper, and we introduce the models used to analyze it. In section 3 the theoretical bit error probability is derived. In the same section some numerical results are given and discussed, even by the light of Montecarlo simulations. Section 4 presents some preliminary results obtained on real videos. Such an analysis will be used both to validate the theoretical results and to evaluate the quality of the attacked video sequence. In section 5 some conclusions are drawn.

2   Problem Setting

Let $\mathbf{f}(t) = \{f_1(t), f_2(t) \ldots f_r(t)\}$ be a set of features extracted from the t-th video frame. For the following analysis to be valid it is necessary that $\mathbf{f}(t)$ is a linear function of the pixel values, so that frame averaging results in averaging $\mathbf{f}(t)$ across t. For instance, $\mathbf{f}(t)$ may correspond to the DCT or wavelet coefficients of the frame, or directly to the grey levels of the pixels. We assume that a single bit b is embedded within $\mathbf{f}(t)$, the extension to the multibit case being straightforward. The same bit is embedded in all the frames interested by the averaging operation performed by the pirate.

According to the ST-DM framework, it is first necessary to define a (secret) direction $\mathbf{s}(t)$ which, in general, may depend on t. In the following we will assume that $\mathbf{s}(t)$ is the same for each frame and that is a unit-norm binary zero-mean[2] sequence taking values $\pm 1/\sqrt{r}$ (this choice causes the watermark distortion to be spread uniformly over all the features).

In order to embed the watermark, the correlation between $\mathbf{f}(t)$ and $\mathbf{s}(t)$ is quantized according to one of two quantizers depending on the to-be-embedded bit. More precisely, let the two codebooks $\mathcal{U}_0$ and $\mathcal{U}_1$ associated respectively to $b = 0$ and $b = 1$ be defined as:

$$\mathcal{U}_0 = \{k\Delta + d, k \in \mathbb{Z}\}, \tag{1}$$

$$\mathcal{U}_1 = \{k\Delta + \Delta/2 + d, k \in \mathbb{Z}\}, \tag{2}$$

where d is an arbitrary parameter that, once chosen, it is equal for each video-frame. Let $\rho(t)$ be the correlation between $\mathbf{f}(t)$ and $\mathbf{s}(t)$, i.e.

$$\rho(t) = \mathbf{f}(t) \cdot \mathbf{s}(t) = \sum_{i=1}^{r} f_i(t) s_i(t). \tag{3}$$

Watermark embedding is achieved by quantizing $\rho(t)$ either with the quantizer $\mathcal{Q}_0$ associated to $\mathcal{U}_0$:

$$\mathcal{Q}_0(\rho(t)) = \arg \min_{u_{0,i} \in \mathcal{U}_0} |u_{0,i} - \rho(t)|, \tag{4}$$

---

[2] Assuming that $\mathbf{s}(t)$ has zero mean does not allow the use of pseudo-random sequences.

where $u_{0,i}$ are the elements of $\mathcal{U}_0$, or the quantizer associated to $b = 1$:

$$\mathcal{Q}_1(\rho(t)) = \arg \min_{u_{1,i} \in \mathcal{U}_1} |u_{1,i} - \rho(t)|. \tag{5}$$

In practice the above quantization is obtained by subtracting the projection of $\mathbf{f}(t)$ on $\mathbf{s}(t)$ from $\mathbf{f}(t)$ and by adding a new component along the direction of $\mathbf{s}(t)$ resulting in the desired quantized autocorrelation:

$$\mathbf{f}_w(t) = \mathbf{f}(t) - \rho(t)\mathbf{s}(t) + \rho_w(t)\mathbf{s}(t), \tag{6}$$

with

$$\rho_w(t) = \begin{cases} \mathcal{Q}_0(\rho(t)) & b = 0 \\ \mathcal{Q}_1(\rho(t)) & b = 1 \end{cases} \tag{7}$$

To read the watermark, a minimum distance decoder is used:

$$b^* = \arg \min_{b \in \{0,1\}} \min_{u_{b,i} \in \mathcal{U}_b} |u_{b,i} - \rho'(t)|, \tag{8}$$

where by $\rho'(t)$ we indicate the correlation between the watermarked and possibly attacked features and the spreading vector $\mathbf{s}(t)$.

In order to evaluate the effect of a collusion attack on ST-DM, it is necessary that the host feature sequence $\mathbf{f}(t)$ is properly modelled. In the sequel, we will adopt the following assumptions

1. $\mathbf{f}(t)$ is a sequence of identically (not necessarily independent) distributed random variables.
2. The dependence between host feature sequences extracted from different frames is modelled by splitting $\mathbf{f}(t)$ into two parts, a constant part which does not depend on t and a varying part whose content does not depend on the previous and subsequent frames. Specifically we will let

$$\mathbf{f}(t) = \mathbf{f}_0 + \mathbf{v}(t), \tag{9}$$

where $\mathbf{f}_0$ and $\mathbf{v}(t)$ are two zero-mean, i.i.d. sequences independent of each other, and where $\mathbf{v}(t)$ does not depend on $\mathbf{v}(\tau)$ for any $\tau \neq t$. We also assume that $\mathbf{f}_0$ and $\mathbf{v}(t)$ are stationary with respect to t, with variance equal to σ_0^2 and σ_v^2 respectively.

Assumption 1 is easily verified if $\mathbf{f}$ is drawn from a transformed domain such as the DCT or wavelet domain. If $\mathbf{f}$ is taken in the pixel domain, it is necessary that the pixels contributing to it are chosen randomly within the frame. If this is the case, we assume that the same subset of pixels is chosen for all the video frames[3]. Assumption 2 is very important since it allows to distinguish between the time varying part of the video and the constant part; the video sequence is considered as composed by a static frame with some noise superimposed to it. In

---

[3] Of course this is not a necessary assumption. We introduced it to preserve robustness against temporal frame averaging.

spite of its simplicity, that, for instance, does not allow to model video sequences with fast motion, this way of separating the contribution of $\mathbf{f}_0$ and $\mathbf{v}(t)$ allows to embrace under a unique umbrella the TFA attack and the WER attack. The TFA attack, in fact, exploits the high correlation between neighboring frames, hence it must be dealt with by assuming that $\mathbf{f}_0$ is predominant with respect to $\mathbf{v}(t)$. On the contrary, for the WER attack, the pirate must use scenes with independent contents. This can be easily taken into account by making the $\mathbf{v}(t)$ term predominant with respect to $\mathbf{f}_0$, or by simply neglecting the presence of $\mathbf{f}_0$.

As we said in the introduction, here we are only interested in the case of a constant watermark, i.e. we will assume that $\mathbf{s}(t)$ does not depend on t. Note, though, that due to the characteristics of ST-DM watermarking, the actual watermarking signal embedded within each frame is not constant, hence even if a constant $\mathbf{s}$ is used, robustness against TFA is not automatically granted.

3   Computation of Bit Error Probability

TFA works as explained in the following. The attacker replaces each watermarked frame $\mathbf{f}_w(t)$ with an average frame computed as follows

$$\overline{\mathbf{f}}_w(t) = \frac{1}{N_c} \sum_{l=1}^{N_c} \mathbf{f}_w(t+l), \tag{10}$$

where N_c indicates the number of frames used for the TFA attack. In our analysis we do not consider the case that a colluder also could add noise when performing his action.

The ST-DM decoder correlates $\mathbf{f}_w(t)$ with $\mathbf{s}$ and applies the decoding rule (8). We want to investigate the probability that a decoding error occurs ($\Pr\{b \neq b^*\}$). Note that we focus on single-bit decoding, i.e. we do not consider the possibility that channel coding or the repetition of the same bit in subsequent frames is exploited to improve the performance of the decoder.

Due to linearity, the correlation between the averaged features and $\mathbf{s}$ can be calculated as follows:

$$\overline{\rho}(t) = \overline{\mathbf{f}}_w(t) \cdot \mathbf{s} = \frac{1}{N_c} \sum_{l=1}^{N_c} \rho_w(t+l), \tag{11}$$

i.e. the correlation after the TFA attack is the average of the quantized correlation values. It is clearly seen that whether the averaged correlation belongs to the right decoding region or not depends on the particular quantized values $\rho_w(t+l)$, $l = 1 \ldots N_c$. Let us consider, for example, the simple case of $N_c = 2$, and let us focus on the embedding of $b = 0$. We have $\rho_w(t) = k(t)\Delta + d$ and $\rho_w(t+1) = k(t+1)\Delta + d$, leading to:

$$\overline{\rho}(t) = \frac{k(t) + k(t+1)}{2} \Delta + d. \tag{12}$$

It is immediate to verify that the decoder will correctly decide for $b = 0$ if and only if $k(t) + k(t + 1)$ is an even number. This is the the case, for example, if $k(t) = k(t + 1)$, but in general there is no assurance that this condition holds.

In order to derive the exact bit error probability, it is necessary that the pdf of the correlation vector $\boldsymbol{\rho}(t) = \{\rho(t), \rho(t + 1) \ldots \rho(t + N_c)\}$ is computed. To do so, we will assume that $\boldsymbol{\rho}(t)$ is a vector of jointly Gaussian variables. This assumption surely holds if the host features follow a Gaussian pdf, since in this case each element of $\boldsymbol{\rho}(t)$ is nothing but a linear combination of Gaussian variables. Obviously, $\boldsymbol{\rho}(t)$ has to be intended Gaussian conditionally to $\boldsymbol{s}(t)$ which is fixed. On the contrary, if we can not assume that the $f_i(t)$'s follow a Gaussian pdf, the Joint Gaussianity of $\boldsymbol{\rho}(t)$ can still be justified by resorting to the multidimensional central limit theorem [6]. Of course, in this last case, the analysis holds only if we do not consider too small error probability values, otherwise a Large-Deviation analysis should be needed.

In order to fully specify the pdf of $\boldsymbol{\rho}(t)$ we need to calculate its covariance matrix (the mean vector is clearly null since we assumed that $\boldsymbol{s}$ is a zero mean sequence). Let us focus on a generic element of $\boldsymbol{\rho}(t)$. We have:

$$\rho(t + l) = \mathbf{f_0} \cdot \mathbf{s} + \mathbf{v}(t + l) \cdot \mathbf{s} = \rho_0 + \rho_v(t + l), \tag{13}$$

where the first term depends on the stationary part of $\mathbf{f}$ and the second on the variable part. By reasoning as before we can assume that both ρ_0 and $\rho_v(t + l)$ follow a zero-mean Gaussian pdf with variance σ_0^2 and σ_v^2 respectively. In addition, ρ_0 and $\rho_v(t + l)$ are independent on each other. We then have:

$$E[\rho(t + l)\rho(t + m)] = \begin{cases} \sigma_0^2 & l \neq m \\ \sigma_0^2 + \sigma_v^2 & l = m. \end{cases} \tag{14}$$

By introducing the correlation coefficient α

$$\alpha = \frac{Cov[\rho(t + l)\rho(t + m)]}{\sqrt{Var[\rho(t + l)]Var[\rho(t + m)]}} = \frac{\sigma_0^2}{\sigma_0^2 + \sigma_v^2}, \tag{15}$$

and by letting $\sigma_f^2 = \sigma_0^2 + \sigma_v^2$ indicate the variance of the host features, the covariance matrix of $\boldsymbol{\rho}(t)$ can be written as:

$$C_{\boldsymbol{\rho}(t)} = \sigma_f^2 \cdot \begin{pmatrix} 1 & \alpha & \ldots & \alpha \\ \alpha & 1 & \ldots & \alpha \\ \cdot & \cdot & & \cdot \\ \cdot & \cdot & & \cdot \\ \alpha & \alpha & \ldots & 1 \end{pmatrix} \tag{16}$$

Interestingly, the above formulation permits to cover various scenarios by simply varying the correlation coefficient α. In the TFA case, for instance, colluders rely on the availability of highly correlated scenes hence calling for high values of α. On the contrary, when fast moving objects are present in the scene, colluder uses less correlated frames thus justifying the adoption of very small values of α, leading to an approximately diagonal covariance matrix.

3.1   Two-Frame Collusion

In this section we focus on the simple case of $N_c = 2$. Despite it simplicity, this is a very important case, first of all because it provides a considerable insight into the behavior of ST-DM against TFA. Secondly, because, due to the presence of motion, the attacker can not use a large number of frames, since averaging a large number of scenes would result in a very low quality video (see section 4). Of course, the pirate can use motion compensation in order to avoid the problems due to the presence of moving objects. In so doing, though, the attacker will average non-aligned feature vectors hence resulting in a scenario which is closest to a system with a varying $s(t)$.

We have already noted that if the embedded bit is equal to zero (see equation (12)) a decoding error occurs whenever the quantity $k(t) + k(t + 1)$ is odd: it is easy to verify that the same condition holds when $b = 1$. With this idea in mind, and by assuming bits 0 and 1 are equiprobable, the probability of a decoding error can be written as

$$P_e = P_{e|b=0}\text{Pr}\{b = 0\} + P_{e|b=1}\text{Pr}\{b = 1\} = \frac{P_{e|b=0} + P_{e|b=1}}{2}, \tag{17}$$

with

$$P_{e|b=0} = \sum_k \text{Pr}\{\rho_w(t) = u_{0,k}\} \sum_h \text{Pr}\{\rho_w(t + 1) = u_{0,k+2h+1}|\rho_w(t) = u_{0,k}\}$$

$$= \sum_k \sum_h \text{Pr}\{\rho_w(t) = u_{0,k}, \rho_w(t + 1) = u_{0,k+2h+1}\}$$

$$= \sum_k \sum_h \text{Pr}\{\rho(t) \in [k\Delta + d - \Delta/2, k\Delta + d + \Delta/2] \cap$$

$$\rho(t + 1) \in [(k + 2h + 1)\Delta + d - \Delta/2, (k + 2h + 1)\Delta + d + \Delta/2]\}, \tag{18}$$

and

$$P_{e|b=1} = \sum_k \text{Pr}\{\rho_w(t) = u_{1,k}\} \sum_h \text{Pr}\{\rho_w(t + 1) = u_{1,k+2h+1}|\rho_w(t) = u_{1,k}\}$$

$$= \sum_k \sum_h \text{Pr}\{\rho_w(t) = u_{1,k}, \rho_w(t + 1) = u_{1,k+2h+1}\}$$

$$= \sum_k \sum_h \text{Pr}\{\rho(t) \in [k\Delta + d, k\Delta + d + \Delta] \cap$$

$$\rho(t + 1) \in [(k + 2h + 1)\Delta + d, (k + 2h + 1)\Delta + d + \Delta]\}. \tag{19}$$

As it can be seen, the error probability depends on three parameters, the quantization step Δ, the parameter d and α. The correlation among video frames is not a parameter that can be controlled by the watermark designer. The value of Δ depends on the allowed distortion, i.e. on the required Document to Watermark

Ratio (DWR) defined as

$$\text{DWR} = \frac{\sum_{i=1}^{r} E[f_i^2]}{\sum_{i=1}^{r} E[w_i^2]}, \tag{20}$$

where $\mathbf{w} = \mathbf{f}_w - \mathbf{f}$ is the actual watermarking signal added to the host feature sequence. The dependence between DWR, r and Δ has been derived in [7] and assumes the form

$$\Delta = \sqrt{\frac{ar\sigma_f^2}{\text{DWR}}}, \tag{21}$$

where a is a parameter ranging from 12 to 16, and whose exact value depends on the ratio Δ/σ_f. In the end, then, the dependence of P_e on Δ turns out to be a dependence on DWR and r.

3.2   Numerical Results

We evaluated the probability of errors given by equations (18) and (19) by means of numerical integration leading to the results reported in Figures 1 and 2. As a first test we plotted the error probability as a function of d/Δ, computed for different values of DWR (Fig. 1(a)) and of α (Fig. 1(b)). As it can be seen, the error probability is minimized when $d/\Delta = 1/4$. This is not surprising since for this value of d a symmetrical arrangement of the centroids belonging to $\mathcal{U}_0$ and $\mathcal{U}_1$ is obtained, thus balancing the probability of errors conditioned to $b = 0$ and $b = 1$. For this reason in the following experiments we always used $d/\Delta = 1/4$. By observing Figure 1(a), it can be noticed, as expected, that the lower the DWR the lower the error probability for any value of d/Δ; in particular, when the DWR is closer to values usually adopted for ST-DM (e.g about 10-20 dB), the error probability quickly reaches an acceptable level around 10^{-4}. In Figure 1(b), a similar trend is obtained by fixing the DWR to 25 dB and varying the correlation between frames: a high correlation (e.g α near to 1) yields a lower error probability, because it is probable that host features belonging to two different frames will be quantized on the same value and do not swap on the other quantizer when collusion is performed.

As a second test, in Figure 2(a) the bit error probability was plotted as a function of r. The basic result that we obtained is that the performance of the system improves for increasing values of r. The reason for this behavior is very simple. When r increases the variance of $\rho(t)$ remains constant (see equation (14), this is due to the fact that s is composed by elements $\pm 1/\sqrt{r}$), whereas the quantization step Δ increases linearly with $\sqrt{r}$ (see equation (21)). As a result, for increasing values of r is more and more likely that both $\rho(t)$ and $\rho(t+1)$ are quantized into the same codeword, i.e. the codeword of $\mathcal{U}_0$ ($\mathcal{U}_1$) which is closest to the origin.

Finally we plotted the bit error probability as a function of α. The results we obtained (Figure 2(b)) show that the performance of ST-DM improve for higher values of α. Again this is an expected result since the higher the correlation between subsequent video frames, the higher the probability that $\rho(t)$ and $\rho(t+1)$ are quantized into the same codeword.

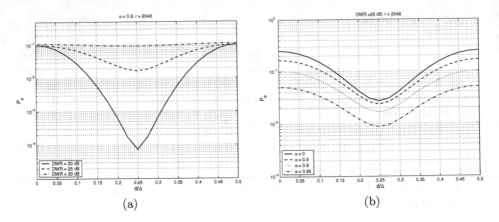

Fig. 1. The error probability as a function of d/Δ for different values of DWR (a) and of α (b)

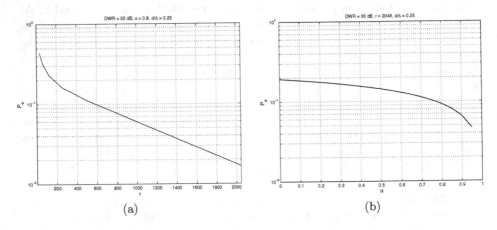

Fig. 2. The error probability as a function of r (a) and of α (b)

3.3   Higher Order Collusion

When TFA involves a higher number of frames the simple odd-even rule outlined in section 3 does not hold, thus making the computation of the exact bit error probability more difficult. A lower bound of the probability of a correct decision can be obtained by assuming that a correct decision is made if all the components of $\rho(t)$ are quantized into the same codeword, hence permitting to upper bound the probability of error. In formulas we have:

$$P_e = \frac{P_{e|b=0} + P_{e|b=1}}{2},$$

(22)

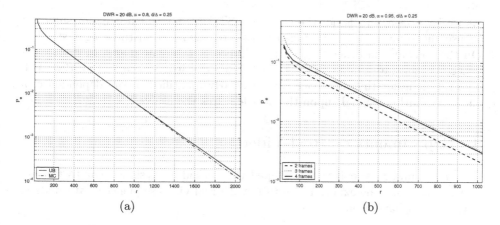

Fig. 3. The error probability as a function of r: (a) comparison between the upper bound(UB) computed by applying the theoretical approach and by Monte Carlo simulations (MC), and (b) Monte Carlo simulations in the case of TFA attack when 2, 3 or 4 consecutive frames are averaged.

$$P_{e|b=0} \leq 1 - P_{c|b=0}$$
$$= 1 - \sum_k \Pr\{\rho_w(t) = u_{0,k}, \rho_w(t+1) = u_{0,k} \ldots \rho_w(t+N_c) = u_{0,k}\}$$
$$= 1 - \sum_k \Pr\{\rho(t) \in [k\Delta + d - \Delta/2, k\Delta + d + \Delta/2] \cap$$
$$\cdots \cap \rho(t+N_c) \in [k\Delta + d - \Delta/2, k\Delta + d + \Delta/2]\}. \qquad (23)$$

A similar expression holds for $P_{e|b=1}$. It is worth noticing that the upper bound tends to be tighter for high values of α, since highly correlated frames are likely to result into close quantized correlations. In Figure 3(a) results obtained for the upper bound of the error probability with respect to r, in the case of $N_c = 3$ and $d/\Delta = 1/4$, are plotted. This theoretical bound is compared with the results achieved with the Monte Carlo simulation and it can be appreciated how its slope actually limits the slope of the empirical results. In Figure 3(b), the error probability computed through Monte Carlo simulation when 2, 3 or 4 consecutive frames are colluded is given. All of these circumstances get to similar trends, but the case of 2 averaged frames is less damaging with respect to the others. Anyway, on the other side, as it will be highlighted in the next section, visual quality degradation of colluded frames when collusion happens among more than 2 frames is quite high.

3.4   Comparison with SS Watermarking

It is instructive to compare the effect of TFA on ST-DM with the effect on a conventional SS system. It is known, in fact, that an SS system adopting the same spreading sequence for all the video frames is intrinsically immune to TFA [1].

As we have seen, this is not the case with ST-DM, for which it is not sufficient to use the same s in all the video frames to ensure robustness against TFA. On the contrary, in order to get some degree of robustness against TFA, it is necessary that large values of r are used. Moreover it is advisable that $d = \Delta/4$. The rationale for this difference can be clearly identified in the dependence of the watermarking signal[4] upon the host features themselves.

4   Experiments on Real Video

To further understand if the developed theoretical analysis is near to the numerical results, some experimental tests with real video sequences watermarked with ST-DM have been carried out.

Table 1. The error probability as a function of r, calculating the effective bit error rate on the attacked video sequence *Basket* (Basket) and theoretically computed

Comparison on error probability		
r	*Real video sequence* Basket	*Theoretical computation*
64	0.386	0.490
128	0.297	0.328
256	0.216	0.183
512	0.147	0.090
1024	0.031	0.048

Hereafter some results referring to the sequence named *Basket* are debated.

In Table 1 the theoretical error probability for different values of r is compared to that obtained on a real video. In both cases only two frames were averaged. In addition the average correlation factor between the frames of the *Basket* was computed leading to $\alpha = 0.98$. As it can be seen the theoretical analysis is in good agreement with the experiments.

To evaluate the visual degradation occurring in presence of watermarking as well as in the case of TFA attack, in Figure 4 the frame number 80 of the video sequence *Basket* is shown. In particular, the original frame is depicted in Figure 4(a), and the watermarked one in Figure 4(b). The watermark has been embedded by setting $r = 2048$ and $DWR = 30dB$, and the resulting visual quality, both frame-by-frame and of the whole sequence, is high. Moreover, to be aware of how TFA attack can harm the colluded video sequence, the colluded frame obtained by averaging frame 80 with the following one, number 81, is shown in Figure 4(c); furthermore the average among frame 79, 80 and 81 is pictured in Figure 4(d). As it can be seen, the TFA attack degrades the visual quality of the video frame already in case of averaging only two frames, thus confirming the rightness of the assumption done in the previous section with regard to the importance of the case of collusion with $N_c = 2$. When $N_c > 2$

---

[4] The signal actually added to the host features.

Fig. 4. A frame belonging to the video sequence *Basket*: the original frame (a), the watermarked one(b); the averaging of the frame with the following one (c), and the averaging of the frame with the previous and the following ones (d).

the visual quality is significantly reduced. In this analysis, motion-compensated frame averaging has not been considered yet but it will be studied in the next developments.

5   Concluding Remarks

In this paper we have moved a first step towards the analysis of the effect that collusion attacks have on QIM watermarking. The analysis we carried out is admittedly limited, since we considered only ST-DM watermarking with a temporally constant spreading sequence subject to Temporal Frame Averaging. In spite of the above limitations, our analysis can give some useful insights. In particular the following lessons were learned:

- **ST-DM (QIM) behaves differently than spread spectrum.** In fact, with SS watermarking it is sufficient that a constant spreading sequence is used to ensure invariance against TFA. This is no more the case with ST-DM (QIM).
- **Choice of dithering factor** d. The choice of the dithering factor d has some influence on the robustness of ST-DM against TFA.
- **Spreading gain.** Robustness against TFA can be improved (at the expense of watermark capacity) by augmenting the spreading gain r.
- **Quality of colluded video.** In the case of intra-video TFA without motion compensation the number of frames that can be used in the collusion is fairly limited.

Some directions for future research follow directly from the limits of the current analysis, in that it will be necessary to extend the analysis to non-constant spreading sequences, and to the WER attack. The extension to a wider class of techniques that go beyond ST-DM is also be required.

Acknowledgements

The work described in this paper has been supported in part by the European Commission through the IST Programme under Contract IST-2002-507932 ECRYPT. The information in this document reflects only the author's views, is provided as is and no guarantee or warranty is given that the information is fit for any particular purpose. The user thereof uses the information at its sole risk and liability. This work was also partially supported by MIUR (Italian Ministry for Education, University and Research) under grant no. 2003094459.

References

1. G. Doerr, J.D.: Security pitfalls of frame-by-frame approaches to video watermarking. IEEE Trans. on Signal Processing **52** (2004) 2955–2964
2. Su, K., Kundur, D., Hatzinakos, D.: Statistical invisibility for collusion-resistant digital video watermarking. IEEE Trans. on Multimedia **7** (2005) 43–51
3. Su, K., Kundur, D., Hatzinakos, D.: Spatially localized image-dependent watermarking for statistical invisibility and collusion resistance. IEEE Trans. on Multimedia **7** (2005) 52–56
4. Chen, B., Wornell, G.: Quantization index modulation: a class of provably good methods for digital watermarking and information embedding. IEEE Trans. on Information Theory **47** (2001) 1423–1443
5. Perez-Gonzalez, F., Balado, F., Hernandez, J.R.: Performance analysis of existing and new methods for data hiding with known-host information in additive channels. IEEE Trans. on Signal Processing **51** (2003) 960–980
6. Breiman, L.: Probability. SIAM, Philadelphia (1992)
7. Bartolini, F., Barni, M., Piva, A.: Performance analysis of ST-DM watermarking in presence of non-additive attacks. IEEE Trans. on Signal Processing **52** (2004) 2965–2974

Oracle Attacks and Covert Channels

Ilaria Venturini

École Nationale Supérieure des Télécommunications (ENST/TSI)
c/o Laboratoire des Signaux et Systèmes (LSS)
École Supérieure d'Électricité (Supélec)
3, rue Joliot Curie
91192 Gif sur Yvette Cedex, France
venturi@tsi.enst.fr, ilaria.venturini@lss.supelec.fr

Abstract. In this paper, well-known attacks named *oracle attacks* are formulated within a realistic network communication model where they reveal to use suitable covert channels, we name *oracle channels*. By exploiting information-theoretic notions, we show how to modify detection/authentication watermarking algorithms in order to counteract oracle attacks. We present three proposals, one based on randomization, another one based on time delay and a third one based on both randomization and delay.

Keywords: Oracle attacks, Covert channels, Watermarking.

1 Introduction

In this paper, we focus on oracle attacks for watermarking schemes. Selective integrity verification via watermarking on signals substantiates our paper as an application where oracle attacks can succeed. Other watermarking applications could indeed be adequate exemplifications as well. Following an information-theoretic approach, oracle attacks reveal here as giving rise to particular covert channels. The covert channels we consider are such that they allow us to set up three countermeasures. Such countermeasures are obtainable by suitably modifying detection/authentication algorithms. We sketch three modifications of authentication algorithms: the first one is based on randomness increasing, the second one, already present in a preliminary version in [16], is based on time delay, and the third one is based on both randomness and delay. The performance of the proposed algorithms is addressed simply to show that an acceptable compromise between security enhancement and authentication reliability is achievable. Our proposals assume a realistic and simplified communication model and do not need to work in an interactive network environment, as it is typical of communication protocols. Moreover, each proposal is stand-alone since it constructs a hash table memory, whose dimension can be adapted to different situations, and thus does not need to gain access to a huge database.

We recall that watermarking communication, after a previous oversimplified modeling where the watermark is the information that codes an external message

M. Barni et al. (Eds.): IWDW 2005, LNCS 3710, pp. 171–185, 2005.

concerning the host signal, which is the channel, has been considered as communication with side information at the embedding. Finally, it has been modeled as a communication channel having a covert channel for transmitting the watermark with side information (the host signal and a key). Such a side information is available at the embedding phase and can be available also at the detection phase, as e.g. in [11]. However, such a covert channel is desired by the scheme designer, is publicly known to exist and does not violate the scheme security. Therefore the known notion of subliminal channel [14] seems to be more adequate than that of covert channel. A formulation following the theory of games has also been given, where the scheme designer wants to maximize the rate of reliable transmission whereas the attacker wants to minimize it [11,12].

The paper is organized into three sections. In the first section we address oracle attacks. In the second section we define oracle channels. Counteracting oracle channels is focused in the third section. A brief conclusion comment concludes the paper.

2   Some Known Oracle Attacks

Well-known oracle attacks are the *sensitivity analysis attack* and the *gradient descendent attack*, described for symmetric schemes designed for copy protection [8,6]. There the attacker has a general knowledge of the detection algorithm, usually of linear correlation type, has one watermarked digital media y as available and has unlimited access to the detector. The watermark is bipolar, i.e. each watermark component w_n is such that $w_n \in \{-1, 1\}$, and it is private as well as the decision thresholds. In the gradient descendent attack, the detector reports the actual detection values rather than its binary decision answer (*yes* or *no*) as in the sensitivity analysis case.

If the attacker starts with a right decision answer by the detector stating that the watermark is present, both attacks use the detector's responses to find the threshold value. To this aim, a short path out of the detection region (geometrically represented), i.e. the region where the detection values are greater than the threshold, is exploited. If the detection statistics decreases monotonically towards the boundary of the detection region, as it is the case for correlation statistics, the local detection statistics turns out to be oriented towards the boundary of the detection area. Once such a direction has been determined, the considered digital media is modified by the attacker so as to be forced to move along it by some amount, iteratively, until the detection region boundary is crossed. Thus an *oracle attack* succeeds if the attacker forces the black box detector to return a wrong decision answer on a digital media. Those oracle attacks are linear in the size N of the input to the detector.

A noniterative formulation of the sensitivity analysis attack, at a copyright protection setting, requiring at most $N + 1$ operations is in [2]. There the watermark is an arbitrary vector of real numbers and is directly reconstructed by exploiting the linearity property, with respect to N, of the detection formula.

In [13] an iterative sensitivity attack is formulated for quantization-based watermarking.

In order to counteract oracle attacks, the authors of [8,6] propose:

1. A decision interval, i.e. two thresholds thr and Thr, with $thr < Thr$. Any detection value below thr denotes that the watermark misses; any detection value above Thr denotes that the watermark is present. Within the interval $[thr, Thr]$, values are either 0 or 1 randomly, based on the probability distribution function of a squared sine function. The larger the interval, the lower the information leakage as well as the detector reliability.
2. Strongly nonlinear ingredients in the detection formula.

In line with increasing non-linearity, T. Furon has shown in [5] that if, at the detection, linear correlation is replaced by a quadratic one, more generally by a quadratic form, the most favorable case of an oracle attack has $O(N^2)$ computational complexity (and, in a subsequent work, that a nth-order detection process increases security over a second-order one).

More effectively, in [15] a decision boundary with a fractal dimension has been exploited.

2.1   Oracle Attacks for Integrity Watermarking

Here we show that oracle attacks can be formulated also for integrity verification watermarking schemes. We focus on integrity verification schemes where a host dependent watermark w is transmitted covertly, but publicly, within a host signal x from a sender Se (i.e. a watermarker as well as a net publisher or a sender site of a network) to a receiver Re, i.e. a Public in the sense we are going to point out. A *Public* is here a common pirate/user model who

i) has a general knowledge of the algorithms used in the watermarking scheme;
ii) receives only some answers from the black box software authenticator. Such an authenticator is a software which has been downloaded at a terminal of the *Public*'s DHN (Digital Home Network). As an alternative, the verification service could be offered by a trusted web site.
iii) has unlimited access to the software black box authenticator considered in item ii).

Our *Public* is not allowed to implement any authentication algorithm, and therefore needs to know no key. This stems from the fact that the *Public* is intended to be a party who changes as the situation changes. For instance, a *Public* might be as follows.

– An unauthorized party who intentionally tampers with some digital media and possibly re-transmits a non-authentic version of it.
– An intruder who alters multimedia contents at a web site.

- A honest end-user who should be interested in receiving authentic products and possibly in verifying their integrity. A honest end-user may be a customer who typically freely downloads a digital media, for instance an MP3 file. Such an end-user is not protected from receiving altered products.
- An authorized party who produces altered copies of a digital media. In case such a party receives information useful for the integrity verification process, either may tamper with or may help a pirate to access the secret information.

Side information at the embedding phase, in the form of a key and of informations about the host signal, is available to Se. Writing $y = x[w]$ we want to denote that w has been added in some way to x. We underline that in the integrity context the imperceptible w does not codify an external message concerning x and its presence means that the signal is integer. Hence w is supposed to be *semi-fragile* in the sense that it is robust until a predetermined level. Erasing the watermark is not the final aim of an attacker; rather it may be an intermediate step only. At the embedding phase, the watermarked $y = x[w]$ is subject to a distortion constraint under a threshold δ_1 (suitably small to guarantee that y is perceptually indistinguishable from x). At the authentication phase, y is subject to a distortion constraint, under a threshold δ_2, between itself and the signal r received by Re.

Let the authenticator consist of a software implemented authentication algorithm $A(r, k) = a$ to be used as a black box, with inputs r and the secret key k. Its output is a binary decision response a, say either $a = 1$ or $a = 0$, with 1 meaning 'integer' and 0 meaning 'altered', i.e. not integer.
$A(r, k)$ is here also simply denoted by A. Let

$$\alpha = \alpha_N = (a_0, a_1, \ldots, a_N)$$

be a finite sequence of decision responses by A. Thus $\alpha_0 = a_0$, $\alpha_1 = (a_0, a_1)$ and so on.

We do not take into account particular probability distribution of sequence α_N because α_N depends on the attacker requests to the black box and it is not realistic that the attacker follows a particular distribution. Therefore the attack we here describe works for any distribution of α_N.

Let us suppose that r is integer. Thus the right decision answer is $A(r, k) = 1$. Let us also suppose that Re first significantly modifies the integer signal $r = y = r_0$ into r_1, say

$$r_1 = f_1(r_0, \alpha_0), \text{ with } \alpha_0 = 1.$$

where $f_1(r_0, \alpha_0)$ also includes the successful finding the detection region boundary. Then, starting from r_1, Re performs slight modifications $f_i(.,.)$ on r_{i-1}, $i = 2, 3, ..., N$, some of which may be the same, such that

$$r_2 = f_2(r_1, \alpha_1), \quad \ldots, \quad r_N = f_N(r_{N-1}, \alpha_{N-1}) \tag{1}$$

until an r_N is constructed that the authenticator reports as integer, i.e. r_N is such that A returns a wrong decision response on r_N (what is $A(r_N, k) = 1$, that is false because r_N is supposed to be quite different from $r = r_0 = y$). We suppose that for $n = 2, 3, \ldots, N$, r_n is such that

$$d(r_{n-1}, r_n) \leq \delta_3$$

with $d(.,.)$ a distance that is a similarity measure and δ_3 a threshold. Moreover

$$d(r_{N-2}, r_N) > \delta_3 \text{ though } d(r_{N-1}, r_N) \leq \delta_3$$

being r_{N-1} in the "borderline" between the family of signals that force A to answer 1 and the family of signals that force A to answer 0.

Being r_1 significantly modified with respect to $r = y$, $A(r_1, k) = a_1 = 0$. The modifications on $r_1, r_2, \ldots, r_{N-1}$ are supposed to be sufficiently smooth so that a sequence of $N - 1$ right decision answers

$$A(r_1, k) = A(r_2, k) = \ldots = A(r_{N-1}, k) = 0 \tag{2}$$

are returned by A. Finally we suppose that r_N is significantly modified with respect to $r = y$ and nevertheless the wrong response $A(r_N, k) = 1$ is obtained from A.

The described general attack procedure may be either iterative or noniterative. The authenticator A may use either a linear or a nonlinear authentication formula. The gained information is here the crucial point for the success of the attack. We are going to investigate about it.

3   Oracle Channels

Here we address oracle attacks as particular covert channels. The covert channel notion received several definitions [9]. All of them agree in considering it as a communication channel that exploits another communication channel in a covert way. Classical distinctions into *storage covert channel*, *timing covert channel* and *mixed channel* can be found for instance in [10]. Being exploitable for getting secret informations not allowed to access to, a covert channel has the following characteristic properties:

1. it violates security;
2. it is allowed to exist with a rate far below an agreed upon upper bound.

A *distinguo* is in order here between a covert channel and a *subliminal channel* [14]: a covert channel exists outside of the scheme/system design, while a subliminal channel is foreseen by the scheme designer as hidden in a publicly known communication channel and moreover does not violates the channel security. We consider a simplified model that stems from real life networks (as the Internet or home networks).

Figure 1 synthesizes the scenario we consider in case the receiver downloads the signal y and the software authenticator A to be used as a black box at his DHN. We suppose that A is integer (for instance A could be transmitted as an *obfuscated* program).

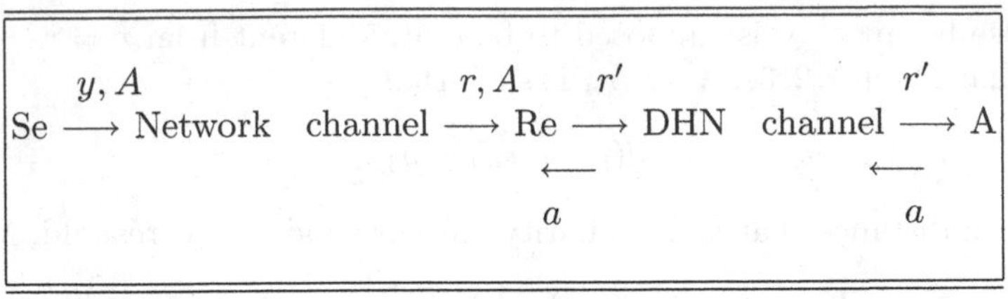

$$y, A \qquad\qquad r, A \quad r' \qquad\qquad r'$$
$$\text{Se} \longrightarrow \text{Network} \quad \text{channel} \longrightarrow \text{Re} \longrightarrow \text{DHN} \quad \text{channel} \longrightarrow \text{A}$$
$$\longleftarrow \qquad\qquad\qquad \longleftarrow$$
$$a \qquad\qquad\qquad a$$

Fig. 1. *Se* is the sender of the watermarked signal $y = x[w]$ and of the software authenticator A through a network channel. *Re* is the receiver of A and of y as r. The input r' to A is transmitted through a channel of the DHN of *Re*. The decision answer a by A on r is returned to *Re* through the DHN channel

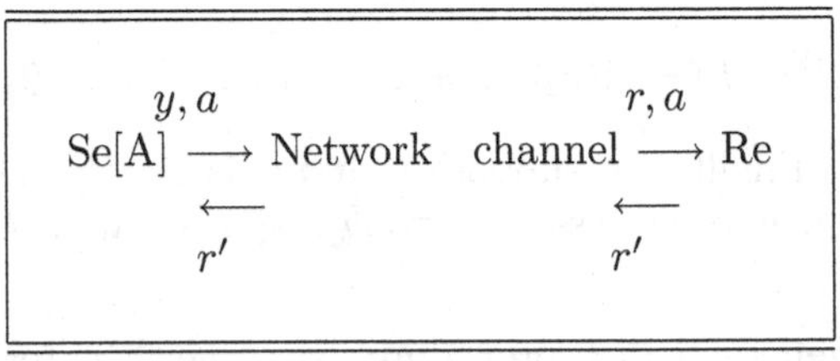

$$y, a \qquad\qquad\qquad r, a$$
$$\text{Se}[A] \longrightarrow \text{Network} \quad \text{channel} \longrightarrow \text{Re}$$
$$\longleftarrow \qquad\qquad\qquad \longleftarrow$$
$$r' \qquad\qquad\qquad r'$$

Fig. 2. *Se* is the sender, through a network channel, of y, and later of each decision response a given by the software authenticator A (which is at the site of *Se*, that is denoted by *Se*[A]) once such responses are requested on signal r' by the receiver *Re*

Figure 2 synthesizes the scenario in case the *Public* utilizes a site of a public network which offers the integrity verification service.

In both the previous cases the *Re*, as a *Public*, freely inquires about the integrity of the signal r, by using A as a black box software authenticator.

Now let us suppose that the same *Re* becomes the attacker and that the oracle attack *Re* performs starts on the integer signal r. We distinguish:

i) the channel from *Se* to *Re*.

ii) the channel between *Re* and A, as the authentication channel. In case of Figure 1, the authentication channel is in the DHN of *Re*. In case of Figure 2, the authentication channel is in the public network.

iia) the channel from A to *Re*, that we name Q, within the bidirectional channel in item ii). For simplicity, we suppose that Q is noiseless. Let Q_n, with n having a finite range, denote Q at its nth usage. Since Q is a binary noiseless channel, any transmitted decision answer a by A (either 1 or 0) is received without error. At each Q_n, A can send one bit reliably to *Re*. The indirect information exploited by *Re* flows through

iib) a covert channel Q_o in Q we name *oracle channel*. In fact, the particular channel Q_o has both properties 1) and 2) we have seen in Section 3 as typical of a covert channel, in as much as it violates the scheme security and may exist also with a low rate. Moreover, it has the following peculiar properties.

- Q_o is not foreseen by the watermarking scheme designer or by the watermarker.
- The authenticator A, as a process, only passively collaborate with Re to set up Q_o, in the sense that Re forces A to collaborate in as much as A returns decision responses.

Since A can return a finite number of short responses to Re within a finite time interval, Re can use A as an oracle and utilize indirect information derived from the received responses from A. Short messages and time duration are crucial for the existence of the covert channel Q_o. A rate R_t is achievable for Q and a rate $R_{o,t}$ is achievable for Q_o.

3.1 Information-Theoretic Setting

To make this paper self-contained we here recall the information-theoretic notions we use.

Let $x = \{x_1, \ldots, x_{L_x}\}$ be a discrete vector-valued random variable, with probability mass function $p(x)$. Let the random variable k be the side information in the form of a key available to the embedder and to the integrity verification algorithm A (the authenticator) but not available to the receiver Re (i.e. a *Public* who may be also the attacker, as we here suppose). In the marked signal $y = x[w] = \{y_1, \ldots, y_{L_x}\}$, let also $w = \{w_1, \ldots, w_{L_x}\}$ be a discrete vector-valued random variable. Any dependency between x, k and w is modeled using a joint distribution $P(x, k, w)$. Let $r = \{r_1, \ldots, r_{L_x}\}$ be the signal received by Re. Let the thresholds of the constraints on the admissible distortion levels at the embedding and at the content authentication phases be δ_1 and δ_2 respectively, with δ_1 suitably small to guarantee that y is perceptually indistinguishable from x, and $\delta_2 \geq \delta_1$.

By the Shannon's definition [3], the entropy of w is $H(w) = -\sum_j p(w_j) log(p(w_j))$, where $p(w_j) = P(w = w_j)$ with $w_j = \{w_{j_1}, \ldots, w_{j_{L_x}}\}$; log stands for log_2 (with $0log0 = 0$), being understood that the unit of information is in bit. $H(w)$ measures the average uncertainty in the random variable w. It is also the lower bound on the average number of bits required to describe w or to read w, as well as the lower bound on the average number of questions needed to identify w (the minimum expected number of binary questions required to determine w lies between $H(w)$ and $H(w) + 1$).

The *conditional entropy*, that is the uncertainty associated with w given r, is

$$H(w|r) = \sum_j p(r_j) H(w|r = r_j)$$

with $r_j = \{r_{j_1}, \ldots, r_{j_{L_x}}\}$. $H(w|r) \leq H(w)$, where equality holds if r and w are independent. Thus $H(w|r)$ reduces $H(w)$ on the average.

The *mutual information* shared between w and r is the symmetric notion $I(w; r)$

$$I(w; r) = H(w) - H(w|r) .$$

$I(w; r) \geq 0$ expresses that the information r reveals about w is the prior uncertainty in w less the posterior uncertainty about w after r is given. Thus $I(w; r)$ is the reduction in uncertainty concerning w due to r, i.e. the reduction in entropy that r provides about w.

The Shannon's perfect secrecy condition for w is $I(w; r) = 0$, which can be approximated if w and r can be considered as each other independent. $I(w; r)$ has to be minimized in case, as in watermarking, less than perfect secrecy is of great interest. On the contrary, $I(w; y|k)$ has to be maximized to obtain a good detection reliability.

A communication channel is characterized by a probability transition matrix that determines, given the input, the conditional distribution of the output. The capacity $C = \max\limits_{p(w)} I(w; r)$ is the maximum rate at which w can be transmitted over the channel and recovered at the output with a vanishing low error probability.

We recall also that results on the hiding capacity have been obtained for different watermarking settings, essentially stating that the hiding capacity is independent from the knowledge the detector has about the media item. It has also been shown that existing watermarking systems operate far below capacity.

For a sequence α of decision responses, the conditional mutual information $I(w; r|\alpha) \geq 0$, with equality only in case w and r are conditionally independent given α, is the reduction in the uncertainty of w due to the knowledge of r when α is given. Each response in α statistically depends on w because each authenticator's decision response depends on the presence of w in its input signal.

For decision response sequences α_1 with probability distribution $p(\alpha_1)$ and α_2 with probability distribution $p(\alpha_2)$, the *relative entropy* or *information discrimination* or *Kullback-Leibler distance* is

$$D(p(\alpha_1)//p(\alpha_2)) = \sum_j p(\alpha_1(j)) log \frac{p(\alpha_1(j))}{p(\alpha_2(j))}$$

where $p(\alpha_1) > 0$, $p(\alpha_2) \geq 0$, $p(\alpha_1) log \frac{p(\alpha_1)}{0} = +\infty$.
The information discrimination has no upper bound being

$$0 \leq D(p(\alpha_1)//p(\alpha_2)) = \begin{cases} 0 \text{ if and only if } p(\alpha_1) = p(\alpha_2) \\ +\infty \text{ if and only if } \exists j \text{ such that } p(\alpha_2)(j)) = 0 . \end{cases}$$

It is well-known that though the information discrimination is not a distance (since, though it is ≥ 0 and 0 only in case $p(\alpha_1) = p(\alpha_2)$, it is not symmetric and moreover it does not enjoy the triangular equality) it is often used as a pseudo-distance.

4   Counteracting Oracle Attacks

Whereas a communication channel designer aims at maximizing the information rate and minimizing the influence of noise, a secure scheme designer aims at maximizing security and minimizing the mutual information. To decrease mutual information the following methods can help.

1) Increasing randomness.

The amount of mutual information varies inversely with the degree of randomness. Moreover the degree of randomness is obviously in trade-off with detection authentication reliability. Therefore a good reliability does not allow increasing randomness to a degree such that mutual information becomes negligible.

We will propose, in Subsection 4.1, a modification of authentication algorithms by increasing the degree of randomness only in some suitable cases.

2) Limiting capacity.

As pointed out in [10], having capacity an asymptotic character, it is fine for very long files or documents sent over a long period of time. In [10], a covert channel is exemplified where small messages are sent without errors through a zero capacity channel. Thus capacity zero does not guarantee security.

Although capacity under average distortion constraints is very low, A can send a finite number of short (one bit) responses to Re within a finite time interval. Hence Re can use A as an oracle and utilize indirect information derived from the received responses through a covert channel Q_o from A to Re, within a finite time interval. Such a covert channel Q_o is allowed to exist with a low information rate.

For $\alpha = \alpha_N = (a_0, a_1, \ldots, a_N)$, let $|a_n| = t_n > 0$, with $n = 0, 1, \ldots, N$, denote the time duration, measured by the assumed time unit, to obtain each decision response a_n. For $T = t_0, t_1, \ldots, t_N$, let $\mu\{T\}$ be the average value of T, i.e.

$$\mu\{T\} = \mu\{|\alpha|\} = \frac{1}{N} \sum_{n=0}^{N} |a_n| \,.$$

The random variable T has a distribution depending on the distribution of α. The temporal conditional mutual information is

$$I_t(w; r|\alpha) = \frac{I(w; r|\alpha)}{\mu\{T\}} \tag{3}$$

where the average time response of the authenticator at the denominator of (3) makes $I_t(w; r|\alpha)$ to decrease as time increases. Capacity C_t is

$$C_t = \max \frac{I(w; r|\alpha)}{\mu\{T\}} = \max \frac{H(w) - H(w|r, \alpha)}{\mu\{T\}} \tag{4}$$

the maximum now being taken over the different distributions of α.

The perfect secrecy condition $I_t(w; r|\alpha) = 0$ is approximated as long as $H(w|r, \alpha)$ is near to $H(w)$ or as $\mu\{T\}$ increases.

A rate $R_t < C_t$ is achievable for Q and a rate $R_{o,t} < C_{o,t}$ is also achievable for the oracle channel sequence $\{Q_{o,n}\}$, with $Q_{o,n}$ the oracle channel Q_o at its nth usage.

3) A combination of the previous two methods, i.e. increasing randomness as well as decreasing rate.

To contrast Re in getting indirect information from A, the scheme designer can modify A so that the modified A changes its behavior only on inputs similar to already authenticated ones by the same A. To this aim, A needs to get a memory.

4.1 Authenticators with Hash Table Memory

As an alternative to suitable interactive communication protocols, the scheme designer can counteract the unknown Q_o by acting on the known Q via a modification of the algorithm A. $A(r, k)$ can be modified to become either algorithm $A_1^+(r, k, \mu)$ or algorithm $A_2^+(r, k, \mu)$ or algorithm $A_3^+(r, k, \mu)$ we are going to describe, each having a hash table μ as its own memory.

Given a set of hashed vectors in the hash table μ and a vector r as input, first of all each A_i^+, $i = 1, 2, 3$, has to verify whether there exists a hashed vector $h(u) \in \mu$ which matches with $h(r)$. We write $h(r) \in \mu$ to express that some $h(r')$, with r' a signal, such that $d_{ham}(h(r), h(r')) \leq \delta_4$, with $d_{ham}(.,.)$ the Hamming distance and δ_4 a predetermined threshold, is in μ. Dependently on this fact, A_i^+ continues to work accordingly.

Algorithm A_1^+: A_1^+ randomizes its decision responses only on suitable inputs r. To this aim $A_1^+(r, k, \mu)$ works as follows on r:

i) if $h(r) \notin \mu$, then $A_1^+(r, k, \mu)$ works as $A(r, k)$ and then stores $h(r)$ in μ;
ii) if $h(r) \in \mu$, then stores $h(r)$ in μ and returns $A_1^+(r, k, \mu) = 0$ or $A_1^+(r, k, \mu) = 1$, randomly.

Algorithm A_2^+: A_2^+ honours the following temporal constraint where $|A_2^+(.,.,.)|_{Q_n}$ stands for the time duration of the response given by A_2^+ at the channel usage Q_n.

$$|A_2^+(r, k, \mu)|_{Q_{m+j}} > |A_2^+(r', k, \mu)|_{Q_m} \quad \text{if} \quad d_{ham}(h(r), h(r')) \leq \delta_4 \qquad (5)$$

for $j \geq 1$, $Q_m, Q_{m+j} \in \{Q_n\}$.

To this aim we extend the answers of A with a new prefix symbol $*$ which means *wait*. Algorithm $A_2^+(r, k, \mu) = a_2^+$, with $a_2^+ \in \{0, 1, *a\}$, where the prefix $*$ means that the answer expressed by the adjacent symbol a has been delayed, works as follows on r:

i) if $h(r) \notin \mu$, then $A_2^+(r, k, \mu)$ works as $A(r, k)$ and then stores $h(r)$ in μ;
ii) if $h(r) \in \mu$, then A_2^+ stores $h(r)$ in μ, then $A_2^+(r, k, \mu) = *a$, i.e. it works as $A(r, k)$ after $c > 1$ time units.

Algorithm A_3^+: A_3^+ works as A_2^+ and as A_1^+. This means that $A_3^+(r, k, \mu)$ works as follows on r:

i) if $h(r) \notin \mu$, then $A_3^+(r, k, \mu)$ works as $A(r, k)$ and then stores $h(r)$ in μ;

ii) if $h(r) \in \mu$, then $A_3^+(r, k, \mu) = *\underline{a}$, with $\underline{a} \in \{\underline{1}, \underline{0}\}$, stores $h(r)$ in μ and works as $A_1^+(r, k, \mu)$, i.e. $A_3^+(r, k, \mu) = 0$ or $A_3^+(r, k, \mu) = 1$ randomly, after $c > 1$ time units.

We point out that:

- Parameter c's values can be tuned to obtain the desired time delay, being $c = |*|$.

- A_1^+ generates also random binary sequences composed of $a_1^+ = \underline{a}$. We denote by $\underline{1}$, $\underline{0}$ numbers 1, 0, respectively, randomly generated. Although we here deal with random sequences, we do not detail about the chosen random/pseudo-random bit generation and allow different techniques to be possibly used by A_1^+.

- Let Δ represent the expected time interval during which an $h(r)$ remains in memory μ. Having memory μ a finite dimension, A_i^+ deletes an allocated $h(r)$ from its full hash table, by following a suitable strategy. Δ depends on the dimension of the hash table (which is secret). Each A_i^+ differs from A only on those signals r whose verification requests have been iterated within the expected time interval Δ.

- In a traditional hash function $h(.)$, in order to guarantee that it is difficult to find $y \neq x$ such that $h(y) = h(x)$, one bit modification in x forces modification of more than half of the bits in $h(x)$. Thus $h(.)$ is not *stable*, in the sense that even if y is obtained from x by a small change, $h(y)$ is very different from $h(x)$. Known cryptographic hash functions are not *stable*. It is nowadays widely recognized that also a notion of hashing is desired to be *stable* (e.g. the *perceptual hash functions* as reviewed in [7]).

Following for instance [1], choosing a random vector ran from the L-dimensional Gaussian distribution, where L is the common length of u and v, a hash function $h_{ran}(u)$ is defined as follows:

$$h_{ran}(u) = \begin{cases} 1 \text{ if } ran \cdot u \geq 0 \\ 0 \text{ if } ran \cdot u < 0 \end{cases}$$

where the product between ran and u is the scalar product. Let F be a family of stable *similarity preserving hash functions* $h_{ran}(.)$ in [1] with the following probability

$$P(h_{ran}(u) = h_{ran}(v)) = |1 - \frac{\theta(u, v)}{\pi}|$$

where the similarity function

$$sim(u, v) = |1 - \frac{\theta(u, v)}{\pi}| = \begin{cases} 1 \text{ if } u \text{ and } v \text{ are identical} \\ 0 \text{ if } u \text{ and } v \text{ are quite different} \end{cases} \tag{6}$$

with $\theta(u, v)$ the angle between u and v, maps a pair of vectors u, v in the interval $[0, 1]$. Since the output of each $h_{ran}(.) \in F$ is one bit, by concatenating the output of t such hash functions, the following hash composed of t bits

$$\begin{cases} h(u) = h_{ran_1}(u)\dots h_{ran_t}(u) \\ h(v) = h_{ran_1}(v)\dots h_{ran_t}(v) \end{cases}$$

are obtained.

For sake of simplicity, here we use the classical Hamming distance under a suitable threshold to deal with similarity of such binary strings. Thus similarity between u and v is finally measured.

We suppose that the error probability $P_e(h(u) = h(v)|u \neq v)$ is negligible as soon as $sim(u, v) > thr$, with thr a threshold value in $[0, 1]$.

- For a similarity preserving hash function $h(.)$, an hash table can be used to store its results such that vectors that are similar to vector u have their hashed values stored in a δ-*neighbor* of $h(u)$, with δ a predetermined value, as in Figure 3.

h(x)
h(y)
0
h(u)-δ
h(v)
h(u)
h(u)+δ
h(z)
0
0
...

Fig. 3. Typical hash table for a similarity preserving hash function h(.) with one similarity neighbor put in evidence in it as $(h(u) - \delta, h(u) + \delta)$

Each address in such a hash table is either empty, and then contains a null element, or contains a hash value obtained by $h(.)$. The dimension of the hash table has not to be large in order the hash table to be practical. The table can be seen as segmented into (possibly overlapping) similarity intervals. $h(r)$ is similar to all elements within the δ-*neighbor* of $h(u)$. $h(r)$ is mostly similar to the elements (at most two) having the minimal distance within the δ-*neighbor* of $h(u)$. If $h(.)$ maps most of the signals onto unique integers, i.e. the number of collisions is sufficiently small, an element $h(r)$ can be searched in $O(1)$ time. Otherwise collisions have to be handled in a standard way. We do not detail here on this subject matter.

4.2 Trade-off Between Attack Counteracting and Authentication Reliability

Let Re use an A_i^+, $i = 1, 2, 3$, instead of A, as a black box to perform the attack procedure we described in Section 2.1. Let α_i^+ be the obtained sequence instead of the sequence α obtained under A. If we suppose that each verification request by Re occurs within the interval Δ related to the hash table, α_i^+ is obtained from signals whose hashed versions are in the memory of A_i^+.

The following Propositions, whose proofs are only sketched, show that each A_i^+ determines the expected modification on the conditional mutual information in case of an oracle attack and does not practically change the authentication reliability of A in case no oracle attack occurs.

Proposition a - *Let w, r, α_i^+ and α be as previously defined.*
Under each algorithm A_i^+, $i = 1, 2, 3$, used as a black box during an oracle attack, the conditional mutual information $I(w; r|\alpha_i^+)$ through Q_o^+ is less than the conditional mutual information $I(w; r|\alpha)$ through Q_o.

<u>Proof sketch</u> - Let $A_i^+(r, k, \mu) = a_i^+$ with :

$$a_1^+ \in \{1, 0, \underline{1}, \underline{0}\}$$

$$a_2^+ \in \{1, 0, *a\}$$

$$a_3^+ \in \{1, 0, *\underline{a}\} \ .$$

In the following sequences

$$\alpha_{1,N}^+ = (1, 0, \underline{a}, \ldots, \underline{a}, \underline{a})$$

$$\alpha_{2,N}^+ = (1, 0, *0, \ldots, *0, *1)$$

$$\alpha_{3,N}^+ = (1, 0, *\underline{a}, , \ldots, *\underline{a}, *\underline{a})$$

the first element $1 = A_i^+(r, k, \mu) = A(r, k)$ is the answer on the integer signal r; the second element $0 = A_i^+(r_1, k, \mu) = A(r_1, k)$ is obtained on r_1 as in (2); the last element is obtained on r_N, that is on a signal significantly modified with respect to y.

The information discrimination $D(p(\alpha)//p(\alpha_i^+)) > 0$ compares α with α_i^+.

- A_1^+ has an error rate value greater than the error rate of A.

- A_2^+ has the same error rate A has, but the information rate of Q_2^+ is less than that of Q_2 because of the time duration $|a_2^+| = g(c) \cdot |\alpha|$, with $g(c) \geq c$ and c as in item ii) of the description of A_2^+. In fact, $R_{2,t}^+ < R_t$ because $\mu\{T^+\} > \mu\{T\}$, with $\mu\{T^+\}$ the average value of the random variable $T^+ = t_0^+, t_1^+, \ldots, t_N^+$, where each time duration t_n^+ includes the delay determined by $*$.

$$R_{2,t}^+ < C_{2,t}^+ = \max \frac{I(w; r|\alpha_2^+)}{\mu\{T^+\}} = \max \frac{H(w) - H(w|r, \alpha_2^+)}{\mu\{T^+\}} < C_t \ .$$

$Q_{2,o}^+$, the covert channel in Q_2^+, has a rate $R_{2,o,t}^+$ such that $R_{2,o,t}^+ < R_{o,t}$.
- A_3^+, like A_1^+, has a greater error rate than A and moreover decreases the information rate as A_2^+ does, i.e. $R_{3,o,t}^+ < R_{o,t}$.   □

On the other hand, for a signal that has to be authenticated and no oracle attack is being performed, there may be a hashed signal in the memory of A_i^+, $i = 1, 2, 3$, such that a match in the hash table is found. Thus the following *caveat* arises:
A_i^+, $i = 1, 2, 3$, might be less reliable than A on signals which are not modified because of an oracle attack.

Proposition b - *Let A_i^+, $i = 1, 2, 3$, be used as a black box to authenticate r without performing an oracle attack.*
The authentication reliability of A_i^+ and of A are practically the same, for every $i = 1, 2, 3$.

Proof sketch - Under the assumption that the error probability of the used hash function is negligible, each α_i^+ is a sequence obtained on signals very few of which have their hash versions that match with elements in the hash table of A_i^+. Then, for each $i = 1, 2, 3$, the information discrimination is quite small, i.e. it is such that $D(p(\alpha)//p(\alpha_i^+)) \sim 0$.
- A_2^+ has the same error rate of A. The error rates of A_1^+ and A_3^+ do not differ from the error rate of A significantly.
- Since A_2^+ and A_3^+ do not delay their decision answers on signals that are not already in their respective memory,

$$|\alpha_2^+| \sim |\alpha| \quad \text{and} \quad R_{2,t}^+ \sim R_t$$

as well as

$$|\alpha_3^+| \sim |\alpha| \quad \text{and} \quad R_{3,t}^+ \sim R_t$$

and for what concerns A_1^+,

$$|\alpha_1^+| = |\alpha| \quad \text{and} \quad R_{1,t}^+ = R_t.$$ □

5   Conclusion

In this paper, oracle attacks for watermarking schemes have been focused. A general formulation for an integrity verification watermarking scheme is exemplified. A covert channel turns out to be set up during an oracle attack, in a realistic communication channel from the authenticator to the attacker. Countermeasures to oracle attacks are then obtainable by modifying authentication algorithms into algorithms with a hash table memory which exploit random decision answers or delayed decision answers. Three algorithms are accordingly outlined such that they need neither interactive connections, typical of communication protocols, nor utilizing huge databases. An acceptable compromise between authentication reliability and enhanced security against oracle attacks can be achieved by using each of the proposed algorithms.

Acknowledgment. We thank an unknown Referee for useful comments.

References

1. M. Charikar. Similarity estimation techniques from rounding algorithms. In *Proceedings of STOC'02*, pages 380–388. ACM, May 2002.
2. M. E. Choubassi and P. Moulin. New sensitivity analysis attack In *Proceedings of International Symposium on Electronic Imaging, Security and Watermarking of Multimedia Contents VII*, pages 734–745. IS&T/SPIE, March 2005.
3. T. Cover and J. Thomas. *Elements of Information Theory*. John Wiley and Sons, New York, 1991.
4. I. Cox, M. Miller, and J. Bloom. *Digital Watermarking*. Morgan Kaufmann Pub., Academic Press, 2002.
5. T. Furon, I. Venturini, and P. Duhamel. An unified approach of asymmetric watermarking schemes. In *Proceedings of International Symposium on Electronic Imaging, Security and Watermarking of Multimedia Contents III*, pages 269–279. IS&T/SPIE, January 2001.
6. T. Kalker, J.-P. Linnartz, and M. van Dijk. Watermark estimation through detector analysis. In *Proceedings of ICIP'98*, pages 1:425–429. IEEE, October 1998.
7. T. Kalker, J. Haitsma and J. Oosteveen. Issues with digital watermarking and perceptual hashing. 2001.
8. J.-P. Linnartz and M. van Dijk. Analysis of the sensitivity attack against electronic watermarks in images. In *Proceedings of Workshop on Information Hiding*, pages 258–272, April 1998.
9. J. Millen. 20 years of covert channel modeling and analysis. In *Proceedings of Symposium on Security and Privacy*, pages 113–114. IEEE, May 1999.
10. I. Moskowitz and M. Kang. Covert channels - here to stay? In *Proceedings of COMPASS'94*, pages 235–243. IEEE, June-July 1994.
11. P. Moulin and J. O'Sullivan. Information-theoretic analysis of watermarking. In *Proceedings of ICASSP'00*. IEEE, June 2000.
12. P. Moulin and J. O'Sullivan. Information-theoretic analysis of information hiding. *IEEE Trans. on Information Theory*, 49(3):563–593, March 2003.
13. L. Perez-Freire, P. Comesana-Alfaro and F. Perez-Gonzales. Detection in quantization-based watermarking: performance and security issues. In *Proceedings of International Symposium on Electronic Imaging, Security and Watermarking of Multimedia Contents VII*, pages 721–733. IS&T/SPIE, March 2005.
14. G.J. Simmons. Subliminal channels; past and present. *European Trans. on Telecommunications*, 5(4): pages 459–473, July 1994.
15. A. Tewfik and M. Mansour. Secure watermark detection with non-parametric decision boundaries. In *Proceedings of ICASSP'02*, pages 2089–2092. May 2002.
16. I. Venturini. Counteracting oracle attacks. In *Proceedings of MM&Sec'04*, pages 187-192. ACM, September 2004.

Security of DM Quantization Watermarking Schemes: A Practical Study for Digital Images

Patrick Bas[1] and Jarmo Hurri[2]

[1] Laboratoire des Images et des Signaux de Grenoble , 961 rue de la Houille Blanche
Domaine universitaire, B.P. 46 38402, Saint Martin d'Hères cedex, France
Laboratory of Computer and Information Science, Helsinki University of Technology,
P.O. Box 5400, FI-02015 HUT, Finland
[2] Helsinki Institute for Information Technology, Basic Research Unit, P.O. Box 68,
FIN-00014 University of Helsinki Finland

Abstract. In this paper, the security of Dither Modulation Quantization Index Modulation schemes for digital images is analyzed. Both pixel and DCT coefficient quantization schemes are investigated. The related works that deal with the security of spread spectrum and quantization schemes are presented and their limits are outlined. The use of independent component analysis (ICA) for natural image is introduced. We show that ICA can be an efficient tool to estimate the quantization noise which is by definition independent of the host signal. We present both a method for estimating the carrier, and an attack that relies on the ICA decomposition of patches of images; our attack scheme is also compared with another classical attack. The results reported in this paper demonstrate how changes in natural image statistics can be used to detect watermarks and devise attacks. Such natural image statistics-based attacks may pose a serious threat against watermarking schemes which are based on quantization techniques.

1 Introduction

After ten years of active development by the watermarking scientific community, many of the proposed watermarking techniques are considered to be mature because they are robust while preserving the quality of the host data. However, if robustness and fidelity are mandatory requirements for an usable watermarking scheme, security is also a very important issue that is not very often addressed. Robustness commonly denotes an ability to decode the watermark after various operations such as compression, filtering, noise addition or geometric transforms. A scheme is considered secure if it is not possible to extract, remove or change the watermark[1][2]. Many watermarking schemes claim to be secure because they use a secret key during the embedding and detection process. However, this hypothesis is often too weak in real application scenarios and several security attacks have been already proposed based on for example a full access to the detection process [3], the use of a symmetric detection scheme [4], or information leakage when a database of hosts is watermarked using the same secret key[2].

M. Barni et al. (Eds.): IWDW 2005, LNCS 3710, pp. 186–200, 2005.

This paper focuses on the security of an important class of watermarking schemes based on quantization called Dither-Modulation (DM) Quantization. The contribution of this paper is to show how changes in natural image statistics can be used to detect watermarks and devise attacks against watermarking schemes. In general, watermarking may change the statistical properties of images, and this can be used to devise detection and attack schemes. Here we show how a method called Independent Component Analysis (ICA) can be used to separate the watermark component when DM Quantization has been used to watermark images. As demonstrated by the results of our paper, such natural image statistics-based attack schemes may pose a serious threat against watermarking schemes.

The rest of the paper is divided in five sections. First, principles of DM Quantization watermarking schemes are presented in section 2. Two different scenarios are presented: secrecy is either established by a secret location selection or by the use of a dither vector. In section 3, the solution proposed by Cayre *et. al* for the Dither-Modulation techniques based on spread transforms is presented, and its limitations with natural images are outlined. We also motivate the use of ICA as a tool to separate the watermark component from the features of the image. Decomposition of natural images into independent basis vectors is presented in section 4. Section 5 presents the two main ideas of the paper: the estimation and identification of the secret carrier and the attack that is used to remove the watermark. These two methods both use decomposition of image blocks into a basis of independent vectors. The performance of the presented scheme against other attacks in term of introduced distortion is also compared. Finally section 6 draws conclusions and gives directions of upcoming works.

2   DM Quantization Schemes

2.1   Principles of DM Quantization

The class of Quantization Index Modulation (QIM) watermarking schemes was first presented by Chen and Wornell [5]. The principle of the basic QIM technique is to embed a binary message $b(m)$ in an host sample x by applying a quantizer on a modified component to obtain the watermarked component x_w:

$$x_w(x; b) = q(x + d(b)) - d(b)$$

where $q(x)$ is a quantization function with a quantization step equal to Δ, and $d(b)$ is called the dither vector that is function of the transmitted bit b:

$$d(b = 1) = \begin{cases} d(b = 0) + \Delta/2 & \text{if} \quad d(b = 0) < 0 \\ d(b = 0) - \Delta/2 & \text{if} \quad d(b = 0) \geq 0 \end{cases}$$

One basic solution is to choose $d(b = 0) = 0$ which is equivalent to have a set of two disjoint quantizers where each quantizer has a quantization step equal to Δ and each quantization cell is distant from $\Delta/2$ with the closest one. Such

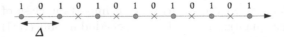

Fig. 1. Quantization grid obtained after applying QIM and a null dither component

embedding quantization grid is illustrated in Fig.1. The main problem of this basic and very simple embedding scheme is that it is public, consequently everybody can access to the watermarked components and decode the watermark once the quantization step Δ is known. Computing the pdf of the watermarked components, or in the practical case, a histogram allows one to estimate the parameter Δ. Two solutions have been used to achieve secrecy, either by taking a pseudo-random dither vector, or by selecting the watermarked coefficients at secret locations.

2.2 Secrecy by the Use of a Dither Vector

In [5] the authors propose to use a pseudo-random dither component $d(b = 0)$ that depends on a secret key (the seed of the random number generator for example). In this case, the scheme is the called QIM with Dither Modulation (DM). The dither sequence may for example represent a uniform distribution between $[-\Delta/2; \Delta/2]$. Under the hypothesis that the host signal is locally uniform around the quantization cell, the watermarked signal will stay uniform after the embedding. If we consider samples such as image pixels, the quasi-invariance of the pdf after DM-QIM embedding can also be presumed for smooth distributions and small quantization steps as illustrated on Fig.2. When considering the information available in the pdf, secrecy has then been achieved because the quantization cells are no more disclosed and it is not possible to access the watermarked components without knowing the dither sequence.

Howerver in this case, due to the quantization process, the embedding can be modelled as the addition of uniform noise between $[-\Delta/2; \Delta/2]$ (this property is true even if the dither component is null) and this noise is independent of the host signal. This last property, independence between the watermark signal and the host image, is the main idea of this paper.

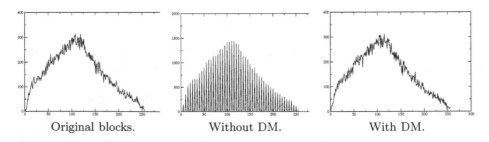

Original blocks.   Without DM.   With DM.

Fig. 2. Histograms of 40000 pixels randomly choosen from different images. After DM, the embedding cannot be observed.

2.3   Secrecy by Location Selection

Another simple way that is used to achieve secrecy in a number of watermarking schemes, including the QIM scheme, is to watermark only a set of selected coefficients of the host image. The selection can be done using a secret key that is used to generate the position of the embedded coefficients. Without this knowledge, the attacker will have to process all of the coefficients to perform a successful attack. This security measure can be of course combined with dither modulation.

2.4   Studied Practical Scenarios

This paper addresses both of the previous security measures but with different practical hypotheses. It is important to point out that we assume that the watermark is embedded in a block, and only one "component" of the block is watermarked using the DM-QIM algorithm. By the term "component" we mean either a pixel of the block (which is often the case when the location is secret) or a DCT coefficient of the DCT transform of the block (which can also be used for robust DM-QIM watermarking).

The "database and location" scenario: if secrecy is based on the position of the watermarked coefficients, we assume that we have a large collection of watermarked images that have been watermarked using the same secret key, which is equivalent to assume that for each host vector, the samples have been watermarked at the same locations. We also assume that the watermarked coefficients are randomly distributed in each host signal and that in one block of size $N \times N$ there is only zero or one watermarked coefficient. We call this the database and location scenario. The goal here is to find the position of the watermarked pixels (see Fig.3) by processing one block per image, each block being taken at the same location. When the location is found, we also aim to remove the watermark. Such a scenario can result from an entity using its private key to watermark all the images in its database.

The "one coefficient" per block scenario: in this case we assume that we have only one watermarked host image that is partitioned into blocks of size $N \times N$ and in each vector only one component is modified using DM-QIM. This scenario is for example used by watermarking schemes working in the JPEG compressed domain where only one coefficient is modified.

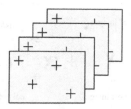

Fig. 3. Database and location scenario: our objective is to find the position of watermarked blocks considering a database of images

It is important to notice that these two scenarios provide similar outputs: in both cases we have to process a set of blocks of size $N \times N$, and the goal is to estimate the position of the watermarked coefficient and subsequently to remove the watermark.

3 Motivation

3.1 Related Research on Watermarking Security

A consequent work on watermarking security has been done by Cayre *et. al.*[2][6]. The authors have analyzed both the theoretical and practical securities of blind spread spectrum (BSS) watermarking schemes and quantization schemes. In this context the watermark is embedded using a set of pseudo random and orthogonal carriers (one carrier for each transmitted bit) that is modulated and added to the host signal. One part of the mentioned work is devoted to estimate the carriers using a collection of images that have been watermarked using the same carriers but different messages. The authors have expressed such a situation by the following equation:

$$\mathbf{Y} = \mathbf{X} + \alpha \mathbf{U} \mathbf{A}$$

where α is a scale proportional to the power of the watermark and the meaning of the other matrices $\mathbf{Y}$, $\mathbf{X}$, $\mathbf{U}$ and $\mathbf{A}$, that compose this equation is explained in Fig.4. Each image is considered as a realization of independent and identically distributed (iid) gaussian process. The authors have proposed to estimate the matrices $\mathbf{U}$ (the carriers) and $\mathbf{A}$ (the embedded messages) using only the matrix $\mathbf{Y}$ (the set of watermarked images) by using Independent Component Analysis [7]. In this case, the independent sources are given by the embedded messages that are supposed to be different in each watermarked image and therefore independent. Thus ICA is the appropriate tool to estimate both $\mathbf{U}$ and $\mathbf{A}$. The only limitation of this technique is the fact that both the decoded message and the carriers are estimated up to sign (or bit flipping), this is due to the ICA technique itself. If it is not possible to decode the watermark, it is however possible to remove it and the authors have successfully used this technique to remove watermarks embedded in images.

In [6] the authors have also proposed to deal with the case of one unique carrier and to apply their methodology on quantization schemes. Because independence can not be exploited anymore in this particular case, the authors

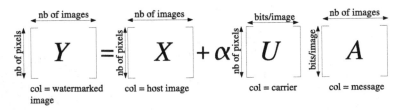

Fig. 4. Details of the model equation proposed by Cayre *et. al.* to model BSS watermarking for a database of images

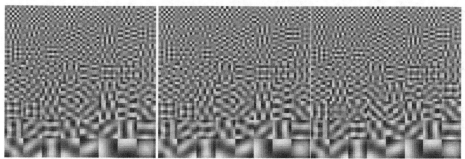

Principal components of original blocks.   Principal components of watermarked blocks, spatial embedding.   Principal components of watermarked blocks, DCT embedding.

Fig. 5. PCA basis vectors for 20000 original and watermarked image blocks. For spatial embedding, the embedding is done on one pixel of each 8×8 block and the resulting PSNR is equal to 51.1dB. For DCT embedding, the embedding is done on the coefficient (5,5) and the resulting PSNR is equal to 43.8dB. No difference is noticeable between the three sets, only several principal components have been displayed with an opposite signe.

propose to use classical principal component analysis (PCA) to estimate the carrier. PCA is a method that estimates *principal components*, i.e., uncorrelated components along which the data has variance optima (including the components with the largest and smallest variances)[7]. Considering the host as an iid process, the principal component of the host should be negligible in comparizon with the component given by the carrier.

However in practice the assumption of an iid host is not realistic in the case of natural images when the carrier has the size of a small block (8x8, 16x16, 32x32). For small patches of natural images, the host can not be modelled by and iid process and the PCA give high energies components looking like a DCT basis (cf Fig.5). Consequently the carrier can not be estimated using PCA on small image blocks.

3.2   Carrier Estimation and Blind Source Separation

Estimating and removing a carrier can be seen has a blind source separation problem where one might have a decomposition of the watermarked image into two subspaces: one representing the watermark and an other one representing the features of the original images. This paper proposes to estimate the secret carrier by exploiting the fact that the carrier is statistically independent of the features of natural images. This property enables firstly to use the decomposition in independent vectors to estimate the secret carrier and secondly to design an attack by processing the independent signal related to the watermark. The next section introduces the model that is used to generate a basis of independent vectors from blocks of images.

4   Independent Basis Vectors of Natural and Watermarked Images

4.1   Estimation of Independent Basis Vectors

Independent component analysis has been proposed to be used as a generative model of image data [7]. In this model each image block $\mathbf{x}$ can be expressed as a linear combination of independent components referred as the source signals $\{s_i\}$:

$$\mathbf{x} = \mathbf{As} = \sum_i \mathbf{a}_i s_i$$

where $\mathbf{A}$ is a constant matrix called the mixing matrix and the vector $\mathbf{a}_i$ denotes the ith column of $\mathbf{A}$. These vectors are called the features or basis vectors. The decomposition of images patches (blocks) into independent basis vectors has been widely used for both image processing and computational modeling of the visual system. The independent basis vectors are similar to edge and lines detectors; neurons performing similar feature detection have been found in the mammalian visual system[8]. Moreover, because in natural image data the distribution of basis vectors is often sparse, the decomposition of images into independent components has also been used for image denoising [9] and image coding [10]. ICA techniques can be used to estimate the mixing matrix $\mathbf{A}$ from a set of N image blocks $\{\mathbf{x}_1, ..., \mathbf{x}_N\}$ (which are unfolded into vectors) using the matrix formulation:

$$\mathbf{X} = \mathbf{AS}$$

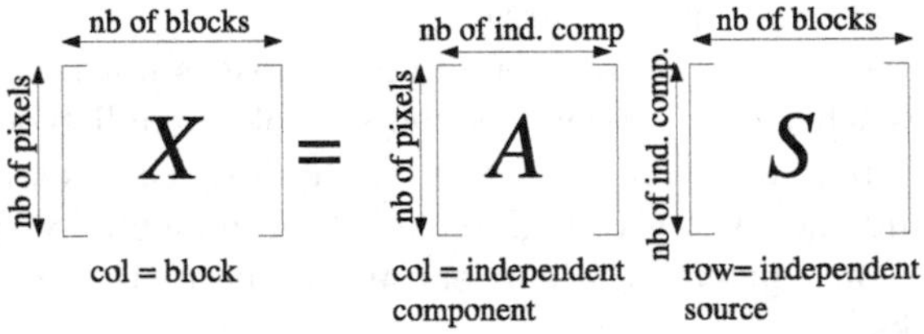

Fig. 6. Details of the equation used for computing independent basis vectors based on images patches

For purpose of illustration each term of this equation is explained in Fig.6. The estimation of the matrices $\mathbf{X}$ and $\mathbf{A}$ can be performed using different ICA algorithms; we have decided to use FastICA because this algorithm achieves good performance both in computational cost and reliability of the extracted basis vectors [7]. An example of a set of ICA basis vectors obtained from 8×8 blocks of natural images is given in Fig.7. Verbally, these basis vectors are typically described as localized, oriented and band-pass filters.

Fig. 7. A complete set of 64 ICA basis vectors, computed from 20000 8×8 pixel samples taken from natural images

4.2 Independent Basis Vectors for Watermarked Images

The main idea of this paper is to use the decomposition of blocks of images into independent basis vectors to estimate the secret carrier that has been used during DM-QIM watermarking. Note that if the image has been watermarked in the pixel domain, the carrier corresponds to the position of the quantized pixel, and if the image has been watermarked in the DCT domain, the carrier then corresponds to a representation of a DCT basis in the pixel domain. Because these carriers are related to the quantization noise, and we can assume that the

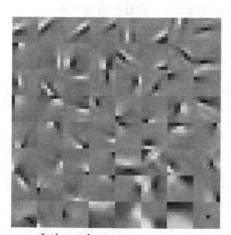
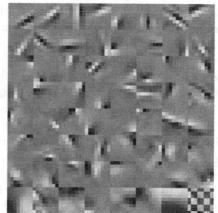

Independent components of   Independent components of
watermarked blocks in the pixel domain. watermarked blocks in the DCT domain.

Fig. 8. ICA outputs for 8 × 8 watermarked blocks. ICA is able to estimate the secret carrier, located at the bottom right block in each set of vectors.

quantization noise in independent of the other independent basis vectors, we can estimate the carriers using independent component analysis.

Fig.8 illustrates the capability of ICA to estimate the secret carrier for both the pixel and DCT DM-QIM. In the pixel domain embedding, we have watermarked the central pixel of 20 000 blocks taken from natural images; the resulting PSNR after the embedding was 51.1dB. The estimation of the basis vectors by FastICA using the tanh nonlinearity[11] shows that the secret carrier has been detected in the basis vector that is located on the bottom right of the set of patches. The same test has been completed for DCT embedding. For illustration purposes, we have chosen to watermark the (4,4) coefficient. The resulting PSNR is equal to 43.8 dB. As illustrated in Fig. 8, the spatial representation of this DCT component is also clearly identified on the bottom right corner of the set of basis vectors.

5   Estimating and Removing the Watermark

The goal of this section is to present a simple scheme to automatically identify the secret carrier and to remove the associated watermark.The estimation of the carrier relies on the decomposition in a basis of independent vectors, as described in the previous section. The removal of the watermark is performed by processing the independent component related to the watermark and applying the mixing operation to generate the attacked image.

5.1   Carrier Estimation

Estimation of a secret carrier is a necessary step to perform a successful attack. The carrier will be estimated as a vector that is included in the set of basis vectors obtained using an ICA algorithm. Note that the proposed method estimates the carrier without any a-priori information about the nature of the transformed coefficient.

Detection criterium: We firt need to select the carrier from the set of basis vectors obtained using the ICA algorithm, e.g. the columns of the mixing matrix **A**. Using the deflationary algorithm which works by estimating the independent vectors one by one, the carrier is extracted ias one of the last estimated vectors. This property is due to the fact that the watermark is the 'least nongaussian' of the independent components, as measured by the objective function maximized by the ICA algorithm. Consequently we have decided to choose the basis vector related to the carrier by taking into account the negentropy of its related component. Negentropy of a source **x** is the difference between the entropy of a gaussian source and the entropy of the considered source. It is given by $J(\mathbf{x}) = H(\mathbf{x}_{gauss}) - H(\mathbf{x})$. The negentropy of subgaussian component is lower than the negentropy of the components of natural images which are sparse and have an large negentropy. Consequently, we select the vector with the lowest negentropy as the estimate of the carrier.

Table 1. Mean Square Error between the estimated and true carrier as a function of the watermarked DCT coefficient ($\Delta = 200$)

Coeff	(1,1)	(2,2)	(3,3)	(4,4)
MSE	0.0209	0.0216	0.0047	0.0037

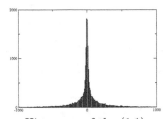

Histogram of the (1;1)
DCT component, original image.

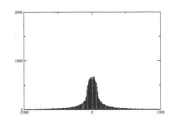

Histogram of the (1;1)
DCT component, watermarked image.

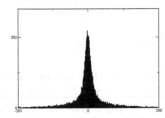

Histogram of the (4,4)
DCT component, original image.

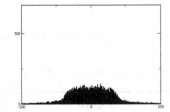

Histogram of the (4,4)
DCT component, watermarked image.

Fig. 9. Histograms of original DCT coefficients and watermarked coefficients ($\Delta = 200$). The subgaussianity is more pronounced for the high frequency component (4,4) than for the low frequency one (1,1) .

Using this criterion, we have noticed that, in the case of the DCT embedding, this estimation of the carrier gives a low estimation error for high frequency components, but gives an high estimation error for low frequency components (see Table 9). This is due to the fact that, for low pass components, the energy of the watermark is too small in comparison with the energy of the host component (see Fig.1). This problem is only present when the embedding is done in a low-frequency DCT coefficient; the selection criterion is successful for pixel embedding and high-frequency DCT embedding.

Improvements using pre-filtering of the DCT components: To improve the estimation of the carrier when the embedding is done using a carrier which has low-frequency component, we have reduced the impact of DCT coefficients having high values by only considering coefficients that are under a given threshold (for example Δ). This operation consists of computing the DCT coefficient of each blocks, zeroing the DCT coefficients that are above the threshold, and

Table 2. Mean Square Error between the estimated and true carrier when the pre-filtering of DCT component is used. The DM algorithm was applied to different DCT components (as denoted by column heading in the table).

Coeff	(1,1)	(2,2)	(3,3)	(4,4)
MSE	0.0009	0.0015	0.0015	0.0014

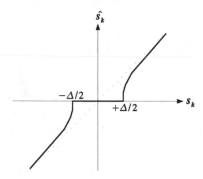

Fig. 10. Shape of the used shrinkage function

finally computing the inverse DCT transform of the block before applying the ICA algorithm using the whole set of blocks. Consequently ICA is performed considering only the centre of the distributions of the DCT coefficients, where difference between the original and watermarked component is the most important. Such a pre-filtering technique enables us to achieve low estimations errors (cf. Table 2).

5.2   Removing the Watermark

Once the carrier $\mathbf{a}_k$ that has been used to convey the watermark has been estimated, we have access to the communication channel. It is then possible to design a specific attack to reduce as much as possible the quantization noise produced in DM-QIM and to destroy the watermark. If we denote with $\mathbf{s}_k$ the kth row of matrix $\mathbf{S}$, $\mathbf{s}_k$ contains all the information that is related to the watermark vector. One straightforward way to remove the watermark is to simply reset $\mathbf{s}_k$. However, if we consider that the component $\mathbf{s}_k$ may contain image information especially for heavy textured patches, we may apply a softer function by keeping high values. This leads to the application of a shrinkage function to each sample of the vector $\mathbf{s}_k$. The used function is depicted in Fig.10; and similar functions have been used for image denoising applications [12] or blind watermarking removal [13]. Our watermark identification and removal procedure can be summarized as follows:

- Build the **X** matrix from the set of watermarked image blocks (each block in a column of **X**).

- Using FastICA, compute **A** and **S** such as $\mathbf{X} = \mathbf{AS}$.
- Estimate the watermark carrier $\mathbf{a}_k$ and the related source $\mathbf{s}_k$.
- Modify $\mathbf{s}_k$ using a shrinkage function to obtain $\hat{\mathbf{s}}_k$.
- Substitute $\mathbf{s}_k$ by $\hat{\mathbf{s}}_k$ to obtain $\hat{\mathbf{S}}$.
- Compute the matrix $\mathbf{X}_a = \mathbf{A}\hat{\mathbf{S}}$ that represents the attacked set of blocks.

5.3 Attack Performance

The goal of this section is to evaluate the performance of the presented denoising attack as a function of the number of observed watermarked blocks. To test the denoising quality we have computed the PSNR between the original and watermarked image and the PSNR between the original and attacked image. We have also computed the resulting Bit Error Rate relative to the attack. For purposes of comparison we have also calculated the PSNR after a straightforward attack that consists of adding $\pm(\Delta/4 + \epsilon)$ on several watermarked coefficients to achieve the same BER. The principle of this attack is to move quantized coefficient just to border of the quantization cell that code the opposed bit as illustrated in Fig.11.

The results are depicted in Table 3. Both pixel domain and DCT domain DM-QIM embedding have been tested. For the DCT embedding, the coefficient (4,4) has been watermarked ((0,0) is the DC coefficient). Due to the fact that the modification of a DCT coefficient affects the whole block, the distortion introduced by the DCT embedding is larger (PSNR=42.8dB) than for embedding in the pixel domain (PSNR=50.9dB). In both cases, the denoising attack is able to increase the PSNR between the attacked and original image in comparison with the PSNR between the watermarked and original image. This means that the power of the watermark has been decreased, and corresponds to a reliable estimation of the watermark component. These results highlight the fact that the estimation error of the secret carrier $\mathbf{a}_k$ and also the independent source $\mathbf{s}_k$ (which depends on the estimation of all the basis vectors) depends on the number of observations which is here represented by the number of blocks that is used to build the matrix **X**. A gain of 2dB for the PSNR can be achieved using 19000 blocks instead of 1200. Comparison of the presented denoising attack against the moving attack confirms the superiority of independent source estimation in comparison with this additive blind attack which always yields to a PSNR that is above the PSNR between the original and watermarked image.

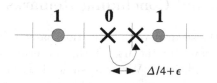

Fig. 11. Principle of the moving attack

Table 3. Denoising performance as a function of different number of blocks

	Pixel domain				DCT domain			
Initial PSNR	50.9 dB				42.8 dB			
	Denoising attack		Moving attack		Denoising attack		Moving attack	
Nb of blocks	BER	PSNR	BER	PSNR	BER	PSNR	BER	PSNR
19000	37%	54.4dB	37%	49.6dB	41%	46.1dB	41%	40.3dB
4800	42%	53.9dB	42%	49.3dB	43%	45.7dB	43%	40.2dB
1200	40%	52.3dB	40%	49.2dB	37%	44.3dB	37%	40.8dB

5.4 Remarks on the Security of DCT Quantization Schemes

In this section, the ability to erase the watermark is studied as a function of the position of the watermarked DCT coefficient. We have applied the watermark removal procedure has described previously, for different positions of the DCT coefficient. The resulting distortion between the attacked and original image is illustrated in Table 4. As a general rule, the efficiency of the proposed attack is lower for the low-frequency coefficient than for the high-frequency ones. For example, if the coefficient (1,0) is watermarked, the PSNR is only 34.1 dB vs. 46.5dB for an embedding in the coefficient (3,3). Such a result is due to the fact that low frequency coefficients convey more information in natural images than high-frequency ones. Consequently it is more difficult to separate the information relative to the image and to the watermark in the first case. This remarks confirms the motivation given in [14] which suggests to watermark low-frequency components for security purposes. Nevertheless it is also important to point out that a compromise between the security and the perceptibility has to be considered by the embedder: the perturbation of low-frequency DCT coefficients produce a more significant impact of the visual system than high frequency ones.

Table 4. Attack performance for different coefficients (4800 blocks, PSNR=45.29 dB, $\Delta = 150$)

Coeff	(0,1)	(1,0)	(0,2)	(1,1)	(2,0)	(1,2)	(2,1)	(0,3)	(2,2)	(1,3)	(3,0)	(3,1)	(2,3)	(3,2)	(3,3)
PSNR	34.1	35.9	38.9	39.1	40.3	41.5	42.6	42.7	43.7	43.9	44.3	44.8	45.2	45.6	46.5

6   Future Work and Concluding Remarks

This paper addresses the security of quantization-based schemes which are supposed to be secure because of the use of the dithering vector and/or secret location of quantized coefficients. We have show that, under several hypothesis (natural images where one coefficient per block has been watermarked, small blocks) it is possible to estimate the secret carrier. Because Principal Component Analysis is not a suitable tool in this case, we have proposed to use Independent Component Analysis (ICA) to estimate the secret carrier and then to perform a removing attack. This is due to the fact that the DM-QIM watermarking process can be seen as the addition of an independent uniform noise that can be extracted using ICA. We have also outlined that the ability to separate the watermark from the original image increases as a function of the position of the DCT coefficient and as a function of the number of processed blocks.

In the future, we would like to see if such an approach can be used for other popular substitutive schemes working in the DCT domain such as the scheme proposed by [15]. In general, we expect that attacks utilizing the statistics of natural images will play an important role in the security of image watermarking schemes.

Acknowledgments

The work described in this paper has been supported (in part) by the European Commission through the IST Programme under Contract IST-2002-507932 ECRYPT, the National French project Fabriano and by the Academy of Finland (project # 205742).

References

1. Kalker, T.: Considerations on watermarking security. In: Proc. of MMSP, Cannes, France (2001) 201–206
2. Cayre, F., Fontaine, C., Furron, T.: Watermarking security part I: Theory. In: Proceedings of SPIE, Security, Steganography and Watermarking of Multimedia Contents VII. Volume 5681., San Jose, USA (2005)
3. Kalker, T.: A security risk for publicly available watermark detectors. In: Proc. Benelux Inform. Theory Symp., Veldhoven, The Netherlands (1998)
4. Furon, T., Duhamel, P.: An asymmetric watermarking method. IEEE Trans. on Signal Processing 51 (2003) 981–995 Special Issue on Signal Processing for Data Hiding in Digital Media and Secure Content Delivery.
5. Chen, B., Wornell, G.W.: Quantization index modulation: A class of provably good methods for digital watermarking and information embedding. IEEE Transactions on Information Theory 47 (2001) 1423–1443
6. Cayre, F., Fontaine, C., Furron, T.: Watermarking security part II: Practice. In: Proceedings of SPIE, Security, Steganography and Watermarking of Multimedia Contents VII. Volume 5681., San Jose, USA (2005)
7. Hyvärinen, A., Karhunen, J., Oja, E.: Independent Component Analysis. John Wiley & Sons (2001)
8. van Hateren, J.H., Ruderman, D.L.: Independent component analysis of natural image sequences yields spatiotemporal filters similar to simple cells in primary visual cortex. Proc. Royal Society B (1998) 2315–2320
9. Hyvärinen, A.: Sparse code shrinkage: Denoising of nongaussian data by maximum likelihood estimation. Neural Computation 11 (1999) 1739–1768
10. J.Ferreira, A., Figueiredo, M.: Class-adapted image compresion using independent component analysis. In: Proc. ICIP, Barcelona (2003)
11. Hyvärinen, A.: Fast and robust fixed-point algorithms for independent component analysis. IEEE Transactions on Neural Networks 10 (1999) 626–634

12. Hyvärinen, A., Hoyer, P.O., Oja, E.: Sparse code shrinkage: Denoising by nonlinear maximum likelihood estimation. In: Proc. of Advances in Neural Information Processing Systems 11 (NIPS*98). (1999) 473–479
13. Voloshynovskiy, S., Pereira, S., Herrigel, A., Baumgärtner, N., Pun, T.: Generalized watermark attack based on watermark estimation and perceptual remodulation. In Wah Wong, P., Delp, E.J., eds.: EI'2000: Security and Watermarking of Multimedia Content II. Volume 3971 of SPIE Proceedings., San Jose, California USA (2000) 358–370
14. Cox, I., Killian, J., Leighton, T., Shamoon, T.: Secure spread sprectrum watermarking for images, audio and video. In: Int. Conf. on Image Processing (ICIP). Volume 3., IEEE (1996) 243–246
15. Zhao, J., Koch, E.: Embedding robust labels intro images for copyright protection. In: Int. Congress on Intellectual Property Rights for Specialized Information, Knowledge and New Technologies, Vienne, Autriche (1995)

A Survey of Watermarking Security

Teddy Furon*

TEMICS project, INRIA Campus de Beaulieu, 35042 Rennes, France
teddy.furon@irisa.fr

Abstract. Digital watermarking studies have always been driven by the improvement of robustness. Most of articles of this field deal with this criterion, presenting more and more impressive experimental assessments. Some key events in this quest are the use of spread spectrum, the invention of resynchronization schemes, the discovery of side information channel, and the formulation of the opponent actions as a game.

On the contrary, security received little attention in the watermarking community. This paper presents a comprehensive overview of this recent topic. We list the typical applications which requires a secure watermarking technique. For each context, a threat analysis is purposed. This presentation allows us to illustrate all the certainties the community has on the subject, browsing all key papers. The end of the paper is devoted to what remains not clear, intuitions and future studies.

1 Introduction

Watermarking is the art of hiding metadata in content in a robust manner. 'Hiding' has unfortunately many meanings. Some understand that the embedding of metadata doesn't cause any perceptual distortion. Watermarking is then the art of creating a communication channel inside a piece of content without spoiling its entertainment. Others cast a security requirement in the word 'hiding'. This surprisingly happened at the very beginning of the digital watermarking story.

1.1 Historical Point of View

This very early relationship between security and watermarking might be explained from a historical perspective. In the analog age, content was protected by copyright laws included in intellectual property treaties dating back from the 50's [1]. There was a balance between conflicting issues like the copyright holders interests and the user-friendly usage of content. The digital age and the merging of formats from the entertainment and computer industries broke this balance in the 90's, spoiling copyright holders. Technical barriers have been created to enforce the copyright laws[1]. As cryptography leaves insecure protected content once decrypted by users, a recent technology named digital watermarking was

---

* This work is partially funded by the national ACI project FABRIANO.
[1] Technical barriers have been existing for a longer time, but the 90's have seen the generalization of their use, especially with DRM (Digital Right Management).

M. Barni et al. (Eds.): IWDW 2005, LNCS 3710, pp. 201–215, 2005.

perceived as the last line of defense. It allows to firmly bound content with metadata such as the copyright holder identity (copyright protection [2]) or the copy status (copy protection [3]). At that time, the naïve rationale was: "If you can't see it, and if it is not removed by common processing, then it must be secure".

Unfortunately, digital watermarking was too young a science to support such an adventurous assertion. The technique was even lacking sufficient robustness to fulfill the requirements of these first applications. Defeats happened very soon [4], so that the watermarking community envisaged applications where security is not an issue (e.g. content enhancement). On the front of copyright and copy protection, new laws has been promoted in the 2000's forbidding the circumvention of DRM system [1]. In a way, this new legal framework patches the security flaws of technical barriers, including digital watermarking. There are now three walls of defense: new laws protect the technical barriers which protect the enforcement of old copyright law which protect content's use and exploitation. On the other hand, absolute security does not exist (not even in cryptography) and a high security level has a cost which nobody wants to pay for (copyright holders, device manufacturers, users?). The goal of the entertainment industry is not to erase piracy but to maximize their incomes. To this end, weak security is better than no security [5], and a slightly secure but cheap protection system is enough to "keep honest people honest".

This historical point of view shows that security of digital watermarking has clearly lost interest in real life applications. However, it becomes a hot issue in the watermarking community [6,7]. We believe that researchers have stretched the limit of robustness to almost its maximum so that new attacks pertain more to security than classical robustness. Because a secure but non robust watermarking technique would be useless, robustness is the weakest link and it was the priority to be fixed. Huge improvements have been done in this field, and security now appears as the next issue on the list. Even if it is less important for real applications, it is also theoretically challenging because very few certainties are known about watermarking security.

1.2   Elements to Define Security

Does a short and concise definition of watermarking security exist? This question stems from two facts: watermarking security has different implications according the targeted application, and security is too close to robustness to be clearly distinguished [8]. Note that, so far, we have discussed about security understanding it as security of robust watermarking. It is time now to broaden our scope.

In copy protection, copyright protection and fingerprinting, we need to assess that dishonest users cannot remove the watermark signal. However, note that in copy protection, a pirate should not be able to change content status to a less restrictive one (e.g., from 'Copy Never' to 'Copy Once')[3]. In fingerprint, a collusion (group of pirates) should not frame an innocent user, i.e. they should not change their hidden message into the identifier of an honest user [9]. In copyright protection, an author should not copy and paste his watermark (possibly issued by a trusted third party) in content he didn't create [10]. In authentication, the goal of the pirate is not to remove the authenticating watermark signal but to sign content in place of the secret key holder [11]. In steganography[2], the pirate does not remove watermark signal but detects the presence of hidden data, and the watermarking technique used for it [12].

This suggests criteria to make a clear cut between robustness and security:

Intention. In security, there obviously exists a pirate. In robustness, a classical content processing made without any malicious intention, might delude the watermark decoder.

General. Robustness usually considers classical content processing. In security, pirates apply malicious attacks dedicated to one watermarking technique.

Removal. In robustness, the effect of the attack is to mure the watermarking decoder. The attack succeeds in removing enough watermarking energy or it has desynchronized the embedder and the decoder. In security, we have seen that pirates' goals are different according to the targeted application.

Number of steps. In robustness, the pirate applies a processing to the watermarked piece of content. This is a single step process. In security, the pirate observes several watermarked pieces of content. He gains from these observations some information about the watermarking technique and the secret key in use. Then, with this 'stolen' knowledge, he attacks protected content. This is a two-step process. Some say the pirate is not fair, in the sense that he is not contented with the official instruction (e.g. the watermarking technique according to the Kerckhoffs' principle), but he tries to access all the information which may be of any help for his goal (e.g. the secret key) [13, Sect. 2].

Probability of success. In robustness, an attack is usually not always successful, but it leads to a given Bit Error Rate (decoding) or probability of a miss (detection). In security, a successful hack is almost granted when the pirate has an accurate estimation of the secret key (if this is his goal).

However, T. Kalker formulated very elegant definitions of robustness and security [14, Sect. 2]. These may not encompass all cases, but they are the only concise attempts we are aware of. *"Robust watermarking is a mechanism to create a communication channel that is multiplexed into original content [...]. It is required that, firstly, the perceptual degradation of the marked content [...] is minimal and, secondly, that the capacity of the watermark channel degrades as a smooth function of the degradation of the marked content. [...]. Watermarking security refers to the inability by unauthorized users to have access to the raw watermarking channel. [...] to remove, detect and estimate, write or modify the raw watermarking bits."*

2   Theories of Watermarking Security

This section deals with the recent attempts to fund a theory of watermark security. What is the role of this theory? Before its existence, the security assessment

---

[2] We only consider passive steganography in this paper.

of a watermarking technique was fuzzy in the sense that the analysts had to think about an attack and to see how dangerous it was. In other words, the security assessment was clearly dependent on the cleverness of the analysts. Maybe, later on, one will discover a more powerful attack which will lower the security level of the watermarking technique. In a way, the role of a watermarking security theory is to assess the security level once for all.

2.1   Steganography

Steganography was the first field in data hiding to benefit from a theory of security. This happens very early in 1998-99 compared to robust watermarking.

The first attempt was made by C. Cachin and it is the most famous theory of steganography security [15]. In steganography, the attacker's goal is to detect a hidden communication in content Z that Alice sends to Bob. This job is a hypothesis test: either the piece of content is a stego-content ($\mathcal{H}_1 : Z = Y$), either it is a natural image ($\mathcal{H}_0 : Z = X$). Performances of the test are measured by the probability of false alarm P_{fa} (i.e. probability of wrongly accusing Alice) and the power of the test P_p (i.e. probability of rightly accusing Alice). An efficient test yields $P_p \sim 1$ for $P_{fa} \sim 0$. However, whatever the structure of the test, its performances are limited by the discrimination between the statistics of Y and of X. This is stated by the data processing theorem [16, Th. 4.4.1]:

$$D_{KL}(p_X, p_Y) \geq D_{KL}(P_{fa}, P_p) \geq 0 \qquad (1)$$

where $D_{KL}(.,.)$ is the Kullback-Leibler distance (aka discrimination or relative entropy). For instance, if Alice succeeds to produce stego-content Y statistically similar to original content X (i.e. pdf p_X and p_Y are identical almost everywhere but possibly on sets of zero p_X-probability), then $D_{KL}(p_X, p_Y) = 0$, which implies $P_{fa} = P_p$. The test is null because it is equivalent of a random decision discarding the observation for flipping a coin to take the decision. If the coin is not biased, this yields $P_{fa} = P_p = 0.5$. C. Cachin argues that if Alice is able to show that $D_{KL}(p_X, p_Y) < \epsilon$, then she limits the performances of the attacker, whatever his test. For $\epsilon = 0$, we have unconditional security. This rationale was applied to build stego-systems with ϵ as small as possible in papers [17,18].

The second attempt was made by T. Mittelholzer and it surprisingly remains unknown [19]. The security is related to the amount of information about the stego-message M that leaks from the stego-content Y when ignoring the secret key. This amount is measured by the mutual information $I(M;Y)$. Perfect steganography (or unconditional security) is achieved when $I(M;Y) = 0$. Examples of such schemes are given in [19, Sect. 3].

2.2   Robust Watermarking

The theory of robust watermarking security, when successfully applied, gives a lower bound on the secret key estimation accuracy depending on the figure of observed contents. Assume that the pirate knows the watermarking technique except the secret key (i.e., assuming the Kerckhoff's principle). The core idea is that pirates observing watermarked content can derive some knowledge about the secret key. In other words, information about secret parameters leaks from one watermarked content. This amount of leakage is certainly very small. Yet, if pirates observe many pieces of content watermarked with the same key, each of them leaking some information, then their knowledge increase. It reaches a point where an accurate estimation of the secret key allows powerful attacks.

This magnitude of order defines in a way the security level of the watermarking technique as a number of contents: if one watermarks with the same secret key more pieces of content than allowed by the security level, then a pirate can disclose this later one. As the pirate cannot extract more information about the secret than foreseen by the theory, this guarantees a lower bound.

These recent attempts setting a theoretical framework for watermarking security analysis are indeed the adaptation of the fundamental work of C.E. Shannon, which is considered as the theoretical basis of cryptanalysis [20]. There is nothing new here except the adaptation. Ideas of this adaptation work firstly appeared in [21, Sect. 2.6], [22, Sect. 4.1.1]. The key idea of this theory is to measure this amount of information leakage. Shannon mutual information [23, Sect. 3][24, Sect. 3] or Fisher information matrix [23, Sect. 4] are tools used for this purpose. We will not address the differences between this two tools (see [24, Sect. 2]). There are pros and cons, and even other ways to measure information (Kullback Leibler distance or Renyi information [25]), and also relations between them [26]. What is of utmost importance is that the measurement tool provide a physical interpretation.

The physical interpretation in the Shannon paradigm links the mutual information with the equivocation [20, Sect. 12]. This term is a synonym for the uncertainty or ignorance the pirate has about the secret key. It is measured by the entropy of secret key, regarding it as a random variable:

$$h(K|\mathbf{Y}^{N_o}) = h(K) - I(K; \mathbf{Y}^{N_o}). \qquad (2)$$

The watermarker has selected a technique and a secret key, the pirate knows the technique but not the key K. Entropy $h(K)$ measures the a priori equivocation, which is the amount of uncertainty before the game starts. The watermarker has produced N_o watermarked pieces of content $\mathbf{Y}^{N_o} = \{\mathbf{Y}_1, \ldots, \mathbf{Y}_{N_o}\}$, each of them leaking some information. Entropy $h(K|\mathbf{Y}^{N_o})$ is the a posteriori equivocation, the amount of uncertainty when the game has started: The total information leakage is $I(K; \mathbf{Y}^{N_o}) \geq 0$. We see that the a posteriori equivocation decreases thanks to the total leakage. A watermarking technique is perfectly secure if $I(K; \mathbf{Y}^{N_o}) = 0$: The pirate will never improve his knowledge about K, whatever the figure of produced watermarked pieces of content.

The physical interpretation provided by the Fisher information $FIM(K, \mathbf{Y}^{N_o})$ is less theoretical. It is given by the Cramer-Rao Bound, which states that whatever the unbiased estimator $\hat{K}$ of the secret key, its accuracy is bounded by[3]:

---

[3] For simplicity reason, we explain here the CRB in the scalar case.

$$\sigma_K^2 \geq \mathrm{FIM}(K, \mathbf{Y}^{N_o})^{-1}. \tag{3}$$

The smaller the leakage $\mathrm{FIM}(K, \mathbf{Y}^{N_o})$ is, the less accurate is the estimator.

2.3 Contextual Studies

C. Shannon gives a theory of encryption security where the attacker observes cipher texts. This describes what might happen in military communication. However, in the 70's, cryptography broadens its activities to different fields such as the security of financial transactions. In these new applications, the attacker might not only access cipher texts. At that time, Diffie and Hellman suggest to encompass different contexts in the security level assessment [27, Sect. 2]. These contexts are classified according to the type of observations.

The same terminology was applied in watermarking because this tool is used in many different applications leading to different contexts of attack [22, Sect. 3.3]. All we have to do is to replace $\mathbf{Y}^{N_o}$ by $\mathbf{O}^{N_o}$, where $\mathbf{O}$ is an observation: Watermarked Only Attack ($\mathbf{O} = \mathbf{Y}$), Known Original Attack ($\mathbf{O} = \{\mathbf{Y}, \mathbf{X}\}$), Estimated Original Attack ($\mathbf{O} = \{\mathbf{Y}, \hat{\mathbf{X}}\}$), Known Message Attack ($\mathbf{O} = \{\mathbf{Y}, \mathbf{M}\}$). This list is absolutely not closed nor exhaustive. Some other ideas can be:

- Chosen Watermarked Attack: This is another name for the sensitivity attack. The pirate has a sealed watermark detector. His goal is to disclose the secret key inside by feeding it with chosen contents while noting the output. The observations in this attack are pairs of content and detection output.
- Chosen Original Attack: The pirate has a sealed watermark embedder. His goal is to disclose the secret key inside by feeding it with chosen original contents and saving the watermarked version. The observations here are pairs of original and watermarked content (with the hidden messages).
- Single Original, Multiple Watermarked Attack: This tackles the threat in fingerprinting application: collusion. One original piece of content is watermarked several times with different hidden messages. A collusion of c pirates shares their version noticing differences. Observations are c-tuples watermarked contents.
- Multiple Original, Multiple Watermarked Attack: This is the same idea, but this time, there are N_o original pieces of content which have been watermarked and distributed to the clients. Observations is a matrix of $c \times N_o$ watermarked contents. Note that a column of this matrix yields a Known Message Attack, and a line a Single Original, Multiple Watermarked Attack.

The security level assessment of a watermarking technique has to be done context by context, decoupled from application considerations. Then, for a given application, the watermark designer selects the most suitable technique depending on which contexts the threats in this scenario relate.

3 Practical Tools

These theories do not say anything on the way how to extract and exploit the information leakage. Another crucial point is the complexity of such an algorithm.

This notion was already present in [20, Sect. 21] and denoted as *work*. It might be theoretically possible to extract enough information in order to estimate the secret key, while, in practice, demanding too much computing power. Cryptographers distinguish unconditional security (it is proven that no information leaks from the observations) and computational security (the best known algorithm requires an unreasonable amount of computing power) [28, Sect. 1.13.3].

Whereas theory is just the adaptation of Shannon's security model, practice of watermarking security consists in inventing original and efficient algorithms. Their cores are often known signal processing tools from fields which have a priori nothing in common with watermarking. This extremely interesting part of the job proves once again that watermarking is a multi-field science.

3.1   Steganalysis

The theory of C. Cachin basically says that an alarm should be raised when a suspicious content does not comply with the statistical model of original images. This raises at least three issues:

Feature Extraction. First, images gather in the order of one million of pixels. If the random variable Y is an image, then its definition set $\mathcal{Y}$ is extremely big, and indeed, too huge to lie a statistical model on top. Steganalysers usually extract a feature vector $\tilde{Y}$ from image Y. This reduces the definition space: $|\tilde{\mathcal{Y}}| < |\mathcal{Y}|$. Yet, this also reduces the discrimination between stego and original content: $D_{KL}(p_{\mathcal{H}_0}(\tilde{Y}), p_{\mathcal{H}_1}(\tilde{Y})) \leq D_{KL}(p_X, p_Y)$. One must take care of extracting the most discriminative features. This strategy is certainly possible when the stego technique is a priori known. However, it is far more difficult when the steganalyser is universal (to spot stego-contents, whatever the stego-system).

The theory provides some clues. If extracted features are modeled as independent under assumption $\mathcal{H}_0$, then $p_{\mathcal{H}_0}(\tilde{Y}) = \prod_i p_{\mathcal{H}_0}(\tilde{Y}_i)$, and [29, Sect. 2.1]:

$$D_{KL}(p_{\mathcal{H}_1}(\tilde{Y}), p_{\mathcal{H}_0}(\tilde{Y})) = I(\tilde{Y}) + \sum_i D_{KL}(p_{\mathcal{H}_1}(\tilde{Y}_i), p_{\mathcal{H}_0}(\tilde{Y}_i)) \qquad (4)$$

where $I(\tilde{Y}) = D_{KL}(p_{\mathcal{H}_1}(\tilde{Y}), \prod_i p_{\mathcal{H}_1}(\tilde{Y}_i))$ measures the dependency between the features, and the second term is the KL distance between the pdf of the marginals. This decomposition seems to justify the use of features extracted from wavelet coefficients such as i) prediction errors to measure the dependency between these coefficients and ii) high order statistics (mean, variance, skewness, kurtosis...) to measure the last summand [30, Sect. 2].

Classifier. Once the definition space is set, a second problem is the statistical model. Such a model is required because theorems of hypothesis testing state that optimal tests are based on a sufficient statistic $T = p_{\mathcal{H}_1}(\tilde{Y})/p_{\mathcal{H}_0}(\tilde{Y})$ [31, Chap. 2]. A simple statistical model might be derived for a given stego-system. Yet, this strategy is not possible for universal steganalysers. Usually, a SVM (Support Vector Machine) is trained on databases of features extracted from stego-contents and original contents [30, Sect. 3]. The SVM learns a way to distinguish the two cases, observing samples of $\hat{Y}$ under both hypothesis $\mathcal{H}_1$ or $\mathcal{H}_0$. In a way, it experimentally learns a statistical model for each hypothesis.

Conditioning. A third problem stems from the fact that Cachin theorem need a model for $p_{\mathcal{H}_0}(\tilde{Y})$. Yet, natural images are so diverse that $p_{\mathcal{H}_0}(\tilde{Y})$ is a kind of smooth and large function spreading all over the definition set $\tilde{\mathcal{Y}}$. Assuming a parametric model $p(\tilde{Y}|\theta)$, we have $p_{\mathcal{H}_0}(\tilde{Y}) = \int p(\tilde{Y}|\theta)p(\theta)d\theta$. Some universal steganalysers, for instance, are confused with noisy original images or sharp contour original images as this corresponds to unusual parameter θ.

However, for one particular image, the sufficient statistic of the stego-content is usually higher than the one of the original image. In other words, if the steganalyser could observe the original content and then its stego version, it would notice an increase of the sufficient statistic. Or, within this statistical model, if the steganalyser knows θ, it could be based on more accurate statistics. This gives birth to a very general idea [32, Sect. 3]: the suspicious image Z is slightly transformed to yield an estimation $\hat{\theta}$. Features are extracted and used to build the pdf $p_{\mathcal{H}_0}(\tilde{X}|\hat{\theta})$. A mathematical model foresees $p_{\mathcal{H}_1}(\tilde{Y}|\hat{\theta})$, and thus the sufficient statistic can be calculated $T = p_{\mathcal{H}_1}(\tilde{Z}|\hat{\theta})/p_{\mathcal{H}_0}(\tilde{Z}|\hat{\theta})$. If the suspicious image is a natural image, then $T \sim 1$, otherwise $T > 1$. This leads to better steganalysers even in the universal mode. This is not surprising as conditioning always improves discrimination on average [16, Th. 4.3.6].

3.2   Watermarking

Here are some useful signal processing tools to hack watermarking schemes.

Maximum Likelihood Estimator. Let us consider the watermarking embedder as a system to be identified. Hence, in the Known Message Attack, we observe pairs of input (i.e. message $\mathbf{m}$) and output (watermarked content $\mathbf{y}$). In other words, we have the framework of a input-output identification. If it possible to write the likelihood $p(\mathbf{y}^{N_o}, \mathbf{m}^{N_o}|K)$, the opponent can use the Maximum Likelihood Estimator (MLE), which finds $\hat{K}$ maximizing the likelihood or nullifying its derivative. The MLE is known to be unbiased and consistent, *i.e.* it asymptotically achieves the CRB derived in 2.2. This has been applied to spread spectrum scheme in [33, Sect. 1.1].

Expectation Maximization Algorithm. Unknown messages can be considered as hidden data. The MLE based on $p(\mathbf{y}^{N_o}, \mathbf{m}^{N_o}|K)$ is not practical in this case. But, the EM algorithm approaches it by the iteration of a two-step process:

- Expectation. Having an estimation of the key $\hat{K}(i)$, we estimate the messages $\hat{\mathbf{m}}^{N_o}(i)$. This basically corresponds to the decoding algorithm, known by the pirate according to Kerckhoff's principle.
- Maximization. Having an estimate of the messages $\hat{\mathbf{m}}^{N_o}(i)$, we estimate the secret key $\hat{K}(i+1)$. This step uses for instance the MLE seen above.

This has been applied to spread spectrum schemes in [33, Sect. 1.3].

Principal Component Analysis. Many watermark schemes uses projection onto N_c orthonormal private vectors or carriers $\mathbf{u}_\ell$ in order to increase the SNR at the decoding side. In general, one can write: $\mathbf{y} = \mathbf{x} + \mathbf{w}$, with $\mathbf{x}$ the host signal, and $\mathbf{w} = \sum_{i=1}^{N_c} \gamma_i \mathbf{u}_i$. The coefficients γ_i carry the message to be hidden and tackle the perceptual constraint. We asssume they are independent from $\mathbf{x}$, i.i.d and centered. It means that the watermark signal $\mathbf{w}$ lives in a small subspace whose dimension is N_c, whereas $\mathbf{x}$ belongs to $\mathbb{R}^{N_v}$. This leaves clues for the pirate as the energy of the watermark is focused on a small subspace. For instance, if $\mathbf{x}$ is a white noise, the covariance matrix of $\mathbf{y}$ is $R_y = \sigma_x^2 \mathcal{I} + \sum_{i=1}^{N_c} E\{\gamma_i^2\} \mathbf{u}_i \mathbf{u}_i^T$, whereas $R_x = \sigma_x^2 \mathcal{I}$. This means that R_x has one eigenvalue σ_x^2 with order N_v, whereas R_y has one eigenvalue σ_x^2 with order $N_v - N_c$, and N_c other eigenvalues equaling $\sigma_x^2 + E\{\gamma_i^2\}$. Moreover, these N_c biggest eigenvalues are related to eigenvectors $\mathbf{u}_i$. Consequently, it is very easy for the pirate to estimate these private carriers: i) estimate the covariance matrix R_y with $\hat{R}_y = \sum_{i=1}^{N_o} \mathbf{y}(i) \mathbf{y}(i)^T / N_o$, ii) make an eigen-decomposition of this matrix, iii) isolate the eigen-vectors corresponding to the N_c biggest eigenvalues. Figure 1 illustrates this for toy examples. Ellipses show that the watermarked signals are no more white signals.

This Principal Component Analysis has been applied to spread spectrum based schemes in [33, Sect. 1.3] and also in [34, Sect. V.C].

Independent Component Analysis. In the case where $E\{\gamma_i^2\} = cst$, then R_y has one eigenvalue $\sigma_x^2 + E\{\gamma_i^2\}$ with associated subspace of dimension N_c. When successful, the PCA reveals this subspace and gives a basis, which is not the one used by the embedder: $\{\mathbf{u}_1, \ldots, \mathbf{u}_{N_c}\}$. The pirate can focus his attack

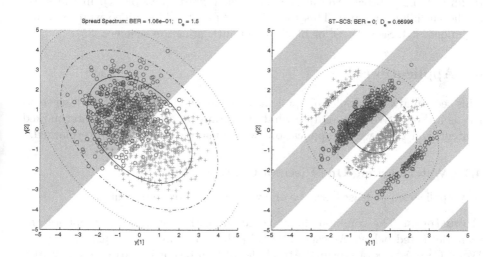

Fig. 1. A collection of watermarked signals ($N_v = 2$, $N_c = 1$) with the Spread Spectrum technique (left) and the Spread Transform Scalar Costa Scheme (right). Red circles (green crosses) represent signals hiding symbol '0' (resp., '1'). The grey area (white area) is the decoding region associated to symbol '0' (resp. '1'). Matlab source code available at www.irisa.fr/temics/Equipe/Furon/iwdw05.m.

noise on this subspace, or remove the watermark signal nullifying the projection of **y** onto this subspace. Yet, he cannot have a read and write access on the watermarking channel.

If symbols γ_i are statistically independent, an Independent Component Analysis rotates the PCA basis until the estimated symbols 'look like' independent. When successful, the ICA yields estimated carriers which correspond to the real basis up to permutation $\pi(.)$ and change of sign: $\hat{\mathbf{u}}_i = \pm\mathbf{u}_{\pi(i)}$. This ambiguity prevents the pirate to embed/decode messages, but he can check if two watermarked contents have the same hidden message or he can flip bits of hidden messages. This was applied to spread spectrum based schemes in [33, Sect. 1.3].

Clustering. The authors of [34] have tested clustering tools to break a video watermarking technique. This technique randomly embeds one of n watermark signals in one video frame. An average attack does not work as it only estimates a mixture of these n signals. However, if a spatial filter succeeds to isolate enough watermark energy, the pirate obtains noisy estimations of the n watermark signals. His goal is now to split this set of estimations in n clusters of estimations corresponding to one watermark signal, and whose centroids would be good estimates of the n watermark signals. This is a typical task for the k-means algorithm (see [34, Sect. IV.D]).

Vector Quantization. A closely related tool is the vector quantization, which is used for replacement attack. The pirate as a database of signal blocks and he wishes to replace a block in a watermarked content by a similar block of the database. The word similar is here important. The vector quantization is used to find in the database the most similar 'codeword' (i.e., block), in the sense of the euclidian distance. This tools is used for attacking video watermarking techniques [34, Sect. IV.D] or block based authentication schemes [35].

4   Applications

This section gives examples of application where the lack of watermarking security is a threat. We first analyze what the pirate can do with one watermarked content, and then, we see applications where many contents are watermarked.

4.1   Watermarking One Piece of Content

Any application at least discloses one watermarked piece of content.

Robustness. The common threat comes from the robustness, except for the scenarios listed below. We especially think here of malicious attack such as the Worst Case Attack or Optimal Attack detailed in recent literature about watermarking robustness [36,37,38]. Another weakness stems from classical synchronization tricks used in watermarking: templates [39] or geometrically redundant watermarking signals [40, Sect. 6.2] are easy to defeat. The block replacement attack is also a threat: the database is constituted from blocks of non-watermarked contents, or even blocks from the watermarked piece of content [34].

Deadlock Attack and Copy-Paste Attack. The deadlock attack concerns copyright protection and illustrates the impossibility to prevent somebody to watermark content with his own technique and key (by embedding a watermark signal or by creating a fake original) [41]. This ruins the identification of the owner because two watermarking channels interfere in the same piece of content.

Multiple problems in the field of copyright protection and authentication stems from the copy attack, where the attacker first copies a watermark and then pastes it in a different piece of content [10].

These two last attacks pertain to the protocol layer, in the sense that it questions the link between the presence (or absence) of watermark and the signification at the application layer. We believe that these attacks stem from a misunderstanding of the watermark designers about the targeted application.

In copyright protection, the presence of a watermark has no legal value. The only receivable proof is the belonging of the content to the database of a trusted third party (i.e., an author society). The authors must register their works in this database in order to be protected. It is absolutely useless, from a legal point of view, for the authors to watermark their works on their own. If watermarking is used in copyright protection, it will be embedded by the trusted third party during the registration process.

However, suppose this resort to a trusted third party is not possible (e.g., it is too expensive for the author). At least, the choice of the watermarking technique shall not be given to the author, but somehow imposed by a standard. This standard should select a non-invertible watermarking technique to avoid the deadlock attack. For instance, the secret key should depend on a hash of the original image to prevent the forgery of fake original. Note that this also prevents the copy-paste attack. In the same way, the copy attack is now a nonsense in authentication application. It is true that the very first watermarking authentication schemes were using a constant watermark. But, nowadays, it is well established that the watermark must depend on the original content like a digital signature in cryptography.

4.2   Watermarking Several Pieces of Content

Some application discloses several watermarked pieces of content using the same key. This is also the case of video watermarking as the embedder watermarks consecutive blocks of video, whence several pieces.

Copy Protection. In copy protection, the set of hidden messages is very small (typically 'Copy Never', 'Copy Once', and 'Copy no more'). Moreover, the pirate knows the status of the content. A Known Message Attack is then a real threat.

Another point is that watermark decoders are released in an hostile environment. For instance, they are embedded in consumer electronic devices such as DVD recorders. Pirates can then test watermark decoding as many times as they wish. They do not do this to remove the watermark content by content, but in order to disclose the secret key of the detector [42,43].

Authentication. The assessment of the authentication schemes is sometimes naïve: researchers check that even slight modification of the signed image is indeed detectable. However, in an authentication scenario, it is likely that many images have to be signed. The threat is that a pirate can sign an image without knowing the secret key: he replaces every block of this image by blocks from already signed images. This is indeed a Vector Quantization attack. Counter attacks exist which render the probability of a successful hack extremely small unless the codebooks of replacement blocks are extremely huge [44].

Fingerprinting. The typical assessment of fingerprinting schemes is that a collusion of pirates cannot frame an innocent user and that the detector can trace at least one pirate. However, a more complex scenario is the following one: video fingerprinting. In this framework, there are many original contents fingerprinted in different versions, because a watermarking technique embeds hidden messages in a video block by block. For a given user, all these blocks are watermarked with the same secret key and the same hidden message (i.e., the user's codeword). This is a Constant Message Attack (or a Multiple Original, Multiple Watermarked Attack), which is very closed to a Known Message Attack. As watermarking techniques are very weak against it [24, Sect. 4.1],[23, Sect. 4.3], it seems for the moment that secure video fingerprinting is not possible.

5   Conclusion: What We Do Not Know Yet

Robust Watermarking. From a theoretical point of view, the security levels of classical schemes such as spread spectrum and QIM have been well established [45]. However, trellis coding schemes [46] or orthogonal dirty paper codes [47] have not been studied yet. From a practical point of view, algorithms to disclose secret dithering in QIM scheme have not been proposed yet. This might be a complex task especially with a QIM based on VQ. Watermarking techniques usually used an Error Correction Code, which brings redundancy and thus a security flaw. But, no study has been done on this topic.

Steganalysis. Good steganalyzers appeared recently, but they have been tested on simple stego-systems (LSB or +1/-1). No one knows how do they perform against more advanced stego-systems based on QIM.

References

1. Maillard, T., Furon, T.: Towards digital rights and exemptions management systems. Computer Law and Security Report **20** (2004) 281–287
2. Craver, S., Memon, N., Yeo, B.L., Yeung, M.: Resolving rightful ownership with invisible watermarking techniques: limitations, attacks, and implications. IEEE Journal of selected areas in communications **16** (1998) 573–87 Special issue on copyright and privacy protection.
3. Bloom, J., Cox, I., Kalker, T., Linnartz, J.P., Miller, M., Traw, C.: Copy protection for DVD video. Proc. of the IEEE **87** (1999) 1267–1276 Special issue on identification and protection of multimedia information.

4. Stern, J., Craver, S.: Lessons learned from the SDMI. In Dugelay, J.L., Rose, K., eds.: Proc. of the Fourth Workshop on Multimedia Signal Processing (MMSP), Cannes, France, IEEE (2001) 213–218
5. Cox, I., Miller, M.: Electronic watermarking: The first 50 years. In Dugelay, J.L., Rose, K., eds.: Proc. of Fourth Workshop on Multimedia Signal Processing (MMSP), Cannes, France, IEEE (2001) 225–230
6. Bartolini, F., Barni, M., Furon, T.: Special session on watermarking security. In: Proc. of 11th European Signal Processing Conference (EUSIPCO). Volume 1., Toulouse, France (2002) 283–302, 441–461
7. Barni, M., Pérez-González, F.: Special session on watermarking security. In Delp, E.J., Wong, P.W., eds.: Security, Steganography, and Watermarking of Multimedia Contents VII. Volume 5681 of Proceedings of SPIE-IS&T Electronic Imaging., San Jose, CA, USA, SPIE (2005) 685–768
8. Doërr, G., Dugelay, J.L.: Collusion issue in video watermarking. In Delp, E.J., Wong, P.W., eds.: Security, Steganography, and Watermarking of Multimedia Contents. Volume 5681 of Proceedings of SPIE-IS&T Electronic Imaging., San Jose, CA, USA, SPIE (2005) 685–696
9. Trappe, W., Wu, M., Wang, Z., Liu, K.: Anti-collusion fingerprinting for multimedia. IEEE Trans. on Signal Processing 51 (2003) 1069–1087 Special Issue on Signal Processing for Data Hiding in Digital Media and Secure Content Delivery.
10. Kutter, M., Voloshynovskiy, S., Herrigel, A.: Watermark copy attack. In P.W. Wong, E. Delp, eds.: Security and Watermarking of Multimedia Contents II. Volume 3971., San Jose, Cal., USA, SPIE Proceedings (2000)
11. Wong, P.W., Memon, N.: Secret and public key image watermarking schemes for images authentication and ownership verification. IEEE Trans. on Image Processing 10 (2001) 1593–1601
12. Anderson, R., Petitcolas, F.: On the limits of steganography. IEEE Journal of Selected Areas in Communications 16 (1998) 474–481 Special issue on copyright & privacy protection.
13. Barni, M., Bartolini, F., Furon, T.: A general framework for robust watermarking security. Signal Processing 83 (2003) 2069–2084 Special issue on Security of Data Hiding Technologies, invited paper.
14. Kalker, T.: Considerations on watermarking security. In Dugelay, J.L., Rose, K., eds.: Proc of the Fourth Workshop on Multimedia Signal Processing (MMSP), Cannes, France, IEEE (2001) 201–206
15. Cachin, C.: An information-theoretic model for steganography. In Aucsmith, D., ed.: Proc. of the 2nd Int. Workshop on Inf. Hiding. Volume 1525 of LNCS. Portland, Oregon, U.S.A., Springer Verlag (1998) 306–318
16. Blahut, R.: Principes and practice of information theory. Addisson-Wesley (1987)
17. Guillon, P., Furon, T., Duhamel, P.: Applied public-key steganography. In P.W. Wong, E. Delp, eds.: Security and Watermarking of Multimedia Contents IV, San Jose, Cal., USA, SPIE (2002)
18. Wang, Y., Moulin, P.: Steganalysis of block-structured stegotext. In Delp, E., Wong, P.W., eds.: Security, steganography and watermarking of multimedia contents VI. Volume 5306 of Proceedings of SPIE-IS&T Electronic Imaging., San Jose, CA, USA, SPIE (2004) 477–488
19. Mittelholzer, T.: An information-theoritic approach to steganography and watermarking. In Pfitzmann, A., ed.: Proc. of the 3rd Int. Workshop on Inf. Hiding, Dresden, Germany, Springer Verlag (1999) 1–17
20. Shannon, C.: Communication theory of secrecy systems. Bell system technical journal 28 (1949) 656–715

21. Hernandez, J., Pérez-González, F.: Throwing more light on image watermarks. In: Proc. of 2nd Int. Workshop on Inf. Hiding (IH98). Volume 1525 of LNCS, Portland, OR, USA, Springer-Verlag (1998) 191–207

22. Furon, T.: Security analysis. Techn. report, Certimark European Project (2002)

23. Cayre, F., Fontaine, C., Furon, T.: Watermarking security part I: Theory. In Delp, E.J., Wong, P.W., eds.: Proc. SPIE-IS&T Electronic Imaging, SPIE. Volume 5681., San Jose, CA, USA, Security, Steganography, and Watermarking of Multimedia Contents VII (2005) 746–757

24. Comesana, P., Pérez-Freire, L., Pérez-González, F.: Fundamentals of data hiding security and their application to spread-spectrum analysis. In: Proc. of 7th Inf. Hiding Workshop (IH05). LNCS, Barcelona, Spain, Springer Verlag (2005)

25. Cachin, C.: Entropy Measures and Unconditional Security in Cryptography. Volume 1 of ETH Series in Inf. Security and Cryptography. H.-Gorre Verlag (1997)

26. Cedilnik, A., Kosmelj, K.: Relations among Fisher, Shannon-Wiener and Kullback measures of information for continuous variables. In Mrvar, A., Ferligoj, A., eds.: Developments in Statistics. Volume 17 of Metodoloski zvezki (ISSN 1318-1726)., FDV, University of Ljubljana (2002) 55–62

27. Diffie, W., Hellman, M.: New directions in cryptography. IEEE Trans. on Inf. Theory 22 (1976) 644–54

28. Menezes, A., Van Oorschot, P., Vanstone, S.: Handbook of applied cryptography. Discrete mathematics and its applications. CRC Press (1996)

29. Cardoso, J.F.: Dependence, correlation and gaussianity in independent component analysis. Journal of Machine Learning Research 4 (2003) 1177–1203

30. Lyu, S., Farid, H.: Detecting hidden messages using higher-order statistics and support vector machine. In Petitcolas, F., ed.: Proc. of the 5th Int. Work. on Inf. Hiding. Volume 2578 of LNCS., Noordwijkerhout, The Netherlands, Springer Verlag (2002) 340–354

31. Poor, H.V.: An introduction to signal detection and estimation. Springer (1994 (2nd edition))

32. Fridrich, J., Goljan, M., Hogea, D.: New methodology for breaking steganographic techniques for JPEGs. In Delp, E., Wong, P.W., eds.: Security and watermarking of multimedia contents V. Volume 5020 of Proc. of SPIE-IS&T Electronic Imaging., Santa Clara, CA, USA, SPIE (2003) 143–155

33. Cayre, F., Fontaine, C., Furon, T.: Watermarking security part II: Practice. In Delp, E.J., Wong, P.W., eds.: Proc. of SPIE-IS&T Electronic Imaging, SPIE. Volume 5681., San Jose, CA, USA, Security, Steganography, and Watermarking of Multimedia Contents VII (2005) 758–768

34. Doërr, G., Dugelay, J.L.: Security pitfalls of frame-by-frame approaches to video watermarking. IEEE Trans. Sig. Proc. 52 (2004) 2955–2964

35. Holliman, M., N. Memon: Counterfeiting attacks on oblivious block-wise independent invisible watermarking schemes. IEEE Trans. Image Proc. 9 (2000) 432–441

36. Vila-Forcen, J., Voloshynovskiy, S., Koval, O., Pérez-González, F., Pun, T.: Worst case additive attack against quantization-based data-hiding methods. In Delp, E., Wong, P.W., eds.: Security, Steganography, and Watermarking of Multimedia Contents VII. Volume 5681 of Proceedings of SPIE-IS&T Electronic Imaging., San Jose, CA, USA, SPIE (2005) 136–146

37. Pateux, S., Le Guelvouit, G.: Practical watermarking scheme based on wide spread spectrum and game theory. Signal Proc.: Image Communication 18 (2003) 283–296

38. Moulin, P., Ivanovic, A.: The zero-rate spread-spectrum watermarking game. IEEE Trans. on Signal Processing 51 (2003) 1098–1117 Special Issue on Signal Processing for Data Hiding in Digital Media and Secure Content Delivery.

39. Herrigel, A., Voloshynovskiy, S., Rystar, Y.: The watermark template attack. In P.W. Wong, E. Delp, eds.: Security and Watermarking of Multimedia Contents, San Jose, Cal., USA, SPIE Proceedings (2001)

40. Topak, E., Voloshynovskiy, S., Koval, O., Mihcak, M., Pun, T.: Security analysis of robust data-hiding with geometrically structured codebooks. In Delp, E., Wong, P.W., eds.: Security, steganogrpahy, and watermarking of multimedia content VII. Volume 5681 of Proceedings of SPIE-IS&T Electronic Imaging., San jose, CA, USA, SPIE (2005) 709–720

41. Craver, S., N. Memon, B.-L. Yeo, M.M. Yeung: On the invertibility of invisible watermarking technique. In: Proc. of Int. Conf. on Image Processing, Washington, DC, USA, IEEE (1997) 540–543

42. Linnartz, J., van Dijk, M.: Analysis of the sensitivity attack against electronic watermarks in images. In Aucsmith, D., ed.: Proc. of the 2nd Int. Workshop on Inf. Hiding. Volume 1525 of LNCS, Portland, Oregon, USA, Springer Verlag (1998)

43. Choubassi, M.E., Moulin, P.: New sensitivity attack. In Delp, E., Wong, P.W., eds.: Security, steganography, and watermarking of multimedia contents VII. Volume 5681 of Proceedings of SPIE-IS&T Electronic imaging., San Jose, CA, USA, SPIE (2005) 734–745

44. Barreto, P.S., Kim, H.Y., Rijmen, V.: Toward a secure public-key blockwise fragile authentication watermarking. IEE Proc. Vision, Image and Signal Processing **149** (2002) 57–62

45. Pérez-Freire, L., Comesana, P., Pérez-González, F.: Information-theoretic analysis of security in side-informed data hiding. In: Proc. of 7th Inf. Hiding Workshop (IH05). LNCS, Barcelona, Spain, Springer Verlag (2005)

46. Miller, M., Doërr, G., Cox, I.: Applying informed coding and informed embedding to design a robust, high capacity watermark. IEEE Tran. Image Processing **13** (2004) 792–807

47. Abrardo, A., Barni, M.: Orthogonal dirty paper coding for informed data hiding. In Delp, E., Wong, P.W., eds.: Security, steganography, and watermarking of multimedia content VI. Volume 5306 of Proceedings of SPIE-IS&T Electronic Imaging., San Jose, CA, USA, SPIE (2004) 274–286

Countermeasures for Collusion Attacks Exploiting Host Signal Redundancy

Gwenaël Doërr and Jean-Luc Dugelay

Eurécom Institute, Multimedia Communications Department,
2229 route des Crêtes – B.P. 193 06904 Sophia-Antipolis Cédex, France
{doerr, dugelay}@eurecom.fr
http://www.eurecom.fr/~image

Abstract. Multimedia digital data is highly redundant: successive video frames are very similar in a movie clip, most songs contain some repetitive patterns, etc. This property can consequently be exploited to successively replace each part of the signal with a similar one taken from another location in the same signal or with a combination of similar parts. Such an approach is all the more pertinent when video content is considered since such signals exhibit both temporal and spatial self-similarities. To counter such attacking strategies, it is necessary to ensure that embedded watermarks are coherent with the redundancy of the host content. To this end, both motion-compensated watermarking and self-similarities inheritance will be surveyed.

1 Introduction

Digital watermarking was initially introduced in the early 90's as a complementary protection technology [1] since encryption alone is not enough. Indeed, sooner or later, encrypted multimedia content is decrypted to be eventually presented to human beings. At this very moment, multimedia content is left unprotected and can be perfectly duplicated, manipulated and redistributed at a large scale. Thus, a second line of defense has to be added to address this issue. This is the main purpose of digital watermarking which basically consists in hiding some information into digital content in an imperceptible manner. Up to now, research has mainly investigated how to improve the trade-off between three conflicting parameters: imperceptibility, robustness and capacity. Perceptual models have been exploited to make watermarks less perceptible, benchmarks have been released to evaluate robustness, channel models have been studied to obtain a theoretical bound for the embedding capacity.

A lot of attention has focused on security applications such as Intellectual Property (IP) protection and Digital Rights Managements (DRM) systems. Digital watermarking was even thought of as a possible solution to combat illegal copying which was a forthcoming issue in the mid-90's. However the few attempts to launch watermarking-based copy-control mechanisms [2,3] have resulted in partial failures, which have significantly lowered the initial enthusiasm

M. Barni et al. (Eds.): IWDW 2005, LNCS 3710, pp. 216–230, 2005.

related to this technology. These setbacks were in part due to the claim that embedded watermarks would survive in a highly hostile environment even if very few works addressed this issue. Indeed, if the survival of the watermark against common signal processing primitives - filtering, lossy compression, global desynchronization - has been carefully surveyed, almost no work has considered that an attacker may try to learn some knowledge about the watermarking system to defeat it. Nevertheless, in applications such as copy control or fingerprinting, digital watermarking is usually seen as a disturbing technology. Therefore, it is likely to be submitted to strong hostile attacks when it is released to the public.

Security evaluation is now a growing concern and collusion attacks have often been mentioned as a possible mean to do it [4,5]. Collusion consists in collecting several watermarked documents and combining them to obtain unwatermarked content. Such attacks are all the more relevant in video since each individual frame can be regarded as a single watermarked document. In Section 2, a specific kind of collusion attack is reviewed. When similar contents carry uncorrelated watermarks, colluders can average them so that watermark samples sum to zero. In this perspective, an attacker can exploit both the temporal and spatial redundancy of the video signal to design efficient attacks. Next, signal coherent watermarking is introduced in Section 3 to circumvent the previously exhibited threats. The goal is basically to make the embedded watermark have the same redundancy as the host signal. To this end, motion-compensated watermarking and self-similarities inheritance will be studied. Finally, conclusions are drawn in Section 4 and tracks for future work are given.

2   Combine Similar Contents Carrying Uncorrelated Watermarks

Previous works have stressed the fact that using a redundant watermarking structure is likely to induce some information leakages [6,7,8]. Considering multiple watermarked contents, a hostile attacker is able to gain some knowledge about the embedded watermark signal and exploit it to confuse the detector. Nevertheless, completely independent watermarks are not the solution either. If an attacker can collect similar contents carrying uncorrelated watermarks, averaging them will usually sum the watermark samples to zero. Since video material is highly redundant, such a strategy can lead to powerful attacks. In Subsection 2.1, the correlation between successive frames is exploited to estimate the background in each frame using the neighbor ones. Furthermore, spatial self-similarities will also be considered in Subsection 2.2 to elaborate efficient Block Replacement Attacks (BRA).

2.1   Temporal Frame Averaging After Registration

One of the pioneering algorithm for video watermarking basically considers video content as a mono-dimensional signal and simply adds a pseudo-random sequence as a watermark [9]. From a frame-by-frame point of view, such a strategy can be seen as always embedding a different watermark[1]. The drawback of this approach is that temporal frame averaging usually succeeds in confusing the watermark detector [4]. In static scenes, video frames are highly similar and can be averaged without introducing strong visible artifacts. On the other hand, since successive watermarks are uncorrelated, temporal averaging significantly decreases the power of the embedded watermark $\mathbf{w}_t$ in the frame $\mathbf{f}_t$. Nevertheless, in practice, video material usually contains dynamic components such as fast moving objects and/or camera motion. Therefore, this simple attack needs to be improved to ensure that the quality of the video is not destroyed.

Each video frame is a projection of a single 3D movie set and different video frames from a shot can be seen as different 2D projections of the same scene. As a result, even if some dynamic components are present, successive frames are still highly correlated. However, they need to be aligned to enable efficient averaging [11,12]. The goal is to register the video frames, so that all the projections of a given 3D point overlap, to enable large temporal averaging without introducing much visual distortion. In other words, Temporal Frame Averaging after Registration (TFAR) aims at estimating a given video frame $\mathbf{f}_t$ from its neighboring ones $\mathbf{f}_{t+\delta}$ thanks to frame registration as depicted in Figure 1. Moving objects are difficult to predict from one frame to the other. This is the reason why segmentation is used to separate two alternative Video Object Planes (VOP) [13]: the background $\mathbf{b}_t$ on one side and the moving objects $\mathbf{o}_t$ on the other side. Video objects are then ignored for the rest of the attack, which simply comes down then to estimate the current background $\mathbf{b}_t$ from the neighbor ones.

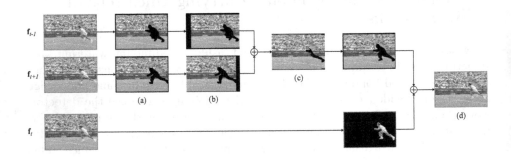

Fig. 1. Temporal Frame Averaging after Registration (TFAR): Once the video objects have been removed (a), neighbor frames are registered (b) and combined to estimate the background of the current frame (c). Next, the missing video objects are inserted back (d).

---

[1] Frame-by-frame watermarking is a commonly used strategy in video [10]. The following notation will be used in the remainder of this article: $\check{\mathbf{f}}_t = \mathbf{f}_t + \alpha \mathbf{w}_t$, where $\mathbf{f}_t$ is the original video frame at instant t, $\check{\mathbf{f}}_t$ its watermarked version, α the embedding strength and $\mathbf{w}_t$ the embedded watermark which is normally distributed with zero mean and unit variance.

To this end, it is necessary to find a registration function which *pertinently* associates to each pixel position (x_t, y_t) in the current frame $\mathbf{f}_t$ a position $(x_{t'}, y_{t'})$ in a neighboring frame $\mathbf{f}_{t'}$ i.e. which minimizes for example the mean square error between the target background $\mathbf{b}_t$ and the registered one $\mathbf{b}_{t'}^{(t)}$. In other words, the goal is to define a model which describes the apparent displacement generated by the camera motion. Physically, camera motion is a combination of traveling displacements (horizontal, vertical, forward and backward translations), rotations (pan, roll and tilt) and zooming effects (forward and backward). As the background of the scene is often far from the camera, pan and tilt rotations can be assimilated, for small rotations, to translations in terms of 2D apparent motion. Thus, the zoom, roll and traveling displacements can be represented, under some assumptions, by a first order polynomial motion model [14] as follows:

$$\begin{cases} x_{t'} = t_x + z(x_t - x_o) - z\theta(y_t - y_o) \\ y_{t'} = t_y + z(y_t - y_o) + z\theta(x_t - x_o) \end{cases} \tag{1}$$

where z is the zoom factor, θ the 2D rotation angle, (t_x, t_y) the 2D translational vector and (x_o, y_o) the coordinates of the camera optical center. Obviously, this simple model may be inaccurate when the camera displacement or the scene structure is very complicated. In this case, more complex motion representations can be introduced [14,15,16].

The registered backgrounds $\mathbf{b}_{t+\delta}^{(t)}$, obtained from the video frames in the considered temporal window, are averaged to obtain an estimation $\tilde{\mathbf{b}}_t$ of the background in the current frame. The moving objects $\mathbf{o}_t$ are then inserted back to obtain the attacked video frame $\tilde{\mathbf{f}}_t$. It should be noted that this attack does not affect the moving objects $\mathbf{o}_t$. As a result, if such objects occupy most of the video scene, the attack is not likely to trap the detector. However, since the background is usually the main part in a video shot, the attack remains pertinent. From a coding perspective, TFAR can be seen as encoding the background with an advanced forward-backward predictive coder e.g. B-frames in MPEG. Alternatively, it can also be considered as temporal averaging along the motion axis. Whatever, since most watermarking algorithms do not consider the evolution of the structure of the scene during embedding, this attack has been shown to confuse several watermark detectors [12]. The only exception is when the same watermark pattern $\mathbf{w}$ is embedded in all the video frames in a static scene. In this case, TFAR has no impact. Skeptical people might argue that such attacks are too computationally intensive to be realistic. However, video mosaics or sprite panoramas are expected to be exploited for efficient background compression in the upcoming video standard MPEG-4 and such video coding algorithms will have a similar impact on embedded watermarks [17].

2.2   Block Replacement Attack

If similarities can be easily exhibited in successive video frames as noticed in the previous subsection, less obvious ones are also present at a lower resolution level: the block level. Such self-similarities have already been exploited to obtain efficient image compression tools [18]. The signal to be processed is first partitioned into a set of blocks $\mathbf{b}_T$ of size S_T. Those blocks can overlap or not. The asset of using overlapping blocks is that it prevents strong blocking artifacts on the border of the blocks by averaging the overlapping areas. The Block Replacement Attack (BRA) processes then each one of these blocks sequentially. For each block, a search window is defined. It can be chosen in the vicinity of the block $\mathbf{b}_T$ or randomly to prevent system designers to systematically invert the attack. This search window is partitioned to obtain a codebook $\mathcal{Q}$ of blocks $\mathbf{b}_{Q_i}$ of size S_Q. Once again, these blocks can overlap or not. Next a candidate block for replacement $\mathbf{b}_R$ is computed using the blocks present in the codebook. Of course, the larger the codebook $\mathcal{Q}$ is, the more choices there are to compute a replacement block which is *similar* enough to the input block $\mathbf{b}_T$ so that it can be substituted without introducing strong visual artifacts. On the other hand, the larger the codebook $\mathcal{Q}$ is, the higher the computational complexity is and a trade-off has to be found. The Mean Square Error (MSE) can be used to evaluate how similar are two blocks. The lower the MSE is, the more similar are the two blocks. Thus, the original block $\mathbf{b}_T$ is substituted by the replacement block $\mathbf{b}_R$ associated with the lowest MSE.

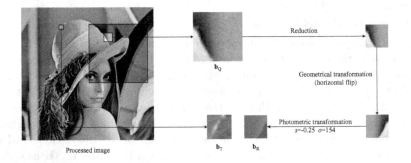

Fig. 2. Block Replacement Attack (BRA) implementation using a fractal coding strategy: each block is replaced by the one in the search window which is the most similar modulo a geometrical and photometric transformation.

There are many ways of computing the replacement block $\mathbf{b}_R$. One of the first proposed implementation was based on fractal coding [19] and is illustrated in Figure 2. The codebook is first artificially enlarged by also considering geometrically transformed versions of the blocks within the search window. For complexity reasons, a small number of transformations are considered e.g. downsampling by a factor 2 and 8 isometries (identity, 4 flips, 3 rotations). Next, the candidate replacement blocks are computed with a simple affine photometric compensation. In other words, each block $\mathbf{b}_{Q_i}$ of the codebook is transformed in $s\mathbf{b}_{Q_i} + o\mathbf{1}$, where $\mathbf{1}$ is a block containing only ones, so that the MSE with the target block $\mathbf{b}_T$ is minimized. This is a simple least squares problem and the scale s and offset o can be determined as follows:

$$s = \frac{(\mathbf{b}_T - \mathrm{m}_T \mathbf{1}) \cdot (\mathbf{b}_{Q_i} - \mathrm{m}_{Q_i} \mathbf{1})}{|\mathbf{b}_{Q_i} - \mathrm{m}_{Q_i} \mathbf{1}|^2} \qquad (2)$$

$$o = \mathrm{m}_T - s.\mathrm{m}_{Q_i} \qquad (3)$$

where m_T (resp. m_{Q_i}) is the mean value of block $\mathbf{b}_T$ (resp. $\mathbf{b}_{Q_i}$), $\cdot$ the linear correlation and $|\mathbf{b}|$ the norm defined as $\sqrt{\mathbf{b} \cdot \mathbf{b}}$. At this point, the transformed blocks $s\mathbf{b}_{Q_i} + o\mathbf{1}$ are sorted in ascending order according to their similarity with the target block $\mathbf{b}_T$ and the most similar one is retained for replacement. In the same fashion, an alternative approach consists in building iteratively sets of similar blocks and randomly shuffling their positions [20,21] until all the blocks have been replaced.

The main drawback of this implementation is that it is not possible to modify the strength of the attack. Furthermore, the computation of the replacement block is not properly managed: either it is too close from the target block $\mathbf{b}_T$ and the watermark is reintroduced, or it is too distant and strong visual artifacts appear. Optimally, one would like to ensure that the distortion $\Delta = \mathrm{MSE}(\mathbf{b}_R, \mathbf{b}_T)$ remains within two bounds τ_{low} and τ_{high}. To this end, several blocks $\mathbf{b}_{Q_i}$ can be combined to compute the replacement block instead of a single one i.e. $\mathbf{b}_R = \sum_{i=1}^N \lambda_i \mathbf{b}_{Q_i}$ where the λ_i's are mixing parameter chosen in such a way that Δ lies within the specified interval. This combination can take into account a fixed number of blocks [22] or also adapt the number of considered blocks for combination according to the nature of the block to be reconstructed [23]. Intuitively, approximating flat blocks requires to combine fewer blocks than for highly textured ones.

However, the computational load induced by computing optimal mixing parameters for each candidate replacement block has motivated the design of an alternative implementation which is described in Table 1. First, for each block $\mathbf{b}_T$, the codebook $\mathcal{Q}$ is built and photometric compensation is performed. Next, Principal Component Analysis (PCA) is performed considering the different blocks $\mathbf{b}_{Q_i}$ in the codebook. This gives a centroid $\mathbf{c}$ defined as follows:

$$\mathbf{c} = \frac{1}{|\mathcal{Q}|} \sum_{\mathbf{b}_{Q_i} \in \mathcal{Q}} \mathbf{b}_{Q_i} \qquad (4)$$

and a set of eigenblocks $\mathbf{e}_i$ associated with their eigenvalues ϵ_i. These eigenblocks are then sorted by descending eigenvalues i.e. there are more variations in direction e_1 than in any other one. Then, a candidate block for replacement $\mathbf{b}_R$ is computed using the N first eigenblocks so that the distortion Δ is minimized. In other words, the block $\mathbf{b}_T - \mathbf{c}$ is projected onto the subspace spanned by the N first eigenblocks and $\mathbf{b}_R$ can be written:

$$\mathbf{b}_R = \mathbf{c} + \sum_{i=1}^{N} \frac{(\mathbf{b}_T - \mathbf{c}) \cdot \mathbf{e}_i}{|\mathbf{e}_i|^2} \mathbf{e}_i \qquad (5)$$

Of course, the distortion Δ gracefully decreases as the number N of combined eigenblocks increases. Thus, an adaptive framework is introduced to identify

Table 1. BRA procedure using block projection on a PCA-defined subspace

For each block $\mathbf{b}_T$ of the signal

1. Build the block codebook $\mathcal{Q}$
2. Perform photometric compensation
3. Performs the PCA of the blocks in $\mathcal{Q}$ to obtain a set of orthogonal eigenblocks $\mathbf{e}_i$ associated with their eigenvalues ϵ_i
   Set $N = 1$ and flag $= 0$
4. While (flag $= 0$) AND ($N \leq S_T$)
   (a) Build the optimal replacement block $\mathbf{b}_R$ using the eigenblocks $\mathbf{r}_i$ associated with the N first eigenvalues
   (b) Compute $\Delta = \mathrm{MSE}(\mathbf{b}_R, \mathbf{b}_T)$
   (c) If $\tau_{\text{low}} \leq \Delta \leq \tau_{\text{high}}$, set flag $= 1$
   (d) Else increment N
5. Replace $\mathbf{b}_T$ by $\mathbf{b}_R$

which value N should have so that the distortion Δ falls within the range $[\tau_{\text{low}}, \tau_{\text{high}}]$. It should be noted that the underlying assumption is that most of the watermark energy will be concentrated in the last eigenblocks since the watermark can be seen as details. As a result, if a valid candidate block can be built without using the last eigenblocks, the watermark signal will not be reintroduced. In fact, BRA has been shown to defeat both Spread Spectrum (SS) and Quantization Index Modulation (QIM) watermarks [21,23].

3   Signal Coherent Watermarking

On one hand, using a redundant watermarking structure is not secure since it can be estimated when several watermarked uncorrelated documents are colluded. On the other hand, uncorrelated watermarks can be removed by averaging similar watermarked documents. These observations intuitively lead to the intuitive embedding principle: *watermarks embedded in distinct contents should be as correlated as the host contents themselves*. Alternative approaches have been proposed to meet this specification e.g. the embedded watermark can be made frame-dependent [24], a frame-dependent binary string can be exploited to generate a watermark pattern which degrades gracefully with an increased number of bit errors [25,26], the watermark can be embedded in some frame-dependent positions [4]. However, those methods are likely to be still defeated by the attacks presented in Section 2. Indeed, the watermark needs to be coherent with the redundancy of the host signal. First, camera motion should be carefully considered to resist to TFAR. Optimally, the embedding process should ensure that *the watermark moves with the camera*. Second, the embedded watermark should exhibit the same spatial self-similarities as the host video frames to make sure it is immune to BRA. If a pattern is repeated in a frame, it should always carry the same watermark.

3.1   Motion Compensated Watermarking

For a given scene, backgrounds of video frames can be considered as several 2D projections of the same 3D movie set. The weakness of common embedding strategies against TFAR is due to the fact that camera motion is not considered at all. These watermarking systems are completely *blind* with respect to camera motion. As a result, a given 3D point, which is projected in different locations in different video frames, is associated with uncorrelated watermark samples. Thus, averaging registered video frames succeeds in confusing the watermark detector. A remedy would be to inform the embedder about camera motion and to find an embedding strategy which forces each 3D point to carry the same watermark sample whenever it is visible in the video scene. In other words, the basic idea is to simulate a utopian world where the movie set would already be watermarked. In this perspective, video mosaicing can be considered to design such a motion compensated watermarking scheme.

Video mosaicing consists in aligning all the frames of a video sequence to a fixed coordinate system [27]. The resulting mosaic image provides a snapshot view of the video sequence i.e. an estimation of the background of the scene if the moving objects have been removed. A straightforward and naive approach would consist in embedding a digital watermark in the mosaic representation of the considered video scene. Next, the resulting watermarked mosaic would be used as the background of the video frames. However, such a process requires double interpolation for the background (frame → mosaic → frame) which is likely to alter the quality of the video. Therefore, an alternative but somewhat equivalent approach is depicted in Figure 3. First of all, warping parameters are computed for each video frame with respect to the considered motion model. For instance, if the motion model defined in Equation (1) is exploited, the warping parameters θ, z, (x_o, y_o) and (t_x, t_y) are computed for each video frame. Hence, each frame

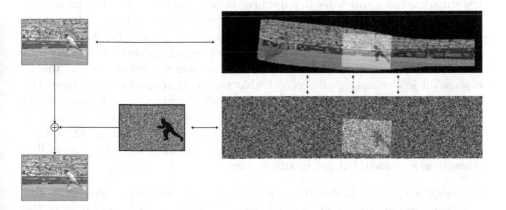

Fig. 3. Embedding procedure for camera motion coherent watermarking: The part of the watermark pattern which is associated with the current video frame is retrieved and registered back. Next, it is embedded in the background portion of the video frame.

$\mathbf{f}_t$ is associated with a set of warping parameters i.e. the frame background $\mathbf{b}_t$ is associated with a portion $\mathbf{b}_m^{(t)}$ of the video mosaic. Next, a key-dependent watermark $\mathbf{w}_m$ is generated which has the same dimensions as the mosaic representation of the video shot. Now, using the same warping parameters as the ones used for building the mosaic, a portion $\mathbf{w}_m^{(t)}$ of this watermark can be associated to each video frame $\mathbf{f}_t$. Finally, the resulting watermark portion only has to be registered back to obtain the watermark signal $\mathbf{w}_t$ to be embedded in the video frame. Similarly to TFAR, object segmentation can be performed to separate moving objects from the background. Next, the embedder only watermarks the background to follow the embedding philosophy: *a 3D point carries the same watermark sample all along the video scene*. In this case, alternative mechanisms have to be deployed to protect moving objects. Previous works have watermarked MPEG-4 video objects according to their main directions [28], their animation parameters [29] or their texture [30]. On the detector side, the procedure is very similar. In a first step, warping parameters are computed for each frames of the video scene to be verified and the watermark $\mathbf{w}_m$ is generated using the shared secret key. Next, the detector only checks whether the portion $\mathbf{w}_t$ associated with each incoming frame $\tilde{\mathbf{f}}_t$ has been effectively embedded in the background or not using for instance a correlation score.

As expected, this novel embedding strategy has exhibited very good performances against TFAR [12]. Furthermore, this method also produces interesting results in terms of watermark imperceptibility. Evaluating the impact of distorting a signal as perceived by a human user is a great challenge. The amount and perceptibility of distortions, such as those introduced by lossy compression or digital watermarking, are indeed tightly related to the actual signal content. This has motivated the modeling of the human perception system to design efficient metrics. For example, when considering an image, it is now admitted that a low-frequency watermark is more visible than a high-frequency one or that a watermark is more noticeable in a flat area than in a texture one. The knowledge of such a behavior can then be exploited to perform efficient perceptual shaping. In the context of video, the Video Quality Experts Group (VQEG) [31] was formed in 1997 to devise objective methods for predicting video image quality. In 1999, they stated first, that no objective measurement system at test was able to replace subjective testing and second, that no objective model outperforms the others in all cases. This explains while the Peak Signal to Noise Ratio (PSNR) is still the most often used metric today to evaluate the visibility of a video watermark. However, from a subjective point of view, previous works [32,33] have isolated two kinds of impairments which appear in video, when the embedding strength is increased, but not in still frames:

1. *Temporal flicker*: Embedding uncorrelated watermarks in successive video frames usually results in annoying twinkle or flicker artifacts similar to the existing ones in video compression,
2. *Stationary pattern*: Embedding the same watermark pattern in all the video frames is visually disturbing since it gives the feeling that the scene has been filmed with a camera having a dirty lens when it pans across the movie set.

With the proposed motion compensated embedding strategy, different water-marks are still embedded in successive video frames. However, these differences are coherent with the camera motion and the user is no longer annoyed by flick-ering. In fact, the user has the feeling that the noise was already present in the filmed movie set and find it more *natural*.

3.2   Host Self-similarities Inheritance

For each signal block, BRA look for a linear combination of neighboring blocks resulting in a block which is similar enough to the current block so that a sub-stitution does not introduce strong visual artifacts. Since watermarking systems do not perform today anything specific to ensure that the embedded watermark is coherent with the self-similarities of the host signal, most of them are defeated by such attacks. Intuitively, to ensure that a watermark will survive to BRA, the embedding process should guarantee that *similar signal blocks carry similar wa-termarks* or alternatively that *pixels with similar neighborhood carry watermark samples with close values*.

Let us assume for the moment that it is possible to associate to each pixel position $\mathbf{p} = (x, y)$ with $1 \leq x \leq X$ and $1 \leq y \leq Y$ in the image $\mathbf{i}$ a feature vector $\mathbf{f}(\mathbf{i}, \mathbf{p})$ which characterizes *in some sense* the neighborhood of the image around this specific position. Thus, this function can be defined as follows:

$$\mathbf{f} : \mathcal{I} \times \mathcal{P} \to \mathcal{F}$$
$$(\mathbf{i}, \mathbf{p}) \mapsto \mathbf{f}(\mathbf{i}, \mathbf{p}) \tag{6}$$

where $\mathcal{I}$ is the image space, $\mathcal{P} = [1 \ldots X] \times [1 \ldots Y]$ the position space and $\mathcal{F}$ the feature space. From a very low-level perspective, generating a digital watermark can be regarded as associating a watermark value $\mathrm{w}(\mathbf{i}, \mathbf{p})$ to each pixel position in the image. However, if the embedded watermark is required to be immune against BRA, the following property should also be verified:

$$\mathbf{f}(\mathbf{i}, \mathbf{p}_0) \approx \sum_k \lambda_k \mathbf{f}(\mathbf{i}, \mathbf{p}_k) \Rightarrow \mathrm{w}(\mathbf{i}, \mathbf{p}_0) \approx \sum_k \lambda_k \mathrm{w}(\mathbf{i}, \mathbf{p}_k) \tag{7}$$

In other words, if at a given position $\mathbf{p}_0$, the local neighborhood is similar to a linear combination of neighborhoods at other locations $\mathbf{p}_k$, then the watermark sample $\mathrm{w}(\mathbf{p}_0)$ embedded at position $\mathbf{p}_0$ should be close to the linear combination (with the same mixing coefficients λ_k) of the watermark samples $\mathrm{w}(\mathbf{p}_k)$ at these locations. A simple way to obtain this property is to make the watermarking process be the composition of a feature extraction operation and a linear form φ.

Hence, one can write $\mathrm{w} = \varphi \circ \mathbf{f}$ where $\varphi : \mathcal{F} \to \mathbb{R}$ is a linear form which takes F-dimensional feature vectors in input. Next, to completely define this linear form, it is sufficient to set the values $\xi_f = \varphi(\mathbf{b}_f)$ for a given orthonormalized basis $\mathcal{B} = \{\mathbf{b}_f\}$ of the feature space $\mathcal{F}$. Without loss of generality, one can consider the canonical basis $\mathcal{O} = \{\mathbf{o}_f\}$ where $\mathbf{o}_f$ is a F-dimensional vector filled with 0's except the fth coordinate which is equal to 1. The whole secret of the algorithm is contained in the values ξ_f and they can consequently be pseudo-randomly generated using a secret key K. Now, assuming that feature vectors have an isotropic distribution, the probability density function of the linear form over the unit sphere $\mathcal{U}$ is given by [34]:

$$f_{\varphi|\mathcal{U}}(w) = \frac{1}{\Xi\sqrt{\pi}}\frac{\Gamma\left(\frac{F}{2}\right)}{\Gamma\left(\frac{F-1}{2}\right)}\left[1 - \left(\frac{w}{\Xi}\right)^2\right]^{\frac{F-3}{2}} \tag{8}$$

where $\Xi^2 = \sum_{f=1}^{F} \xi_f^2$ and $\Gamma(.)$ is the Gamma function. When the dimension F of the feature space $\mathcal{F}$ grows large, this probability density function tends towards a Gaussian distribution with zero mean and standard deviation $\Xi/\sqrt{F}$. Thus if the ξ_f's are chosen to have zero mean and unit variance, this ensures that the values of the linear form restricted to the unit sphere $\mathcal{U}$ are normally distributed with also zero mean and unit variance. Then, keeping in mind that φ is linear and that the following equation is valid,

$$w(\mathbf{i}, \mathbf{p}) = \varphi\left(\|\mathbf{f}(\mathbf{i}, \mathbf{p})\|\frac{\mathbf{f}(\mathbf{i}, \mathbf{p})}{\|\mathbf{f}(\mathbf{i}, \mathbf{p})\|}\right) = \|\mathbf{f}(\mathbf{i}, \mathbf{p})\|\varphi(\mathbf{u}(\mathbf{i}, \mathbf{p})) \quad \text{with } \mathbf{u}(\mathbf{i}, \mathbf{p}) \in \mathcal{U} \tag{9}$$

it is straightforward to realize that the obtained watermark is equivalent to a Gaussian watermark with zero mean and unit variance multiplied by some local scaling factors. The more textured is the considered neighborhood, the more complicated it is to characterize it and the greater the norm $\|\mathbf{f}(\mathbf{i}, \mathbf{p})\|$ is likely to be. Looking back at Equation 9, it results that the watermark is amplified in textured area whereas it is attenuated in smooth ones. This can be regarded as some kind of perceptual shaping [35].

A practical implementation of this strategy using Gabor features has clearly demonstrated its superiority with respect to BRA in comparison to common SS watermarks [36]. Furthermore, this implementation exhibited an unexpected relationship with earlier multiplicative watermarking schemes in the frequency domain. The watermark sample obtained at position $\mathbf{p}$ is simply given by:

$$w(\mathbf{i}, \mathbf{p}) = \sum_{f=1}^{F} \xi_f \mathbf{g}_f(\mathbf{i}, \mathbf{p}) \tag{10}$$

where $\mathbf{g}_f(\mathbf{i}, \mathbf{p})$ is the f-th coordinate of the F-dimensional Gabor feature vector $\mathbf{g}(\mathbf{i}, \mathbf{p})$. In other words, the watermark is a linear combination of different Gabor responses $\mathbf{g}_f$. However, when the number of filters in the Gabor filterbank grows, more and more Gabor responses need to be computed which can be quickly computationally prohibitive. Hopefully, when the Fourier domain is considered, the watermark can be computed as follows:

$$\mathbf{W}(\mathbf{i},\mathbf{q}) = \sum_{\mathbf{p}\in\mathcal{P}} \left(\sum_{f=1}^{F} \xi_f\, \mathbf{g}_f(\mathbf{i},\mathbf{p})\right) \omega_{\mathbf{p},\mathbf{q}}$$

$$= \sum_{f=1}^{F} \xi_f \left(\sum_{\mathbf{p}\in\mathcal{P}} \mathbf{g}_f(\mathbf{i},\mathbf{p})\, \omega_{\mathbf{p},\mathbf{q}}\right) = \sum_{f=1}^{F} \xi_f\, \mathbf{G}_f(\mathbf{i},\mathbf{q})$$

$$= \sum_{f=1}^{F} \xi_f\, \mathbf{H}_f(\mathbf{q})\, \mathbf{I}(\mathbf{q}) = \mathbf{H}(K,\mathbf{q})\, \mathbf{I}(\mathbf{q}) \tag{11}$$

$$\text{with} \quad \mathbf{H}(K,\mathbf{q}) = \sum_{f=1}^{F} \xi_f\, \mathbf{H}_f(\mathbf{q})$$

where $\omega_{\mathbf{p},\mathbf{q}} = \exp\left[-j2\pi\left((x-1)(u-1)/X + (y-1)(v-1)/Y\right)\right]$, capital letters indicate FFT-transformed variables and $\mathbf{q} = (u,v)$ denotes a frequency position with $1 \leq u \leq U$ and $1 \leq v \leq V$. The Gabor response $\mathbf{G}_f$ is given in the frequency domain by the multiplication of the image spectrum $\mathbf{I}$ with some filter $\mathbf{H}_f$. In summary, Equation 11 means that the watermark can be generated in one row in the Fourier domain by computing $\mathbf{H}$. It is now straightforward to realize that the watermark generation process comes down to a simple multiplication between the image spectrum $\mathbf{I}$ and some pseudo-random signal $\mathbf{H}(K)$. Following this track, multiplicative watermarks in the FFT [37] and the DCT [38] domains have been shown to be also resilient against BRA. At this point, it is interesting to note that multiplicative watermarking in the frequency domain was initially motivated by contrast masking properties: larger coefficients can convey a larger watermark value without compromising invisibility [39]. This can be related with the natural perceptual shaping of signal coherent watermarks exhibited in Equation (9).

4   Conclusion

The partial failure of initiatives to launch copy control mechanisms using digital watermarking has recently triggered an effort in the watermarking community to evaluate security. Security is basically related with the fact that, in many applications, consumers do not benefit from the introduction of digital watermarks: they can be used to identify customers, to prevent playback of illegal content, etc. As a result, customers are likely to attack the protection system. In this perspective, researchers try to anticipate their hostile behaviors to propose efficient countermeasures. In this paper, two collusion attacks have been introduced which exploit the redundancy of the host signal to remove the embedded watermark. In order to circumvent those threats, two remedies have been proposed to make the embedded watermark coherent with the spatio-temporal redundancy of the host video signal. The first one considers camera motion during embedding to ensure immunity against TFAR. The second one takes the self-similarities of the host signal into account to cope with BRA at the block level. However, at this stage it is not possible to assert how secure the obtained schemes are. One can only claim that they resist BRA but nothing ensures that another attack will not defeat them. Recent studies have defined some kind of *security metric* to determine how much information leaks when a redundant watermarking structure is used [6]. It could be interesting to investigate in the near future whether this approach can be extended to also consider the case when non redundant watermarks are used. The resulting metric would then be useful to quantify the security level of signal coherent watermarking.

Acknowledgment

This work has been supported in part by the European Commission through the IST Program under Contract IST-2002-507932 ECRYPT.

References

1. Cox, I., Miller, M., Bloom, J.: Digital Watermarking. Morgan Kaufmann Publishers (2001)
2. DVD Copy Control Association: (http://www.dvdcca.org)
3. Secure Digital Music Initiative: (http://www.sdmi.org)
4. Su, K., Kundur, D., Hatzinakos, D.: A novel approach to collusion resistant video watermarking. In: Security and Watermarking of Multimedia Contents IV. Volume 4675 of Proceedings of SPIE. (2002) 491–502
5. Doërr, G., Dugelay, J.L.: Collusion issue in video watermarking. In: Security, Steganography and Watermarking of Multimedia Contents VII. Volume 5681 of Proceedings of SPIE. (2005) 685–696
6. Cayre, F., Fontaine, C., Furon, T.: Watermarking security, part I: Theory. In: Security, Steganography and Watermarking of Multimedia Contents VII. Volume 5681 of Proceedings of SPIE. (2005) 746–757
7. Cayre, F., Fontaine, C., Furon, T.: Watermarking security, part II: Practice. In: Security, Steganography and Watermarking of Multimedia Contents VII. Volume 5681 of Proceedings of SPIE. (2005) 758–768
8. Doërr, G., Dugelay, J.L.: Security pitfalls of frame-by-frame approaches to video watermarking. IEEE Transactions on Signal Processing, Supplement on Secure Media **52** (2004) 2955–2964
9. Hartung, F., Girod, B.: Watermarking of uncompressed and compressed video. Signal Processing **66** (1998) 283–301
10. Doërr, G., Dugelay, J.L.: A guide tour of video watermarking. Signal Processing: Image Communication, Special Issue on Technologies for Image Security **18** (2003) 263–282
11. Doërr, G., Dugelay, J.L.: New intra-video collusion attack using mosaicing. In: Proceedings of the IEEE International Conference on Multimedia and Expo. Volume II. (2003) 505–508
12. Doërr, G., Dugelay, J.L.: Secure background watermarking based on video mosaicing. In: Security, Steganography and Watermarking of Multimedia Contents VI. Volume 5306 of Proceedings of SPIE. (2004) 304–314

13. Smolic, A., Lorei, M., Sikora, T.: Adaptive kalman-filtering for prediction and global motion parameter tracking of segments in video. In: Proceedings of the Picture Coding Symposium. (1996)

14. Nicolas, H., Labit, C.: Motion and illumination variation estimation using a hierarchy of models: Application to image sequence coding. Journal of Visual Communication and Image Representation **6** (1995) 303–316

15. Szeliski, R., Shum, H.Y.: Creating full view panoramic image mosaics and environment maps. In: Proceedings of the International Conference on Computer Graphics and Interactive Techniques. (1997) 251–258

16. Sun, Z., Tekalp, M.: Trifocal motion modeling for object-based video compression and manipulation. IEEE Journal on Circuits and Systems for Video Technology **8** (1998) 667–685

17. Koenen, R.: MPEG-4 overview. In: JTC1/SC29/WG11 N4668, ISO/IEC (2002)

18. Fisher, Y.: Fractal Image Compression: Theory and Applications. Springer-Verlag (1994)

19. Rey, C., Doërr, G., Dugelay, J.L., Csurka, G.: Toward generic image dewatermarking? In: Proceedings of the IEEE International Conference on Image Processing. Volume III. (2002) 633–636

20. Petitcolas, F., Kirovski, D.: The blind pattern matching attack on watermarking systems. In: Proceedings of the IEEE International Conference on Acoustics, Speech, and Signal Processing. Volume IV. (2002) 3740–3743

21. Kirovski, D., Petitcolas, F.: Blind pattern matching attack on watermarking systems. IEEE Transactions on Signal Processing **51** (2003) 1045–1053

22. Kirovski, D., Petitcolas, F.: Replacement attack on arbitrary watermarking systems. In: Proceedings of the ACM Digital Rights Management Workshop. Volume 2696 of Lecture Notes in Computer Science. (2003) 177–189

23. Doërr, G., Dugelay, J.L., Grangé, L.: Exploiting self-similarities to defeat digital watermarking systems - a case study on still images. In: Proceedings of the ACM Multimedia and Security Workshop. (2004) 133–142

24. Holliman, M., Macy, W., Yeung, M.: Robust frame-dependent video watermarking. In: Security and Watermarking of Multimedia Contents II. Volume 3971 of Proceedings of SPIE. (2000) 186–197

25. Fridrich, J., Goljan, M.: Robust hash functions for digital watermarking. In: Proceedings of the International Conference on Information Technology: Coding and Computing. (2000) 178–183

26. Delannay, D., Macq, B.: A method for hiding synchronization marks in scale and rotation resilient watermarking schemes. In: Security and Watermarking of Multimedia Contents IV. Volume 4675 of Proceedings of SPIE. (2002) 548–554

27. Irani, M., Anandan, P., Bergen, J., Kumar, R., Hsu, S.: Mosaic representations of video sequences and their applications. Signal Processing: Image Communication **8** (1996) 327–351

28. Bas, P., Macq, B.: A new video-object watermarking scheme robust to object manipulation. In: Proceedings of the IEEE International Conference on Image Processing. Volume II. (2001) 526–529

29. Hartung, F., Eisert, P., Girod, B.: Digital watermarking of MPEG-4 facial animation parameters. Computers & Graphics **22** (1998) 425–435

30. Garcia, E., Dugelay, J.L.: Texture-based watermarking of 3D video objects. IEEE Transactions on Circuits and Systems for Video Technology **13** (2003) 853–866

31. Visual Quality Expert Group (VQEG): (http://www.vqeg.org)

32. Macy, W., Holliman, M.: Quality evaluation of watermarked video. In: Security and Watermarking of Multimedia Contents II. Volume 3971 of Proceedings of SPIE. (2000) 486–500
33. Winkler, S., Gelasca, E., Ebrahimi, T.: Towards perceptual metrics for video watermark evaluation. In: Applications of Digital Image Processing. Volume 5203 of Proceedings of SPIE. (2003) 371–378
34. Doërr, G.: Security Issue and Collusion Attacks in Video Watermarking. PhD thesis, Université de Nice Sophia-Antipolis, France (2005)
35. Voloshynovskiy, S., Herrigel, A., Baumgärtner, N., Pun, T.: A stochastic approach to content adaptive digital image watermarking. In: Proceedings of the Third International Workshop on Information Hiding. Volume 1768 of Lecture Notes in Computer Science. (1999) 211–236
36. Doërr, G., Dugelay, J.L.: How to combat block replacement attacks? In: Accepted for publication in the 7th Information Hiding Workshop. (2005)
37. Barni, M., Bartolini, F., De Rosa, A., Piva, A.: A new decoder for optimum recovery of nonadditive watermarks. IEEE Transactions on Image Processing 10 (2001) 755–766
38. Cox, I., Kilian, J., Leighton, T., Shamoon, T.: Secure spread spectrum watermarking for multimedia. IEEE Transactions on Image Processing 6 (1997) 1673–1687
39. Foley, J., Legge, G.: Contrast masking in human vision. Journal of the Optical Society of America 70 (1980) 1458–1470

Fingerprinting Schemes. Identifying the Guilty Sources Using Side Information

Miguel Soriano, Marcel Fernandez, and Josep Cotrina*

Departament d'Enginyeria Telemàtica, Universitat Politècnica de Catalunya,
C/ Jordi Girona 1 i 3. Campus Nord, Mod C3, UPC. 08034 Barcelona, Spain
{soriano, marcel, jcotrina}@entel.upc.es

Abstract. In a fingerprinting scheme a distributor places marks in each copy of a digital object. Placing different marks in different copies, uniquely identifies the recipient of each copy, and therefore allows to trace the source of an unauthorized redistribution. A widely used approach to the fingerprinting problem is the use of error correcting codes with a suitable minimum distance. With this approach, the set of embedded marks in a given copy is precisely a codeword of the error correcting code. We present two different approaches that use side information for the tracing process. The first one uses the Guruswami-Sudan soft-decision list decoding algorithm and the second one a modified version of the Viterbi algorithm.

1   Introduction

With the increasing availability of copying devices for digital data, the need to restrain illegal redistribution of multimedia objects is becoming an important issue. The fingerprinting technique consists in inserting a different set of marks, called fingerprint, in each copy of a digital object, using a watermarking scheme [7,22,6]. The watermarking scheme imperceptibly embeds the fingerprint in a way that it can only be recovered using a secure key. Therefore, if a user redistributes his fingerprinted object without modification, he can be incriminated in an unambiguous way. Nevertheless, a group of dishonest users, called traitors, can collude to create a pirate copy that hides their identities, by comparing their copies. If the set of marks to be embedded are the codewords of an error correcting code, it is possible to obtain efficient algorithms to trace the traitors.

If the code is a traceability code, then the traitor tracing algorithm reduces to search for the codewords that agree in most symbol positions with the pirate. For this search, list decoding algorithms are optimal when all traitors contribute with the same amount of information in the construction of the pirate copy. The use of soft-decision list decoding allows extending the tracing capabilities. In this paper, we present two different approaches, whose output is a list containing all traitors that have positively been involved in the construction of the pirate:

- By means of the Guruswami-Sudan soft-decision decoding algorithm. The output of one decoding is changed into side information that is used as the input to the next decoding.

* This work has been supported in part by the Spanish Research Council (CICYT) Project TIC2002-00249 (DISQET) and Project TIC2003-01748 (RUBI) and by the IST-FP6 Project 506926 (UBISEC).

M. Barni et al. (Eds.): IWDW 2005, LNCS 3710, pp. 231–243, 2005.

– Applying the Viterbi algorithm to the trellis representation of a cyclic traceability code to find all possibly identifiable traitors.

1.1   Related Work

The idea of error correcting codes having traceability properties, as discussed in this paper, is due to the work of Chor, Fiat and Naor in [4] (see also [5]), where the term *tracing traitors* first appeared. The schemes in [4], work as long as the number of colluders is less than a prefixed threshold, and can only guarantee the identification of one of the traitors.

The collusion attack introduced above, is modeled by the following *marking assumption*: In the positions where they detect a mark, the colluders have to choose between placing one of their marks or making the mark unreadable, whereas all the undetected marks will remain unchanged. This marking assumption is extended in [12], by allowing some of the undetected marks to also be erased.

The previous marking assumption is assumed in [1,2,3,18,15], and in almost all of the work that deals with traceability from an information-theory, media-independent point of view, as this paper does. A more practical approach, to the collusion secure fingerprinting problem, can be found in [20].

1.2   Organization of the Paper

The paper is organized as follows. Section 2 gives the required background in coding theory and traceability codes. Our soft-decision tracing algorithm is presented in Section 3. The soft-decision tracing algorithm is extended to traceability codes tolerating erasures in Section 4. In Section 5 we show how a modified version of the Vitebi algorithm can also be used in the tracing process. We present our conclusions in Section 6.

2   Background on Coding Theory and Traceability Codes

2.1   Codes and Traceability Codes

Reed-Solomon and cyclic codes. We use the terminology in [19] to describe *traceability codes*. Let $\mathbb{F}_q^n$ be a vector space, then $C \subseteq \mathbb{F}_q^n$ is called a *code*. The set of symbols, $\mathbb{F}_q$ is called the *code alphabet*. A vector in $\mathbb{F}_q^n$ is called a *word* and the elements of C are called *codewords*. A code C is a *linear code* if it forms a subspace of $\mathbb{F}_q^n$. A code with length n, dimension k and minimum distance d is denoted as a $[n, k, d]$-code.

For a linear $[n, k, d]$-code C, we have that the inequality $d \leq n-k+1$ always holds. This inequality is called the *Singleton bound* [14]. Codes with equality in the Singleton bound are called *maximum distance separable codes* or just MDS codes. A well known class of linear MDS codes are Reed-Solomon codes, that can be defined as follows:

Take n distinct elements $P = \{\nu_1, \ldots, \nu_n\} \subseteq \mathbb{F}_q$. Then a *Reed-Solomon code* of length n and dimension k, consists of all the codewords $(f(\nu_1), \ldots, f(\nu_n))$ where f takes the value of all polynomials of degree less than k in $\mathbb{F}_q[x]$

$$\mathrm{RS}(P, k) = \{(f(\nu_1), ..., f(\nu_n)) | f \in \mathbb{F}_q[x] \wedge \deg(f) < k\}$$

A code is said to be *cyclic* if, for every codeword $\mathbf{c} = (c_0, c_1, \ldots, c_{n-1})$, the cyclically shifted word $\mathbf{c}' = (c_1, c_2, \ldots, c_{n-1}, c_0)$ is also a codeword. An $[n, l, d]$ cyclic code can be defined using a generator polynomial $g(D) = g_0 + g_1 D + \cdots + g_l D^{n-l}$. Using this definition, we can associate a codeword to a *code polynomial*: $\mathbf{c} = (c_0, c_1, \ldots, c_{n-1}) \Rightarrow c(D) = c_0 + c_1 D + \cdots + c_{n-1} D^{n-1}$.

This association provides a very elegant way to obtain the codewords. We say that a word $\mathbf{c}$, is a codeword in the code defined by $g(D)$, if and only if its associated code polynomial $c(D)$ is a multiple of $g(D)$. So, if $\mathbf{u} = (u_0, u_1, \ldots, u_{l-1})$ is a block of information symbols, then we can express $\mathbf{u}$ as the polynomial $u(D) = u_0 + u_1 D + u_2 D^2 + \cdots + u_{k-1} D^{l-1}$. Encoding is then a multiplication by $g(D)$, $c(D) = u(D)g(D)$.

Traceability codes. If $C_0 = \{\mathbf{w}^1, \ldots, \mathbf{w}^c\}$, $C_0 \subseteq C$, is any subset of codewords, the set of *descendants* of C_0, denoted $\mathbf{desc}_c(C_0)$, is defined as

$$\mathbf{desc}_c(C_0) = \{\mathbf{z} \in \mathbb{F}_q^n : z_i \in \{w_i^1, \ldots, w_i^c\}\}.$$

If at most s erasures are allowed then the *extended* set of descendants is defined as $\mathbf{desc}_c^*(C_0; s) = \{\mathbf{z} = (z_1, \ldots, z_n)\}$, where

$$z_j \in \{w_j^1, \ldots, w_j^c\} \cup \{*\} \text{ and } |j : z_j = \{*\}| \leq s.$$

The symbol $\{*\}$ denotes an erasure.

For a code C and an integer $c \geq 2$, let $C_i \subseteq C$, $i = 1, 2, \ldots, t$ be all the subsets of C such that $|C_i| \leq c$.

Definition 1. *Let C be a code, then C is a c-traceability code if for all i and for all $\mathbf{z} \in \mathbf{desc}_c(C_i)$, there is at least one codeword $\mathbf{a} \in C_i$ such that $|j : z_j = a_j| > |j : z_j = b_j|$ for any $\mathbf{b} \in C \backslash C_i$. The elements of C_i are called the parents of $\mathbf{z}$.*

Theorem 1 ([19]). *Let C be a $[n,k,d]$-code, if $d > n(1 - 1/c^2)$ then C is a c-traceability code.*

In [15] Definition 1 and Theorem 1 are extended for the case of erasure tolerance.

Definition 2 ([15]). *Let C be a code. C is called a c-traceability code tolerating s erasures if for all i and for all $\mathbf{z} \in \mathbf{desc}_c^*(C_i; s)$, there is at least one codeword $\mathbf{a} \in C_i$ such that $|j : z_j = a_j| > |j : z_j = b_j|$ for any $\mathbf{b} \in C \backslash C_i$.*

Theorem 2 ([15]). *Let C be a $[n,k,d]$-code, if $d > n(1 - 1/c^2) + s/c^2$ then C is a c-traceability code tolerating s erasures.*

3 Soft-Decision Tracing of Traceability Codes

In this section we present our soft-decision tracing process. Since this process uses as its underlying routine the improvement made by Koetter and Vardy [13] of the Guruswami-Sudan (GS) soft-decision decoding algorithm [11], the needed results are briefly detailed below.

3.1   The Guruswami-Sudan Soft-Decision Decoding Algorithm

When a codeword is transmitted through a communications channel, the received word is usually a corrupted version of the sent codeword due to the inherent presence of noise in the channel. If the number of errors e is greater than $\lfloor \frac{d-1}{2} \rfloor$, then there can be more than one codeword within distance e from the received word and the decoder may either decode incorrectly or fail to decode. This leads to the concept of *list decoding* [11], were the decoder outputs a list of all codewords within distance e of the received word, thus offering a potential way to recover from errors beyond the error correction bound of the code.

In *soft-decision* decoding, the decoding process takes advantage of "side informa-tion" generated by the receiver and instead of using the received word symbols, the decoder uses probabilistic reliability information about these received symbols.

Without loss of generality, we take $\alpha_1, \alpha_2, \ldots, \alpha_q$ as the ordering of the elements of the field $\mathbb{F}_q$. A q-ary symmetric erasure channel with error probability δ, erasure probability σ, input alphabet $\mathcal{X} = \mathbb{F}_q$ and output alphabet $\mathcal{Y} = \mathbb{F}_q \cup \{*\}$, can be characterized by a *transition probability matrix* $\mathcal{T}_{X|Y}$, that has the following expression

$$
\mathcal{T}_{X|Y}(x,y) = \begin{cases} \sigma & y = \{*\} \\ (1-\sigma)(1-\delta) & y = x \\ (1-\sigma)\dfrac{\delta}{q-1} & y \neq x \text{ and } y \neq \{*\} \end{cases}
\tag{1}
$$

To construct the reliability matrix $\mathcal{R}$, suppose that codeword $\mathbf{u}$ is transmitted and word $\mathbf{v}$ is received. Then the entries in the $q \times n$ matrix over the reals, $[\mathbf{v}]$, are defined by

$$
[\mathbf{v}]_{i,j} = \begin{cases} 1 & \text{if } v_j = \alpha_i \\ 1/q & \text{if } v_j = \{*\} \\ 0 & \text{otherwise} \end{cases}
\tag{2}
$$

and we have

$$
\mathcal{R} = (1-\delta)[\mathbf{v}] + \frac{\delta}{q-1}(1 - [\mathbf{v}])
\tag{3}
$$

In [13] Koetter and Vardy show that the GS algorithm when applied to the q-ary symmetric erasure channel, achieves the following performance

$$
\frac{l^2}{m} + \frac{(m-l)^2}{m(q-1)} + \frac{n-m}{q} \geq (k-1)
\tag{4}
$$

This means that upon receiving a word $\mathbf{v}$, with $n - m$ erased symbols, for every value of l that satisfies (4) the GS algorithm will output codeword $\mathbf{u}$. Therefore the algorithm can handle $(n - m)$ erasures and $(m - l)$ errors.

3.2   Soft-Decision Tracing Process

For a c-traceability Reed-Solomon code, the goal of a tracing algorithm is to output a c-bounded list that contains all parents of a given descendant. We cannot expect to find all parents, since some of them may contribute with too few positions and cannot be traced. This happens for example, when a parent contributes with only $k - 1$ positions where k is the dimension of the code. So given a descendant, we call any codeword that is involved in the construction of the descendant in an unambiguous way a *positive parent*. The condition for a codeword to be a positive parent is given in Theorem 3 below.

Lemma 1. *Let C be a c-traceability Reed-Solomon code. Given a descendant there always exists a codeword in C that agrees with the descendant in at least $c(k - 1) + 1$ positions.*

Proof. Since there are at most c parents, one of them must contribute with at least $\lceil n/c \rceil$ symbols in the creation of the descendant, so it suffices to prove that $c(k - 1) + 1 \leq \lceil n/c \rceil$. Since $d > n - n/c^2$ this is clearly the case.   ∎

Theorem 3. *Let C be a c-traceability Reed-Solomon code with parameters $[n, k, d]$, if a codeword agrees in at least $c(k - 1) + 1$ positions with a given descendant then this codeword must be involved in the construction of the descendant.*

Proof. The existence of the codeword follows from Lemma 1. If the code has minimum distance d, then two codewords can agree in at most $n - d$ positions. Therefore, a coalition of size c, is able to create a descendant that agrees in at most $c(n-d)$ positions with any other codeword not in the coalition. Then any codeword that agrees with the descendant in at least $c(n-d)+1$ positions is a positive parent of the descendant. Since Reed-Solomon codes are MDS then $c(n - d) + 1 = c(k - 1) + 1$.   ∎

For a codeword $\mathbf{u}$ and a descendant $\mathbf{z}$ the set $M(\mathbf{u}, \mathbf{z}) = \{i : u_i = z_i\}$ is called the set of *matched positions*. Now we have the following corollary.

Corollary 1. *Let C be a c-traceability Reed-Solomon code with parameters $[n, k, d]$. Let $\mathbf{p}$ be a descendant of some coalition. Suppose that j already identified positive parents $(j < c)$ jointly match less than $n - (c - j)(k - 1)$ positions of $\mathbf{p}$, then any codeword that agrees with $\mathbf{p}$ in at least $(c - j)(k - 1) + 1$ of the unmatched positions is also a positive parent.*

Intuitively our algorithm works as follows:

Since given a descendant word there is no side information available, the reliability matrix is constructed as if the channel were a q-ary symmetric channel. A first run of the decoding algorithm is made.

Once some positive parents are identified, the algorithm computes the number of remaining parents to be found. All symbol positions where these already identified parents match the descendant are erased. Then to construct the reliability matrix, the situation is modeled as a *q-ary symmetric erasure channel*. Another run of the GS algorithm is made. This step is repeated until it becomes clear that there are no more positive parents.

Algorithm:

Input: c: positive integer; C: Reed-Solomon code of length n where $n > c^2(k - 1)$; Descendant $\mathbf{z} \in \mathbf{desc}_c(U)$, $|U| \leq c$.

Output: A list L of all positive parents of $\mathbf{z}$.

1. Set $i := 1$, $c_i := c$ and $M_i := \{\emptyset\}$.
2. $j := 0$.
3. Using the descendant $\mathbf{z}$, compute the entries of the $q \times n$ matrix $[\mathbf{z}]$ as follows:

$$[\mathbf{z}]_{a,b} := \begin{cases} 1/q & \text{if } b \in M_i \\ 1 & \text{if } z_b = \alpha_a \text{ and } b \notin M_i \\ 0 & \text{otherwise} \end{cases}$$

so the reliability matrix is: $\mathcal{R}_i = (1 - \delta)[\mathbf{z}] + \dfrac{\delta}{q-1}(1 - [\mathbf{z}])$

4. Compute the value of l closest to $(c_i(k-1)+1)$ that satisfies (4) and set $\delta = \dfrac{(n - |M_i|) - l}{n - |M_i|}$.

5. Apply $\mathcal{R}_i$ to the GS soft-decision algorithm. From the output list take all codewords $\mathbf{u}_{i_1}, \ldots, \mathbf{u}_{i_{j_w}}$, that agree with $\mathbf{z}$ in at least $(c_i(k-1)+1)$ of the positions not in M_i, and add them to L. Set $j := j + j_w$.

6. If $j_w \neq 0$ then: $M_i := \{t : (z_t = u_t) \forall \mathbf{u} \in L\}$. Go to step 3

7. Set $i := i + 1$, $c_i := c_{i-1} - j$ and $M_i = \{t : (z_t = u_t) \forall \mathbf{u} \in L\}$.

8. If $j = 0$ or $c_i = 0$ or if $|M_i| \geq (n - c_i(k-1))$ output L and quit, else go to step 2.

4   Soft-Decision Tracing of Traceability Codes Tolerating Erasures

4.1   Extension of the Marking Assumption

We now model the collusion attack by the following marking assumption [2]: In the positions where they detect a mark, the colluders have to choose between placing one of their marks or making the mark unreadable, whereas all the undetected marks will remain unchanged. This marking assumption is extended in [12] by allowing some of the undetected marks to also be erased. In both cases it is clear that as before, upon finding a pirate copy, the goal of the distributor is to identify as many traitors as possible.

To see the motivation for the extension our tracing algorithm, consider the following scenario from [15]. The distributor assigns a codeword from a q-ary fingerprinting code to each user. To embed the codeword into each users object, the object is first divided into blocks. The distributor then picks a set of these blocks at random. This set of blocks is kept secret and will be the same for all users. Then using a watermarking algorithm a mark of the fingerprint codeword is embedded in each block. Such a watermarking approach is presented in [8] for the binary case, whereas [7] deals with the case of watermarking algorithms that can embed more than one bit. Note that a given user will have one of the q versions of the block.

The colluding traitors compare their copies, detect the blocks where their copies differ and with this information at hand, they construct a pirate copy where each block belongs to the corresponding block of one of the traitors. Since each mark is embedded using a different random sequence and these sequences are unknown to the traitors, they cannot create a version of the block that they do not have, but they can modify the block as to make the mark unreadable. Traitors are also allowed to erase some of the marks in the undetected positions by using attacks such as averaging. This is a q-ary version of Guth and Pfitzmann's marking assumption [12].

If the fingerprinting code is a *traceability code tolerating erasures*, then tracing the traitors can be successful provided the number of erased positions is bounded and it reduces to search for the codewords that agree in most symbol positions with the pirate.

4.2   Soft-Decision Tracing Algorithm Tolerating Erasures

The conditions for a codeword to be a positive parent in the case of erasure tolerance are given in the following theorem and its corollary.

Theorem 4. *Let C be a c-traceability Reed-Solomon code tolerating s erasures with parameters $[n, k, d]$. If a codeword and a descendant agree in at least $c(k - 1) + 1$ of the non-erased positions, then this codeword must be involved in the construction of the descendant.*

Proof. If there are no erased positions in the descendant, then $s = 0$ and from the proof of Theorem 3, we have that the number of positions in which a descendant and a codeword not in the coalition that created the descendant agree, is at most $c(k - 1)$. Erasing symbols in the descendant (at most s), only makes this number smaller.

From the above reasoning, and again from the proof of Theorem 3, it follows that any codeword that agrees with the descendant in at least $c(k - 1) + 1$ of the *non-erased* positions, is a positive parent. ∎

Corollary 2. *Let C be a c-traceability Reed-Solomon code tolerating s erasures with parameters $[n, k, d]$, and let $\mathbf{z}$ be a descendant of some coalition, having s symbols erased. Suppose that j already identified positive parents ($j < c$) jointly match less than $n - s - (c - j)(k - 1)$ positions of $\mathbf{z}$, then any codeword that agrees with $\mathbf{z}$ in at least $(c - j)(k - 1) + 1$ of the unmatched positions is also a positive parent.*

The development of the algorithm follows that given previously in Section 3, with the exception that, since the descendant may have some symbols erased, the reliability matrix is constructed as if the channel were a q-ary symmetric erasure channel, right at the initialization step of the algorithm.

Algorithm:
Input: c, s: positive integers; C: Reed-Solomon code of length n and minimum distance $d > n(1 - 1/c^2) + s/c^2$; Descendant $\mathbf{z} \in \mathbf{desc}_c^*(U; s)$, $|U| \leq c$.
Output: A list L of all positive parents of $\mathbf{z}$.

1. Set $i := 1$, $c_i := c$ and $M_i := \{m : z_m = *\}$.
2. $j := 0$.
3. Using the descendant $\mathbf{z}$, compute the entries of the $q \times n$ matrix $[\mathbf{z}]$ as follows:

$$[\mathbf{z}]_{r,t} := \begin{cases} 1/q & \text{if } t \in M_i \\ 1 & \text{if } z_t = \alpha_r \text{ and } t \notin M_i \\ 0 & \text{otherwise} \end{cases}$$

so the reliability matrix is: $\mathcal{R}_i = (1 - \delta)[\mathbf{z}] + \dfrac{\delta}{q - 1}(1 - [\mathbf{z}])$

4. Compute the value of l closest to $(c_i(k-1)+1)$ that satisfies (4) and set $\delta = \dfrac{(n-|M_i|)-l}{n-|M_i|}$.

5. Apply $\mathcal{R}_i$ to the GS soft-decision algorithm. the output list take all codewords $\mathbf{u}_{i_1}, \ldots, \mathbf{u}_{i_{j_w}}$, that agree with $\mathbf{z}$ in at least $(c_i(k-1)+1)$ of the positions not in M_i, and add them to L. Set $j := j + j_w$.

6. If $j_w \neq 0$ then: $M_i := \{m \ : \ (z_m = u_m) \ \forall\, \mathbf{u} \in L\} \cup \{m : z_m = *\}$. Go to step 3

7. Set $i := i+1$, $c_i := c_{i-1} - j$ and $M_i = \{m \ : \ (z_m = u_m) \ \forall\, \mathbf{u} \in L\} \cup \{m : z_m = *\}$.

8. If $j = 0$ or $c_i = 0$ or if $|M_i| \geq (n - c_i(k-1))$ output L and quit, else go to step 2.

The correctness and one example can be found in [9].

5   Tracing Viterbi Algorithm for Traceability Codes

In order to apply the Viterbi [10] algorithm to a block code, we first need a way to obtain its trellis representation. An elegant way to graphically represent such a trellis can be found in [21], as is shown below.

5.1   Trellis Representation of Cyclic Block Codes

For a linear block $[n, l, d]$ code over $\mathbb{F}_q$, a *trellis* is defined as a graph in which the nodes represent states, and the edges represent transitions between these states. The nodes are grouped into sets S_t, indexed by a "time" parameter t, $0 \leq t \leq n$. The parameter t indicates the *depth* of the node. The edges are unidirectional, with the direction of the edge going from the node at depth t, to the node at depth $t + 1$. Each edge is labeled using an element of $\mathbb{F}_q$.

It can be shown [21] that, in any depth t, the number of states in the set S_t is at most $q^{(n-l)}$. The states at depth t are denoted by $\mathbf{s}_t^i$, for certain values of i, $i \in \{0, 1, \ldots, q^{(n-l)} - 1\}$. The states will be identified by q-ary $(n-l)$-tuples. In other words, if we order all the q-ary $(n-l)$-tuples from 0 to $q^{(n-l)} - 1$, then $\mathbf{s}_t^i$ corresponds to the ith tuple in the list. Using this order, for each set of nodes S_t, we can associate the set I_t that consists of all the integers i, such that $\mathbf{s}_t^i \in S_t$. We denote the edge going from node $\mathbf{s}_t^i$ to node $\mathbf{s}_{t+1}^j$ as $\theta_t^{i,j}$.

In the trellis representation of a code C, there are q^l different paths in the trellis starting at depth 0 and ending at depth n, each different path corresponding to a different codeword. The labels of the edges in the path are precisely the codeword symbols. The correspondence between paths and codewords is therefore one to one, as it will be readily seen from the construction process of the trellis, that we now present following the ideas in [21].

The encoding process for a cyclic code with generator polynomial $g(D) = g_0 + g_1 D + \cdots + g_{n-l} D^{n-l}$, can be described as follows: We express the information digits by the polynomial $u(D) = u_{n-1} D^{n-1} + u_{n-2} D^{n-2} + \cdots + u_{n-l} D^{n-l}$. By the Euclidean division algorithm we have that $u(D) = a(D)g(D) + r(D)$, where $r(D)$ is a polynomial of degree at most $n - l - 1$. Therefore, the polynomial $u(D) - r(D) = a(D)g(D)$ is a codeword.

We first show how to construct the polynomial $u(D)$. We start with the zero polynomial $s_0(D, 0) = 0$ and perform the iteration

$$s(D, i) = D \cdot s(D, i - 1) + u_{n-i} D^{n-l} \qquad (5)$$

for $1 \leq i \leq l$. Note that this iteration yields a polynomial of degree at most $n - 1$, that is precisely $u(D)$, in other words, $s(D, l) = u(D)$.

Since we have to obtain $r(D) = u(D) \mod g(D)$, from the properties of the modulo operation, the recursion (5) can be expressed as

$$s_g(D, i) \equiv (D \cdot s_g(D, i - 1) + u_{n-i} D^{n-l}) \mod g(D) \qquad (6)$$

for $1 \leq i \leq l$, where $s_g(D, i)$ denotes the reduction of $s(D, i)$ modulo $g(D)$ and therefore $r(D) = s_g(D, l)$.

As a consequence of the above reasoning, we have that the trellis of a block cyclic code can be intuitively constructed as follows: Encode each possible l-tuple over $\mathbb{F}_q$, and associate each encoder state at time t with a trellis state (node) at depth t. We now summarize these ideas more formally.

The algorithm uses a function **coefs**, defined as follows: let $p(D) = p_0 + p_1 D + p_2 D^2 + \cdots + p_n D^n$ then $\mathbf{coefs}[p(D)] = (p_0, p_1, p_2, \ldots, p_n)$.

Block Cyclic Codes: Trellis Construction Algorithm.

1. Initialization (depth $t = 0$):
   $S_0 = \{\mathbf{coefs}[s_g(D, 0)]\}$, where $s_g(D, 0)$ is the zero polynomial.
2. Iterate for each depth $t = 0, 1, \ldots, (n - 1)$.

   (a) if $t \leq l - 1$ then
   - Construct $S_{t+1} = \{s_{t+1}^0, \ldots, s_{t+1}^{|I_{t+1}|}\}$, where
     $s_{t+1}^j = \mathbf{coefs}[s_g^j(D, t + 1)]$
     and $s_g^j(D, t + 1) \equiv (D \cdot s_g^i(D, t) + u_m \cdot D^{n-l}) \mod g(D)$
     $\qquad \forall i \in I_t$ and $\forall u_m \in \mathbb{F}_q$.

   else ($l \leq t \leq n - 1$)
   - Construct $S_{t+1} = \{s_{t+1}^0, \ldots, s_{t+1}^{|I_{t+1}|}\}$, where
     $s_{t+1}^j = \mathbf{coefs}[s_g^j(D, t + 1)]$
     and $s_g^j(D, t + 1) \equiv D \cdot s_g^i(D, t) \mod g(D)$
     $\qquad \forall i \in I_t$.

   (b) For every $i \in I_t$, according to 2a:
   - Draw a connecting edge between the node s_t^i and the nodes it generates at depth $(t + 1)$, according to 2a.
   - Label each edge $\theta_t^{i,j}$, with the value of $c_j \in \mathbb{F}_q$ that appeared at the output of the decoder when s_{t+1}^j was generated from s_t^i.

From Step 2b, for every edge $\theta_t^{i,j}$ we define the function $\mathbf{label\_of}(\theta_t^{i,j})$ that, given a codeword $\mathbf{c} = (c_1, c_2, \ldots, c_n)$, returns the c_j that generated s_{t+1}^j from s_t^i.

5.2 Modified Viterbi Tracing Process

In [21] it is shown that maximum likelihood decoding of any $[n, l, d]$ block code can be accomplished by applying the VA to a trellis representing the code. However, the algorithm discussed in [21] falls into the category of unique decoding algorithms since it outputs a single codeword, and is therefore not fully adequate for our purposes. In this section we present a modified version of the Viterbi algorithm that when applied to a descendant, outputs a list that contains the codewords corresponding to the positive parents of the descendant. As we said in the introduction, the algorithm we present falls into the category of serial list Viterbi decoding algorithms [16].

We first describe the algorithm in an intuitive manner. Suppose C is a c-traceability $[n, l, d]$ code. Our goal is to find all positive parents of a descendant $\mathbf{z} = (z_1, z_2, \ldots, z_n)$. Let $\boldsymbol{\theta}_u = \{\theta_0^{0,l}, \ldots, \theta_{t-1}^{i,j}, \ldots \theta_{n-1}^{k,0}\}$ be the sequence of edges in the path associated with codeword $\mathbf{u} = (u_1, \ldots, u_t, \ldots, u_n)$. According to the definition in Section 5.1, we have that $\mathbf{label\_of}(\theta_{t-1}^{i,j}) = u_t$. Since each distinct path of the trellis corresponds to a distinct codeword, and since we need to search for codewords within a given distance of $\mathbf{z}$, it seems natural to define the "*length*" $l[\theta_{t-1}^{i,j}]$, of the edge $\theta_{t-1}^{i,j}$, as

$$l[\theta_{t-1}^{i,j}] := \mathbf{d}(z_t, u_t) = \mathbf{d}(z_t, \mathbf{label\_of}(\theta_{t-1}^{i,j})). \tag{7}$$

We expect the tracing algorithm to return all positive parents of $\mathbf{z}$, this implies that we will possibly have more than one "*survivor*" for each node. For node $\mathbf{s}_t^j$, we denote the mth "survivor" as $\mathbf{surv}_t^{j,m}$.

Let $\mathbf{path}_t^{j,m}$ denote the mth path starting at node $\mathbf{s}_0^0$ and ending at node $\mathbf{s}_t^j$, and let $|\mathbf{s}_t^j|$ denote the number of such paths. Using the above "length" definition for $l[\theta_{t-1}^{i,j}]$, we define the length $L[\mathbf{path}_t^{j,m}]$, of the path $\mathbf{path}_t^{j,m}$, as

$$L[\mathbf{path}_t^{j,m}] := \sum_{w=1}^{t} \mathbf{d}(z_w, \mathbf{label\_of}(\theta_{w-1}^{i,j})) = \sum_{w=1}^{t} l[\theta_{w-1}^{i,j}].$$

where z_w is the wth position of the descendant and $l[\theta_{w-1}^{i,j}]$ is defined as (in 7).

The tracing algorithm obtains all positive parents by passing (iterating) multiple times through the trellis. Let M_i be the set of erased positions in the descendant at the ith iteration. In the same fashion, let c_i be the number of remaining parents to be found in the ith iteration. Note that at the beginning of the algorithm $M_i = \{\emptyset\}$ and $c_i = c$. Since given only a descendant word, there is no "soft information" available, we make a first pass through the trellis, and we search for all codewords within distance $\leq n - [c(n-d)+1]$ of the descendant. This implies that whenever the length of a path, say $\mathbf{path}_t^{j,m}$, satisfies $L[\mathbf{path}_t^{j,m}] > n - [c(n-d)+1]$ we can remove this path from consideration.

Once some positive parents are identified, all symbol positions where these already identified parents match the descendant are erased. This is how "soft information" is introduced in the decoding process. Then we make another pass through the trellis. Now, according to Corollary 2, whenever $L[\mathbf{path}_t^{j,m}] > n - |M_i| - [c_i(n-d)+1]$ we remove the path $\mathbf{path}_t^{j,m}$ from consideration. This step is repeated until it becomes clear that there are no more positive parents to be found. Note that, for a given node (state) the different "survivors" do not necessarily need to have the same length. Therefore, for each node s_t^j, in the trellis, we maintain a list SL_t^j of tuples $(\mathbf{surv}_t^{j,k}, L[\mathbf{surv}_t^{j,k}])$, $k \in \{1, \ldots, |SL_t^j|\}$, where $\mathbf{surv}_t^{j,k} := \{\mathbf{path}_t^{j,v} : L[\mathbf{path}_t^{j,v}] \leq n - |M_i| - [c_i(n-d)+1]\}$.

In the case that the symbol in position t of $\mathbf{z}$ is erased ($z_t = \{*\}$), we define the "*length*" of the edge $\theta_{t-1}^{i,j}$ as $l[\theta_{t-1}^{i,j}] := \mathbf{d}(z_t, c_t) = \mathbf{d}(*, \mathbf{label\_of}(\theta_{t-1}^{i,j})) = 0$. This is clearly the appropriate definition for our purposes, since if a position is erased is because this position is already matched by a positive parent and therefore (using Corollary 2) is irrelevant to the identification of other parents.

Tracing Viterbi Algorithm. (TVA) *Variables:*

$\mathbf{z}$	descendant of a c-traceability code.
t	time index.
$\mathbf{surv}_t^{j,m}, \forall j \in I_t$	mth survivor terminating at s_t^j.
$L[\mathbf{surv}_t^{j,m}], \forall j \in I_t$	mth survivor length.
$L[\mathbf{path}_t^{j,m}]$	Length of the path $(\mathbf{surv}_{t-1}^{i,k} || \theta_{t-1}^{i,j})$.
$SL_t^j, \forall j \in I_t$	List of "survivors" terminating at s_t^j.
$\mathcal{P}$	List of positive parents terminating at s_n^0.

Initialization:

$t = 0$; $\mathbf{surv}_0^{0,1} = s_0^0$; $L[\mathbf{surv}_0^{0,1}] = 0$;
$SL_0^0 = \{(\mathbf{surv}_0^{0,1}, L[\mathbf{surv}_0^{0,1}])\}$; $SL_t^j = \{\emptyset\} \, \forall t \neq 0$; $\mathcal{P} = \{\emptyset\}$;
Set $i = 1$, $c_i = c$ and $M_i = \{\emptyset\}$.

Recursion: $(1 \leq t \leq n)$
1. For every node s_t^j do
   Reset "survivor" counter $\Rightarrow m := 0$
   2. For every node s_{t-1}^i that is connected to s_t^j through an edge $\theta_{t-1}^{i,j}$ do
      3. For every "survivor" $\mathbf{surv}_{t-1}^{i,k} \in SL_{t-1}^i$ do
         Compute the length of the path that extends "survivor" $\mathbf{surv}_{t-1}^{i,k}$
         from node s_{t-1}^i to node s_t^j:
         $$L[\mathbf{path}_t^{j,m}] = L[\mathbf{surv}_{t-1}^{i,k}] + l[\theta_{t-1}^{i,j}]$$
         if $L[\mathbf{path}_t^{j,m}] \leq n - |M_i| - [c_i(n-d)+1] \Leftrightarrow$ the path is a "survivor":
            add $(\mathbf{path}_t^{j,m}, L[\mathbf{path}_t^{j,m}])$ to the list of survivors of s_t^j, SL_t^j
         else discard $\mathbf{path}_t^{j,m}$.

Identification:
   Identify as positive parents the codewords $\mathbf{u}_{i_1}, \mathbf{u}_{i_2}, \ldots, \mathbf{u}_{i_j}$, associated with each surviving path $\mathbf{surv}_n^{0,m}$ at node s_n^0 and add them to $\mathcal{P}$.
   (Note that j is the number of identified parents in this iteration).
Update:
   Set $i = i + 1$, $c_i = c_{i-1} - j$ and $M_i = \{m : (z_m = u_m) \, \forall \, \mathbf{u} \in \mathcal{P}\}$.
   Erase the symbols in $\mathbf{z}$ corresponding to the positions in M_i.
Termination:
   If $j = 0$ or if $c_i = 0$ or if $|M_i| \geq (n - c_i(n - d))$ output $\mathcal{P}$ and quit,
   else go to *Recursion*.

6   Conclusions

In [17,18] Silverberg, Staddon and Walker, apply hard-decision list decoding techniques to traceability codes. They use the Guruswami-Sudan algorithm, that corrects up to the necessary number of errors that allow to identify all parents that contribute with at least n/c positions to the descendant, where n is the codeword length and c is the maximum coalition size. Their approach is optimal when all parents contribute equally to the parent construction, and it guarantees to find at least one of the parents.

As it is shown in this paper, the results of Silverberg, Staddon and Walker can be extended, on one hand by considering traceability codes tolerating erasures [15], and on the other hand by using soft-decision decoding techniques that introduces back into a decoding process step, the tracing information obtained in the previous steps. Both extension can be achieved either by using the KV improvement of the GS algorithm or by using a modified version of the Viterbi algorithm.

References

1. A. Barg, G. R. Blakley, and G. Kabatiansky. Digital fingerprinting codes: Problem statements, constructions, identification of traitors. *IEEE Trans. Inform. Theory*, 49(4):852–865, 2003.
2. D. Boneh and J. Shaw. Collusion-secure fingerprinting for digital data. *Advances in Cryptology-Crypto'95, LNCS*, 963:452–465, 1995.
3. D. Boneh and J. Shaw. Collusion-secure fingerprinting for digital data. *IEEE Trans. Inform. Theory*, 44(5):1897–1905, 1998.
4. B. Chor, A. Fiat, and M. Naor. Tracing traitors. *Advances in Cryptology-Crypto'94, LNCS*, 839:480–491, 1994.
5. B. Chor, A. Fiat, M. Naor, and B. Pinkas. Tracing traitors. *IEEE Trans. Inform. Theory*, 46:893–910, 2000.
6. C. S. Collberg and C. Thomborson. Watermarking, tamper-proofing, and obfuscation - tools for software protection. *IEEE Trans. Software Eng.*, 28(8):735–746, 2002.
7. I. Cox, J. Killian, T. Leighton, and T. Shamoon. Secure spread spectrum watermarking for multimedia. *IEEE Trans. Img. Process.*, 6(12):1673–1687, 1997.
8. J. Dittmann, A. Behr, M. Stabenau, P. Schmitt, J. Schwenk, and J. Ueberberg. Combining digital watermarks and collusion secure fingerprinting for digital images. *Proceedings of SPIE*, 3657:171–182, 1999.
9. M. Fernandez and M. Soriano. Soft-decision tracing in fingerprinted multimedia contents. *IEEE Multimedia*, 11:36–40, 2004.
10. G. D. Forney. The Viterbi algorithm. *Proc. IEEE*, 61:268–278, 1973.
11. V. Guruswami and M. Sudan. Improved decoding of Reed-Solomon and algebraic-geometry codes. *IEEE Trans. Inform. Theory*, 45(6):1757–1767, 1999.
12. H. Guth and B. Pfitzmann. Error and collusion-secure fingerprinting for digital data. *IHW'99 LNCS*, 1768:134–145, 1999.
13. R. Koetter and A. Vardy. Algebraic soft-decision decoding of Reed-Solomon codes. *Proceedings IEEE ISIT 2000.*, page 61, 2000.
14. F. J. MacWilliams and N. J. A. Sloane. *The Theory of Error-Correcting Codes*. North Holland, 1977.
15. R. Safavi-Naini and Y. Wang. Collusion secure q-ary fingerprinting for perceptual content. *Security and Privacy in Digital Rights Management (SPDRM'01), LNCS*, 2320:57–75, 2002.

16. Nambirajan Seshadri and Carl-Erik W. Sundberg. List Viterbi decoding algorithms with applications. *IEEE Trans. Comm.*, 42:313–323, 1994.
17. A. Silverberg, J. Staddon, and J. Walker. Efficient traitor tracing algorithms using list decoding. *Advances in Cryptology - ASIACRYPT 2001*, 2248:175 ff., 2001.
18. A. Silverberg, J. Staddon, and J. Walker. Applications of list decoding to tracing traitors. *IEEE Trans. Inform. Theory*, 49(5):1312–1318, 2003.
19. J. N. Staddon, D. R. Stinson, and R. Wei. Combinatorial properties of frameproof and traceability codes. *IEEE Trans. Inform. Theory*, 47(3):1042–1049, 2001.
20. W. Trappe, M. Wu, Z. Wan, and K.J.R. Liu. Anti-collusion fingerprinting for multimedia. *IEEE Trans. on Signal Processing*, 51(4):1069–1087, April 2003.
21. Jack K. Wolf. Efficient maximum likelihood decoding of linear block codes using a trellis. *IEEE Trans. Inform. Theory*, 24:76–80, 1978.
22. In-Kwon Yeo and Hyoung Joong Kim. Modified patchwork algorithm: a novel audio watermarking scheme. *IEEE Trans. Speech Audio Process.*, 11(4):381–386, 2003.

Practical Data-Hiding: Additive Attacks Performance Analysis

J.E. Vila-Forcén[1], S. Voloshynovskiy[1], O. Koval[1],
F. Pérez-González[2], and T. Pun[1]

[1] University of Geneva, Department of Computer Science.
24 rue Général-Dufour, CH 1211, Geneva, Switzerland
{vila, svolos, koval, pun}@cui.unige.ch
[2] University of Vigo, Signal Theory and
Communications Department. E-36200 Vigo, Spain
fperez@gts.tsc.uvigo.es

Abstract. The main goal of this tutorial is to review the theory and design the worst case additive attack (WCAA) for $|\mathcal{M}|$-ary quantization-based data-hiding methods using as performance criteria the error probability and the maximum achievable rate of reliable communications. Our analysis focuses on the practical scheme known as distortion compensation dither modulation (DC-DM). From the mathematical point of view, the problem of the worst case attack (WCA) design using probability of error as a cost function is formulated as the maximization of the average probability of error subject to the introduced distortion for a given decoding rule. When mutual information is selected as a cost function, a solution to the minimization problem should provide such an attacking noise probability density function (pdf) that will maximally decrease the rate of reliable communications for an arbitrary decoder structure. The obtained results demonstrate that, within the class of additive attacks, the developed attack leads to a stronger performance decrease for the considered class of embedding techniques than the additive white Gaussian or uniform noise attacks.

1 Introduction

Data-hiding techniques aim at reliably communicating the largest possible amount of information under given distortion constraints. Their resistance against different attacks determine the possible application scenarios. An extensive review of various application of digital data-hiding techniques is given in [21]. The knowledge of the WCA allows to create a fair benchmark for data-hiding techniques and makes it possible to provide reliable communications with the use of appropriate error correction codes.

In general, the digital data-hiding can be considered as a game between the data-hider and the attacker. This three-party two-players game was already investigated by Moulin and O'Sullivan [12] where two set-ups are analyzed. In the first one, the host is assumed to be available at both encoder and decoder prior

M. Barni et al. (Eds.): IWDW 2005, LNCS 3710, pp. 244–259, 2005.
© Springer-Verlag Berlin Heidelberg 2005

to the transmission, the so-called *private game*. In the second one, the host is only available at the encoder as in Fig. 1, i.e., the *public game*. The performance is analyzed with respect to the maximum achievable rate when the decoder is aware of the attacking channel and therefore *maximum likelihood* (ML) decoding is applied. A similar game-theoretic analysis of the $|\mathcal{M}|$-ary information detection problem, the so-called zero-rate spread spectrum watermarking problem, is performed in [11]. As in the previous case, it is assumed that the detector has the possibility to learn the statistics of the attacking channel.

In both cases [11,12], the results were obtained under the assumption of continuous input alphabets. They lead to the conclusion that the optimal attacker strategy in the class of additive blockwise memoryless attacks corresponds to the application of the Gaussian test channel from the rate-distortion theory.

The knowledge of the attacking channel at the decoder is not a realistic case for most practical applications. Somekh-Baruch and Merhav considered the data-hiding problem in terms of maximum achievable rates and error exponents. They assumed that the host data is available either at both encoder and decoder [1] or only at the encoder [16] and supposed that neither encoder nor decoder is aware of the attacker strategy. In their consideration, the class of potentially applied attacks is significantly broader than in the previous study case [12] and includes any conditional pdf that satisfies a certain energy constraint. Although the solution of the problem is classically presented in terms of the achievable rate establishing the maximum number of messages $|\mathcal{M}|$ that can be reliably communicated, the error exponents solution is interesting in many practical applications where the objective is to minimize the probability of error at a given communications rate.

Quantization-based data-hiding methods have attracted attention in the watermarking community. They are a practical implementation of a binning technique for channels whose state is non-causally available at the encoder considered by Gel'fand-Pinsker [8]. Recently it has been also demonstrated [13] that quantization-based data-hiding performance coincides with the spread-spectrum (SS) data-hiding at the low-WNR by taking into account the host statistics and by abandoning the assumption of an infinite image to watermark ratio.

The quantization-based methods have been widely tested against a fixed channel and assuming that the channel transition pdf is available at the decoder. A *minimum Euclidean distance* (MD) decoder is implemented as a low-complexity equivalent of the ML decoder under the assumption of a channel pdf created by the symmetric extension of a monotonically non-increasing function [2].

It is a common practice in the data-hiding community to measure the performance in terms of the error rate for a given decoding rule as well as the maximum achievable rate of reliable communications. In this tutorial we will analyze the WCAA using both criteria. We restrict the encoding to the quantization-based one and the channel to the class of additive attacks only. We assume that the attacker might be informed of the encoding strategy and also of the decoding one for the error exponent analysis, while both encoder and decoder are uninformed of the channel. Furthermore, the encoder is aware of the host image but not of the attacking strategy.

It is important to note that the optimality of the attack critically relies on the input alphabet even under power-limited attacks. McKellips and Verdu showed that the additive white Gaussian noise (AWGN) is not the WCAA for discrete input alphabets such as pulse amplitude modulation in digital communications [10]. Similar conclusion for data-hiding was obtained by Pérez-González et al. [14], who demonstrated that the uniform noise attack performs worse than the AWGN attack for some watermark-to-noise ratios (WNRs). In [15], Pérez-González demonstrated that the AWGN cannot indeed be the WCAA because of its infinite support. Vila-Forcén et al. [19] and Goteti and Moulin [9] solved independently the min-max problem for distortion-compensated dither modulation (DC-DM) [3] in terms of probability of error for the fixed decoder, binary signaling, the subclass of additive attacks in data-hiding and detection-formulation, respectively. The additional difference between the two approaches consists in the definition of the cost function. While in the former case explicit computation of the probability of error is performed for the selected class of embedding strategies, in the latter one the Bhatacharyya bound is exploited in order to reduce the complexity of the considered game optimization problem. Simultaneously, Vila-Forcén et al. [20] and Tzschoppe et al. [18] derived the WCAA for DC-DM using the mutual information as objective function for additive attacks and binary signaling.

The goal of this paper is to provide an overview of the WCAA against quantization-based data-hiding techniques, focusing on the core principles and basic performance measures used in the data-hiding community. We did not attempt to provide a comprehensive overview of all possible attacking strategies that could be applied against quantization-based methods. All these classes of attacks are rather broad for this review and include various geometrical transformation and signal processing attacks as well as attacks that combine prior information about scheme design with security leakages revealed by the attacker. The last group is the most dangerous one besides the fact that it requires some specific information about the data-hiding technique. The geometrical attacks are quite generic and can be applied to any data-hiding method disregarding any prior information about the codebook design. Signal processing attacks are generally based on the statistical priors about the host data and the watermark. The group of WCAA conforms to the signal processing attacks and directly exploits the knowledge of the watermark statistics caused by the structured codebook design. We refer the interested readers to [23,24] for more information about attacks classification. More recent studies [4,17,22] address the impact of security leakages in the scope of information-theoretic analysis for geometrically structured and quantization-based codebooks and general reversibility of watermark embedding.

This paper aims at establishing the information-theoretic limits of $|\mathcal{M}|$-ary quantization-based data-hiding techniques and developing a benchmark that can be used for the fair comparison of different quantization-based methods.

The selection of the distortion compensation parameter α' (see Section 2.2) fixes the encoder structure for the quantization-based methods. Although the optimal α' can easily be determined when the power of the noise is available at the encoder prior to the transmission [6], this is not always feasible for various practical scenarios. Nevertheless, the availability of the attacking power and of the attacking pdf is a very common assumption in most data-hiding schemes. We will demonstrate that for a specific decoder (MD decoder) it is possible to calculate the optimal α' independently of the attack variance and pdf for the block error probability as a cost function.

Notations. We use capital letters to denote scalar random variables X, bold capital letters to denote vector random variables $\mathbf{X}$ and corresponding small letters x and $\mathbf{x}$ to denote the realizations of scalar and vector random variables, respectively. An information message and a set of messages with cardinality $|\mathcal{M}|$ is designated as $m \in \mathcal{M}, \mathcal{M} = \{1, 2, \ldots, |\mathcal{M}|\}$, respectively. A host signal distributed according to the pdf $f_{\mathbf{X}}(\mathbf{x})$ is denoted by $\mathbf{X} \sim f_{\mathbf{X}}(\mathbf{x})$; $\mathbf{Z} \sim f_{\mathbf{Z}}(\mathbf{z})$, $\mathbf{W} \sim f_{\mathbf{W}}(\mathbf{w})$ and $\mathbf{V} \sim f_{\mathbf{V}}(\mathbf{v})$ represents the attack, the watermark and the received signal, respectively. The step of quantization is equal to Δ and the distortion-compensation factor is denoted as α'. The variance of the watermark is σ_W^2 and the variance of the attack is σ_Z^2. The watermark-to-noise ratio (WNR) is given by WNR $= 10 \log_{10} \xi$, where $\xi = \frac{\sigma_W^2}{\sigma_Z^2}$. The set of natural numbers is denoted as $\mathbb{N}$ and $\mathbb{I}_N$ denotes the $N \times N$ identity matrix.

2   Problem Formulation

2.1   Data-Hiding Formulation of the Gel'fand-Pinsker Problem

The Gel'fand-Pinsker problem [8] has been recently revealed as the appropriate theoretical framework of data-hiding communications with side information. The Gel'fand-Pinsker data-hiding set-up is presented in Fig. 1. The random variable $\mathbf{X}$ stands for the host signal, which is independent and identically distributed (i.i.d.) according to $p(\mathbf{x}) = \prod_{i=1}^{N} p(x_i)$ and available non-causally at the encoder. The encoder is a mapping $\phi : \mathcal{M} \times \mathcal{X}^N \times \mathcal{K} \to \mathcal{W}^N$, where the key $K \in \mathcal{K}, \mathcal{K} = \{1, 2, \ldots, |\mathcal{K}|\}$. The stego data $\mathbf{Y}$ is obtained using the embedding mapping: $\varphi : \mathcal{W}^N \times \mathcal{X}^N \to \mathcal{Y}^N$. The decoder estimates the embedded message as $\psi : \mathcal{V}^N \times \mathcal{K} \to \mathcal{M}$. According to this scheme, a key is available at both encoder and decoder. Nevertheless, key management is outside of the scope of this paper and will not be considered further.

Two constraints apply to the Gel'fand-Pinsker in the data-hiding scenario: the embedding and the channel distortion constraints [12]. Let $d(\cdot, \cdot)$ be a non-negative function and σ_W^2, σ_Z^2 be two positive numbers, the embedder and the channel are said to satisfy the embedding and channel distortion constraints if:

$$\sum_{\mathbf{x} \in \mathcal{X}^N} \sum_{\mathbf{y} \in \mathcal{Y}^N} d(\mathbf{x}, \mathbf{y}) f_{\mathbf{X}, \mathbf{Y}}(\mathbf{x}, \mathbf{y}) \leq \sigma_W^2; \quad \sum_{\mathbf{y} \in \mathcal{Y}^N} \sum_{\mathbf{v} \in \mathcal{V}^N} d(\mathbf{y}, \mathbf{v}) f_{\mathbf{Y}, \mathbf{V}}(\mathbf{y}, \mathbf{v}) \leq \sigma_Z^2, \quad (1)$$

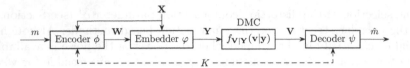

Fig. 1. Gel'fand-Pinsker data-hiding set-up

where $d(\mathbf{x}, \mathbf{y}) = \frac{1}{N} \sum_{i=1}^{N} d(x_i, y_i)$.

Costa considered the Gel'fand-Pinsker problem for the i.i.d. Gaussian case and mean square error distance [5]. The embedder φ produces $\mathbf{Y} = \mathbf{W} + \mathbf{X}$, $\mathbf{X} \sim \mathcal{N}(\mathbf{0}, \sigma_X^2 \mathbb{I}_N)$ and the channel output is obtained as: $\mathbf{V} = \mathbf{X} + \mathbf{W} + \mathbf{Z}$, where $\mathbf{Z} \sim \mathcal{N}(\mathbf{0}, \sigma_Z^2 \mathbb{I}_N)$. The estimate of the message $\hat{m}$ is obtained at the decoder as in the Gel'fand-Pinsker set-up.

2.2 Quantization-Based Data-Hiding Techniques

Aiming at reducing the Costa codebook exponential complexity, a number of practical data-hiding algorithms exploit *structured codebooks* instead of random ones. The most famous discrete approximations of Costa problem are known as DC-DM [3] and scalar Costa scheme (SCS) [6]. The structured codebooks are designed using quantizers (or lattices [7]) in order to achieve host interference cancellation. In the case of DC-DM, the stego data is obtained as follows:

$$\phi_{\text{DC-DM}}(m, x, \alpha') = y = x + \alpha'(Q_m(x) - x), \tag{2}$$

where $Q_m(\cdot)$ denotes a vector or scalar quantizer for the message m and $0 < \alpha' \leq 1$ is the analogue of the Costa optimization parameter α. If $\alpha' = 1$, the DC-DM simplifies to the DM: $\phi_{\text{DM}}(m, x) = \phi_{\text{DC-DM}}(m, x, 1)$.

3 Error Probability as a Cost Function

When the average error probability is selected as a cost function, we formulate the problem of Fig. 1 as:

$$P_B^{*(N)} = \min_{\phi, \psi} \max_{f_{V|Y}(\cdot|\cdot)} P_B(\phi, \psi, f_{V|Y}(\cdot|\cdot)). \tag{3}$$

The error probability depends on the particular encoder/decoder pair (ϕ, ψ) and the attacking channel $f_{\mathbf{V}|\mathbf{Y}}(\mathbf{v}|\mathbf{y})$, i.e., $P_B(\phi, \psi, f_{V|Y}(v|y)) = \Pr[\hat{m} \neq m | M = m]$. Here, we assume that the attacker knows both encoder and decoder strategies and selects its attacking strategy accordingly. Both encoder and decoder choose their strategy without knowing the attack in advance. Although this is a very conservative set-up, it is also important for various practical scenarios.

The more advantageous set-up for the data-hider is based on the assumption that the decoder selects its strategy knowing the attacker choice:

$$\min_{\phi} \max_{f_{V|Y}(\cdot|\cdot)} \min_{\psi} P_B(\phi, \psi, f_{V|Y}(\cdot|\cdot)). \tag{4}$$

Here, the attacker knows only the encoding function, which is fixed prior to the attack, and the decoder is assumed to be aware of the attack pdf.

In the general case, Somekh-Baruch and Merhav [1] have shown that the following inequalities apply for the above scenarios :

$$\min_{\phi,\psi} \max_{f_{V|Y}(\cdot|\cdot)} P_B(\phi,\psi,f_{V|Y}(\cdot|\cdot)) \geq \min_{\phi} \max_{f_{V|Y}(\cdot|\cdot)} \min_{\psi} P_B(\phi,\psi,f_{V|Y}(\cdot|\cdot)) \qquad (5)$$

$$= \min_{\phi} \max_{f_{V|Y}(\cdot|\cdot)} P_B(\phi,\psi^{ML},f_{V|Y}(\cdot|\cdot)), \qquad (6)$$

where (6) assumes that the decoder is aware of the attacking pdf and therefore the minimization at the decoder results in the optimal ML decoding strategy ψ^{ML}. Using (6) one can write:

$$\min_{\phi} \max_{f_{V|Y}(\cdot|\cdot)} P_B(\phi,\psi^{MD},f_{V|Y}(\cdot|\cdot)) \geq \min_{\phi} \max_{f_{V|Y}(\cdot|\cdot)} P_B(\phi,\psi^{ML},f_{V|Y}(\cdot|\cdot)), \qquad (7)$$

with equality if, and only if, the MD decoder coincides with the optimal ML decoder. In the class of additive attacks, the attacking channel transition pdf is only determined by the pdf of the additive noise $f_Z(z)$. Finally, in this analysis we assume independence of the error probability on the quantization bin where the received signal v lies (because the error decision region $\overline{R}_m$ has periodical structure and the host pdf $f_X(x)$ is assumed to be asymptotically constant within each quantization bin).

The problem (3) implies that the attacker might know both encoding and decoding strategy. Here, we target finding the WCAA pdf and the optimum fixed encoding strategy independently of the particular attacking case which guarantees reliable communications and provides an upper bound on the error probability.

3.1   Additive White Gaussian Noise Attack

The probability of error is determined using the equivalent noise pdf given by the convolution of the self-noise (a delta in the DM case and a uniform in the DC-DM one) with the attacking noise. The analytical expression for the error probability does not exist, and it is evaluated numerically. The error probability for the DM and the DC-DM under the AWGN attack is depicted in Fig. 2.

3.2   Uniform Noise Attack

It was shown [14] that the uniform noise attack produces higher error probability than the AWGN attack for some particular WNR in the binary signaling case. This fact contradicts the common belief that the AWGN is the WCAA for all data-hiding methods since it has the highest differential entropy among all pdfs with bounded variance.

As for the AWGN attacking case, we assume that the MD decoder is used and the probability of error is calculated as the integral of the equivalent noise pdf over the error region. The corresponding performance of the DC-DM under the uniform noise attack is presented in Fig. 3. Since we are assuming fixed decoder, the error probability for the binary case can be higher than 0.5.

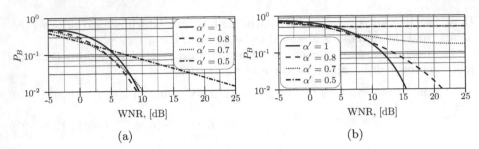

Fig. 2. Error probability analysis results for the AWGN attack case: (a) binary signaling and (b) quaternary signaling

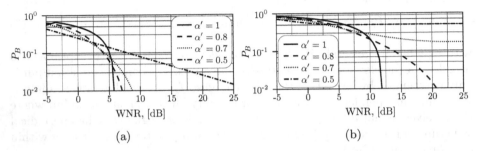

Fig. 3. Error probability for the uniform noise attack case: (a) binary signaling and (b) quaternary signaling

3.3   The Worst Case Additive Attack

The problem of the WCAA for digital communications based on binary pulse amplitude modulation (PAM) was considered in [10] using the error probability under attack power constraint. In this paper, the problem of the WCAA is addressed for the quantization-based data-hiding methods.

The problem (4) for the DM with the fixed MD decoder is given by:

$$\min_{\alpha'} \max_{f_Z(\cdot)} P_B(\alpha', \psi^{\mathrm{MD}}, f_Z(\cdot)), \tag{8}$$

where the encoder is optimized over all α' such that $0 < \alpha' \leq 1$, and the attacker selects the attack pdf $f_Z(\cdot)$ maximizing the error probability P_B. Since the encoder must be fixed in advance in the practical set-ups, we will first solve the above min-max problem as an internal maximization problem for a given encoder/decoder pair:

$$\max_{f_Z(\cdot)} P_B(\alpha', \psi^{\mathrm{MD}}, f_Z(\cdot)) = \max_{f_Z(\cdot)} \int_{\mathcal{R}_m} f_V(v|M = m)dv, \tag{9}$$

where $0 < \alpha' \leq 1$, subject to the constraints:

$$\int_{-\infty}^{\infty} f_Z(z)dz = 1, \quad \int_{-\infty}^{\infty} z^2 f_Z(z)dz \leq \sigma_Z^2, \tag{10}$$

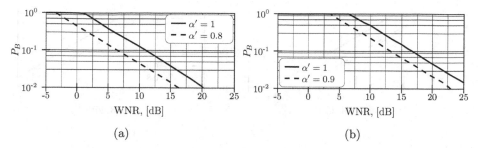

(a)   (b)

Fig. 4. WCAA error probability optimization results: (a) binary signaling and (b) quaternary signaling

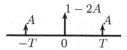

Fig. 5. $3 - \delta$ attack, $0 \leq A \leq 0.5$

where the first constraint follows from the pdf definition and σ_Z^2 constrains the attack power. The obtained error probabilities are depicted in Fig. 4, where the maximum is equal to 1 since we are assuming that the decoder is fixed (MD decoder) and it is completely known to the attacker. In a different decoding case when it is possible to invert the bit values, the maximum error probability will be equal to 0.5.

We approximate the performance of the WCAA by a so-called $3 - \delta$ attack whose pdf is presented in Fig. 5. The $3 - \delta$ attack provides a simple and powerful attacking strategy, which approximates the performance of the WCAA and might be used for testing different data-hiding algorithms. In order to demonstrate how accurate this approximation is, one needs to compare the average error probability caused by this attack versus the numerically obtained results.

The corresponding performance for the DM and the DC-DM under the 3-δ attack is presented in Fig. 6. The comparison between Fig. 4 and Fig. 6 demonstrates that the 3-δ attack produces asymptotically the same error probability as the optimization results. The presented results (Fig. 2, Fig. 3 and Fig. 4) demonstrate that the gap between the AWGN attack and the real worst case attack can be larger than 5dB in terms of the WNR.

The error probability as a function of the distortion compensation parameter for a given WNR demonstrates that the $3 - \delta$ attacking scheme is worse than either the uniform or Gaussian ones (Fig. 7). If the noise attack is known, it is possible to select such an α' that minimizes the error probability for the given WNR in Fig. 7. For example, if WNR = 0dB and Gaussian noise is applied, the optimal distortion compensation factor is $\alpha' = 0.53$, resulting in $P_B = 0.23$. Nevertheless, the encoder and the decoder are in general uninformed of the attacking strategy in advance and a mismatch in the attacking scheme may

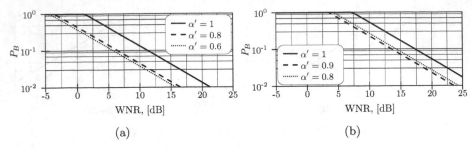

Fig. 6. Error probability analysis results for the $3 - \delta$ attack case: (a) binary signaling and (b) quaternary signaling

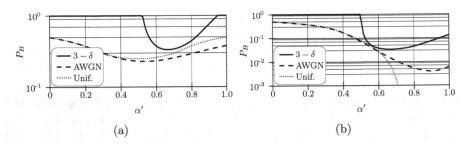

Fig. 7. Error probability comparison as a function of the distortion compensation parameter for the $3 - \delta$, Gaussian and uniform attacks and binary signaling: (a) WNR = 0dB, (b) WNR = 10dB

cause a bit error probability[1] of 1, while for $\alpha' = 0.66$ the maximum bit error probability is $P_B = 0.33$.

In order to find the optimal compensation parameter value that will allow the data-hider to upper bound the error probability introduced by the WCAA, we analyzed the error probability given by the 3-δ attack. Surprisingly, it was found that, independently of the operational WNR, $\alpha' = \alpha'_{\text{opt}} = \frac{2(|\mathcal{M}|-1)}{2|\mathcal{M}|-1}$ guarantees the lowest error probability of the analyzed data-hiding techniques under the WCAA (Fig. 8). Having this bound on the error probability, it is possible to guarantee reliable communications using proper error correction codes. Therefore, one can select such a fixed distortion compensation parameter $\alpha' = \alpha'_{\text{opt}}$ at the uninformed encoder and the MD decoder, which guarantees a bounded error probability. Substituting $\alpha' = \alpha'_{\text{opt}}$ into the error probability, one obtains the upper bound on the error probability:

$$P_B(\alpha'_{\text{opt}}) = \frac{1}{6}|\mathcal{M}|(|\mathcal{M}| - 1)\xi^{-1}. \tag{11}$$

---

[1] In general the maximum bit error probability is equal to 1 for the fixed MD decoder.

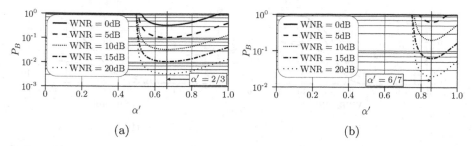

Fig. 8. Error probability analysis results as a function of the distortion compensation parameter α' for the $3 - \delta$ attack: (a) binary signaling and (b) quaternary signaling

4   Mutual Information as a Cost Function

The analysis of the WCAA with mutual information as a cost function is crucial for the fair evaluation of quantization-based data-hiding techniques. It provides the information-theoretic performance limit (in terms of achievable rate of reliable communications) that can be used for benchmarking of different practical robust data-hiding algorithms. Moulin *et al.* [12] considered the maximum achievable rate in the Gel'fand-Pinsker set-up as a max-min problem:

$$C = \max_{\phi} \min_{f_{V|Y}(\cdot|\cdot)} \left[I(U; V) - I(U; X) \right], \tag{12}$$

for a blockwise memoryless attack, the embedder distortion constraint σ_W^2 and the attacker distortion constraint σ_Z^2. In the case of quantization-based methods the mutual information is measured between the communicated message M and the channel output V [15] and the above problem is given by:

$$\max_{\phi} \min_{f_{V|Y}(\cdot|\cdot)} I_{\phi, f_{V|Y}(\cdot|\cdot)}(M; V'). \tag{13}$$

where $V' = Q_\Delta(V) - V$, since it was shown in [15] that modulo operation does not reduce the mutual information between V and M if the host is assumed to be flat within the quantization bins.

Rewriting the inequalities (5)–(6) for the mutual information we have:

$$\max_{\phi} \min_{f_{V|Y}(\cdot|\cdot)} I_{\phi, f_{V|Y}(\cdot|\cdot)}(M; V') \leq \max_{\phi} I_{\phi, \tilde{f}_{V|Y}(\cdot|\cdot)}(M; V'), \tag{14}$$

with equality if, and only if, the fixed attack $\tilde{f}_{V|Y}(\cdot|\cdot)$ coincides with the WCAA. Thus, the decoder in Fig. 1 is not fixed and we assume that the channel attack pdf $f_{V|Y}(\cdot|\cdot)$ is available at the decoder (informed decoder) and, consequently, ML decoding is performed. Under previous assumptions of quantization-based embedding and additive attack, it is possible to rewrite (13) as:

$$\max_{\alpha'} \min_{f_Z(\cdot)} I_{\alpha', f_Z(\cdot)}(M; V'). \tag{15}$$

Assuming equiprobable symbols, one obtains [15,20]:

$$I_{\alpha', f_Z(\cdot)}(M; V') = D\left(f_{V'|M}(v'|M = 1) \| f_{V'}(v') \right), \tag{16}$$

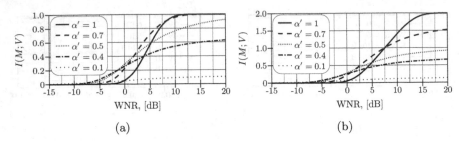

Fig. 9. Mutual information analysis results for the AWGN attack case and different α' and WNR values: (a) binary signaling and (b) quaternary signaling

where $D(\cdot\|\cdot)$ denotes the Kullback-Leibler distance (KLD). The next section is dedicated to the analysis of the DM and the DC-DM under the AWGN attack, the uniform noise attack and the WCAA.

4.1 Additive White Gaussian Noise Attack

When the DM and the DC-DM undergo the AWGN, no closed analytical solution to the mutual information minimization problem exists; the minimization was therefore performed using numerical computations. The results of this analysis for the binary and quaternary cases are shown in Fig. 9.

4.2 Uniform Noise Attack

It was shown [14] that the uniform noise attack is stronger than the AWGN attack for some WNRs when the error probability is used as a cost function. One of the properties of the KLD measure states that it is equal to zero if, and only if, the two pdfs are equal. In case the uniform noise attack is applied, this condition holds for some particular values of WNR for the mutual information given by (16). It can be demonstrated that $I(M; V') = 0$ when $\xi = \frac{\alpha'^2}{k^2}, k \in \mathbb{N}$ for the $|\mathcal{M}|$-ary signaling. The mutual information of quantization-based data-hiding techniques for the uniform noise attacking case with binary and quaternary signaling is depicted in Fig. 10.

The uniform noise attack guarantees that it is not possible to communicate using the DC-DM at $\xi \leq \alpha'^2$, and therefore distortion compensation parameter α' has a strong influence on the performance at the low-WNR. As a consequence, $\xi = \alpha'^2$ represents the WNR corresponding to zero rate communication, if the attacking variance satisfies $\sigma_Z^2 \geq \frac{D_w}{\alpha'^2}$.

For example (binary signaling, Fig. 10(a)), if the data-hider anticipates a WNR = -6dB, he/she could select $\alpha' = 0.7$ to maximize the mutual information. Nevertheless, at the WNR = -3dB the mutual information is zero for $\alpha' = 0.7$. Therefore, it is possible for the attacker to inhibit reliable communications by applying an attack 3dB lower in power than the data-hider prediction in this example. This forces the data-hider to decrease the value of α'. Therefore, the

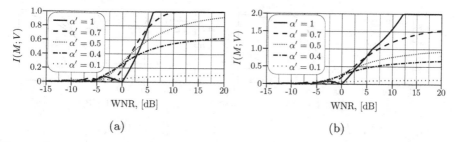

Fig. 10. Mutual information analysis results for the uniform noise attack case: (a) with binary signaling and (b) quaternary signaling

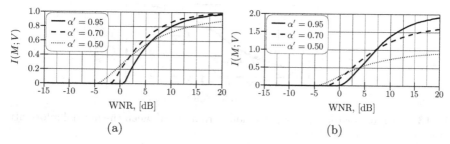

Fig. 11. Mutual information analysis results for the WCAA case: (a) binary signaling and (b) quaternary signaling

attacker can inhibit communications by making less efforts. In this example, to reduce the power of the attack on 3dB from the embedder prediction is favorable for the attacker.

4.3   The Worst Case Additive Attack

The problem of the WCAA using the mutual information as a cost function can be formulated using (15). Since the encoder must be fixed in advance as for the probability of error analysis case, we solve the max-min problem as a constrained minimization problem:

$$\min_{f_Z(\cdot)} I_{\alpha', f_Z(\cdot)}(M; V') = \min_{f_Z(\cdot)} D\left(f_{V'|M}(v'|M = 1||f_{V'}(v'))\right), \qquad (17)$$

where $0 < \alpha' \leq 1$. The constraints in (17) are the same as with the error probability oriented analysis case (10). Unfortunately, this problem has no closed form solution and it was solved numerically. The obtained results are presented for different α' values in Fig. 11. In comparison with the AWGN and the uniform noise attacks, they demonstrate that the developed attack produces the maximum possible loss in terms of the mutual information for all WNRs (Fig. 12).

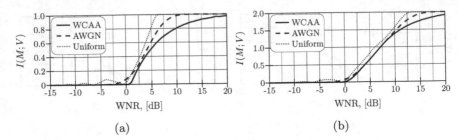

Fig. 12. Comparison of different attacks using mutual information as a cost function: (a) $\alpha' = 0.95$, binary signaling and (c) $\alpha' = 0.95$, quaternary signaling

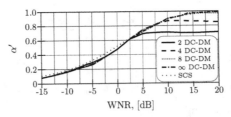

Fig. 13. Optimum distortion compensation parameter α' when the mutual information is selected as a cost function

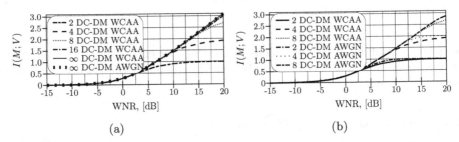

Fig. 14. Maximum achievable rate for different cardinality of the input alphabet under the WCAA compared to the AWGN (a) for $|\mathcal{M}| \to \infty$ and (b) for $|\mathcal{M}| < \infty$

In the analysis of the WCAA using the error probability as a cost function, the optimal α' parameter was found. Unfortunately, it is not the case in the mutual information oriented analysis, and its value varies with the WNR. In Fig. 13 the optimum α' values as a function of the WNR are presented for different input distributions in comparison with the optimum SCS parameter [6]. It demonstrates that SCS optimum distortion compensation parameter designed for the AWGN is also a good approximation for the WCAA case.

Using the optimum α' for each WNR, the resulting mutual information (17) is presented in Fig. 14(a) for different cardinality of the input alphabet compared to the performance of the AWGN using the optimized $\alpha = \alpha_{opt}$ parameter [12]. The obtained performance demonstrates that the developed WCAA is worse than the AWGN whenever the optimum α' is selected.

It is possible to observe in Fig. 14(a) that the impact of the WCAA is very similar to the AWGN and that the difference in terms of the mutual information is negligible. Although the AWGN is not the WCAA, its performance is an accurate and practical approximation to the WCAA in the asymptotic case when $|\mathcal{M}| \to \infty$. For $|\mathcal{M}| < \infty$, the difference might be important for some WNRs and it is needed to consider the real WCAA as it is presented in Fig. 14(b).

5 Conclusions

In this tutorial we analyzed the performance of quantization-based data-hiding techniques from the probability of error and mutual information perspectives. The comparison between the analyzed cost functions demonstrated that in a rigid scenario with a fixed decoder, the attacker can decrease the rate of reliable communication more severely than by using either the AWGN or the uniform noise attacks. We showed that the AWGN attack is not the WCAA in general, and we obtained an accurate and practical analytical approximation to the WCAA, the so-called $3 - \delta$ attack, when the cost function is the probability of error for the fixed MD decoder. For the $3 - \delta$ attack, $\alpha' = \frac{2(|\mathcal{M}|-1)}{2|\mathcal{M}|-1}$ was found to be the optimal value for the MD decoder that allows to communicate with an upper bounded probability of error for a given WNR. This value could be fixed without prior knowledge of the attacking pdf.

The analysis results obtained by means of numerical optimization showed that there exists a worse attack than the AWGN when the mutual information was used as a cost function. Contrarily to the error probability analysis case, the optimal distortion compensation parameter (α') depends on the operational WNR for the mutual information analysis case. The particular behaviour of the mutual information under uniform noise attack was considered, achieving zero-rate communication for attacking variances σ_Z^2 such that $\sigma_Z^2 \geq \frac{D_w}{\alpha'^2}$. The presented results should serve as a basis for the development of fair benchmarks for various data-hiding technologies under the assumptions of high rate and $\sigma_X^2 \gg \sigma_W^2$.

Acknowledgment

This paper was partially supported by SNF Professorship grant No PP002-68653/1, Interactive Multimodal Information Management (IM2) project and by the European Commission through the IST Programme under Contract IST-2002-507932 ECRYPT. The authors are thankful to the members of the Stochastic Image Processing group at University of Geneva and to Pedro Comesaña and Luis Pérez-Freire of the Signal Processing in Communications Group at University of Vigo for many helpful and interesting discussions. The information in this document reflects only the author's views, is provided as is and no guarantee or warranty is given that the information is fit for any particular purpose. The user thereof uses the information at its sole risk and liability.

References

1. A. Somekh-Baruch and N. Merhav. On the error exponent and capacity games of private watermarking systems. *IEEE Trans. on Information Theory*, 49(3):537–562, March 2003.

2. Mauro Barni and Franco Bartolini. *Watermarking Systems Engineering*. Marcel Dekker, Inc., New York, 2004.

3. B. Chen and G. W. Wornell. Quantization index modulation: A class of provably good methods for digital watermarking and information embedding. *IEEE Trans. on Information Theory*, 47:1423–1443, 2001.

4. P. Comesaña-Alfaro, L. Pérez-Freire, and F. Pérez-González. An information-theoretic framework for assessing security in practical watermarking and data hiding scenarios. In *WIAMIS 2005, 6th International Workshop on Image Analysis for Multimedia Interactive Services*, Montreux, Switzerland, April 13-15 2005.

5. M. Costa. Writing on dirty paper. *IEEE Trans. on Information Theory*, 29(3):439–441, 1983.

6. Joachim J. Eggers, Robert Bäuml, Roman Tzschoppe, and Bernd Girod. Scalar costa scheme for information embedding. *IEEE Transactions on Signal Processing*, 51(4):1003–1019, April 2003.

7. U. Erez and R. Zamir. Lattice decoding can achieve 0.5 log(1+snr) over the additive white gaussian noise channel using nested codes. In *Proceedings of IEEE International Symposium on Information Theory*, page 125, Washington DC, USA, June 2001.

8. S.I. Gel'fand and M.S. Pinsker. Coding for channel with random parameters. *Problems of Control and Information Theory*, 9(1):19–31, 1980.

9. A. K. Goteti and P. Moulin. Qim watermarking games. In *Proc. ICIP*, Oct. 2004.

10. A. McKellips and S. Verdu. Worst case additive noise for binary-input channels and zero-threshold detection under constraints of power and divergence. *IEEE Transactions on Information Theory*, 43(4):1256–1264, July 1997.

11. P. Moulin and A. Ivanovic. The zero-rate spread-spectrum watermarking game. *IEEE Transactions on Signal Processing*, 51(4):1098–1117, April 2003.

12. P. Moulin and J. O'Sullivan. Information-theoretic analysis of information hiding. *IEEE Trans. on Information Theory*, 49(3):563–593, October 2003.

13. L. Peréz-Freire, F. Peréz-González, and S. Voloshynovskiy. Revealing the true achievable rates of scalar costa scheme. In *IEEE International Workshop on Multimedia Signal Processing (MMSP)*, Siena, Italy, September 29 - October 1 2004.

14. F. Peréz-González, F. Balado, and J. R. Hernández. Performance analysis of existing and new methods for data hiding with known-host information in additive channels. *IEEE Trans. on Signal Processing, Special Issue on Signal Processing for Data Hiding in Digital Media and Secure Content Delivery*, 51(4), April 2003.

15. Fernando Pérez-González. The importance of aliasing in structured quantization modulation data hiding. In *International Workshop on Digital Watermarking*, Seoul, Korea, 2003.

16. A. Somekh-Baruch and N. Merhav. On the capacity game of public watermarking systems. *IEEE Trans. on Information Theory*, 49(3):511–524, March 2004.

17. E. Topak, S. Voloshynovskiy, O. Koval, M.K. Mihcak, and T. Pun. Towards geometrically robust data-hiding with structured codebooks. *ACM Multimedia Systems Journal, Special Issue on Multimedia and Security*, 2005. submitted.

18. R. Tzschoppe, R. Bäuml, R. Fischer, A. Kaup, and J. Huber. Additive Non-Gaussian Attacks on the Scalar Costa Scheme (SCS). In *Proceedings of SPIE Photonics West, Electronic Imaging 2005, Security, Steganography, and Watermarking of Multimedia Contents VII (EI120)*, volume 5681, San Jose, USA, January 16-20 2005.

19. J. E. Vila-Forcén, S. Voloshynovskiy, O. Koval, F. Peréz-González, and Thierry Pun. Worst case additive attack against quantization-based watermarking techniques. In *IEEE International Workshop on Multimedia Signal Processing (MMSP)*, Siena, Italy, September 29 - October 1 2004.

20. J. E. Vila-Forcén, S. Voloshynovskiy, O. Koval, F. Peréz-González, and Thierry Pun. Worst case additive attack against quantization-based data-hiding methods. In *Proceedings of SPIE Photonics West, Electronic Imaging 2005, Security, Steganography, and Watermarking of Multimedia Contents VII (EI120)*, San Jose, USA, January 16-20 2005.

21. S. Voloshynovskiy, F. Deguillaume, O. Koval, and T. Pun. Information-theoretic data-hiding: Recent achievements and open problems. *International Journal of Image and Graphics*, 5(1):1–31, 2005.

22. S. Voloshynovskiy, O. Koval, E. Topak, J.E. Vila-Forcén, P. Comesaña, and Thierry Pun. On reversibility of random binning techniques: multimedia perspectives. In *9th IFIP TC-6 TC-11 Conference on Communications and Multimedia Security (CMS 2005)*, Salzburg Austria, September 2005.

23. S. Voloshynovskiy, S. Pereira, V. Iquise, and T. Pun. Attack modelling: Towards a second generation benchmark. *Signal Processing*, 81(6):1177–1214, June 2001. Special Issue: Information Theoretic Issues in Digital Watermarking, 2001. V. Cappellini, M. Barni, F. Bartolini, Eds.

24. S. Voloshynovskiy, S. Pereira, T. Pun, J. Eggers, and J. Su. Attacks on digital watermarks: Classification, estimation-based attacks and benchmarks. *IEEE Communications Magazine (Special Issue on Digital watermarking for copyright protection: a communications perspective)*, 39(8):118–127, 2001. M. Barni, F. Bartolini, I.J. Cox, J. Hernandez, F. Pérez-González, Guest Eds. Invited paper.

The Return of the Sensitivity Attack

Pedro Comesaña, Luis Pérez-Freire, and Fernando Pérez-González*

Signal Theory and Communications Department,
University of Vigo, Vigo 36310, Spain
{pcomesan, lpfreire, fperez}@gts.tsc.uvigo.es

Abstract. The sensitivity attack is considered as a serious threat to the security of spread-spectrum-based schemes, since it provides a practical method of removing watermarks with minimum attacking distortion. This paper is intended as a tutorial on this problem, presenting an overview of previous research and introducing a new method based on a general formulation. This new method does not require any knowledge about the detection function nor any other system parameter, but just the binary output of the detector, being suitable for attacking most known watermarking methods. Finally, the soundness of this new approach is tested by attacking several of those methods.

1 Introduction

In its early years, digital watermarking was conceived as a solution to the problems of illegal copy control and intellectual property rights (IPR) protection. Perhaps for this reason and the analogies commonly made to the field of cryptography, watermarking was declared as synonymous to security [1]. However, watermarking research until now has much more to do with *robustness* than with *security*: roughly speaking, watermarking security [2] may be related to attacks which try to gain knowledge about certain secret parameters of the watermarking system, whereas robustness is more concerned with attacks whose aim is to degrade the performance of the watermarking system.

In watermarking for IPR protection and copy control, the aim is to distinguish whether the digital media at hand contains a certain watermark or not. This problem is known as *watermark detection*,[1] and is commonly modeled as a binary hypothesis testing problem. In a general setup, the watermarking of a

* This work was partially funded by *Xunta de Galicia* under projects PGIDT04 TIC322013PR and PGIDT04 PXIC32202PM; MEC project DIPSTICK, reference TEC2004-02551/TCM; FIS project IM3, reference G03/185 and European Comission through the IST Programme under Contract IST-2002-507932 ECRYPT. ECRYPT disclaimer: The information in this paper is provided as is, and no guarantee or warranty is given or implied that the information is fit for any particular purpose. The user thereof uses the information at its sole risk and liability.

[1] Watermark detection and *watermark decoding* must be regarded as different problems, since in the latter (which is often referred to as *data hiding*) the objective is to decode the embedded message.

M. Barni et al. (Eds.): IWDW 2005, LNCS 3710, pp. 260–274, 2005.

digital document $\mathbf{x}$, which is arranged as a column vector of dimension n, can be expressed as $\mathbf{y} = \mathbf{x} + \mathbf{w}$, with $\mathbf{w}$ the watermark. Hence, the hypothesis testing problem can be written as

$$
\begin{aligned}
H_0 &: \mathbf{y} = \mathbf{x} \\
H_1 &: \mathbf{y} = \mathbf{x} + \mathbf{w}
\end{aligned}.
$$

In detection, we must adapt this test to take into account that the watermarked signal could have been attacked; this attack will be modeled as the addition of a vector $\mathbf{t}$, yielding a signal $\mathbf{z} = \mathbf{y} + \mathbf{t}$. Note that $\mathbf{w}$ may be made key-dependent in order to improve the security of the system. The optimal solution to the hypothesis test is given by the likelihood ratio test, i.e.,

$$
l(\mathbf{z}) = \frac{f_{\mathbf{Z}|H_1}(\mathbf{z}|H_1)}{f_{\mathbf{Z}|H_0}(\mathbf{z}|H_0)} \underset{H_0}{\overset{H_1}{\underset{\leq}{>}}} \eta, \tag{1}
$$

where $f_{\mathbf{Z}|H_i}(\mathbf{z}|H_i)$ is the pdf of $\mathbf{Z}$ conditioned to hypothesis H_i and η is a threshold which can be adjusted so as to optimize a certain criterion (Neyman-Pearson, Bayes, etc.). We will denote by $D \in \mathcal{H} = \{H_0, H_1\}$ the output of the detector. The detection function given by (1) divides the subspace $\mathbb{R}^n$ in two disjoint regions, $\mathcal{R}$ and $\mathcal{R}^c$, termed *acceptance* or *detection region* and *rejection region*, respectively, such that $\mathbb{R}^n = \mathcal{R} \cup \mathcal{R}^c$, which are defined as

$$
\mathcal{R} = \{\mathbf{z} \in \mathbb{R}^n : l(\mathbf{z}) > \eta\}; \mathcal{R}^c = \{\mathbf{z} \in \mathbb{R}^n : l(\mathbf{z}) \leq \eta\}.
$$

Unfortunately, an analytical derivation of the likelihood ratio test is not always feasible, so we will consider instead a more general family of detection functions. Thus, the test performed by the detector is

$$
g(\mathbf{z}, \boldsymbol{\theta}) \underset{H_0}{\overset{H_1}{\underset{\leq}{>}}} \eta,
$$

where $\boldsymbol{\theta}$ is the secret key used in the detection process. Be aware that the resulting detector will be optimal only when $g(\mathbf{z}, \boldsymbol{\theta})$ coincides with the likelihood ratio $l(\mathbf{z})$.

In the considered scenarios, the watermark detector is often made public, generally in the form of a tamper-proof black box which only provides binary outputs, in such a way that an observer can check whether $g(\mathbf{a}, \boldsymbol{\theta})$ is larger or smaller than η, but he can not know its actual value. This scenario gives raise to the so-called *oracle attacks*, where the attacker can use the detector outputs to some selected inputs in order to gain knowledge about secret information used in the detection process (for instance, the detection key). Intuitively speaking, the detector acts as an oracle, responding *yes* or *no* to the inputs provided by the attacker. The most popular oracle attack is the so-called *sensitivity attack*, introduced for the first time in [3]. At the time this attack was proposed, *additive spread spectrum* methods [4] constituted the state of the art in digital watermarking, so this attack was suited to this particular scenario. For additive spread spectrum under the assumption of a Gaussian host, the likelihood ratio has a well-known closed-form solution, given by $l(\mathbf{z}) = \mathbf{z}^T\mathbf{w}$, so the optimal detector in this case must apply the following test:

$$\mathbf{z}^T\mathbf{w} \underset{H_0}{\overset{H_1}{\underset{\leq}{>}}} \eta. \tag{2}$$

Detectors that implement the test given by (2) are termed *linear correlator detectors*. Essentially, the sensitivity attack (specialized to the case of digital images) for this kind of detectors consists of the following steps [3]:

1. The algorithm starts from a watermarked image $\mathbf{y}$ of dimension n. The first step is the modification of $\mathbf{y}$ so as to obtain a new image $\mathbf{z}$ near the boundary of $\mathcal{R}$, which according to (2) is a hyperplane in an n-dimensional subspace, perpendicular to $\mathbf{w}$.
2. For the i-th pixel of $\mathbf{z}$, a random vector $\mathbf{t}^i = [0, \cdots, 0, t_i, 0, \cdots, 0]^T$ is added to $\mathbf{z}$ observing how the sign of t_i affects the outputs of the detector and, hence, gaining knowledge about the polarity of the watermark in each pixel. Since $\mathbf{z}$ is near the detection boundary, small changes are likely to toggle the detector response. This procedure is repeated for all $i = 1, \cdots, n$.
3. At the end of the previous step, by combining the results for all pixels, the attacker has a rough estimate $\hat{\mathbf{w}}$ of the watermark vector and, thus, of the detection boundary, which in the considered case is perpendicular to $\mathbf{w}$.

According to the classification introduced at the beginning of this section, the sensitivity attack clearly falls into the category of attacks to security, since the attacker is trying to disclose the boundary of the detection region (which is supposed to be secret to unauthorized users). Of course, once the attacker has estimated this boundary, he can use his knowledge to devise smart attacks against watermarked contents: for instance, once the estimate $\hat{\mathbf{w}}$ has been obtained, the attacker can generate an attacked image $\mathbf{z}$ with small distortion, capable of fooling the detector, just by subtracting a suitably scaled version of $\hat{\mathbf{w}}$. Before the sensitivity attack was proposed, it was believed that the complexity of an attack disclosing the watermark was $O(2^n)$ (by means of a *brute force* approach), but the proposed strategy showed that it would be feasible in a number of iterations which is linear with the dimensionality of the watermarked image, i.e., the complexity of the attack was reduced to $O(n)$. Hence, it is easy to realize that this attack represented a serious threat to any watermarking scheme with a public detector available, and it raised up the problem of security in watermarking.

This paper is concerned with a generalization of the sensitivity attack, providing a formulation that encompasses most known watermark detection scheme with parameterizable and differentiable (but unknown to the attacker) detection boundaries; in fact, our approach is suitable even for attacking QIM schemes, whereas the sensitivity attacks that had been devised so far were only aimed against spread spectrum methods. The rest of the paper is organized as follows: Section 2 provides an overview of previous works dealing with the characterization of this attack and the countermeasures proposed to increase the security of a watermarking system where public detectors are available. In Section 3, our new formulation of the problem is presented, and its application to some examples is given in Section 4.

2   Previous Work and Improvements

The sensitivity attack for detectors based on linear correlation, i.e., those given by (2), was extensively studied in [5] and [6]. Starting from the formulation of the attack given in [4], which was explained in the Introduction, the work in [5] proposes a countermeasure based on the randomization of the detection boundary: the basic idea is to define a region around the points that satisfy $\mathbf{z}^T\mathbf{w} = \eta$ where the decision of the detector is made random, in order to reduce the sensitivity of the detector to small changes in its inputs. Thus, the detection function is modified as follows:

$$D = \begin{cases} H_1, & \text{if } \mathbf{z}^T\mathbf{w} > \eta_2 \\ H_0, & \text{if } \mathbf{z}^T\mathbf{w} < \eta_1 \\ H_1 \text{ with probability } p(\mathbf{z}^T\mathbf{w}), & \text{if } \eta_1 \leq \mathbf{z}^T\mathbf{w} \leq \eta_2 \end{cases}, \qquad (3)$$

where the two new thresholds η_1 and η_2 must be close to η so as not to degrade significantly the performance of the detector, and $p(r)$ verifies $p(\eta_1) = 0$ and $p(\eta_2) = 1$. The internal behavior of the detector is such that its outputs are deterministic, i.e., the response of the detector is always the same for a fixed input signal $\mathbf{z}$, in order to avoid the estimation of $p(r)$ simply by feeding the same $\mathbf{z}$ to the detector repeatedly. Anyway, estimation of the watermark is still possible. Let $\mathbf{z}'$ be a vector such that $\eta_1 \leq (\mathbf{z}')^T\mathbf{w} \leq \eta_2$, and ϵ a random vector. For sufficiently small $\epsilon_i, i = 1 \cdots n$, and $\mathbf{z} = \mathbf{z}' + \epsilon$, we have that $p(\mathbf{z}^T\mathbf{w}) = p((\mathbf{z}')^T\mathbf{w} + \epsilon^T\mathbf{w}) \approx p((\mathbf{z}')^T\mathbf{w})$, so after trying a sufficiently large number of different vectors ϵ, the value of $p((\mathbf{z}')^T\mathbf{w})$ can be estimated simply by counting the number of outcomes that yield $D = H_1$. Similarly, for $\mathbf{t}^i = [0, \cdots, 0, t_i, 0, \cdots, 0]^T$ and $\mathbf{z}^i = \mathbf{z}' + \mathbf{t}^i + \epsilon$, we have $(\mathbf{z}^i)^T\mathbf{w} = (\mathbf{z}')^T\mathbf{w} + t_i w_i + \epsilon^T\mathbf{w} \approx (\mathbf{z}')^T\mathbf{w} + t_i w_i = (\mathbf{z}')^T\mathbf{w} \pm t_i\delta$, where in the last equality we have assumed that $w_i \in \{\pm\delta\}$. By means of a first order approximation, and assuming that $p(r)$ is differentiable, we can write $p((\mathbf{z}^i)^T\mathbf{w}) \approx p((\mathbf{z}')^T\mathbf{w} \pm t_i\delta) \approx p((\mathbf{z}')^T\mathbf{w}) \pm t_i\delta p'((\mathbf{z}')^T\mathbf{w})$, where $p'(r) \triangleq \frac{\partial p(r)}{\partial r}$ is the derivative of $p(r)$. Again, using enough different vectors ϵ, an estimate of $p((\mathbf{z}^i)^T\mathbf{w})$ can be obtained. By comparing this estimate to the previous estimate of $p(\mathbf{y}^T\mathbf{w})$, the sign of w_i can be inferred (as long as $p(r)$ is a monotically increasing function). In [5], the information leakage about the watermark provided by the detector outputs is quantified in an information-theoretic sense, and the shape of the optimum function $p(r)$ for $\eta_1 \leq r \leq \eta_2$ that minimizes the information leakage is given. It is easy to see that this countermeasure complicates the sensitivity attack, but its complexity still remains linear with the dimensionality of the images. In fact, a practical method for estimating the watermark in this framework was devised in [6]. The method basically consists of the following steps:

1. Starting from a valid watermarked image $\mathbf{y}$, an image $\mathbf{z}'$ which yields $\eta_1 \leq (\mathbf{z}')^T \mathbf{w} \leq \eta_2$ is constructed by iteratively degrading $\mathbf{y}$.
2. The image $\mathbf{z}'$ is perturbed by the addition of zero-mean random vectors $\mathbf{t}$ with $t_i = \{\pm\delta\}$. If $\mathbf{w}$ and $\mathbf{t}$ are positively correlated, the detector will return $D = H_1$ with higher probability, so $\mathbf{t}$ will be taken as an approximation of $\mathbf{w}$; otherwise, if $D = H_0$, then $-\mathbf{t}$ will be taken as an estimate of $\mathbf{w}$.
3. By averaging the estimates obtained in the previous step, an approximation of $\mathbf{w}$ is obtained.

Following this approach it is possible to obtain reliable estimates of $\mathbf{w}$ in a number of iterations which is a small multiple of n, as it was shown in [6].

Another approach for performing a successful sensitivity attack was presented in [7]. The method is able to estimate the boundary of the acceptance region by modeling the attack as a classical adaptive filtering problem: it is easy to realize that the linear detection function given in (2) for additive spread spectrum can be thought of in terms of filtering $\mathbf{z}$ with a filter $\tilde{\mathbf{w}}$ such that $\tilde{w}_i = w_{n+1-i} \; \forall \; i = 1, \cdots, n$; furthermore, the attacker knows that $\mathbf{z} * \tilde{\mathbf{w}} = g(\mathbf{z}, \boldsymbol{\theta})$, where $*$ denotes the convolution operator, so if he/she can access the values of $g(\mathbf{z}, \boldsymbol{\theta})$, then using this signal as reference he can manage to construct an estimate of $\tilde{\mathbf{w}}$. The authors propose in [7] the use of the Least Mean Squares (LMS) algorithm in order to iteratively construct these estimates. Let $\hat{\mathbf{w}}_k$ be the estimate of $\tilde{\mathbf{w}}$ in the k-th iteration and $\{\mathbf{z}_k\}$ a set of vectors near the detection boundary; each iteration of the LMS algorithm consists of the following steps:

$$
\begin{aligned}
&1. \quad r_k = \mathbf{z}_k * \tilde{\mathbf{w}}, \\
&2. \quad e_k = g(\mathbf{z}_k, \boldsymbol{\theta}) - r_k, \\
&3. \quad \mathbf{w}_{k+1} = \mathbf{w}_k + \mu e_k \mathbf{z}_k,
\end{aligned}
$$

where μ is the step-length. In a more realistic situation, the attacker only has access to the detector outputs, D, so this algorithm must be properly modified. In this situation, the attacker must restrict the set $\{\mathbf{z}_k\}$ to those vectors lying near the detection boundary, because he still knows that $g(\mathbf{z}_k, \boldsymbol{\theta}) \approx \eta$; thus, the algorithm is complicated by the fact of computing the appropriate set $\{\mathbf{z}_k\}$. The authors also propose some modifications in order to cope with the countermeasure introduced in [5], which was explained above.

In view of the security flaws presented by traditional spread spectrum methods under sensitivity-like attacks, researchers put their effort in the design of *asymmetric* schemes [8].[2] One of the advantages offered by asymmetric schemes

---

[2] Watermarking techniques can be roughly classified according to the role of the secret key in the embedding/detection processes: those methods which use different keys for embedding and detection are termed *asymmetric*, otherwise they belong to the category of *symmetric schemes*.

against sensitivity attacks is the fact that the embedding and detection keys are different, thus the impact of a successful attack revealing the detection boundary is minimized (recall that disclosure of the watermark in traditional spread spectrum methods allows to unwatermark legal contents, as well as generating forged illegal documents). The other advantage of asymmetric watermarking is the use of more involved detection regions, complicating the description of the detection boundary; for instance, in [8], four asymmetric methods are analyzed under a unified framework, showing that the detection function can be written in terms of a quadratic form in $\mathbb{R}^n$ for all cases, i.e.

$$\frac{\mathbf{z}^T \mathbf{A} \mathbf{z}}{n} \underset{H_0}{\overset{H_1}{\underset{\leq}{>}}} \eta.$$

The idea of increasing the security of the system against sensitivity attacks by complicating the detection region is exploited by the family of detection functions called JANIS [9], which use N-th order polynomial detection functions, i.e.

$$g(\mathbf{z}, \boldsymbol{\theta}) = \frac{1}{n} \sum_{k=1}^{n/N} \prod_{j=1}^{N} z_{p[(k-1)\cdot N+j]} \cdot a_{p[(k-1)\cdot N+j]},$$

where $\mathbf{a}$ is secret random ± 1 vector and $\mathbf{p}$ is a secret random permutation vector. Based on this detection function the watermark is obtained as $\mathbf{w} = \gamma \nabla g(\mathbf{x}, \boldsymbol{\theta})$, where γ is a parameter to adjust the embedding distortion. Indeed it makes more difficult the sensitivity attack, but obviously this is not the ultimate solution: for example, a N-th order detection boundary can still be described by estimating n^N points on the detection boundary. This point was addressed in [7], showing that the LMS attack can be properly modified in order to cope with this kind of detection boundaries. A possible solution to this problem was proposed also in [7] by means of non-parametric decision boundaries, i.e., by using decision boundaries that can not be described by a finite number of parameters. An example of such decision boundaries are those given by fractal curves like the Peano curve, which is used in [7] to replace the original linear detection boundary in a spread spectrum scheme. With a proper design, the proposed method can invalidate sensitivity attacks with slight degradations in robustness.

Recently, an attempt to give a rigorous formulation of the sensitivity attack was presented in [10]: first, the convergence of the algorithm proposed in [6] is proven, using the law of large numbers; thereafter, a new non-iterative sensitivity attack for detectors based on linear correlation is presented.[3] The main steps of this new algorithm are outlined in the following:

1. As in the former algorithms, the first step is the construction of a signal $\mathbf{z}'$ near the boundary of the detection region.

---

[3] As a further contribution, this new algorithm is also suitable for estimating continuous-valued watermarks, whereas the algorithms previously proposed in [5] and [6] assumed that the watermark could only take discrete values.

2. Now consider the set of vectors $\{\mathbf{t}^i\}$, $i = 1, \cdots, n$, defined by the canonical basis of $\mathbb{R}^n$. For each $\mathbf{t}^i$, a signal $\mathbf{z}'' = \mathbf{z}' + \alpha_i \mathbf{t}^i$ on the detection boundary is constructed, by properly selecting the scaling factor α_i. The search for this value of α_i must be accomplished by means of some numerical algorithm, so it will be surely the most costly part of the algorithm.

3. For the detector under consideration, it holds that $(\mathbf{z}'')^T \mathbf{w} = \sum_{k=1}^n z_k'' w_k + \alpha_i w_i = \eta, i = 1, \cdots, n$ where η is the detection threshold and $w_i = (\mathbf{t}^i)^T \mathbf{w}$. Thus, a linear system with n equations and n unknowns has been defined. By taking into account the special structure of this system, it is easy to show that it can be solved in $n + 1$ elemental operations.

Another remarkable contribution of [10] is the extension of the sensitivity attack in order to work with a more generic family of detection functions of the form $g(\mathbf{y}, \mathbf{w})$; furthermore, this method has the advantage of return an estimate of the watermark. Nevertheless, this approach presents several drawbacks: the attacker needs to know the detection function and even the inverse of the gradient of the detection function. Thus, the need for a new formulation which overcomes these problems is justified; in the next section we will try to solve this problem, achieving a solution which will be shown to work with a wider range of detection functions. The method proposed has the following characteristics:

- It does not require knowledge about the detection function; it just needs to know the binary output of the detection function for a given input. Due to this, our method is indeed able to deal with watermarking methods which use a secret detection key (different from the embedding key), in such a way that the attacker has no access to the decoding function; these methods are known under the generic name of *asymmetric watermarking* (see [8] and [11]).
- The gradient of the detection function does not need to be inverted. As it was said in the previous point, sometimes the detection function will not be known by the attacker, so he/she will not be able to invert its gradient.

3   The Blind Newton Sensitivity Attack (BNSA)

Focusing on watermark detection, we will describe the detector output through the function $f_{\text{binary}} : \mathbb{R}^n \to \mathcal{H}$, with $\mathcal{H} = \{H_0, H_1\}$. Without loss of generality, we can define the following functions

$$f : \mathbb{R}^n \to \mathbb{R}^m \text{ and} \tag{4}$$

$$g_{\text{binary}} : \mathbb{R}^m \to \mathcal{H},$$

with $m \leq n$, in such a way that $f_{\text{binary}} = g_{\text{binary}} \circ f$, and f is parameterized by the secret key $\boldsymbol{\theta}$. This decomposition will be shown to be useful in the next sections, since some of the most popular watermarking techniques perform embedding/detection in a projected domain so f can be seen as the projection function. Furthermore, in the schemes studied in this paper the output of g_{binary}

will be based on the output of a real function g and a threshold η, in such a way that

$$g_{\text{binary}}(\mathbf{x}) = \begin{cases} H_0, & \text{if } g(\mathbf{x}) \leq \eta \\ H_1, & \text{if } g(\mathbf{x}) > \eta \end{cases}, \tag{5}$$

with $g : \mathbb{R}^m \to \mathbb{R}$.

On the other hand, a distorsion measure has to be defined in order to quantify the impact of the attacking signal $\mathbf{t}$ on the watermarked signal $\mathbf{y}$: [4]

$$d_{\mathbf{y}} : \mathbb{R}^n \to \mathbb{R}^+$$
$$\mathbf{t} \to d_{\mathbf{y}}(\mathbf{t}).$$

This distortion measure could be based on perceptual criteria (depending on the nature of the host signal), although very often, and due to simplicity, the squared Euclidean norm of $\mathbf{t}$ is chosen (i.e., $d_{\mathbf{y}}(\mathbf{t}) = \|\mathbf{t}\|_2^2$).

Recalling that the attacker tries to find the vector $\mathbf{t}$ which yields a "no watermark" decision (i.e., $f_{\text{binary}}(\mathbf{y} + \mathbf{t}) = H_0$) while minimizing the distortion measure $d_{\mathbf{y}}(\mathbf{t})$, his/her target can be formalized as

$$\arg \min_{\mathbf{t}: g \circ f(\mathbf{y}+\mathbf{t}) \leq \eta} d_{\mathbf{y}}(\mathbf{t}). \tag{6}$$

Let us assume that $d_{\mathbf{y}}(\mathbf{t})$ is a continuous and convex function of $\mathbf{t}$ (for a given watermarked signal $\mathbf{y}$), which achieves its absolute minimum value at $\mathbf{t}_0$ (the squared Euclidean norm obviously fulfills these conditions), a vector that belongs the set of attacking vectors yielding H_1 (which we will denote by $\mathcal{B}$),[5] i.e., $\mathbf{t}_0 \in \mathcal{B} \triangleq \{\mathbf{t} : g \circ f(\mathbf{t} + \mathbf{y}) > \eta\}$. Then, replacing $\mathcal{B}$ in (6), and denoting by $\partial \mathcal{B}$ its boundary and by $\mathcal{B}^c$ its complement, it is straightforward to show that $\arg \min_{\mathbf{t} \in \mathcal{B}^c} d_{\mathbf{y}}(\mathbf{t}) \in \partial \mathcal{B}$, so (6) is tantamount to

$$\arg \min_{\mathbf{t}: g \circ f(\mathbf{y}+\mathbf{t}) = \eta} d_{\mathbf{y}}(\mathbf{t}). \tag{7}$$

This is a typical Lagrange's multipliers problem, so the attacker could find a theoretical solution if both d and $g \circ f$ were known by him/her; nevertheless, this is not the case, since the last one depends on the secret key, which is unknown for the attacker. Actually, he/she will have only access to the binary output of the decoder. In Appendix A we will show that this is equivalent to

$$\arg \min_{\mathbf{s} \in \mathbb{R}^n} d_{\mathbf{y}}^{\star}(h_{\mathbf{y}}(\mathbf{s})), \tag{8}$$

---

[4] Ideally this measure should quantify the differences between the original host signal and its attacked version; nevertheless, the attacker will have to design his/her strategy taking into account the watermarked signal, since he/she has not access to the original one.

[5] Be aware that in most cases it is reasonable to consider that $\mathbf{t}_0 = \mathbf{0}$, since in that case the attacked signal will be the watermarked one, so the distortion is minimized; furthermore $\mathbf{t}_0$ is in $\mathcal{B}$, since $g \circ f(\mathbf{y})$ will yield H_1.

where $d_{\mathbf{y}}^{\star}$ the restriction of $d\mathbf{y}$ to the boundary of $\mathcal{B}$, and $h\mathbf{y}$ is a surjection which maps $\mathbb{R}^n$ onto the boundary of the decision region.

Since theoretical solutions to (8) are not in general possible due to the lack of knowledge of the boundary of the decision region, numerical iterative methods should be applied (in general) by the attacker in order to find the solution. Concretely, in this paper we will use an adaptation of Newton's method [12], where the considered vector in the $(k + 1)$-th iteration is computed as

$$\mathbf{s}_{k+1} = \mathbf{s}_k - \xi_k \cdot \left[\nabla^2 (d_{\mathbf{y}}^{\star} \circ h\mathbf{y})(\mathbf{s}_k) \right]^{-1} \cdot \nabla (d_{\mathbf{y}}^{\star} \circ h\mathbf{y})(\mathbf{s}_k), \tag{9}$$

where $\xi_k \in \mathbb{R}^+$ is the step-length, whose computation requires (in general) a line search [12]: a small value of ξ_k will imply a slow convergence, but with a large one convergence cannot be assured. When the boundary to be estimated is known to be an hyperplane we can adopt $\xi_k = 1$.

It is straightforward to see that $\nabla (d_{\mathbf{y}}^{\star} \circ h\mathbf{y})(\mathbf{s}_k)$ and $\nabla^2 (d_{\mathbf{y}}^{\star} \circ h\mathbf{y})(\mathbf{s}_k)$ cannot be obtained in an analytic way, therefore they must be numerically approximated by taking into account that

$$\frac{\partial (d_{\mathbf{y}}^{\star} \circ h\mathbf{y})}{\partial s_i}(\mathbf{s}) = \frac{(d_{\mathbf{y}}^{\star} \circ h\mathbf{y})(\mathbf{s} + \delta \mathbf{e}_i) - (d_{\mathbf{y}}^{\star} \circ h\mathbf{y})(\mathbf{s})}{\delta} + O(\delta), \text{ and}$$

$$\frac{\partial^2 (d_{\mathbf{y}}^{\star} \circ h\mathbf{y})}{\partial s_i \partial s_j}(\mathbf{s}) = \frac{(d_{\mathbf{y}}^{\star} \circ h\mathbf{y})(\mathbf{s} + \delta \mathbf{e}_i + \delta \mathbf{e}_j) - (d_{\mathbf{y}}^{\star} \circ h\mathbf{y})(\mathbf{s} + \delta \mathbf{e}_i)}{\delta^2}$$
$$+ \frac{-(d_{\mathbf{y}}^{\star} \circ h\mathbf{y})(\mathbf{s} + \delta \mathbf{e}_j) + (d_{\mathbf{y}}^{\star} \circ h\mathbf{y})(\mathbf{s})}{\delta^2} + O(\delta),$$

with $\mathbf{e}_i$ the i-th vector of the canonical basis. Another choice, which is especially suitable for large-scale problems, is based on replacing the Hessian by a diagonal matrix keeping the diagonal elements; in that way, an iteration of the algorithm just requires $(2 \cdot n + 1)$ evaluations of $(d_{\mathbf{y}}^{\star} \circ h\mathbf{y})(\mathbf{s})$ and (9) is computed with n scalar divisions (if the complete matrix were used, a linear system with n equations and n variables should be solved).

On the other hand, $h\mathbf{y}(\mathbf{s})$ is usually based on scaling $\mathbf{s}$ by a factor $\alpha \in \mathbb{R}$, such that $\alpha \cdot \mathbf{s} \in \partial \mathcal{B}$. The existence of such an α is based on the fact that for most of the known detection functions $\mathbf{0} \in \mathcal{B}$ and $\beta \cdot \mathbf{s} \in \mathcal{B}^c$ for large values of β, so α can be found by a dicothomy algorithm. Be aware that this method is based on the binary output of the detector, without any other knowledge about the detection function; this is why the algorithm is said to be *blind*.

4   Application to Real Methods

In this section we will particularize the proposed algorithm to some of the most popular watermarking methods, showing the practical usefulness of this new attack and comparing the performance of the different methods. In order to

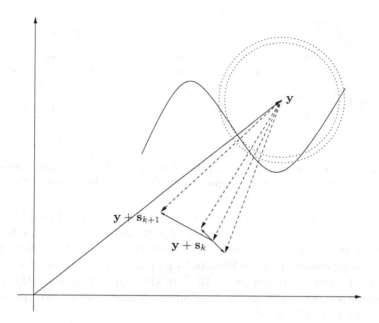

Fig. 1. Example of an iteration of the algorithm. Given a watermarked signal $\mathbf{y}$ and the attacking vector in the k-th iteration $\mathbf{s}_k$, the last one is slightly modified to estimate the gradient and Hessian of $d_{\mathbf{y}}^* \circ h_{\mathbf{y}}(\mathbf{s}_k)$. Once the descent direction and the step-length have been computed, $\mathbf{s}_{k+1}$ is obtained. It can be seen that $\mathbf{y} + \alpha_{k+1}\mathbf{s}_{k+1}$ is closer to the boundary than $\mathbf{y} + \alpha_k\mathbf{s}_k$.

make a fair comparison, the value of the probability of false alarm $P_{fa}{}^6$ will be fixed to 10^{-4}, $n = 2048$ and the document to watermark ratio to 16 dB (with $\sigma_W^2 = 1$) in order to ensure a reasonable probability of missed detection for all the studied methods.[6]

4.1   Spread Spectrum

Detection of standard Spread Spectrum methods is based on the correlation between the received signal $\mathbf{z}$ and the watermark $\mathbf{w}$. Therefore, the function f, defined in (4), projects $\mathbf{z}$ onto a one-dimensional domain ($m = 1$), i.e. $f(\mathbf{z}) = \mathbf{z}^T \cdot \mathbf{w}$, and g in (5) will be the identity function ($g(x) = x$, for all $x \in \mathbb{R}$), so the detection is given by

$$\mathbf{z}^T \cdot \mathbf{w} \underset{H_0}{\overset{H_1}{\underset{\leq}{\gtrless}}} \eta,$$

---

[6] The probability of false alarm P_{fa} is defined as $\Pr\{g_{\text{binary}} \circ f(\mathbf{x} + \mathbf{t}) = H_1\}$. On the other hand, the probability of missed detection P_m is defined as $\Pr\{g_{\text{binary}} \circ f(\mathbf{x} + \mathbf{w} + \mathbf{t}) = H_0\}$.

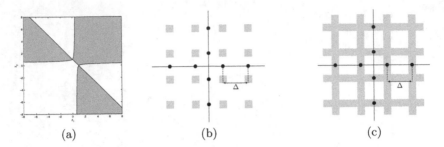

Fig. 2. Examples of decision regions: (a) Decision regions obtained taking into account a l_c-norm when $c = 0.5$. (b) AND Region for QPD. (c) OR Region for QPD.

in such a way that the boundary of the decision region ($\partial\mathcal{B}$) will be a hyperplane and just one iteration will be needed to estimate its orthogonal vector, i.e. the projecting vector, which is a scaled version of the watermark itself. Nevertheless, due to the approximation of the Hessian by a diagonal matrix, about 4 iterations are needed to meet a tolerance of 10^{-6} in the squared norm of the optimal attacking vector. As it was said in Section 3, the line search is not necessary in this case and ξ_k can be fixed to 1.

Comparing the cost of this method with that proposed by El Choubassi and Moulin [10], the latter requires the knowledge of only n points in the border to estimate the watermark, whereas we need $8 \cdot n$ points.

Another alternative for the detection function is that proposed by Cox *et al.* in [13]; in that case, f quantifies the angle between the received signal $\mathbf{z}$ and the watermark vector $\mathbf{w}$, i.e. $f(\mathbf{z}) = \frac{\mathbf{z}^T \cdot \mathbf{w}}{||\mathbf{z}|| \cdot ||\mathbf{w}||}$, and g is again the identity function, yielding a decision region $\mathcal{B}$ which is a n-dimensional cone.

4.2   Side-Informed Methods

In Section 2 the JANIS methods were introduced. In order to make a comparison with the other existing methods, we have fixed the order of the detection function to 4, so

$$f(\mathbf{z}) = \frac{1}{n} \sum_{k=1}^{n/4} \prod_{j=1}^{4} z_{p[(k-1)\cdot N+j]} \cdot a_{p[(k-1)\cdot N+j]}.$$

Quantization-based methods have been shown to be useful for data hiding applications; nevertheless, and despite of their success in that application, very little has been said about their use in detection scenarios. To the best of our knowledge, the first work addressing the problem from this point of view was [14], where the Scalar Costa Scheme is adapted to authentication purposes by embedding a fixed message, yielding the detection function $g(\mathbf{z}, \boldsymbol{\theta}) = \frac{f_{\mathbf{Y}}(\mathbf{z})}{f_{\mathbf{X}}(\mathbf{z})}$. Note that in this case the sensitivity attack is straightforward, since it can be done componentwise.

On the other hand, in [15] the received signal $\mathbf{z}$ is quantized with a lattice Λ and the decision is made upon the squared norm of the quantization error.

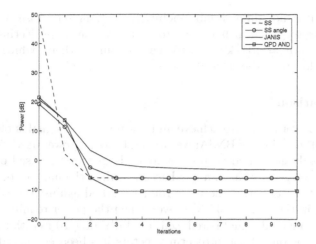

Fig. 3. Power needed to yield an unwatermarked signal (in dB) averaged over 100 watermarked Gaussian vectors as a function of the number of iterations (0 when there is not attack), for different decision regions: SS based on a hyperplane, SS based on the angle, JANIS and QPD for AND regions. Iteration 0 corresponds to random attacking vectors (without applying the proposed algorithm).

Formalizing it, we can write $f(\mathbf{z}) = ||\mathbf{z} \mod \Lambda||^2$, and g is the identity function again. In this way, the acceptance region is the union of n-dimensional hyperspheres centered at the centroids of Λ. From the point of view of attacking such a system, this decision region assures that the attacker can produce a signal yielding H_0 by adding *any* noise vector with a given variance, as far as that noise vector is independent of the self noise. Therefore, a sensitivity attack is not really necessary in this case.

Another approach to this problem is Quantized Projection based Detection (QPD) [16], where uniform scalar quantizers are used to quantify a m-dimensional projected version of the received signal $\mathbf{z}$ and the detection function depends on the quantization error, introducing two different strategies: the AND and OR detection regions, which can be formalized as

$$f_i(\mathbf{z}) = \sum_{j=1}^{n} a_{ij} z_j, \ 1 \le i \le m,$$

$$g_{\text{AND}}(f(\mathbf{z})) = \max_{1 \le i \le m} |(f_i(\mathbf{z}) \mod \Delta) - \Delta/2|, \text{and}$$

$$g_{\text{OR}}(f(\mathbf{z})) = \min_{1 \le i \le m} |(f_i(\mathbf{z}) \mod \Delta) - \Delta/2|,$$

where Δ is the quantization step, a_{ij} are the secret projection matrix coefficients and m the dimensionality of the projected subspace. Obviously, the optimal attacking strategy will depend on the chosen decision region. The convergence of the algorithm introduced in Section 3 for finding the optimal attacking vector will be very much slower for the OR region, since the cost function has its min-

imum value at a non-differentiable point. In fact, in such case we will follow
a different strategy in which we try to estimate the m projecting vectors to
compute the optimal attacking vector as the sum of them, which implies the
complete disclosure of the secret key.

4.3   Comparison

In Fig. 3 the power needed to achieve an unwatermarked signal is plotted versus
the number of iterations of BNSA; we can see that the power needed at iteration
0 (just randomly generated vectors) is much larger for SS based on an hyperplane, but converges to that of angle-based SS when the number of iterations is
increased. In the same way, the most robust method against the BNSA among
those plotted in the figure is JANIS, even when the power required for producing an unwatermarked signal is reduced in 24 dB after 10 iterations. For QPD-
AND, as soon as one of the projecting vectors has been estimated, the power
needed to yield an unwatermarked signal is significantly smaller than in the other
studied cases. Finally, for QPD-OR, the power required after 10 iterations is only
-38 dB.

5   Final Remarks

Following are some guidelines on how to measure the robustness of watermarking
methods against BNSA, the design of practical watermarking methods which are
BNSA-resistant, and the application of BNSA to new scenarios:

- The power needed to push a watermarked signal out of the detection region
  after the BNSA can be seen as a measure of the robustness of a watermarking
  method against this attack: the larger the power needed, the more robust the
  method is. In this sense, JANIS could be said to be the most robust among
  the studied methods, whereas the QPD methods show quite poor performance. Note, however, that this measure does not provide full information
  on the behavior of a particular method; for instance, QPD methods, which
  been shown here to be quite weak against BNSA, have a very good Receiver
  Operating Characteristic (see [16] for a comparison with SS).
- As a countermeasure against BNSA, one could design detection functions
  for which component-wise modifications produce bounded increments, since
  for this kind of functions the task of finding vectors on the boundary of
  the detection function is considerably complicated. Interestingly, the ML
  detection function for Generalized Gaussian distributed hosts (which is a
  l_c-norm, see [17]), fulfills this requirement whenever the shape parameter c
  is such that $c < 1$.
- Taking into account that it just needs the binary output of the detector, the
  BNSA is also suitable for zero-knowledge protocols [18], where, at the end,
  regardless of the domain where the detection function is computed, there is
  a detection region which can be estimated by the proposed algorithm.

– As a final remark, the approach presented in this paper can be also used in the case of data-hiding systems, since the decoding process is nothing but a multiple hypothesis test. In this case, any change of the decoder output should be interpreted as if it were done by a change in the detector output; this is equivalent to have the following binary hypothesis: a) the decoded message is changed; b) the decoded message is unaltered.

A   Appendix

In this Appendix we will show that (7) is equivalent to

$$\arg\min_{\mathbf{s}\in\mathbb{R}^n} d_{\mathbf{y}}^{\star}(h_{\mathbf{y}}(\mathbf{s})),\tag{10}$$

with $d_{\mathbf{y}}^{\star}(\mathbf{t})$ the restriction of $d_{\mathbf{y}}(\mathbf{t})$ to those $\mathbf{t}\in\partial\mathcal{B}$, i.e.,

$$d_{\mathbf{y}}^{\star}(\mathbf{t}):\partial\mathcal{B}\to\mathbb{R}^+$$
$$\mathbf{t}\to d_{\mathbf{y}}(\mathbf{t}),$$

and $h_{\mathbf{y}}(\mathbf{s})$ is a surjection from $\mathbb{R}^n$ to $\partial\mathcal{B}$, i.e.,[7] $h_{\mathbf{y}}(\mathbf{s}):\mathbb{R}^n\to\partial\mathcal{B}$, such that $h_{\mathbf{y}}(\mathbb{R}^n)=\partial\mathcal{B}$, verifying that $h_{\mathbf{y}}(\mathbf{s})=\mathbf{s}$ for all $\mathbf{s}\in\partial\mathcal{B}$; we will also assume that $h_{\mathbf{y}}(\mathbf{s})\in C^2$, i.e., its second derivative exists and is continuous, in a neighborhood of $\mathbf{s}$ (this last point is related to the differentiability of $g\circ f$). Note that $h_{\mathbf{y}}(\mathbf{s})$ just maps the vector $\mathbf{s}$ to a point on $\partial\mathcal{B}$; following this approach the constraint in (7) is straightforwardly verified and we no longer have to care about it. In this way, if $\mathbf{t}_1^*$ is a solution to (7), it will verify $g\circ f(\mathbf{y}+\mathbf{t}_1^*)=\eta$, so $\mathbf{t}_1^*\in\partial\mathcal{B}$ and we can define the set of vectors $\mathcal{S}_1\triangleq\{\mathbf{s}_1^*\in\mathbb{R}^n:h_{\mathbf{y}}(\mathbf{s}_1^*)=\mathbf{t}_1^*\}$. Taking into account that $h_{\mathbf{y}}$ is a surjection there will be at least one such vector $\mathbf{s}_1^*\in\mathcal{S}_1$, so $d_{\mathbf{y}}^{\star}(h_{\mathbf{y}}(\mathbf{s}_1^*))=d_{\mathbf{y}}(\mathbf{t}_1^*)$, and $\mathbf{s}_1^*$ is a solution to (10). On the other hand, if $\mathbf{s}_2^*$ is a solution to (10), we can define $\mathbf{t}_2^*=h_{\mathbf{y}}(s_2^*)$, which minimizes $d_{\mathbf{y}}^{\star}(\mathbf{t})$ over $\partial\mathcal{B}$, so $\mathbf{t}_2^*$ also minimizes $d_{\mathbf{y}}(\mathbf{t})$ for all $\mathbf{t}\in\partial\mathcal{B}$, and is a solution to (7).

Therefore, a vector $\mathbf{s}$ is a solution to (10) if and only if $h_{\mathbf{y}}(\mathbf{s})$ is a solution to (7), in such a way that we can restrict our problem to look for a function $h_{\mathbf{y}}$ and an algorithm which finds a solution to (10).

References

1. Kalker, T.: Considerations on watermarking security. In: IEEE International Workshop on Multimedia Signal Processing, MMSP'01, Cannes, France (2001) 201—-206
2. Comesaña, P., Pérez–Freire, L., Pérez–González, F.: Fundamentals of data hiding security and their application to Spread–Spectrum analysis. In: 7th Information Hiding Workshop, IH05. Lecture Notes in Computer Science, Barcelona, Spain, Springer Verlag (2005)
3. Cox, I.J., Linnartz, J.P.M.G.: Public watermarks and resistance to tampering. In: IEEE International Conference on Image Processing ICIP'97. Volume 3., Santa Barbara, California, USA (1997) 3–6

---

[7] This means that for all $\mathbf{b}\in\partial\mathcal{B}$, there is an $\mathbf{a}\in\mathbb{R}^n$ such that $h_{\mathbf{y}}(\mathbf{a})=\mathbf{b}$.

4. Cox, I.J., Killian, J., Leighton, T., Shamoon, T.: Secure spread spectrum watermarking for multimedia. IEEE Transactions on Image Processing 6 (1997) 1673-1687
5. Linnartz, J.P.M.G., van Dijk, M.: Analysis of the sensitivity attack against electronic watermarks in images. In Aucsmith, D., ed.: 2nd International Workshop on Information Hiding, IH'98. Volume 1525 of Lecture Notes in Computer Science., Portland, OR, USA, Springer Verlag (1998) 258-272
6. Kalker, T., Linnartz, J.P., van Dijk, M.: Watermark estimation through detector analysis. In: IEEE International Conference on Image Processing, ICIP'98, Chicago, IL, USA (1998) 425-429
7. Mansour, M.F., Tewfik, A.H.: LMS–based attack on watermark public detectors. In: IEEE International Conference on Image Processing, ICIP'02. Volume 3. (2002) 649-652
8. Furon, T., Venturini, I., Duhamel, P.: An unified approach of asymmetric watermarking schemes. In Edward J. Delp III, Wong, P.W., eds.: Security and Watermarking of Multimedia Contents III. Volume 4314., San Jose, California, USA, SPIE (2001) 269-279
9. Furon, T., Macq, B., Hurley, N., Silvestre, G.: JANIS: Just Another N–order side–Informed watermarking Scheme. In: IEEE International Conference on Image Processing, ICIP'02. Volume 3., Rochester, NY, USA (2002) 153-156
10. El Choubassi, M., Moulin, P.: New sensitivity analysis attack. In Edward J. Delp III, Wong, P.W., eds.: Security, Steganography and Watermarking of Multimedia contents VII, SPIE (2005) 734-745
11. Furon, T., Duhamel, P.: An asymmetric watermarking method. IEEE Trans. on Signal Processing 51 (2003) 981-995 Special Issue on Signal Processing for Data Hiding in Digital Media and Secure Content Delivery.
12. Nocedal, J., Wright, S.J.: Numerical Optimization. Springer (1999)
13. Cox, I.J., Miller, M.L., Bloom, J.A.: Digital watermarking. Multimedia Information and Systems. Morgan Kauffman (2002)
14. Eggers, J.J., Girod, B.: Blind watermarking applied to image authentication. In: Int. Conf. on Acoustics, Speech and Signal Processing (ICASSP). Volume 3. (2001) 1977-1980
15. Liu, T., Moulin, P.: Error exponents for one–bit watermarking. In: Int. Conf. on Acoustics, Speech and Signal Processing (ICASSP). Volume 3. (2003) 65-68
16. Pérez-Freire, L., Comesaña, P., Pérez–González, F.: Detection in quantizationbased watermarking: performance and security issues. In Edward J. Delp III,Wong, P.W., eds.: Security, Steganography, and Watermarking of Multimedia Contents VII. Volume 5681., San Jose, California, USA, SPIE (2005) 721-733
17. Hernández, J.R., Amado, M., Pérez–González, F.: DCT–domain watermarking techniques for still images: Detector performance analysis and a new structure. IEEE Trans. on Image Processing 9 (2000) 55-68 Special Issue on Image and Video Processing for Digital Libraries.
18. Adelsbach, A., Sadeghi, A.R.: Zero–knowledge watermark detection and proof of ownership. In Moskowitz, I.S., ed.: 4th International Workshop on Information Hiding, IH'01. Volume 2137 of Lecture Notes in Computer Science., Pittsburgh, PA, USA, Springer Verlag (2001) 273-288

Look Up Table(LUT) Method for Halftone Image Watermarking*

InGook Chun

School of Information Technology Engineering, Soonchunhyang University,
Asan-si, Choongchungnam-do, Republic of Korea
chunik@sch.ac.kr

Abstract. In this paper, we introduce a LUT based watermarking method for a halftone image. Watermark bits are hidden at pseudo-random locations of halftone image during halftoning process which is based on LUT method. The pixel values of the halftone image are determined from the LUT entry indexed by both the neighborhood halftone pixels and current grayscale value. The LUT is trained by a set of grayscale images and halftone images. The advantage of LUT method is that it can be executed very fast compared with other watermarking method for a halftone image. Therefore LUT watermarking algorithm can be embedded in a printer. Experiments using real scanned images show that the proposed method is feasible method to hide the large amount of data within a halftone image without noticeable distortion and the watermark is robust to cropping and rotation.

1 Introduction

Digital watermarking of image is a technique to protect the copyright of a image by embedding of copyright information in a image. Watermark methods should enable a sufficient amount of embedded information but introduce only minimal distortion to the image and its visual quality. So far, a lot of watermarking methods have been developed. The most common approaches of watermarking are to embed watermark in the spatial domain or frequency domain and target images are primarily digital images.

In this paper, we deal with watermarks for printed images rather than digital images. Printed image watermarking means that watermarks are inserted into hardcopy images generated by printers. Potential application might be secure printing, authentication of printed tickets and picture ID cards. In the proposed method, watermarks are inserted performed by exploiting the printing process itself i.e. halftoning. Halftoning is a process to convert continuous-tone images to two-tone images [1]. It is widely used in printing process because most printers have limited numbers of colors. Most previous watermarking methods which are designed for grayscale images, can not be applied directly to halftone images because halftone images have only two tones: black and white.

---

* This work is supported by the Korea Science and Engineering Foundation (KOSEF-R05-2004-000-10894-0) and Korea Research Foundation.

M. Barni et al. (Eds.): IWDW 2005, LNCS 3710, pp. 275–285, 2005.
© Springer-Verlag Berlin Heidelberg 2005

There are a lot of halftoning methods, but most popular methods are ordered dithering and error diffusion [2]. In ordered dithering, a continuous-tone image is thresholded with a spatially periodic screen. Ordered dithering requires only simple pointwise computations but the quality of halftone image suffers from periodic patterns. In error diffusion, the halftone error between the actual pixel intensity and halftone value is fed back to its neighboring pixels. The quality of error diffusion is fairly good but the operation is inherently serial and slow. Recently Mese has developed a new halftoning method using Look Up Table (LUT) [14]. The main advantage of LUT halftoning method, is that it requires no arithmetic operation rather than memory access. Moreover, we can train the LUT using a sample set of images and halftones which are halftoned with any halftoning method.

In this paper, a new watermarking method for halftone images using LUT, is proposed. There have been some researches in halftone image watermarking. There are two popular methods. The first method is to use two different halftone screens and switch the halftone screen according to the binary value of watermark bits [3], [4], [5]. The problem here is how to design an optimal halftone screen pair which allows minimal distortion and easy extraction of watermark bits. The second method is to change directly the pixel value of the halftone image according to the watermark bits. Ming and Oscar have proposed a data hiding method for halftone image generated by error diffusion method [6], [7], [8], [9]. Data Hiding Error Diffusion (DHED) integrates the data hiding into the error diffusion operation. DHED hides data by forced complementary toggling at pseudo-random locations within a halftone image. But their method shows some artifacts due to the watermark insertion. The main reason is that the data hiding error is only compensated by the future pixel, that is, the next pixels in the scanning order.

In this paper, a very fast watermarking method for printed image using LUT halftoning method is described. The proposed method can reduce the distortion by finding an appropriate halftone value at each pixel location using LUT. Moreover, the required computation is minimal, that is, just one memory access is sufficient. The watermark pattern is designed to be robust to cropping and geometric distortion. The watermark extraction procedure is designed to handle real scanned images. The proposed method is a true blind watermarking scheme which requires no information from the encoder except the seed of random number generator.

2   Watermarking Algorithm

2.1   Watermark Embedding

Because both of halftone image and watermark are binary, the pixels of halftone images can carry the watermark information. Some pixels in halftone image are forced to have watermark information. The candidate pixel locations are generated by a random number generator with a specific seed value. The pixel values of candidates are set to be black or white dot according to the watermark bits as shown in Figure 1. If this seed value is sent to the watermark decoder, one can extract the watermark bits just by reading the value of these random locations generated by received seed value.

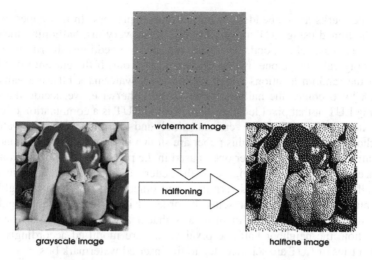

Fig. 1. The watermark bits are inserted into the random locations of halftone image in the process of halftoning

In order to provide robustness to cropping and geometrical robustness, the same watermarks are inserted multiple times at periodic shifted locations. This redundancy can be used to identify the parameters of geometrical affine transformation [12]. Since the watermark has been embedded multiple times, the autocorrelation of watermarked image has multiple peaks. If the image has undergone a geometrical transformation, the peaks in the autocorrelation function will reflect the same transformation. Hence using these point pairs, we can compute the parameter of the geometrical transformation parameters. The Figure 2 shows that the same watermarks are embedded four times in four non-overlapping blocks. The first P bits of base watermark block are preset to known values. These preset bits act like a reference mark which can be used in order to compute the amount of translation. Note that the values of preset bits are known but the positions of preset bits are not preset. The positions are determined according to the secret key.

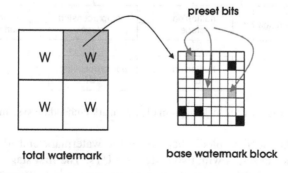

Fig. 2. The concept of periodic watermark with preset bits

The watermarks are embedded during halftoning process. In this paper, grayscale image is halftoned using LUT method because it is a very fast halftoning method and its quality is reasonably good. The watermarking embedding algorithm processes pixels of grayscale image one by one in raster scan order. If the current pixel location is one of the random locations which should carry watermark bits, the value of the watermark bit becomes the halftone pixel value. Otherwise, we decide the halftone value using LUT at that pixel location. The input to LUT is a combination of carefully selected neighborhoods of the current pixel and current grayscale value. The neighborhood templates used in this paper are shown in Figure 3. The first one is used in halftoning stage [14]. The other one is used in the postprocessing of halftone image to enhance its quality. In the Figure 3, the letter "O" denotes the current location whose halftone value is being determined and other numbers denote neighborhood pixel locations. The number represents the order of importance of the neighborhood pixels to the chosen pixel. The main idea is that if a watermark bit is inserted into some location, the neighbor halftone pixel values are modified accordingly because different entries of LUT are selected due to the inserted watermark bits.

	15			14	
	11	9	6	8	
13	7	3	2	4	12
10	5	1	O		

(a)

		11		
13	5	3	7	
9	1	O	2	10
	6	4	8	14
		12		

(b)

Fig. 3. LUT template used in halftoning. (a) LUT template used in halftoning   (b) LUT template used in postprocessing

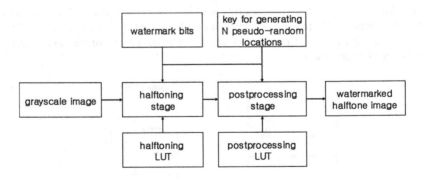

Fig. 4. The block diagram of watermark embedding system

Figure 4 is the detailed block diagram of the watermark embedding system. We have two processing stages with two different LUTs. The first stage is called as halftoning stage. In the halftoning stage, a grayscale image is halftoned in a raster-scan order. In a postprocessing LUT, the halftoning result of the previous stage is enhanced. Note that two LUTs have different neighborhood configurations. In the halftoning stage, we can not consult the future pixel beyond current pixel but in postprocessing stage, we can. Note that two LUTs can be trained using the same set of grayscale images and halftone images at the same time.

We assume that there are N pixels in the neighborhood template and they are ordered in a specific way as in the Figure 3. The halftone pixels in the neighborhood template, are denoted as $h_0, h_1, ..., h_{N-1}$ and the grayscale value of the current pixel as g. The combination $p=(h_0, h_1, ..., h_{N-1}, g)$ can be considered as a pattern, and it is given to the LUT as input and the output value is generated from the corresponding entry of LUT. The neighborhood pixel values $h_0, h_1, ..., h_{N-1}$ should be 0 or 1 because a halftone image is a binary image and the gray value g is represented by $2^8 = 256$ gray levels. Therefore there can be $2^N 2^8$ possible different patterns in the LUT. The LUT return a binary value for a pattern p and denoted as $T(p)$.

The LUT is trained using a set of grayscale images and corresponding halftone images. A sample set of images is selected and they are halftoned using any halftoning algorithm. We select the error diffusion halftoning algorithm. We will first obtain the expected halftone value for each pattern. Then this halftone value will be assigned to the corresponding LUT position for that pattern. Let us denote the number of occurrences of pattern $p=(h_0, h_1, ..., h_{N-1}, g)$ in the sample halftone images, M_p and its corresponding halftone values as

$$H_p(i) \quad for \quad i = 0, 1, ..., M_p - 1.$$

If $M_p > 0$, the LUT halftone value for that pattern $p = (h_0, h_1, ..., h_{N-1}, g)$ will be the closest quantization point to the mean of the corresponding halftone values, i.e.,

$$T(p) = \begin{cases} 1 & if \ m_p \geq 0.5 \\ 0 & if \ m_p < 0.5 \end{cases} \tag{1}$$

where

$$m_p = \frac{\sum_{i=0}^{M_p-1} H_p(i)}{M_p}. \tag{2}$$

If $M_p = 0$ then the pattern $p=(h_0, h_1, ..., h_{N-1}, g)$ dose not exist. In this case, the halftone value should be estimated in a different way. We use the simplest one which is to find the nearest pattern which does exist [14]. The following pseudo-code summarizes our algorithm.

```
for all pixel location (x,y) in halftone image {
    if h(x,y) is watermark pixel
        h(x,y) = watermark bit;
    else {
        p = (h_0, h_1, ..., h_{N-1}, g);
        find T_p and M_p from LUT with input pattern p;
        if(M_p == 0)
            find the nearest T_p with M_p != 0;
        h(x,y) = T_p;
    }

}
```

2.2 Watermark Extraction

We assume that the input is a scanned image which is obtained by scanning the printed halftone image containing watermark. The resolution of scanner is set to be higher than that of printer. We process the scanned image using image processing technology such as Hough transform, in order to get an original binary halftone image. The watermark extraction algorithm consists of two major modules. The first module is called pre-processing module which generates the binary halftone image from the scanned image. The second module is called watermark extraction module which extracts the watermark from the binary halftone image. Figure 5 shows the overall block diagram of watermark extraction system [15].

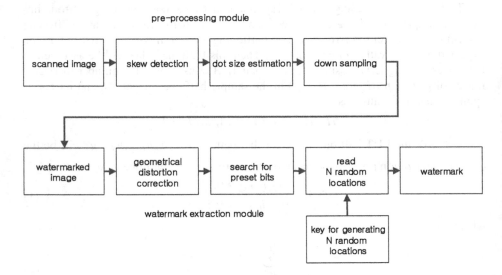

Fig. 5. The block diagram of watermark extraction system

In order to determine the watermark block size, autocorrelation function of binary halftone image is computed. If there are any periodic data in the watermarked image, there would be multiple peaks in autocorrelation function as shown Figure 6. To detect the peaks, the gradient of autocorrelation value is computed. These peaks are used to compute the block size and parameters of geometrical transformation.

After the watermark block size is determined, N pseudo-random locations are generated by a same key which was used in the embedding process. Knowing the information of these random locations, the corrected image is scanned sequentially to find the preset bits of the watermark. The concept of preset bits is used in order to be robust to translation and cropping. The first P bits of watermark are preset to known values. After finding the preset bits, the remaining watermark bits can be recovered simply by reading the pixel values at next random locations.

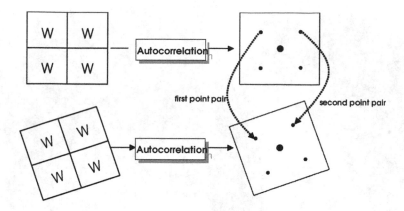

Fig. 6. The peaks of autocorrelation function can be used as reference points in computing transformation parameters

3 Experimental Results and Discussion

The proposed algorithm is tested with several test images in order verify its performance. We have chosen $N_1 = 15$ for halftoning LUT, $N_2 = 14$ for postprocessing LUT, therefore we need $2^{N_1}2^8 = 2^{23}$ (1Mbytes) to store the halftoning LUT and $2^{N_2}2^8 = 2^{22}$ (0.5Mbytes) to store the postprocessing LUT. We have trained our LUTs with 11 images including Lena, pepper and cameraman. The halftone images in the training set were halftoned with error diffusion halftoning algorithm. After training stage, we applied our algorithm to a 256 x 256 image called "Debbie" with the previously trained LUTs. Figure 7(a) shows the "Debbie" image. Note that "Debbie" was not in the training set. The watermark image consists of non-overlapping 32 x 32 blocks containing 8 watermark bits in each block as shown in Figure 7(b). The watermark bit "0" is shown as a black dot and "1" as a white dot. Figure 7(c) is the LUT-generated halftone image without watermark. In LUT halftoning method, there are some no-dot areas in the regions of very high grey level, especially in the nose area of "Debbie" image. It is mainly due to the limited size of LUT window template. It can be solved by tree structure LUT halftoning [14]. Figure 7(d) is the halftone image generated by our watermarking algorithm. As you can see, there is no significant distortion in the watermarked image.

We compared our results with that of DHED(Data Hiding Error Diffusion) which was proposed by Ming. DHED inserts watermark by toggling the pixel value of halftone image during error diffusion halftoning process. In their method, the data hiding error is compensated by future pixels, which are the next pixels in the scanning order. For comparison, we increased the watermark rate to about 0.0312 bits/pixel. As you can see from the comparison of Figure 8(a) and Figure 8(b), the result of our algorithm shows slightly less salt and pepper type artifacts than that of DHED.

(a)   (b)

(c)   (d)

Fig. 7. The results of 256 x 256 "Debbie" image watermarking. (a) grayscale image (b) watermark image (c) halftone image generated from LUT halftoning method(no watermark) (d) halftone image generated from the proposed algorithm(watermark rate is 0.0078 bits/pixel).

To compare the results of the proposed method with that of DHED, we use MPSNR (Modified Peak Signal-to-Noise Ratio) between the original continuous-tone image and halftone image [8]. The idea is that we apply a lowpass filtering to the halftone image before computing the normal PSNR. Table 1 shows the MPSNR values. Generally MPSNR of the results of the proposed method is slightly lower than that of results of DHED. This can be approved if we generate training samples using a more powerful halftoning method, such as DBS [2].

Fig. 8. The comparison results of 256 x 256 "Debbie" image watermarking. (a) halftone image generated from DHED watermarking method(watermark rate is 0.0312 bits/pixel) (b) halftone image generated from the proposed algorithm(watermark rate is 0.0312 bits/pixel).

Table 1. MPSNR of result haltone images. Watermark rate is 0.0312 bits/pixel and the sizes of images are 256 x 256.

	"Debbie" image	"butterfly" image	"Lena" image
DHED	23.52dB	21.92dB	22.16dB
Proposed method	23.05dB	21.51dB	21.50dB

Table 2 compares the processing time of the proposed algorithm with that of DHED. The proposed algorithm is much faster than DHED.

Table 2. Comparison of processing time. Watermark rate is 0.0312 bits/pixel and the sizes of images are 256 x 256.

	"Debbie" image	"butterfly" image	"Lena" image
DHED	6.890 sec.	6.860 sec.	6.920 sec.
Proposed method	0.471 sec.	0.460 sec.	0.490 sec.

To test the robustness of the proposed algorithm to geometrical cropping and rotation, the final halftone was printed by HP LaserJet at 600 dpi and it was scanned by HP scanjet at 2400 dpi as shown in Figure 9(a). During scanning, it was deliberately rotated and cropped. In Figure 9(b), the skew was corrected using edge information and Hough transform. The binary halftone image was recovered by reading the value of each dot in Figure 9(c). The final halftone image is scanned sequentially to find the preset bits of the watermark block. Once we find the preset bits, the remaining watermark bits can be recovered simply by reading the pixel values at next random locations as shown Figure 9(d).

Fig. 9. Watermark extraction steps. (a) scanned halftone image (b) skew-corrected image (c) recovered binary halftone image (d) detected watermark bits.

4 Conclusion

In this paper, a new watermarking method for halftone images is proposed. The proposed method is based on LUT halftoning technique. It hides data at pseudo-random locations within a halftone image. The method should remove the artifacts and distortions due to the embedded watermark data effectively. The proposed method achieves the improved visual quality by finding the appropriate halftone value from the neighborhood template through LUT. Because LUT chooses most appropriate halftone value considering the surrounding halftone pixels, the watermark data within the halftone images is not easily detectable by the eye. The main advantage of LUT watermarking method is that it requires no arithmetic operations other than memory access. Therefore it can be executed very fast, which will enable us to embed the proposed algorithm inside a printer very easily. Moreover the LUT can be trained by any halftoning algorithm. Therefore we can train our LUT using the computation intensive halftoning algorithms which give the best halftone quality.

To be robust to cropping and distortion, the watermark consists of several non-overlapping blocks. Each block contains the same watermark data. Using autocorrelation function, we can determine the watermark block size and finally we can extract the watermark information form the watermark block. Experiments using real scanned images were conducted and experimental results show that the proposed algorithm generates halftone images with good visual quality and robust to the unintentional geometrical attacks. This new technique has great potential in printing security documents such as currency, coupon, on-line tickets and ID card as well as confidential documents

References

1. Ulichney, R. A.: Digital Halftoning. MIT Press, Cambridge, MA(1987)
2. Allebach, J. P.: DBS: Retrospective and Future Direction. Proceedings of SPIE Vol. 4300 (2001) 358-376
3. Hel-Or, H. Z.: Copyright Labeling of Printed Images. Proceedings of IEEE Int. Conf. on Image Processing (2000) 702-705
4. Wang, S.G. and Knox, K.T.: Embedding digital watermarks in halftone screens. Proceedings of SPIE Vol. 3971(2000) 218-227
5. Baharav, Z. and Shaked, D.: Watermarking of dither halftoned images. Proceedings of SPIE Vol. 3657 (1999) 307-316
6. Fu, M.S. and Au, O.C.: Data Hiding in Halftone Images by Stochastic Error Diffusion. Proceedings of IEEE Int. Conf. on Acoustics, Speech, and Signal Processing (2001) 1965-1968
7. Fu, M.S. and Au, O.C.: Hiding Data in Halftone Image using Modified Data Hiding Error Diffusion. Proceedings of SPIE Vol. 4067 (2000) 1671-1680
8. Fu, M.S. and Au, O.C.: Data Hiding for Halftone Images. Proceedings of SPIE Vol.3971, (2000) 228-236
9. Fu, M.S. and Au, O.C.: Halftone image data hiding with intensity selection and connection selection. Signal Proceeding: Image Communication 16(2001) 909-930
10. Kacker, D. and Allebach, J. P.: Joint Halftoning and Watermarking. Proceedings of IEEE Int. Conf. on Image Processing (2000) 69-72
11. Mese, M., Vaidyanathan, P. P.: Look-Up Table (LUT) Method for Inverse Halftoning. IEEE Trans. on Image Processing, Vol. 10 (2001) 1566-1578
12. Kutter, M.: Watermarking Resisting to Translation, Rotation, and Scaling. Proceedings of SPIE Vol. 3528 (1998) 423-431
13. Parker, J.R.: Algorithms for Image Processing and Computer Vision. John Wiley & Sons, Hoboken, NJ (1996)
14. Mese, M., Vaidyanathan, P. P.: Look-Up Table (LUT) Method for Image Halftoning. Proceedings of ICIP, Vancouver, Canada, (2000)
15. InGook, Chun and Sanho, Ha: A Watermarking Method for Halftone Images Based on Iterative Halftoning Method, LNCS 2738(2003) Springer-Verlag 165-175.

New Public-Key Authentication Watermarking for JBIG2 Resistant to Parity Attacks

Sergio Vicente Denser Pamboukian[1] and Hae Yong Kim[2]

[1] Universidade Presbiteriana Mackenzie, São Paulo, Brazil,
sergiop@mackenzie.com.br
http://meusite.mackenzie.com.br/sergio
[2] Escola Politécnica, Universidade de São Paulo, Brazil,
hae@lps.usp.br
http://www.lps.usp.br/~hae

Abstract. An authentication watermark is a hidden data inserted into an image that allows detecting any alteration made in the image. AWTs (Authentication Watermarking Techniques) normally make use of secret- or public-key cryptographic cipher to compute the authentication signature of the image, and inserts it into the image itself. Many previous public-key AWTs for uncompressed binary images can be attacked by an image adulterating technique named "parity attack." JBIG2 is an international standard for compressing bi-level images (both lossy and lossless). The creation of secure AWTs for compressed binary images is an important practical problem. However, it seems that no AWT for JBIG2 resistant to parity attacks has ever been proposed. This paper proposes a new data-hiding method to embed information in the text region of JBIG2 files. Then, we use this technique to design a new AWT for JBIG2-encoded images resistant to parity attacks. Both the secret- and public-key versions of the proposed AWT are completely immune against parity attacks. Moreover, watermarked images are visually pleasant, without visible salt and pepper noise. Image authenticity verification can be performed in either JBIG2 file itself or in the binary image obtained by decoding the JBIG2 file.

1 Introduction

Steganography (also known as data/information hiding) is the study of techniques used to hide secret information inside another kind of information, without loss of quality of the host information. For example, a sequence of bits can be embedded inside an image by modifying some of its pixels, without perceptible degradation in image quality. The steganography is not concerned about the usefulness of the hidden information or the facility of removing it. A digital watermark makes use of data hiding techniques to insert, into a digital data, a signal that can be extracted later to make an assertion about the host data. Digital watermarks are usually classified as either "robust" or "fragile," depending on the difficulty of removal.

Robust watermarks cannot be easily removed and are designed to resist common image-manipulation procedures (rotation, scaling, cropping, lossy compression, printing/scanning, etc.) This kind of watermark is normally used for copyright verification and fingerprinting.

M. Barni et al. (Eds.): IWDW 2005, LNCS 3710, pp. 286–298, 2005.
© Springer-Verlag Berlin Heidelberg 2005

On the other hand, fragile watermarks (or authentication watermarks) are easily corrupted by any image processing procedure. However, watermarks for checking image integrity and authenticity can be fragile because if the watermark is removed, the watermark detection algorithm will correctly report the corruption of the image.

Only recently, some secure authentication-watermarking techniques (AWTs) for uncompressed binary images have been proposed [1, 2, 3]. We mean by "secure AWT" a scheme that has two properties: (1) it must detect *any* image alteration (both accidental and malicious); (2) its security must not lie on the secrecy of the algorithm but only on the secrecy of the key. Hence, a secure AWT usually relies upon cryptography.

Many previous AWTs for uncompressed binary images can be assaulted by an image adulterating technique named "parity attack" [2, 3]. For secret-key AWTs, some general methods for preventing parity attacks have been identified [3]. However, for public-key AWTs, no general parity attack preventing method has been discovered. Only very recently, one of the authors of this paper has proposed a particular AWT for uncompressed binary images completely immune against parity attacks, named AWTC (Authentication Watermarking by Template ranking with symmetrical Central pixels) [4].

JBIG2 is an international standard for compressing bi-level images (both lossy and lossless) [5, 6]. In this standard, the image is decomposed in several regions (text, halftone and line-art) and each region is compressed using the most appropriate method. The creation and implementation of secure AWTs for compressed binary images (such as JBIG2) seems to be an important practical problem. Scanned documents are largely binary images, which may be protected against fraudulent alterations. Besides, binary document images must be stored in a compressed format in order to save storage space.

Queiroz and we have very recently proposed an AWT for JBIG2-encoded images (possibly lossy-compressed), named AWTRJ (Authentication Watermarking by Template Ranking for JBIG2) [7]. Unfortunately, AWTRJ (especially its public-key version) can be assaulted by parity attacks. To the best of our knowledge, no AWT for JBIG2 resistant to parity attacks has ever been proposed.

This paper proposes a new data-hiding method, inspired by AWTC and AWTRJ, to embed information in the text region of JBIG2 files (both lossy and lossless). The embedded data can be extracted from either JBIG2 file itself or the binary image obtained by decoding the JBIG2 file. Then, we use the proposed data-hiding technique to design a new AWT for JBIG2-encoded images resistant to parity attacks. This AWT can be used to protect any JBIG2 file (both lossy and lossless) that has a text region large enough to bear the authentication signature. Both secret-key and public-key versions of this AWT are completely immune against parity attacks.

We did not apply any perceptual distortion measure to quantify the quality of watermarked images, because this analysis is beyond the scope of this paper. However, the suggested template ranking can be adapted to minimize the distortion according to a specific perceptual model.

2 JBIG2 Format

The Joint Bi-level Image Experts Group (JBIG), a "collaborative team" established in 1988, prepared JBIG2 standard. This standard defines a compression method for bi-level images (usually black and white) and was explicitly prepared for lossy, lossless, and lossy-to-lossless image compression [5, 6]. A JBIG2-encoded image is composed by several regions (text, halftone and line-art). Each region is encoded using the most appropriate method. A JBIG2 text region has two kinds of segments:

- Symbol dictionary segment – contains bitmaps of the characters present in the text region.
- Text region segment – describes locations of characters within the text region, with references to the symbol dictionary.

There are many researches on symbol dictionary design [8, 9]. Many instances of a character can refer to the same symbol in the dictionary, what increases the compression rate. In lossy compression, similar instances of a symbol can refer to the same symbol in the dictionary. This happens, for example, in scanned documents where several instances of the same character may differ slightly. If these similar characters refer to a unique symbol in the dictionary, the image quality decreases but the compression rate increases.

3 Previous Techniques

3.1 Data Hiding in Uncompressed Binary Images

There are three basic ways of embedding a sequence of bits in uncompressed binary/halftone images:

- **Pixel-wise**: Change the values of (usually pseudo-randomly chosen) individual pixels [10, 11]. This approach is well suited for dispersed-dot halftone images. However, visible salt and pepper noise will appear when applied to other types of binary images. It can be applied to the binary image or directly to the halftone screen in its design step [12].
- **Component-wise**: Change the characteristics of pixel groups (for example, the position or the area of connected components) [13]. Unfortunately, the success of this approach depends on the type of the host image.
- **Block-wise**: Divide the host image into blocks and modify some characteristics of each block. Some works [14, 15] suggest alternating between two different weight matrices to halftone an image such that the matrix used in each block can be determined in the future by analyzing the statistical properties. Other works suggest modifying slightly the content of the block so that it hides the desired sequence of bits [16, 17].

3.2 Authentication Watermarking for Uncompressed Binary Images

Authentication watermarking techniques (AWTs) make use of data-hiding techniques and cryptography theory to check the image integrity and authenticity. In a typical cryptography-based AWT, an authentication signature (AS) is computed from the whole image and inserted into the image itself. An AS contains information about the host image content that may be checked to verify its integrity. In cryptography, an AS is called message authentication code (MAC) using a secret-key cipher or digital signature (DS) using a public/private-key cipher.

The chosen AS must be long enough to assure the security. Too small an AS does not withstand birthday attacks. Usually, a MAC with 128-bits is considered computationally secure. The best-known DS, RSA, is considered computationally secure with 1024 bits. A newer scheme, DSA, is considered computationally secure with 320 bits. A brand new scheme, BLS, is computationally secure with only 160 bits [18]. The reader is referred to introductory books on Cryptography for more details (for example, [19]).

In a secret-key AWT, the same secret-key is used in both watermark insertion and verification. In a public-key AWT, only the owner of the private-key can insert the valid watermark, and anyone can verify the image authenticity and integrity using the corresponding public-key. However, inserting the AS into the image alters the image itself, hence modifying its AS and invalidating the watermark. Typically, the image has to be somehow divided into at least two parts: a portion to maintain the image integrity and another portion to carry the AS. However, dividing the image in two parts makes possible the occurrence of a "parity attack."

3.3 Parity Attack

Many data hiding schemes for binary images can be transformed into AWTs by simply dividing the host image Z in two regions: the first region Z_1 where the AS is to be stored, and the second region Z_2 from where the AS is to be computed. This idea was used to design AWST (Authentication Watermarking by Self Toggling) for dispersed-dot halftone images [1] and AWTR (Authentication Watermarking by Template Ranking) for generic binary images [2, 3].

However, some caution must be taken when transforming a data-hiding scheme into an AWT, because although the region Z_2 is well protected (with the security assured by the cryptography theory), the region Z_1 is not. For example, let us take the component-wise data-hiding scheme that inserts one bit per connected component, forcing it to have an even or odd number of pixels. A connected component can be forced to have the desired parity by toggling one of its boundary pixels. This scheme can be transformed into an AWT by dividing the host image in regions Z_1 and Z_2, computing the AS of Z_2 and inserting it in Z_1. Yet, a malicious hacker can arbitrarily alter the region Z_1 without being noticed by the AWT, as long as all the parities of its connected components remain unaltered. For example, a character "a" in Z_1 region can be changed into an "e" (or any other character that contains only one connected component) as long as its parity remains unchanged. We refer to this as a "parity attack."

3.4 AWTC

Very recently, a new AWT for uncompressed binary images, called AWTC (Authentication Watermarking by Template ranking with symmetrical Central pixel), was proposed [4]. This technique is completely immune against parity attacks, and consequently both its secret- and public-key versions are secure. This technique can detect *any* image alteration, even a single pixel flipping. An image watermarked by AWTC does not present visible salt-and-pepper noise. We will use the ideas used to design AWTC to create an AWT for JBIG2-encoded images immune against parity attacks.

Fig. 1. A 3×3 template ranking with symmetrical central pixels in increasing visual impact order. Hatched pixels match either black or white pixels (note that all templates have hatched central pixels). The score of a given pattern is that of the matching template with the lowest impact. Mirrors, rotations and reverses of each pattern have the same score.

AWTC keeps the visual scores of flippable pixels unaltered after embedding the data. It is possible because the template ranking used assigns the same visual impact score to the patterns that differ only by the colors of their central pixels. Figure 1 depicts a 3×3 template ranking with symmetrical central pixels. Note that all patterns have hatched central pixels. To simplify the explanation, let us assume that 3×3 patterns are used, although larger patterns may be used:

1. Divide the uncompressed binary image Z to be watermarked in a sequence v of non-overlapping 3×3 pieces of image Z. The simplest of such sequence is the division of Z into regular 3×3 pieces (incomplete pieces at image borders are discarded), scanned in raster sequence (figure 2). Only the central pixels of the pieces of v can have their colors changed by the watermark insertion.
2. Sort the sequence v in increasing order using the visual scores as the primary-key and non-repeating pseudo-random numbers as the secondary-key. The secondary-key prevents from embedding the data only in the upper part of the image.
3. Clear the central pixels of the first n pieces of the sorted v, where n is the length of the AS. Compute the AS of the now-cleared image Z.
4. Embed n bits of the AS by flipping (if necessary) the central pixels of the first n pieces of the sorted v.

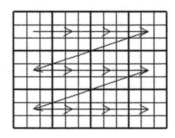

Fig. 2. A 9×12 image divided into regular 3×3 pieces and scanned in raster order

To extract the AS, the sequence v of non-overlapping 3×3 pieces is constructed again and sorted as in the insertion step. The result is exactly the same sequence v used in the insertion. Then, the values of the n first central pixels are the hidden data.

Why do parity attacks not apply to AWTC? Because the number of data-bearing Z_1 pixels is exactly equal to the length of the adopted AS. All image pixels (except the n pixels that will bear the n bits of the AS) are taken into account to compute the AS. Consequently, any alteration of Z_2 region can be detected because it changes the AS of the watermarked image, and any alteration of Z_1 region can also be detected because it changes the stored AS.

3.5 AWTRJ

To the best of our knowledge, Queiroz and we have proposed the only AWT for JBIG2-encoded binary images (possibly lossy-compressed) [7]. This technique is named AWTRJ (Authentication Watermarking by Template Ranking for JBIG2). Only the secret-key AWTRJ has been proposed, because the public-key version can be assaulted by parity attacks. The goal of this paper is to obtain another AWT for JBIG2 immune to parity attacks and consequently secure in both secret- and public-key versions.

AWTRJ embeds the MAC in the text region of a JBIG2-encoded image, more precisely in the symbol dictionary segment. AWTRJ can authenticate any JBIG2 binary image with a text region large enough to bear the MAC. Image authenticity verification can be performed in either JBIG2 file itself or in the binary image obtained by decoding the JBIG2 file. AWTRJ consists of:

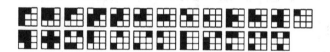

Fig. 3. Set of 3×3 templates that do not disconnect symbols

1. Selects pseudo-randomly, using the secret-key as the seed, an appropriate number of symbols of the text region to bear the data.
2. Remove the selected symbols from the image and compute the MAC of the resulting image (that includes not only the text region but also halftone and line-art regions) using the secret-key.
3. As each dictionary symbol can be referred by several instances in the text region, an alteration of a symbol will have its effect multiplied. To avoid this problem, duplicate the symbols that will bear data in the *symbol dictionary segment* and modify the *text region segment* so that only one instance of the symbol (the one selected pseudo-randomly) refers to the data-bearing symbol (DBS). All others instances continue referring to the original symbol.
4. Shuffle pseudo-randomly the set of all pixels of all DBSs of the symbol dictionary.
5. Divide the set of shuffled pixels of DBSs into small blocks (e.g., each block with 64 pixels).

6. Analyze the neighborhood (usually 3×3) of each shuffled pixel to rate its visual significance.
7. Insert one bit of the MAC in each block by forcing it to have even or odd number of black pixels. Only pixels that do not disconnect symbols can be flipped (figure 3).

In the watermark verification, the same pseudo-random number generator detects the marked symbols. The MAC S is extracted from these symbols. After that, the marked symbols are removed from the watermarked image and the check MAC C is computed using the secret-key. If the extracted MAC S is equal to the check MAC C, the authentication is verified. Otherwise, the image was modified.

The secret-key AWTRJ is protected against parity attacks because it uses the secret-key as the seed of the pseudo-random selection in step 1, and uses the secret-key as the seed of the pseudo-random shuffling in step 4. Unfortunately, the same ideas cannot be applied to the public-key version, because anyone must be able to extract completely the hidden bits without knowing the private-key.

4   The Proposed Technique

We propose a new AWT for JBIG2-encoded images resistant to "parity attacks," called AWTCJ (Authentication Watermarking by Template ranking with symmetrical Central pixels for JBIG2). AWTCJ is inspired by both AWTC and AWTRJ. For the sake of clarity, we first describe the data-hiding technique DHTCJ (Data Hiding by Template ranking with symmetrical Central pixels for JBIG2), which will be transformed into AWTCJ using the idea described in subsections 3.2 and 3.3.

4.1   DHTCJ

DHTCJ data insertion algorithm is:

1. Let be given a JBIG2-encoded image Z' and n bits of data to be inserted into Z'. Decode the text region of Z', obtaining the uncompressed binary image Z.
2. Divide Z in a sequence v of non-overlapping pieces of image and sort v as in AWTC.
3. Identify in the *text region segment* the symbols that contain the n first central pixels of the sorted sequence v and its references to the Data Bearing Symbols (DBSs) in the *symbol dictionary segment*. Note that the number of DBSs can be smaller than n, because each symbol can bear more than one bit of AS.
4. Verify how many times each DBS is referenced in the *text region segment*. If there's only one reference, the data will be stored in the original symbol. If there's more than one reference, the symbol must be duplicated and inserted at the end of *symbol dictionary segment*. The reference to the symbol in the *text region segment* should also be modified. The data will be inserted in the duplicated symbol, instead of the original.
5. Insert n bits of data in the DBSs by flipping, if necessary, the n first central pixels of the sorted sequence v.
6. Verify the possibility of connection or disconnection of the DBSs. If a black pixel was transformed to white, a disconnection can occur separating the symbol in two

parts (figure 4(b)). If a white pixel was transformed to black, two symbols can become united (figure 4(c)). In these cases, the DBS(s) must be eliminated from *symbol dictionary segment* and the new symbol(s) must be inserted. Also the reference(s) in the *text region segment* must be modified.

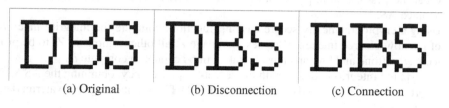

(a) Original   (b) Disconnection   (c) Connection

Fig. 4. A symbol may become disconnected or two symbols may become connected by the watermark insertion

In order to simplify the implementation, we suggest using a new template ranking (figure 5) instead of the template ranking designed for AWTC (figure 1). The new set does not contain templates that can cause the connection or disconnection of symbols. Using the new template ranking, the last step of the DHTCJ insertion algorithm (that is too hard to implement) can be ignored.

Every possible 3×3 pattern has a matching template in the old template ranking (figure 1). On the contrary, there are many 3×3 patterns that do not have a matching template in the new template ranking (figure 5). This means that there may exist some small images that can hide a certain number of bits using the old template ranking (although probably some high visual impact pixels have to flipped), but that cannot hide the same number of bits using the new template ranking.

Fig. 5. Set of 3×3 template designed to be used with AWTCJ in increasing visual impact order. Only the templates that cannot cause symbol connection or disconnection are listed. Hatched pixels match either black or white pixels (note that all templates have hatched central pixels). The score of a given pattern is that of the matching template with the lowest impact. Mirrors, rotations and reverses of each pattern have the same score.

DHTCJ data extraction algorithm is straightforward:
1. Let be given a JBIG2-encoded image Z' with n bits of data to inserted by DHTCJ. Decode the text region of Z', obtaining the uncompressed binary image Z.
2. Divide the binary image Z in a sequence v of non-overlapping pieces of image and sort v as in the insertion.
3. Extract the hidden data from the n first central pixels of the sorted sequence v.

4.2 AWTCJ

DHTCJ can be easily transformed in a secure AWT resistant to "parity attacks" named AWTCJ (Authentication Watermarking by Template ranking with symmetrical Central pixels for JBIG2). AWTCJ insertion algorithm is:

1. Let be given a JBIG2-encoded image Z'. Decode the text region of Z', obtaining the uncompressed binary image Z.
2. Divide Z in a sequence v of non-overlapping pieces of image and sort v as in DHTCJ.
3. Clear the first n central pixels of the sorted sequence v, where n is the size of the adopted AS.
4. Using a cryptographically secure hashing function, compute the integrity-index H of the now-cleared image Z. Besides the image Z, all other regions of Z' to be protected (halftone and line-art) must be taken into account to compute H.
5. Encrypt the integrity-index H with the secret- or private-key, obtaining the AS S.
6. Insert n bits of S in the DBSs as explained in DHTCJ, obtaining the watermarked image.

AWTCJ verification algorithm is:

1. Let be given an AWTCJ-watermarked JBIG2-encoded image Z'. Decode the text region of Z', obtaining the uncompressed binary image Z.
2. Divide Z in a sequence v of non-overlapping pieces of image and sort v as in the insertion.
3. Extract the AS S from the n first central pixels of the sorted sequence v.
4. Decrypt S with the secret- or public-key, obtaining the extracted integrity-index H.
5. Clear the first n central pixels of the sorted sequence v.
6. Compute the check integrity-index C of the now-cleared image Z, using the same hashing function used in insertion. Besides the image Z, all other protected regions of Z' must be taken into account to compute C.
7. If the extracted integrity-index H and the check integrity-index C are the same, the watermark is verified. Otherwise, the image was modified.

Parity attacks do not be apply to AWTCJ because the number of data-bearing pixels is exactly equal to the length of the adopted AS. All image pixels (except the pixels that will bear the bits of the AS) are used to compute the AS. In this way, any alteration of pixels used to compute the AS can be detected because it changes the AS, and any alteration of data-bearing pixels can also be detected because it changes the stored AS.

5   Experimental Results

AWTCJ was applied in several scanned and software-generated binary images at different resolutions. The resulting watermarked images have pleasant visual quality, even when a small image is watermarked.

The image depicted in figure 6 has 626×240 pixels, 93 symbols instances and was scanned at 300×300 dpi. It was watermarked by AWTCJ using a 128-bits long MAC, which was stored in 61 DBSs.

The image depicted in figure 7 has 194×74 pixels, only 56 symbol instances and was scanned at 81×81 dpi. It was watermarked with a 128-bits long MAC, which was stored in 42 DBSs.

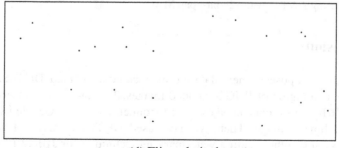

(a) Part of original image.

(b) Watermarked image.

(c) Watermarked image – flipped pixels are printed in color.

(d) Flipped pixels.

Fig. 6. An image scanned at 300 dpi, with 626×240 pixels, 93 symbols instances and water-marked using AWTCJ with 128-bits long MAC

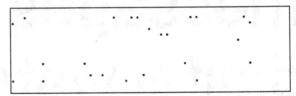

(a) Part of original image.

(b) Watermarked image.

(c) Watermarked image – flipped pixels are printed in color.

(d) Flipped pixels.

Fig. 7. An image scanned at 81×81 dpi, with only 194×74 pixels, 56 symbol instances and watermarked using AWTCJ with 128-bits long MAC

6 Conclusions

This paper has proposed a new data-hiding technique, named DHTCJ, to embed data into the text region of JBIG2-encoded images. The data can be inserted in lossy or lossless JBIG2 files and can be extracted from either the JBIG2 file itself or from the decoded binary image. Then, we have used DHTCJ to create a new crypto-graphically secure authentication watermarking technique for JBIG2 files, resistant to "parity attacks," named AWTCJ. In this method, the authentication signature of the whole image is inserted into the text region of the JBIG2 file. AWTCJ can detect *any* alteration made in the image, even a single pixel flipping. The water-marked images present excellent visual quality, even for small images, because only low-visibility pixels are flipped in the watermark insertion.

Acknowledgements

The authors would like to thank FAPESP and CNPq for the partial financial supports of this work under grants 2003/13752-9 and 305065/2003-3, respectively.

References

[1] H. Y. Kim, and A. Afif, "Secure Authentication Watermarking for Halftone and Binary Images," *Int. J. Imaging Systems and Technology*, vol. 14, no. 4, pp. 147-152, 2004.

[2] H. Y. Kim and R. L. Queiroz, "A Public-Key Authentication Watermarking for Binary Images", in *Proc. IEEE Int. Conf. on Image Processing*, (Singapore), pp. 3459-3462, 2004.

[3] H. Y. Kim and R. L. de Queiroz, "Alteration-Locating Authentication Watermarking for Binary Images," Int. Workshop on Digital Watermarking 2004, (Seoul), *Lecture Notes in Computer Science* 3304, pp. 125-136, 2004.

[4] H. Y. Kim, "A New Public-Key Authentication Watermarking for Binary Document Images Resistant to Parity Attacks", submmitted to *IEEE Int. Conf. on Image Processing*, (Italy), 2005.

[5] P. G. Howard, F. Kossentini, B. Martins, S. Forchhammer, and W.J. Rucklidge, "The Emerging JBIG2 Standard," *IEEE Trans. Circ. Syst. Video Tech.*, vol. 8, no. 7, pp. 838-848, 1998.

[6] JBIG - Final Committee Draft for ISO/IEC International Standard 14492, available at site: http://www.jpeg.org/jbig/jbigpt2.html, 1999.

[7] S. V. D. Pamboukian, H. Y. Kim and R. L. de Queiroz, "Watermarking JBIG2 text region for Image Authentication", submmitted to *IEEE Int. Conf. on Image Processing*, (Italy), 2005.

[8] Yan Ye, D. Schilling, P. Cosman and Hyung Hwa Ko, "Symbol Dictionary Design for the JBIG2 Standard", in *Proc. Data Compression Conference*, pp. 33-42, 2000.

[9] Yan Ye and P. Cosman, "Dictionary Design for Text Image Compression with JBIG2", *IEEE Trans. Image Processing*, vol. 10, no. 6, pp. 818-828, June 2001.

[10] I. G. Chun and S. Ha, "A Robust Printed Image Watermarking Based on Iterative Half-toning Method," 2nd Int. Workshop on Digital Watermarking, *Lecture Notes in Computer Science* 2939, pp. 200-211, 2003.

[11] M. S. Fu and O. C. Au, "Data Hiding Watermarking for Halftone Images," *IEEE Trans. Image Processing*, vol. 11, no. 4, pp. 477-484, 2002.

[12] K. T. Knox and S. Wang, "Digital Watermarks Using Stochastic Screens, Color Imaging: Device-Independent Color, Color Hard Copy, and Graphic Arts II," *SPIE Proc.*, vol. 3018, pp.316-322, Feb. 1997.

[13] N. F. Maxemchuk and S. Low, "Marking Text Documents," *Int. Conf. Image Processing*, vol. 3, pp. 13-17, 1997.

[14] Z. Baharav and D. Shaked, "Watermarking of Dither Halftone Images," *Hewlett-Packard Labs. Tech. Rep.* HPL-98-32, 1998.

[15] S. C. Pei and J. M. Guo, "Hybrid Pixel-Based Data Hiding and Block-Based Watermarking for Error-Diffused Halftone Images," *IEEE Trans. on Circuits and Systems for Video Technology*, vol. 13, no. 8, pp. 867-884, 2003.

[16] Y.-C. Tseng, Y.-Y. Chen and H.-K. Pan, "A Secure Data Hiding Scheme for Binary Images," *IEEE Trans. on Communications*, vol. 50, no. 8, Aug. 2002, pp. 1227-1231.

[17] M. Wu, and B. Liu, "Data Hiding in Binary Image for Authentication and Annotation," *IEEE Trans. on Multimedia*, vol. 6, no. 4, pp. 528-538, 2004.

[18] D. Boneh, B. Lynn and H. Shacham, "Short signatures from the Weil pairing," Advances in Cryptology - Asiacrypt'2001, *Lecture Notes in Computer Science* 2248, pp. 514-532, 2002.

[19] B. Schneier, *Applied Cryptography*, John Wiley & Sons, 1996.

Software Watermarking as a Proof of Identity: A Study of Zero Knowledge Proof Based Software Watermarking

Balaji Venkatachalam

Department of Computer Science,
Iowa State University, Ames, IA 50011, USA
balaji@cs.iastate.edu

Abstract. Software watermarking has been proposed as a way to prove ownership of software intellectual property in order to contain software piracy. In this paper, we propose a novel watermarking technique based on Zero Knowledge Proofs. The advantages are multi-fold. The watermark recognizer can now be distributed publicly. This helps in watermark being used as a proof for both authorship and authentication of the software. The watermark is shown as a mathematical proof which varies with every run instead of the watermark string as in the previous techniques. This watermarking scheme not only has a high degree of tamper resistance but also allows the protocol to point out the tampered subset of the embedded secret data. We present potential attacks on the protocol and discuss the strength of the watermarking scheme. We present empirical results based on our implementation.

1 Introduction

Software can be easily copied without permission. Protecting software against misuse and illegal copying is an important problem. The actual creator of the software can established his authorship by *software watermarking*. Software watermarking refers to the process of embedding secret data called *watermark* in a software application by the creator of the software so that the authorship of the software can be proven where the presence of the secret data is demonstrated by a watermark recognizer. Since the watermark is secret, only the true author knows its value.

An important consideration in watermarking is protecting the watermark from the adversary. The adversary might tamper with the program and modify or completely remove the watermark so that the watermark recognition would fail; in the existing watermarking schemes, by modifying even one bit of the watermark key, the recognizer would fail to recognize the correct secret data. The knowledge of the secret key to the adversary will render the whole scheme ineffective. These reasons constrain the watermark recognizer from being available in public.

In this paper, we propose a solution based on Zero Knowledge Proofs (ZKPs) that allows the watermark recognizer to be available publicly. In the ZKP based

M. Barni et al. (Eds.): IWDW 2005, LNCS 3710, pp. 299–312, 2005.

watermarking scheme, the presence of the watermark is conveyed to the end user or the adversary without revealing the actual keys by means of a protocol. In other words, the end-user (or an adversary) is convinced about the authenticity of the software but has gained *zero* knowledge about the secret keys.

Zero Knowledge Proofs introduced by Goldwasser, Micali, Rackoff [18], provide a solution in a situation where a *prover* wants to prove its knowledge of the truth of a statement to another party, called the *verifier*. However, the prover wants to convey the its knowledge of the proof without conveying the actual proof. The proof is provided by the *interaction* between the two parties, at the end of which the verifier is convinced of the prover's knowledge of the proof. However, the verifier has not gained any knowledge in the interaction. In our case, we show the watermark by a zero knowledge proof.

Let C be the actual creator of the software s. Let A be a malicious adversary who steals (claims authorship) s. C should prove its true *authorship* of s. If A sells a fake software s' as s to the end-user B, B would like to verify the *authenticity* of s. s can be a large program (for e.g., a text editor) or a smaller software component (for e.g., a spell checker for a text editor). For authentication, the end-users require a recognizer. Existing watermarking techniques provide proof of authorship only. We show the application of zero knowledge based watermarking system to solve both these problems.

We propose two different zero knowledge protocols to achieve these goals and discuss their relative merits and demerits.

Contributions: The main thesis of this paper is that zero knowledge based software watermarking has a number of advantages over the existing watermarking systems including novel applications to the problems of authentication and authorship. The novelty in this paper is the application of ZKP to software watermarking. Since the proof of the watermark is given in zero knowledge the software watermark recognizer can be made public, which is not possible in the existing models of software watermarking.

The goal of the paper is to show the natural connections between ZKPs and software watermarking. We show that the proof is independent of watermarking scheme used. We describe software watermarking using the ZKP of the "quadratic residue problem". We use this ZKP here for its ease of exposition. ZKPs of other languages and other cryptographic protocols can be applied to software watermarking (see discussion in section 8).

This scheme builds robustness to the authorship problem by tamper-proofing and detecting the exact bits that were tampered. In addition, it also provides a solution to the new problem of software authentication, due to the public distribution of the recognizer.

This paper is the first paper in applying cryptographic protocols to *software* watermarking to the best of our knowledge. This claim needs some clarification. There has been work to apply zero knowledge proofs to media watermarking and steganography [3,13,1]. However, the issues of media watermarking are different from software watermarking (for e.g. statistical profiling of static media objects, dynamic nature of software etc.). The current work was done independently of these results; with the initial goal to improve robustness of the software watermarking schemes. The results we achieve (the computational difficulty for the adversary, public recognizer etc.) are different from the results of the media watermarking papers (more details in section 2).

Roadmap: Section 2 discusses existing watermarking schemes. In section 3, we describe the model and the terminology. We also discuss the problems of authorship and authenticity, and the attacks against these problems. Section 4 provides a specific zero knowledge protocol that we use for software watermarking. The application of ZKP to software watermarking – the two protocols and the related issues are described in sections 5 We discuss the advantages of our scheme in section 6. We describe the experimental results in section 7.2. Section 8 has a discussion on extensions to the scheme described.

2   Related Work

Watermarking media objects has been an active area of research since the 1990s, with a large amount of literature [12,20,6] and many different techniques for watermarking audio, video and images. *Software watermarking* [10] is a relatively recent research topic. Existing software watermarking schemes can be classified on the basis of watermark embedding and recognition techniques. *Static* watermarking [14,22] refers to embedding the watermark in the executable text or data segments of the software application such that it does not change the application semantically. In *dynamic* watermarking schemes [9], the watermark exploits the dynamic change of state of the software program. The instructions that generate the watermark are embedded in the software application. The watermark is generated at run time.

For example, in *dynamic graph-based watermarking* [9] the watermark string is represented as a graph. The instructions to generate this graph are embedded at various locations in the software application. At run time the embedded instructions execute along with the application code and generates the watermark graph on the heap. The encoding of the graph and the location of embedding are unknown to the adversary. During program execution, the time of watermark creation and heap structure vary in every run. The added stealth makes it difficult for the adversary to detect and tamper the watermark.

Sandmark[11] is a Java-based watermarking software that implements many static and dynamic watermarking schemes. Palsberg et al. [21] describe an implementation of the dynamic watermarking scheme [9] to show its practicality.

Media data is static, as opposed to, the dynamic change of state of software. The issues that arise in the software watermarking systems are different from the issues in media watermarking systems [10]. For example, statistical tests on media objects can detect some possible watermarking structures, whereas detecting software watermarks involve analyzing the heap space which is a hard problem [9]. Various papers [3,13,1,2] discuss the application of various zero knowledge proofs to watermark media. These papers deal with the statistical distinction of an actual proof from a spurious proof, which is a natural problem in media watermarking. However, in the current paper, we are concerned with knowing the secret data and we discuss the computational difficulty to break the ZKP based watermarking system and its practical implications.

3   Models and Notation

In security systems it is essential that the threat model, the trust and power assumptions about the various agents, be made explicit to test the limitations of the system [19]. In this section, we will describe the model and definitions used in this paper.

A *watermark* can be viewed as secret data stored in an application. The secret data could be a string, a number, or other secret data that is hidden in some format in the application. We will call the secret data the *watermark value* and the secret format of the watermark representation its *encoding*. The creator of the software *embeds* the watermark into the software to obtain the *watermarked software*.

For example, in graph encoding of a dynamic watermark the secret data or the watermark value is a number, which is encoded in the form of a graph. The structure of the graph represents the watermark value in some radix. This method of representing the watermark string as a graph is called graph-based watermark encoding. The instructions that generate this watermark graph are embedded in the application program in an appropriate way to obtain a watermarked software.

The existence of the watermark is demonstrated by a watermark *recognizer*. When the watermark is *dynamic*, the recognizer executes the watermarked application; it observes the program execution trace to identify or recognize the embedded watermark. In this paper we propose to enhance the recognizer to facilitate an interactive session for the ZKP.

Prover and Verifier: To describe ZKPs, we need the notion of a prover and a verifier. The *prover* is an agent or entity who claims the *knowledge of the proof of a statement* and tries to prove it. The *verifier* is an agent or entity who tries to learn the proof from the verifier. At the end of the interaction, called a *protocol*, a prover convinces the verifier about his knowledge of the proof (but not any additional knowledge). If the prover does not know the proof, he is called a *cheating* prover. The protocol is designed so that the verifier would not accept the proof of a cheating prover. A *cheating* verifier, is the one who tries to gain knowledge from the prover through the protocol executions.

3.1   Threat Model

The end user of the software is the potential adversary in the software piracy world. In many cases, the end user/adversary also has supervisory privileges on the host machine where the software is executed. That is, we consider an *all powerful* adversary who can observe and modify the software that is available.

The adversary has access only to the watermarked application but does not know the encoding scheme or the location of the watermark within the application. As mentioned before, decoding a dynamic watermark is hard for an adversary. The adversary tampers with the application for two reasons – to learn the watermark value, or to modify or completely remove the watermark so that the watermark recognition would fail. Availability of the watermark recognizer publicly brings in extra difficulty of hiding the watermark, because it allows the adversary to observe the execution and tamper the recognizer. This helps the adversary to gain significant knowledge about the watermark.

The adversary tampering and removing the watermark are called *distortive and subtractive* attacks. The adversary can also add an additional watermark, which is called an *additive* attack. Adding an extra watermark does not interfere with the recognizer in recognizing the existing watermark. Therefore we do not consider additive attacks in this paper. Dispute resolving which arise due to additive attacks are not considered in this work.

3.2   Watermarking Problems and Their Attacks

In this subsection, we describe the main problems of software copy protection addressed in this paper and the attacks on those watermarking systems. Separating the concerns of the problems and the corresponding attacks is helpful, because the attacks on one system (say, authentication) are completely ineffective on the other watermarking system (say, authorship, and vice versa). For the rest of this subsection, let C be the actual creator of the software s, let A be the malicious adversary, and B the end user.

Proof of Authenticity: C creates a software s. The malicious adversary A sells a fake product s' as the original software s. B on buying a software from A, would like to ensure its *authenticity* – the creator of the software is indeed A. If the watermark recognizer of s is available publicly, B can use C's recognizer to test the authenticity. A fake software s' should not be able to cheat and should fail the protocol.

Proof of Authorship: The malicious adversary A sells the original software of C as his own. Now C claims the true authorship, and proves this by showing the presence of his secret data. If A is to prevent the proof of C's claims, he should remove the secret data in s.

In the authentication problem, we need a public recognizer. The authorship problem does not need a public recognizer but the watermark recognition is done in the presence of a trusted third party. The attack for the proof of authorship is the removal of watermark in the original software, which was not relevant in the authentication problem. The adversary needs to replicate the watermark in s' to provide a proof of authenticity.

4   ZKP of Quadratic Residue Problem

The ZKP of quadratic residue problem [18,15] is described as follows. Consider a number n that is a product of 2 large primes. The size of n, $|n| = b$ bits, is a security parameter. Initially, the prover chooses k-random numbers, $s_1, s_2, \ldots, s_k$ in Z_n^* (Z_n^* is the *multiplicative field* relative to n, that is, $Z_n^* = \{x | 1 \leq x \leq n \wedge gcd(x, n) = 1\}$). The numbers $v_1, v_2, \ldots, v_k$ are chosen such that $v_i = \frac{1}{s_i^2}$ (That is, v_i is the inverse of the square of s_i in the field Z_n^*).

At the start of the protocol, the modulus, n,the number of residues k, and the inverses, $v_1, \ldots, v_k$, are known to both the parties. However, $s_1, \ldots, s_k$ are known only to the prover. This protocol is pictorially represented in Figure 1.

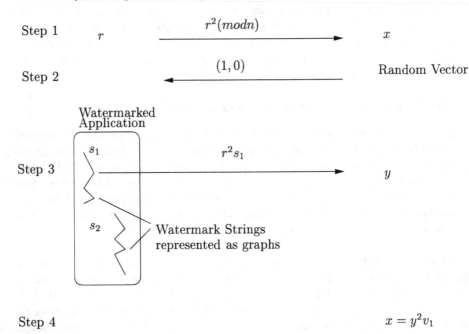

Fig. 1. Pictorial representation of Protocol 1 with a dynamic graph based encoding

Protocol:

1. Prover picks a random number $r \in [0, n)$ and sends $x = r^2 (\bmod\, n)$ to verifier
2. Verifier sends a random bit vector $(e_1, e_2, \ldots, e_k)$ to prover, (that is $e_i \in \{0, 1\}$)
3. Prover sends to verifier

$$y = r \prod_{e_i=1} s_i (\bmod\, n)$$

4. Verifier computes that

$$z = y^2 \prod_{e_i=1} v_i (\bmod\, n)$$

and checks that $z = x$.

Note that, the proof varies in every run based on the values of r and e_i. The verifier does not know the value of r in an execution and the prover does not have control over the random bits, e_i. It is hard for the verifier to compute the values of r and the residues. The computation needed for the verifier – the multiplication in step 4 – is easy.

5   ZKP for Watermarking

In this section, we present two zero knowledge protocols to show the application of ZKPs to software watermarking. The first protocol is based on the natural connection between software authentication and smart card authentication. This protocol is expository and helps in understanding the modeling issues and the threat model better. This also helps us to understand the advantages of ZKP over traditional watermarking systems. Protocol 2 intends to resolve the issues of Protocol 1. While these are not the most optimal protocol or the best solution for all software applications, but this ZKP was chosen for the ease of exposition.

Fiat and Shamir [15] show the application of ZKPs to smart card authentication. The smart-card is the prover which proves its authenticity to the end-user, who is the verifier, and the smart-card reader supports the interaction. Analogously, for software watermarking, the software is the prover (who has access to secret data), the watermark recognizer helps in the interaction, and the end-user is the verifier. This correspondence leads to Protocol 1.

5.1   Protocol 1:

The quadratic residues $s_1, \ldots, s_k$ are stored in the software application as the secret key (watermark). The creator of the software embeds these in the application using any of the dynamic watermarking schemes. The numbers n and $v_1, \ldots, v_k$ are embedded in the public recognizer. (They can be generated by a random function [15]). The recognizer provides the interface between the prover (the application) and the verifier (the user). During the watermark recognition phase, the recognizer performs the computation needed for the protocol. The recognizer performs the following operations for each of the steps of the protocol – it receives the random bits e_i from the user, it reads s_i and computes y etc.

Advantages: It is easy to see that Protocol 1 solves the authorship problem (when the recognizer is not available in public). The relative merits of this scheme over the existing watermarking techniques are discussed in the next section. When the recognizer is distributed publicly to solve the authentication problem we have the following issues.

Attacks on Protocol 1: The adversary can fix the random string in round 1 and observe the change of state of the recognizer. These attacks are considered in the context of smart-cards – *Reseting attack* and *Concurrent Reset – CR1, CR2 attacks* [8] respectively. The solutions proposed in Bellare et al. [8] to overcome these attacks can be used in the context of watermarking. In general, any attack on the protocol is similar to attack on a general ZKP and the solutions to those attacks apply to watermarking too.

Drawback of Protocol 1: Although Protocol 1 provides the most natural mapping for a prover and verifier among the candidate set of software creator, application software, and the end user, as we discussed before, the recognizer being available publicly helps the adversary. In addition to the attacks on the protocol the adversary can observe changes and tamper with the recognizer. The adversary can potentially learn the s_i values when there will be no other secrets left. To prevent these attacks on the recognizer, we can use an *obfuscator* [10,5].

Barak, Goldreich et al. [7] show the impossibility of obfuscating programs. However, their impossibility result is for a generic obfuscator which obfuscates all programs and does not leak even one bit of information. Obfuscation of a smaller program (the recognizer) is more difficult (than a very large program) owing to the smaller space of combinatorial richness. On the other hand, there is some recent work towards efficient [5] and hardware-based obfuscators [4] which are very hard to crack. Obfuscation will be easier on a platform like *Palladium*. We do not know the practicality of "breaking" an obfuscator or the use of obfuscation to protect the recognizer.

5.2   Protocol 2

We now present an alternate protocol, to address the drawback of Protocol 1. The basic premise in the design of Protocol 2 is that a compromise of the inverses (v_i), is less harmful than a compromise of the residues (s_i). The following protocol allows for the authentication to happen over the Internet. The end user authenticates the software using the (server of the) creator of the software.

The creator picks numbers, n, $s_1, \ldots, s_k$ and $v_1, \ldots, v_k$ as before. The creator embeds the v_i values in the application (instead of the s_i as before), and the protocol is run with the creator of the software as the prover and the software as the verifier and the recognizer helping in the interaction between the prover and verifier. The public recognizer, which can be obtained from the creator, neither contains the residues nor the inverses. The protocol is as before – the software creator sends x, the recognizer receives the random vector from the end-user etc.

Advantages: Protocol 2 augments the existing watermarking schemes. Hence it is easy to see that Protocol 2 solves the authorship problem. Protocol 2 also solves the authentication problem as the user can verify z which changes with every run. Since r is chosen by the creator and the adversary cannot control the random source, the Resettable, CR1 & CR2 attacks are *not possible*. The adversary can observe the data in the network stream between the recognizer and the creator. But this provides only x and y which do not help the adversary to learn the secrets.

If the recognizer is not obfuscated, the adversary can see the change of state of the recognizer and the location in the application where the watermark is stored. (Recall that removal of watermark is not a solution for the authentication problem.) At best, the adversary will only learn the values of v_is from all this information. For the adversary computing the s_i values is hard.

If an adversary sells a fake software s' as the original software s, the end-user can verify the authenticity of s' by using the software creator's publicly available recognizer. Therefore s' not only needs to know all the data-structures but it should also replicate them in s' (also ensuring that, the data-structures of s' are not (mis)recognized as a watermark).

The creator of the software can pick different values $(v_1, \ldots, v_k, s_1, \ldots, s_k)$ for different copies of the software. We assume that the watermark recognizer which is available from the creator's web-page through a secure channel, is parameterized for every copy (say, using the registration key). Since the creator of the software is involved in the watermarking protocol, it can detect any suspicious protocol requests, (for e.g. too many requests from the same client, too many requests with the same v_i values etc.) and detect an attack.

6   Advantages

In this section, we discuss the advantages of using Protocol 2 for software watermarking. It is easy to see that most of the advantages for the proof of authorship hold for Protocol 1 too.

Proof of Authorship: When the recognizer is not distributed publicly using ZKPs for watermarking has a few advantages to solve the problem of authorship. In the current watermarking schemes, there is only one query for the watermark which displays the watermark string. Tampering even one bit of the watermark will destroy the watermark and the true creator cannot prove his claim of authorship.

With the zero knowledge protocol, the claim for authorship is proved (and substantiated) in multiple ways (1) When one or a few bits are tampered, only some of the residues are affected, and the watermarking protocol would work for the queries involving other residues. Suppose the residue v_i is tampered, v_i is used (in Step 4) only when $e_i = 1$. Therefore, the tampering does not affect the correctness of the proof for all random vectors generated in Step 2 where $e_i = 0$. There are 2^k possible distinct vectors that can be generated in Step 2. When f bits are tampered, in the worst case, f different residues v_i are tampered. These tampered residues do not affect the validity of the proof for all vectors for which the corresponding bit $e_i = 0$. The remaining $(k - f)$ bits can take on any values. We have $2^{(k-f)}$ vectors in which the tampered residues would be unused. The fraction of valid proof vectors as a fraction of all the 2^k vectors then is $\frac{2^{k-f}}{2^k}$ which is $1/2^f$. Note that, we are counting only the number of queries and not the number of different proofs shown (which are larger due to the choice of random numbers). (2) Based on the successful queries, the creator can exactly point to the bits that are tampered and the other bits that are tampered. (3) The creator has knowledge of the numbers s_i which are not easily computable by the adversary. The knowledge of the secret keys, hardness of computing the values and the mathematical proof for the bits tampered strongly support the claim for authorship.

Collberg and Thomborson watermarking scheme [9,21], is not resilient to tampering. Even when one bit of the string is tampered, the watermark recognizer will fail to retrieve the correct watermark. When the same key is replicated k times, there is only one query that returns same the watermark string. Once the secret value is known the scheme becomes ineffective [19]. Moreover, there is no (mathematical) proof for the third-party to believe the claim.

In terms of hardness of learning the secret watermark values, we achieve the best of both worlds – the stealth of the dynamic watermarks (difficulty of locating and decoding the watermark) and the computational difficulty of learning the secret values from the proof.

Proof of Authentication: One of the main advantages of using zero knowledge proofs for watermarking is the public distribution of the recognizer. In the existing watermarking schemes, the embedded key is shown during the watermark recognition process. This is because the watermarking process is symmetric. This hinders the distribution of watermark recognizer. Knowledge of the embedded key allows the adversary to create a "dummy recognizer", which always outputs the same key during all runs for watermark recognition. The adversary can also claim the knowledge of the key to the arbitrator and therefore claim to be the actual creator of the software. The original creator cannot prove his authorship as the creator does not have extra knowledge over the adversary.

With the ZKP watermarking scheme, however, the creator of the software can safely distribute/share the watermark recognizer to/with the end users. This is possible since the recognition protocol does not reveal the values $s_1, \ldots, s_k$. The information revealed are x and y (which change in every run). This still makes it computationally difficult to derive s_is. This is similar to the case of smart-cards where both smart-card and the smart-card verifier are publicly available. The computational difficulty of reversing the proof makes it hard for the adversary to break this scheme. As mentioned in the previous section, since the creator is involved in the verification process it is difficult for the adversary to cheat. As the watermark recognizer is available to the user, the watermark can be used as a proof of authenticity of the software.

Computation and Storage costs: We now show that the computation and the extra storage space needed for the protocol are not very high. The total number of bits that need to be encoded depends on the number of stored values, k, and the size of each value, b. We cab choose these values to exceed an acceptable vale of robustness for the watermarking scheme.

Let us consider $k = 20$, and n and the residues to be $512-$bit numbers. The total embedded key size is about $20 \times 512 -$ bits $\approx 1.3KB$. The average number of multiplications needed per recognition is 10. The communication complexity (the number of bits used during the interaction) is about $1000-$bits per proof – 512 bits for each of x and y and the random vector $(e_1, \ldots, e_{20})$. This protocol computation is much cheaper than RSA where many more multiplications need to be performed by each party[15].

If the watermark string is about 50 characters long, the number of stored bits in a traditional dynamic watermarking method such as Sandmark is about

400 bytes. The space overhead compared to Sandmark is a factor of about 2-3 times. If only one 512-bit number (9-character string) is embedded, the space overhead is about 10 times. The computation overhead is about 10 extra multiplications. Note that even for a medium sized application, the 1.3KB watermark storage space and the computation is dwarfed by the application's own requirements.

7   Experimental Evaluation

7.1   Design and Implementation

The security parameters, n – the product of two large primes, k – and the number of quadratic residues can be chosen according to the degree of security needed for the protocol. In the Collberg-Thomborson model, only one number is stored, and it is stored as a graph. However, we need to encode and embed the residues of numbers. In ZKP based watermarking scheme, in addition to recognizing the watermark (as done in the earlier schemes), the recognizer acts as the interface between the prover and the verifier.

We extend Sandmark [11] class hierarchy and methods. We reuse the graph-based encoding methods and represent each quadratic residue as a separate graph (each with a different encoding radix). Since each residue is stored as a different graph knowing one graph to obtain one residue does not yield any information about the encoding of the other graphs. Each of these graphs is split into a number of parts so that, even if some subgraph of one of the graphs is identified, the entire watermark is not revealed. In fact even the graph to which this particular subgraph belongs to, is not known.

7.2   Empirical Results

In this section, we show that the experimental results follow the theoretical expectations. We find that the amount of heap space used and byte-codes size of the program increase linearly with the number of bits of the quadratic residue.

Building a recognizer and the time to embed the residues in the program does not impact the normal program execution in this model, because it is a one time cost (similar to compilation) incurred by the creator of the software.

The time to recognize the watermark depends on the program flow and the watermark data structure identification instructions. We observe that, once all the watermark data structures are recognized, the time to compute the product (for Step 3 of the protocol) is negligible. The degree of tamper resistance would also be as expected theoretically. The two factors that would affect in a program and which could possibly provide clues to an adversary are the heap space usage and the increase in the static program size.

To benchmark the results, we ran the watermarking process on a simple test program that does not allocate any memory for any object other than the watermark on the heap. We calculate the increase in the amount of heap space as

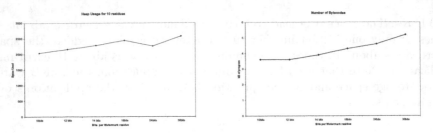

Fig. 2. Experimental Results: **(a)** Heap Space Overhead **(b)** Program Size Overhead

the number of bits of the quadratic residues increases. To obtain the worst case usage, we set all bits (e_i) to 1, and the resulting heap space sizes are averaged over experiments. This would give us the exact memory requirements of the watermark. This is a reasonable assumption because the amount of heap space used by the program is only for the watermark. The increase in memory usage due to the watermark is additive and independent of the program, and therefore we should observe similar heap overhead for other programs as well. Using larger programs for benchmarking would not give us consistent values across runs as the heap usage may vary due to program flow, garbage collection (by the virtual machine) and other program idiosyncrasies. Similarly we measure the increase in program size.

We embedded 10 residues. We repeat the experiment for residues of various sizes as shown in the graphs in Figures 2. (a) and 2. (b). We observe that the increase in program size is linear in the number of bits used to represent the residues (Figure 2. (a)). The heap space overhead also grows linearly with the number of bits in the residues as seen in Figure 2. (b).

Since we are using existing watermark encoding techniques, it is a reasonable conclusion that the overhead of space and heap usage are linear in the number of residues.

8   Discussion

As we mentioned before, we used ZKP of the quadratic residue problem mainly for the ease of exposition. More robust protocols can be used for software watermarking. For e.g. $v = \frac{a}{s^2} + b \pmod{n}$ for some $a, b \in Z_n^*$ would be harder function to break than the one described [16]. ZKP of other languages,interactive proofs, one-way functions and public-key schemes can also be used. For instance, the ZKP of *Graph non-Isomorphism* problem [17]. This is well suited for software watermarking as graphs are good, well-obfuscatable watermark representations.

Other watermark or birthmark encoding and embedding methods can also be used for watermarking.

The zero knowledge proof is independent of the encoding and embedding. As mentioned above various encoding schemes and cryptographic protocols can be used for watermarking. The choice of encoding scheme and the cryptographic protocol is an interesting design issue. For example, for a small application, a graph based representation may be a bad choice. This is since the graph based representations are generally large, and might reveal more than they hide! An encoding and protocol to suit the application attributes can be chosen.

As noted in section 5, any improvement in obfuscation technology will help in securing the watermark. In the absence of obfuscation an extremely powerful adversary (who can read, modify, and tamper the entire watermark), *no* watermarking scheme is completely secure! However, our watermarking scheme has a higher degree of tamper resistance and prevents the creation of new identities (new pairs of values for $s_1, \ldots, s_k$ and the corresponding $v_1, \ldots, v_k$) easily.

9 Conclusions

We have presented a new watermarking paradigm for software watermarking based on zero knowledge proof systems (ZKPs). The proof of the watermark is provided in zero-knowledge, and therefore the recognizer can be distributed publicly. We show two protocols for problems of authenticity and authorship and discuss attacks on protocols. Both the protocols work best when obfuscated. However, when used without obfuscation, it is computationally hard to obtain all the secrets from the values learnt in Protocol 2.

With our watermarking scheme we obtain best of both worlds – stealth of dynamic watermarks and computational hardness of ZKPs, which makes it hard for the adversary to learn the watermark keys. One of the main advantages in the proof of authorship is in tamper detection and resistance. Moreover, a mathematical proof of which bits are tampered can be provided.

This watermarking environment was implemented as an extension to Sandmark. The memory usage of the heap and watermarking code size overheads are characterized experimentally. Both the heap space and byte-code size overhead are linear in the number of bits to represent the embedded secret data as predicted theoretically.

This is the first application of a cryptographic protocol for software watermarking to the best of our knowledge.

Acknowledgments. This work was supported by AFRL/OUSD under contract number F33615-02-C-1238 through Software Protection Initiative program. Thanks to Akhilesh Tyagi for some useful discussions, suggestions and help in editing some early drafts of the manuscript. Thanks also to Curt Clifton for some helpful feedback on the manuscript and to the anonymous reviewers for their critical comments which have helped in improving the presentation.

References

1. André Adelsbach, Stefan Katzenbeisser, Ahmad-Reza Sadeghi, "Watermark detection with zero-knowledge disclosure", *Multimedia Systems*, 9(3), pp. 266-278 2003.
2. André Adelsbach, Ahmad-Reza Sadeghi, "Zero-Knowledge Watermark Detection and Proof of Ownership", *Information Hiding 2001*, pp. 273-288, 2001.

3. André Adelsbach, Stefan Katzenbeisser and Ahmad-Reza Sadeghi, "Cryptography Meets Watermarking: Detecting Watermarks with Minimal- or Zero-Knowledge Disclosure", *XI European Signal Processing Conference*, Volume I, pp. 446-449.

4. M. Gomathisankaran, A. Tyagi, "3D Obfuscation Architecture", *under submission*, 2005.

5. D. Aucsmith, "Tamper Resistant Software: An Implementation", *Information Hiding 1996*, pp. 317-333, 1996.

6. Mauro Barni, Franco Bartolini, "Watermarking systems engineering : enabling digital assets security and other applications", *Marcel Dekker*, 2004.

7. Boaz Barak, Oded Goldreich, Russell Impagliazzo, Steven Rudich, Amit Sahai, Salil P. Vadhan, Ke Yang, "On the (Im)possibility of Obfuscating Programs", *CRYPTO 2001*, pp. 1-18, 2001.

8. Mihir Bellare, Marc Fischlin, Shafi Goldwasser, Silvio Micali, "Identification Protocols Secure against Reset Attacks", *EUROCRYPT 2001*, pp, 495–511, 2001.

9. Christian Collberg, Clark Thomborson, "Software watermarking: Models & dynamic embeddings", *POPL'99*, 1999.

10. Christian S. Collberg, Clark Thomborson, "Watermarking, Tamper-Proofing, and Obfuscation - Tools for Software Protection", *IEEE Transactions on Software Engineering*, 28:8, pp. 735-746, August 2002.

11. Christian Collberg, Ginger Myles, Andrew Huntwork, "SandMark - A Tool for Software Protection Research", *IEEE Security and Privacy*, Vol. 1, Num. 4, July/August 2003.

12. Ingemar Cox, Matthew Miller, Jeffrey Bloom, "Digital watermarking", *Morgan Kaufmann*, 2002.

13. Scott Craver, "Zero Knowledge Watermark Detection", *Information Hiding 1999*, pp. 101-116, 1999.

14. R. L. Davidson and N. Myhrvold,, "Method and system for generating and auditing a signature for a computer program". *US Patent 5,559,884*, Sept. 1996.

15. A. Fiat, A. Shamir, "How to prove yourself: Practical solutions to identification and signature problems", *CRYPTO '86*, LNCS 263, pp. 186-194.

16. A. Fiat, U. Fiege A. Shamir, "Zero-Knowledge Proofs of Identity", *STOC 87*, 1987.

17. Oded Goldreich, "Foundations of Cryptography: Basic Tools", *Cambridge University Press*, 2001.

18. S. Goldwasser, S. Micali, and C. Rackoff, "The Knowledge Complexity of Interactive Proof Systems", *SIAM Journal of Computing*, 18(1), pp. 186-208, February 1989.

19. Stefan Katzenbeisser, "On the Integration of Watermarks and Cryptography", *Digital Watermarking 2003*, pp. 50-60, 2003.

20. Stefan Katzenbeisser, Fabien A.P. Petitcolas(editors), "Information hiding techniques for steganography and digital watermarking", *Artech House*, 2000.

21. Palsberg, J., Krishnaswamy, S., Minseok, K., Ma, D., Shao, Q., and Zhang, Y, "Experience with software watermarking", ACSAC '00, pp. 308–316, 2000.

22. R. Venkatesan, V. Vazirani, S. Sinha, "A Graph Theoretic Approach to Software Watermarking", *Information Hiding Workshop 2001*, LNCS vol. 2137, 2001.

Watermarking of 3D Irregular Meshes Based on Wavelet Multiresolution Analysis[*]

Min-Su Kim[1,2], Sébastien Valette[3], Ho-Youl Jung[2,**], and Rémy Prost[1]

[1] CREATIS, INSA-Lyon, France
{kim, prost}@creatis.insa-lyon.fr
[2] MSP Lab, Yeungnam University, Korea
Tel.: +82-53-810-3545, Fax: +82-53-810-4742
hoyoul@yu.ac.kr
[3] Informatics & Telematics Institute, Thessaloniki, Greece
valette@iti.gr

Abstract. In this paper, we propose a robust watermarking method for 3-D triangle surface meshes. Most previous methods based on the wavelet analysis can process only semi-regular meshes. Our proposal can be applied to irregular as well as regular meshes by using recently introduced irregular wavelet analysis scheme. L2-Norm of the wavelet coefficients is modified in various multi-resolution levels to embed the watermark. We also introduced a vertex and face re-ordering process as pre-processing in both watermark embedding and extraction for the robustness against connectivity reordering attacks. In addition, our proposal employs blind watermark detection scheme, which can extract the watermark without reference of cover mesh model. Through the simulations, we prove that our approach is robust against connectivity reordering as well as various kinds of geometrical attacks such as lossy compression and affine transform.

1 Introduction

Outstanding progress of digital multimedia data has eased its reproduction and retransmission. Such trend also increases the need for copyright protection. Traditional data protection techniques such as encryption are not adequate for copyright enforcement, because the protection cannot be ensured after the data is decrypted. Unlike the encryption, digital watermarking does not restrict access to the host data, but ensures the hidden data to remain inviolated and recoverable [1,2]. Watermarking is a copyright protection technique to embed information, so-called watermark, into host data.

[*] This work was supported by the Ministry of Information & Communications, Korea, under the Information Technology Research Center (ITRC) Program (204-B-000-215), and was supported by both Korea Science and Engineering Foundation (KOSEF, 000-B-105-898) and Centre National de la Recherche Scientifique, France (CNRS, 14894).
[**] Corresponding author.

M. Barni et al. (Eds.): IWDW 2005, LNCS 3710, pp. 313–324, 2005.

Most of previous watermarking technologies have focused on traditional media data, such as digital text, audio, image, and video data. Recently, 3-D geometric models including Computer Aided Design (CAD) based 3-D data, Virtual Reality Modeling Language (VRML), and MPEG-4, have been receiving a lot of attention, due to powerful computational performance of today's computer and the demand for a better representation of virtual worlds and scientific data. Despite such popularity, few watermarking methods have been proposed for 3-D geometric model. This is caused in part by the watermarking technology that has emerged for image, video, and audio which cannot be easily adapted to work for 3-D geometric models [3].

Since the watermarking technique for 3D meshes was introduced in [4], there have been several trials to improve the performance in terms of capacity, invisibility and robustness. Praun *et al.* [3] generalized the spread-spectrum approach commonly used in 2D image watermarking [1] to 3D surface meshes. Yin *et al.* [5] extends [3] by using the half-edge collapse method. It has lower complexity than edge collapse to build multiresolution meshes. They can embed 250 bits into coarser mesh while having robustness against several attacks including geometrical and topological attacks. However, it requires a registration before an extraction to be robust against similarity transform: rotation, uniform scaling and translation. It also needs resampling of both the original mesh and the watermarked after simplification, vertex reordering or cropping attacks. It is a non-blind watermarking because the registration and the resampling need the original mesh. It is encouraged not to use the original mesh in detection for copyright protection systems. Cho *et al.* [6] proposed a blind watermarking method. They modify the distribution of vertex norms which is invariant to similarity transform and vertex reordering. The method is robust against various attacks.

Kanai *et al.* [7], in 1998, proposed the first watermarking method based on wavelet analysis with non-blind detection scheme. Uccheddu *et al.* [8] extends [7] to detect the watermark without the original mesh. Both of them cannot process irregular meshes directly because of the limitation of Lounsbery's scheme [9]. They can embed the watermark into an irregular mesh by using remeshing that converts an irregular mesh into a semi-regular one. But, the remeshed model cannot be seen as identical to the original, as it corresponds to a different sampling of the underlying 3D surface : the mesh connectivity is different from the original.

In this paper, we propose a watermarking method for 3D meshes, which allows to embed the information data at various resolution levels, and to detect the watermark without the original mesh. Our multiresolution approach is more effective than spatial domain one in the viewpoint of invisibility, capacity and robustness. Our proposal is based on irregular wavelet analysis scheme, recently introduced as wavelet analysis technique for both regular and irregular meshes [10], so that our watermarking method can be applied to both regular and irregular 3D triangular meshes. In our proposal, the watermark is embedded by modifying L2-norm of the wavelet coefficients.

The rest of this paper is organized as follows. In Section 2.1, we describe briefly wavelet based multiresolution analysis for irregular 3-D surface meshes.

We explain the synchronization issue caused from the wavelet approach of 3-D meshes and give our approach to overcome the problem in Section 2.2. Section 2.3 and 2.4 presents the embedding and the extraction method. Simulation results show the effectiveness of our proposal in Section 3. Finally, we draw a conclusion.

2   Our Approach

2.1   Wavelet Multiresolution Analysis of Irregular Meshes

Irregular wavelet analysis scheme [10] simplifies the original mesh by reversing an irregular subdivision scheme. The simplification is repeated until the resulting mesh cannot be simplified anymore. For meshes homeomorphic to a sphere, the simplest mesh is a tetrahedron. We obtain a hierarchy of meshes from the simplest one M^0, called base mesh, to the original mesh M^J. Following [10], the wavelet decomposition can be applied to the geometrical properties of the different meshes which are linked by the following matrix relations:

$$C^{j-1} = A^j C^j \tag{1}$$

$$D^{j-1} = B^j C^j \tag{2}$$

$$C^j = P^j C^{j-1} + Q^j D^{j-1} \tag{3}$$

where C^j is the $v^j \times 3$ matrix representing the coordinates of the vertices of M^j, v^j is the number of vertices for each mesh M^j. D^{j-1} is the $(v^j - v^{j-1}) \times 3$ matrix of the wavelet coefficients at level j. A^j and B^j are the analysis filters, P^j and Q^j are the synthesis filters. Valette's scheme [10] attempt to inverse the connectivity simplification to 1:4 subdivision as much as possible. This is for semi-regular regions in the irregular input meshes. If 4:1 simplification is not

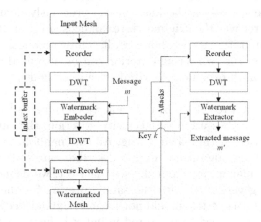

Fig. 1. Watermark embedding and extraction of our approach

possible, it will be merged in groups of three or two faces, or leave some faces unchanged. Edge flips are performed when needed.

Fig. 1 shows the general concept of our approach. It is inspired from Kanai *et al.* [7] and Uccheddu [8]. In contrast with the previous approaches where the watermarking method was based on regular wavelet multiresolution analysis which was limited to meshes with 4:1 subdivision connectivity, we use the irregular wavelet analysis scheme [10], which supports 4:1, 3:1, 2:1, 1:1 merging. In addition, starting from the Lazy wavelet filter-bank (Eq. (1) - (3)) following [9] we build new filters A^j, Q^j by the Lifting scheme in order to make the wavelet functions more orthogonal to the scaling functions in the 1-ring. By using irregular wavelet analysis scheme, our method can embed the watermark for both regular and irregular 3-D triangular meshes.

2.2   Preprocessing for DWT of 3D Surface Meshes

Unlike discrete wavelet transform (DWT) of 2D images, the wavelet coefficients of 3D meshes depend on the seed-triangle group merged during connectivity graph simplification. This artifact results from both irregular sampling and unusual scanning of the 3D surface. In addition, although the lossless reconstruction of integer coordinates meshes is possible and the reconstructed mesh from M^0 to M^J is exact in terms of geometry, the original vertex indices were lost when processing with the irregular wavelet analysis [10].

Such a problem can be overcome by reordering the original model before irregular wavelet analysis. Our walking algorithm for reordering an irregular mesh is inspired both from Touma-Gotsman connectivity coder [11] and from the well-known backtracking algorithm for the visit of tree nodes. The reordering starts from a seed triangle which is determined from geometry criteria such as the triangle with the largest area, the farthest triangle from the model centroid. Connectivity information, for example, the triangle which has the greatest number of neighboring triangles within its n-ring, also could be good to use. After having processed the reordered mesh by watermark embedder, the resulting mesh should be reordered on the basis of the previously defined seed triangle group in order to recover the original vertex indices (Fig. 1). Reordering brings an additional computational cost, however, it can be an another interest for watermarking, because the reordering criterion can be also used as a secret key to protect the watermark over unauthorized erasing or multiple watermarking of wavelet coefficients.

It is very important to select the criterion which is insensitive against various attacks. In this paper, we use a connectivity criterion: the sum of the number of neighboring vertices within their 4-ring. All the manifold meshes can be processed by our walking algorithm. Fig. 2 describes our walking algorithm for reordering an irregular mesh. From the seed-face $f1$, we define both focus vertex $v1$ and walking vertex $v3$ with the same criterion for the seed-face $f1$. In addition, the first focus vertex should not have a boundary edge. All the visited faces and edges indices need to be stored in index buffers to process the exception handling, for example, a visited face, a boundary edge. Then, we walk to

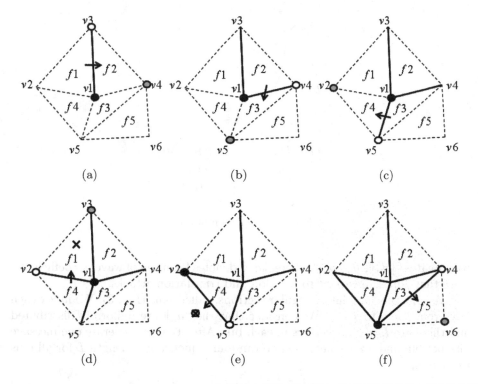

Fig. 2. Our walking algorithm for reordering where dark point is focus vertex, white point is walking vertex and gray point is the next vertex. The arrow means the direction to walk. Solid line depicts visited edges and dashed line is unvisited edges.

the neighbor face $f2$ which shares $v1$ and $v2$ in $f1$ and store $f2$ and the edge $(v1, v2)$ (see Fig. 2(a)). The next vertex $v4$ will be the next walking vertex. $f3$ can be found with the same rule with the focus vertex $v1$ and the new walking vertex $v4$ (Fig. 2(b), Fig. 2(c)). If the neighbor face has been visited as shown in Fig. 2(d), we need to backtrace the last ordered face $f4$ in the index buffer. For backtracing the buffer, we also need to switch the focus and the walking vertices. Boundary edges also can be treated by the same way as visited faces.

2.3   Embedding Method

Following Eq. (2), D is the vector of wavelet coefficients.

$$D^{j-1} = [\, d_0, \ d_1, \dots, \ d_{N-1} \,]^t \tag{4}$$

where, $d_n = [x_n \ y_n \ z_n]^t$ and N is the number of wavelet coefficients. We omit the resolution level $j-1$ for the sake of notational simplicity.

After we compute forward DWT of the mesh, we obtain the wavelet coefficient vector D. We convert the Cartesians coordinates of the coefficient d_n to spherical

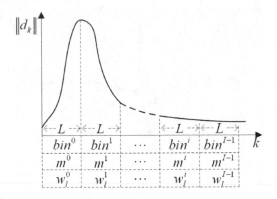

Fig. 3. Generation of *bins*

coordinates $[\ \|d_n\|,\ \theta_n,\ \phi_n\ ]^t$ where, $\|d_n\|$ denotes L2-norm of wavelet coefficients. Note that $\|d_l\|$ is invariant to rotation and translation attacks.

We split the $\|d_n\|$ into I regular sections, called bins (Fig. 3). We index each bin^i from $i = 0$ to $I - 1$. We consider that the $\|d_n\|$ are uniformly distributed and there are $L = N/I$ vectors in each bin. After that we generate one message bits per bin and a zero mean pseudo random sequence p_l of length L for all bins as follows,

$$m^i \in \{-1, 1\}, 0 \leq\ i\ < I \tag{5}$$

$$p_l \in \{-1, 1\}, 0 \leq\ l\ < L \tag{6}$$

The watermark w_l^i is generated from Eq. (5) and Eq. (6).

$$w_l^i = m^i p_l\ ,\quad 0 \leq i < I, 0 \leq l < L \tag{7}$$

We embed w_l^i into $\|d_l\| \in bin^i$ in proportion to $\|d_l\|$ and the global strength factor β. β can help to extract the watermark easily, but it has to be selected carefully because it also controls the visual quality after embedding the watermark.

$$\left\|\tilde{d}_l^i\right\| = \|d_l\| + \beta\,\|d_l\|\,w_l^i \tag{8}$$

Then, spherical coordinates $[\ \|\tilde{d}_l^i\|,\ \theta_l\ \phi_l\ ]^t$ are changed into Cartesian coordinates $[\tilde{x}_l,\ \tilde{y}_l,\ \tilde{z}_l]^t = \tilde{d}_l^i$. Finally, we can get the watermarked mesh $\tilde{M}^J$ after inverse DWT (Eq. (3)) with $\tilde{d}_l^i$. Note that the inverse reordering of $\tilde{M}^J$ is required to recover the original indices of both vertices and faces as we mentioned in Section 2.2.

2.4   Extraction Method

We use a blind extraction scheme based on cross-correlation of the norm of wavelets coefficients of the attacked mesh $\tilde{M}^J$ with the pseudo random sequence.

For the sake of notational simplicity we do not change the notation of wavelet coefficients. In other words the following can be considered as a mesh free of attack. According to Eq. (8) the cross correlation results in,

$$\sum_{l \in bin^i} \left\| \tilde{d}_l^i \right\| p_l = \sum_{l \in bin^i} \|d_l\| p_l + \beta \sum_{l \in bin^i} \|d_l\| w_l^i p_l \tag{9}$$

From Eq. (5) and Eq. (6), $w_l^i p_l = m^i p_l^2 = m^i$. In addition, due to both the zero mean pseudo random sequence and the uniform distribution in a bin, the first term of Eq. (9) cancels. Then, we can recover m^i by computing the sign of Eq. (9).

$$sign\left[\sum_{l \in bin^i} \left\| \tilde{d}_l^i \right\| p_l \right] = m^i \tag{10}$$

The components of wavelet coefficients follow a generalized Gaussian pdf [12]. Then the pdf of the wavelet coefficient norms is close to a χ_3^2 distribution [12]. It means that the distribution in the bins is not uniform. However, our approach remains effective in practice when the watermarked wavelet coefficient norms were limited to the minimum number of wavelet coefficients in the overall bins $L_{\min}$. It can be enhanced by removing the first bin which is clearly out of the uniform hypothesis.

3   Experimental Results

In this section, we demonstrate the experimental results to show the effectiveness of our proposal. Since wavelet based approach is specific of the synchronization of the order of vertices and faces, we do not consider the topological attacks such as re-triangulation, simplification or remeshing [8]. We use four meshes in Fig. 3. Three of them are irregular meshes: Stanford Bunny (34834 vertices, 69451 faces), Davidhead (24085 vertices, 47753 faces), Hand (10196 vertices, 20261 faces), and the other is an semi-regular mesh, Head (6737 vertices, 13408 faces).

We first embedded one bit into $Head$ to present the efficiency of transparency and robustness according to the watermark strength factor β in both Fig. 5 and

Table 1. $corr$ and RMS distances without an attack

Embedding Level	β, I	Bunny		Davidhead		Hand		Head	
		corr	RMS	corr	RMS	corr	RMS	corr	RMS
$J-1$	0.3, 125	1.000	0.005	1.000	0.018	1.000	0.007	1.000	0.014
$J-1$	0.4, 125	1.000	0.007	1.000	0.024	1.000	0.009	1.000	0.019
$J-1$	0.4, 265	1.000	0.007	1.000	0.024	1.000	0.009	1.000	0.019
$J-2$	0.2, 50	1.000	0.009	1.000	0.020	1.000	0.010	1.000	0.035
$Multilevel^a$	—	1.000	0.011	1.000	0.032	1.000	0.014	1.000	0.040

^a Both level $J-1$ with $\beta = 0.4$ and $I = 265$, $J-2$ with $\beta = 0.2$ and $I = 50$.

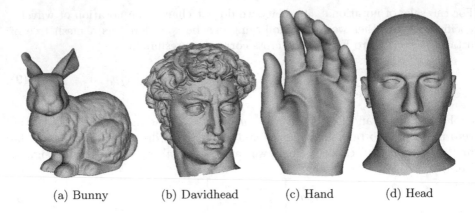

(a) Bunny   (b) Davidhead   (c) Hand   (d) Head

Fig. 4. Test models

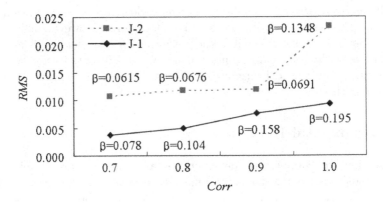

Fig. 5. Efficiency of transparency and robustness versus the strength factor β

Table 1. Root mean square (RMS) distance between the original mesh and the watermarked in % of the bounding box diagonal [13], estimates the visual quality. We use linear correlation ($corr$) between extracted message bits ($\tilde{m}^i$) and designated message bits (m^i) to measure the robustness. In the same level, robustness ($corr$) increases according to β, but RMS distance also increases with β. Fig. 5 also shows that the wavelet coefficients of lower resolution level $J-2$ (dashed line) is more affected than higher resolution level $J-1$ (solid line).

To compare the transparency between two resolution levels, we embedded the watermark with different strength factor at each levels. In Fig. 6, although two models have similar RMS distances, the watermark in the higher resolution level is more visible than in the lower resolution level, because the modification in the lower frequency component is less affected to high curvature area. It proves that the methods based on frequency domain are more effective than spatial domain methods when the application needs a good visual quality of the model after the watermarking.

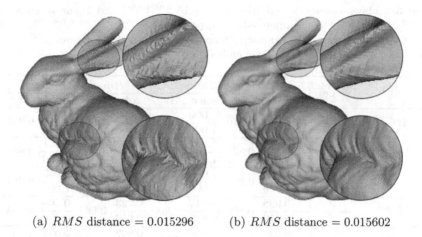

(a) RMS distance = 0.015296   (b) RMS distance = 0.015602

Fig. 6. RMS distance for *Bunny* according to embedding level (a) $J-1$ where $\beta = 0.8$, and (b) $J-4$ where $\beta = 0.1$

Table 2. Robustness against additive noise and laplacian smoothing attacks of single level at $J-1$

(β, I)	corr			
	Bunny	*Davidhead*	*Hand*	*Head*
$Noise^{0.2\%}$				
0.3, 125	0.952	1.000	0.984	0.890
0.4, 125	1.000	1.000	1.000	0.968
0.4, 265	0.940	1.000	1.000	0.903
$Noise^{0.45\%}$				
0.3, 125	0.744	1.000	1.000	0.615
0.4, 125	0.856	1.000	1.000	0.744
0.4, 265	0.751	1.000	0.992	0.601[a]
$Smooth^{20}$				
0.3, 125	0.920	1.000	0.906	0.936
0.4, 125	1.000	1.000	1.000	1.000
0.4, 265	0.947	1.000	0.970	0.962
$Smooth^{40}$				
0.3, 125	0.795	0.968	0.744	0.588
0.4, 125	0.888	1.000	0.808	0.728
0.4, 265	0.706	0.917	0.753	0.751

[a] 0.518 in Yin *et al.* [5].

$$corr(\tilde{m}^i, m^i) = \frac{\sum\limits_{i=0}^{I-1} (\tilde{m}^i - \bar{\tilde{m}}^i)(m^i - \bar{m}^i)}{\sqrt{\sum\limits_{i=0}^{I-1} (\tilde{m}^i - \bar{\tilde{m}}^i)^2}\sqrt{\sum\limits_{i=0}^{I-1} (m^i - \bar{m}^i)^2}} \tag{11}$$

The capacity I is dependent on the number of wavelet coefficients N in our approach. It also can be varied by β. For the fair analysis of robustness, we embed the same number of bits with the same strength factor to all models. We

Table 3. Robustness against additive noise ($AN^{amplitude}$) and laplacian smoothing ($LS^{numbers\ of\ iteration}$) and progressive compression ($PC^{numbers\ of\ bitplane}$), random connectivity reordering (RR), similarity transform (ST), uniform scaling ($US^{(x,\ y,\ z)}$), affine transform (RST) of *multilevel* embedding

	Level	Bunny		DavidHead		Hand		Head	
		corr	Avg.	corr	Avg.	corr	Avg.	corr	Avg.
$AN^{0.2\%}$	$J-1$	0.940	0.970	1.000	1.000	1.000	1.000	0.903	0.951
	$J-2$	1.000		1.000		1.000		1.000	
$AN^{0.45\%}$	$J-1$	0.751	0.876	1.000	1.000	1.000	1.000	0.601	0.801 [a]
	$J-2$	1.000		1.000		1.000		1.000	
LS^{20}	$J-1$	0.955	0.977	1.000	1.000	0.962	0.902	0.962	0.981
	$J-2$	1.000		1.000		0.842		1.000	
LS^{40}	$J-1$	0.698	0.809	0.917	0.900	0.723	0.666	0.766	0.863
	$J-2$	0.919		0.883		0.610		0.960	
PC^{8}	$J-1$	0.992	0.996	1.000	1.000	0.992	0.996	0.584	0.792
	$J-2$	1.000		1.000		1.000		1.000	
PC^{9}	$J-1$	0.947	0.974	1.000	1.000	1.000	1.000	0.940	0.970
	$J-2$	1.000		1.000		1.000		1.000	
RR	$J-1$	1.000	1.000	1.000	1.000	1.000	1.000	1.000	1.000 [b]
	$J-2$	1.000		1.000		1.000		1.000	
ST	$J-1$	1.000	1.000	1.000	1.000	1.000	1.000	1.000	1.000 [c]
	$J-2$	1.000		1.000		1.000		1.000	
$US^{(2.0,1.0,1.0)}$	$J-1$	1.000	1.000	1.000	1.000	1.000	1.000	1.000	1.000
	$J-2$	1.000		1.000		1.000		1.000	
$US^{(1.0,2.0,1.0)}$	$J-1$	1.000	1.000	1.000	1.000	1.000	1.000	1.000	1.000
	$J-2$	1.000		1.000		1.000		1.000	
$US^{(1.0,1.0,2.0)}$	$J-1$	0.992	0.996	0.992	0.996	1.000	0.980	1.000	0.980
	$J-2$	1.000		1.000		0.960		0.960	
RST^{d}	$J-1$	1.000	1.000	1.000	1.000	1.000	1.000	1.000	1.000
	$J-2$	1.000		1.000		1.000		1.000	
RST^{e}	$J-1$	0.992	0.996	0.992	0.996	1.000	1.000	1.000	1.000
	$J-2$	1.000		1.000		1.000		1.000	

[a] 0.518 in Yin *et al.* [5],
[b] 0.786 in Yin *et al.* [5].
[c] Similarity Transform from user's random input. 0.779 in Yin *et al.* [5].
[d] $R^{(30°,60°,90°)}, S^{(2.0,1.1,1.7)}, T^{(5,10,15)}$
[e] $R^{(90°,30°,60°)}, S^{(1.1,1.7,2.0)}, T^{(-5,10,-15)}$

give the result from single level at $J-1$ in Table 2. For noise attack, we add a noise vector to each vertex. The amplitudes of the noise vectors are 0.2% and 0.45%. We applied laplacian smoothing with the relaxation factor of 0.03 and the iteration 20 and 40 times each. *corr* increases according to β. But, if we increase β, it makes the watermark more visible. A small number of embedded bits gives better robustness.

Table 3 presents the result of multilevel embedding. We embedded 315 bits, (265 bits at level $J-1$ and 50 bits at level $J-2$), into all test models. The strength factors are $\beta = 0.4$ at $J-1$ and $\beta = 0.2$ at $J-2$, respectively. The

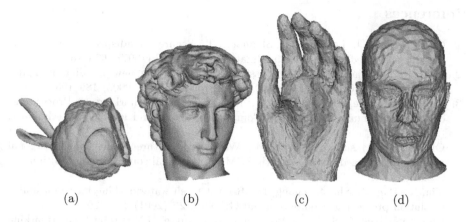

(a)   (b)   (c)   (d)

Fig. 7. Attacked models: (a) Affine transform, (b) Laplacian smoothing 0.03 × 40, (c) Progressive compression 8 bitplanes, (d) Additive noise 0.45%

table gives *corr* at each level and the average of both levels. For compression attack, we applied progressive geometry compression proposed by Valette [14]. It encodes the wavelet coefficients using a zerotree coder with a bitplane approach and reconstructs the mesh geometry progressively while the connectivity is kept unchanged. The numbers of bitplanes for compression were 8 and 9, and a small number of bitplanes gives lower quality of the model. $J - 2$ results a better robustness comparing with $J - 1$ cause D^{J-2} is less affected than D^{J-1} on the other attacks. The table shows that the given strength factors are not sufficient to explain the robustness against all the attacks, but the capacity is still effective comparing with the previous work in Yin *et al.* [5] which uses non-blind detection.

We also tested similarity transform (ST) and affine transform and random connectivity reordering of both faces and vertex indices. Since L2-norm of wavelet coefficients is invariant to rotation and translation, our method that embeds into wavelet coefficient norms gives error-free detection on rotation and translation for both single level and multilevel. In addition, it is also effective on scaling attacks including non-uniform scaling. Random reordering attack can be recovered by the reordering before the DWT.

4   Conclusion

In this paper, we proposed a multiresolution analysis based watermarking method for 3D irregular meshes. The proposed embeds the watermark into L2-norm of wavelet coefficients in various multiresolution levels. Through the experiment, we proved that a vertex and face re-ordering process as pre-processing in both watermark embedding and extraction make our proposal be robust against connectivity reordering attacks. We also showed that multiresolution embedding has more capacity while keeping the robustness against connectivity reordering as well as various kinds of geometrical attacks such as lossy compression and affine transform.

References

1. Cox, I., Kilian, J., Leighton, T., Shamoon, T.: Secure spread spectrum watermarking for multimedia. IEEE Trans. Image Processing **6** (1997) 1673–1687
2. Fridrich, J., Goljan, M., Du, R.: Lossless data embedding–new paradigm in digital watermarking. EURASIP J. Appl. Signal. Process. **2002** (2002) 185–196
3. Praun, E., Hoppe, H., Finkelstein, A.: Robust mesh watermarking. In: Proceedings of the 26th annual conference on Computer graphics and interactive techniques. (1999) 49–56
4. Ohbuchi, R., Masuda, H., Aono, M.: Watermarking three-dimensional polygonal models. In: Proceedings of the fifth ACM international conference on Multimedia, ACM Press (1997) 261–272
5. Yin, K., Pan, Z., Shi, J., Zhang, D.: Robust mesh watermarking based on multiresolution processing. Computers and Graphics **25** (2001) 409–420
6. Cho, J.W., Kim, M.S., Prost, R., Chung, H.Y., Jung, H.Y.: Robust watermarking on polygonal meshes using distribution of vertex norms. In Cox, I.J., Kalker, T., Lee, H.K., eds.: IWDW. Volume 3304 of Lecture Notes in Computer Science., Springer (2004) 283–293
7. Kanai, S., Date, D., Kishinami, T.: Digital watermarking for 3d polygon using multiresolution wavelet decomposition. In: Proc. Sixth IFIP WG 5.2 GEO-6, Tokyo, Japan (1998) 296–307
8. Uccheddu, F., Corsini, M., Barni, M.: Wavelet-based blind watermarking of 3d models. In: MM&Sec '04: Proceedings of the 2004 multimedia and security workshop on Multimedia and security, ACM Press (2004) 143–154
9. Lounsbery, M., DeRose, T.D., Warren, J.: Multiresolution analysis for surfaces of arbitrary topological type. ACM Transactions on Graphics **16** (1997) 34–73
10. Valette, S., Prost, R.: Multiresolution analysis of irregular surface meshes. IEEE Trans. Visual. Comput. Graphics **10** (2004) 113–122
11. Touma, C., Gotsman, C.: Triangle mesh compression. In: Graphics Interface. (1998) 26–34
12. Payan, F., , Antonini, M.: Multiresolution 3d mesh compression. In: IEEE Int. Conf. on Image Processing ICIP'02. Volume 2. (2002) 245–248
13. Aspert, N., Santa-Cruz, D., Ebrahimi, T.: Mesh: Measuring errors between surfaces using the hausdorff distance. In: Proceedings of the IEEE International Conference on Multimedia and Expo. Volume I. (2002) 705 – 708 `http://mesh.epfl.ch`.
14. Valette, S., Gouaillard, A., Prost, R.: Compression of 3d triangular meshes with progressive precision. Computer & Graphics, Special Issue on Compression **28** (2004) 35–42

Digital Watermarking Robustness and Fragility Characteristics: New Modelling and Coding Influence

Marcos de Castro Pacitti[1] and Weiler Alves Finamore[2]

[1] Brazilian Air Force
pacitti@ciscea.gov.br
[2] CETUC/ PUC - Rio, Brazil
weiler@cetuc.puc-rio.br

Abstract. This paper, introduces a new methodology for the design and analysis of digital watermarking systems which, from an information theoretic point of view, incorporates robustness and fragility. The proposed methodology is developed by focusing on the probability of error versus watermark-to-noise ratio curve, describing the technique performance, and a scenario for coded techniques which takes into account not only the coding gain, but also the robustness or fragility of the system. This new concept requires that coded digital watermarking systems design be revisited to also include the robustness and fragility requirements. Turbo codes, which appropriately meet these requirements, can be used straightforwardly to construct robust watermarking systems. Fragile systems can also be constructed by introducing the idea of polarization scheme. This new idea has allowed the implementation of hybrid techniques achieving fragility and robustness with a single watermark embedding. We moreover, present (turbo) coded techniques which can also be used in a semi-fragile mode.

1 Introduction

Watermarking refers to the process of embedding in a host information an information mark which is not immediately discernible upon examining the embedded host information. These techniques have been used as a way of reducing counterfeiting in documents, currency, and other applications for centuries. With the widespread use of digital representation of images, video, audio, and other signals, the copyright protection by using an "invisible" digital watermarks became a very active area of research. Naturally many new watermarking applications have become of great interest in this new digital perspective, including national security applications such as integrity and authenticity verification, covert communication and traitor tracing (finger printing) applications. Several other digital watermarking applications are still emerging, bringing a wide perspective for research [1].

Watermarking in this new context is a complex problem, with issues that involve not only the watermarking techniques themselves, but also system design,

M. Barni et al. (Eds.): IWDW 2005, LNCS 3710, pp. 325–335, 2005.

cryptography, and a series of economical and legal aspects that have to be taken into account, considering the specific application and business model as well. In this paper we only deal with a single aspect of the problem: the modelling and analysis of the *robustness* and *fragility* characteristics of the embedded digital watermark.

Digital watermarking robustness and fragility are intimately connected to, respectively, the copyright protection and the authenticity/integrity of the host information (digital media). Therefore, the investigation of these characteristics modelling is of great interest in order to support techniques design for a wide application scenario.

This paper is organized as follows: in Section II, we present the coded digital watermark embedding problem model, including a brief discussion on the main parameters involved on the embedding techniques design. In Section III, we introduce our model for robustness and fragility characteristics. In Section IV we analyze the coding influence on these characteristics proprieties, specially considering the turbo code technique for robust operation. In Section V, a polarization scheme is introduced for fragile operation, and in Section VI a semi-fragile operation approach is discussed. In Section VII, our conclusions are presented.

2   Problem Model

The digital watermarking problem has many aspects and steps to be considered: embedding domain and coefficients selection; human perception system (auditory or visual) model; possible attacks; security; specific application requirements. In this work we will only consider the embedding (modulation) step, where the digital watermark is to be robustly or fragilely embedded in a given host domain.

Coded binary modulation phase is generically modelled as illustrated on fig. 1. In this diagram, the digital watermark informational bits, represented by the block of bits b, are encoded (with code rate R) before being embedded in the host signal. Each set of N samples from the host signal, represented by the vector $\mathbf{x} \in \mathbb{R}^N$ [1], together with $1/R$ bits (output coded bits for each input watermark - informational - bit) from the encoder output, are processed to produce the marked signal $\mathbf{s}$. Because of the similarity to the communication model, we also refers to the embedding process as modulation. The modulator processing outputs vector $\mathbf{s}(b, \mathbf{x}) \in \mathbb{R}^N$.

We say that the informational bit modulation rate (or watermark rate) is $1/N$ bits per sample. The difference between vectors $\mathbf{x}$ and $\mathbf{s}$ are measured according to a distortion criteria, and should not exceed a maximum value. Naturally, among other requirements, the modulation technique shall be designed to maximize the watermark (information) embedding rate, minimizing vector length N

---

[1] The vector $\mathbf{x}$ is any adequate representation of part of the host signal. In the case of a host image, it could be a vector of pixel values, discrete cosine transform (DCT) coefficients or discrete wavelet transform (DWT) coefficients, for example. In the case of a host audio waveform, this vector could be a vector of samples, spectral parameters, or linear prediction coding (LPC) coefficients, for example.

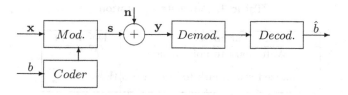

Fig. 1. Problem model for coded digital watermarking modulation techniques

necessary to embed each bit. That is the primary reason to use coding techniques (error correcting codes) in the watermark embedding scheme. For a given performance (error probability), the "coding gain" will allow operation at lower signal (watermark) to noise (attack) ratio, which is proportional to host vector length N, as we will see next.

The introduced distortion (D_b) in signal $\mathbf{s}$ in relation to $\mathbf{x}$ due to the modulation with bit b, is defined as:

$$D_b = \frac{1}{N} \sum_{i=1}^{N} E\{(s_i - x_i)^2\} \tag{1}$$

where $E\{.\}$ denotes expectation. Note that D_b also represents the watermark power (σ_{wm}^2). Therefore, it is possible to interpret the bit energy (E_b), responsible for the corresponding distortion (due to modulation), as

$$E_b = N D_b = N \sigma_{wm}^2 \tag{2}$$

Many innocent or intentional (malicious) signal processing, as compression and additive noise, can be applied to the digital watermarked signal $\mathbf{s}$, and may remove the digital watermark. These processing are generally called as attacks, and they are also constrained to the maximum allowed distortion induced on the signal. In this work, the attack model is resumed to an additive gaussian noise $\mathbf{n} \in \mathbb{R}^N$ with uncorrelated components, zero mean, and variance $\sigma_n^2 = N_0/2$. Therefore, at demodulator input $\mathbf{y} = \mathbf{s} + \mathbf{n}$ is present, representing the attacked watermarked signal.[2] Considering the noise $\mathbf{n}$ statistically independent to the other problem's variables, we can express the distortion of signal $\mathbf{y}$ in relation to $\mathbf{x}$ as

$$D_{\mathbf{y}} = \sigma_{wm}^2 + \sigma_n^2 . \tag{3}$$

The demodulator/decoder objective is to produce the best estimate of the digital watermark from the attacked digital watermarked signal. The demodulator objective is to produce the best estimate of the coded bits, and the decoder

---

[2] Another class of attacks do not aim the watermark itself but the detector synchronization capability. For demodulation, the detector needs to find where each watermark bit is hidden in the host signal. Segmentation and geometric transforms in images are examples of detector synchronization attack . This type of attacks are not considered in our model.

Table 1. Parameters Notation

Parameter	Definition
Watermark to noise ratio	$WNR = \frac{D_b}{\sigma_n^2}$
Normalized watermark to noise ratio	$WNR_N = \frac{E_b}{\sigma_n^2}$

objective is to produce the best estimate $\hat{b}$ of the informational (watermark) bits b. The technique is said to be "non blind" or "blind" when $\mathbf{x}$ is available or not, respectively, at demodulation. Blind techniques are generally considered, since most practical applications requires this condition.

Table 1 introduces some parameters notations and definitions for future analysis support. Note that, from WNR_N definition, yields $WNR_N = 2E_b/N_0$.[3]

Next, robustness and fragility behavior analysis will be focused on their dependency to the performance of the digital watermarking technique. Technique performance is taken here as the detection error probability (p_e) as a function of WNR_N. In practice, p_e is estimated by the bit error rate (BER) measurement, corresponding to the number of wrongly estimated bits, from the attacked signal, over the total number of embedded bits.

3   Analysis and Design Model for Digital Watermark Robustness and Fragility Characteristics

Two key concepts are central to our discussion: robustness and fragility. Digital watermark robustness refers to the technique ability to reliably extract the watermark information (keeping the watermark detection error probability low) even when the amount of noise introduced by the attacker is high. This robustness condition is mostly desired on host copyright protection applications. On the other hand, fragility of a digital watermark scheme refers to the ability to prevent the digital watermark from being detected even when the intensity of the attack is low. This fragility condition is mostly desired on host authenticity/integrity verification applications.

We now introduce some design parameters that take into account the robustness and fragility. The first parameter establishes an upper bound to the maximum allowed host distortion D^M. Above this distortion, for many copyright protection verification applications, the received signal is considered useless. In a covert communication application scenario, if this distortion is exceeded, the user will easily notice that a third part tried to jam the secret communication.

A second parameter establishes a threshold p_e^M for the error detection probability. Above this threshold the recovered watermark is no longer considered reliable.

---

[3] One advantage on using the normalized watermark to noise ratio (WNR_N) parameter is to consolidate the analysis of single host sample and spread bit modulation techniques. When single host sample bit modulation is considered, it is just necessary to make $N = 1$. WNR_N also has a simple relation with the E_b/N_0 parameter widely used in information and communication theory.

We can then state that a scheme is designed for a robust operation mode when the digital watermark detection error probability $p_e < p_e^M$, yet $D_y > D^M$. On the same vein the scheme is designed for a fragile operation mode when the digital watermark detection error probability $p_e > p_e^M$, yet $D_y < D^M$.

The concepts above described will be developed next in order to derive mathematical expressions for robustness and fragility analysis.

The maximum host distortion condition is

$$D_{\mathbf{y}} = \sigma_{wm}^2 + \sigma_n^2 < D^M ,\tag{4}$$

Let the robustness factor (ρ) be defined as $\rho = \sigma_{wm}^2 / D^M$. This factor ($0 < \rho < 1$) expresses the ratio of digital watermark distortion and the maximum allowed distortion. Condition 4 can now be written as

$$WNR_N > N\rho/(1-\rho) = WNR_N^{D^M} ,\tag{5}$$

meaning that for a useful (not critically damaged) host, WNR_N shall be greater than the value $WNR_N^{D^M}$ (above defined).

For the maximum allowed detection error probability (p_e^M) we have the condition

$$p_e < p_e^M .\tag{6}$$

It should be noticed that $p_e = f(WNR_N)$, which expresses the scheme performance, is a decreasing function on WNR_N. Condition 6 now becomes

$$WNR_N > f^{-1}(p_e^M) = WNR_N^{p_e^M} ,\tag{7}$$

meaning that for reliable watermark detection, WNR_N shall be greater than the value $WNR_N^{p_e^M}$ (above defined). We emphasize that inequalities (5) and (7) represent design conditions.

The following discussion illustrates the use of these design parameters. In the absence of an attack (no noise) the normalized watermark to noise ratio (WNR_N) is infinite and the error probability, assuming a sided-informed scheme, is zero. As the attack intensity increases, the signal to noise ratio decreases, describing the WNR_N versus p_e performance curve of the scheme. If, when WNR_N decreases, the value $WNR_N^{D^M}$, is reached before the value $WNR_N^{p_e^M}$ the scheme is said to be a robust, otherwise if the value $WNR_N^{p_e^M}$ is reached first the scheme is said to be a fragile.

In summary:

- Robustness : Even after critical host distortion it is still possible to recover the digital watermark.
- Fragility : Reliable digital watermark detection is lost before critical host distortion, i.e., watermarked host authenticity/integrity is sensed as the ability to detect the digital watermark, and tampering (adulteration) is sensed as digital watermark detection loss.

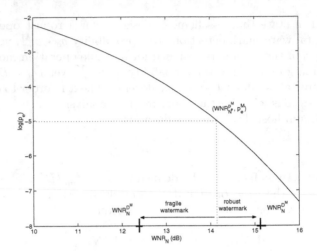

Fig. 2. STDM digital watermarking technique performance with design parameters represented

Also, the value $WNR_N^{D^M} - WNR_N^{p_e^M}$ can be used to represent a robustness or fragility measure. So if one wish to project a very robust system $WNR_N^{D^M}$ shall be much greater than $WNR_N^{p_e^M}$, and for a very fragile system, $WNR_N^{D^M}$ shall be much smaller than $WNR_N^{p_e^M}$.

Fig. 2 illustrates the above discussion. The performance of a an uncoded STDM [2] was used to plot this figure. The parameter p_e^M was chosen to be 10^{-5}, yielding to $WNR_N^{p_e^M} = 14.1dB$. The design can now be pursued by selecting appropriate values for the parameters N and ρ. If a robust system is to be designed the value of $WNR_N^{D^M}$ should be set, according to equation 5, such that $WNR_N^{D^M} > 14.1dB$. If on the other hand a fragile system is desired, this value should be set such that $WNR_N^{D^M} < 14.1dB$. Fig. 2 illustrates the two design possibilities. The right(left) oriented arrow length from $14.1dB$ to $WNR_N^{D^M}$ measure the robustness(fragility) of the scheme. So we have seen that the performance function of the technique can be used to set up either a fragile or a robust scheme as desired.

4   Coding Influence on Digital Watermarking Robustness and Fragility

An important aspect of the robustness or the fragility is its sensitivity, as measured by the steepness of the p_e^M versus WNR_N performance function. The idea can be better understood when we compare two systems A and B operating in the robust (fragile) mode. A watermarking system A is said to be more robust (fragile) than system B if an attack that decreases the value of WNR_N, by the

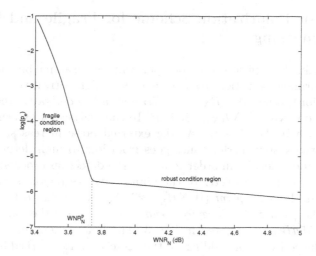

Fig. 3. Performance function of a typical turbo coded digital watermarking technique with rate 1/2

same amount on both systems, results in a smaller (greater) p_e increase for system A than the corresponding increase for system B.

Therefore, the curve p_e^M versus WNR_N has a prominent influence not only on the operation mode (robust or fragile) definition (as described on Section (3)) but also on the mode sensitivity. Recalling that coding techniques can strongly affect the shape of the performance function, lead us to consider that the investigation of the influence of coding technique on the mode (robust or fragile) sensitivity is important — in fact, as it will be next discussed, this influence can be used in the system design not only to obtain the so called coding gain (on WNR_N), but also to attain appropriately the operational mode sensitivity. Therefore coding techniques design shall be revisited to also consider this new digital watermarking scenario.

To deepen this discussion further let us consider, as an example, that the coder used in Fig. 1 is a typical turbo code [4] with the p_e versus WNR_N performance illustrated on Fig. 3 (for digital watermarking coded implementations refer to [3]).

From Fig. 3 we can deduct that the turbo code technique is very convenient in providing robustness characteristics to the digital watermarking technique, since it has a flat shape for $WNR_N > 3.75dB$, for this typical performance. If we assume that the system is required to operate in the robust mode, with $p_e^M < 10^{-6}$, we can then adjust the design parameters such that $WNR_N^{D^M} > 3.75dB$.

At a first glance, turbo code is not directly appropriate, when fragile digital watermark application is sought, the difficulty being that a high intensity attack is required in order to disrupt the system (forcing the system into a high derivative region with large p_e excursion) — a solution to overcome this difficulty (the fragility goal is to loose watermark detection for small intensity attack) will be presented next.

5   Detector Polarization Scheme for Fragile and Hybrid Watermarking

Observing again the typical turbo code performance example on Fig. 3 we note that the performance function has two regions, a high derivative region (fragile condition region), where $WNR_N < 3.75dB$ and, a low derivative region (robust condition region) with $WNR_N > 3.75dB$. In the absence of external noise (no attack) we have $WNR_N \rightarrow \infty$. As the external noise increases, WNR_N decreases, and the system performance goes from low to high derivative region. Noise can be added locally in order to adjust the detection processing, bringing the system performance directly to the high derivative region, such that operation starts at the *knee point* (WNR_N^p, p_e^p). We will refer to the component WNR_N^p as the *polarized watermark-to-noise ratio* — for the current example $WNR_N^p = 3.75dB$ as illustrated in Fig. 3. The before mentioned adjustment, can be introduced by simply adding, to the attacked watermarked host signal **y**, a gaussian polarization noise (zero mean and variance $\sigma_{n_p}^2$) with power

$$\sigma_{n_p}^2 = \frac{\sigma_{wm}^2}{WNR_N^p} = \frac{\rho D^M}{WNR_N^p}. \tag{8}$$

Therefore, the polarized (adjusted) receiver is ready to process the watermark detection in a fragile condition region, i.e., such that any incremental attack will severely degrade the p_e.

It should be noticed that in spite of having embedded a single watermark only, the system, at the reception, can be set to operate either in a robust or fragile mode. If fragile operation mode is desired, adding the polarization noise, in the receiver premisses, is all that is required. Fig. 4 illustrates this idea. Techniques such as the one just described, are referred to, in the literature [5], as hybrid techniques. For instance, for copyright verification, the robust mode processing should be selected, while for authenticity verification, the fragile mode processing (polarized) should be selected.

For applications other than authenticity/integrity verification, the polarization may be performed at the modulator side (transmitter). For example, if the digital watermark to be embedded is a sensitive information (covert communication), the polarization at modulation will guarantee that this sensitive information is lost (auto destructed) if threatened by some external interfer-

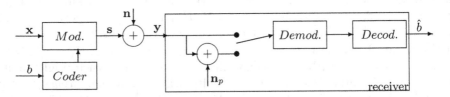

Fig. 4. Watermarking polarization scheme where input to detection processing is selected according to the desired operation mode (fragile or robust)

ence. Generally, for any application in which host distortion is not a strong requirement, allows the polarization to be performed at transmission. Finally, it shall be noted that if this polarization (at transmission) is not reversible at the receiver side, only fragility (but not robustness) can be achieved.

6 A Semi-fragile Coded Watermark Technique

The aim of this section is the investigation of how to assess the intensity of the attack that a host has been subject to. A technique which allows to measure the intensity of the attack, by taking advantage of the above proposed polarization scheme, will next be addressed.

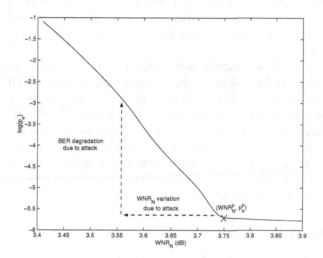

Fig. 5. BER variation due to external attack for a typical turbo code polarized scheme

Such technique, which is to be used when digital media (host) authenticity/integrity verification is required, can be classified as a *semi-fragile* tamper detection technique [5] and can be seen as a "soft" evaluation technique.[4]

To better explain the technique, let us consider our typical turbo code example, illustrated on Fig. 3 and let us say that the system is polarized to the "knee point" ($WNR_N^p = 3.75$, $p_e^p = 10^{-5.5}$). If no attack occurs the BER^p, measured by comparing the blocks of bits $\hat{b}$ and b, will be close to p_e^p — it should be noticed that, in order to avoid the actual BER^p measurement, p_e^p is being used instead of BER^p. On the other hand, if an attack $\mathbf{n}$, with unknown power, changes the normalized watermark-to-noise ratio, from its current value WNR_N^p, to a

---

[4] It will not be considered in our discussion, techniques aiming at attack localization (in the host domain) and neither those where the goal is to distinguish malicious attacks (intentional) from innocent attacks (non intentionally harmful image processing operations, for instance).

new value WNR_N^*, it will correspondingly change the bit-error-rate to a value $BER^* \in [10^{-5.5}, 10^{-1}]$ in a range which can be easily measured.[5]

We now propose that a soft evaluation of the attack intensity be defined by $WNR_N^p - WNR_N^*$, the normalized watermark-to-noise ratio variation which can be obtained by measuring the variation $BER^* - p_e^p$ thus observed.

The idea just described is illustrated in Fig. 5. It should be noticed in this example that while the attack intensity (smaller than $0.2dB$) obtained when $WNR_N^p = 3.75$ changes to $WNR_N^* = 3.55$, the corresponding BER variation experiments a reduction by a factor greater than 300.

The polarization scheme, by forcing the BER excursion into the fragile condition region, where small intensity attacks produce large increase in the BER, increases the precision with which the attack intensity can be measured.[6] Polarization which brings the BER excursion into the robust condition region results in a poor (if not impossible) attack intensity precision measurement, while no polarization do not allow a meaningful definition for the attack intensity $(WNR_N^p \rightarrow \infty)$.

As a final remark one should notice that the measure of attack intensity is polarization scheme dependent. It shall also be noticed that BER excursion in the fragile condition region falls in the practical BER measurement range (in our typical turbo code example, for instance, $BER \in [10^{-5.5}, 10^{-1}]$)). For different implementations (coded or non-coded), it can happens that the fragile condition region corresponds to an impractical BER measurement range (for instance, $BER < 10^{-10}$). The turbo coded implementation together with the polarization scheme proposed in this section provides the practical means to implement a semi-fragile attack intensity measurement system.

7   Conclusions

In this paper, we have introduced a new methodology for the design and analysis of digital watermarking systems which incorporates two important characteristics, robustness and fragility. The proposed methodology has been developed by focusing on the curve which describes the performance of the watermarking technique. By considering that error correcting coding techniques directly influences the performance curve shape, we have also developed these ideas in a new application scenario, which takes into account not only the coding gain, but also the robustness or fragility of the system. This new concept requires that digital watermarking coded systems design be revisited to also include the robustness and

---

[5] Of course this requires that, at the receiver, the true digital watermark block (b) be used as reference. Alternatively, one could use $\hat{b}$ (a good estimate of b) as reference, obtained by selecting the robust processing mode. This alternative turns the authenticity verification into a more practical and secure implementation since the watermark block b is no longer needed at the receiver.

[6] Some application may require reduced fragility sensitivity, in other words, with performance curve derivative in the fragile condition region not so steep. For the turbo code implementation, this sensitivity (steepness) decrease can be simply achieved by reducing the number of iterations of turbo decoding algorithm.

fragility requirements. Turbo codes which have been found to be very appropriated to meet these requirements have been investigated. Robust watermarking systems can be constructed with straightforward use of turbo codes. Fragile systems can also be constructed by introducing the idea of polarization scheme. This new idea has allowed the implementation of hybrid techniques achieving fragility and robustness with a single watermark embedding. We have moreover, presented (turbo) coded techniques which can also be used in a semi-fragile mode.

This work, introduces concepts which, among others system requirements, we believe are important for the development of watermarking techniques and system architecture. We also believe that there is a wide field for practical application architecture implementations to be investigated, considering the concepts here introduced.

References

1. M. Barni, F. Bartolini and J. Fridrich, "EDITORIAL - EURASIP Journal of applied signal processing" *[online]. Available: http://www.hindawi.co.uk/open-access/asp/volume-2002/S1110865702001981.pdf*, 2002.
2. B. Chen and G. W. Wornell, "Quantization Index Modulation: A class of provably good methods for digital watermarking and information embedding" *IEEE Trans. Inform. Theory*, v. 47, No. 4, p. 1423-1443, May 2001.
3. J. Eggers and B. Girod, "Informed Watermarking" *Kluwer Academic Publishers*, 2002, ISBN 1-4020-7071-3.
4. C. Berrou, A. Glavieux, and P. Thitimajshima, "Near Shannon limit error-correcting coding and decoding: Turbo-codes" *in ICC'93*,Geneva, Switzerland,p. 1064-1070, May 1993.
5. J. Fridrich, "Methods for Tamper Detection in Digital Images," *ACM Workshop on Multimedia and Security*, Orlando, FL, October 30-31, 1999, pp. 19-23.

New Geometric Analysis of Spread-Spectrum Data Hiding with Repetition Coding, with Implications for Side-Informed Schemes

Félix Balado

University College Dublin,
Belfield Campus, Dublin 4, Ireland

Abstract. In this paper we initially provide a new geometric interpretation of additive and multiplicative spread-spectrum (SS) watermarking with repetition coding and ML decoding. The interpretation gives an intuitive rationale on why the multiplicative scheme performs better in front of additive independent attacks, and it is also used to produce a novel quantitative performance analysis. Furthermore, the geometric considerations which explain the advantages of multiplicative SS with repetition afford the proposal of a novel side-informed STDM-like method, which we name Sphere-hardening Dither Modulation (SHDM). This method is the side-informed counterpart of multiplicative SS with repetition coding, in the same sense that STDM is the side-informed counterpart of additive SS with repetition coding.

1 Introduction

Until the advent of quantization methods, based on the host signal interference cancellation principle, spread spectrum (SS) watermarking techniques largely dominated the watermarking field. Special attention has been given to those schemes based on repetition coding, due to their relatively simple analysis and practical applicability. Also, additive SS with this type of coding has led to the side-informed method STDM [1] through the application of the new quantization paradigm. Different authors have tackled the analysis of additive or multiplicative SS, but it is perhaps more pertinent to this work to point out the comparative analyses of additive and multiplicative SS with repetition given by Barni, Bartolini *et al* [2,3]. In those works the authors have shown that multiplicative SS is superior to additive SS when both are decoded using maximum likelihood (ML) decoding. The strategy followed therein consists in modeling the ML decision statistic according to the specific conditions assumed, in order to derive analytical expressions of the probability of error.

In this work we initially aim at giving a geometric interpretation of those previous comparisons. As we will see, former comparisons were constrained to a particular best case for multiplicative SS; in this paper we provide a discussion of the general case. For the comparison we will assume, as in prior works, a conveniently restricted scenario with Gaussian host and additive independent

M. Barni et al. (Eds.): IWDW 2005, LNCS 3710, pp. 336–350, 2005.
© Springer-Verlag Berlin Heidelberg 2005

Gaussian distortion, but we will also discuss the implications of our analysis for non-Gaussian sources. Subsequently, we will show that the geometric interpretation given may also be used to obtain new analytical expressions of the probability of error, which strengthen the validity of our interpretation. These expressions are obtained along completely new guidelines, although they lead basically to the same findings of previous authors. In the case of multiplicative SS we provide a normal-based approximation tighter than the usual one using the central limit theorem (CLT), and we show why this expression is also valid asymptotically for an arbitrary key.

Lastly, the geometric perspective obtained on the operation of multiplicative SS affords the proposal of a new side-informed scheme with bears a strong resemblance to Spread Transform Dither Modulation (STDM). This novel scheme, which we name Sphere Hardening Dither Modulation (SHDM), performs similarly as STDM in front of additive distortions.

2   Spread Spectrum with Repetition Coding

In the following, capital letters denote random variables and lowercase letters their realizations. Except otherwise indicated, all vectors are L-dimensional and arranged column-wise, and are denoted by boldface types. The notation $\|\mathbf{x}\|_c$ refers to the ℓ_c-norm of $\mathbf{x}$; if the subscript is omitted then $\|\mathbf{x}\| = \|\mathbf{x}\|_2$.

For the best part of our exposition we will consider that the host signal $\mathbf{x}$ is a realization of an L-dimensional Gaussian random variable $\mathbf{X} \sim \mathcal{N}(0, \sigma_X^2 I_L)$, with I_L the $L \times L$ identity matrix. The analysis will be undertaken for the most common modulation found in the SS watermarking literature, that is, binary antipodal Pulse Amplitude Modulation (PAM). As we are considering repetition coding, the same binary information symbol $b \in \{\pm 1\}$ is embedded at each of the L host signal samples of $\mathbf{x}$, yielding an embedding rate $R = 1/L$ bit/sample. After generating a key-dependent pseudorandom sequence $\mathbf{s}$, with $s_i \in \{\pm 1\}$ for all $i = 1, \cdots, L$, the watermark at the sample i is given for that modulation by

$$w_i = b\, s_i \cdot \alpha_i, \tag{1}$$

for all $i = 1, \cdots, L$. The perceptual mask vector $\boldsymbol{\alpha}$ is a parameter used to control the watermark power. For real hosts $\boldsymbol{\alpha}$ can be computed from the host signal in order to perceptually shape the watermark power in a more efficient way.

The SS watermark $\mathbf{w}$ has to be embedded in the host signal $\mathbf{x}$ before being sent through a given attack channel. This operation forms part of the overall communications channel "seen" by the SS signal $\mathbf{w}$. Usually the watermark is just added to the host signal and we have then that

$$y_i = x_i + w_i, \tag{2}$$

which is termed *additive* SS watermarking. In our analysis of additive SS we will assume for simplicity that $\alpha_i = \alpha > 0$ for all $i = 1, \cdots, L$. In this case, the average embedding distortion (power) per sample is just $D_E = \alpha^2$. We will assume in this case that $\mathbf{W}$ is completely independent from $\mathbf{X}$, although this might not be exact in real cases due to possible dependencies introduced by $\boldsymbol{\alpha}$.

If the perceptual mask happens to be proportional to the host signal, i.e., $\boldsymbol{\alpha} = \gamma \mathbf{x}$, then the watermark is no longer independent from the host. The embedding scheme amounts in this case to what is called *multiplicative* SS watermarking, because substituting (1) in (2) we have that

$$y_i = x_i \cdot (1 + \gamma\, b\, s_i). \tag{3}$$

The embedding distortion is now just $D_E = \gamma^2 \sigma_X^2$. As for perceptual reasons $\alpha_i^2 \ll \sigma_X^2$ we also have that $\gamma^2 \ll 1$, and we will assume $\gamma > 0$ without loss of generality.

Finally, we assume that the watermarked signal $\mathbf{y}$ may undergo an additive independent and identically distributed (i.i.d.) Gaussian attack channel with variance σ_Z^2, i.e., $\mathbf{Z} \sim \mathcal{N}(\mathbf{0}, \sigma_Z^2 I_L)$, and independent of $\mathbf{Y}$. Therefore, for a given realization $\mathbf{z}$ of $\mathbf{Z}$ the signal at the decoder is $\mathbf{v} = \mathbf{y} + \mathbf{z}$. In order to make fair comparisons between the methods we will make use of the customary working points host-to-watermark power ratio (HWR) and watermark-to-noise power ratio (WNR), which are just the quotients of the corresponding signal powers.

3   ML Decoding of SS Watermarking with Repetition

The optimum decoder retrieves an estimate $\hat{b}$ of b from $\mathbf{v}$, such that $P_e \triangleq \Pr\{\hat{b} \neq b\}$ is minimized. This is accomplished through maximum likelihood (ML) decoding, assuming that the binary information symbols are equally likely. In obtaining the decoding rule we will assume that the perceptual mask and the channel model are known. The ML decoder may be then written as

$$\hat{b} = \underset{b \in \{-1,1\}}{\arg\max}\, f_{\mathbf{V}}(\mathbf{v}|b, \mathbf{s}) \tag{4}$$

$$= \underset{b \in \{-1,1\}}{\arg\max} \prod_{i=1}^{L} f_V(v_i|b, s_i), \tag{5}$$

where the second equality is due to the elements of $\mathbf{V}$ being i.i.d. according to the assumptions. The decision rule (4) divides the L-dimensional space where $\mathbf{V}$ lies into two decisions regions, which we can define as

$$\mathcal{R}_b \triangleq \left\{ \mathbf{t} \in \mathbb{R}^L : f_{\mathbf{V}}(\mathbf{t}|b, \mathbf{s}) > f_{\mathbf{V}}(\mathbf{t}| - b, \mathbf{s}) \right\}. \tag{6}$$

Additive SS. Defining $\mathbf{Z}' \triangleq \mathbf{X} + \mathbf{Z}$ we have that $\mathbf{Z}' \sim \mathcal{N}(\mathbf{0}, (\sigma_X^2 + \sigma_Z^2)I_L)$. Using the notation $\mathbf{w}_b$ to indicate that b is the symbol encoded by the watermark, i.e., $\mathbf{w}_b = b \cdot \boldsymbol{\alpha}\mathbf{s}$ then (4) just chooses the maximum of $f_{\mathbf{V}}(\mathbf{v}|b, \mathbf{s}) = f_{\mathbf{Z}'}(\mathbf{v} - \mathbf{w}_b|\mathbf{s})$. Taking logarithms in the maximization (4) and using the fact that the two possible watermarks have the same power, it is straightforward to see that

$$\hat{b} = \underset{b \in \{-1,1\}}{\arg\max}\, \mathbf{v}^T \mathbf{w}_b, \tag{7}$$

that is, the maximum of the cross-correlation decoder. The expression (7) can also be written as

$$\hat{b} = \operatorname{sgn}\left\{r^{\mathrm{add}}\right\},\qquad(8)$$

with the sufficient statistic defined as

$$r^{\mathrm{add}} \triangleq \sum_{i=1}^{L} v_i \cdot s_i = \mathbf{v}^T\mathbf{s}.\qquad(9)$$

For sgn{0} = 0 any arbitrary decision may be made without any performance loss.

Multiplicative SS. We assume next that the embedding equation takes the form (3). As the multiplicative watermark is clearly not independent of the host signal we cannot apply the previous decoding approach. Consider first the case in which there is no attack distortion and then $\mathbf{v} = \mathbf{y} = \mathbf{x} \cdot (1 + b \cdot \gamma \mathbf{s})$. In order to obtain the ML decoder we just need the probability density function (pdf) of Y conditioned to an arbitrary embedded symbol and the secret key. The pdf of Y can be straightforwardly obtained from that of X using a change of variable that yields

$$f_Y(y|b, s) = \frac{1}{|1 + b \cdot \gamma s|} \cdot f_X\left(\frac{y}{1 + b \cdot \gamma s}\right).\qquad(10)$$

In practice we can remove the absolute value in the denominator of (10), as $\gamma < 1$ and then $1 + b_i \cdot \gamma s_i$ is always positive. Then (10) is a zero-mean Gaussian pdf with variance $\sigma_X^2(1 + b \cdot \gamma s)^2$, and taking again logarithms on the maximization it is easy to show that the ML decision is

$$\hat{b} = \operatorname{sgn}\left\{r^{\mathrm{mul}}\right\},\qquad(11)$$

with the sufficient statistic defined as

$$r^{\mathrm{mul}} \triangleq \sum_{i=1}^{L} \left\{ \frac{v_i^2}{\sigma_X^2} \cdot \frac{2\gamma s_i}{(1 - \gamma^2)^2} + \log \frac{1 - \gamma s_i}{1 + \gamma s_i} \right\}.\qquad(12)$$

using $s_i^2 = 1$ for all i. With an AWGN attack with variance σ_Z^2, $f_V(y|b, s_i)$ is still Gaussian but with variance $\sigma_Z^2 + \sigma_X^2(1 + b \cdot \gamma s_i)^2$, and an expression similar to (12) can be easily obtained.

We can simplify conveniently the ML decision rule by defining $\bar{r}^{\mathrm{mul}} \triangleq r^{\mathrm{mul}}$ $\sigma_X^2(1 - \gamma^2)^2/2\gamma$. As the multiplicative factor used is positive, then sgn$\{\bar{r}^{\mathrm{mul}}\}$ = sgn$\{r^{\mathrm{mul}}\}$, and the decision (11) remains the same if we use instead the modified statistic. Using now a Taylor expansion around $\gamma = 0$, we have that

$$\frac{(1 - \gamma^2)^2}{2\gamma} \log \frac{1 - \gamma s_i}{1 + \gamma s_i} = s_i \cdot \left(-1 + \frac{5}{3}\gamma^2 - \cdots\right).\qquad(13)$$

Then, as $\gamma^2 \ll 1$, an approximation to the equivalent sufficient statistic is

$$\tilde{r}^{\mathrm{mul}} \approx \sum_{i=1}^{L} s_i \cdot (v_i^2 - \sigma_X^2) \tag{14}$$

$$= \mathbf{v}^T \mathrm{diag}\{\mathbf{s}\} \mathbf{v} - \sigma_X^2 \mathbf{s}^T \mathbf{1}, \tag{15}$$

with $\mathbf{1}$ the all-ones vector $L \times 1$. Notice that, in contrast to the correlator (9), this statistic requires knowledge of σ_X and is not invariant to fixed gain attacks. To conclude this section, it is possible to show, along the same guidelines provided, that for AWGN with power σ_Z^2 we just need to replace σ_X^2 by $\sigma_X^2 + \sigma_Z^2$ in the approximation (15).

4   Geometric Interpretation of Performance

The performance analysis of additive and multiplicative SS with repetition coding and ML decoding can be accomplished using statistical models of the sufficient statistics (9) and (12). The reader interested in expressions for P_e obtained along these lines is referred to [4,2,3], where the authors undertake performance analyses of SS watermarking with repetition coding and ML decoding under different additive channels, and with and without CLT assumptions. A similar analysis is done in [5] for additive SS with repetition coding, with Laplacian host and no attacks, and using the CLT.

Instead, we take here a geometrical approach to assess the performance of additive and multiplicative SS with repetition coding and ML decoding. Notice that several authors have already pursued similar studies in the case of additive SS with repetition coding. Nevertheless, only the shape of the decision region has been taken into account in those works, without considering the asymptotic implications of that geometric setting for performance as we will do here. Initially we will assume that $s_i = 1$ for all $i = 1, \cdots, L$, and that $\mathbf{v} = \mathbf{y}$.

4.1   ML Decision Boundaries

First, we will obtain the shape of the boundaries splitting the space into the decision regions (6). In additive SS, that boundary is given by the sign change of the correlation (9). As $\mathbf{v}^T \mathbf{s} \gtrless 0$ implies $\hat{b} = 1$ and $\hat{b} = -1$, respectively, the decoder decides the symbol sent depending on the side of the hyperplane $\tilde{\mathbf{v}}^T \mathbf{s} = 0$ where $\mathbf{v}$ lies. Then the ML boundary is simply a hyperplane containing the origin and with normal vector $\mathbf{s} = \mathbf{1}$.

Similarly, the boundary between the decision regions in the multiplicative case is given by the change of sign of the sufficient statistic (14). As $\|\mathbf{v}\|^2 - L\sigma_X^2 \gtrless 0$ approximately implies $\hat{b} = 1$ and $\hat{b} = -1$, respectively, the approximate decoder decides the symbol sent depending on $\mathbf{v}$ being outside or inside the sphere $\|\tilde{\mathbf{v}}\|^2 = L\sigma_X^2$. Hence, the ML boundary is a sphere centered at the origin and with radius $\sqrt{L}\sigma_X$. Both decision boundaries are schematically plotted with dashed lines in Figs. 1(a) and (b), respectively, and $\mathcal{R}_{-1}$ is shaded in gray.

4.2   Qualitative Performance Analysis

Now we have all the elements for interpreting geometrically the performance of the SS schemes considered. The interpretation is based on the fact that, for L large, we may consider that $\mathbf{X}$ roughly lies on a sphere of radius

$$E[\|\mathbf{X}\|] \approx \sqrt{L - 1/2}\,\sigma_X \approx \sqrt{L}\,\sigma_X, \tag{16}$$

as we have that

$$\mathrm{Var}[\|\mathbf{X}\|] \le \sigma_X^2/2 \tag{17}$$

for all L (see for instance [6] for more details on this "sphere hardening" effect). Moreover, as $\mathbf{X}$ is Gaussian, it is uniformly distributed on any sphere centered at the origin.

Figures 1(a) and 1(b) depict the behavior of additive and multiplicative SS for two particular realizations of $\mathbf{X}$, therein denoted as $\mathbf{x}'$ and $\mathbf{x}''$. Bear in mind that those plots represent schematically an L-dimensional space in two dimensions, and that the magnitudes of the watermarks are exaggerated for illustration purposes. For simplifying the explanation we assume first that $\mathbf{X}$ lies *exactly* on the sphere and not in an environment of it, as it actually happens. Notice first that, for any finite L, the watermarks $\mathbf{w}_b^{\mathrm{add}} = b \cdot \alpha\,\mathbf{s} = b \cdot \alpha\,\mathbf{1}$ and $\mathbf{w}_b^{\mathrm{mul}} = b \cdot \gamma\,\mathrm{diag}\{\mathbf{s}\} \cdot \mathbf{x} = b \cdot \gamma\,\mathbf{x}$ are always orthogonal (locally in the multiplicative case) to their corresponding ML decision boundaries. Intuitively this orthogonality makes sense in order to set the vector $\mathbf{y} = \mathbf{x} + \mathbf{w}$ as far away as possible from the error region for a given embedded symbol.

- Additive SS: for certain positions of $\mathbf{x}$ on the sphere it will be impossible for the embedder to place $\mathbf{y} = \mathbf{x} + \mathbf{w}_b^{\mathrm{add}}$ at the desired side of the decision hyperplane, because $\|\mathbf{w}_b^{\mathrm{add}}\| = \sqrt{L}\,\alpha \ll \sqrt{L}\,\sigma_X$. This is what happens in Fig. 1(a) to $\mathbf{x}'$ if we try to embed $b = -1$. This phenomenon will take place at any of the two symmetrical polar caps of the sphere spawned by the angle $\beta \triangleq \arccos(\alpha/\sigma_X)$ between the hyperplane director vector $\mathbf{s}$ and any vector $\mathbf{v}$ on the intersection of $\|\tilde{\mathbf{v}}\|^2 = L\,\sigma_X^2$ and $\tilde{\mathbf{v}}^T\mathbf{s} = \pm L\,\alpha$. One of those error caps is schematically shown in Fig. 1(a). Outside these caps, it is possible for additive SS to place $\mathbf{y}$ at any desired decoding region, as it happens for $\mathbf{x}''$ in the figure. Notice that a non-constant perceptual mask would change the director vector of the boundary hyperplane from $\mathbf{s}$ to $\mathrm{diag}\{\mathbf{s}\}\boldsymbol{\gamma}$.
- Multiplicative SS: by symmetry, we may consider the setting radially (i.e., in magnitude) for any arbitrary angle. If $\mathbf{x}$ is on the sphere, we see from Fig. 1(b) that it is possible to embed $\mathbf{y} = \mathbf{x} + \mathbf{w}_b^{\mathrm{mul}}$ without decoding errors for any arbitrary symbol $b = \pm 1$, in particular both for $\mathbf{x}'$ and $\mathbf{x}''$. Unfortunately, the host vector is not always exactly on the sphere since the asymptotic behavior of $\|\mathbf{X}\|$ is $\mathrm{Var}[\|\mathbf{X}\|] \to \sigma_X^2/2$ as $L \to \infty$ [6], and then errors will actually happen also for the multiplicative scheme. Nonetheless, this proximity of the host signal to the decision boundary hints at why multiplicative SS should perform better than additive SS, as for L

large less watermark energy will be used to counteract host signal interference. Actually, as the expected magnitude of the multiplicative watermark is $E[\|\mathbf{W}_b^{\text{mul}}\|] = \sqrt{L}\gamma\sigma_X$ and its variance is always upper bounded, if $\gamma \gg 1/\sqrt{2L}$ (i.e., if L is large enough) the interpretation above becomes more accurate.

It is clear from Fig. 1 that the use of a correlation decoder in multiplicative SS would lead to catastrophic decoding performance, as $P_e \to 1/2$ asymptotically when replacing the decoding sphere by the decoding hyperplane in that case. Notice that this adverse situation happens even though we are also assuming Gaussian host and repetition coding for multiplicative SS. This example highlights the mistake of assuming *a priori* the universality of correlation decoding for SS schemes.

The conclusions drawn may seem at first overly optimistic for multiplicative SS due to the reason we explain next. While the choice of $\mathbf{s}$ does not change the interpretation for the additive case (as the ML boundary $\tilde{\mathbf{v}}^T\mathbf{s} = 0$ is always a hyperplane), its value varies radically the shape of the decision boundary in the multiplicative case. From (15), the general multiplicative ML boundary is given by $\tilde{\mathbf{v}}^T\text{diag}\{\mathbf{s}\}\tilde{\mathbf{v}} = \sigma_X^2\mathbf{s}^T\mathbf{1}$. This family of quadrics includes generalized hyperboloids for most of the values of $\mathbf{s}$, as $s_i \in \{\pm 1\}$, and it only yields a spheric boundary with radius $\sqrt{L}\sigma_X$ for $\mathbf{s} = \pm\mathbf{1}$ ($\mathbf{s} = \mathbf{1}$ was the particular case studied in [4,3]). Contrary to the spheric case, the open decision surfaces given by generalized hyperboloids will no longer coincide with the neighborhood of the sphere in which $\mathbf{x}$ lies, and performance will worsen in consequence. As a simple 2-dimensional example of a possible multiplicative ML decision boundary, if we take $s_1 = +1$ and $s_2 = -1$ the boundary is given by the pair of straight lines $\tilde{v}_2 = \pm\tilde{v}_1$.

In order to grasp geometrically what performance would be expected with a generic $\mathbf{s}$ we define first the two sets of indices $\mathcal{S}^\pm \triangleq \{j \in \{1, \cdots, L\} : s_j = \pm 1\}$. Observe now that the samples of $\mathbf{x}$ can be divided into two subvectors $\mathbf{x}^+$ and $\mathbf{x}^-$, using the indices in those sets to select their samples. Assuming without loss of generality that $b = 1$ is embedded and letting $N \triangleq |\mathcal{S}^+|$, then we see that multiplicative SS positions $\mathbf{w}^+$ as far outside as possible from the sphere with radius $\sqrt{N}\sigma_X$ in the direction of $\mathbf{x}^+$, whereas $\mathbf{w}^-$ is placed as far inside as possible within the sphere with radius $\sqrt{L-N}\sigma_X$ in the direction of $\mathbf{x}^-$. As (15) can be rewritten as

$$\tilde{r}^{\text{mul}} = \left(\|\mathbf{v}^+\|^2 - N\sigma_X^2\right) - \left(\|\mathbf{v}^-\|^2 - (L-N)\sigma_X^2\right), \tag{18}$$

then we first see that the ML decoder for multiplicative SS amounts to "soft decoding" of two spheric decoders (the one corresponding to $\mathcal{S}^-$ with reversed signs). Now consider the typical case for a good pseudorandom sequence in which $N = L/2$ (assuming L even). Then we can write (18) as

$$\tilde{r}^{\text{mul}} = (1+\gamma)^2\|\mathbf{x}\|^2 - 2(1+\gamma^2)\|\mathbf{x}^-\|^2, \tag{19}$$

by just adding and subtracting $(1+\gamma)^2\|\mathbf{x}^-\|^2$ and noting that $\|\mathbf{x}\|^2 = \|\mathbf{x}^+\|^2 + \|\mathbf{x}^-\|^2$. Notice that (19) can be seen as the case $N = L$ in which the spheric

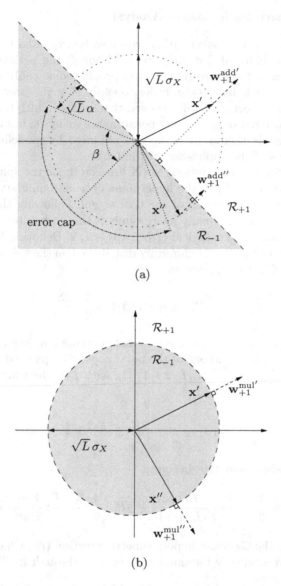

Fig. 1. Geometric interpretation of (a) additive and (b) multiplicative SS with repetition coding and ML decoding (Gaussian i.i.d. host) for large L. The ML decision boundary is plotted with dashed lines in both cases. Watermark vectors $\mathbf{w}_{-1}$ for embedding $b = -1$ (not depicted) would just have opposite directions than the corresponding $\mathbf{w}_{+1}$ ones.

decoder presents a signal dependent radius instead of $\sqrt{L}\,\sigma_X$. As the asymptotic behavior of $\|\mathbf{X}^-\|^2$ is roughly $\frac{L}{2}\sigma_X^2$ then the decoding performance cannot be too different in both cases for $\gamma^2 \ll 1$ (high HWR). The same rationale applies for $b = -1$. For this reason, we will focus our attention in the case $\mathbf{s} = 1$.

4.3   Quantitative Performance Analysis

The preceding geometric considerations can also be exploited to obtain expressions of the probability of decoding error. Although the performance analysis thus obtained is sometimes involved, we will provide some analytical expressions based on the geometric insights, in order to verify that the previous qualitative explanations are correct. We will also see that in the multiplicative case it is possible to produce not only an exact performance analysis, but also an approximation to it that is tighter than the one obtained by modeling the decision statistic by means of the application of the CLT.

For additive SS, the assumption that $\mathbf{X}$ lies exactly on the sphere with radius $\sqrt{L}\,\sigma_X$ is accurate enough, as the hyperplane decision boundary is likely to be far away from most realizations of the host signal. Following the discussion in the preceding section, for equally likely symbols the probability of error on the symmetric L-dimensional spherical error caps is $1/2$. Denoting by $\Omega_L(\beta)$ those two surfaces, and as the host is uniformly distributed on the sphere, we can write the probability of decoding error as

$$P_e^{\text{add}} \approx \frac{1}{2}\Pr\{\mathbf{X} \in \Omega_L(\beta)\} = \frac{1}{2} \cdot \frac{2S_L(\beta)}{S_L}, \tag{20}$$

with S_L and $S_L(\beta)$ the $(L-1)$-dimensional contents (surface areas) of the L-dimensional unit sphere and one of the polar caps of it spawned by the angle β, respectively. As $S_L = L\pi^{L/2}/\Gamma(L/2+1)$ [7], with $\Gamma(\cdot)$ the usual Gamma function, and [8]

$$S_L(\beta) = S_{L-1}\int_0^\beta \sin^{L-2} x \, dx, \tag{21}$$

it is possible to show that (20) becomes

$$P_e^{\text{add}} \approx \frac{1}{2} - \frac{1}{\sqrt{\pi}}\frac{\Gamma(L/2)}{\Gamma(L/2 - 1/2)} \, {}_2F_1\left(\frac{1}{2}, \frac{3-L}{2}; \frac{3}{2}; \frac{\alpha^2}{\sigma_X^2}\right)\frac{\alpha}{\sigma_X}, \tag{22}$$

with ${}_2F_1(\cdot, \cdot; \cdot; r)$ the Gaussian hypergeometric function ([9], Chapter 15), which can be evaluated efficiently for small arguments r through its Taylor series expansion around zero.

It is possible to verify that $P_e^{\text{add}} \to 0$ as $L \to \infty$, which shows the performance improvement afforded by repetition coding. To this end notice that, for large L, we may approximate $S_{L-1}/S_L \approx \sqrt{(L-1)/2\pi}$ (using Stirling's formula) and that the integral in (21) is always upper bounded by $\beta(\sin\beta)^{L-2}$. In these conditions $P_e^{\text{add}} < \sqrt{(L-1)/2\pi}\,\beta(\sin\beta)^{L-2}$, and this bound tends to zero as $L \to \infty$ (as $0 < \beta < \pi/2$, and applying L'Hôpital's theorem). Last, the validity of the analysis is confirmed by the fact that, as shown in Fig. 2, (22) is really close to the much simpler and useful expression $P_e^{\text{add}} = Q(\sqrt{L}\,\alpha/\sigma_X)$ using the Gaussian Q-function, even for low values of L. This last expression, as it is well known, is obtained using a model of the decision statistic.

We analyze next the performance of multiplicative SS. In this case, due to the proximity of $\mathbf{X}$ to the decision boundary, we cannot assume for the analysis that $\mathbf{X}$ is exactly on the sphere, as we have just done for additive SS. For simplicity we assume first that $\|\mathbf{X}\| \sim \mathcal{N}(\sqrt{L}\sigma_X, \sigma_X^2/2)$, and then for equally likely embedded symbols the probability of decoding error is given by

$$P_e^{\mathrm{mul}} = \frac{1}{2}\left[\Pr\left\{\|\mathbf{X}\| > \frac{\sqrt{L}}{1-\gamma}\sigma_X\right\} + \Pr\left\{\|\mathbf{X}\| < \frac{\sqrt{L}}{1+\gamma}\sigma_X\right\}\right] \qquad (23)$$

$$\approx \frac{1}{2}\left[\mathcal{Q}\left(\frac{\gamma}{1-\gamma}\sqrt{2L}\right) + \mathcal{Q}\left(\frac{\gamma}{1+\gamma}\sqrt{2L}\right)\right]. \qquad (24)$$

From (24) we may see that $P_e^{\mathrm{mul}} \to 0$ when $L \to \infty$, showing again the improvement granted by repetition coding. Also, comparing (24) with the expression using the $\mathcal{Q}$-function for additive SS, we see that there is a gain of $\sqrt{2}$ in the argument of $\mathcal{Q}(\cdot)$, for a fixed HWR and using $1\pm\gamma \approx 1$. Although (24) is enough to observe the performance behavior, actually $\|\mathbf{X}\|$ follows a generalized Rayleigh distribution [6][1] from which it is possible to compute the exact probability of error using (23). In this case we have that

$$P_e^{\mathrm{mul}} = \frac{1}{2}\left\{1 - \frac{\Gamma\left(\frac{L}{2}, \frac{L}{2(1+\gamma)^2}\right)}{\Gamma(\frac{L}{2})} + \frac{\Gamma\left(\frac{L}{2}, \frac{L}{2(1-\gamma)^2}\right)}{\Gamma(\frac{L}{2})}\right\}. \qquad (25)$$

Notice that this is basically the expression obtained in [2,3] using a model of the decision statistic without the CLT approximation. Indeed, the ratios of incomplete Gamma and Gamma functions in (25) can also be seen as the evaluations of the cumulative distribution function (cdf) of a sum of χ_L^2 random variables in those works. Then the geometric analysis is also valid for the multiplicative case. Also, as argued in the previous section, (25) is a good approximation for the case $N = L/2$ when the HWR is high. A last remark is that (23) (and then (24) and (25)) can be obviously refined for lower HWRs by not neglecting the term on γ^2 in the approximation (13). The same consideration applies to the decoder in this case.

In Fig. 2 we see a comparison of the multiplicative and additive schemes which shows the superiority of multiplicative SS when the only distortion present is the host signal interference. With respect to the multiplicative case, we may see that the normal approximation (24) is quite good with respect to the exact analysis. As discussed in [3], the CLT approximation of the decision statistic —which is also shown for $\mathbf{s} = 1$ for comparison purposes— is less accurate, but it becomes tighter for higher HWR.

4.4 Geometric Interpretation for Non-gaussian Sources

It is interesting to discuss which are the implications of the geometric considerations for non-Gaussian i.i.d. sources. For these sources, although the host signal

---

[1] $f_{\|\mathbf{x}\|}(\|\mathbf{x}\|) = 2\|\mathbf{x}\|^{L-1}\exp(-\|\mathbf{x}\|^2/2\sigma_X^2)(2\sigma_X^2)^{-L/2}/\Gamma(L/2)$.

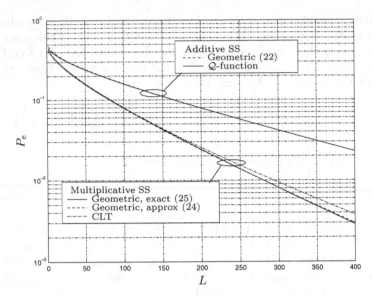

Fig. 2. Performance comparison of additive and multiplicative SS with repetition coding and ML decoding (host to watermark power ratio HWR = 20 dB, no attack)

is also subject to the sphere-hardening effect seen in (16) and (17), in general it does not present uniformity on that sphere[2]. Nevertheless, as the radial component is the only trait relevant for multiplicative SS, we may conjecture that the ML spheric decoder derived for Gaussian host has to be asymptotically optimal regardless of the pdf the of i.i.d. source.

In order to illustrate this issue we take for instance the ML boundary of multiplicative SS for an i.i.d. zero-mean generalized Gaussian host with shape parameter c, which for $\mathbf{s} = \mathbf{1}$ can be seen to be given by

$$\sum_{j=1}^{L} \left(\sigma_X^{-c} \left(\frac{\Gamma(3/c)}{\Gamma(1/c)} \right)^{\frac{c}{2}} |\tilde{v}_j|^c \left[\frac{1}{(1-\gamma)^c} - \frac{1}{(1+\gamma)^c} \right] + \log \frac{1-\gamma}{1+\gamma} \right) = 0, \quad (26)$$

following the same steps as in Sect. 3. We readily see that this region is never a sphere for $c \neq 2$. Nevertheless, if the conjecture is correct, (26) should be asymptotically close to the areas of the sphere where the host is more likely. In order to investigate this hypothesis, it is not difficult to see that if we restrict $\|\mathbf{x}\|_2^2 = L\sigma_X^2$ as an asymptotic approximation of the sphere-hardening effect, then the minimum of $\|\mathbf{x}\|_c^c$ in the positive orthant (enough by symmetry) takes place at $\mathbf{x} = \mathbf{1}\,\sigma_X$ for arbitrary c. One can verify next that this maximum of the

---

[2] Uniformity on the sphere (or, equivalently, on the solid angle) amounts to spherical symmetry of the multidimensional pdf, i.e., the pdf must take the same value for all points of a sphere centered at the mean. For instance, the pdf of a zero-mean i.i.d. generalized Gaussian vector $\mathbf{X}$ depends on $\|\mathbf{x}\|_c^c$, and then for this family of pdfs there is only spherical symmetry for $c = 2$ (Gaussian).

generalized Gaussian pdf at the sphere nearly belongs to (26) for small γ, what shows the near-tangency of both surfaces at this point. Of course, this informal reasoning is far from being a rigorous proof of the conjecture.

On the other hand, and following the same steps as before, for additive SS the ML boundary for generalized Gaussian i.i.d. hosts is

$$\sum_{j=1}^{L} |\tilde{v}_j + \alpha|^c - |\tilde{v}_j - \alpha|^c = 0, \qquad (27)$$

which is never a hyperplane for $c \neq 2$. However, in this case it is easy to check that the decision regions (27) are not close to the hyperplane at the most likely areas of the host on the sphere, which supports the hypothesis that hyperplane is not optimal even in an asymptotic sense for non-Gaussian sources.

5   Sphere-Hardening Dither Modulation

In this section we will show, relying on the insights gleaned from the previous geometric interpretation, that it is possible to draw on the principles operating behind multiplicative SS with repetition in order to design a novel side-informed method similar in many ways to STDM [1]. For the following discussion we assume initially that $\mathbf{v} = \mathbf{y}$.

Let us recall first the close relationship between additive SS with repetition coding and STDM. Considering the sufficient decision statistic in both cases, we see that in additive SS we just *add* a positive or negative amount to $\mathbf{x}^T\mathbf{s}$, as we have that $r^{\mathrm{add}} = \mathbf{x}^T\mathbf{s} + \mathbf{w}_b^T\mathbf{s}$ and $\mathbf{w}_b^T\mathbf{s} = b \cdot \alpha L$. On the other hand, in STDM we *quantize* instead the same projection using one out of two uniform quantizers denoted by $Q_b(\cdot)$, as for that method we have that $r^{\mathrm{STDM}} = Q_b(\mathbf{x}^T\mathbf{s})$. It is well known that both methods exploit the fact that, for a fixed embedding power, the projection $\mathbf{x}^T\mathbf{s}$ affords a gain of $\sqrt{L}$ in the decoding performance P_e (see Sect. 4.3 for additive SS, and [10] for STDM as a particular case of QP). STDM performs of course better than additive SS thanks to the degree of host interference rejection in the projection given by the quantization operation, as, for example, for the case with no attacks considered we will have errorless decoding with STDM.

With this in mind, we turn next our attention to multiplicative SS with repetition coding. From Sect. 4 we know that this method implicitly exploits the so-called sphere-hardening effect given by (16) and (17). Observing (24), this effect also allows a gain of $\sqrt{L}$ in the multiplicative SS scheme. In order to see how this gain could be exploited by a quantization-based scheme, consider again the decision statistic $r^{\mathrm{mul}} = \left[\|\mathbf{x}\| \cdot (1 + \gamma b)\right]^2 - L\sigma_X^2$ (for $\mathbf{s} = \mathbf{1}$). In multiplicative SS with repetition we just *multiply* $\|\mathbf{x}\|$ by a factor greater or less than one. But clearly, as happens with STDM in regard of additive SS with repetition, we can exploit more efficiently the sphere hardening phenomenon if we *quantize* $\|\mathbf{x}\|$ instead of scaling it.

This is the basis for proposing a new data hiding method that we name Sphere-hardening Dither Modulation (SHDM), which is described and analyzed next. As STDM can be deemed the side-informed counterpart of additive SS with repetition coding, SHDM will therefore be the corresponding parallel for multiplicative SS with repetition coding. Also, $\|\mathbf{x}\|$ will approximately play the role of $\mathbf{x}^T \mathbf{s}$. Notice that we are only considering initially the case $\mathbf{s} = \mathbf{1}$ for multiplicative SS; the general case is discussed at the end of this section.

According to the exposition above, the embedding rule for SHDM is just

$$
\begin{aligned}
\mathbf{y} &= \mathbf{x} + \left[Q_b\left(\|\mathbf{x}\| \right) - \|\mathbf{x}\| \right] \cdot \frac{\mathbf{x}}{\|\mathbf{x}\|} \\
&= Q_b\left(\|\mathbf{x}\| \right) \cdot \frac{\mathbf{x}}{\|\mathbf{x}\|},
\end{aligned}
\tag{28}
$$

which amounts to project $\mathbf{x}$ to the closest quantization sphere for the symbol b, with radius $Q_b(\|\mathbf{x}\|)$. The role of the evenly spaced quantization hyperplanes in STDM is played by quantization spheres nested with evenly spaced radii in SHDM. In both cases the quantization function $Q_b(\cdot)$ is given by the points of the scalar lattice $\sqrt{L}\, \Lambda_b$, with $\Lambda_b \triangleq 2\Delta\mathbb{Z} + b\Delta/2 + d$ and d a key-dependent offset. Notice that, for a fixed HWR, we can scale Λ_b by $\sqrt{L}$ thanks to the corresponding gain afforded by sphere hardening in one case and by the linear projection in the other. An additional detail is that in (28) we are neglecting the possibility that the quantized value be less that zero, as this is a highly unlikely event as L increases.

Using the normal approximation of $\|\mathbf{X}\|$ employed in Sect. 4.3, the computation of the embedding distortion proceeds exactly as the computation of the embedding distortion for STDM (QP) undertaken in [10]. As shown therein, for a fixed high HWR we may approximate $D_E \approx \Delta^2/3$ for any L.

In parallel to STDM, in SHDM the simplest minimum distance decoder acts by quantizing the received vector $\mathbf{v} = \mathbf{y} + \mathbf{z}$ to the closest sphere, that is

$$
\hat{b} = \underset{b \in \{-1, +1\}}{\arg\min} \ \left| Q_b\left(\|\mathbf{v}\| \right) - \|\mathbf{v}\| \right|.
\tag{29}
$$

We sketch next the performance analysis of this decoder when $\mathbf{Z} \sim \mathcal{N}(\mathbf{0}, \sigma_Z^2 I_L)$. A decoding error occurs when the noise displaces the vector $\mathbf{y}$ lying on a given quantization sphere corresponding to b to any of the wrong concentric decision regions limited by spheres corresponding to $-b$. If we assume that $\sigma_X \gg \sigma_Z$ then the quantization and decision spheres —which are likely to have radii close to σ_X due to sphere hardening— may be locally approximated by hyperplanes in relation to the noise sphere. Then, an upper bound to the probability of error is just the probability that AWGN applied on any arbitrary point of the quantization "hyperplane" traverses any of the two closest "hyperplanes" corresponding to the limits of the two closest wrong decision regions. As this amounts to viewing SHDM locally as STDM, then the performance has to be the same in the same conditions and then [10]

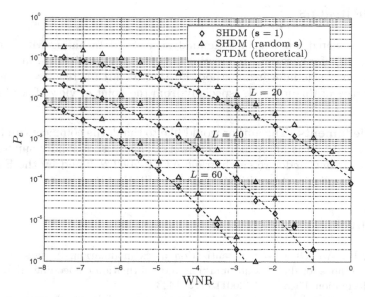

Fig. 3. Performance of SHDM in AWGN, HWR = 40 dB

$$P_e \approx 2\,Q\left(\frac{\sqrt{L}\Delta}{2\,\sigma_Z}\right) \tag{30}$$

for large L. The accuracy of this reasoning is confirmed by Fig. 3, where the empirical performance of SHDM is seen to be correctly predicted by the theoretical prediction (30) for STDM.

The question remains on how to secure SHDM when $\mathbf{s}$ is different than the all ones vector while retaining the same performance. Although it is possible to devise a method based on quantizing $\sqrt{|\mathbf{x}^T \mathrm{diag}(\mathbf{s})\mathbf{x}|}$ which boils down to (28) for $\mathbf{s} = \mathbf{1}$, this strategy poses embedding distortion control problems and exploits poorly sphere hardening. For this reason we do not pursue here this option.

As a suboptimal approach, it is possible to use the strategy (28) separately at each of the subvectors $\mathbf{x}^+$ and $\mathbf{x}^-$ defined at the end of Sect. 4.2. In this case the corresponding watermarked subvectors are obtained as $\mathbf{y}^\pm = \mathbf{x}^\pm Q_b(\|\mathbf{x}^\pm\|)/\|\mathbf{x}^\pm\|$. As in average we will have $N = L/2$ for a good pseudorandom sequence, we will need to scale the lattices by $\sqrt{L/2}$ instead of $\sqrt{L}$ in order to keep the same embedding distortion. Notice that this strategy amounts to quantizing the projection of the host signal onto a bidimensional space —instead of a scalar one—, using scalar DM with repetition rate $1/2$. This approach was explored in [10] under the name of generalized QP, and shown to be suboptimal in terms of decoding performance. In this scheme, decoding is also made by minimum Euclidean distance of the bidimensional vector with components $\|\mathbf{v}^+\|$ and $\|\mathbf{v}^-\|$ to the closest of the two bidimensional lattices given by the Cartesian product $\sqrt{L/2}\,\Lambda_b \times \sqrt{L/2}\,\Lambda_b$. The performance achieved with this scheme, using pseudorandomly generated $\mathbf{s}$ and decoding by minimum distance, can be observed in Fig. 3.

6 Conclusions

We have presented a new geometric analysis of SS data hiding with repetition coding which affords several interesting insights and predictions, and the proposal of a novel side-informed method. Further research is required to assess all the properties of this method, especially from the point of view of security.

Acknowledgments. The author would like to thank the comments and corrections provided by the anonymous reviewers. This work is kindly supported by Enterprise Ireland under research grant ATRP-2002/230 and by the European Commission under contract IST-2002-507609 SIMILAR.

References

1. Chen, B., Wornell, G.W.: Quantization index modulation: A class of provably good methods for digital watermarking and information embedding. IEEE Trans. on Information Theory **47** (2001) 1423–1443
2. Barni, M., Bartolini, F., Rosa, A.D.: Advantages and drawbacks of multiplicative spread spectrum watermarking. In: Procs. of the SPIE. Number 5020 in Security and Watermarking of Multimedia Contents V, San José, USA (2003) 290–299
3. Barni, M., Bartolini, F.: Watermarking Systems Engineering. Enabling Digital Assets Security and Other Applications. Signal Processing and Communications Series. Marcel Dekker (2004)
4. Barni, M., Bartolini, F., Rosa, A.D., Piva, A.: Optimum decoding and detection of multiplicative watermarks. IEEE Trans. on Signal Processing **51** (2003) 1118–1123
5. Balado, F.: Digital Image Data Hiding Using Side Information. PhD thesis, University of Vigo (2003)
6. Hamkins, J., Zeger, K.: Gaussian source coding with spherical codes. IEEE Trans. on Information Theory **48** (2002) 2980–2989
7. Conway, J., Sloane, N.: Sphere Packings, Lattices and Groups. 3rd edn. Volume 290 of Comprehensive Studies in Mathematics. Springer (1999)
8. Hamkins, J., Zeger, K.: Asymptotically dense spherical codes part I: Wrapped spherical codes. IEEE Trans. on Information Theory **43** (1997) 1774–1785
9. Abramowitz, M., Stegun, I.: Handbook of Mathematical Functions. Dover (1974)
10. Pérez-González, F., Balado, F., Hernández, J.R.: Performance analysis of existing and new methods for data hiding with known-host information in additive channels. IEEE Trans. on Signal Processing **51** (2003) 960–980 Special Issue "Signal Processing for Data Hiding in Digital Media & Secure Content Delivery".

Trellis-Coded Rational Dither Modulation
for Digital Watermarking

A. Abrardo[1], M. Barni[1], F. Pérez-González[2], and C. Mosquera[2]

[1] Department of Information Engineering, University of Siena, Italy
{abrardo, barni}@dii.unisi.it
[2] Department Teoría de la Señal y Comunicaciones, ETSI Telecom,
Universidad de Vigo, Spain
{fperez, mosquera}@tsc.uvigo.es

Abstract. Rational Dither Modulation has been proposed as an effective QIM watermarking algorithm which is robust against value-metric scaling. Invariance is obtained by quantizing a rational function of the host features instead of the features themselves. In this paper we propose a vector extension of the basic RDM scheme. Specifically, a sequence of feature ratios is quantized vectorially with the aid of a properly designed dirty trellis code. A fast sub-optimum embedding algorithm is proposed ensuring fast watermark insertion and good distortion properties. Preliminary results show that a significant advantage is obtained with respect to conventional RDM.

1 Introduction

Till its very introduction [1] QIM watermarking has proved to greatly outperform the older spread spectrum algorithms. At the same time, it has been immediately apparent that practical implementations of QIM, such as SCS or ST-DM [1,2], had a main drawback in their vulnerability against valuemetric scaling: it only needs that the features hosting the watermark are multiplied by an unknown gain factor ρ to compromise the possibility of correctly reading the watermark [3]. This is a serious problem, since in most cases multiplication by a constant gain does not damage the quality of the host document at all. On the contrary, sometimes this multiplication has a beneficial effect on the appearance of the watermarked data, as in the image case where multiplication by a factor $\rho > 1$ is often used to increase the image contrast.

Possible remedies include estimation of the gain factor at the decoder, possibly with the aid of a pilot signal [4], use of spherical (equi-energetic) codewords [5,6], or use of an image-dependent quantization step [7]. Recently an effective solution named RDM (Rational Dither Modulation) has been proposed, that achieves invariance to the gain attack, by quantizing a rational function of consecutive features instead of the features themselves [8,9]. In this way gain invariance is obtained at the expense of a minor modification of the classical DM scheme, leading to a very simple, yet effective algorithm. As a matter of fact, it

M. Barni et al. (Eds.): IWDW 2005, LNCS 3710, pp. 351–360, 2005.

can be shown that by properly designing the RDM algorithm the same performance of conventional DM can be achieved asymptotically. A similar approach, though with significant differences and in a different context is described in [10].

Though ensuring good performance, the RDM scheme as described in [8,9] can be improved in many ways, for instance by applying distortion compensation, or by introducing some form of channel coding to increase the robustness of the watermark. In this paper we focus on another aspect of RDM that needs improvement. In its basic form, in fact RDM is an essentially scalar algorithm, since each feature ratio is quantized by itself, by means of a scalar quantizer. Yet it is known that better results can be obtained by means of vector quantization. This is indeed the purpose of this paper: to replace the scalar quantizer of RDM with a, trellis-based, vector quantizer, whereby a set of consecutive ratios are quantized all together. As it is shown in section 5, preliminary simulations on i.i.d. gaussian features demonstrate that the new Trellis-Coded RDM (TC-RDM) scheme permits a gain of about 3.5 dB with respect to plain RDM in standard working conditions ($P_e \simeq 10^{-3}$).

The paper is organized as follows. In section 2 the basic notation used throughout the paper is introduced. In section 3 the classical RDM algorithm is revised. Section 4 describes the new TC-RDM algorithm. Some preliminary results are shown in section 5. Section 6 presents our conclusions.

2   Notation

In this section we introduce the basic notation used throughout the paper. We assume that the features hosting the watermark are arranged into a one-dimensional vector $\mathbf{X} = (x_1 \ldots x_{N_t})$ of length N_t. The to-be-hidden message is indicated by a binary vector $\mathbf{W}$ whose length is equal to N_w. The vector with the watermarked features is indicated by $\mathbf{Y}$, and the actual watermarking signal added to $\mathbf{X}$ by $\mathbf{S}_w$. Clearly $\mathbf{S}_w = \mathbf{Y} - \mathbf{X}$. We assume that the host feature samples are i.i.d. random variables drawn according to a pdf f_x, having zero mean and variance σ_x^2. Note that we will use the same symbol both to indicate a random variable and the specific values assumed by the variable, the exact meaning of each symbol being clearly identified by the context wherein the symbol is used.

We assume that the decoder works on a manipulated version of the watermarked feature vector. We indicate such a manipulated vector by $\mathbf{Z}$. In particular the manipulations addressed here include the multiplication of $\mathbf{Y}$ vector by a constant factor ρ unknown to the decoder (gain attack) and the addition of a white gaussian noise vector $\mathbf{N}$ (AWGN attack).

The evaluation of the performance of the system requires that some other definitions are given. The embedding distortion D_w is defined as the average value of the watermarking signal, that is $D_w = E[\|\mathbf{Y} - \mathbf{X}\|^2]/N$. In a similar way, the attack distortion is defined as $D_a = E[\|\mathbf{N}\|^2]/N$. Note that the presence of the gain factor ρ does not have any influence on D_a whose only goal is to measure the strength of the AWGN part of the attack. It is also useful to introduce the Document to Watermark Ratio, DWR $= \sigma_x^2/D_w$, the Watermark to Noise Ratio,

WNR $= D_w/D_a$ and the Document to Noise Ration, DNR $= \sigma_x^2/D_a$. These quantities are often given in decibels.

3   Rational Dither Modulation

In this section we briefly review the RDM algorithm. For a more detailed description readers are referred to [8,9].

Let $\mathbf{y}_k^h$ denote the vector with samples from y_k to y_h. For example, in the following we will often use the symbol $\mathbf{y}_{k-L}^{k-1} = (y_{k-L}, y_{k-L+1}, \ldots, y_{k-1})$. We consider the set $\mathcal{G}$ of functions $g : \mathcal{Y}^L \to \mathbb{R}$ having the property that for any $\rho > 0$, and any vector $\mathbf{y}$, $g(\rho\mathbf{y}) = \rho g(\mathbf{y})$. Given the k-th bit to be hidden w_k, embedding goes through the application of standard DM watermarking to the ratio $x_k/g(\mathbf{y}_{k-L}^{k-1})$, i.e.

$$y_k = g(\mathbf{y}_{k-L}^{k-1})Q_{w_k}\left(\frac{x_k}{g(\mathbf{y}_{k-L}^{k-1})}\right), \tag{1}$$

where the quantizer $Q()$ is chosen according to the particular bit to be embedded, hence justifying the subscript appearing in the equation. The decoder receives z_k and based on its previous knowledge about $\mathbf{z}_{k-L}^{k-1}$, decodes the hidden bit by applying the standard DM decoding procedure to the ratio between z_k and $g(\mathbf{z}_{k-L}^{k-1})$:

$$\hat{w}_k = \arg \min_{w_k \in \{-1,1\}} \left| \frac{z_k}{g(\mathbf{z}_{k-L}^{k-1})} - Q_{w_k}\left(\frac{z_k}{g(\mathbf{z}_{k-L}^{k-1})}\right) \right| \tag{2}$$

From the above equation, and the properties of the function g, it is immediate to see that RDM is intrinsically immune against the gain attack. Note also that RDM is very close to standard DM watermarking; in embedding, the only difference regards the division of x_k by $g(\mathbf{y}_{k-L}^{k-1})$ prior to quantization, while in decoding, due to the unavailability of $\mathbf{y}_{k-L}^{k-1}$ the divisor becomes $g(\mathbf{z}_{k-L}^{k-1})$. As to the choice of $g()$, the set $\mathcal{G}$ includes, but is not limited to, the l_p vector-norms, given by:

$$g(\mathbf{y}_{k-L}^{k-1}) = \left(\frac{1}{L}\sum_{i=1}^{L}|y_{k-i}|^p\right)^{1/p}. \tag{3}$$

For instance, in [8,9] the squared Euclidean norm is adopted, by letting $p = 2$ in equation (3). Previous works on RDM demonstrated the good performance of the system that approach that of conventional DM for $L \to \infty$. At the same time with respect to other gain invariant schemes such as SS and ISS [11,12], RDM has a great advantage in terms of capacity.

The main weakness of the basic RDM algorithm is its essentially scalar nature, in that the overall quantization codebook is nothing but a rectangular lattice. As we demonstrate in the following sections, better performance can be obtained by using a vector quantization approach.

4   Trellis-Coded RDM

In this section we give a detailed description of TC-RDM watermarking. We first outline the basic ideas behind it, then we pass to a formal description of the algorithm.

4.1   The Basic Idea

The main idea behind TC-RDM is to replace the scalar quantizers used by RDM with a set of vector quantizers built by relying on a dirty trellis mechanism similar to that described in [5,13]. Specifically, we first build a redundant trellis (dirty trellis) by associating several possible paths to each sequence of input bits. This is done by introducing the concept of free bits. In other words, the input of the trellis is composed by a set of informative bits taken from $\mathbf{W}$ and some free bits that can be used to choose the trellis path that results in the lowest embedding distortion. Note that the number of informative bits determines the number of bits conveyed by each host feature, whereas the number of free bits determines the, so to say, dirtiness of the trellis. The output of the trellis is a sequence of ratios $\mathbf{R} = (r_1, r_2 \ldots r_{N_t})$, that can be seen as the vector quantized version of the input ratios $x_k / g(\mathbf{y}_{k-L}^{k-1})$. The quantized ratios are used to build the sequence of watermarked features as in equation (1), i.e. $Q_{w_k}((x_k)/(g(\mathbf{y}_{k-L}^{k-1})))$ is replaced by r_k.

The decoder calculates the sequence of ratios $z_k / g(\mathbf{z}_{k-L}^{k-1})$ and uses it to feed the trellis. By running a standard Viterbi decoding algorithm the path on the trellis that is closest to the sequence of received ratios is selected, and the corresponding bit sequence is given as the output of the decoder.

As it can be readily seen, due to the properties of $g()$, the output of the decoder is invariant with respect to the gain factor ρ, hence ensuring immunity against the gain attack.

4.2   The Algorithm

To present the details of the TC-RDM algorithm we find it useful to describe the trellis as a Discrete-time Finite-state Markov process (DFM). Specifically, let us consider a DFM characterized by an input vector $\mathbf{b}$ of size M, a state λ and an output real vector $\mathbf{o} \in \mathbb{R}^P$, P being the output's dimension. Let $\mathcal{B}$ be the set of all possible inputs, i.e., $\mathbf{b} \in \mathcal{B}$, and $\mathcal{L}$ the set of all possible states, i.e., $\lambda \in \mathcal{L}$.

Let's define the DFM's transition at a generic time instant t as:

$$\lambda_{t+1} = \eta_f(\lambda_t, \mathbf{b}_t)$$
$$\mathbf{o}_t = \gamma(\lambda_t, \mathbf{b}_t) \tag{4}$$

where η_f is the forward state transition function, γ is the input-output function, λ_t and $\mathbf{b}_t$ are the state and the input at time instant t, respectively.

Accordingly, for a sequence of N inputs $\mathbf{B} = (\mathbf{b}_1, \mathbf{b}_1, \ldots, \mathbf{b}_N)$ and for a given initial state of the DFM, say it λ_0, the sequence of outputs $\mathbf{O} = (\mathbf{o}_1, \mathbf{o}_2, \ldots, \mathbf{o}_N)$ and of states $\boldsymbol{\Lambda} = (\lambda_1, \lambda_2, \ldots, \lambda_N)$ are computed as follows:

$$\mathbf{o}_t = \gamma(\lambda_t, \mathbf{b}_t)$$
$$\lambda_{t+1} = \eta_f(\lambda_t, \mathbf{b}_t) \tag{5}$$

Note that, for a given initial state λ_0, the output sequence $\mathbf{O}$ depends only on $\mathbf{B}$, i.e., we can write $\mathbf{O} = \mathbf{O}(\mathbf{B})$.

We also find it convenient to define the partial vectors from time t to $t + t_0$ as:

$$\mathbf{B}_t^{t+t_0} = (\mathbf{b}_t, \mathbf{b}_{t+1}, \ldots, \mathbf{b}_{t+t_0})$$
$$\mathbf{O}_t^{t+t_0} = (\mathbf{o}_t, \mathbf{o}_{t+1}, \ldots, \mathbf{o}_{t+t_0})$$
$$\boldsymbol{\Lambda}_t^{t+t_0} = (\lambda_t, \lambda_{t+1}, \ldots, \lambda_{t+t_0}).$$

We will consider in the following the case of binary inputs, i.e., the input vector at generic time instant t is given by $\mathbf{b}_t = (b_{t,1}, b_{t,2}, \ldots, b_{t,M})$, $b_{t,j}$ being the $j - th$ input bit at $t - th$ transition. Moreover, we assume that k out of M bits of $\mathbf{b}_t$ are the actual information bits to be hidden in the host features at time instant t, while the remaining $M - k$ are free bits. That is, the first k bits are taken (in a sequential fashion) from the message sequence $\mathbf{W}$, whereas the others are left free.

More formally, the message sequence $\mathbf{W}$ is split into $N_t/k = N$ chunks[1] $(\mathbf{w}_1 \ldots \mathbf{w}_N)$, with $\mathbf{w}_i = (w_{(i-1)k+1}, w_{(i-1)k+2} \cdots w_{(i-1)k+k})$, then the DFM input is composed as follows

$$\mathbf{b}_i = (\mathbf{w}_i, \mathbf{v}_i), \tag{6}$$

where $\mathbf{v}_i$ is the vector with the $M - k$ free bits. Hence, for each information sequence of kN bits, a set (bin) of $2^{(M-k)N}$ codewords is obtained.

As we said, the output of the trellis, formed by blocks of P values at a time, is interpreted as the sequence of ratios to be used in equation (1) instead of $Q_{w_k}(x_k/g(\mathbf{y}_{k-L}^{k-1}))$. Note that since for each block of k input bits the trellis produces P output values, and the dimensionality of $\mathbf{Y}$ must be equal to that of $\mathbf{R}$, it is necessary that the length of $\mathbf{W}$ is equal to $k \cdot N_t/P$. In formulas, we first let $\mathbf{R} = \mathbf{O}$, then we define the output of the TC-RDM embedder as

$$y_k = g(\mathbf{y}_{k-L}^{k-1}) \cdot r_k. \tag{7}$$

We must now define a strategy to choose the free bits the output sequence $\mathbf{O}$ depends on. To do so, we consider an MSE informed embedding approach, whereby the free bits are chosen so that the mean squared error between the watermarked sequence (that is a function of $\mathbf{R}$ via equation (7)) and the host features vector $\mathbf{X}$ is minimized.

To proceed, let us remember that $\mathbf{w}_t$ and $\mathbf{v}_t$ represent the vectors of informative and free bits at time instant t, respectively. We define the vector $\mathbf{V}$

---

[1] We neglect border effects for simplicity.

$(\mathbf{v}_1, \mathbf{v}_2, \ldots, \mathbf{v}_N)$. Note that, according to the above notations, we have $\mathbf{B} = (\mathbf{W}, \mathbf{V})$ and $\mathbf{R} = \mathbf{R}(\mathbf{W}, \mathbf{V})$.

The goal of the embedder is to find $\mathbf{V}$, and hence $\mathbf{R}(\mathbf{W}, \mathbf{V})$ so that the transmitted signal $\mathbf{Y}$ defined by means of (7) is as *close* as possible to the side information $\mathbf{X}$. Note that for sake of simplicity we omit the details regarding the initialization of the trellis.

By summarizing, for a given information vector $\mathbf{W}$, the MSE criterion for information embedding consists in evaluating the free bits vector $\mathbf{V} = \tilde{\mathbf{V}}$ as:

$$\tilde{\mathbf{V}} = \arg \min_{\mathbf{V}} \sum_{n=1}^{N_t} (x_n - y_n (\mathbf{W}, \mathbf{V}))^2 \tag{8}$$

In order to actually perform the above minimization, it is essential to note that, due to the feedback introduced in the computation of $\mathbf{Y}$ (see (7)), the term y_n depends on all the previous DFM's inputs, i.e., the memory is infinity. Thus, the only possibility to perform the minimization in (8) is by means of exhaustive search. This means that the embedder should consider the whole encoding tree, with a complexity which increases exponentially with N (and hence with N_t). Of course, this approach is not feasible and alternative sub-optimum strategies must be envisaged. In the next section we describe a trellis-based sub-optimum Viterbi approach with a fixed number of survivors.

4.3   Sub-optimum Embedding Strategy

To start with, let us observe that every path on the trellis results in a transmitted sequence $\mathbf{Y}(\mathbf{W}, \mathbf{V})$ defined by (7). Moreover, for each partial path $\mathbf{Y}_1^t$ it is possible to evaluate the partial path distance:

$$D^2 \left(\mathbf{X}_1^t, \mathbf{Y}_1^t\right) = \sum_{n=1}^{tP} (x_n - y_n)^2, \tag{9}$$

where the sum goes from 1 to tP since at each step t, the trellis outputs P ratio values. The proposed suboptimum approach works by evaluating the partial distance between the host feature sequence $\mathbf{X}_1^t$ and all the sequence $\mathbf{Y}_1^t$ deriving from the partial trellis paths $\mathbf{R}_1^t$, where the various paths differ because of a different choice of the free bits sequence $\mathbf{V}_1^t$. Of course the number of possible paths increases exponentially with t. To avoid such a complexity, each time two or more paths enter the same state the partial distances associated to them are evaluated and only the N_s paths with the smallest distances are retained. In this way the complexity of the algorithm is proportional to N_s, and increases only linearly with the length of the host feature sequence.

It is worth noting again that, though this way of operating closely resembles the classical Viterbi's algorithm [14], it does not lead to an optimum decoding strategy due to the infinite memory of the Trellis. In fact, for each transition the distance between $\mathbf{Y}_t^{t+1}$ and $\mathbf{X}_t^{t+1}$ depends also on the previous transitions due to the intrinsic memory of RDM. Nevertheless, it is expected that the higher the

N_s the closer the solution will be to the optimum one. Of course, if $N_s \to \infty$ the proposed algorithm coincides with the exhaustive approach, thus yielding the optimum MSE solution (with an exponentially high computational complexity). On the contrary, for $N_s = 1$ the proposed scheme works as the classical Viterbi algorithm with only one survivor per node.

5   Simulation Results

In order to verify the performance of the proposed embedding scheme we have carried out computer simulations for different values of N_s. In the proposed encoding scheme, only k input bits are actually encoded by means of a con-volutional encoder, while the remaining $M - k$ input bits yield 2^{M-k} parallel transitions. As to the encoder, we have considered Ungerboeck codes [14] with $M = 8$ and $k = 1$ (i.e., rate one Trellis Coded Modulations - TCM). The memory of the encoder has been set to $\nu = 5$, (i.e., we have considered a 16 states en-coder). Besides, we have generated i.i.d. Gaussian host features with variance σ_x^2 and we have set the minimum squared distance between constellation points of the Ungerboeck code to $d^2 = \frac{\sigma_x^2}{10}$. Finally, we have considered mono-dimensional codewords, i.e., we let $P = 1$.

In Figure 1 we plot the DWR of the watermarked host feature sequence versus the number of survivors N_s, for three different values of L, $L = 1$, $L = 5$, and $L = 10$. Note that for $L = 1$, increasing N_s allows to improve the embedder's performance, even if a floor is quickly achieved for $N_s \simeq 7$. For higher values

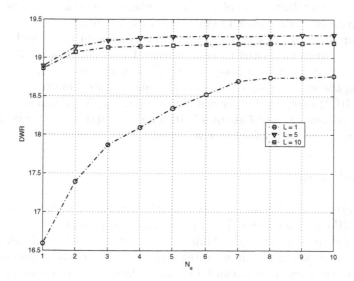

Fig. 1. DWR vs. number of survivors for various L's. As the number of survivor in-creases the suboptimum embedding algorithm tends to the optimum one, in that no further improvement of DWR is expected.

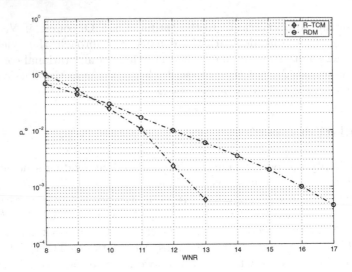

Fig. 2. Comparison between TC-RDM and conventional RDM. For low values of P_e the improvement brought by TC-RDM is evident. The plot has been obtained by embedding one bit for each sample of the host feature sequence, lower bit error rates are expected for lower embedding rates (channel coding).

of L, the floor is achieved even for lower N_s. This is due to the fact that, by increasing L, TC-RDM tends to behave as the classical TCM scheme (due to the lower fluctuations of $g(\cdot)$) where the optimum embedder is already achieved for $N_s = 1$. The lower fluctuation of $g(\cdot)$ also explains why, starting from a certain point, increasing L may result in (slightly) worse performance.

In order to get an insight into the performance gain that can be obtained by TC-RDM when compared to conventional RDM, in Figure 2 the bit error probability P_e is given as a function of WNR in the case of $L = 10$, and by considering the same rate-one Ungerboeck code described above (i.e., both TC-RDM and RDM carry one bit per host feature symbol). We found that TC-RDM allows a performance gain of about 3.5 dB for $P_e = 0.001$, while the performance gain becomes even higher for lower values of P_e.

6   Conclusions

We have presented a vector extension of the basic RDM algorithm for gain-invariant QIM watermarking. The vector extension is obtained by introducing the concept of free bits, i.e. a set of bits at the input of a trellis code which can be adjusted in such a way to minimize the embedding distortion. From a different perspective, the same results can be obtained by means of a redundant trellis (like the dirty trellis described in [5]) whereby several paths can be associated to the same input message. The redundant trellis is used to quantize a sequence of rational functions of the host feature sequence, chosen in the same way of the RDM scheme.

We have observed that, due to the memory introduced by RDM, optimum embedding would require an exhaustive search over all the possible paths on the trellis. This approach is clearly unfeasible, hence we introduced a sub-optimum embedding scheme that permits to approach the performance of the optimum scheme at a reduced computational cost.

We have proved the validity of the proposed approach by testing it on a sequence of i.i.d. normal features, obtaining a gain of about 3.5 dB with respect to the plain RDM algorithm.

Future works will include the introduction of distortion compensation and channel coding to further improve the robustness of the algorithm. The possibility of increasing the security of the system by randomizing the rational function RDM relies on will be investigated. Finally, the gap between theory and practice needs to be covered, by applying the TC-DRM concept to the watermarking of real data such as still images or audio.

References

1. Chen, B., Wornell, G.: Quantization index modulation: a class of provably good methods for digital watermarking and information embedding. IEEE Trans. on Information Theory **47** (2001) 1423–1443
2. Eggers, J.J., Bäuml, R., Tzschoppe, R., Girod, B.: Scalar Costa scheme for information embedding. IEEE Trans. on Signal Processing **4** (2003)
3. Bartolini, F., Barni, M., Piva, A.: Performance analysis of st-dm watermarking in presence of non-additive attacks. IEEE Trans. on Signal Processing **52** (2004) 2965–2974
4. Eggers, J.J., Bäuml, R., Girod, B.: Estimation of amplitude modifications before SCS watermark detection. In Wong, P.W., Delp, E.J., eds.: Security and Watermarking of Multimedia Contents IV, Proc. SPIE Vol. 4675, San Jose, CA (2002) 387–398
5. Miller, M.L., Doerr, G.J., Cox, I.J.: Applying informed coding and embedding to design a robust, high capacity, watermark. IEEE Trans. on Image Processing **13** (2004) 792–807
6. Abrardo, A., Barni, M.: Informed watermarking by means of orthogonal and pseudo-random dirty paper coding. IEEE Trans. on Signal Processing **53** (2005) 824–833
7. Oostven, J., Kalker, T., Staring, M.: Adaptive quantization watermarking. In Wong, P.W., Delp, E.J., eds.: Security, Steganography, and Watermarking of Multimedia Contents VI, Proc. SPIE Vol. 5306, San Jose, CA, USA (2004) 296–303
8. Perez-Gonzalez, F., Mosquera, C., Barni, M., Abrardo, A.: Rational dither modulation: a novel data-hiding method robust to value-metric scaling attacks. In: MMSP 2004, IEEE Workshop on Multimedia Signal Processing, Siena, Italy (2004)
9. Perez-Gonzalez, F., Mosquera, C., Barni, M., Abrardo, A.: Ensuring gain invariance in high-rate data-hiding. In Wong, P.W., Delp, E.J., eds.: Security, Steganography, and Watermarking of Multimedia Contents VII, Proc. SPIE Vol. 5681, San Jose, CA, USA (2005)
10. Liu, T., Venkatesan, R., Mihcak, M.K.: Scale-invariant image watermarking via optimization algorithms for quantizing randomized statistics. In: Proceedings of the ACM Multimedia and Security Workshop, Magdeburg, Germany (2004)

11. Cox, I.J., Kilian, J., Leighton, T., Shamoon, T.: Secure spread spectrum watermarking for multimedia. IEEE Trans. on Image Processing **6** (1997) 1673–1687
12. Malvar, H.S., Florencio, D.A.F.: Improved spread spectrum: a new modulation technique for robust watermarking. IEEE Trans. on Image Processing **51** (2003) 898–905
13. M. L. Miller, G. J. Doerr, I.J.C.: Dirty-paper trellis codes for watermarking. In: Proc. 9th IEEE Int. Conf. on Image Processing, ICIP'02. Volume II., Rochester, NY (2002) 129–132
14. Proakis, J.G.: Digital Communications, 2nd Edition. McGraw-Hill, New York (1989)

Closed-Form Formulas for Private Watermarking Capacities of Laplacian Sources with the Magnitude-Error Distortion Measure and Under Additive Attacks*

Wei Sun and En-hui Yang

Department of Electrical and Computer Engineering,
University of Waterloo, Waterloo, Ontario, Canada, N2L 3G1
{wsun, ehyang}@bbcr.uwaterloo.ca

Abstract. Calculation of watermarking capacities of private Laplacian watermarking systems with the magnitude-error distortion measure under fixed attacks is addressed. First, in the case of an additive Laplacian attack, a nice closed-form formula for the watermarking capacities is derived, which involves only the distortion level and the parameter of the Laplacian attack. Second, in the case of an arbitrary additive attack, a general, but slightly more complicated formula for the watermarking capacities is given. Finally, calculation of the joint compression and private watermarking rate region of Laplacian watermarking systems with an additive Laplacian attack is considered.

1 Introduction

As a technique to protect copyrights for digital content, digital watermarking has been recently one of the most active research fields in signal processing and information theory. A digital watermarking system embeds a watermark into the digital content to be protected, which can be used to identify the copyright owners. The performance of a watermarking system can be evaluated in terms of three parameters: **perceptual transparency**, **robustness** and **information rate**.

From an information-theoretic viewpoint, a few theoretical results about digital watermarking have been reported so far, for example, in [6,2,8] and references therein. The general methodology used is to model a watermarking system as a communication system with side information. A watermarking system is called **private** if the side information (i.e., the covertext) is available to both the transmitter and the receiver, and **public** if it is available only to the transmitter.

---

* This work was supported in part by the Natural Sciences and Engineering Research Council of Canada under Grants RGPIN203035-98 and RGPIN203035-02 and under Collaborative Research and Development Grant, by the Communications and Information Technology Ontario, by the Premier's Research Excellence Award, by the Canadian Foundation for Innovation, by the Ontario Distinguished Researcher Award, and by the Canada Research Chairs Program.

M. Barni et al. (Eds.): IWDW 2005, LNCS 3710, pp. 361–371, 2005.

Watermarking capacities defined as the maximum achievable information rates subject to perceptual transparency and robustness requirements are then determined for both private and public systems and often expressed as a maxmin optimization problem in the information-theoretic research of digital watermarking.

Characterizing watermarking capacities as a maxmin optimization problem, however, does not mean that watermarking capacities can be calculated easily. Indeed, a closed-form formula of watermarking capacities is often difficult to get by solving this optimization problem. So far, closed-form formulas for watermarking capacities are known only for independent and identically distributed (IID) binary covertexts and IID Gaussian covertexts [6,2]. On the other hand, in most applications, source data such as transformed coefficients of image signals can be more or less modeled as Laplacian sources. Therefore, it is important to investigate calculation of watermarking capacities of Laplacian watermarking systems.

Since watermarked signals are likely to be stored and/or transmitted in compressed format, instead of treating watermarking and compression separately, it is interesting and beneficial to look at the joint design of watermarking and compression system. Karakos and Papamarcou [7] and Maor and Merhav [5] studied the tradeoff between watermarking rate, compression rate and distortions for the discrete and Gaussian cases with and without attacks. Their results are extended to the case of abstract alphabets in [9]. Like the problem of determining closed-form formulas for Laplacian watermarking capacities, no description of joint compression and watermarking rate regions of Laplacian sources has been reported.

In this paper, calculation of watermarking capacities of private Laplacian watermarking systems with the magnitude-error distortion measure under fixed attacks is addressed. The setting of private Laplacian watermarking models and main results are given in Section 2, followed by proofs of the main results in Section 3 and Section 4. In Section 5, the description of the joint compression and private watermarking rate region for a Laplacian source with an additive Laplacian attack is discussed, and the last section is the conclusion of the paper.

2   Setting of Watermarking Models and Main Results

The model of private Laplacian watermarking studied in this paper is depicted in Figure 1. Let $S = \{S_i\}_{i=1}^{\infty}$ be an IID Laplacian source with a common Laplacian density function $p(s) = \frac{1}{2\alpha}e^{-|s|/\alpha}$, $\alpha > 0$. Let M, called a **watermark**, be a random variable uniformly distributed over the set $\{1, 2, ..., e^{nR}\}$, and $S^n = (S_1, S_2, ..., S_n) \in \mathbb{R}^n$, called a **covertext**, be a random vector generated by the source S. A watermarking encoder of length n with rate R maps (M, S^n) to $X^n = (X_1, X_2, ..., X_n) \in \mathbb{R}^n$, called a **stegotext**. An attacker uses an additive IID noise vector $V^n = (V_1, V_2, ..., V_n) \in \mathbb{R}^n$ generated by a real-valued random variable V to disturb the stegotext X^n and generates a forgery $Y^n \in \mathbb{R}^n$, that is, $Y^n = X^n + V^n$. Finally, a private watermarking decoder estimates a watermark $\hat{M}$ from Y^n with the help of S^n.

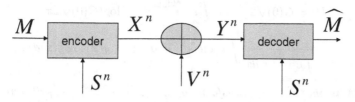

Fig. 1. Model of private Laplacian watermarking system

To satisfy the requirement of perceptual transparency, a distortion level D between the covertexts S^n and the stegotexts X^n is required, that is, $Ed(S^n, X^n) \leq D$, where the magnitude-error distortion measure is employed

$$d(s^n, x^n) = \frac{1}{n} \sum_{i=1}^{n} |x_i - s_i|.$$

A rate R is achievable with respect to a distortion level D if for any arbitrary small number $\epsilon > 0$, there exist a sequence of watermarking encoders and decoders of length n with rate R such that for sufficiently large n, $\Pr\{\hat{M} \neq M\} < \epsilon$ and $Ed(S^n, X^n) < D + \epsilon$. The **watermarking capacity** $C(D)$ of a private watermarking system is defined to be the maximum achievable embedding rate R with respect to the distortion level D.

It is well known [1,2,6,8] that for an IID source $\{S_i\}_{i=1}^{\infty}$ and a distortion level D with respect to a single-letter distortion measure d, the private watermarking capacity is given by

$$C(D) = \max_{Ed(S,X) \leq D} I(X; Y|S) \tag{1}$$

where $Y = X + V$, $I(X; Y|S)$ is the conditional mutual information between X and Y given S, and the maximization is taken over all random variables X such that $Ed(S, X) \leq D$.

Unless otherwise specified, in this paper all logarithms are with respect to base e and the upper and lower limits of all integrals are ∞ and $-\infty$, respectively. Now we are ready to give our main results.

Theorem 1. *Let V be a Laplacian random variable with the density function $g(x) = \frac{1}{2d} e^{-\frac{|x|}{d}}$, $d > 0$. Then, the private watermarking capacity $C(D)$ of an IID Laplacian watermarking system with respect to the distortion level D and under an additive Laplacian noise(ALN) V^n attack is given by*

$$C(D) = \log \left(1 + \frac{2d + D - \sqrt{D^2 + 4d^2}}{\sqrt{D^2 + 4d^2} - D} \right). \tag{2}$$

Theorem 2. *Let V be a real-valued random variable with the density function $g(x)$. Then, the private watermarking capacity $C(D)$ of an IID Laplacian watermarking system with respect to the distortion level D and under an additive noise(AN) V^n attack is given by*

$$C(D) = G(0)\sqrt{2\pi}\left[\log\int e^{-\frac{\lambda_0 l(x)}{\pi\sqrt{2\pi}}}dx - \log(G(0)\sqrt{2\pi})\right]$$

$$+\frac{\lambda_0 G(0)}{\pi\int e^{-\frac{\lambda_0 l(x)}{\pi\sqrt{2\pi}}}dx}\int l(x)e^{-\frac{\lambda_0 l(x)}{\pi\sqrt{2\pi}}}dx + \int g(x)\log g(x)dx,$$

where $G(t)$ is the Fourier transform of $g(x)$, $l(x) = \int\frac{e^{-ixt}}{t^2 G(t)}dt$ and $\lambda_0 < 0$ satisfies

$$\pi D\int e^{-\frac{\lambda_0 l(x)}{\pi\sqrt{2\pi}}}dx = -G(0)\int l(-x)e^{-\frac{\lambda_0 l(x)}{\pi\sqrt{2\pi}}}dx.$$

Particularly, if $g(x)$ is even, then the watermarking capacity is

$$C(D) = -\lambda_0 D + G(0)\sqrt{2\pi}\left[\log\int e^{-\frac{\lambda_0 l(x)}{\pi\sqrt{2\pi}}}dx - \log(G(0)\sqrt{2\pi})\right]$$

$$+\int g(x)\log g(x)dx.$$

Discussion:

- Under an additive Laplacian attack, the capacity given in Theorem 1 has a very nice closed formula, which is independent of the parameter α of the Laplacian source, and determined only by the distortion level D and the parameter d of the Laplacian attack random variable.
- Actually, the watermarking capacity $C(D)$ in (2) can be simplified to be $C(D) = \log\frac{D+\sqrt{D^2+4d^2}}{2d}$. Thus, $C(D) \simeq \log\frac{D}{d}$ if $D \gg d$, and $C(D) \simeq 0$ if $D \ll d$.
- For the Laplacian attack random variable V with parameter d, the variance is $\sigma^2 = 2d^2$. So, $C(D) = \log\frac{D+\sqrt{D^2+2\sigma^2}}{\sqrt{2}\sigma}$.
- It is well known that the watermarking capacity of a Gaussian watermarking system with the mean square distortion measure and under a fixed Gaussian attack with variance σ^2 is $C_G(D) = \log\frac{\sqrt{D+\sigma^2}}{\sigma}$. Therefore,
  - if $\sigma^2 \gg D$, the watermarking capacity of a Laplacian system under an additive Laplacian attack with variance σ^2 is almost equal to that of a Gaussian system under an additive Gaussian attack with the variance σ^2;
  - If $\sigma^2 \ll D$, the watermarking capacity of a Laplacian system under an additive Laplacian attack with variance σ^2 is larger than that of a Gaussian system under an additive Gaussian attack with the variance σ^2 and the difference is $\log(2D)/2$.
- For $D < 0.5$, solving $\frac{D+\sqrt{D^2+2\sigma^2}}{\sqrt{2}\sigma} = \frac{\sqrt{D+\sigma^2}}{\sigma}$ yields $\sigma^2 = 1/2 - D$. So,
  - if $\sigma^2 < 1/2 - D$, then the capacity of a Laplacian system under a Laplacian attack with variance σ^2 is bigger than that of a Gaussian system under a Gauusian attack with variance σ^2;
  - if $\sigma^2 > 1/2 - D$, then the capacity of a Laplacian system under a Laplacian attack with variance σ^2 is smaller than that of a Gaussian system under a Gauusian attack with variance σ^2.

– To determine a closed form of watermarking capacity with an arbitrary additive noise attack, one only needs to solve an equation to get the parameter λ_0.

3   Watermarking Capacities Under Additive Laplacian Noise Attacks

Let V be a real random variable with density function $g(x)$ and independent of all other random variables. Then, from (1), the private watermarking capacity under the additive attack V^n is

$$
\begin{aligned}
C(D) &= \max_{X:E|S-X|\leq D} I(X;Y|S) \\
&= \max_{X:E|S-X|\leq D} [H(Y|S) - H(Y|X,S)] \\
&= \max_{X:E|S-X|\leq D} [H(X+V|S) - H(V)] \\
&= \max_{T:E|T|\leq D} H(T+V|S) - H(V) \\
&= \max_{T:E|T|\leq D} H(T+V) - H(V) \quad\quad (3) \\
&= \max_{T:E|T|=D} H(T+V) - H(V). \quad\quad (4)
\end{aligned}
$$

Now we will compute $\max_{E|T|=D} H(T+V)$ using the method of Lagrange multipliers. Let $f(\cdot)$ be the density function of a real-valued random variable T, and define a functional for $\mu, \lambda < 0$ and $f(\cdot)$

$$
\begin{aligned}
\Delta(f(\cdot), \lambda, \mu) &= \int_{x'} \left(\int_{t'} f(t')g(x'-t')dt' \right) \log \left(\int_{t'} f(t')g(x'-t')dt' \right) dx' \\
&\quad - \lambda \left(\int_{x'} |x'| f(x')dx' - D \right) - \mu \left(\int_{x'} f(x')dx' - 1 \right).
\end{aligned}
$$

Then

$$
\begin{aligned}
\frac{\partial \Delta}{\partial f(x)} &= \int_{x'} g(x'-x) \log \int_{t'} f(t')g(x'-t')dt' dx' + \int_{x'} g(x'-x)dx' - \lambda|x| - \mu \\
&= \int_{x'} g(x'-x) \log h(x')dx' - \lambda|x| - \mu + 1
\end{aligned}
$$

where

$$
h(x) = \int_{t'} f(t')g(x-t')dt'.
$$

Let $\frac{\partial \Delta}{\partial f(x)} = 0$. Then for any $x \in \mathbb{R}$

$$
\int_{x'} g(x'-x) \log h(x')dx' = \lambda|x| + \mu - 1. \quad\quad (5)
$$

Let $G(t)$ and $H(t)$ be Fourier transforms of $g(x)$ and $\log h(x)$, respectively. Then, by the Fourier Convolution Theorem and (5), we have

$$\int_t G(t)H(t)e^{-ixt}dt = \int_{x'} g(x'-x)\log h(x')dx'$$

$$= \lambda|x| + \mu - 1, \forall x. \tag{6}$$

By solving the integral equation (6), one has

$$G(t)H(t) = \frac{1}{2\pi}\int_{-\infty}^{\infty}(\lambda|x| + \mu - 1)e^{ixt}dx$$

$$= -\frac{\lambda}{t^2\pi} + (\mu - 1)Dirac(t), \tag{7}$$

where $Dirac(\cdot)$ is the unit impulse function. Note (7) holds for any additive attack V.

In the following of this section, we assume V is a Laplacian random variable with density function $g(x) = \frac{1}{2d}e^{-\frac{|x|}{d}}$, then the Fourier transform of $g(x)$ is

$$G(t) = \frac{1}{\sqrt{2\pi}}\int_{-\infty}^{\infty}g(x)e^{ixt}dx$$

$$= \frac{1}{\sqrt{2\pi}(1 + t^2d^2)}.$$

Thus, from (7) we have

$$H(t) = \sqrt{2\pi}(1 + t^2d^2)\left[-\frac{\lambda}{t^2\pi} + (\mu - 1)Dirac(t)\right],$$

and appling the inverse Fourier transform to $H(t)$, it is not hard to obtain

$$\log h(x) = \pi(2\lambda x Heaviside(x) + \mu - 1 - 2d^2\lambda Dirac(x) - \lambda x),$$

where $Heaviside(x)$ is the unit step function.

By the definition of $h(x)$ and the Fourier Convolution Theorem, we get

$$h(x) = \int_{-\infty}^{\infty}G(t)F(t)e^{-ixt}dt$$

$$= e^{\pi(2\lambda x Heaviside(x) + \mu - 1 - 2d^2\lambda Dirac(x) - \lambda x)}, \tag{8}$$

where $F(t)$ is the Fourier Transform of $f(x)$. Solving the integral equation (8),

$$G(t)F(t) = \frac{1}{2\pi}\int_{-\infty}^{\infty}h(x)e^{ixt}dx = -\frac{\lambda}{t^2 + \pi^2\lambda^2}e^{\pi(\mu-1)},$$

so

$$F(t) = -\frac{\lambda}{t^2 + \pi^2\lambda^2}\sqrt{2\pi}(1 + t^2d^2)e^{\pi(\mu-1)}.$$

Using the inverse Fourier transform, we obtain

$$f(x) = -\lambda e^{\pi(\mu-1)} \int_{-\infty}^{\infty} \frac{1+t^2 d^2}{t^2 + \pi^2 \lambda^2} e^{-ixt} dt$$

$$= -e^{\pi(\mu-1)}[e^{-\lambda\pi x}(\pi^2\lambda^2 d^2 - 1)Heaviside(-x)$$
$$+ e^{\lambda\pi x}(\pi^2\lambda^2 d^2 - 1)Heaviside(x) \qquad (9)$$
$$+ 2\pi\lambda d^2 Dirac(x)].$$

Since the density function $f(x)$ must satisfy the constraints $\int_x f(x)dx = 1$ and $\int_x |x| f(x)dx = D$, that is,

$$\begin{cases} -\frac{2}{\pi\lambda} e^{\pi(\mu-1)} = 1 \\ -\frac{2(d^2\lambda^2\pi^2-1)}{\pi^2\lambda^2} e^{\pi(\mu-1)} = D \end{cases}$$

one has

$$\begin{cases} \lambda = \frac{D-\sqrt{D^2+4d^2}}{2\pi d^2}, \\ \mu = 1 + \frac{1}{\pi} \log \frac{\sqrt{D^2+4d^2}-D}{4d^2}. \end{cases} \qquad (10)$$

Now we get the optimal real-valued random variable T with the density function $f(x)$ in (9) with (λ, μ) of (10). For this optimal $f(x)$, it is not hard to obtain the entropy of $T + V$

$$H(T + V) = 1 - \log \frac{\sqrt{D^2 + 4d^2} - D}{4d^2}.$$

Therefore, by (3) and $H(V) = 1 + \log(2d)$,

$$C(D) = 1 - \log \frac{\sqrt{D^2 + 4d^2} - D}{4d^2} - H(V)$$

$$= -\log \frac{\sqrt{D^2 + 4d^2} - D}{4d^2} - \log(2d)$$

$$= \log \left(1 + \frac{2d + D - \sqrt{D^2 + 4d^2}}{\sqrt{D^2 + 4d^2} - D} \right).$$

The proof of Theorem 1 is completed.

4 Watermarking Capacities Under Additive Noise Attacks

In this section, we assume the additive noise V^n is generated IID by a real-valued random variable V with density function $g(x)$. Then, from (7), we get

$$H(t) = \frac{\mu - 1}{G(t)} Dirac(t) - \frac{\lambda}{\pi t^2 G(t)},$$

where $G(t)$ is the Fourier transform of $g(x)$.

Since $H(t)$ is the Fourier transform of $\log h(x)$, then by the inverse Fourier transform,

$$\log h(x) = \frac{1}{\sqrt{2\pi}} \int H(t) e^{-ixt} dt$$

$$= \frac{\mu - 1}{\sqrt{2\pi}} \int \frac{Dirac(t)}{G(t)} e^{-ixt} dt - \frac{\lambda}{\pi\sqrt{2\pi}} \int \frac{e^{-ixt}}{t^2 G(t)} dt$$

$$= \frac{\mu - 1}{\sqrt{2\pi} G(0)} - \frac{\lambda}{\sqrt{2\pi}\pi} l(x),$$

where

$$l(x) = \int \frac{e^{-ixt}}{t^2 G(t)} dt. \tag{11}$$

Let $F(t)$ be the Fourier transform of $f(x)$. Then

$$F(t) = \frac{1}{2\pi G(t)} \int h(x) e^{ixt} dx$$

$$= \frac{1}{2\pi G(t)} e^{\frac{\mu - 1}{\sqrt{2\pi} G(0)}} \int e^{-\frac{\lambda}{\sqrt{2\pi}\pi} l(x) + ixt} dx$$

by the Fourier Convolution Theorem. Applying the inverse Fourier transform to $F(t)$ yields

$$f(x) = \frac{e^{\frac{\mu - 1}{\sqrt{2\pi} G(0)}}}{2\pi\sqrt{2\pi}} \int\int \frac{1}{G(t)} e^{-\frac{\lambda l(x_1)}{\pi\sqrt{2\pi}} + ix_1 t - ixt} dx_1 dt. \tag{12}$$

Since $\int f(x) dx = 1$ and $\int |x| f(x) dx = D$, that is,

$$\int f(x) dx = \frac{e^{\frac{\mu - 1}{\sqrt{2\pi} G(0)}}}{2\pi\sqrt{2\pi}} \int\int \left(\int e^{-ixt} dx \right) \frac{1}{G(t)} e^{-\frac{\lambda l(x_1)}{\pi\sqrt{2\pi}} + ix_1 t} dx_1 dt$$

$$= \frac{e^{\frac{\mu - 1}{\sqrt{2\pi} G(0)}}}{2\pi\sqrt{2\pi}} \int\int 2\pi Dirac(t) \frac{1}{G(t)} e^{-\frac{\lambda l(x_1)}{\pi\sqrt{2\pi}} + ix_1 t} dx_1 dt$$

$$= \frac{e^{\frac{\mu - 1}{\sqrt{2\pi} G(0)}}}{\sqrt{2\pi} G(0)} \int e^{-\frac{\lambda}{\pi\sqrt{2\pi}} l(x)} dx = 1$$

and

$$\int |x| f(x) dx = \frac{e^{\frac{\mu - 1}{\sqrt{2\pi} G(0)}}}{2\pi\sqrt{2\pi}} \int\int \left(\int |x| e^{-ixt} dx \right) \frac{1}{G(t)} e^{-\frac{\lambda l(x_1)}{\pi\sqrt{2\pi}} + ix_1 t} dx_1 dt$$

$$= \frac{e^{\frac{\mu - 1}{\sqrt{2\pi} G(0)}}}{2\pi\sqrt{2\pi}} \int\int \left(\frac{-2}{t^2} \right) \frac{1}{G(t)} e^{-\frac{\lambda l(x_1)}{\pi\sqrt{2\pi}} + ix_1 t} dx_1 dt$$

$$= -\frac{e^{\frac{\mu - 1}{\sqrt{2\pi} G(0)}}}{\sqrt{2\pi}\pi} \int l(-x) e^{-\frac{\lambda}{\pi\sqrt{2\pi}} l(x)} dx = D,$$

we obtain

$$\begin{cases} \lambda = \lambda_0 \\ \mu = 1 + \sqrt{2\pi}G(0)\left[\log(G(0)\sqrt{2\pi}) - \log \int e^{-\frac{\lambda_0 l(x)}{\pi\sqrt{2\pi}}} dx\right], \end{cases} \tag{13}$$

where $\lambda_0 < 0$ satisfies

$$\pi D \int e^{-\frac{\lambda_0 l(x)}{\pi\sqrt{2\pi}}} dx = -G(0) \int l(-x) e^{-\frac{\lambda_0 l(x)}{\pi\sqrt{2\pi}}} dx. \tag{14}$$

For this optimal random variable T with the density function $f(x)$ determined by (12), (13) and (14), we can calculate the entropy

$$H(T+V) = G(0)\sqrt{2\pi}\left[\log \int e^{-\frac{\lambda_0 l(x)}{\pi\sqrt{2\pi}}} dx - \log(G(0)\sqrt{2\pi})\right]$$

$$+ \frac{\lambda_0 G(0)}{\pi \int e^{-\frac{\lambda_0 l(x)}{\pi\sqrt{2\pi}}} dx} \int l(x) e^{-\frac{\lambda_0 l(x)}{\pi\sqrt{2\pi}}} dx. \tag{15}$$

In particular, if $g(x)$ is even, then $G(t)$ is even, so $l(x)$ is. Thus, by (14),

$$\int l(x) e^{-\frac{\lambda_0 l(x)}{\pi\sqrt{2\pi}}} dx = \int l(-x) e^{-\frac{\lambda_0 l(x)}{\pi\sqrt{2\pi}}} dx$$

$$= -\frac{D\pi}{G(0)} \int e^{-\frac{\lambda_0 l(x)}{\pi\sqrt{2\pi}}} dx,$$

and the last term in (15) is simplified to be $-\lambda_0 D$. In view of (3), the proof of Theorem 2 is finished.

5 Joint Compression and Watermarking Rate Regions for Private Laplacian Watermarking Systems Under ALN Attacks

Since watermarked signals are likely to be stored and transmitted in compressed format, instead of treating watermarking and compression separately, it is interesting and beneficial to look at the joint design of watermarking and compression system. So, in this section joint compression and watermarking rate regions for private Laplacian watermarking systems under ALN attacks are considered. For details on general joint watermarking and compression systems refer to [5,7,9] and references therein.

For a given watermarking rate R_W and a distortion level D with respect to a distortion measure d, let $R_C(R_W, D)$ denote the minimum compression rate of an IID covertext source of a joint compression and private watermarking system under a fixed attack. It is proved in [5,7,9] that

$$R_C(R_W, D) = R_W + \min_{Ed(S,X)\leq D, R_W \leq I(X;Y|S)} I(S;X). \tag{16}$$

For the IID Laplacian source with the density function $p(s) = \frac{1}{2\alpha}e^{-\frac{|s|}{\alpha}}$, $\alpha > 0$, it is well known that its rate-distortion function

$$R(D) = \begin{cases} \log\frac{\alpha}{D}, & D < \alpha \\ 0, & \text{otherwise,} \end{cases}$$

and the forward test channel is the additive Laplacian noise $f(x|s) = \frac{1}{2D}e^{-\frac{|x-s|}{D}}$. Now assume V^n is generated IID by an additive Laplacian random variable V with the density function $f(v) = \frac{1}{2d}e^{-\frac{|v|}{d}}$. Then, for the forward test channel $f(x|s)$, it is not hard to obtain the entropy of $X + V$ conditioned by S,

$$H(X+V|S) = \log(2D + 2d) + \frac{D^2}{D^2 - d^2}h(D/d) - \frac{d^2}{D^2 - d^2}h(d/D),$$

where $h(\theta) \overset{def}{=} \int_0^1 \frac{x-x^\theta}{x-x^\theta/\theta}dx$. Therefore,

$$\begin{aligned} R_W(0) &\overset{def}{=} I(X+V; X|S) = H(X+V|S) - H(V) \\ &= \log(1 + \frac{D}{d}) + \frac{D^2}{D^2 - d^2}h(D/d) - \frac{d^2}{D^2 - d^2}h(d/D) - 1. \quad (17) \end{aligned}$$

Thus, for a given distortion level D, R_C increases linearly with R_W in the range $0 \le R_W \le R_W(0)$ by (16), that is, $R_C = R_W + R(D)$, and R_C is a increasing convex curve in the range $R_W(0) \le R_W \le R_W(1)$, here $R_W(1)$ is the watermarking capacity $C(D)$ given in (2). The joint compression and watermarking rate region is designated in Figure 2, where $R_C(0) = R_W(0) + \log(\alpha/D)$ and $R_C(1) = I(S; S + T)$, T is the random variable with the density function $f(x)$ in (9) with (λ, μ) of (10).

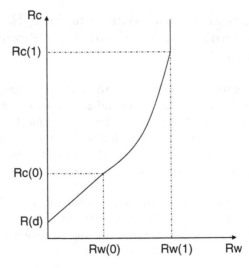

Fig. 2. Watermarking-compression rate region

6   Conclusion

Calculation of watermarking capacities of private Laplacian watermarking systems with the magnitude-error distortion measure under fixed attacks is addressed. First, in the case of an additive Laplacian attack, a nice closed-form formula for the capacities is derived, which involves only the distortion level and the parameter of the Laplacian attack. Second, in the case of an arbitrary additive attack, a general, but slightly more complicated formula for the capacities is given. Finally, calculation of the joint compression and private watermarking rate region of Laplacian watermarking systems with an additive Laplacian attack is considered.

Acknowledgement

The authors are grateful to referees' comments and insights.

References

1. B. Chen and G. W. Wornell, "Quantization index modulation: A class of provably good methods for digital watermarking and information embedding," *IEEE Trans. Inform. Theory*, vol. 47, pp. 1423-1443, May 2001.
2. A. S. Cohen and Amos Lapidoth, "The Gaussian Watermarking Game," *IEEE Trans. Inform. Theory*, vol. 48, pp. 1639-1667, June 2002.
3. T. M. Cover and J. A. Thomas, *Elements of Information Theory*, New York: John Wiley & Sons, 1991.
4. I. Cox, M. Miller and J. Bloom, *Digital Watermarking*, Elsevier Science: Morgan Kaufmann Publishers, 2001.
5. A. Maor and N. Merhav, "On joint information embedding and lossy compression", *Proceedings of International Symposium on Information Theory*, 27 June-2 July 2004 Pages:194.
6. P. Moulin and J. A. O'Sullivan, "Information-theoretic analysis of information hiding," *IEEE Trans. Inform. Theory*, vol. 49, pp. 563–593, March 2003.
7. D. Karakos and A. Papamarcou, "A Relationship Between Quantization and Watermarking Rates in the Presence of Additive Gaussian Attacks", *IEEE Trans. Inform. Theory*, vol. 49, pp. 1970–1982, Augst 2003.
8. A. Somekh-Baruch and N. Merhav, "On the error exponent and capacity games of private watermarking systems," *IEEE Trans. Inform. Theory*, vol. 49, pp. 537-562, March 2003.
9. En-hui Yang and Wei Sun, "On Watermarking and Compression Rates of Joint Compression and Private Watermarking Systems with Abstract Alphabets", *Proceedings of Canadian Workshop on Information Theory*, 5 June-8 June 2005, Montreal, Canada.

Improved QIM Strategies
for Gaussian Watermarking*

Pierre Moulin and Ying Wang

University of Illinois, Beckman Inst., Coord. Sci. Lab & ECE Dept.,
405 N. Mathews Ave., Urbana, IL 61801
moulin@ifp.uiuc.edu

Abstract. This paper revisits the problem of watermarking a Gaussian host, where the embedder and attacker are subject to mean-squared distortion constraints. The worst (nonadditive) attack and unconstrained capacity have been identified in previous work. Here we constrain the encoding function to lie in a given family of encoding functions — such as spread-spectrum or fixed-dimensional Quantization Index Modulation (QIM), with or without time-sharing, with or without external dithering. This gives rise to the notion of constrained capacity. Several such families are considered in this paper, and the one that is best under the worst attack is identified for each admissible value of the watermark-to-noise ratio (WNR) and the noise-to-host ratio (NHR). With suitable improvements, even scalar QIM can outperform any (improved) spread-spectrum scheme, for any value of WNR and NHR. The remaining gap to unconstrained capacity can be bridged using higher-dimensional lattice QIM.

1 Introduction

Quantization-index modulation (QIM) methods, introduced by Chen and Wornell [1], possess attractive practical and theoretical properties for watermarking. On the practical side, they are easy to implement when scalar quantizers or some low-dimensional lattice quantizers are used. On the theoretical side, the *dithered* version of QIM (using an external, uniformly distributed dither vector shared by encoder and decoder) studied by Eggers *et al* [2] and by Erez and Zamir [3,4,5] is mathematically more tractable than the original (nondithered) QIM. It follows from Erez and Zamir's work [4,5] that there exist capacity-approaching lattice QIM coding and decoding schemes for data hiding under additive white Gaussian noise (AWGN) attacks, under some mild technical conditions on the host (*aka* interference) signal statistics. A remarkable byproduct of Erez and Zamir's analysis is that lattice QIM decoding causes no capacity loss vis-a-vis optimal maximum-likelihood (ML) decoding. In other words, the lattice QIM decoder is not penalized (in terms of achievable rates) by not knowing, or ignoring, host signal statistics.

---

* This work was supported by NSF under grant CCR 03-25924.

M. Barni et al. (Eds.): IWDW 2005, LNCS 3710, pp. 372–386, 2005.

Recent research in watermarking [6,7,8] has however raised the concern that for "weak host signals", dithered scalar QIM performs somewhat poorly. In particular, [7] showed that dithered scalar QIM can be outperformed by spread-spectrum modulation (SSM) [9] methods in this scenario, and [8] studied possible improvements. The results in [6,7,8] were however restricted to the case of AWGN attacks. This is a rather restrictive assumption because if the host signal is weak, compression-type attacks are much more effective than additive-noise attacks. More precise formulations of this statement appear in [10,11,12].

This motivated us to revisit the data-hiding game under squared-error distortion constraints studied in [12] (and applied to image watermarking in [13,14]), in which the host signal is Gaussian, and all distortions are measured in an expected sense, *with respect to the host*. In this setup, the worst attack (in the sense of achieving unconstrained capacity) is the *Gaussian test channel* from rate-distortion theory [15], and the AWGN attack may be severely suboptimal. We then ask what is the performance of lattice QIM schemes of arbitrary dimensions, and whether substantial improvements are possible:

- either by exploiting the host signal statistics in the design of the QIM decoder,
- or by using an improved version of the QIM encoder,
- or both.

These lattice QIM schemes are compared with spread-spectrum schemes using linear precancellation of the host signal [16,17,18].

In addition to the standard QIM and SSM, several new or uncommon acronyms are used in this paper. They are summarized in Table 1 for convenience.

Table 1. List of acronyms used in this paper

Acronym	Full name	Equation
WNR	watermark to noise ratio	(7)
NHR	noise to host ratio	(8)
WNR$_{\text{eff}}$	effective WNR	(17)
aSSM	attenuated SSM	(19)
ISS	improved SSM [18]	Sec. 4
aQIM	attenuated QIM	(28)

2   Background: Mutual-Information Game

This section reviews some results from [11,12]. We use uppercase letters for random variables, lowercase for their individual realizations, and boldface for vectors. The symbol $\mathbb{E}$ denotes mathematical expectation. The symbol $f(x) \sim g(x)$ as $x \to x_0$ denotes asymptotic equality: $\lim_{x \to x_0} \frac{f(x)}{g(x)} = 1$.

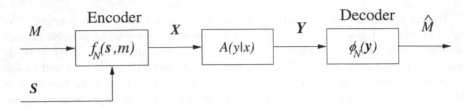

Fig. 1. The blind watermark communication problem

2.1 Mathematical Model

Let $d(x, y) = (x-y)^2$ be the squared-error distortion measure. Referring to Fig. 1, a message m is drawn uniformly from a message set $\mathcal{M}$ and embedded in a length-N host sequence $\mathbf{s} = (s_1, \cdots, s_N)$ using an encoding function $\mathbf{x} = f_N(\mathbf{s}, m)$. The following average-distortion constraint is imposed on f_N:

$$\mathbb{E}\|\mathbf{X} - \mathbf{S}\|^2 = \frac{1}{|\mathcal{M}|} \sum_{m \in \mathcal{M}} \int_{\mathbb{R}^N} \|f_N(\mathbf{s}, m) - \mathbf{s}\|^2 p(\mathbf{s}) d\mathbf{s} \leq ND_1.$$

A *memoryless attack channel, subject to distortion* D_2, is a conditional probability density function (pdf) $A(y|x)$, $x, y \in \mathbb{R}$, subject to distortion constraints. The length-N extension of this channel is defined as $A^N(\mathbf{y}|\mathbf{x}) = \prod_{i=1}^{N} A(y_i|x_i)$. The attack channel is subject to an average-distortion constraint:

$$\mathbb{E}\|\mathbf{Y} - \mathbf{S}\|^2 = \frac{1}{|\mathcal{M}|} \sum_{m \in \mathcal{M}} \int_{\mathbb{R}^N} \int_{\mathbb{R}^N} \|\mathbf{y} - \mathbf{s}\|^2 A^N(\mathbf{y}|f_N(\mathbf{s}, m)) \, p(\mathbf{s}) \, d\mathbf{s} \, d\mathbf{y} \leq ND_2,$$

$$(1)$$

i.e., distortion is measured with respect to the host.

We require $D_2 \geq D_1$, so that the feasible set of attack channels includes $\mathbf{Y} = \mathbf{X}$ (no attack). The distortions for the information hider and the attacker are equal in this special case.

2.2 Watermarking Capacity

Watermarking capacity is defined as the supremum of all achievable transmission rates, where the supremum is taken over all encoding functions subject to distortion D_1. This capacity is the value of a mutual-information game between the information hider and the attacker [11]. First, the information hider designs a *covert channel* $Q(x, u|s)$, where U is an auxiliary real-valued random variable. The covert channel satisfies the distortion constraint

$$\int \int \int (x - s)^2 Q(x, u|s) p(s) \, dx \, ds \, du \leq D_1.$$

$$(2)$$

Next, the attacker designs an attack channel $A(y|x)$ that satisfies the distortion constraint

$$\int \int \int \int (y - s)^2 A(y|x) Q(x, u|s) p(s) \, ds \, dx \, du \, dy \leq D_2.$$

$$(3)$$

Let $\mathcal{A}(Q, D_2)$ and $\mathcal{Q}(D_1)$ be the set of channels that satisfy the constraints (3), and (2), respectively. The dependency of $\mathcal{A}(Q, D_2)$ on Q is via the marginal $p(x|s)$. The capacity is given by [11][1]

$$C = \sup_{Q(x,u|s)\in\mathcal{Q}(D_1)} \min_{A(y|x)\in\mathcal{A}(Q,D_2)} J(Q, A) \tag{4}$$

where

$$J(Q, A) = I(U;Y) - I(U;S). \tag{5}$$

2.3 Gaussian Channels

When the host S is Gaussian, the optimal covert channel admits an elegant closed-form solution: X is the output of a Gaussian test channel with distortion D_1, whose input is S. The optimal attack is the Gaussian test channel with distortion level $D_2 - D_1$. The solution is stated in Theorem 1 below, and the capacity-achieving marginal pdf of (S, X, Y) is depicted in Fig. 2. All capacity expressions in this paper are given in terms of the function

$$C_{AWGN}(SNR) = \frac{1}{2}\log(1 + SNR) \tag{6}$$

which is Shannon's capacity formula for the AWGN channel with signal-to-noise ratio equal to SNR. Moreover, all capacity expressions depend on σ_s^2, D_1 and D_2 only via the *watermark-to-noise ratio*

$$\mathrm{WNR} \triangleq \frac{D_1}{D_2} \leq 1 \tag{7}$$

(where the inequality follows from our discussion below (1)), and the *noise-to-host ratio*

$$\mathrm{NHR} \triangleq \frac{D_2}{\sigma_s^2}. \tag{8}$$

Assuming that $D_2 > 0$, the case $\mathrm{NHR} = 0$ corresponds to the limiting case of a Gaussian host pdf with unbounded variance.

Theorem 1. *[12] Assume blind watermarking of a Gaussian host $S \sim \mathcal{N}(0, \sigma_s^2)$.*
(i) *If $\mathrm{NHR} \geq 1$, the optimal attack channel is given by $Y = 0$, and capacity is $C = 0$.*
(ii) *If $\mathrm{NHR} < 1$, capacity is given by*

$$C(\mathrm{WNR}, \mathrm{NHR}) = C_{AWGN}\left(\frac{\mathrm{WNR}(1 - \mathrm{NHR})}{1 - \mathrm{WNR}}\right). \tag{9}$$

The optimal attack channel $A(y|x)$ is the Gaussian test channel:

$$Y = \frac{1}{\beta}(X + W), \tag{10}$$

---

[1] This theorem was stated in [12] under the assumption that the decoder knows the attack channel A, however this restriction is now known to be unnecessary.

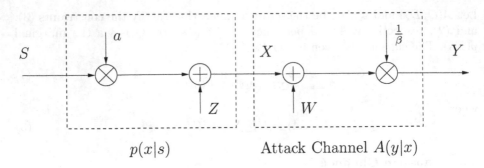

Fig. 2. Minmax-optimal $p(x|s)$ and $A(y|x)$ for i.i.d. Gaussian host data $S \sim \mathcal{N}(0, \sigma_s^2)$ under type-S distortion constraints. Both $p(x|s)$ and $A(y|x)$ are Gaussian test channels.

where $W \sim \mathcal{N}(0, \sigma_w^2)$ is independent of X,

$$\sigma_w^2 = D_2(1 - \text{WNR}) \frac{1 - \text{WNR} * \text{NHR}}{1 - \text{NHR}}, \tag{11}$$

and

$$\beta = \frac{\sigma_x^2}{\sigma_x^2 - (D_2 - D_1)} = \frac{1 - \text{WNR} * \text{NHR}}{1 - \text{NHR}}. \tag{12}$$

The optimal covert channel $Q(x, u|s)$ is given by

$$X = aS + Z \tag{13}$$
$$U = \alpha S + Z \tag{14}$$

where $Z \sim \mathcal{N}(0, \sigma_z^2)$ is independent of S,

$$\sigma_z^2 = aD_1, \quad a = 1 - \text{WNR} * \text{NHR}, \quad \alpha = \frac{\sigma_z^2}{\sigma_z^2 + \sigma_w^2}. \tag{15}$$

Remark 1. For small distortions ($\text{NHR} \to 0$), we have $a, \beta \to 1$ and $C \sim C_{AWGN}(\frac{\text{WNR}}{1-\text{WNR}})$. The AWGN attack is asymptotically optimal as $\text{NHR} \to 0$.

Remark 2. For fixed WNR, the capacity expression (9) is zero for $\text{NHR} \geq 1$ and strictly decreasing in NHR for $0 \leq \text{NHR} \leq 1$. Informally speaking, capacity is zero if the host is too weak; and capacity increases with the randomness of S ($\text{NHR} \to 0$). Based on the discussion above, the range of nontrivial values for (WNR, NHR) is given by

$$0 \leq \text{NHR} \leq 1, \quad 0 \leq \text{WNR} \leq 1. \tag{16}$$

Remark 3. We may write (9) as $C(\text{WNR}, \text{NHR}) = C_{AWGN}(\text{WNR}_{\text{eff}})$ where

$$\text{WNR}_{\text{eff}} = \frac{\sigma_z^2}{\sigma_w^2} = \frac{\text{WNR}(1 - \text{NHR})}{1 - \text{WNR}}. \tag{17}$$

Therefore $C(\text{WNR}, \text{NHR})$ is the capacity of an AWGN channel with input power σ_z^2 and noise power σ_w^2. The formula can be interpreted by referring to Fig. 2 and recalling Costa's result [21]. The known interference aS does not reduce capacity, and neither, of course, does the known constant β.

Remark 4. In (17), WNR_{eff} is a convex, increasing function of WNR. Observe that $\text{WNR}_{\text{eff}} = 0$ for $\text{WNR} = 0$; $\text{WNR}_{\text{eff}} = \text{WNR}$ for $\text{WNR} = \text{NHR}$; and $\text{WNR}_{\text{eff}} = \infty$ for $\text{WNR} = 1$.

Remark 5. The optimal attack when $a = 1$ is the minimum-mean-squared-error (MMSE) estimator of S given X cascaded with a Gaussian test channel. The MMSE operation helps the attacker in reducing the distortion with respect to S, making it possible for the noise source W to have larger variance.

Remark 6. For the optimal choice $a = 1 - \text{WNR} * \text{NHR}$, the MMSE estimator of S given X is X itself. Obviously this choice of a makes the MMSE operation least useful for the attacker.

3   Spread-Spectrum Modulation

Additive SSM is a linear modulation technique, commonly formulated as

$$\mathbf{X} = \mathbf{S} + \mathbf{Z}_m \tag{18}$$

where the vector $\mathbf{Z}_m$ is indexed by the message m to be sent. For weak hosts, a simple but effective enhancement is to attenuate the host prior to embedding [16,17]:

$$\mathbf{X} = a\mathbf{S} + \mathbf{Z}_m \tag{19}$$

where $0 \leq a \leq 1$ is the attenuation factor. This technique was later called *distortion-compensated SSM* [7]. However, since the attenuation mechanism is fundamentally different from the distortion-compensation mechanism used in QIM, we shall simply refer to (19) as *aSSM*.

Remarkably, optimization of the attenuation factor a against the worst attack in class $\mathcal{A}(Q, D_2)$ results in the same solution as in Fig. 2, hence in the same optimal values of a, σ_z^2, σ_w^2, and β. This follows from [17], where, like here, the cost function is effective SNR at the receiver.

For aSSM, the effective noise power is $a^2\sigma_s^2 + \sigma_w^2$, and the effective signal power is σ_z^2. This results in an effective signal-to-noise ratio

$$\begin{aligned}\text{WNR}_{aSSM} &= \frac{\sigma_z^2}{a^2\sigma_s^2 + \sigma_w^2} \\ &= \frac{\text{WNR} * \text{NHR}(1 - \text{NHR})}{1 + (\text{NHR}^2 - 2*\text{NHR})\text{WNR}} \\ &\leq \text{WNR}_{\text{eff}}\end{aligned} \tag{20}$$

(where equality holds only in the trivial cases $NHR = 1$ and $WNR = 0$), and the capacity function

$$C_{AWGN}(\text{WNR}_{aSSM}) < C_{AWGN}(\text{WNR}_{\text{eff}}) = C(\text{WNR}, \text{NHR}). \qquad (21)$$

As expected from such a simple linear modulation scheme, aSSM is not capacity-achieving. Conventional SSM is even worse. However, note from (20) and (17) that $\text{WNR}_{aSSM} \sim \text{WNR}_{\text{eff}}$ as NHR $\to 1$. Therefore we may conclude from (21) that aSSM is asymptotically capacity-achieving as NHR $\to 1$ for all values of WNR $\in [0,1)$. Another way to look at this property follows from (11) and (15): we have

$$\frac{\sigma_w^2}{a^2 \sigma_s^2} \sim \frac{1}{1 - \text{NHR}} \to \infty \quad \text{as NHR} \to 1.$$

That is, the attacker's noise W dominates the host signal aS, and the communication model becomes equivalent to the standard AWGN model without side information at the encoder.

4   Improved Spread Spectrum

One may ask whether further improvements on aSSM are possible using Malvar and Florêncio's Improved Spread Spectrum (ISS) method [18], in which different attenuation factors and watermark powers are allocated to different host signal components (different subliminal channels). The fundamental potential advantage of ISS over aSSM resides in the ability to keep the subliminal channels unknown to the attacker; otherwise an analysis similar to that in [12] shows that there is nothing to be gained by such strategy.

A mathematically tractable version of ISS would be the following. Host signal samples $S_1, \cdots, S_N$ are divided into K (secret) groups with size $N_k = \lfloor r_k N \rfloor$, where $1 \leq k \leq K$ and $\sum_{k=1}^{K} r_k = 1$. For each group a different attenuation factor a_k and watermark power $\sigma_{z,k}^2$ is used, resulting in a per-sample embedding distortion of $D_{1k} = (a_k - 1)^2 \sigma_s^2 + \sigma_{z,k}^2$. Define the random variables $\overline{Z}$ and $\overline{X}$ taking values Z_k and X_k respectively, with probability r_k for $1 \leq k \leq K$. The time-average embedding distortion is $D_1 = \sum_{k=1}^{K} r_k D_{1,k}$, and the variance of $\overline{X}$ (also equal to the time-averaged variance of X) is $\sigma_{\overline{x}}^2 = \sum_k r_k \sigma_{x,k}^2$. Similarly, $\overline{Z}$ has variance $\sigma_{\overline{z}}^2 = \sum_k r_k \sigma_{z,k}^2$; moreover, $\overline{Z}$ and S are independent. We assume that the attacker knows the joint statistics of $(S, \overline{X})$ but not the subliminal channels and implements a *memoryless* Gaussian channel $Y = (\overline{X} + W)/\beta$ subject to the distortion constraint D_2; W is independent of $\overline{X}$. We may not assume that the second-order statistics of $(S, \overline{X})$ and $(\overline{X}, Y)$ are those of Gaussian test channels.

The capacity function for ISS may be written as

$$C_{ISS}(\text{WNR}, \text{NHR}) = \max_{\sigma_{\overline{x}}^2} \min_{\sigma_w^2} \tilde{C}_{ISS}(D_1, \sigma_{\overline{x}}^2, \sigma_w^2) \qquad (22)$$

where

$$\tilde{C}_{ISS}(D_1, \sigma_x^2, \sigma_w^2) = \max_{\mathbf{r}, \{a_k, \sigma_{z,k}^2\}} \sum_{k=1}^{K} r_k C_{AWGN}\left(\frac{\sigma_{z,k}^2}{a_k{}^2 \sigma_s^2 + \sigma_w^2}\right). \qquad (23)$$

The maximization is subject to the constraints

$$\sum_{k=1}^{K} r_k[(a_k - 1)^2 \sigma_s^2 + \sigma_{z,k}^2] = D_1, \quad \sum_{k=1}^{K} r_k[a_k^2 \sigma_s^2 + \sigma_{z,k}^2] = \sigma_x^2.$$

The maximization over $\mathbf{r}$ takes place over the probability simplex. Therefore $\tilde{C}_{ISS}(D_1, \sigma_x^2, \sigma_w^2)$ is the upper convex envelope (with respect to D_1) of the function

$$\tilde{C}(D_1, \sigma_x^2, \sigma_w^2) = \max_{a, \sigma_z^2} C_{AWGN}\left(\frac{\sigma_z^2}{a^2 \sigma_s^2 + \sigma_w^2}\right), \quad 0 \le D_1 \le \sigma_s^2, \qquad (24)$$

where the maximization is subject to the constraints

$$(a - 1)^2 \sigma_s^2 + \sigma_z^2 = D_1, \quad a^2 \sigma_s^2 + \sigma_z^2 = \sigma_x^2.$$

Therefore the feasible set for (a, σ_z^2) is a singleton. After some simple algebra, we can establish that the function $\tilde{C}(D_1, \sigma_x^2, \sigma_w^2)$ is convex in D_1 for all $D_1 \ge D_1^* = \sigma_x^2 + \sigma_s^2 - 2\sigma_s \sigma_w$ but *concave otherwise*. Hence its upper convex envelope is

$$\tilde{C}_{ISS}(D_1, \sigma_x^2, \sigma_w^2) = \begin{cases} D_1 \frac{\tilde{C}(D_1^*, \sigma_x^2, \sigma_w^2)}{D_1^*} & : D_1 < D_1^* \\ \tilde{C}(D_1, \sigma_x^2, \sigma_w^2) & : \text{else.} \end{cases} \qquad (25)$$

At most two subliminal channels are needed to achieve ISS capacity. Observe the following special cases:

- $\frac{\sigma_w}{\sigma_s} \ge \frac{\sigma_x^2 + \sigma_w^2}{2\sigma_s^2}$: in this case, $D_1^* \le 0$, and $\tilde{C}_{ISS}(D_1, \sigma_x^2, \sigma_w^2) = \tilde{C}(D_1, \sigma_x^2, \sigma_w^2)$. This corresponds to the case of high NHR, with WNR not too close to 1.
- $\frac{\sigma_w}{\sigma_s} \le \frac{\sigma_x^2}{2\sigma_s^2}$: in this case, $D_1^* \ge \sigma_s^2$, and $\tilde{C}_{ISS}(D_1, \sigma_x^2, \sigma_w^2) > \tilde{C}(D_1, \sigma_x^2, \sigma_w^2)$ is in the straight-line regime. This corresponds to the case of low NHR.

On the other hand, the capacity function for aSSM is given by

$$C_{AWGN}(\text{WNR}_{aSSM}) = \max_{\sigma_x^2} \min_{\sigma_w^2} \tilde{C}(D_1, \sigma_x^2, \sigma_w^2). \qquad (26)$$

Due to (22) and (25), the aSSM capacity cannnot exceed $C_{ISS}(\text{WNR}, \text{NHR})$. Equality is achieved at high NHR, provided WNR is not too close to 1. A potential advantage of ISS over aSSM[2] appears at low NHR, as illustrated by the numerical results in Fig. 3. Plots are given for a low value of NHR and for a large value of NHR.[3]

---

[2] Also note that ISS presents dramatic advantages over aSSM in terms of error probability for zero-rate watermarking [20].

[3] Some of the values of (NHR, WNR) used in Fig. 3 are likely to be unrealistic in a practical application. We use them to illustrate the limiting performance of the various schemes considered.

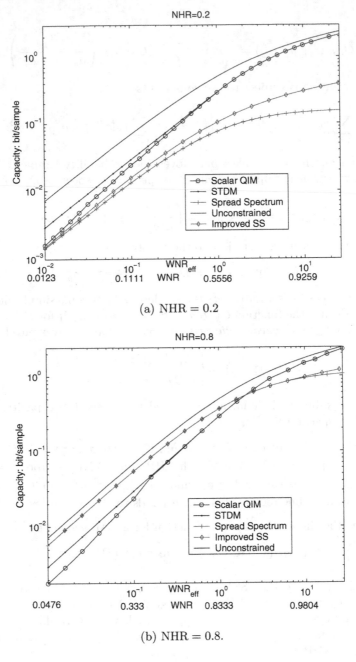

(a) NHR = 0.2

(b) NHR = 0.8.

Fig. 3. Capacity curves: C is plotted on a log scale as a function of $WNR_{eff} \geq 0$ (corresponding values of WNR $\in [0, 1]$ are indicated underneath)

5   Dithered Lattice QIM

Let

Λ = lattice in Euclidean space $\mathbb{R}^L$;

Q = quantization function mapping each point $\mathbf{x} \in \mathbb{R}^L$ to the nearest lattice point in Λ;

$\mathcal{V} = \{\mathbf{x} \in \mathbb{R}^L : Q(\mathbf{x}) = 0\}$ = Voronoi cell of Λ.

Let M be an integer, and $R = \frac{1}{L}\log_2 M$. Consider the problem of embedding a message $m \in \{0, 1, \cdots, M - 1\}$. A rate-$R$ lattice QIM embedding scheme is defined by a set of vectors $\{\mathbf{z}_m, 0 \le m < M\}$, a lattice inflation parameter $0 \le \alpha \le 1$ (aka Costa parameter), and the embedding function

$$\mathbf{x} = Q(\alpha\mathbf{s} + \mathbf{z}_m - \mathbf{d}) + (1 - \alpha)\mathbf{s} - \mathbf{z}_m + \mathbf{d}. \tag{27}$$

The vector $\mathbf{d}$ in (27) is an external dither vector that is randomized uniformly over $\mathcal{V}$ and independent of $\mathbf{s}$ and m, and is known to the decoder. Such randomization achieves two purposes: (1) it facilitates the proof of capacity theorems [4] and error exponent analyses [?,?], and (2) it provides a certain level of security against attackers that are not limited to additive-noise attacks. In the remainder of this section, we assume that $\mathbf{d}$ satisfies the statistical model above. This makes the *self-noise* due to quantization uniformly distributed over the scaled Voronoi cell $(1 - \alpha)\mathcal{V}$ and independent of $\mathbf{s}$ and m.

A natural idea in our problem with nonadditive attacks is to apply lattice QIM to the attenuated signal aS, resulting in the embedding formula

$$\mathbf{x} = Q(\alpha a\mathbf{s} + \mathbf{z}_m - \mathbf{d}) + (1 - \alpha)a\mathbf{s} - \mathbf{z}_m + \mathbf{d}. \tag{28}$$

Analogously to aSSM in (19), this scheme could be termed *aQIM*. The maximum achievable rate for L-dimensional aQIM is given by

$$\tilde{C}_L(\text{WNR}) = C_L(\text{WNR}_{\text{eff}})$$

where

$$C_L(\text{WNR}_{\text{eff}}) \triangleq \max_{0 \le \alpha \le 1} \max_{\Lambda} \max_{p_{\mathbf{Z}}} I(\mathbf{Z}; \tilde{\mathbf{Y}}) \tag{29}$$

is the capacity function for the Erez-Zamir scheme. In (29), $p_{\mathbf{Z}}$ is a pdf over the Voronoi cell $\mathcal{V}$ of Λ, and

$$\tilde{\mathbf{Y}} = \alpha\beta\mathbf{Y} \bmod \Lambda = \alpha\beta\mathbf{Y} - Q(\alpha\beta\mathbf{Y}) \tag{30}$$

is the output of the lattice-reduction step at the decoder. The capacity formula (29) *can be* obtained by analyzing the MAN *vector channel* of Fig. 4.[4] The noise $\mathbf{V}$ in this channel is the sum (mod Λ) of the self-noise and the scaled attacker's noise, $\alpha\mathbf{W} \sim \mathcal{N}(0, \alpha^2\sigma_w^2 I_L)$.

From Remark 3 in Sec. 2, we immediately obtain the following result.

---

[4] The method of proof used by Erez and Zamir [4] is somewhat different.

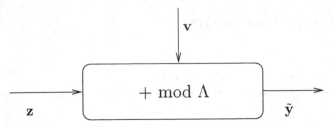

Fig. 4. Modulo Additive Noise (MAN) channel for lattice QIM

Proposition 1. *The aQIM scheme (28) achieves the unconstrained capacity bound (9), in the limit as the lattice dimension L tends to infinity.*

The capacity-achieving p_Z in (29) is uniform over $\mathcal{V}$ [4]. The sequence $C_L(\text{WNR}_{\text{eff}})$ is nondecreasing in L and converges to the unconstrained capacity limit $C_{AWGN}(\text{WNR}_{\text{eff}})$ as $L \to \infty$. It is remarkable that the lattice-reduction step (30), which is information-lossy, does not cause a loss of capacity. Therefore any substantial improvement to QIM would have to be restricted to low-dimensional QIM.

Consider the two extreme values of NHR in (16), and fix WNR.

- For NHR $= 0$ we have $\text{WNR}_{aSSM} = 0$; hence scalar QIM outperforms SSM.
- As NHR $\to 1$, we have $\text{WNR}_{aSSM} \sim \text{WNR}_{\text{eff}}$; both tend to zero.

Fig. 3 compares capacity functions for scalar QIM in (28) and aSSM in (19) to the unconstrained capacity formula (9). These plots illustrate the superiority of scalar QIM over aSSM for low NHR, but also the high performance of aSSM for large NHR. We reemphasize that the advantage of aSSM over scalar QIM in this case is due to the low dimensionality of the lattice QIM scheme used.

6 Time-Shared Lattice QIM

The scalar QIM capacity function $C_1(\text{WNR}_{\text{eff}})$ is nonconvex. Therefore time-sharing can be used to improve capacity performance [5,19]. In a time-shared scheme, transmission takes place during a fraction τ of the time; the transmission power during that time is boosted by a factor of $\frac{1}{\tau}$. The effect of time-sharing is to convexify the capacity function $C_1(\text{WNR}_{\text{eff}})$. The resulting (improved) capacity function is given by[5]

$$
\begin{aligned}
\tilde{C}_{STDM}(\text{WNR}) &= C_{STDM}(\text{WNR}_{\text{eff}}) \\
&= \begin{cases} \text{WNR}_{\text{eff}} \, \frac{C_1(\text{WNR}^*)}{\text{WNR}^*} & : \ 0 \le \text{WNR}_{\text{eff}} < \text{WNR}^* \\ C_1(\text{WNR}_{\text{eff}}) & : \ \text{WNR}_{\text{eff}} \ge \text{WNR}^* \end{cases}
\end{aligned} \tag{31}
$$

---

[5] Recall our assumption that the attacker does not know the subliminal channels and sticks to the memoryless attack of Theorem 1.

i.e., improvements are obtained at all $\mathrm{WNR}_{\mathrm{eff}}$ below a critical value $\mathrm{WNR}^* \approx 1$; the corresponding critical value of WNR is obtained from (17) as $\frac{\mathrm{WNR}^*}{\mathrm{WNR}^*+1-\mathrm{NHR}}$. We also have $C_1(\mathrm{WNR}^*) \approx 0.3$ bits ≈ 0.2 nats. The straight-line portion of the curve (31) is obtained by varying τ from 0 to 1. Time-shared scalar QIM was introduced by Chen and Wornell under the name Spread Transform Dither Modulation (STDM) [1] and further studied by Eggers *et al* [2].

Due to (17), the capacity expression (31), viewed as a function of WNR and measured in nats, has slope at the origin equal to $(1 - \mathrm{NHR}) \frac{C_1(\mathrm{WNR}^*)}{\mathrm{WNR}^*}$. The slope of the spread-spectrum capacity function (21) at $\mathrm{WNR} = 0$ is equal to

$$\left. \frac{d(\mathrm{WNR}_{aSSM})}{d(\mathrm{WNR})} \right|_{\mathrm{WNR}=0} = \frac{1}{2}\mathrm{NHR}\,(1 - \mathrm{NHR}).$$

Therefore a necessary condition for time-shared scalar QIM to outperform SSM *at all* WNR's is

$$\frac{C_1(\mathrm{WNR}^*)}{\mathrm{WNR}^*} \geq \frac{1}{2}\mathrm{NHR}. \tag{32}$$

i.e., $\mathrm{NHR} \leq 0.4$. If the condition above is violated, then aSSM outperforms time-shared scalar QIM at low WNR's, as illustrated in Fig. 3.

This derivation carries to the higher-dimensional case. Lattice QIM can be improved at low WNR's using time-sharing, but WNR^* tends to 0 as $L \to \infty$[6]; therefore $\lim_{L\to\infty} \frac{C_L(\mathrm{WNR}^*)}{\mathrm{WNR}^*} = \frac{1}{2}$. Moreover, equation (32) holds with C_L in place of C_1, and thus in the limit as $L \to \infty$, lattice QIM outperforms SSM *at all* NHR and WNR, in agreement with our earlier analysis.

7   Nondithered Lattice QIM

For scalar QIM subject to AWGN attacks, numerical experiments by Pérez-Freire and Pérez-González [7,8] have revealed possible improvements in communication performance if no external dither is used in (27).[7]

Here we comment upon this interesting result from an analytical perspective. The mutual information $I(\mathbf{Z}; \tilde{\mathbf{Y}})$ for lattice QIM can be written as

$$I(\mathbf{Z}; \tilde{\mathbf{Y}}) = \int_{\mathcal{V}} p_{\mathbf{D}}(\mathbf{d})I(\mathbf{Z}; \tilde{\mathbf{Y}}|\mathbf{D} = \mathbf{d})d\mathbf{d}$$

$$\leq \max_{\mathbf{d}\in\mathcal{V}} I(\mathbf{Z}; \tilde{\mathbf{Y}}|\mathbf{D} = \mathbf{d})$$

$$= \max_{\mathbf{d}\in\mathcal{V}} I(\mathbf{Z} - \mathbf{d}; \tilde{\mathbf{Y}}|\mathbf{D} = 0) \tag{33}$$

---

[6] By convexity of the limiting capacity function $C_{AWGN}(\mathrm{WNR}_{\mathrm{eff}})$.

[7] Additionally, Pérez-Freire and Pérez-González [7,8] discovered that additional improvements – albeit minor ones – are obtained if the lattice-reduction step (30) is omitted at the decoder. The existence of an improvement follows from the data-processing inequality [15]: $I(\mathbf{Z}; \tilde{\mathbf{Y}}) \leq I(\mathbf{Z}; \mathbf{Y})$. As discussed in the Introduction, the improvement vanishes for higher-order QIM, as $L \to \infty$.

where the last line follows from the definition (27) of the dithered QIM scheme. In the Erez-Zamir scheme, $p_{\mathbf{D}}$ is chosen to be uniform over $\mathcal{V}$; as we know, this choice is asymptotically optimal as $L \to \infty$. It is however clear that if one uses $p_{\mathbf{D}}$ as an additional variable to be optimized, one will do at least as well as the Erez-Zamir scheme. Specifically, the upper bound in (33) is achieved by a mass distribution $p_{\mathbf{D}}$ located at some $\mathbf{d}^* \in \mathcal{V}$. Optimizing the left side of (33) over $p_{\mathbf{Z}}$, we obtain

$$\max_{p_{\mathbf{Z}}, p_{\mathbf{D}}} I(\mathbf{Z}; \tilde{\mathbf{Y}}) = \max_{p_{\mathbf{Z}}} \max_{\mathbf{d} \in \mathcal{V}} I(\mathbf{Z} - \mathbf{d}; \tilde{\mathbf{Y}} | \mathbf{D} = 0)$$
$$= \max_{p_{\mathbf{Z}}} I(\mathbf{Z}; \tilde{\mathbf{Y}} | \mathbf{D} = 0),$$

i.e., the cost function is maximized when no external dither is used! Note that the maximizing $p_{\mathbf{Z}}$ above is not necessarily uniform over $\mathcal{V}$ (as was the case in the Erez-Zamir scheme). For any L, α, and Λ, the nondithered design improves over the Erez-Zamir design with uniform dither; however, as mentioned above, the performance gap vanishes for large L.

For small L, the performance gap may be substantial. Indeed Erez and Zamir showed that at high $\mathrm{WNR}_{\mathrm{eff}}$, the gap to capacity for their scheme is equal to the shaping gain of lattice VQ (about 1.53 dB in the scalar case, $L = 1$). In the case NHR $\to 1$, aSSM is capacity-achieving and therefore outperforms (by about 1.53 dB when $L = 1$) dithered L-dimensional QIM.[8] The following proposition shows that nondithered aQIM does *much better*.

Proposition 2. *The capacity function of aSSM cannot exceed that of nondithered aQIM for any value of* NHR, WNR, *and* L.

Sketch of the proof: To prove the claim, it suffices to consider the scalar QIM case $(L = 1)$ and identify a particular value of the lattice inflation parameter α and of the quantizer step size Δ, as well as a pdf p_Z, such that nondithered QIM and aSSM have the same capacity performance. Let $\Delta \to \infty$ and choose $\alpha = 0$ and $p_Z = \mathcal{N}(0, \sigma_z^2)$. Then $Q(a\alpha S + Z) = 0$ with probability tending to 1, and (28) becomes $X = aS - Z$ (with probability one), i.e., coincides almost surely with aSSM. The actual proof is based on the continuity of mutual information with respect to variational norm.   □

From the proposition above, one could numerically optimize α, Δ and p_Z to devise a scalar QIM scheme that outperforms both the aSSM and dithered aQIM schemes. We have not attempted such costly optimization, simply noting that time-sharing between aSSM and aQIM (with time-sharing parameter determined by the values of WNR and NHR) achieves the convex hull of the aSSM and aQIM capacity curves, which may be good enough for practical purposes. Similarly to the proposition above, we also have

Proposition 3. *The capacity function of ISS cannot exceed that of nondithered STDM for any value of* NHR *and* WNR.

---

[8] Some care is needed about the order in which asymptotics are taken. To have both NHR $\to 1$ and $\mathrm{WNR}_{\mathrm{eff}} \to \infty$, we need that $1 - \mathrm{WNR} \ll 1 - \mathrm{NHR}$.

8 Discussion

We have considered Gaussian host signals and studied the effects of NHR $\in [0, 1]$ on the capacity function of constrained watermark embedding schemes, allowing nonadditive attacks with bounded squared distortion. For unconstrained schemes the worst attack is known to be the Gaussian test channel. When NHR $\to 0$ (host signal whose variance tends to infinity), additive attacks are optimal. For NHR $= 1$, the compression attack $Y = 0$ is feasible, and capacity is zero. We have introduced the aQIM scheme, which is a simple variation on the Erez-Zamir scheme [4], and compared its performance with that of the aSSM linear modulation scheme [16,17]. Our results are summarized as follows.

1. Prop. 1: At all NHR's, L-dimensional aQIM with uniform dither and lattice reduction at the decoder is asymptotically capacity-achieving, as $L \to \infty$.
2. In the extreme case NHR $\to 1$, host-signal interference is weak, and attacker's noise dominates at the decoder. aSSM is asymptotically capacity-achieving and outperforms *low-dimensional* aQIM schemes with uniform dither.
3. For any finite choice of L, the aQIM scheme can be improved by eliminating the external dither (and keeping the lattice reduction step at the decoder); the improvement vanishes as $L \to \infty$.
4. Prop. 2: The nondithered aQIM scheme outperforms aSSM [16,17] for all values of L, WNR, and NHR.
5. Prop. 3: The nondithered STDM scheme outperforms ISS [18] for all values of L, WNR, and NHR.

Clearly, the potential for improving the attacker's performance exists in the form of non-Gaussian strategies and strategies with memory.

Acknowledgements. The authors thank Tie Liu and the reviewers for helpful comments and suggestions.

References

1. B. Chen and G. W. Wornell, "Quantization Index Modulation: A Class of Provably Good Methods for Digital Watermarking and Information Embedding," *IEEE Trans. on Information Theory*, Vol. 47, No. 4, pp. 1423—1443, May 2001.
2. J. J. Eggers, R. Bäuml, R. Tzschoppe and B. Girod, "Scalar Costa Scheme for Information Embedding," *IEEE Transactions on Signal Processing*, Vol. 51, No. 4, pp. 1003—1019, Apr. 2003.
3. R. Zamir, S. Shamai (Shitz), and U. Erez, "Nested Linear/Lattice Codes for Structured Multiterminal Binning," *IEEE Trans. Information Theory*, Vol. 48, No. 6, pp. 1250—1276, June 2002.
4. U. Erez and R. Zamir, "Achieving $\frac{1}{2} \log(1 + SNR)$ on the AWGN Channel with Lattice Encoding and Decoding," *IEEE Trans. on Information Theory*, Vol. 50, No. 10, pp. 2293—2314, Oct. 2004.
5. U. Erez and S. ten Brink, "Approaching the dirty paper limit for canceling known interference," *Proc. Allerton Conf.*, Monticello, IL, Sep. 2003.

6. O. Koval, S. Voloshynovskiy, and F. Pérez-González, "Quantization-Based Watermarking Performance Improvement Using Host Statistics: AWGN Attack Case," *Proc. ACM Multimedia and Security Workshop*, Magdeburg, Germany, Sep. 2004.

7. L. Pérez-Freire, F. Pérez-González, and S. Voloshynovskiy, "Revealing the True Achievable Rates of Scalar Costa Scheme," *Proc. IEEE Multimedia Signal Proc. Workshop*, Siena, Italy, Sep.-Oct. 2004.

8. L. Pérez-Freire and F. Pérez-González, "Spread-Spectrum vs Quantization-Based Data Hiding: Misconceptions and Implications," *Proc. SPIE*, San Jose, CA, Jan. 2005.

9. I. J. Cox, J. Killian, F. T. Leighton and T. Shamoon, "Secure Spread Spectrum Watermarking for Multimedia," *IEEE Trans. Image Proc.*, Vol. 6, No. 12, pp. 1673—1687, Dec. 1997.

10. J. A. O'Sullivan, P. Moulin and M. Ettinger, "Information Theoretic Analysis of Steganography," *Proc. Int. Symp. on Information Theory (ISIT'98)*, Boston, MA, Aug. 1998.

11. P. Moulin and J. A. O'Sullivan, "Information–Theoretic Analysis of Information Hiding," *IEEE Trans. on Information Theory*, Vol. 49, No. 3, pp. 563-593, March 2003.

12. P. Moulin and M. K. Mıhçak, "The Parallel-Gaussian Watermarking Game," *IEEE Trans. on Information Theory*, Vol. 50, No. 2, pp. 272-289, Feb. 2004.

13. P. Moulin and M. K. Mıhçak, "A Framework for Evaluating the Data-Hiding Capacity of Image Sources," *IEEE Trans. on Image Processing*, Vol. 11, No. 9, pp. 1029–1042, Sep. 2002.

14. M. K. Mıhçak and P. Moulin, "Information-Embedding Codes Matched to Local Gaussian Image Models," *Proc. IEEE Int. Conf. on Image Processing*, Rochester, NY, Sep. 2002.

15. T. M. Cover and J. A. Thomas, *Elements of Information Theory*, Wiley, 1991.

16. P. Moulin and A. Ivanović, "Game-Theoretic Analysis of Watermark Detection," *Proc. IEEE Int. Conf. on Image Processing*, Thessaloniki, Greece, Oct. 2001.

17. P. Moulin and A. Ivanović, "The Zero-Rate Spread-Spectrum Watermarking Game," *IEEE Trans. on Signal Processing*, Vol. 51, No. 4, pp. 1098-1117, Apr. 2003.

18. H. Malvar and D. Florêncio, "Improved Spread Spectrum: A New Modulation Technique for Robust Watermarking," *IEEE Trans. Signal Processing*, Vol. 51, no. 4, pp. 898—905, April 2003.

19. F. M. J. Willems, "On Gaussian Channels with Side Information at the Transmitter," *Proc. 9th Symp. on Information Theory in the Benelux*, Enschede, The Netherlands, pp. 129—135, May 1988.

20. T. Liu and P. Moulin, "Error exponents for watermarking game with squared-error constraints," *Proc. Int. Symp. Information Theory*, Yokohama, Japan, July 2003.

21. M. Costa, "Writing on Dirty Paper," *IEEE Trans. on Information Theory*, Vol. 29, No. 3, pp. 439—441, May 1983.

On the Achievable Rate of Side Informed Embedding Techniques with Steganographic Constraints

Mark T. Hogan, Félix Balado, Neil J. Hurley, and Guénolé C.M. Silvestre

University College Dublin, Belfield, Dublin 4, Ireland
{markhogan, fiz, neil.hurley, guenole.silvestre}@ihl.ucd.ie

Abstract. The development of watermarking schemes in the literature is generally guided by a power constraint on the watermark to be embedded into the host. In a steganographic framework there is an additional constraint on the embedding procedure. It states that, for a scheme to be undetectable by statistical means, the pdf of the host signal must be approximately or exactly equal to that of the stegotext. In this work we examine this additional constraint when coupled with DC-DM. An analysis of the embedding scheme Stochastic QIM, which automatically meets the condition under certain assumptions, is presented and finally the capacity of the steganographic channel is examined.

1 Introduction

The term steganography refers to the family of techniques used to hide data within a *host* multimedia signal. Ideally, the corresponding modified signal, referred to as a *stegotext*, is perceptually and statistically indistinguishable from the host. The classical representation of steganographic communication is given by the prisoners' problem [1]. Alice produces a stegotext using the message that she wants to communicate and a given host, and sends it to Bob through an insecure communications channel. Usually, Alice and Bob make use of secret keys for their covert communication. The warden Wendy monitors the channel between Alice and Bob, and performs a detection test to decide if the signal being sent includes hidden information by exploiting potential imperfections of the steganographic method used. In an analogous way to cryptanalysis, this detection procedure is known as *steganalysis*.

Some considerations on the nature of Wendy's tests are necessary. Typically Wendy can be either *passive* or *active*. If the warden is passive then a detection test is all that is performed, but on the other hand, if she is active, then the document is deliberately attacked regardless of the outcome of any detection test. In this work we consider only that Wendy is passive. We also assume that the transmitted document undergoes a channel distortion before it is decoded. The nature of the channel is taken to be additive white Gaussian noise (AWGN), for the sake of comparison with previous results.

The success of detection tests lies in the location of statistical differences between the host signal and the stegotext signal. This idea has been formalised

M. Barni et al. (Eds.): IWDW 2005, LNCS 3710, pp. 387–402, 2005.

by Cachin in [2], where the security of a steganographic embedding method has been defined in terms of the Kullback Leibler distance (D_{KL}) between the densities of the host and stegotext signals. D_{KL} is equal to zero iff the two distributions are the same. The implication is that a non-negligible value for D_{KL} for any embedding scheme leads to detectable statistical differences. A major goal of embedding is, therefore, to keep D_{KL} as low as possible, such that the communication passes unhindered.

We now specify two cases of steganographic communication, namely *perfect* and *non-perfect* steganography. The difference lies in the restriction placed on the encoder. If the restriction is such that the $D_{\mathrm{KL}} = 0$ between the host and stegotext densities then the embedding scheme is said to conform to perfect steganography. In this case optimal statistical steganalysis will always be have a probability of error, P_e, no better than 0.5. If a small value for D_{KL} is allowed, such that the results of practical statistical tests are unreliable, then we have non-perfect steganography (c.f. ϵ-secure steganography in [2]).

Statistical differences are, of course, not the only concern when designing embedding schemes. As in the related area of watermarking, it is also desired that the rate of communication be as high as possible. Consider for a moment the case where the host is zero-mean independent identically distributed (iid) Gaussian random vector and the channel noise consists of two sources of additive white Gaussian noise (AWGN), both mutually independent. Assuming power constrained codewords and given knowledge of one of the noise sources at the encoder, the capacity of the channel can be achieved with Costa's codebook [3]. Now, to the authors knowledge, the work of Moulin and Wang in [4], is the only previous work in which the capacity of steganographic communication scenarios is rigorously examined. One of the main starting points in this work is that, for capacity calculations, in addition to the usual power constraint, there is also a pdf constraint which, for $D_{\mathrm{KL}} = 0$ (i.e. perfect steganography), requires that the pdf of the codebook must be equal to the pdf of the host signal.

For the case in which no secret key is used at the encoder, this result implies that Costa's codebook is not suitable for the steganographic channel because the codewords, although Gaussian, are discretely distributed. It can be argued that, if the codewords are unknown to the detector, scaled correctly and only used once, then the system will be perfectly secure. However, if the codewords are used more than once, as is the case in practical methods, then a detector can be designed to exploit this fact and the security is lost.

Considering only the power constraint at the encoder, it has been shown that distortion compensated dither modulation (DC-DM) [5] (or equivalently, the scalar Costa scheme [6]) has an achievable rate close to the capacity of the side informed AWGN channel. It was also shown in [7] that DC-DM can never conform to the restrictions of perfect steganography. However, it is well known that DC-DM requires the optimisation of a parameter, α, for a given noise power over the channel. This parameter can also be tuned for the purposes of reducing the value of D_{KL}, such that non-perfect steganography is still possible. Several authors have adopted this approach in the past [8],[9]. In those works, assuming the key to be leaked to an attacker, the value of α was taken to be 0.5, such that the D_{KL} is kept as low as possible while allowing errorless communication in the absence of any channel noise. Here, in the case where the key has not been leaked, we will show that this is not necessarily the best value. We indicate, using Stein's lemma [10], the optimal value for Alice to choose, such that practical statistical tests have a probability of error, P_e, close to 0.5, and the rate of communication is simultaneously maximised over the AWGN channel. We will also use Stein's lemma to show the penalty in capacity incurred when a non-perfect steganographic constraint is coupled with the power constraint at the encoder.

Given that DC-DM is an approximation to Costa's discrete codebook, the question arises of whether or not there exists an analogous codebook for the steganographic channel. A promising scheme is that of stochastic quantization index modulation (SQIM), proposed by Wang and Moulin [8]. Unlike DC-DM where the codewords are fixed, SQIM uses non-fixed codewords to improve security. Subject to the flat host assumption, the codebook is then formed from the same density as the host pdf and thus statistical steganalysis on SQIM will fail. Here we present an analysis of SQIM and illustrate its performance compared to that of dither modulation (DM) [5]. We will also show that the achievable rate of scalar SQIM is upper bounded by that of DM.

The essential feature of SQIM, from a perfect steganography point of view, is that every point in the host signal space forms an allowable codeword with probability given according to the host signal pdf. Finally, we extend this philosophy to higher dimensions using a sphere packing argument.

The paper is organised as follows. Section 2 is devoted to setting out the problem and the notation we adopt. An analysis of DC-DM with non-perfect steganographic constraints at the encoder is presented in Sect. 3. Section 4 contains an analysis of SQIM and the capacity of perfect steganographic channels is addressed in Sect. 5. Finally, conclusions are drawn in Sect. 6.

2   Problem Set-Up

Notation and Preliminaries. In this work capital letters refer to random variables and vectors respectively, e.g. X, $\mathbf{X}$, with lower case letters the respective realisations, e.g. x, $\mathbf{x}$. Individual elements of $\mathbf{x}$ are indexed as x_j. All vectors are of length N. The probability density function (pdf) of a random variable X is denoted as $f_X(\cdot)$ and the corresponding cumulative density function as $F_X(\cdot)$. The statistical expectation of X is denoted $E_X\{X\}$ and the differential entropy of X is denoted as $H(X) = -\int f_X(x)\log f_X(x)\mathrm{d}x$. The mutual information between X and Y is denoted $I(X;Y) = H(X) - H(X|Y)$.

We assume that the host, $\mathbf{x} = [x_1, \cdots, x_N]$, consists of a realization of a random vector $\mathbf{X}$ formed by independent identically distributed (iid), Gaussian zero-mean random variables for both ease of comparison with previous works, and reasons of analytic tractability. Alice may send either $\mathbf{x}$ to Bob, or modify it before transmission to embed $\mathbf{b} = [b_1, \cdots, b_N]$, $b_i \in \mathcal{B}$, where in experiments we take $|\mathcal{B}| = 2$, giving a sequence of binary digits drawn from a uniform distribution. This produces a stegotext (watermarked) vector $\mathbf{s} = G(\mathbf{x}, \mathbf{b})$, and the watermark $\mathbf{w}$ is then given as $\mathbf{w} \triangleq \mathbf{s} - \mathbf{x}$. We assume that only one information symbol b_j is embedded in one corresponding covertext sample x_j. The embedding process may be secured by using a pseudorandom symmetric key $\mathbf{k}$, shared by Alice and Bob, and then $\mathbf{s} = G_\mathbf{k}(\mathbf{x}, \mathbf{b})$.

Two important parameters for establishing the working point of the steganographic method are the *host to watermark* power ratio (HWR) and the *watermark to noise* power ratio (WNR). The HWR is the average power of the host normalized by the watermark power, which can be written as HWR $\triangleq$ $\mathrm{E}\{\|\mathbf{X}\|^2\}/\mathrm{E}\{\|\mathbf{W}\|^2\} = \sigma_X^2/\sigma_W^2$, where σ_X^2 and σ_W^2 refer to the variances of the host signal and watermark, respectively, assuming that W has zero mean. If X and S are independent and zero-mean then $\sigma_W^2 = \sigma_S^2 - \sigma_X^2$. Notice that the perceptual constraints in any data hiding problem impose very high values for the HWR.

The channel noise $\mathbf{v} = [v_1, \cdots, v_N]$, is assumed to be AWGN with power σ_V^2 such that the received vector $\mathbf{y} = \mathbf{x} + \mathbf{w} + \mathbf{v}$. Correspondingly, the WNR is defined as the watermark power, normalized by the noise power and is written as, WNR $\triangleq \mathrm{E}\{\|\mathbf{W}\|^2\}/\mathrm{E}\{\|\mathbf{V}\|^2\} = \sigma_W^2/\sigma_V^2$.

2.1   Detection Test

Alice transmits either $\mathbf{x}$ or $\mathbf{s}$. Because Wendy does not know the origin of the document she receives, she can only assume it to be an unclassified document $\mathbf{z}$. She must decide if $\mathbf{z}$ sent to Bob by Alice has been drawn either from $f_\mathbf{X}$ or from $f_\mathbf{S}$. Assuming that $f_\mathbf{X}$ is known, then, given $G(\cdot)$, $f_\mathbf{S}$ is also known. This detection problem is then a hypothesis testing problem with two choices, denoted as the null hypothesis H_0 ($\mathbf{z}$ is a host), and the alternative hypothesis, H_1 ($\mathbf{z}$ is a stegotext). To make a decision on $\mathbf{z}$, the optimal test based on the Bayes likelihood ratio [11], and is given by

$$\Lambda(\mathbf{z}) \triangleq \frac{f_\mathbf{X}(\mathbf{z})}{f_\mathbf{S}(\mathbf{z})} \overset{H_0}{\underset{H_1}{\gtrless}} \mu, \tag{1}$$

where $\mu \triangleq (P_0/P_1) \cdot ((C_{10} - C_{00})/(C_{01} - C_{11}))$. The P_i, $i \in \{0, 1\}$ represent the *a priori* probabilities for the null and alternative hypotheses respectively, and C_{ij} the cost of choosing H_i when the true hypothesis is H_j. Letting $C_{ij} = \delta_{ij}$, with δ_{ij} the Kronecker delta function, and choosing the *a priori* probabilities to be uniformly distributed, gives the maximum likelihood (ML) test.

It is desirable to relate the predicted outcome of (1) to some performance property of the embedding process which is directly measurable. One such interesting property is the probability of error in the detection test, P_e, defined as

$$P_e \triangleq P(\mathbf{Z} \sim f_\mathbf{X} | \Lambda(\mathbf{Z}) < \mu) \cdot P_0 + P(\mathbf{Z} \sim f_\mathbf{S} | \Lambda(\mathbf{Z}) > \mu) \cdot P_1 = \frac{P_{fa} + P_m}{2}, \tag{2}$$

where $\mathbf{Z} \sim f_{\mathbf{X}}$ is taken to mean that the random vector $\mathbf{Z}$ follows $f_{\mathbf{X}}$, P_{fa} represents the probability of false alarm and P_m, the probability of a miss. We have again assumed that the *a priori* probabilities are uniform as this is worst case for Wendy. A quantity to relate the P_e and the embedding process, as we will see, is the Kullback-Leibler distance which is defined, in one direction, as

$$D_{\mathrm{KL}}(f_{\mathbf{X}} \| f_{\mathbf{S}}) \triangleq \int f_{\mathbf{X}}(\mathbf{x}) \log \frac{f_{\mathbf{X}}(\mathbf{x})}{f_{\mathbf{S}}(\mathbf{x})} \mathrm{d}\mathbf{x}. \tag{3}$$

In general $D_{\mathrm{KL}}(f_{\mathbf{X}} \| f_{\mathbf{S}}) \neq D_{\mathrm{KL}}(f_{\mathbf{S}} \| f_{\mathbf{X}})$ and $D_{\mathrm{KL}}(f_{\mathbf{X}} \| f_{\mathbf{S}}) = 0$ iff $f_{\mathbf{X}} = f_{\mathbf{S}}$.

In [8] the sum of the Kullback Leibler distances in both directions (the *J*-divergence) was used to lower bound the error probability in Wendy's test. Here, we take a different approach through the use of Stein's lemma [10], which we review next. In [10] the lemma applies to discrete random variables but here we use a direct translation to a continuous domain. Using this lemma the P_e and D_{KL} can be directly related to one another. Firstly let $P_{fa} = \int_{A^c} f_{\mathbf{X}}(\mathbf{z}) \mathrm{d}\mathbf{z}$ and $P_m = \int_A f_{\mathbf{S}}(\mathbf{z}) \mathrm{d}\mathbf{z}$, where $A \subseteq \mathbb{R}^N$ is an acceptance region for H_0 and A^c its complement. Then for $0 < \nu < 0.5$, let $P_{fa}^\nu = \min_{\substack{A \subseteq \mathbb{R}^N \\ P_m < \nu}} P_{fa}$, which leads to

$$\lim_{\nu \to 0} \lim_{N \to \infty} \frac{1}{N} \log(P_{fa}^\nu) = -D_{\mathrm{KL}}(f_{\mathbf{X}} \| f_{\mathbf{S}}). \tag{4}$$

This gives a direct relationship between the errors in detection of (1) and D_{KL} in the limit as N approaches infinity. Alice can readily monitor D_{KL} and as such can approximately predict the outcome of any optimal detection test on the documents she transmits. Hence suitable parameters can be chosen for the embedding scheme such that the P_e in Wendy's detection test will be close to 0.5. This relationship only holds true in the limit but, here, for practical purposes, we assume that N is large and take (4) to approximately hold in this case. It should also be noted that, in inverting (4), a slowly varying function is required which depends on, among other parameters, the P_m [12]. However, in general, this function is not known and as in [12] we will ignore this function for the purposes of simplicity.

2.2 Capacity

For the purposes of this discussion assume that Alice wishes to embed a message in $\mathbf{x}$ and transmits $\mathbf{s}$. Ignoring the detection test, this communication scenario is the standard watermarking channel, see e.g. [6]. It has been noted in [3] that the capacity of this channel is given as $C = \max_{f_{U,Y}(u,y|x)} I(U;Y) - I(U;X)$, where U is an auxiliary random variable. Achieving this capacity is then a problem of choosing a suitable codebook U. For the power constrained case where the host signal is iid Gaussian, and the channel distortion is represented as AWGN, Costa [3] showed that, for $U = W + \alpha X$ and $\alpha = \sigma_W^2/(\sigma_W^2 + \sigma_V^2)$, the capacity of the channel is given as

$$C = \frac{1}{2} \log \left(1 + \frac{\sigma_W^2}{\sigma_V^2} \right). \tag{5}$$

An alternative geometrical approach to calculating the capacity of this channel is contained in [13], which we summarise here because it will be drawn upon in Sect. 5. Noting that N is large consider the following. Around any given $\mathbf{x}$, there is an allowable distortion (embedding power) sphere, denoted T_W, with radius given as $\sqrt{N\sigma_W^2}$, which must contain at least one codeword corresponding to each possible message. For a given achievable rate, R, we then wish to position the 2^{NR} codewords within the sphere such that the noise spheres, T_V, of radius $\sqrt{N\sigma_V^2}$ around each codeword have asymptotically vanishing overlap as $N \to \infty$. To calculate the achievable rate, a ratio of volumes is formed which gives

$$2^{NR} \leq \frac{(N(\sigma_W^2 + \sigma_V^2))^{\frac{N}{2}}}{(N\sigma_V^2)^{\frac{N}{2}}}. \tag{6}$$

A capacity achieving code will achieve this rate for $R = C$ from which it can be seen that (6) reduces to (5).

Finally, for a given coding scheme, host pdf and channel, the achievable rate of communication can be calculated as the following [10],

$$R = I(Y; B) = H(Y) - \frac{1}{|\mathcal{B}|} \sum_{b \in \mathcal{B}} H(Y|b). \tag{7}$$

3   DC-DM

In this section we analyse DC-DM in respect of the constraints imposed by steganography. Firstly a brief review of DC-DM is presented. Then the achievable rate of DC-DM with steganographic constraints at the encoder is examined.

3.1   Embedding Method

DC-DM with uniform scalar quantizers is a practical implementation of distortion-compensated quantization index modulation (DC-QIM), proposed by Chen and Wornell [5]. It has been shown that, for the AWGN channel with side information at the encoder, DC-DM has an achievable rate acceptably close to the capacity of the channel [6]. The embedding technique is based on the quantization of the host samples with a dithered version of a uniform scalar quantizer $Q_\Delta(\cdot)$. We assume that the quantization step Δ is the same for all covertext samples. For example, in the case of binary messages the embedding takes place with two quantizers shifted by $\Delta/2$. In order to embed a binary symbol b_j at the host sample x_j the corresponding stegotext sample s_j is obtained in DC-DM as

$$s_j = G_{k_j}(x_j, b_j) = x_j + \alpha \left[Q_\Delta \left(x_j - k_j - \Delta\frac{b_j}{2} \right) + k_j + \Delta\frac{b_j}{2} - x_j \right], \tag{8}$$

where the additional dither $k_j \in (-\frac{\Delta}{2}, \frac{\Delta}{2}]$ is the secret key shared by Alice and Bob at the jth sample. The distortion compensation factor $0 < \alpha \leq 1$ allows for tuning the method for optimal robustness to channel noise, assuming that its power is known in advance [6], or alternatively, for tuning its detectability properties [9],[8], as we will discuss in Sect. 3.2. DM is a particular case of DC-DM for which $\alpha = 1$.

Assuming that the quantization error is approximately uniform and independent from $\mathbf{X}$, the HWR is for this embedding method is given by

$$\text{HWR} = \frac{12\sigma_X^2}{\alpha^2 \Delta^2}. \tag{9}$$

3.2 Optimal DC-DM Detection

In previous works [7] the optimal detection of DC-DM was presented in the presence and absence of a secret key. Here we limit ourselves to the case of DC-DM in which the secret key has not been leaked to Wendy, as this is the more pertinent case for analysis. In terms of the achievable rate of a particular scheme, the use of a key has no effect, but, of course, the knowledge of the key has implications for the detection of stegotexts. Considering that the key is unavailable to Wendy, then, for her ML detection test she may use the average expression for the pdf, taken over all possible keys. This approach comes down to computing $\tilde{f}_S(s) = E_K\{f(s|K)\} = \int f_S(s|k) \cdot f_K(k) \, dk$, and to use this average pdf, $\tilde{f}_S$, in (1). The result for $\tilde{f}_S$ in the case of DC-DM, for a uniformly distributed key variable $K \sim U(-\Delta/2, \Delta/2]$, is as follows (details in [7]),

$$\tilde{f}_S(s) = f_X(s) * U\left(-\frac{\alpha\Delta}{2}, \frac{\alpha\Delta}{2}\right), \tag{10}$$

where $*$ denotes convolution. Noteworthy here, is the fact that (10) illustrates that perfect steganography is never possible using DC-DM. The only case for which $\tilde{f}_S = f_X$ is when α or Δ is set to zero. In either case no embedding takes place and the achievable rate is consequently zero.

3.3 Achievable Rate of DC-DM

It was noted in [7] that for a fixed HWR the choice of α is irrelevant in respect of the secrecy of the communication. It can be seen from (9) that the HWR is directly dependent on the product of α and Δ. Also, $\tilde{f}_S$ from (10), is directly related to the same product. Thus the actual value of α does not matter in respect of the secrecy of the communication. Then, assuming a given performance constraint, an optimal α can be picked for a given channel noise power.

Now, considering the case of fixed Δ it can be seen that the previous rationale is no longer true. Other authors [8],[9], assuming a fixed Δ and that the attacker has access to $\mathbf{k}$, have proposed the value of $\alpha = 0.5$. This particular value allows for errorless communication in the absence of noise and also has the property that the pdf of the stegotext has full support over $\mathbb{R}$, assuming that X also does. We consider the case where $\mathbf{k}$ has not been leaked to Wendy and will show that $\alpha = 0.5$ is not necessarily the optimal value in this case.

Now, we will fix the value of Δ and use Stein's lemma to set a limit, $\alpha_{\max}$, on the maximum value of α such that, if $\alpha \in (0, \alpha_{\max}]$ is used at the encoder, the P_e in the detection test will be close to 0.5. Firstly, $D_{KL}(f_X \| f_S)$ is calculated using f_X and (10) for all $\alpha \in (0, 1]$ and substituted into (4) to give a value for the P_{fa} as a function of α. These values are then substituted into (2) to give the P_e as a function of α.

It can be seen that in (4), by reversing the probabilities and correspondingly changing the pdfs, the theorem remains essentially unchanged. However the limit now depends on $D_{KL}(f_S \| f_X)$ with the result that the final probability of error may be different. As such, this case is also calculated and the final P_e is taken as the minimum of the two results at each α, as this represents worst case for Alice. Finally $\alpha_{\max}$ is chosen according to

$$\alpha_{\max} = \max_{P_e(\alpha) \geq (0.5 - \epsilon)} \alpha, \tag{11}$$

where ϵ is an arbitrarily small number. Now, due to the nature of the DC-DM transformation an analytic expression is unavailable for D_{KL} in both directions and the results are only available by numerical evaluation.

The limited range of α values, $\alpha \in (0, \alpha_{\max}]$, is then used to find the constrained achievable rate of DC-DM according to

$$R = \arg\max_{\alpha \in (0, \alpha_{\max}]} I(B; Y|k). \tag{12}$$

This rate is calculated by substituting the pdfs $f_Y(y|k)$, $f_Y(y|k, b=0)$ and $f_Y(y|k, b=1)$ into (12). The derivation of these pdfs is performed using (8) and the change of variable theorem, [14] as follows. Assume that message $b \in \mathcal{B}$, corresponds to the reconstruction points denoted as $q_{i,b} = i\Delta + b\Delta/|\mathcal{B}|$ for suitable $i \in \{-\infty, \infty\}$. Then for $x \in (q_{i,b} - \Delta/2, q_{i,b} + \Delta/2]$ we have that $s = x + \alpha(q_{i,b} - x)$. Using the theorem the we obtain the following, $f_{S_{i,b}}(s) = (1/(1-\alpha)) \cdot f_X((s_{i,b} - q_{i,b})/(1-\alpha))$, for $s \in (q_{i,b} - (1-\alpha)\Delta/2, q_{i,b} + (1-\alpha)\Delta/2]$. The dependence on the bin can then be removed by summing over i, giving $f_{S_b}(s) = \sum_{i=-\infty}^{\infty} f_{S_{i,b}}(s)$. Finally we can remove the dependence on b by averaging over the message alphabet (uniformity assumption) and then, $f_S(s) = (1/|\mathcal{B}|) \cdot \sum_{b \in \mathcal{B}} f_{S_b}(s)$. Then it can be seen that $f_Y(y|k) = f_S(y) * f_V(y)$. The conditional pdfs follow easily. Now, these pdfs are such that an analytic expression for R is not available so a numerical evaluation of (12) is performed.

For illustration purposes we take $\Delta = 1$ and assume that $N = 10^5$ for the results. A higher value of N with a corresponding lower value of Δ will lead to similar results. Now consider Fig. 1. Here the achievable rate of DC-DM is plotted as a function of $\alpha \in (0, 1]$ for a range of WNRs. The equivalent value of P_e as a function of α is plotted on the x-axis. First examine the cases of high WNRs. Here it can be seen that the highest value of R is achieved when the P_e is approaching 0. This implies that at these values of WNR there is a significant loss in the achievable rate of the scheme due to the steganographic constraint, as the optimum α in terms of rate cannot be used. A sub-optimal value must be used lowering the rate of the scheme. However, when the low

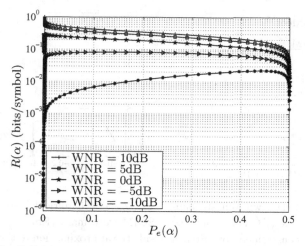

Fig. 1. $R(\alpha)$ for DC-DM plotted against $P_e(\alpha)$ in Wendy's detection test for a range on WNRs. $\sigma_X^2 = 1.0$, $\Delta = 1.0$, $\alpha \in (0, 1]$, $N = 10^5$, HWR varies with α.

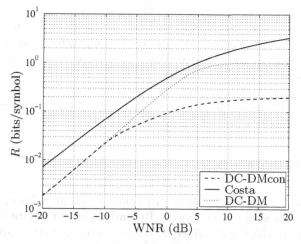

Fig. 2. Achievable rate R for binary, scalar DC-DM under two scenarios. The first plot (DC-DM) gives R, maximised for all $\alpha \in (0, 1]$ while the second (DC-DMcon) gives the constrained value of R maximized over $\alpha \in (0, \alpha_{max}]$, where the value of ϵ in (11) is 0.05. The channel capacity (Costa) is plotted for reference.

WNRs are examined it can be seen that the maximum value of R is obtained within the region where Wendy's detection test will have a probability of error close to 0.5. Now, assuming that a given $P_e > 0.5 - \epsilon$ is acceptable to Alice, it can be observed that there will be no loss in the achievable rate due to the steganographic constraint, and choosing the optimal value of α based on this rate will not allow any significant advantage in the detection test.

Fig. 2 shows plots of (12) alongside the value of R for unconstrained values of α, as discussed above. There is an evident loss in the achievable rate in the

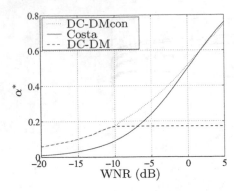

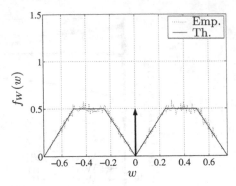

Fig. 3. α^* for DC-DM without steganographic constraints (DC-DM) and the optimal value constrained by Stein's lemma (DC-DMcon). Costa's α [3], is plotted for reference. $\sigma_X^2 = 1.0$, $\Delta = 1.0$, $\epsilon = 0.05$.

Fig. 4. The empirical histogram of the SQIM watermark (Emp.) plotted alongside the approximation to the derived pdf (Th.). $\Delta = 1$

high WNRs whereas at low WNRs the rate is equal for both cases. This is due to the fact that at very low WNRs the optimal value of α is close to zero while it approaches 1 as the WNR increases. The increasing α increases the D_{KL} eventually passing the threshold set as α_{max}.

Finally, in Fig. 3 the optimal values of α (i.e. α^*) are plotted for a number of scenarios. Firstly Costa's α [3] is plotted, alongside the α numerically optimised for DC-DM and finally the α which maximises (12).

4   Stochastic QIM

We have seen in Sect. 3 that the achievable rate of the embedding method is reduced under steganographic conditions. Recently however a data hiding scheme has been proposed which approximately conforms to the perfect steganographic channel. Stochastic QIM is a side informed embedding technique [8] which, under the flat host assumption, maintains $f_S = f_X$. The main idea is that every $x \in \mathbb{R}$ forms a valid codeword s, with probability drawn from f_X. This is of course unlike DC-DM where only certain subsets of $\mathbb{R}$ form the codewords with probability determined by the transformation $G(\cdot)$. In this section an analysis of SQIM is presented. Then the achievable rate of the coding scheme is analysed more closely than previously [8]. This analysis is performed under the assumption that $\mathbf{k} = \mathbf{0}$.

4.1   Analysis of SQIM Watermark

The binary one dimensional SQIM embedding scheme can be summarised as follows. The host space $\mathbb{R}$ is tiled into disjoint regions of length $\Delta/2$. Each region contains codewords corresponding to either $b = 0$ or $b = 1$. Let the union of all the regions of $\mathbb{R}$ corresponding to $b = 0$ be denoted A_0 and similarly for A_1. Now assume that $x \in A_0$ and that $b = 0$. In this case x already forms a required codeword so $s = x$.

Now again assume that $b = 0$ but that this time $x \in A_1$. Then s is formed as follows. Firstly the nearest correct code region to x (in a Euclidean sense) is chosen. Then s is chosen randomly from this region with probability given by the host pdf truncated to said region and scaled accordingly. Thus $w = s - x$ is the watermark in this case. Now assuming that x has equal probability of lying in either A_0 or A_1 we have, with probability, $P(x \in A_0, b = 0) + P(x \in A_1, b = 1) = P(x \in A_0)P(b = 0) + P(x \in A_1)P(b = 1) = 0.5$, that $s = x$ and with probability 0.5 a watermark w is added to x to form s.

We must now consider the effect of the above embedding on the pdf of the stegotext. Without loss of generality consider a generic quantization point $i\Delta$ with corresponding decision region $(i\Delta - \Delta/4, i\Delta + \Delta/4]$. It is clear that, for equiprobable symbols, the weight of $f_S(s)$ over this region should be

$$a_i \triangleq P\left(x \in \left(i\Delta - \frac{\Delta}{4}, i\Delta + \frac{\Delta}{4}\right]\right) = F_X\left(i\Delta + \frac{\Delta}{4}\right) - F_X\left(i\Delta - \frac{\Delta}{4}\right). \quad (13)$$

This weight is composed of three components, namely a portion equal to $a_i/2$ formed from host points falling in the region already associated with the correct corresponding message bit (i.e. $s = x$) and two other portions formed by transformations from the adjacent decision regions, which, it can be seen, are equal in expectation to $a_{i-1}/4$ and $a_{i+1}/4$.

We now have that for the embedding to be perfect, the following must hold, $a_i = a_{i-1}/2 + a_{i+1}/2 \ \forall \ i \in \mathbb{Z}$. In general, for a given f_X this is not the case with the result that $D_{\mathrm{KL}} > 0$. If f_X is uniform then the problem is avoided but this, of course, is a generally not the case. Now, under the flat host assumption the difference in weights between adjacent bins is zero and this holds as a good approximation if $\sigma_X^2 \gg \sigma_W^2$. As such we adopt this approximation in all further analysis with the result that $f_S(s) = f_X(s)$.

In practice the problem can be circumvented by calculating a_i for each bin. When the normalised number of samples in the bin reaches this amount any remaining points must be either embedded in a bin further away (increasing the embedding distortion) or embedded with the wrong bit (increasing the errors in the communication). Either option results in a loss in achievable rate for the scheme. Hence the flat host assumption gives an upper bound for calculation of the rate of this steganographic method.

Now, to analyse this watermark we first assume that x is not lying in the correct region for the corresponding b. The embedding can be considered as a standard DM embedding with an additional stochastic element which we denote as D. We can therefore write the following transformation for the jth sample, s_j,

$$s_j = x_j + \left(Q_\Delta\left(x_j - \Delta\frac{b_j}{|\mathcal{B}|}\right) - x_j + \Delta\frac{b_j}{|\mathcal{B}|}\right) + d_j, \quad (14)$$

where d_j has support range $(-\Delta/4, \Delta/4]$ and where we assume from here on that, without loss of generality, $b_j = 0$. Let $Q_\Delta(x) = i\Delta$ with the appropriate value of i, and the probability of the host lying in the region around this reconstruction point be given as a_i, from (13). Then the pdf of D can be seen to be

$$f_D(d) = \frac{1}{a_i} \cdot f_X(i\Delta + d), \ d \in \left[-\frac{\Delta}{4}, \frac{\Delta}{4}\right). \tag{15}$$

Next we have the quantization error, $e = Q_\Delta(x) - x$, usually taken to be uniform over a quantization bin. Here however we have a slightly different scenario. It has been noted that quantization only takes place if $\frac{\Delta}{2} \geq |x - i\Delta| > \frac{\Delta}{4}$. Then the pdf of the quantization error is given as the following,

$$f_E(e) = \begin{cases} \frac{2}{\Delta}, e \in \left\{ \begin{array}{l} [i\Delta - \Delta/2, i\Delta - \Delta/4) \\ (i\Delta + \Delta/4, i\Delta + \Delta/2] \end{array} \right., \\ 0, \ \text{otherwise}. \end{cases}$$

Given that the quantization error is independent of D, this portion of the watermark pdf is given as $f_E(w) * f_D(w)$. This calculation is straightforward but the resulting pdf depends on the absolute value of x. However, the effect is minimal if $\Delta^2 \ll \sigma_X^2$. In this case an approximation of uniformity in the quantization bin is adopted in (15), simplifying the analysis considerably. To finalise, the pdf of the watermark the case when $s = x$ must be considered. It can be easily seen that this contributes a Dirac δ-function to f_W. We therefore obtain f_W as $f_W(w) = \frac{1}{2}(\delta(w) + f_E(w) * f_D(w))$.

4.2   Comparison of SQIM and DM

Here we discuss the tradeoff in achievable rate and statistical transparency between DM and SQIM. In Fig. 4 an example of the pdf $f_W(w)$ for SQIM is presented for the theoretical simplification alongside an empirically obtained histogram. This pdf has the shape of two trapeziums either side of a Dirac δ-function centred at zero. Using the approximate pdf the power of the watermark can be easily obtained as $E\{w^2\}$ which after some calculus gives $\sigma_W^2 = \Delta^2/12$. This power is the same as DM embedding power (i.e. the power of the quantization noise) and leads to a direct, fair comparison between DM and SQIM. In terms of capacity it results in the fact that SQIM can never outperform DM. This is due to the fact that in DM all of the embedding power is used to transmit the message but in SQIM only a proportion of the same total power in used for the message. The remaining power is used to compensate the shape of the pdf. To see what this proportion is we can simply compare f_D and f_E above (the δ-function in f_W contributes no energy). It can be seen that $\sigma_D^2 = \Delta^2/96$ while $\sigma_E^2 = 7\Delta^2/96$. The total power is of course the addition of the two variances as both signals are independent. It can now be seen that in SQIM 1/8 of the embedding power is used in the pdf compensation while the remaining 7/8s is actually used in the message transmission. Thus the capacity of DM acts as an upper bound to that of SQIM.

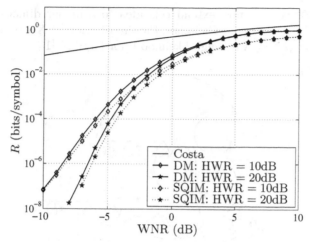

Fig. 5. The achievable rate R, calculated using (7), for SQIM (dashed lines) and DM (continuous lines). Two separate HWRs are plotted to emphasize the fact that the rate is a function of the host signal power. $\sigma_X^2 = 1.0$.

Another important observation is the fact that DM does not achieve complete host signal rejection in the presence of noise whereas DC-DM almost does. It can be seen that under moderately high noise conditions the performance of DM falls off considerably in comparison to DC-DM. This indicates that there is a threshold noise level below which the achievable rate of DM tends to zero. It also indicates that reducing the HWR for DM and SQIM will increase the achievable rate of these embedding techniques. This fact can be seen in Fig. 5. The implication of this is that it is not possible to communicate using SQIM in high noise scenarios. In the next section we will se how the same effect can be seen to apply to a generic N dimensional scheme designed along the same lines without the use a secret key.

5   Capacity of Perfectly Secure Steganography

In previous sections we have seen that the achievable rate of some scalar side-informed embedding schemes is reduced when steganographic security is required. Here we will examine the capacity of the steganographic channel with the use of a sphere packing argument in the case where non-fixed codewords are used at the encoder.

5.1   Stochastic QIM Analogy in N Dimensions

As described in Sect. 4 the basic premise of one dimensional SQIM is that every point in $\mathbb{R}$ is a possible codeword with a probability of each $s \in \mathbb{R}$ given by f_X (i.e. the codewords are random, not fixed). The transformation (14) contained a stochastic element, D, which compensated the pdf of the stegotext such that $f_S = f_X$. We now extend this idea to a higher dimensional space. Consider $\mathbf{X} \in \mathbb{R}^N$. For $f_{\mathbf{X}}$ iid Gaussian, the distribution of $\mathbf{X}$ is uniform on the sphere of radius $\sqrt{N\sigma_X^2}$ with high likelihood, for large N [15].

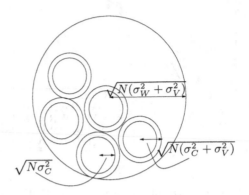

Fig. 6. A schematic representing the sphere packing argument for steganography. All points in T_W are valid codewords but only those contained within the spheres of radius $\sqrt{N\sigma_C^2}$ are reliable.

Let the sphere of radius $\sqrt{N\sigma_W^2}$ around $\mathbf{x}$ be denoted T_W as before. All points on the surface of T_W have the same probability as $\mathbf{x}$ so any point in T_W can be transmitted without altering the host pdf. Now, applying the procedure outlined in Sect. 2.2 we can fill the sphere, T_{W+V}, of radius $\sqrt{N(\sigma_W^2 + \sigma_V^2)}$, with codewords to calculate the capacity. Following the SQIM idea, it can be seen that all points $\mathbf{s}$ lying on T_W must be codewords, with the result that none of said codewords are reliable for a noise variance $\sigma_V^2 > 0$.

To manufacture reliable codewords we do the following for a particular message $\mathbf{b}$. Consider a noise sphere, T_V, of radius $\sqrt{N\sigma_V^2}$ in T_{W+V}. Now, form a sphere at the centre of T_V such that all codewords in the new sphere, T_C of radius σ_C^2, are reliable. We now have that T_W is filled with spheres of radius $\sqrt{N(\sigma_V^2 + \sigma_C^2)}$. The idea is illustrated in Fig. 6.

Assume for a moment that σ_C^2 is known such that reliable communication is possible. Then the achievable rate of the channel is given as $2^{NR} = (N(\sigma_W^2 + \sigma_V^2))^{N/2}/(N(\sigma_C^2 + \sigma_V^2))^{N/2}$, which gives $R = \frac{1}{2}\log\left((\sigma_W^2 + \sigma_V^2)/(\sigma_C^2 + \sigma_V^2)\right)$. This suggests, for $\sigma_C^2 > 0$, that Costa's capacity is not achievable under steganographic conditions when non-fixed codewords are used at the encoder. It also implies that there is a vertical asymptote in the achievable rate curve, similar to those seen in the rate plots for SQIM, Fig. 5.

Now consider the value of the parameter σ_C^2. It must be chosen such that the probability of error at the decoder vanishes as N tends to infinity. Simple limits on the actual value of σ_C^2 are formed as $0 \leq \sigma_C^2 \leq \sigma_W^2$. It can be seen that this upper limit corresponds to the case of all codewords in the allowable distortion region corresponding to just one message. This will give a zero achievable rate which goes some way to explaining the sharp falloff in the achievable rate of SQIM shown previously.

6 Conclusion

The issue of robust embedding for the steganographic channel has been examined. It was seen that the achievable rate of DC-DM is constrained when steganographic secrecy is required. The optimum value of the Costa parameter α was also seen to be restricted for this channel.

An analysis of an approximately statistically undetectable technique, namely Stochastic QIM was also undertaken. It was shown that the achievable rate of this technique is bounded by that of DM. Also noteworthy is a vertical asymptote in the achievable rate at a particular WNR. The location of this asymptote was shown to be dependent on the HWR.

Extending the idea behind SQIM to N dimensions indicated that a similar asymptote exists for a more general steganographic embedding scheme utilising non fixed codewords. The location of the asymptote however remains an open topic.

Acknowledgements. The authors wish to thank Pedro Comesaña for interesting remarks and corrections on an early version of this manuscript. This work is supported by Enterprise Ireland under research grant ATRP–2002/230 and the European Commission through the IST Programme under contract IST-2002-507609 SIMILAR.

References

1. Simmons, G.: The prisoner's problem and the subliminal channel. In: Advances in Cryptology, Crypto '83. Volume 20., Plenum Press (1984) 51–67
2. Cachin, C.: An information-theoretic model for steganography. In: Information Hiding: Second International Workshop. Volume 1525., Springer (1998) 306–318
3. Costa, M.: Writing on dirty paper. IEEE Trans. on Information Theory **29** (1983) 439–441
4. Moulin, P., Wang, Y.: New results on steganographic capacity. In: Proc. CISS Conference, Princeton, USA (2004)
5. Chen, B., Wornell, G.: Quantization index modulation: A class of provably good methods for digital watermarking and information embedding. IEEE Trans. on Information Theory **47** (2001) 1423–1443
6. Eggers, J., Girod, B.: Informed watermarking. Kluwer Academic Publishers (2002)
7. Hogan, M.T., Hurley, N.J., Silvestre, G.C., Balado, F., Whelan, K.M.: ML detection of steganography. In: Security, Steganography and Watermarking of Multimedia Contents. Volume 5681 of Proc. Electronic Imaging., SPIE (2005)
8. Wang, Y., Moulin, P.: Steganalysis of block structured stegotext. In: Security, Steganography and Watermarking of Multimedia Contents. Volume 5306 of Proc. Electronic Imaging., SPIE (2004)
9. Guillon, P., Furon, T., Duhamel, P.: Applied public-key steganography. In: Security and Watermarking of Multimedia Contents. Volume 4675 of Proc. Electronic Imaging., SPIE (2002) 38–49
10. Cover, T., Thomas, J.: Elements of Information Theory. J. Wiley & Sons (1991)
11. Van Trees, H.L.: Detection, Estimation and Modulation Theory. J. Wiley & Sons (1968)

12. Johnson, D.H., Orsak, G.C.: Relation of signal set choice to the performance of optimal non-Gaussian detectors. IEEE Trans. on Communications **41** (1993)
13. Barron, R.J., Chen, B., Wornell, G.W.: The duality between information embedding and source coding with side information and some applications. IEEE Trans. on Information Theory **49** (2003) 1159–1180
14. Pérez-Freire, L., Pérez-González, F., Voloshinovskiy, S.: Revisiting scalar quantization-based data hiding: Exact analysis and results. IEEE Trans. on Signal Processing (2005) To appear.
15. Hamkins, J., Zeger, K.: Gaussian source coding with spherical codes. IEEE Trans. on Information Theory **48** (2002) 2980–2988

Performance Lower Bounds for Existing and New Uncoded Digital Watermarking Modulation Techniques

Marcos de Castro Pacitti[1] and Weiler Alves Finamore[2]

[1] Brazilian Air Force
pacitti@ciscea.gov.br
[2] CETUC/ PUC - Rio, Brazil
weiler@cetuc.puc-rio.br

Abstract. Many coded digital watermarking systems development requires first the selection of a (uncoded) modulation technique to be part of a coded architecture. Therefore, performance bounds for uncoded techniques are an important tool for coded system optimization, aiming at operation close to capacity. This paper introduces a new performance lower bound for uncoded binary watermarking modulation techniques, based on a simple equivalence with a binary communication system, considering an additive gaussian attack model. When compared to others results, we observe that the proposed performance lower bound is more accurate and general. New M-ary unidimensional and multidimensional Spread Spectrum based modulation techniques are introduced, including their improved forms. The performances of the proposed techniques are determined, and the performance lower bounds for the corresponding techniques classes are determined as well.

1 Introduction

Watermarking refers to the process of embedding, in a host information, an information mark which is not immediately discernible upon examining the embedded host information. These techniques have been used for centuries as a tool to reduce counterfeiting in documents, currency, and other applications. With the widespread use of digital representation of images, video, audio, and other signals, the copyright protection by using "invisible" digital watermarks became a very active area of research. Naturally many new watermarking applications have become of great interest in this new digital perspective, including national security applications such as integrity and authenticity verification, covert communication and traitor tracing (finger printing) applications. Several other digital watermarking applications are still emerging, widening the perspective for research [1].

Watermarking in this new context is a complex problem, with issues that involve not only the watermarking techniques themselves, but also system design, cryptography, and a series of economical and legal aspects that have to

M. Barni et al. (Eds.): IWDW 2005, LNCS 3710, pp. 403–417, 2005.

be taken into account, considering the specific application and business model as well. In this paper we only deal with a single aspect of the problem: uncoded watermark embedding (modulation) techniques and performance lower bounds for some modulation classes. A watermarking application generally requires an appropriate modulation class to be used, then the knowledge of its performance lower bound is important to evaluate the efficiency of a specific modulation technique implementation. If an uncoded technique is not optimized to operate close to the corresponding lower bound performance, even the subsequent use of a coding technique (in a coded architecture) will not achieve operation close to system capacity. The advantage of operating close to capacity is to reduce as much as possible the required watermark energy (or, equivalently, the introduced host distortion) for a given performance (detection error probability).

Modelling watermark process as a communication task, in which the watermark is the signal to be transmitted, the host signal is an interference and the external attack is the channel noise, is very helpful when analysising watermarking performance. In this context, digital watermarking performance lower bounds have been investigated in [2], [3] and [4], and generally, they are limited by the system capacity, requiring a coded system architecture in order to approach this capacity. Still it is important to investigate performance lower bounds, for *uncoded* digital watermarking techniques using other modulation classes, rather than the binary unidimensional modulation technique.

Based on Costa's *Writing on Dirty Paper* article [5], and on its equivalence to the digital watermarking problem, a new performance lower bound for uncoded binary watermarking techniques is proposed in this article. We also introduce new M-ary, unidimensional and multidimensional, improved SS-based modulation techniques, increasing the set of available techniques to be considered for system design. Their performances and corresponding lower bounds are derived as well.

In Section II, we present the digital watermark embedding problem model, and in Section III, we introduce our proposal for the binary non-coded modulation performance lower bound. In Section IV we analyze our proposed lower bound with relevant existing non-coded binary watermarking techniques. Then on Section V new M-ary unidimensional and multidimensional Spread Spectrum based modulation techniques are introduced, their performances are evaluated, and the performance lower bounds for these new techniques classes are determined as well. In Section VI, we present some conclusions.

2   Problem Model

The digital watermarking problem has many aspects and steps to be considered: embedding domain and coefficients selection; human perception system (auditory or visual) model; possible attacks; security; specific application requirements. In this work we will only consider the embedding (modulation) step, where the digital watermark is to be embedded in a given host domain.

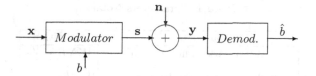

Fig. 1. Digital watermarking bit modulation/demodulation problem model

The block diagram on Fig. 1 illustrates the general model for uncoded binary watermark modulation. In this diagram each bit b, from the block of watermark informational bits, is to be embedded in N distinct samples from the host signal[1], vector $\mathbf{x} \in \mathbb{R}^N$, to produce the watermarked signal $\mathbf{s}$. Because of the similarity to the communication model, we also refer to the embedding process as modulation. The modulator processing outputs vector $\mathbf{s}(b, \mathbf{x}) \in \mathbb{R}^N$.

We say that the informational bit modulation rate (or watermark rate) is $1/N$ bits per sample. Naturally, among other requirements, the modulation technique shall be designed to maximize the watermark (information) embedding rate, minimizing vector length N necessary to embed each bit.

The distortion between the marked signal $\mathbf{s}$ and the host $\mathbf{x}$, due to the modulation with bit b, can be measured by

$$D_b = \frac{1}{N} \sum_{i=1}^{N} E\{(s_i - x_i)^2\}. \tag{1}$$

where $E\{.\}$ denotes expectation. Note that D_b also measure the watermark power (σ_{wm}^2). Therefore, it is possible to interpret the bit energy, E_b, responsible for introducing the corresponding distortion (due to modulation), as

$$E_b = ND_b = N\sigma_{wm}^2. \tag{2}$$

Many innocent signal processing (such as compression) or malicious (such as additive noise), can be applied to the digital watermarked signal $\mathbf{s}$ which may, unintentionally or intentionally, remove the digital watermark. These processing are generally called as attacks. In this work, the attack is modeled by a sequence of uncorrelated, additive, gaussian noise $\mathbf{n} \in \mathbb{R}^N$ with zero mean, and variance $\sigma_n^2 = N_0/2$. Therefore, the demodulator input is $\mathbf{y} = \mathbf{s} + \mathbf{n}$, corresponding to the watermarked signal under attack[2].

The demodulator objective is to produce, by observing $\mathbf{y}$, the best estimate $\hat{b}$ of the digital watermark. Techniques are said to be "non blind", when $\mathbf{x}$ is available at the receiver end or, "blind", otherwise. Most practical applications make general use of blind techniques.

---

[1] Vector $\mathbf{x}$ is any adequate representation of part of the host signal. In the case of a host image, for example, $\mathbf{x}$ could be a vector of pixels values or a vector of discrete cosine transform (DCT) coefficients.

[2] Other class of attacks which do not aim at the watermark itself, but rather at the detector synchronization capability, are not considered in our model. Segmentation and geometric transforms, are examples of detector synchronization attacks.

Table 1. Parameters Notation

Parameter	Definition
Watermark to noise ratio	$WNR = \frac{D_b}{\sigma_n^2}$
Normalized watermark-to-noise ratio	$WNR_N = \frac{E_b}{\sigma_n^2}$
Document-to-watermark ratio	$DWR = \frac{\sigma_x^2}{D_b}$
Document-to-noise ratio	$DNR = \frac{\sigma_x^2}{\sigma_n^2}$

Table 1 lists some parameters, notations and definitions, which will be used in this paper. It should be noticed that the normalized watermark-to-noise ratio $WNR_N = 2E_b/N_0$. Using this parameter is useful when analyzing single host sample and spread bit modulation techniques (for single host sample bit modulation, $N = 1$). Also, WNR_N has a simple relation with the parameter E_b/N_0, widely used in information and communication theory.

3   Binary Modulation Performance Lower Bound

An alternative model for the blind digital watermarking problem is presented in Fig.2. This model, which is equivalent to the model on Fig.1 when the distortion $e(\mathbf{x}, b) \triangleq s(\mathbf{x}, b) - \mathbf{x}$ is defined, as noticed in [2], casts the watermark problem, more clearly, in the framework of communication systems, as explained next. Signal $\mathbf{e}$ is interpreted as the input to a "super-channel" subject to an additive interference $\mathbf{x}$, cascaded with a true channel. The signal $\mathbf{x}$, taken to be the state of this "super-channel", is known at the modulator. In this representation the distortion is given by $\frac{1}{N} \| \mathbf{e} \|^2$.

The importance of this equivalent model is to allow the introduction of Costa's *Writing on Dirty Paper* article [5] result. Costa proved that, under some conditions, the capacity of the "super channel" shown on Fig. 2, surprisingly, is independent of the channel interference (state) $\mathbf{x}$, which is not known at the demodulator. It can be shown that this capacity is $C = \frac{1}{2} \log_2(1 + WNR)$ bits/sample, the same as that of a system with zero interference.

The understanding of the concept above discussed naturally allow us to conjecture that an ideal, uncoded, binary, digital watermarking system performance can be, at best, identical to that of a system with no host signal interference. In

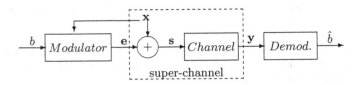

Fig. 2. Super-channel equivalent model for the digital watermarking problem

this sense, for performance analysis purposes, this ideal, binary watermarking modulation technique, can be taken to be equivalent to a binary input communication system[10] corrupted by gaussian noise. For the watermark model with gaussian noise (attack) under consideration, the corresponding error probability (p_e), obtained by exploiting the equivalence to a BPSK communication system with an antipodal signal constellation, is

$$p_e = \frac{1}{2}\text{erfc}(\sqrt{E_b/N_o}) = \frac{1}{2}\text{erfc}(\sqrt{WNR_N/2}). \tag{3}$$

We therefore propose above expression to be used as the performance lower bound for uncoded, binary, digital watermarking modulation under additive gaussian noise attack. This proposal is validated on the next section by examining the performance of existing binary watermarking modulation techniques against the proposed lower bound.

4   Lower Bound Comparison and Analysis with Existing Digital Watermarking Techniques

Several binary watermarking modulation techniques performances considered in this paper are summarized in Table 2. This includes the traditional spread spectrum (SS) modulation [6] and the corresponding improved (ISS) modulation technique [7], where the host interference is significantly reduced. Also considered were the techniques derived from the quantization index modulation (QIM) [2]: The "*Spread-Transform Dither Modulation*" ($STDM$) and the "*Low Bit Modulation*" (LBM). The quantized projection (QP) [8] combines elements from both SS and QIM methods. All performances curves ($\log(p_e)$ x $WNR_N(dB)$) listed in Table 2 are plotted in Fig. 3, where the proposed lower bound is also shown. One can assess the efficiency of each technique by examining, the asymptotic distance $\Delta WNR_N(dB)$ from the corresponding curve to the lower bound curve. Table 3 summarizes the results for each considered technique.

Table 2. Digital watermarking modulation techniques performances

Technique	p_e
lower bound	$\frac{1}{2}\text{erfc}\left(\sqrt{WNR_N/2}\right)$
SS	$\frac{1}{2}\text{erfc}\left(\sqrt{WNR_N/2(1+DNR)}\right)$
linear ISS	$\frac{1}{2}\text{erfc}\left(\sqrt{WNR_N-DNR)/2}\right)$
$STDM$	$erfc\left(\sqrt{\frac{3}{8}WNR_N}\right)$
LBM	$erfc\left(\sqrt{\frac{3}{14}WNR_N}\right)$
QP	$\frac{1}{2}\text{erfc}\left(\sqrt{WNR_N/2(1+DWR/N)}\right)$

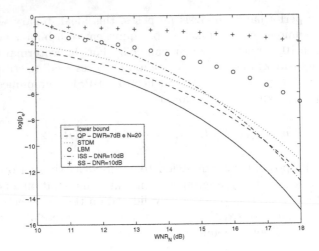

Fig. 3. Lower bound and existing uncoded modulation performances curves

Table 3. Technique performance distance from lower bound

Technique	$\Delta \mathbf{WNR_N(dB)}$	Conditions
SS	$10 \log(1 + DNR)$	$\forall \, p_e$
ISS	0	$WNR_N \gg DNR$ e $\forall \, p_e$
STDM	1.25	$p_e \to 0$
LBM	3.68	$p_e \to 0$
QP	0	$N \gg DWR$ e $\forall \, p_e$

From Table 3 one can see that there is a strong host interference for the SS technique while for ISS and QP techniques this interference is significantly reduced (even arbitrarily approaching to zero). For the $STDM$ and LBM techniques a gap is always observed.

The 1.25 dB gap between the $STDM$ performance and the proposed lower bound, shown in this table, was also the gap reported in [2] when analyzing the best advantage of the binary SS techniques class over the $STDM$ technique. In [2], however, the analysis was restricted to $STDM$ and to the limit case when $p_e \to 0$. The proposed lower bound allows this distance (advantage) measure to be extended to other techniques and to the entire range of error probabilities as well. Also in [7] the ISS performance was analyzed by considering that the performance of $STDM$ was 1.25 dB away from the optimum performance — rendering a discrepancy of more than 0.5 dB, for medium error probabilities, when compared to the here proposed lower bound (this discrepancy is even higher when lower WNR_N is considered).

It is also worth to point out that the performance of distortion-compensated (DC) techniques is also bounded by the proposed lower bound. In [9] this technique is incorporated to $STDM$ (DC-$STDM$) resulting in $1\ dB$ improvement as compared to the original $STDM$, at $p_e = 10^{-6}$ — bringing, therefore, the performance of DC-$STDM$, close to $0.5\ dB$ of the proposed lower bound. As observed in [4] we shall note that the DC-$STDM$ technique can also be understood as a particular scalar Costa scheme (SCS) implementation.

Therefore, we understand that the proposed uncoded binary modulation performance lower bound for digital watermarking techniques is consistent with many existing results, and corresponds to a more precise and general reference for any technique.

It is important to mention that the watermarking technique design can be broken in two distinct steps. The first step, called embedding (or modulation) gain step, aims at the development of an uncoded modulation technique with performance as close as possible to the corresponding uncoded performance lower bound (we may call this modulation step as *dirty paper coding*). Then, traditional (channel) coding should be introduced to achieve performance close to capacity, providing the so called coding gain.

5 M-Ary SS-Based Modulation Techniques

5.1   Traditional Approach for Binary SS-Based Watermarking

SS-based watermarking is illustrated in Fig. 4. A secret key K is used by a pseudo random vector generator (PRV) to produce a vector $\mathbf{u}$ with energy $E_b = \sum_{i=1}^{N} u_i^2 = N\sigma_u^2$. Specifics constraints shall be considered for the vector generator depending on the watermarking application requirements. Then, vector $\mathbf{u}$ is added or subtracted from signal $\mathbf{x}$, according to the value of variable $b \in \{\pm1\}$. The signal $\mathbf{s}$ is the watermarked signal.

Analysis of SS-based watermarking leads to a simple formula for the probability of error (technique performance). The bit embedding (modulating) yields

$$\mathbf{s} = \mathbf{x} + b\mathbf{u} \tag{4}$$

with $D_b = \sigma_u^2$.

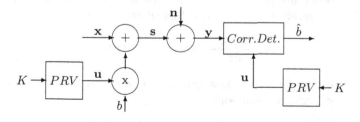

Fig. 4. Spread Spectrum digital watermarking modulation model

Considering the inner product $< \mathbf{x}, \mathbf{u} > = \frac{1}{N} \sum_{i=1}^{N} x_i u_i$, the detection is performed by first computing the normalized sufficient statistic

$$r = \frac{< \mathbf{y}, \mathbf{u} >}{\sigma_u^2} = \frac{< b\mathbf{u} + \mathbf{x} + \mathbf{n}, \mathbf{u} >}{\sigma_u^2} = b + x + n \tag{5}$$

and estimating the embedded bit by

$$\hat{b} = \text{sign}(r) \tag{6}$$

where $x = < \mathbf{x}, \mathbf{u} > /\sigma_u^2$ and $n = < \mathbf{n}, \mathbf{u} > /\sigma_u^2$.

We assume that $\mathbf{x}$ and $\mathbf{n}$ are vectors of uncorrelated samples from white Gaussian random process. Therefore $x_i \sim N(0, \sigma_x^2)$ and $n_i \sim N(0, \sigma_n^2)$ and it is easy to show that performance is given by

$$p_e = \frac{1}{2} \text{erfc} \left(\sqrt{WNR_N/2(1 + DNR)} \right). \tag{7}$$

5.2   Revisiting the Improved Binary Spread Spectrum (ISS)

The main idea behind the ISS modulation performance presented in [7] is that by using the modulator knowledge about signal $\mathbf{x}$, performance enhancement is obtained by modulating the energy of the inserted watermark to compensate for the host signal interference. The ISS embedding approach, a slight modification of the plain SS embedding, consists on controlling the amplitude of the inserted vector $\mathbf{u}$, by a function $\mu(x, b)$

$$\mathbf{s} = \mathbf{x} + \mu(x, b)\mathbf{u} \tag{8}$$

where, as before, $x = < \mathbf{x}, \mathbf{u} > /\sigma_u^2$. Note that plain SS is a particular case of ISS, where the function μ is made independent of x. The general problem of finding the optimum $\mu(x, b)$ is discussed in [7]. In this work we will consider only the linear approximation, since it is very effective and also yields simple expressions for analysis. The linear ISS modulation is defined as

$$\mathbf{s} = \mathbf{x} + (\alpha b - \lambda x)\mathbf{u}. \tag{9}$$

The parameters α and λ control, respectively, the distortion level and the removal of the host interference on the detection statistic. With the same channel noise model as before, receiver normalized sufficient statistic is

$$r = \frac{< \mathbf{y}, \mathbf{u} >}{\sigma_u^2} = \alpha b + (1 - \lambda)x + n. \tag{10}$$

To make distortion D_b of the new system to equal that of the plain SS, we enforce $D_b = \sigma_u^2$, which results on

$$\alpha = \sqrt{\frac{N\sigma_u^2 - \lambda^2 \sigma_x^2}{N\sigma_u^2}}. \tag{11}$$

Considering that $\hat{b} = \text{sign}(r)$, the linear ISS performance is easily derived as

$$p_e = \frac{1}{2}\text{erfc}\left(\sqrt{\frac{WNR_N - DNR\,\lambda^2}{2(1 + DNR(1-\lambda)^2)}}\right) \qquad (12)$$

The expression for the optimum value of parameter λ (λ_{opt}) can be computed through error probability minimization, by setting $\partial p_e / \partial \lambda = 0$, yielding

$$\lambda_{opt} = \frac{1}{2}\left(1 + \frac{1}{DNR} + \frac{WNR_N}{DNR} - \sqrt{(1 + \frac{1}{DNR} + \frac{WNR_N}{DNR})^2 - 4\frac{WNR_N}{DNR}}\right)$$
$$(13)$$

In addition, note, from this expression, that large DNR and $WNR_N > DNR$, yields $\lambda_{opt} \approx 1$. These assumptions result on performance expression approximation for linear ISS as shown in Table 2. Note also that, again for large DNR but with $WNR_N < DNR$, we have $\lambda_{opt} \approx E_b/\sigma_x^2$.

5.3 *M*-Ary Unidimensional *SS* Modulation

Up to now, all presented digital watermarking modulation techniques correspond to binary modulation, where one informational bit is embedded in N samples of the host signal $\mathbf{x}$. When higher watermarking rate is aimed, specially when higher watermark-to-noise ratio is considered, performance closer to capacity can be obtained by embedding more than one bit in signal $\mathbf{x}$ at once. M-ary unidimensional SS modulation can be achieved by

$$\mathbf{s} = \mathbf{x} + m\mathbf{u}, \qquad (14)$$

where $m \in \{\pm 1, \pm 3, ..., \pm(M-1)\}$, M is the number of symbols (levels) available and $\log_2(M)$ is the number of informational bits to be embedded in $\mathbf{x}$.

The normalized sufficient statistic is

$$r = \frac{<\mathbf{y}, \mathbf{u}>}{\sigma_u^2} = m + x + n. \qquad (15)$$

The above detection problem is equivalent to the M-ASK (Amplitude Shift Keying) communication detection problem, where the normalized sufficient statistic signals m form a collinear constellation. A slight difference is that in the M-ary unidimensional SS detection problem, not only the channel noise n influences the decision but also x added to that noise. Therefore we can obtain easily the performance for this technique, and its corresponding lower bound, from the M-ASK performance [10]

$$p_e = \frac{M-1}{M}\text{erfc}\left(\frac{d}{2\sqrt{N_0}}\right), \qquad (16)$$

where d is the distance between consecutive signals from the collinear M-ASK constellation, and total gaussian noise power is $\sigma_{nt}^2 = N_0/2$. Note that later on, the total noise power shall be considered as resulting from host interference and attack (channel) noise contributions.

Each embedded symbol introduces an average distortion (also representing the watermark symbol power) $D_s = E_s/N$, where E_s is the average symbol energy. The average bit energy is $E_b = E_s/\log_2(M)$, and its contribution to distortion (also representing average bit power) is $D_b = E_b/N$. Note that the average bit energy is not $N\sigma_u^2$ anymore as for the binary case. The average bit energy is now given by $E_b = \frac{M^2-1}{3\log_2(M)}N\sigma_u^2$, where $N\sigma_u^2$ is vector $\mathbf{u}$ energy.

Now let us first consider the performance lower bound for the class of M-ary unidimensional modulation techniques. The same argument used before, for the binary case, can also be used here to support that the ideal non coded M-ary unidimensional modulation technique will allow detection without host interference. In this sense, we shall consider the channel noise only, and then the M-ASK communication model is directly equivalent to this one, and its performance will represent the lower bound for these techniques class. [3] As mentioned before, the signal constellation to be considered for performance determination is represented by m, resulting in $d = 2$. The normalized channel noise power interfering at detection is $\sigma_n^2/(N\sigma_u^2)$. Therefore, from Eq. 16, the performance lower bound (symbol error probability), for an ideal modulation technique, is

$$p_e = \frac{M-1}{M}\text{erfc}\left(\sqrt{\frac{3\log_2(M)}{M^2-1}\frac{E_b}{N_0}}\right) = \frac{M-1}{M}\text{erfc}\left(\sqrt{\frac{3\log_2(M)}{M^2-1}\frac{WNR_N}{2}}\right).$$
(17)

Now we can derive the performance of the M-ary unidimensional SS modulation technique considering the "full" host interference, i.e., the total normalized noise power interfering at detection is $(\sigma_n^2 + \sigma_x^2)/(N\sigma_u^2)$. Therefore, as before, from Eq. 16, we can easily derive the performance of the M-ary unidimensional SS modulation technique to be

$$p_e = \frac{M-1}{M}\text{erfc}\left(\sqrt{\frac{3\log_2(M)}{M^2-1}\frac{WNR_N}{2(1+DNR)}}\right).$$
(18)

In order to reduce host interference at detection, we introduce now the M-ary unidimensional ISS, where modulation is defined as

$$\mathbf{s} = \mathbf{x} + (\alpha m - \lambda x)\mathbf{u},$$

following the same approach as for the binary ISS. The parameter α, computed as before in order to keep the same average distortion, is

$$\alpha = \sqrt{\frac{3}{M^2-1}\frac{(\frac{M^2-1}{3})N\sigma_u^2 - \lambda^2\sigma_x^2}{N\sigma_u^2}}.$$
(19)

---

[3] Techniques class refers to all possible M-ary unidimensional uncoded modulation techniques implementations, not restricted to the SS-based ones.

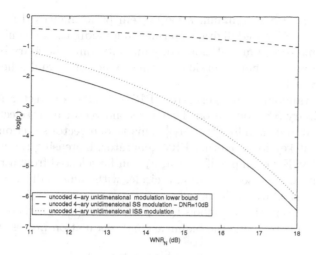

Fig. 5. 4-ary unidimensional uncoded modulation performance lower bound and the corresponding SS-based techniques performances

The normalized sufficient statistic is given by

$$r = <\mathbf{y}, \mathbf{u}> /\sigma_u^2 = \alpha m + (1 - \lambda)x + n$$

at the demodulator. Therefore the total normalized noise power interfering at detection is $(\sigma_n^2 + (1-\lambda)^2\sigma_x^2)/(N\sigma_u^2)$, and now the distance d between consecutive signals is 2α. From Eq. 16, the M-ary unidimensional ISS performance is

$$p_e = \frac{M-1}{M}\text{erfc}\left(\sqrt{\frac{3}{2(M^2-1)}\frac{\log_2(M)WNR_N - \lambda^2 DNR}{(1 + (1-\lambda)^2 DNR)}}\right). \quad (20)$$

The optimum parameter λ for error probability minimization is also obtained as for the traditional ISS and is determined to be

$$\lambda_{opt} = \frac{1}{2}\left(1 + \frac{1}{DNR} + \frac{\log_2(M)WNR_N}{DNR}\right)$$
$$- \frac{1}{2}\left(\sqrt{(1 + \frac{1}{DNR} + \frac{\log_2(M)WNR_N}{DNR})^2 - 4\frac{\log_2(M)WNR_N}{DNR}}\right). \quad (21)$$

Observe that for large DNR, λ_{opt} depends only on the value $(E_b/\sigma_x^2)\log_2(M)$.

Fig. 5 shows unidimensional SS-based techniques performances when $M = 4$. Note the significant modulation gain obtained when using the ISS technique.

5.4 M-Ary Multidimensional SS Modulation

In communication systems, M-ary modulation performance can be improved using multidimensional modulation, as can be observed when comparing the

M-ASK and M-PSK communication system performances [10]. Now we will introduce a new SS-based digital watermarking modulation technique considering a multidimensional modulation. For simplicity, only the 4-ary bidimensional case will be analyzed, but extension to other values of M and other dimensions is straightforward.

A pseudo random vector generator (PRV) produces a vector $\mathbf{u_1}$ as for the traditional binary SS modulation. Then a second vector $\mathbf{u_2}$ is selected such that it is orthogonal to $\mathbf{u_1}$ and $||\mathbf{u_2}|| = ||\mathbf{u_1}||$. This second vector selection can be done with a different key for a another PRV generator, increasing the watermarking system security. For example, if $N = 3$, $\mathbf{u_1}$ can be selected from a radius $\sqrt{N}\sigma_u$ sphere, and $\mathbf{u_2}$ can be selected from a circle, with same radius, belonging to a plane orthogonal to $\mathbf{u_1}$ at the origin.

We will represent the 4 symbols by a pair of bits (b_1, b_2) where $b_i \in \{-1, 1\}$. Then, we are able to define the bidimensional modulation process to be

$$\mathbf{s} = \mathbf{x} + b_1\mathbf{u_1} + b_2\mathbf{u_2}. \tag{22}$$

This specific 4-ary orthogonal bidimensional SS modulation technique implementation will be called QSS (quaternary SS) modulation. Note that symbol power (distortion) is $D_s = 2\sigma_u^2$ and that the average bit power is $D_b = \sigma_u^2$. The channel noise is the same as for the plain SS model.

At the demodulator, detection is performed computing the normalized sufficient statistic r_i for each dimension:

$$r_1 = \frac{<\mathbf{y}, \mathbf{u_1}>}{\sigma_u^2} = b_1 + x_1 + n_1 \tag{23}$$

and

$$r_2 = \frac{<\mathbf{y}, \mathbf{u_2}>}{\sigma_u^2} = b_2 + x_2 + n_2 \tag{24}$$

and estimating each embedded symbol (pair of bits) by

$$(\hat{b_1}, \hat{b_2}) = (\text{sign}(r_1), \text{sign}(r_2)) \tag{25}$$

where $x_i = <\mathbf{x}, \mathbf{u_i}>/\sigma_u^2$ e $n_i = <\mathbf{n}, \mathbf{u_i}>/\sigma_u^2$.

The above detection problem is equivalent to the $QPSK$ communication detection problem, where the normalized sufficient statistic signals forms a square constellation, and total noise is composed by host interference and attack contributions. The performance of the $QPSK$ modulation [10], with square constellation and side length d, is

$$p_e = \text{erfc}\left(\frac{d}{2\sqrt{N_0}}\right) - \frac{1}{4}\left(\text{erfc}(\frac{d}{2\sqrt{N_0}})\right)^2, \tag{26}$$

where the total interfering gaussian noise power is, for each dimension, $\sigma_{nt}^2 = N_0/2$. Note that on later discussion, the total noise power shall be considered as resulting from host interference and attack (channel) noise contributions.

We now consider the performance lower bound for this class of 4-ary bidimensional uncoded modulation techniques.[4] The same argument used before, can also be used here to support that an ideal technique will allow detection without host interference. In this sense, we shall consider only the normalized channel noise power $(\sigma_n^2/(N\sigma_u^2))$ as the total noise power interfering at detection, for each dimension, and the square constellation side length to be $d = 2$. Therefore, from Eq. 26, the performance lower bound (symbol error probability), for an ideal modulation technique, is

$$p_e = \text{erfc}\left(\sqrt{WNR_N/2}\right) - \frac{1}{4}\left(\text{erfc}(\sqrt{WNR_N/2})\right)^2. \tag{27}$$

Now we can derive the performance of the QSS modulation technique considering the "full" host interference, i.e., the total normalized noise power interfering at detection is $(\sigma_n^2 + \sigma_x^2)/(N\sigma_u^2)$, for each dimension. Therefore, again from Eq. 26, we can easily derive the performance of the QSS watermarking modulation technique to be

$$p_e = \text{erfc}\left(\sqrt{WNR_N/2(1+DNR)}\right) - \frac{1}{4}\left(\text{erfc}(\sqrt{WNR_N/2(1+DNR)})\right)^2. \tag{28}$$

In order to reduce host interference at detection, we introduce now the improved QSS ($IQSS$), where modulation is defined as

$$\mathbf{s} = \mathbf{x} + (\alpha_1 b_1 - \lambda_1 x_1)\mathbf{u_1} + (\alpha_2 b_2 - \lambda_2 x_2)\mathbf{u_2},$$

following the same approach as for the binary ISS. The normalized sufficient statistic for each dimension is given by

$$r_i = \frac{<\mathbf{y}, \mathbf{u_i}>}{\sigma_u^2} = \alpha_i b_i + (1 - \lambda_i)x_i + n_i$$

at the demodulator. The parameters α_i are computed as before, and both parameters are also given by equation 11. However, now the normalized sufficient statistic square constellation side length is $d = 2\alpha$, and the total normalized noise power interfering at detection is $(\sigma_n^2 + (1-\lambda)^2\sigma_x^2)/(N\sigma_u^2)$, for each dimension. The optimum parameters λ_i (for p_e minimization) are also expressed as in equation 13. Then, again from Eq. 26, the optimized $QISS$ performance is given by

$$p_e = \text{erfc}\left(\sqrt{\frac{(WNR_N - \lambda_{opt}^2 DNR)}{2(1+(1-\lambda_{opt})^2 DNR)}}\right) - \frac{1}{4}\left(\text{erfc}(\sqrt{\frac{(WNR_N - \lambda_{opt}^2 DNR)}{2(1+(1-\lambda_{opt})^2 DNR)}})\right)^2. \tag{29}$$

Fig. 6 shows the QSS and $QISS$ techniques performances together with the lower bound for quaternary orthogonal techniques class. Note the significant modulation gain obtained when using the $IQSS$ technique.

---

[4] Techniques class refers to all possible 4-ary bidimensional uncoded modulation techniques implementations, not restricted to the SS-based ones.

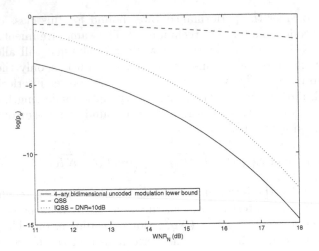

Fig. 6. Quaternary bidimensional uncoded modulation lower bound performance and the corresponding SS-based techniques performances

6   Conclusions

In this paper, we have proposed a performance lower bound for non-coded binary watermarking techniques. We have verified that this lower bound is consistent with existing non-coded binary watermarking techniques performances, representing a precise and generic bound. Then we have introduced the uncoded M-ary unidimensional and multidimensional SS-based modulation techniques, including the corresponding improved forms. The M-ary SS and ISS unidimensional technique performances were determined based on the equivalence with the M-ASK communication detection problem. The performances of the 4-ary SS and ISS bidimensional orthogonal techniques, namely QSS and $QISS$, respectively, were also determined based on the equivalence with the $QPSK$ communication detection problem. Finally, the performance lower bounds for these two new classes of watermarking techniques were determined as well. For further investigation, the performance lower bounds of new digital watermarking technique classes, with signal constellations equivalent to others communication system detection problems, is of interest.

References

1. M. Barni, F. Bartolini and J. Fridrich, "EDITORIAL - EURASIP Journal of applied signal processing" *[online]. Available: http://www.hindawi.co.uk/open-access/asp/volume-2002/S1110865702001981.pdf,* 2002.
2. B. Chen and G. W. Wornell, "Quantization Index Modulation: A class of provably good methods for digital watermarking and information embedding" *IEEE Trans. Inform. Theory,* v. 47, No. 4, p. 1423-1443, May 2001.

3. F. Perez-Gonzàlez, F. Balado, and J. R. Hernndez, "Performance analysis of existing and new methods for data hiding with known-host information in additive channels" *IEEE Trans. on Signal Processing*, v. 51, No. 4, p. 960-980, April 2003. Special Issue on Signal Processing for Data Hiding in Digital Media & Secure Content Delivery.

4. J. Eggers and B. Girod, "Informed Watermarking" *Kluwer Academic Publishers*, 2002, ISBN 1-4020-7071-3.

5. M. H. M. Costa, "Writing on dirty paper" *IEEE Trans. Inform. Theory*, v. IT-29, p. 439-441, May 1983.

6. I. J. Cox, J. Killian, F. T. Leighton, and T. Shamoon, "Secure spread spectrum watermarking for mutimedia" *IEEE Trans. Image Processing*, v. 6, p. 1673-1687, Dec 1997.

7. H. S. Malvar and D. A. F. Florêncio, "Improved Spread Spectrum: A new modulation Technique for robust watermarking" *IEEE Trans on Signal Processing*, v. 51, No. 4, p. 898-905, April 2003.

8. F. Perez-Gonzàlez and F. Balado, "Quantized projection data hiding" *In Proc. of the IEEE International Conference on Image Processing (ICIP)*, Rochester (NY), USA, September 2002.

9. B. Chen and G. W. Wornell, "Implementations of Quantization Index Modulation methods for digital watermarking and information embedding of multimedia" *J. VLSI Signal Processing Syst. Signal, Image, and Video Technol. (Special Issue on Multimedia Signal Processing)*, v. 27, p. 7-33, Feb 2001.

10. S. Benedetto and E. Biglieri, "Principles of Digital Transmission with Wireless Applications" *Kluwer Academic / Plenum Publishers*, 1999, ISBN 0-306-45753-9.

Evaluation of Feature Extraction Techniques for Robust Watermarking

Hae-Yeoun Lee[1], In Koo Kang[1], Heung-Kyu Lee[1], and Young-Ho Suh[2]

[1] Department of EECS, Korea Advanced Institute of Science and Technology,
Guseong-dong, Yuseong-gu, Daejeon, Republic of Korea
hytoiy@casaturn.kaist.ac.kr
[2] Digital Content Research Division, Electronics and Telecommunications Research Institute
Guseong-dong, Yuseong-gu, Daejeon, Republic of Korea

Abstract. This paper addresses feature extraction techniques for robust watermarking. Geometric distortion attacks desynchronize the location of the inserted watermark and hence prevent watermark detection. Watermark synchronization, which is a process of finding the location for watermark insertion and detection, is crucial to design robust watermarking. One solution is to use image features. This paper reviews feature extraction techniques that have been used in feature-based watermarking: the Harris corner detector and the Mexican Hat wavelet scale interaction method. We also evaluate the scale-invariant keypoint extractor in comparison with other techniques in aspect of watermarking. After feature extraction, the set of triangles is generated by Delaunay tessellation. These triangles are the location for watermark insertion and detection. Redetection ratio of triangles is evaluated against geometric distortion attacks as well as signal processing attacks. Experimental results show that the scale-invariant keypoint extractor is appropriate for robust watermarking.

1 Introduction

Digital technologies have grown over the last decades, wherein all kinds of multimedia such as image, video, and audio have been digitalized. However, digital multimedia can be copied, manipulated, and reproduced illegally without any quality degradation and protection.

Digital watermarking is an efficient solution for copyright protection of multimedia, which inserts copyright information into contents itself. This information is used as evidence of ownership. Digital watermarking has many applications, in which robustness has been an important issue. There have been many watermarking researches inspired by methods of image coding and compression. Most previous algorithms perform well against signal processing attacks. Nevertheless, in blind watermarking, these algorithms show severe weakness to geometric distortion attacks that desynchronize the location of the inserted copyright information and prevent watermark detection.

In order to resist geometric distortion attacks, watermark synchronization, a process for finding the location for watermark insertion and detection, should be per-

M. Barni et al. (Eds.): IWDW 2005, LNCS 3710, pp. 418–431, 2005.
© Springer-Verlag Berlin Heidelberg 2005

formed. Through this paper, we call this location *the patch*. There have been several solutions for watermark synchronization. The use of periodical sequences [1], the insertion of templates [2], and the use of invariant transforms [3, 4, 5, 6] have been reported among others. One solution to synchronize the watermark location is to use image features. Generally, image features represent an invariant reference for geometric distortion attacks so that referring features can solve watermark synchronization problems.

Kutter *et al.* [7] describe a feature-based synchronization method. First, they extract feature points using a scale interaction technique based on 2D continuous wavelet. Then, they use these points to segment the image, using a Voronoi diagram partitioning of the image. These segments are used as the patches for watermarking. Bas *et al.* [8] extract feature points by applying the Harris corner detector and then decompose the feature points into a set of disjoint triangles by Delaunay tessellation. These triangles are used as the patches for watermarking. Nikolaidis and Pitas [9] describe an image-segmentation based synchronization method. By applying an adaptive k-mean clustering technique, they segment images and select several of the largest regions. The bounding rectangles of these regions are used as the patches for watermarking. Tang and Hang [10] extract feature points using the Mexican Hat wavelet scale interaction method. Disks of fixed radius *R,* whose centers is the feature points are normalized, because objects in the normalized image are invariant to image distortions. The normalized disks are used as the patches for watermarking.

In watermark synchronization by reference to image features, feature extraction is important for achieving robustness of the watermark. This paper reviews feature extraction techniques that have been used in feature-based watermarking: the Harris corner detector and the Mexican Hat wavelet scale interaction method. We also evaluate an affine-invariant feature extractor called as the scale-invariant keypoint extractor in comparison with other techniques. It is important to redetect the patches in attacked images, which have been detected in the original image for robust watermarking, so we measure redetection ratio of the patches against geometric distortion attacks as well as signal processing attacks. Results show that the scale-invariant keypoint extractor is useful and robust against attacks.

The following section reviews feature extraction techniques and describes the scale-invariant keypoint extractor. Section 3 explains the way to synchronize the location of the watermark. Evaluation results are shown in Section 4. Section 5 concludes this paper.

2 Feature Extraction Techniques

There have been many feature extraction techniques in image processing and computer vision applications. Bas *et al.* [8] compared major feature extraction techniques that consider image gradients: the Harris corner detector, the SUSAN detector, and the Achard-Rouquet detector. The Harris corner detector performed well against image attacks. However, they just focus on the redetection of each feature point, not the patches for watermarking. Image segmentation is commonly used for feature extraction, because segmented regions are expected to be invariant to image distortions. However, the number of regions depends on image contents and its texture. Moreover, their location is sensitive to image distortions [9]. In our opinions, regions from image segmentation are not useful for watermarking purpose. The Mexican Hat wavelet scale interaction method is an intensity-based feature extraction technique and has been used for robust watermarking [7, 10]. In this section, we review two feature extraction techniques: the Harris corner detector and the Mexican Hat wavelet scale interaction method and then describe the scale-invariant keypoint extractor.

2.1 Harris Corner Detector

The Harris corner detector is initially developed for 3D reconstruction [8] and uses image gradients. This detector calculates locally averaged moment matrix computed from image gradients and then combines eigenvalues of the moment matrix to compute a corner-strength, whose local maximums indicate corner locations.

The locally averaged moment matrix $E_{x,y}$ is expressed by

$$E_{x,y} = (x,y)H(x,y)^T \text{ with } H = \begin{bmatrix} D_{x,x} & D_{x,y} \\ D_{x,y} & D_{y,y} \end{bmatrix}. \tag{1}$$

$E_{x,y}$ can be considered as a local auto-correlation function with a shape factor H. D represents image gradient of x- and y-axis. The corner-strength R_H is acquired by combining the eigenvalues as follows.

$$R_H = Det(H) - kTr^2(M), \text{ where } Tr(H) = D_{xx} + D_{yy}, Det(H) = D_{xx}D_{yy} - D_{xy}^2. \tag{2}$$

k is an arbitrary constant. An example of the corner-strength is shown in Fig. 1. Corner points are extracted by searching local maximums on this corner-strength R_H. The Harris corner detector shows high accuracy in corner locations. However, the set of corner points is sensitive to image noise.

Fig. 1. (a) original image and (b) corner-strength R_H

2.2 Mexican Hat Wavelet Scale Interaction

The Mexican Hat wavelet scale interaction method is initially used in Manjunath *et al.* [11]. Feature points are determined by identifying significant intensity changes that occur at different scaled version of the same image. This method applies two different scale of the Mexican Hat wavelet to the same image and calculates a scale interaction image between two scaled images. Local maximums of the scale interaction image indicate feature points. The Mexican Hat wavelet, called as Marr wavelet, is invariant to rotation because it has a circularly symmetric frequency response.

The Mexican Hat wavelet at location x is defined as

$$\varphi(\vec{x}) = (2 - |\vec{x}|^2) e^{-|\vec{x}|^2/2} \text{ with } |\vec{x}| = (x^2 + y^2)^{1/2}. \tag{3}$$

The 2D Fourier transform of $\varphi(\vec{x})$ is given as follows.

$$\varphi(\vec{k}) = (\vec{k} \cdot \vec{k}) e^{-|\vec{k}|^2/2}, \tag{4}$$

where $\vec{k}$ represents 2D spatial frequency.

The scale interaction image is acquired by the following quantities.

$$P_{ij}(\vec{x}) = \left| M_i(\vec{x}) - \gamma \cdot M_j(\vec{x}) \right|, \tag{5}$$

$M_i(\vec{x})$ represents response of the Mexican Hat wavelet at the image location $\vec{x}$ for scale i and j respectively. γ is a normalizing constant. $P_{ij}(\vec{x})$ is the scale interaction between two different scale i and j. Local maximums of $P_{ij}(\vec{x})$ are determined as the set of potential feature points and the points whose strength exceed a threshold are used as the feature points. Fig. 2b and 2c show images filtered by the Mexican Hat wavelet operator with different scale. Fig. 2d shows the scale interaction image between two filtered images and their local maximums are feature points.

2.3 Scale-Invariant Keypoint Extractor

In object recognition and image retrieval applications, affine-invariant features have been recently researched [12, 13, 14]. These features are highly distinctive and matched with high probability against a large case of image distortions, such as viewpoint changes, illumination condition changes, partial visibility, and image noise. In watermark synchronization using image features, the robustness of features is related to that of watermarking systems. We introduce an affine-invariant feature extractor called as the scale-invariant keypoint extractor [12].

The scale-invariant keypoint extractor considers local image characteristics and retrieves feature points with properties of each point such as the location, the scale, and the orientation. These feature points are invariant to image rotation, scaling, translation, partly illumination changes, and projective transform.

The scale-invariant keypoint extractor detects feature points through a staged filtering approach that identifies stable points in the scale-space. To generate a scale-space, we use a difference of Gaussian function, in which we successively smooth an image with a variable scale (σ_1, σ_2, and σ_3) Gaussian filter and calculate difference images by subtracting two successive smoothed images. In this scale-space, we retrieve all local maximums and minimums by checking 8 closest neighborhoods in the same scale and 9 neighborhoods in the scale above and below (see Fig. 3). These locations are invariant to the scale change of images.

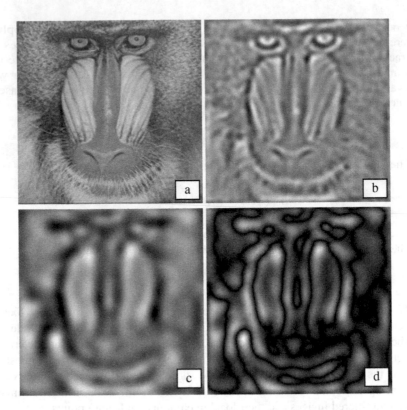

Fig. 2. (a) original image, (b) image filtered by Mexican Hat wavelet scale 3.0, (c) image filtered by Mexican Hat wavelet scale 4.0, and (d) scale interaction image between two different scales

After candidate points are found, the points that have a low contrast or are poorly localized are removed by measuring stability of each feature point at its location and scale. The stability of each feature point is calculated from a 2 by 2 Hessian matrix H as follows.

$$Stability = \frac{(D_{xx} + D_{yy})^2}{D_{xx}D_{yy} - D_{xy}^2} < \frac{(r+1)^2}{r}, \text{ where } H = \begin{bmatrix} D_{xx} & D_{xy} \\ D_{xy} & D_{yy} \end{bmatrix}. \tag{6}$$

r is the ratio between the largest and smallest eigenvalues and controls the stability. D represents image gradient of x- and y-axis.

Orientation of each feature point is assigned by considering local image properties. Orientation histogram is formed from gradient orientations at all sample points within the circular window of a feature point. Gradient magnitude m and orientation θ are computed by using pixel differences as follows.

$$m = \sqrt{(L_{x+1,y} - L_{x-1,y})^2 + (L_{x,y+1} - L_{x,y-1})^2}$$

$$\theta = \tan^{-1}\left(\frac{L_{x,y+1} - L_{x,y-1}}{L_{x+1,y} - L_{x-1,y}}\right) \qquad (7)$$

L is a Gaussian filtered image with the closest scale, in which each feature point is found. Peak in this histogram corresponds to dominant direction of the feature point. Scale-invariant keypoints obtained through this process are invariant to rotation, scaling, translation, and illumination changes of images. Therefore, scale-invariant keypoints may be useful to design robust watermarking.

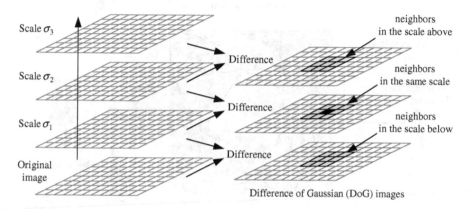

Fig. 3. Scale-space from the difference of gaussian function and the closest neighborhoods of a pixel.

3 Watermark Synchronization Using Feature Extraction

Watermarking algorithms are divided into two processes, watermark insertion and detection. Watermark insertion is a process of inserting the watermark into contents imperceptibly. Watermark detection is a process of detecting the inserted watermark from contents to prove ownership. General framework of feature-based watermarking is shown in Fig. 4 [8].

The first step for watermark insertion and detection is analyzing contents to extract features and then features are relatively related to generate the patches for watermarking. During watermark insertion, several patches are extracted from an image and the watermark is inserted into all patches. During watermark detection, there are several patches and all patches are tried to detect the watermark. We can prove ownership successfully if the watermark is detected correctly from at least one patch. Correlation-based detector is used to determine whether or not the watermark is inserted. Because the watermark is inserted multiple times into the image, it is highly likely that this method has high probability to detect the watermark even after attacks.

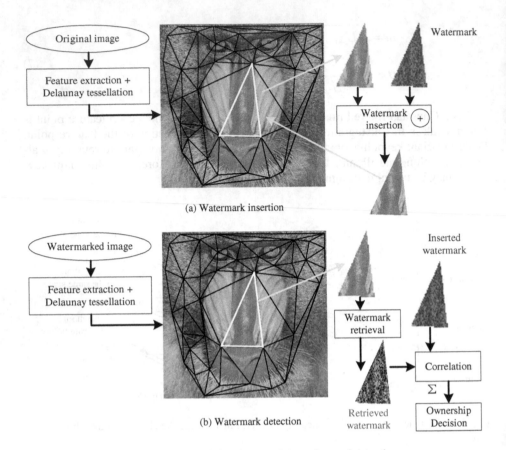

Fig. 4. Framework for watermark insertion and detection

As explained in Section 2, feature points are extracted by analyzing media contents. The feature points should be relatively related to generate the patches for watermark insertion and detection. Delaunay tessellation is commonly used to formulate the patches by decomposing the feature points into a set of disjoint triangles. Given a set of feature points, Delaunay tessellation is the straight line dual of the corresponding Voronoi diagram which partitions the image into segments such that all points in one segment are closer to the location of the feature points. This tessellation is independent of rotation, scaling, and translation of images. Moreover, computational cost is low. The extracted triangles are shaped irregularly. During watermarking, we require warping between the right-handed triangular watermark and the extracted triangles, which is affine transformation as follows.

$$\begin{pmatrix} x_n \\ y_n \end{pmatrix} = \begin{pmatrix} a_{11} & a_{12} \\ a_{21} & a_{22} \end{pmatrix} \begin{pmatrix} x_o \\ y_o \end{pmatrix} + \begin{pmatrix} s_1 \\ s_2 \end{pmatrix}. \tag{8}$$

(x_o, y_o) and (x_n, y_n) are coordinates of the original points and warped points respectively. This affine transformation is composed of 6 unknown parameters and mathematically calculated using three corner points of a triangle.

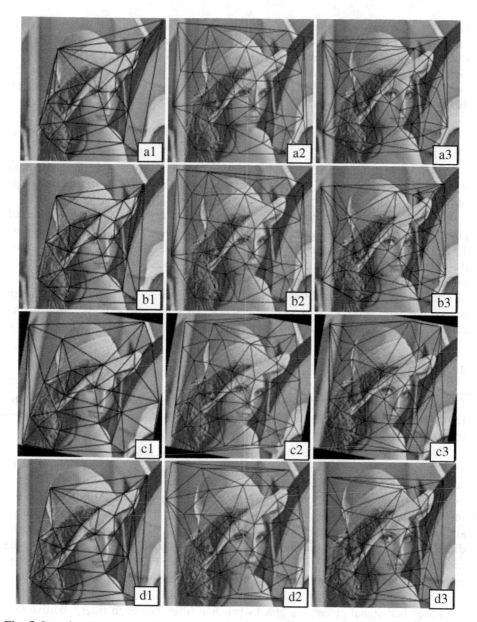

Fig. 5. Location for watermark insertion and detection against image attacks: (a) original image, (b) image with additive uniform noise, (c) image with rotation 10°, and (d) image with scaling 1.1x

As described in Bas *et al.* [8], the distribution of feature points is an important factor to design robust watermarking. In other words, the distance between adjacent feature points should be selected carefully. If the distance is too short, the distribution of the feature points is concentrated on textured areas. Furthermore, the size of the patch for watermark insertion is too small to insert the watermark efficiently because the watermark should be sampled. If the distance is too long, feature points become isolated. In order to obtain the homogeneous distribution of feature points, we apply a circular neighborhood constraint, in which the feature points whose strength is the largest are selected [8]. The neighborhood size D is dependent on image dimension and quantized by r as follows.

$$D = \frac{w+h}{r}. \qquad (9)$$

w and h represent the width and height of images, respectively. r is a constant to control the size. Circle diameter depends on image dimensions to be against scale change of images.

For feature extraction methods described in Section 2, Fig. 5 shows the extracted patches for watermarking against additive uniform noise, rotation 10°, and scaling 1.1x. The first column is from the Harris corner detector. The second column is from the Mexican Hat wavelet scale interaction method. The last column is from the scale-invariant keypoint extractor. Although signal processing attacks and geometric distortion attacks result in different tessellation by modifying relative position of the feature points, there are several corresponding patches. Therefore, we can synchronize successfully the location for watermark insertion and detection.

4 Evaluation Results

This section evaluates three feature extraction methods for robust watermarking: the Harris corner detector (method 1), the Mexican Hat wavelet scale interaction method (method 2), and the scale-invariant keypoint extractor (method 3).

We have used 15 images with the size of 512 by 512 pixels including commonly used images in image processing applications (see Fig. 6). Because our research focuses on watermarking of remote-sensing imagery, we include satellite images such as IKONOS (1.1m resolutions), SPOT (10m resolutions), and KOMPSAT (6.6m resolutions). Differently from natural images, satellite images contain much noise, similar patterns are repeated multiple times and that make feature extraction to be difficult. The quantization parameter r of the neighborhood size is set as 24, i.e. the minimum distance between adjacent feature points is about 42 pixels. The patches from this parameter may be small to watermark efficiently. On future works, we are going to adjust this parameter during applying watermarking scheme to the patches.

We applied signal processing attacks (median filter, Gaussian filter, additive uniform noise, and JPEG compression) and geometric distortion attacks (rotation, scaling, and cropping) listed in Stirmark 3.1.

For each method, the number of extracted patches is shown in Table 1. The averaged number from method 1, method 2, and method 3 were 73 patches, 79 patches, and 71 patches, respectively.

We measured redetection ratio of the patches, which represents how many patches that have been detected in the original image are correctly redetected in the attacked images. If the difference between the patches from the original image and the patches from attacked images was less than two pixels, we regarded the patches as having been correctly redetected. These small misalignments can be compensated by searching some pixels around position of the patches originally founded during watermark detection. In particular, prior to comparison, we reversed coordinates of the patches in attacked images into coordinates in the original image by calculating their inverse transform.

Fig. 6. Test images: Baboon, Boat, Lake, Bridge, Couple, Pepper, Lena, Indian, Plane, Pentagon, Girl, IKONOS, KOMPSAT, SPOT1, and SPOT2

Table 1. Number of extracted patches for each method

	Babo.	Boat	Lake	Brid.	Coup.	Pepp.	Lena	Indian	Plane	Penta.	Girl	Ikono.	Kom.	Spot1	Spot2
Method1	67	63	86	89	58	61	40	60	53	60	41	81	114	113	102
Method2	60	73	86	79	71	72	67	77	71	106	66	90	98	80	87
Method3	57	46	65	69	56	71	65	77	56	55	51	81	122	91	97

Table 2. Redetection ratios under signal processing attacks (unit %)

		Baboon	Lake	Bridge	Lena	Indian	Plane	Penta.	Ikonos	Komp.	Spot2	Total
Median 2×2	Method1	25	35	25	58	28	47	35	20	21	50	34
	Method2	50	57	76	85	88	77	56	82	68	78	73
	Method3	40	51	39	46	21	45	36	36	24	48	41
Median 3×3	Method1	39	33	28	55	35	17	28	25	13	52	35
	Method2	50	64	67	66	64	77	53	70	54	90	66
	Method3	19	17	36	29	27	55	36	17	37	32	34
Median 4×4	Method1	19	22	11	40	42	21	20	9	11	35	25
	Method2	23	41	52	67	48	24	47	29	23	82	48
	Method3	21	22	35	29	45	50	24	32	15	36	31
Gaussian filter	Method1	57	42	34	53	67	43	25	33	38	45	44
	Method2	90	77	92	85	78	90	64	84	92	90	85
	Method3	75	62	59	74	51	86	58	54	52	62	64
Uniform noise	Method1	45	38	30	58	25	28	27	23	35	43	41
	Method2	72	78	81	75	75	79	71	78	86	91	81
	Method3	42	62	51	72	44	59	29	52	57	47	53
JPEG comp. 40	Method1	67	36	37	58	47	38	27	21	40	45	46
	Method2	85	81	90	88	84	100	68	88	87	93	87
	Method3	60	80	59	57	35	89	64	58	53	61	61
JPEG comp. 50	Method1	48	47	37	60	37	32	37	32	41	56	46
	Method2	87	85	81	69	88	100	82	89	91	93	87
	Method3	72	57	51	77	64	88	55	62	62	81	65
JPEG com. 60	Method1	46	36	39	60	48	30	57	25	52	51	46
	Method2	85	78	95	90	74	97	81	97	87	93	89
	Method3	65	63	59	65	53	82	47	67	62	70	62
JPEG comp. 70	Method1	45	42	38	58	45	47	37	27	39	55	45
	Method2	97	81	91	88	87	100	78	89	91	93	90
	Method3	74	63	59	52	58	86	56	54	63	78	64
JPEG comp. 80	Method1	46	36	42	58	48	38	40	33	47	51	47
	Method2	92	78	97	94	77	100	84	82	90	93	90
	Method3	70	71	61	69	49	93	53	53	67	76	67
JPEG comp. 90	Method1	52	38	43	60	48	43	40	31	46	48	47
	Method2	98	78	95	90	77	100	81	92	90	93	90
	Method3	74	72	61	72	58	82	58	54	57	79	67

Table 2 shows redetection ratios under signal processing attacks and Table 3 shows redetection ratios under geometric distortion attacks. We represent results of several images. The last column represents the averaged detection ratios of 15 images.

Against signal processing attacks, method 2 based on the Mexican Hat wavelet scale interaction method outperformed than other methods. Because the Mexican Hat wavelet considers image intensity distributed to the wide area, small distortions in intensity do not affect performance. Because the Harris corner detector uses image gradients that are sensitive to image noise, method 1 based on the Harris corner detector showed relatively low performance and worked poorly in images which included complex texture like Baboon or contained much noise like satellite images: IKONOS and KOMPSAT. Method 3 using scale-invariant keypoints showed higher performance than method 1, but relatively lower performance than method 2.

Table 3. Redetection ratios under geometric distortion attacks (unit %)

		Baboon	Lake	Bridge	Lena	Indian	Plane	Penta.	Ikonos	Komp.	Spot2	Total
Crop 5%	Method1	34	27	30	40	25	34	40	10	26	28	30
	Method2	18	22	25	31	23	21	19	24	27	24	25
	Method3	25	38	42	42	23	63	38	27	39	51	38
Crop 10%	Method1	21	24	26	38	25	28	42	7	25	27	26
	Method2	15	16	23	18	22	13	15	11	14	22	18
	Method3	25	34	28	42	27	48	36	21	33	36	31
Crop 15%	Method1	22	23	18	38	28	23	38	4	19	25	24
	Method2	7	15	19	15	14	7	13	8	13	17	14
	Method3	19	28	20	26	17	43	25	14	32	30	25
Crop 20%	Method1	13	20	12	40	22	17	37	5	20	24	21
	Method2	5	5	11	7	16	3	8	4	11	15	9
	Method3	16	23	19	18	13	39	25	9	23	23	21
Crop 25%	Method1	9	16	11	38	18	15	32	1	18	23	18
	Method2	3	5	5	6	12	3	6	6	7	9	6
	Method3	9	18	17	15	13	29	20	10	20	21	17
Rotation 0.5° +Cropping	Method1	52	26	36	40	38	40	35	23	27	40	37
	Method2	80	53	58	55	52	48	47	48	58	70	57
	Method3	40	58	39	63	38	54	40	54	40	48	45
Rotation 1.0° +Cropping	Method1	31	21	28	40	32	34	23	25	18	35	32
	Method2	52	50	56	52	40	44	44	43	54	59	50
	Method3	47	38	38	42	38	61	44	51	33	44	42
Rotation 5.0° +Cropping	Method1	34	16	15	40	33	40	25	12	18	32	29
	Method2	27	33	34	39	39	23	26	29	44	40	33
	Method3	32	26	35	46	25	36	35	32	25	35	32
Rotation 10.0° +Cropping	Method1	33	21	27	33	27	26	22	11	19	22	25
	Method2	23	22	25	36	34	25	23	26	21	34	27
	Method3	21	23	35	38	21	45	47	41	25	33	33
Rotation 15.0° +Cropping	Method1	27	24	20	45	32	30	15	12	12	32	26
	Method2	17	24	30	36	23	17	21	24	22	30	25
	Method3	23	29	29	42	19	36	27	40	15	33	29
Rotation 30.0° +Cropping	Method1	25	17	19	40	23	30	25	14	12	34	24
	Method2	17	15	22	28	25	17	23	24	24	26	23
	Method3	26	18	17	23	18	21	29	33	16	25	23
Scaling 0.8×	Method1	10	10	6	20	3	15	42	11	4	19	19
	Method2	0	0	0	0	0	0	2	0	0	0	0
	Method3	11	9	13	8	8	11	13	12	7	8	10
Scaling 0.9×	Method1	33	20	18	23	40	34	35	22	6	37	29
	Method2	0	0	0	1	1	0	8	0	1	0	1
	Method3	19	22	30	12	5	11	35	23	11	21	19
Scaling 1.1× +Cropping	Method1	27	15	30	45	25	43	32	19	11	36	27
	Method2	5	0	13	4	1	3	24	0	4	6	5
	Method3	25	9	26	38	12	29	29	16	7	22	20
Scaling 1.2× +Cropping	Method1	12	15	13	43	22	30	17	4	5	25	20
	Method2	0	0	4	0	0	0	5	0	2	0	1
	Method3	11	11	7	15	5	11	13	4	5	7	8

Against most geometric distortion attacks except scaling attacks, method 3 performed relatively well. However, the performance differences were small to be ignorable. Method 1 worked better than other methods in scaling attacks because image gradients were preserved in scale change of images. Method 2 showed severe weakness in scaling attacks. In scale changes of images, the response of the Mexican Hat wavelet is different, feature points are extracted in different position, and hence method 2 failed to redetect the patches. Method 3 showed relatively lower perform-ance than method 1 in scaling attacks. However, overall performance is acceptable for watermarking purposes. We can prove the ownership if the watermark is detected from at least one patch.

5 Conclusion and Future Works

Watermark synchronization is crucial to design robust watermarking. One solution to find the location for watermark insertion and detection is by reference to image fea-tures. In feature-based watermarking, feature extraction is important to design robust watermarking, so feature extraction method should be selected carefully. This paper reviewed major feature extraction techniques: the Harris corner detector and the Mexican Hat wavelet scale interaction method. We evaluated the scale-invariant key-point extractor in comparison with other techniques in aspect of watermarking. First, we extracted feature points. Then, the feature points were decomposed into a set of triangles by Delaunay tessellation. We measured the redetection ratio of the patches against geometric distortion attacks as well as signal processing attacks. The scale-invariant keypoint extractor showed acceptable performance for robust watermarking. Nevertheless, the redetection ratio in scaling attacks was relatively low. Our future research focuses on increasing robustness against geometric distortion attacks and applying the watermarking scheme to the patches.

References

1. M. Kutter: Watermarking resisting to translation, rotation and scaling. Proc. of SPIE, Vol. 3528 (1998) 423-431
2. S. Pereira, T. Pun: Robust template matching for affine resistant image watermark. IEEE Trans. on Image Processing, Vol. 9 (2000) 1123-1129
3. J.J.K.O. Ruanaidh, T. Pun: Rotation, scale and translation invariant spread spectrum digi-tal image watermarking, Signal Processing, Vol. 66 (1998) 303-317
4. C. Lin, I.J. Cox: Rotation, scale and translation resilient watermarking for images. IEEE Trans. on Image Processing, Vol. 10 (2001) 767-782
5. D. Simitopoulos, D.E. Koutsonanos, M.G. Strintzis: Robust image watermarking based on generalized radon transformation, IEEE Trans. on Circuits and Systems for Video Tech-nology, Vol. 13 (2003) 732-745
6. M. Arghoniemy, A.H. Twefik: Geometric invariance in image watermarking. IEEE Trans. on Image Processing, Vol. 13 (2004) 145-153
7. M. Kutter, S.K. Bhattacharjee, T. Ebrahimi: Towards second generation watermarking schemes. Proc. of ICIP, Vol. 1, (1999) 320-323
8. P. Bas, J-M. Chassery, B. Macq: Geometrically invariant watermarking using feature points. IEEE Trans. on Image Processing, Vol. 11 (2002) 1014-1028
9. A. Nikolaidis, I. Pitas: Region-based image watermarking. IEEE Trans. on Image Process-ing, Vol. 10 (2001) 1726-1740

10. C.W. Tang, H-M. Hang: A feature-based robust digital image watermarking scheme. IEEE Trans. on Signal Processing, Vol. 51 (2003) 950-959
11. B.S. Manjunath, C. Shekhar, R. Chellappa: A new approach to image feature detection with applications, Pattern Recognition, Vol. 4 (1996) 627-640
12. D.G. Lowe: Distinctive image features from scale-invariant keypoints. International Journal of Computer Vision, Vol. 60 (2004) 91-110
13. K. Mikolajczyk, C. Schmid: Scale and affine invariant interest point detectors. International Journal of Computer Vision, Vol. 60 (2004) 63-86
14. T. Tuytelaars, L.V. Gool: Matching widely separated views based on affine invariant regions. International Journal of Computer Vision, Vol. 59 (2004) 61-85

Perceptual Video Watermarking in the 3D-DWT Domain Using a Multiplicative Approach

Patrizio Campisi and Alessandro Neri*

University of Roma TRE, Rome, Italy
{campisi, neri}@uniroma3.it

Abstract. A video watermarking method operating in the three-dimensional discrete wavelet transform (3D DWT) relaying on the use of a novel video perceptual mask, applied in the 3D DWT domain, is here proposed. Specifically the method consists in partitioning the video sequence into spatio-temporal units of fixed length. Then the video shots undergo a one level 3D DWT. The mark is embedded by means of a multiplicative approach using perceptual masking on the 3D DWT coefficients in order to trade off between the mark robustness and its imperceptibility. The mask we propose takes into account the spatio-temporal frequency content by means of the spatio-temporal contrast sensitivity function, the luminance, and the variance of the 3D subbands which host the mark. The effectiveness of the proposed mask is verified experimentally, thus guaranteeing a high imperceptibility of the mark. Moreover, experimental results show the robustness of the proposed approach against MPEG2 compression, MPEG4 compression, gain attack, collusion, and transcoding.

1 Introduction

The dramatic growth of the digital multimedia market we have experienced in the last few years has risen the need to protect the media content. In this paper we focus on the issue of copyright protection of digital video sequences by using digital watermarking.

A review of many video watermarking techniques, attacks, and applications can be found in [1], [2]. The first proposed video watermaking techniques where the straightforward extention of existing algorithms designed for still image watermaking. In fact, in these approaches, the video is considered as a succession of still digital images, which are marked independently of the others. However, the use of these algorithms does not allow exploiting the temporal dimension of a video thus leading to methods which are not robust to both non-hostile and hostile video processing operations such as temporal desynchronization, video format conversion, video editing and video collusion [3]. To counteract these attacks some approaches operating in three dimensional domains have been recently proposed, which, although computationally more intensive, offer greater resilience to attacks with respect to analogous embedding methods operating in both 1D and 2D domain.

---

* This work was partially supported by the Italian MIUR project WAtermarking for Video and imagEs COpyright Protection (WAVECOP).

M. Barni et al. (Eds.): IWDW 2005, LNCS 3710, pp. 432–443, 2005.

Among the most recent developed watermarking methods operating in the 3D domains, we cite the following. The 3D discrete Fourier transform domain has been exploited in [4]. A spread spectrum approach operating in the 3D wavelet domain, obtained by first performing a 2D spatial wavelet transform and then a temporal 1D wavelet transform, has been presented in [5]. In [6] a discrete wavelet transform based video watermarking method based on the use of BCH codes, 3D interliving, incorporating an effective temporal synchronization technique has been presented. In [7] the mark is embedded in the 3D Wavelet domain, by using the pseudo random linear statistics of pseudo random connected regions in the DC subband of the 3D wavelet domain. A video watermarking technique using the 3D discrete cosine transform has been described in [8]. In order to make the embedding of the mark imperceptible, methods exploiting perceptual information have been presented in the recent past (see for example [9], [10]).

In this paper, we propose a perceptual based video watermarking technique operating in the 3D DWT domain. In order to compromise between robustness and imperceptibility we propose a novel perceptual mask that jointly exploits both the spatial and the temporal dimension of a video sequence by weighting the 3D wavelet coefficients by means of a three dimensional spatio-temporal frequency mask, a luminance, and a variance mask. The mark embedding is performed by weighing the watermark by means of the obtained mask, and then by using the well known muliplicative embedding approach. The paper is organized as follows. In Section 2 the 3D DWT is briefly reviewed. The watermark embedding is detailed in Section 3. The perceptual mask is derived in Section 4. In Section 5 the watermark detection is detailed. Eventually, experimental results and conclusions are drawn in Section 6.

2   Three Dimensional Discrete Wavelet Transform

The 3D discrete wavelet transform we consider is a separable dyadic tree-structured transform. Given a video shot $\{v[n_1, n_2, n_3] | 0 \leq n_1 < N_1-1, 0 \leq n_2 < N_2-2, 0 \leq n_3 < N_3-3\}$, composed by N_3 frames of dimension $N_1 \times N_2$ pixels, its one level 3D DWT is obtained by performing a 1D temporal transform followed by 2D spatial transform. The signal so obtained is indicated as $v_{\alpha\beta\gamma}^{(1)}[n_1, n_2, n_3]$ with $(\alpha, \beta, \gamma) \in \{L, H\}$, where α, β, and γ refer to the lowpass (L) and to the highpass (H) representation of the given signal along the rows, columns, and the third dimension respectively. A multilevel 3D DWT $v_{\alpha\beta\gamma}^{(l)}[n_1, n_2, n_3]$, with $l > 1$, is obtained by recursively applying the aforementioned procedure on the lowest frequency subband $v_{LLL}^{(l-1)}[n_1, n_2, n_3]$.

3   Watermark Embedding

The proposed watermarking method (see Fig. 1), can be summarized as follows:

- the video sequence is segmented into non-overlapping spatio-temporal plot units, namely *shots*, of fixed length;

- each shot undergoes a one level 3D discrete wavelet transform;
- a perceptual mask on the different subbands is evaluated;
- perceptual multiplicative watermarking is performed in the wavelet domain;
- the subbands are recomposed and the 3D IDWT is performed, thus obtaining the marked shot.

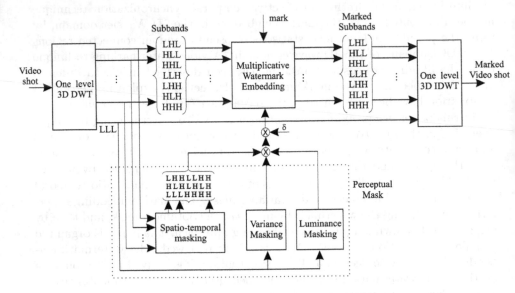

Fig. 1. Flow graph of the proposed multiplicative watermark embedding using perceptual mask in the 3D-DWT domain

Specifically, let us consider a video shot $\{v[n_1, n_2, n_3]\}$, composed by N_3 frames of dimension $N_1 \times N_2$ pixels belonging to the given video sequence. Let us consider its 1-level 3D DWT, $v^{(1)}_{\alpha\beta\gamma}[n_1, n_2, n_3]$, with $(\alpha, \beta, \gamma) \in \{L, H\}$. The mark is a pseudorandom binary sequence with values in the set $\{-1, +1\}$. Perceptual weighting is performed in order to guarantee the imperceptibility of the mark as well as its robustness. Therefore, the strength of the mark embedding is not uniform but it is dependent on the masking characteristics of the human visual system (HVS). Specifically, the embedding is performed according to the following rule:

$$\tilde{v}^{(1)}_\theta[n_1, n_2, n_3] = v^{(1)}_\theta[n_1, n_2, n_3] + \delta|v^{(1)}_\theta[n_1, n_2, n_3]|m[n_1, n_2, n_3]w_\theta[n_1, n_2, n_3] \tag{1}$$

where θ represents the considered subband belonging to the ensemble $\Theta = \{LHL, HLL, HHL, LLH, LHH, HLH, HHH\}$, δ represents the watermark strength, $m[n_1, n_2, n_3]$ the watermark rearranged in 3D, and $w_\theta[n_1, n_2, n_3]$ the weighting function that is obtained as described in Section 4.

4   Perceptual Masking

The weighting function $w_\theta[n_1, n_2, n_3]$ is designed as the product of three terms taking into account:

- the spatio-temporal frequency content of the different subbands by means of the spatio-temporal contrast sensitivity function (CSF),
- the image brightness,
- the eye sensitivity to noise.

4.1   Spatio-temporal Contrast Sensitivity Function

The spatio-temporal CSF characterizes the varying sensitivity of the human visual system to spatial and temporal frequencies. Specifically, the spatio-velocity CSF is defined in [12] as follows:

$$CSF(\rho, \nu_R) = k \cdot c_0 \cdot c_2 \cdot \nu_R \cdot \left(\frac{c_1\rho}{2\pi}\right)^2 \exp\left(\frac{-c_1\rho}{\pi \cdot \rho_{max}}\right) \tag{2}$$

with

$$\begin{cases} k = s_1 + s_2 |\log(c_2\nu_R/3)|^3 \\ \rho_{max} = p_1/(c_2\nu_R + 2), \end{cases} \tag{3}$$

where ρ is the horizontal spatial frequency in cyc/deg and ν_R is the retinal velocity in deg/sec. Following the indication given in [12] we set the constants as $s_1 = 6.1$, $s_2 = 7.3$, $p_1 = 45.9$, $c_0 = 1.14$, $c_1 = 0.67$, and $c_2 = 1.7$. Moreover, ν_R, that represents the retinal image velocity, is expressed as

$$\nu_R = \nu_I - \min[g_{sp}\nu_I + \nu_{MIN}, \nu_{MAX}] \tag{4}$$

being ν_I the image plane velocity, ν_{MIN} the drift velocity of the eye, which is assumed to be equal to 0.15 deg/sec, ν_{MAX} the maximum velocity beyond which the eye cannot track moving objects efficiently (80 deg/sec), and g_{sp} is the gain of the smooth pursuit eye movements set equal to 0.82. The spatio-temporal $CSF(\rho, \omega)$ can be obtained from (2) by using the relation $\omega = \nu\rho$, where ω is the temporal frequency in cy/sec, ν is the velocity in deg/sec, and ρ represents the spatial frequency in cy/sec.

The CSF curve is a continuous function of the spatio-temporal frequencies. However, for a discrete wavelet transform, in order to simplify the implementation, we choose one CSF weight for each subband. Specifically, given $CSF(\rho, \omega)$, the spatio-temporal frequency domain is partitioned according to the wavelet decomposition performed on the video shot into regions corresponding to low (L) and to high (H) horizontal spatial and temporal frequencies. We thus resort to partition the $CSF(\rho, \omega)$ into four functions $CSF_{st}(\rho, \omega)$ with $(s, t) \in \{L, H\}$ where s, t refer to the horizontal spatial and temporal frequencies respectively. Then the average value is evaluated for each of the four subbands thus obtaining the weights $\overline{CSF}_{st}$ with $(s, t) \in \{L, H\}$. However, since a CSF function that

Table 1. Weights derived from the spatio-temporal CSF for the different video subbands

Subband	Weight
LLH	$\overline{CSF}_{LH}$
HLL	$(\overline{CSF}_{HL} + \overline{CSF}_{LL})/2$
HLH	$(\overline{CSF}_{HH} + \overline{CSF}_{LH})/2$
LHL	$(\overline{CSF}_{HL} + \overline{CSF}_{LL})/2$
LHH	$(\overline{CSF}_{HH} + \overline{CSF}_{LH})/2$
HHL	$\overline{CSF}_{HL}$
HHH	$\overline{CSF}_{HH}$

takes into account the temporal frequency and both the horizontal and the vertical spatial frequency is not available we resort to weight the horizontal and the vertical spatial frequencies of the video shot at the same manner. Therefore, for a given video subband $v_{\alpha\beta\gamma}^{(1)}[n_1, n_2, n_3]$ with $(\alpha, \beta, \gamma) \in \{L, H\}$ a weight defined as follows is considered:

$$v_{\alpha\beta\gamma}^{(1)}[n_1, n_2, n_3] \Leftrightarrow \overline{CSF}_\theta = \frac{\overline{CSF}_{\alpha\gamma} + \overline{CSF}_{\beta\gamma}}{2} \qquad (5)$$

with $\theta \in \Theta$. Specifically, in Table 1 the weights used for the different video subbands are specified.

4.2   Luminance Masking

As for the sensitivity of the HVS to the luminance level, it is worth pointing out that the human eye is less sensitive to noise in the image's regions with high or low brightness levels. In [13] an expression that gives the visibility threshold due to background luminance is provided. Specifically, with reference to the spatio-temporal low-pass version $v_{LLL}[n_1, n_2, n_3]$ of the video shot under examination, according to [13] the visibility threshold is given by:

$$LM[n_1, n_2, n_3] =$$
$$\frac{1}{20} \begin{cases} 17 \left[1 - \left(\frac{B(v_{LLL})[n_1, n_2, n_3]}{127} \right)^{0.5} \right] + 3 & \text{if } B(v_{LLL}) < 127 \\ \frac{3}{128} [B(v_{LLL})[n_1, n_2, n_3] - 127] + 3 & \text{if } B(v_{LLL}) \geq 127 \end{cases} \qquad (6)$$

where $B(\cdot)$ represents the average background luminance calculated by using the operator

$$O(i, j) = \begin{pmatrix} 1\,1\,1\,1\,1 \\ 1\,2\,2\,2\,1 \\ 1\,2\,0\,2\,1 \\ 1\,2\,2\,2\,1 \\ 1\,1\,1\,1\,1 \end{pmatrix}$$

as follows:

$$B(v_{LLL})[n_1, n_2, n_3] = \frac{1}{32} \sum_{i=1}^{5} \sum_{j=1}^{5} v_{LLL}[n_1 - 3 + i, n_2 - 3 + j, n_3]O(i, j). \quad (7)$$

Subjective tests have verified the effectiveness of the visibility threshold to well representing the relationship between the sensitivity to noise and the background luminance.

4.3 Variance Masking

As for the sensitivity of the HVS to noise, it is well known that the eye is less sensitive to noise in high activity regions. The eye sensitivity to noise is taken into account by evaluating the variance on the different subbands. However, in order to limit the computational complexity, the mask is evaluated on the LLL subband and then some corrective factors are introduced to weight differently the high frequency subbands. Specifically a three dimensional sliding window of dimension $2 \times 2 \times 2$ is applied on $v_{LLL}[n_1, n_2, n_3]$ to evaluate the local variance $VAR[n_1, n_2, n_3]$. Then a corrective factor is applied to use this mask for the high frequency subbands as specified in the following:

$$VAR_\theta[n_1, n_2, n_3] = \quad (8)$$
$$VAR[n_1, n_2, n_3] \cdot \begin{cases} \sqrt{2} & \text{if } \theta = \text{HHL, LHH, HLH, HHH} \\ 1 & \text{if } \theta = \text{LLH, LHL, HLL} \end{cases}$$

4.4 Global Mask

To summarize the spatio-temporal mask $w_\theta[n_1, n_2, n_3]$ is obtained as the product of the terms given by (5), (6), and (8), that is:

$$w_\theta[n_1, n_2, n_3] = \overline{CSF}_\theta^{-1} \cdot LM[n_1, n_2, n_3] \cdot VAR_\theta[n_1, n_2, n_3] \quad (9)$$

Then, given the 1-level 3D DWT of the video shot under examination, apart the spatio temporal low pass version (subband LLL), the mark is embedded in every other subband according to (1) to obtain imperceptibility. Eventually the 3D IDWT is performed thus obtaining the marked video.

5 Watermark Detection

Watermark detection is accomplished by evaluating the correlation ρ between the marked 3D DWT coefficients and the watermark to be tested:

$$\rho = \frac{1}{C} \sum_{\theta \in \Theta} \sum_{n_1=0}^{M_1-1} \sum_{n_2=0}^{M_2-1} \sum_{n_3=0}^{M_3-1} \tilde{v}_\theta^{(1)}[n_1, n_2, n_3]m[n_1, n_2, n_3] \quad (10)$$

being $M_i = N_i/2, i = 1, 2, 3$, and C a normalization term. In case we need to determine whether the mark is present or not, ρ is compared to a threshold T, that is determined by applying the Neyman-Pearson criterion following the same arguments presented in [14]. Specifically, the threshold T is determined by minimizing the probability of not detecting the mark given a probability of false detection. In order to face the problem some assumptions have been made. Specifically we assume that ρ is normally distributed, the mark $m[n_1, n_2, n_3]$ is zero mean and independent of the host signal, and that $\tilde{v}_\theta^{(1)}[n_1, n_2, n_3]$ are zero mean and independent variables. With this assumptions it is straightforward to verify that the probability of false detection is:

$$P_f = \frac{1}{2}\text{erfc}\left(\frac{T}{\sqrt{2\sigma_\rho^2}}\right),\tag{11}$$

where σ_ρ^2 represents the variance of ρ. By requiring a probability of false detection $P_f \leq 10^{-8}$ a threshold

$$T = 3.97\sqrt{2\sigma_\rho^2}\tag{12}$$

is obtained, where the correlation variance σ_ρ^2 is obtained by means of the following estimator:

$$\sigma_\rho^2 \approx \frac{1}{C^2}\sum_{\theta\in\Theta}\sum_{n_1=0}^{M_1-1}\sum_{n_2=0}^{M_2-1}\sum_{n_3=0}^{M_3-1}\left(\tilde{v}_\theta^{(1)}[n_1, n_2, n_3]\right)^2.\tag{13}$$

6   Experimental Results and Conclusions

The method has been widely tested using uncompressed videos where each frame is of size $(N_1 \times N_2) = (352 \times 288)$ pixels (CIF format). Although several video segmentation algorithms which detect the abrupt scene changes [15] have been proposed in literature, for the sake of simplicity, we have segmented the video sequence into shots of fixed lenght equal to 32 frames.

The effectiveness of the proposed perceptual mask (9) has been tested using the Video Quality Metric (VQM) [16]. Different VQM models which can be applied to specific scenarios such as television, videoconferencing, as well as to a generic scenario. In our tests we have used the general VQM model, denoted as VQM_G, which has been designed to track subjective quality judgments of video scene with a wide range of quality levels. It uses objective parameters which measure the perceptual effects on both the luminance component and the chrominance components of impairment such as blurring, block distortion, jerky/unnatural motion, noise and error blocks. The values of the VQM_G metric can follow in the interval $[0, 1]$, although for extremely distorted scenes they can assume values greater than one. In order to test the effectiveness of the proposed mask in Fig.2 the VQM_G behavior $vs.$ the watermark strength δ for the same

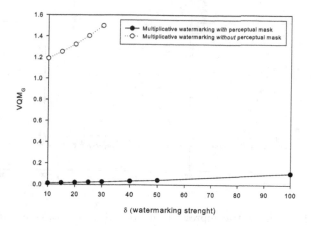

Fig. 2. VQM_G vs. the watermark strength δ for watermarked video and using the perceptual mask

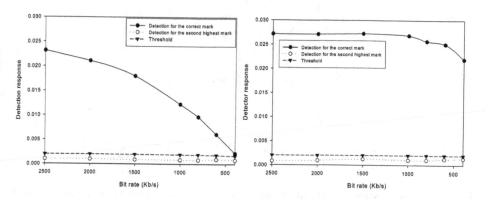

Fig. 3. Left: detector response for MPEG-2 compression attack at different bit rates. Right: detector response for MPEG-4 compression attack at different bit rates.

video marked using the multiplicative approach without and with the perceptual mask is reported. As enlightened in Fig.2, the perceptual mask allows us using heavy strength watermark without affecting the video visual appearance. Whereas, the VQM_G reaches unbearable values even for low energy watermarks when the mask is not used.

The performances of the proposed approach have been tested against video attacks such as MPEG-2 compression, MPEG-4 compression, transcoding, and collusion. Moreover, the gain attack and multiple embedded marks have been tested as well. The videos have been MPEG-2 and MPEG-4 compressed at differ bit rates. In Fig.3 the detection response *vs.* the bit rate is given, along with the estimated threshold at the different bit rates. In Figs. 3-8, the detection response to 200 random generated marks are considered. The actual mark is the one at position 100. Specifically, in Fig.4 the detector response when MPEG-2

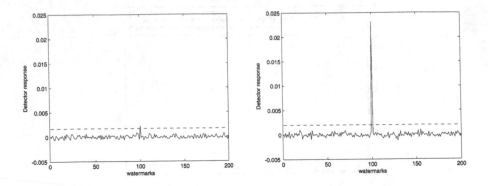

Fig. 4. MPEG-2 attack. Left: compression at 400 Kb/s. Right: compression at 2500 Kb/s.

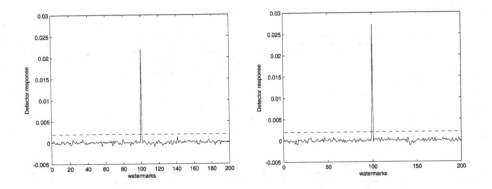

Fig. 5. MPEG-4 attack. Left: compression at 400 Kb/s. Right: compression at 2500 Kb/s.

compression at 400 Kb/s and 2500 Kb/s is applied, is depicted along with the threshold value (dotted line). The detector response when MPEG-4 compression at 400 Kb/s and 2500 Kb/s is applied is reported in Fig.5. In Fig. 6 the robustness of the proposed approach to transcoding attacks (MPEG-2 2500 Kb/s → MPEG-4 600 Kb/s, and MPEG-2 1000 Kb/s → MPEG-4 600 Kb/s) is reported. Moreover, Type I and Type II collusion attacks are considered. Specifically, for Type I collusion, a subsequence obtained by picking one frame belonging to the marked video sequence every ten is generated. An estimation of the mark is obtained by averaging the subsequence's frames. As for Type II collusion, the attack is performed by averaging two consecutive frames in a subsequence of ten consecutive frames drawn from the marked video. Then the watermark is estimated by applying the decoding procedure to the so obtained nine frames sequence. Experimental results pertaining both Type I and Type II collusion attacks are reported in Fig.7. As it is evident the method is robust against both types of collusion, in fact the detector response for the actual embedded

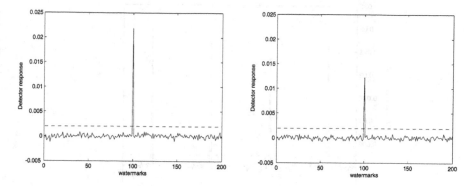

Fig. 6. Transcoding attack. Left: MPEG2 2500 Kbps → MPEG4 600 Kbps. Right: MPEG2 1000 Kbps → MPEG4 600 Kbps. Detector response to 200 different watermarks for watermark strength $\delta = 15$.

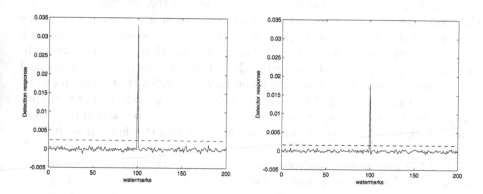

Fig. 7. Left: Type I collusion attack. Right: Type II collusion attack.

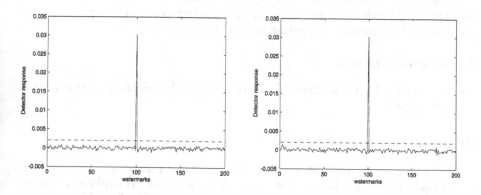

Fig. 8. Gain attack. Left: gain attack = 0.5. Right: gain attack = 1.5.

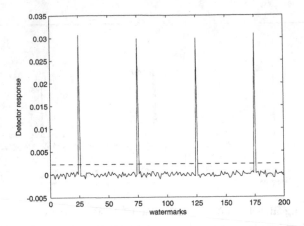

Fig. 9. Detector response for multiple embedded marks

watermark exceeds the threshold whereas the value of the detector responses for the remaining marks are beyond the computed threshold. In order to increase security the shot length, within the same video, can be modified according to a secret key known at the receiver. A minimum shot length must be guaranteed to provide enough capacity. Moreover the shots lengths sequence can be changed from video to video. As an alternative approach, the video segmentation can be performed using a content dependent segmentation approach. In Fig.8, the robustness of the proposed approach to the gain attack is also taken into account. When multiple marks are embedded into the same data the detector is still able to recover them as pointed out in Fig. 9 where four marks at position 25, 75, 125, and 175 have been considered. For the sake of completeness it is necessary to point out that temporal desynchronization attacks, such as frame dropping, frame rate conversion, seriously affect the mark detection. Countermeasures to provide temporal synchronization at a block as well as at a frame level are currently under investigation. In summary, the experimental results have outlined that proposed method allows obtaining an excellent perceptual invisibility still maintaining high robustness against most video attacks.

Acknowledgments

The authors would like to thank L. Sordini and L. Indelicato for their help in computer simulations.

References

1. D. Kundur, K. Su, and D. Hatzinakos, "Digital Video Watermarking: Techniques, Technology and Trends," in **Intelligent Watermarking Techniques,** Chapter 10, P. J.-S. Pan, H.-C. Huang and L. Jain, eds., World Scientific Publishing Company, pp. 265-314, 2004.
2. G. Doërr, J.-L. Dugelay "A guided tour to video watermarking," *Sig. Proc.: Image Comm.* 18 (2003) pp.263-282.

3. G. Doërr, J.-L. Dugelay "Security pitfalls of frame-by-frame approaches to video watermarking," *IEEE Transactions on Signal Processing* Vol. 52, Issue 10, Oct. 2004, pp. 2955 - 2964.
4. F. Deguillaume, G. Csurka, J. O'Ruanaidh, T. Pun, "Robust 3D DFT video watermarking," *Proc. SPIE, Security and Watermarking of Multimedia Content II*, vol. 3971, pp. 346-357, 2000.
5. Y. Li, X. Gao, and H. Ji, "A 3D wavelet based spatial-temporal approach for video watermarking," *Proc. of 5th Int. Conf. on Computational Intell. and Multimedia Applications*, (ICCIMA) pp.260-265, Sept. 2003.
6. H. Liu, N. Chen, J. Huang, X. Haung, Y. Q. Shi, "A robust DWT-based video watermarking algorithm," *IEEE International Symposium on Circuits and Systems*, pp.631-634, 2002.
7. M. Kucukgoz1, Ö. Harmanci, M. K. Mihçak and R. Venkatesan, "Robust Video Watermarking via Optimization Algorithm for Quantization of Pseudo-Random Semi-Global Statistics" *Proc. SPIE, Security, Steganography, and Watermarking of Multimedia Contents VII*, vol. 5681, 2005.
8. J.H. Lim, D.J. Kim, H.T. Kim, C.S. Won "Digital video watermarking using 3D-DCT and Intra-Cubic Correlation," *Proc. SPIE, Security and Watermarking Contents III* Vol. 4314 pp.54-72, 2001.
9. R. Wolfgang, C. I. Podilchuk, and E. J. Delp, "Perceptual watermarks for digital images and video," *Proc. of the IEEE* Vol. 87, No.7, pp. 1108-1126, July 1999.
10. C. De Vleeschouwer, J.-F. Delaigle, B. Macq, " Invisibility and application functionalities in perceptual watermarking an overview," *Proc. of the IEEE* Vol. 90, No.1, pp. 64-77, Jan. 2002.
11. M. Swanson, B. Zhu, and A. T. Tewfik, "Multiresolution scene-based video watermarking using perceptual models," *IEEE J. Sel. Areas in Comm.* Vol. 16, No. 4, 1998.
12. S. Daly, "Engineering observations from spatiovelocity and spatiotemporal visual models," *Proc. SPIE, Conference on Human Vision and Electronic Imaging III* Vol. 3299, pp.180-191, 1998.
13. Chun-Hsien Chou, Yun-Chin Li, "A perceptually tuned subband image coder based on the measure of just-noticeable-distortion profile" *IEEE Trans. on Circuits and Systems for Video Technology*, Vol. 5, No. 6, pp. 467-476, Dec. 1995.
14. M. Barni, F. Bartolini, and A. Piva, "Improved wavelet-based watermarking through pixel-wise masking" *IEEE Trans. on Im. Proc.*, Vol. 10, No. 5, pp. 783-791, May 2001.
15. N. Vasconcelos, and A. Lippman, "Statistical models of video structure for content analysis and characterization", *IEEE Transactions on Image Processing*, vol. 9, no.1, pp. 3-19, January 2000.
16. Video Quality Metric (VQM) Software Download, v. 2.0. *http://www.its.bldrdoc.gov/n3/video/*.

Robustness Enhancement of Content-Based Watermarks Using Entropy Masking Effect

Amir Houman Sadr[1] and Shahrokh Ghaemmaghami[2]

[1] Electrical Engineering Department,
Sharif University of Technology, Azadi st., Tehran, Iran
houmansadr@mehr.sharif.edu
[2] Electronic Research Center, Sharif University of Technology, Azadi st., Tehran, Iran
ghaemmag@sharif.edu

Abstract. Image-Adaptive watermarking systems exploit visual models to adapt the watermark to local properties of the host image. This leads to a watermark power enhancement, hence an improved resilience against different attacks, while keeping the mark imperceptible. Visual models consider different properties of the human visual system, such as frequency sensitivity, luminance sensitivity and contrast masking. Entropy masking is another human visual system's characteristic, which rarely has been addressed in visual models. In this paper we have utilized this masking effect to improve the robustness of Image-Adaptive watermarks while keeping their transparency. Experimental results show a significant amount of enhancement to the power of watermark. The work has been expanded to video watermarking, considering special properties of the entropy masking effect.

1 Introduction

The extreme development of Internet has made the transmission, distribution and access to digital media very convenient. As a result, media producers are more frequently dealing with illegal and unauthorized usage of their productions. Amongst all digital media, video files could be the most valuable products that are being used vastly, while violating copyright laws that could impose huge damage to filmmaking industry.

Over the last two decades digital watermarking has been addressed as an effective solution to safeguard copyright laws, and an extensive research activity has been done on the area. Generally speaking, a digital watermark is an invisible mark that is inserted into a digital media such as audio, image or video and could be utilized to identify illegal distributions of copyright protected digital media and also lawbreaking customers. A digital watermark must have special features to make its desired functionalities. The embedded mark should be robust enough against various watermarking attacks while keeping the perceived quality of the host signal unchanged (the imperceptibility requirement). Watermarking attacks consist of deliberate attacks made maliciously to remove or change the mark sequence by lawbreakers and unintentional attacks caused as a result of different kinds of coding and compression made to the digital media prior to transmission and/or storage and

M. Barni et al. (Eds.): IWDW 2005, LNCS 3710, pp. 444–458, 2005.

also errors occurred during the transmission of the media through the transmission networks. In addition, inserted watermark must prohibit the malicious insertion of additional marks by embedding the maximum possible watermark power, exploiting the maximum affordable capacity of the digital media.

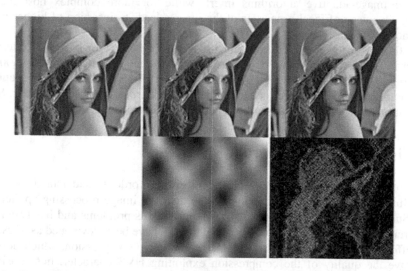

Fig. 1. Comparison of *Cox* scheme (Image-Independent) and *IA-DCT* scheme (Image-Adaptive): (a) top-left: Original image, (b) top-middle: watermarked image by *Cox* scheme, (c) top-right: watermarked image by *IA-DCT* scheme, (d) bottom-middle: Cox's watermark and (e) bottom-right: IA-DCT's watermark (watermarks are scaled to be visible)

Watermarking algorithms, as far as digital images are concerned, can be classified into two different categories: Image-Independent watermarking schemes and Image-Adaptive watermarking schemes. Watermarking schemes of the first class embed the mark discarding Human Visual System (HVS) characteristics and without using any visual model. In other words, watermark insertion algorithm performs the same for every host image without considering its special characteristics. *Cox* watermarking scheme [1] is a well-known scheme, which belongs to this category and is based on the spread spectrum communications. In this scheme, a DCT (Discrete Cosine Transform) transform is performed on the whole image and then the watermarking sequence is embedded in the predetermined perceptually significant DCT coefficients (low frequency components except DC coefficient). On the other hand, Image-Adaptive watermarking schemes exploit visual models to adapt the mark sequence to the local properties of the host image providing an optimal transparency and robustness. *Podilchuk et al* proposed two watermarking algorithms, which are classified in this category of image watermarking scheme [2]. Their *IA-DCT* scheme is the modified version of the Cox scheme using *Watson visual model* [3], in which DCT transform is performed on non-overlapping 8*8 blocks of the host image and then the mark sequence is inserted in each block considering its visual characteristics according to Watson's visual model. Figure 1 shows the watermarked images of *Lena* using Cox algorithm and IA-DCT algorithm in addition to their corresponding watermarks. As shown in the figure, the second class of image watermarking schemes allocates watermark positions according to local characteristics of the host image with respect to a visual model. As a result, for images with fairly uniform perceptual characteristics, image-adaptive watermarks provide a watermark power close to what the non-image-adaptive algorithms insert, while for more complex host images, taking advantage of local properties of the images leads to insertion of higher power and more watermark bits.

In this paper, we will use a rarely used masking effect to improve watermark power in Image-Adaptive watermarking schemes. In section 2, the concept of *entropy masking* is described, following a general introduction to visual models. In section 3, the mentioned masking effect is exploited in the watermark insertion process. Some simulation results are given in section 4 and the paper is concluded in section 5.

2   Visual Models and Entropy Masking

Over recent years, there has been tremendous effort in order to understand and model the Human Visual System and applying it to different image processing applications [2]. Such effort has been examined for solving various problems and has resulted in different levels of success. Recently, visual models have been developed as a result of the efforts taken place in the field of image and video compression, which desire to improve the quality of the compression exploiting HVS characteristics. Basically, both image watermarking and image compression are concerned of the image redundancy, which is to be reduced in the case of compression, while is employed to insert the mark in the case of watermarking. As a result, visual models devised in the area of image compression can also be suited to the watermarking problem.

In compression applications, a common approach to perceptual coding is to derive an image dependent mask containing the *JND*'s (Just Noticeable Difference) to gain perceptual based quantizers and to perceptually allocate the bit positions. The same approach can be utilized in the case of watermarking problem to find upper bounds of the watermark intensity levels in different regions of the image to assure the watermark's transparency, while providing the maximum affordable robustness of the mark.   Also, JND's can be used to determine an upper bound of the number of watermarks that can be inserted in a particular image with a low error probability, which can be referred to as the *watermark capacity*.

In contrast with compression applications, watermarking algorithms can fully utilize the local information extracted from the visual models since the original image is available at the receiver [2].   As an example of visual models, we consider two perceptual models which have been applied to the baseline of the JPEG coder. *Watson* model [3] and *Safranek-Johnston* model [4] are based on the same image independent component, utilizing *frequency sensitivity,* which is the human's eye sensitivity to sine wave grating at various frequencies. This component is based on the work done in [5] with a minimum viewing distance of four picture heights and a D65 monitor white point. As a result, a frequency threshold value is obtained for each DCT basis function that we mention it by $t_{u,v}^{F}$ where u and v are the indexes of the block and in the case of the work done for JPEG compression, this results in an 8*8 matrix of threshold values. Frequency sensitivity provides a static JND, which only depends on the viewing conditions and is independent from the image. Generally speaking, HVS decreases its sensitivity to very low and very high frequencies. Furthermore, Watson refined his model by adding a *luminance sensitivity* and *contrast masking* component [3]. Luminance sensitivity states the detecting threshold of noise on a constant background. This is a nonlinear parameter, which depends on the local characteristics of the image. Watson estimated luminance sensitivity in [3] by the formula

$$t_{u,v,b}^{L} = t_{u,v}^{F} \left(\frac{X_{0,0,b}}{X_{0,0}} \right)^{a}, \tag{1}$$

where $X_{0,0,b}$ is the DC coefficient of the DCT transform over the b's block, $X_{0,0}$ is the DC coefficient of the DCT transform over the whole image and a is a parameter for controlling the degree of luminance sensitivity which was set to 0.649 by the authors in [5]. *Contrast masking* is the third component that Watson used in his model, which states that a signal can be masked in the presence of another signal especially when the both signals have the same spatial frequency, orientation and location. This allows for a more dynamic JND threshold allocation. Considering $X_{u,v,b}$ as the DCT coefficients of block b and $t_{u,v}^{L}$ as the threshold values derived from the viewing conditions and also the luminance masking, a contrast masking threshold is derived as

$$t_{u,v,b}^{C} = Max \left[t_{u,v,b}^{L}, \left| X_{u,v,b} \right|^{\omega_{u,v}} \left(t_{u,v,b}^{L} \right)^{1-\omega_{u,v}} \right], \tag{2}$$

where $\omega_{u,v}$ assumes a different value for each DCT basis function, where a value of 0.7 was derived for it in [3].

Here, we address another masking effect that was first introduced by *Watson et al* [6]. Watson classified all the previous studies on visual masking into two classes: *contrast masking* and *noise masking* depending primarily on whether the mask is deterministic or random. Generally, contrast masking refers to a decrease in the effective gain of the early visual system. On the other hand, noise masking is explained by an increased variance in some internal decision variable [6]. Clearly, contrast masking is the one which plays the role in image quality models. Watson et al. introduced a third type masking effect, which is *deterministic* but *unfamiliar* and called it *entropy masking*. Watson performed a number of experiments to determine the detectability threshold of an especial Gabor function added to various backgrounds by some observers. Each trial of the experiment consists of two intervals, which in one of them the single background is shown to the observer and in the other the background containing the target (Gabor function) is shown to the observer, from which he/she must detect the background containing the target. The mean results of the Watson's experiments are shown in table 1, where *none* represents the condition without any background, *cos* represents the situation with a cosine background having the same frequency and orientation as the Gabor function, *random* represents the situation that a new sample of a bandpass noise (with a bandwidth equal to Gabor function's frequency) was used in each interval of each trial, *twin* is a especial case of *random* experiment, in which the same background is used in two intervals of each trial and the *fixed* experiment is the case where the bandpass noise background is fixed for all the trials.

Table 1. Mean threshold and threshold elevation for different experimental conditions. Elevations are relative to no mask condition. (Table from [6]).

	None	Cos	Random	Twin	Fixed
Threshold(dB)	-27.59	-24.92	-14.08	-12.80	-19.34
Elevation(dB)	0	2.67	13.51	14.79	8.24

The small threshold elevation in the *cos* case is as a result of contrast masking. As stated, all the experiments are under the same contrast masking effect, so the 10.84 dB threshold elevation of *random* experiment in comparison to *cos* experiment must be due to *noise masking*. Surprisingly, threshold elevation in the *twin* condition is approximately the same as that in the random condition while we have no more *noise masking* because of utilizing the same background for the both intervals of every trial. Watson et al stated that this threshold elevation is due to unfamiliarity of the observer to background which they called it entropy masking to reflect the notion that the masking is a function of the degree to which the mask is unknown. Entropy is a measure of information in a signal which is by definition that which we do not know.

An interesting phenomenon was observed dealing with entropy masking. In the *fixed* condition of the experiments (where the bandpass noise is fixed for all the trials), as we raise the number of observations, the detectability threshold decreases (see Table 1). This is called *learning* characteristic upon it entropy masking decreases if the complexity of the background is *learned* by the observers. Other experiments utilizing *white noise*, *fixed white noise* and *fixed image* as a background showed that learning ability and speed of learning of the background is a function of its *simplicity* [6]. In other words, an image is learned very rapidly while a fixed white noise either not learned or learned very slowly.

In the next sections of this paper, we consider the entropy masking effect in the Watson's visual model in order to improve watermarking power of the IA-DCT scheme [2] (which is an Image-Adaptive watermarking scheme), and then implement this power enhancement on video streams with respect to learning characteristic of the entropy masking effect.

3 Watermark Insertion and Detection

As mentioned earlier, Watson in [6] introduced a new masking effect and called it entropy masking. The goal of this paper is to exploit this masking effect to increase watermark power in content based (image adaptive) watermarking schemes, hence to improve their resilience against various intentional and unintentional attacks.

For the aim of representing and measuring the amount of complexity, we define a *spatial complexity* parameter. To avoid massive computational complexity (especially when dealing with video host signals) we define this parameter for $n*n$ blocks of pixels (rather than for each pixel). On the other hand, spatial complexity for each pixel of an $n*n$ block b is defined as the entropy of the block

$$En_b = -\sum_x p(x).\log p(x) \, ,$$

(3)

where $p(x)$ is the ratio of the number of x'th symbol occurrence in block b over the block size. Before computing the spatial complexity as above, pixel values must be quantized. Figure 2 shows the complexity parameter for pixels of an 8bit image for different number of quantization levels (block size is set to 4). With no quantization (256 levels of quantization), the complexity parameter is uniform (high) for almost all the pixels (figure2b). On the other hand, a 2-level quantization yields the complexity function representing the edges in the image (figure 2d). Our simulation results show that for an 8bit image, 32 levels of quantization make the defined complexity parameter to represent high entropy regions of the image, which is affected by the entropy masking effect (figure 2b).

Fig. 2. Sketching the defined complexity function for different number of quantizing levels: (a) top-left: original image, (b) top-right: no quantization, (c) bottom-left: 32 levels of quantization and (d) bottom-right: 2 levels of quantization.

Figure 3 shows our complexity function on *Lena* image for different values of size of the block n. It can be seen that for large n (figure 3a) our complexity parameter returns a high value for some non-complex pixels in the neighborhood of the edges and this will lead some impairment in this regions after applying watermark utilizing entropy masking effect. On the other hand, figure 3c returns a more realistic value for all the pixels but leading to more computational complexity. Our simulations showed that choosing n equal to *4*, will make an acceptable tradeoff between precision and complexity (figure 3b). An alternative approach in defining a complexity parameter will be similar to what *Kim et al* [7] done in the DCT domain. In this manner, the entropy of eight neighbors of a pixel is defined as a measurement for its complexity. Figure 3d shows this measure for the same image. Clearly, here we have a more precise measure of complexity for all the pixels but this will impose about 8 times more complexity to our watermarking algorithm than our simple complexity parameter. We do not need such accuracy, so we do not suffer such a high computational complexity.

Fig. 3. Sketching the defined complexity parameter for different values of block size: (a) top-left: original image, (b) top-middle: block size equals 8, (c) top-right: block size equals 4, (d) bottom-left: block size equals 3 and (e) bottom-middle: a different complexity parameter

As an example of content based watermarking schemes, we first introduce *IA-DCT* watermarking scheme [2] and then apply our power improvement idea on it using complexity function which we defined above. In IA-DCT method, the host image is first divided into 8*8 non-overlapping blocks and 8*8 DCT transforms are performed on these blocks. Then watermark will be inserted into each DCT coefficient as below

$$X'_{u,v,b} = X_{u,v,b} + jnd_{u,v,b} * \omega_{u,v,b} \quad \text{if } X_{u,v,b} \geq jnd_{u,v,b}$$
$$X'_{u,v,b} = X_{u,v,b}, \quad\quad\quad\quad\quad\quad \text{if } X_{u,v,b} < jnd_{u,v,b} \tag{4}$$

where $X_{u,v,b}$ is the (u,v)-th coefficient of DCT transform over b'th block, *jnd* is the corresponding Just Noticeable Difference, $\omega_{u,v,b}$ is the corresponding watermark bit and $X'_{u,v,b}$ is the resulted watermarked DCT coefficient. *jnd* is the contrast masking that was defined by Watson and mentioned in the previous section. Considering En_b as the complexity parameter of block b, we modify this JND considering entropy masking effect as below

$$jnd^*_{u,v,b} = jnd_{u,v,b} * f(En_b) \qquad \text{if } En_b > k$$
$$jnd^*_{u,v,b} = jnd_{u,v,b} , \qquad\qquad \text{if } En_b < k$$

(5)

where $jnd^*_{u,v,b}$ is the modified JND, f is a function of defined complexity parameter and k is a threshold discussed in the following. We keep the JND of the three low-frequency components of each block unchanged to avoid changes to image luminance.

Through a meticulous inspection of a set of images of various degrees of complexity, we found out that choosing the threshold, k, equal to 2 would lead our complexity function revealing complex regions affected by the entropy masking phenomenon. Figure 4 illustrates regions of Lena image whose entropy (as defined by the complexity parameter) is greater than k, for different values for k. It is observed that regions having entropy more than 1 covers a vast area of the image (fig 4b). On the other hand, regions with entropy more than 3 are restricted to neighborhoods of the edges (fig 4d), while a reasonable result is obtained with $k=2$ (figure 4c).

Fig. 4. Regions having entropy more than k threshold: (a) top-left: original image, (b) top-right: k=1, (c) bottom-left: k=2 and (d) bottom-right: k=3

According to our subjective experiments on images with various degrees of complexity, it is concluded that a simple linear function, constructed by a line connecting highest affordable entropy (which is six) and the minimum entropy masking capability (which is two), yields a reliable imperceptibility margin in the entropy space. This is expressed as:

$$f(x) = 0.2 * x + 0.8 \ . \tag{6}$$

This means that making the mark's intensity twice in regions having the maximum entropy keeps the mark still imperceptible due to the entropy masking effect, where we can have just a 20% intensity increment for regions of minimum entropy, as two extremes over the margin. Selection of a linear function for $f(x)$ minimizes the computational complexity, as compared to possibly more accurate non-linear alternatives.

The detection process is the same as that introduced in [2] for a typical IA-DCT scheme. The original image is subtracted from the received possibly distorted image that results in a difference image. The correlation between this difference and the watermark sequence is then evaluated, based on a certain threshold, to check if the image contains a watermark. The detection scheme based on normalized correlation can be expressed as [1]:

$$\omega^{*}_{s,u,v,b} = X^{*}_{u,v,b} - X_{u,v,b} \ , \tag{7}$$

$$\omega^{*}_{u,v,b} = \frac{\omega^{*}_{s,u,v,b}}{JND_{u,v,b}} \ , \tag{8}$$

$$\rho_{\omega\omega^{*}} = \frac{\omega \, . \omega^{*}}{\sqrt{E_{\omega} . E_{\omega^{*}}}} \ , \tag{9}$$

where $\omega^{*}.\omega$ denotes the dot product, $JND_{u,v,b}$ is the corresponding JND threshold, $\omega^{*}_{u,v,b}$ is the received possibly distorted watermark, E_{ω} represents the $\omega.\omega$ and $\rho_{\omega\omega^{*}}$ is the normalized correlation coefficient between the two signals ω^{*} and ω. If ω is normally distributed and identical to ω^{*}, the correlation coefficient approaches to one. Independence of ω^{*} and ω leads a normally distributed correlation coefficient with zero mean. A blind detection also can be performed by estimating the JND thresholds from the received image. The estimated JND form the watermarked image highly resembles the JND used for the mark insertion; however, the blind detection scheme is less robust to various watermarking attacks.

At this point, we want to perform our power enhancement method to video frames. Because of the *learning* effect mentioned in section 2, we should act a little conservatively when applying entropy masking JND elevation to still images. Similarly, for video frames, we consider that the JND elevation of a complex scene resulted from entropy masking will vanish if the scene is being repeated on consecutive frames. So, we have to define a *motion* parameter to reflect how much the components of a video frame have been changed in respect to another frame. This parameter could be defined as the absolute difference or square difference of the frame components and could be performed pixel-wise or block-wise. By spending the price of more complexity, a BMA block search yields to more accurate results. For convenience, we defined the *motion* parameter to be the pixel-wise square difference between the selected video frames. Figure 5 shows the result of our motion parameter on two video frames. Our simulations on various video sequences showed that regions having motion parameter lower than 0.1 represent the *static* regions. Regions which remain static over a number of frames will be *learned* and its increased JND due to entropy masking will be retreated.

Fig. 5. Our motion parameter on two video frames. (Left): first video frame, (Middle): seventh video frame of the *momdaughter* sequence and (Right): the corresponding motion parameter.

Motion parameter can be used to repair the JND thresholds in different manners. One can evaluate the motion parameter between the interested frame and a number of its followers to determine the static regions of that frame. But, this will yield a huge computational complexity in the watermark insertion and detection processes of a video sequence. Our experiments showed that a motion parameter evaluation between the interested frame and only two frames located 6 and 12 frames later will give a similar measurement. So, in the case of video watermarking, after evaluating entropy of the pixels (as defined earlier) the following algorithm refines them before being performed on the JND threshold of the frame pixels:

```
For every pixel p of the i'th frame
If motion_p(i,i+6)<0.1 then En_p=En_p-Th
If motion_p(i,i+12)<0.1 then En_p=En_p-Th
```

where $motion_p(i,j)$ is our motion parameter for pixel p between i'th and j'th frames and En_p is the defined complexity parameter for pixel p. *Th* is the amount of entropy decrement which we set it to be 0.3 after a number of experiments.

4 Results

As described in the previous section, we exploit entropy masking effect to improve the watermark power in IA-DCT scheme [2] which is one paradigm of Image-Adaptive watermarking schemes. We used different host images with various degrees of complexity to simulate the proposed power-improved watermarking scheme. Figure 6 comprises our power improved watermarking method with the normal IA-DCT scheme for two types of host images (a high-entropy image and a medium-entropy image). As shown in the figure, we have strengthened the watermark power in high entropy regions of the host image by relying on the entropy masking effect.

As mentioned in the previous section, we have an extra power of the mark in regions that are being masked by the entropy masking effect. Expectedly we expect an improved resilience against various intentional and unintentional watermarking attacks due to this power enhancement. Table 2 shows the amount of improved mark power for two kinds of the images. Clearly, more power enhancement can be done for high-entropy host images.

Table 2. Power enhancement percentage for medium-entropy and high-entropy images

Image Type	*Lena* (a medium-entropy image)	*Baboon* (a high-entropy image)
Power Enhancement	35%	84%

Fig. 6. Comparison between the typical IA-DCT method and its power improved version using our method for a medium-entropy (Lena) and a high-entropy image (Baboon). (left): original image, (middle): IA-DCT watermark and (right): the corresponding power improved watermark. (Watermarks are scaled to be visible.)

There are three kinds of attacks to the IA-DCT scheme considered in [2]: JPEG Compression, Cropping, and Scaling. We investigated the robustness of the improved IA-DCT scheme to the same attacks to compare the proposed method to the typical IA-DCT scheme.

JPEG Compression acts as a low-pass filtering, which zeros out frequency components. We marked different images using the typical IA-DCT scheme and its improved version, and then performed JPEG compression with various quality factors

(Q) on the marked images. Subsequently, we verified the existence of the watermark in the compressed images, evaluating the correlation coefficient as in (9). In the power-improved method, the correlation coefficient showed different amounts of elevation depending on the complexity of the host image, while the false correlation value (correlation by a non-relevant watermark) remained the same. Table 3 depicts the ratio of the correlation coefficient of the improved IA-DCT scheme over the typical IA-DCT scheme's correlation coefficient. As shown, there is not a significant elevation in the correlation coefficient, especially for low-entropy images. This is due to the fact that the improved-power mark has been inserted in high-frequency (complex) regions of the image, which are highly degraded by the JPEG compression.

Table 3. Enhancement in the detection value of the power-improved method to JPEG compression

Q factor	80	60	40	20	10	5
Baboon	1.22	1.22	1.22	1.20	1.37	1.15
Lena	1.06	1.05	1.08	1.09	1.03	1.10

Cropping can be taken as the dual of the JPEG Compression, which zeros out spatial components of the image. Because of its structure, the typical IA-DCT scheme is quite robust to only-cropping attack. We cropped several images to one-sixteenth of their original size (keeping the central part of the image) and performed JPEG compression with various quality factors. Table 4 shows the ratio of the correlation coefficient of the improved method to the typical IA-DCT's correlation coefficient, stating higher robustness of the power-improved method to the cropping attack.

Table 4. Enhancement in the detection value of the power-improved method to Cropping (one-sixteenth) followed by the JPEG compression

Q factor	80	60	40	20	10	5
Baboon	1.49	1.43	1.34	1.48	1.09	1.29
Lena	1.97	1.46	1.55	1.18	1.13	0.98

Table 5. Enhancement in the detection value of the power-improved method to Scaling

Scaling factor	2	4
Baboon	2.38	1.41
Lena	1.53	1.42

Pudlichuk et al. also investigated the robustness of the IA-DCT method to the *Scaling* of a watermarked image. Similar to the procedure given in [2], we lowpass filtered the watermarked image using four-tap filter prior to downsampling by 2 in each direction. The resulting image is upsampled prior to calculation of the correlation coefficient. Table 5 shows the ratio of the correlation coefficient of the improved method to the typical IA-DCT's correlation coefficient. A high amount of improvement in the correlation coefficient is achieved, while the false correlation exhibits no elevation.

To prove the watermarking imperceptibility, we performed a number of subjective tests employing three independent observers. Each trial was composed of a typical IA-DCT watermarked image and its power-improved version in a random order. In every trial, each observer had to distinguish the image with more impairment (due to the watermark insertion) or remark his ambiguity. By changing the time each observer has to make his decision, three different kinds of experiments conducted: fast-decision experiment, medium-decision experiment and slow-decision experiment with two, five and ten seconds permitted for each trial respectively. Table 6 shows the success percentage of different kinds of experiments for two kinds of high-entropy and medium entropy images. By definition, an experiment is done successfully if the observer chooses the typical IA-DCT watermarked image as the image with more impairment or reveals his ambiguity.

As the results show, while enhancing a significant amount of watermark power, the mark remains truly imperceptible for fast-decision and medium-decision experiments as a result of entropy masking phenomenon. Logically, awarding a habit-time to observers gives them more chance to distinguish the power-improved mark because of *learning* property. On the other words, *learning* the complex background leads its entropy masking effect to decline as stated in section 2. As a result, we have to do our treatment more conservatively when exploiting the entropy masking effect for still images in respect to their functionalities.

We also implemented our method to improve the watermark power in video sequences. As explained in section 3, we have considered the *Learning* property of entropy masking in the process of mark insertion in video frames. Figure 7 shows the mark's power enhancement for a medium-entropy video frame. Obviously, our method strengthens the mark power in regions having a large amount of spatial entropy and/or motion entropy with respect to the temporal activity.

Table 6. Success percentage for three kinds of experiments performed on medium-entropy and high-entropy images

Image Type	*Lena* (a medium-entropy image)	*Baboon* (a high-entropy image)
Fast-decision Experiment	100%	100%
Medium-decision Exper.	95%	97%
Slow-decision Experiment	87%	91%

Table 7. Power enhancement percentage for medium-entropy and high-entropy video sequences

Video Sequence	*Momdaughter* (medium-entropy)	*Coastguard* (high-entropy)
Power Enhancement	28%	57%

Table 7 shows the average power enhancement per frame for two kinds of the video streams. Again, more power enhancement can be achieved for high-entropy sequences.

Fig. 7. Comparison between the typical IA-DCT watermarking scheme on video sequences and its power improved version using our method for a medium-entropy video sequence (Momdaughter). (left): video frame watermarked with the IA-DCT method and its corresponding watermark and (right): our power improved version. (Watermarks are scaled to be visible)

Similar to what was done for still images a number of subjective experiments were done to assure the imperceptibility of the power increased mark. Again, each trial of the experiments consisted of an IA-DCT frame by frame marked video sequence and its power improved twin (according to our method) in an unknown ordering, and the observers had to distinguish the sequence having more impairment or claim their ambiguity. Table 8 shows the success percentage of the experiments for two kinds of the sequences (high-entropy and medium-entropy sequences). Results promise a high assurance of imperceptibility while achieving the valuable mark's power improvement. Because of considering the *learning* property, there is no more need to perform conservatively similar to what concluded for the still images.

Table 8. Success percentage of our experiments performed on medium-entropy and high-entropy video sequences.

Video Sequence	*Momdaughter* (medium-entropy)	*Coastguard* (high-entropy)
Experiment's Success Percentage	94%	97%

5 Conclusions

In this paper, we have discussed the entropy masking effect, which was initially introduced by Watson et al. [3], and utilized it to improve the watermark power in content-based watermarking schemes. The proposed method leads to enhancement of the watermark's robustness against various intentional and unintentional attacks. As an example of IA watermarking scheme, we have implemented our method on the IA-DCT scheme [2] and have shown that a significant amount of power enhancement can be achieved exploiting the mentioned masking effect. In fact, we have increased the power of the mark in the regions that are being masked by the entropy masking effect. Because of the learning effect of the entropy masking effect, we must act a little conservatively (not using all the power enhancement of the method) when applying our method on still images, depending on how the marked image is used. However, exploiting this masking effect will result in a more assurance of the mark's imperceptibility with the same watermark power, if there is an upper bound limitation on the mark's power.

We also applied our method to video sequences. The same power enhancement achieved while keeping the marked sequence imperceptible. As cited, we considered the learning property in the watermark embedding process of the video frames, so there is no more need for working conservatively. We tried our method to be as simple as possible, because of the computational constraints in video watermarking. So, different approaches can be implemented with varying degrees of complexity.

Acknowledgements. The authors would like to thank Professor F. Marvasti, director of the Advanced Communications Research Institute for his cooperation and M. Sohizadeh Abianeh for his reviews.

References

1. I. J. Cox, J. Kilian, T. Leighton, and T. Shamoon, "Secure spread spectrum watermarking for multimedia," NEC Research Institute Tech. Rep. 95-10, 1995.
2. C. I. Podilchuk and W. Zeng, "Image-Adaptive Watermarking using visual models", *IEEE Journal on selected areas in communications,* vol. 16, no. 4, May 1998, pp. 525-539
3. A. B. Watson, "DCT quantization matrices visually optimized for individual images," in *Proc. SPIE Conf. Human Vision, Visual Processing, and Digital Display IV,* Feb. 1993, vol. 1913, pp. 202–216.
4. R. J. Safranek and J. D. Johnston, "Perceptually based prequantization for image compression," in *Proc. SPIE Conf. Human Vision, Visual Processing, and Digital Display V, 1994.*
5. H. A. Peterson, A. J. Ahumada, Jr., and A. B. Watson, "Improved detection model for DCT coefficient quantization," in *Proc. SPIE Conf. Human Vision, Visual Processing, and Digital Display IV,* Feb. 1993, vol. 1913, pp. 191–201.
6. A. B. Watson, R. Borthwick and M. Taylor, "Image quality and entropy masking", in *Proc. SPIE Conf.,* vol. 3016, 1997
7. S. W. Kim and S. Suthaharan, "An entropy masking model for multimedia content watermarking", in *Proc. 37th Hawaii International Conference on System Sciences, 2004*

Secure Mutual Distrust Transaction Tracking Using Cryptographic Elements

Angela S.L. Wong[1], Matthew Sorell[1], and Robert Clarke[2]

[1] School of Electrical & Electronic Engineering,
The University of Adelaide, SA 5005, Australia
awong@eleceng.adelaide.edu.au, matthew.sorell@adelaide.edu.au
[2] School of Mathematical Sciences (Pure Mathematics),
The University of Adelaide, SA 5005, Australia
rclarke@maths.adelaide.edu.au

Abstract. This paper presents a novel approach to secure transaction tracking. The focus of the proposed scheme is on preventing insider attacks particularly prevalent in multimedia transactions, assuming both parties involved in a transaction are mutually distrustful. To achieve authentication and non-repudiation, the proposed system, called *staining*, is composed of two key components: public-key cryptography and basic watermarking. The concept is to watermark after encryption, thereby introducing a *stain* on the watermark due to decryption. Watermarking and cryptography are not usually combined in such a manner, due to several issues involved, which are also discussed.

1 Introduction

Protecting content ownership has always been an important issue. However, recent advancements in digital technology, allowing easier sharing of information such as images, music and video, have also brought about an increase in copyright violations. One particular problem arises from the ability to generate perfect copies of video content. This problem has made video piracy very popular, since high quality illegal copies can be obtained easily and are considerably less expensive than a legal copy.

The entertainment industry's response to this increase in piracy has been to target end-users and consumers, including researchers and scholars [3,7,17]. Instead of targeting end users, another option is to identify the sources of illegal distribution. A recent study has shown that 77% of DVD piracy occurred through insider sellout, originating from among pre-market-release organisations [4], such as multimedia processing companies, review committees, advertising agencies, airlines, cinemas, television networks, and even from the film studios themselves.

The approach taken here focuses on the latter problem of insider sellout by providing a system for tracking transactions which occur before mass distribution. Since there is a risk that the supposedly trustworthy pre-mass-distribution parties could be unreliable, we assume a state of mutual distrust between all parties involved in the transactions.

M. Barni et al. (Eds.): IWDW 2005, LNCS 3710, pp. 459–469, 2005.

The outline of this paper is as follows. In Section 2, we present the intuitive approach to watermarking with encryption, and identify a weakness, motivating our proposed solution. We then discuss our proposed approach, which we call *staining*, in Section 3. In Section 4, we make use of cryptographic elements, and then present simulation results to illustrate our staining system. In Section 5, we discuss the associated problems with such a system, and outline why the cryptographic aspect will be the main difficulty of the approach. Finally we give our conclusion in Section 6.

2   Problem Statement

2.1   The "Intuitive" Scenario

Consider a system in which digital steganographic watermarking is used to identify a particular copy of a digital content file, and encryption is used to prevent interception, either during transmission or from the premises of either party. The intuitive approach is to watermark the copy and then encrypt, as shown in Figure 1 below.

In this scenario, party A wishes to pass a document to party B. Party A is explicitly trusted. A embeds the distributed cover work with a secret watermark uniquely identifying B's copy to prevent betrayal by B. Should the cover work be intercepted en route from A to B, B is protected from being blamed for the leak by A encrypting the watermarked cover work (to be decipherable only by B) before transmission.

However, it has been established that party A is capable of betrayal [4]. Assuming mutual distrust, we have identified a weakness in the scenario in Figure 1, indicated by the star. At the two indicated positions, assuming no information is lost in transition, the documents produced are identical. It is at the point to the left of the star that A could deliver the cover work to an enemy E to copy and illegally redistribute, protecting itself by implicating B. Conversely, B would falsely be able to repudiate the charge of supplying E with a copy, since the same watermarked copy is also available through A.

2.2   The Staining Approach

To avoid the above problem, we require a system which ensures B's copy is unique. B's copy must be altered irreversibly after decryption. However, it is not in B's interest to embed a receipt voluntarily, signifying that the copy has reached B. Such a mechanism must then be compulsory.

Hence we propose the following: instead of embedding the watermark before encryption, embedding should occur *after* encryption. This is shown in Figure 2. After decryption, B would possess a copy containing a distorted watermark, altered by the cryptographic process. Then to discover which party leaked the copy to E, the watermark need only be detected. If it is undistorted or missing, A was the culprit. B can be implicated only if a distorted watermark is detected.

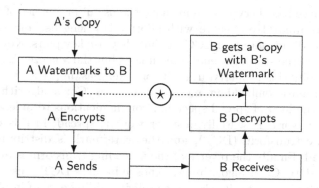

Fig. 1. Trust-distrust copy transfer process. At the point labeled ⋆ both A and B have access to the same version of the document.

This protocol, which we call *staining*, embeds a secret in B's copy which contains elements from both parties, A and B. The stain can only be generated by B's private decipher key (unknown to A, which is given B's public key for encryption), together with A's watermark (not known to B). In the event of a copy being found in E's possession, A has sufficient information to identify the stain (B's public key and A's watermark), but not enough information to frame B. If A and B are in dispute, a third party could be given all secrets to verify the existence of the stain in the copy recovered from E.

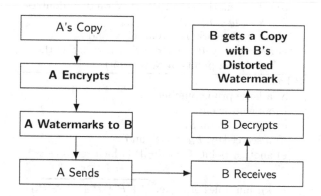

Fig. 2. Mutual distrust copy transfer process

3   Experimental Results

Our primary aim is to demonstrate the feasibility of our solution by considering the simpler problem of staining a digital photographic image. After considering various types of public-key cryptosystems, such as RSA [14], El Gamal [10], Rabin as well as McEliece [13], we chose an Elliptic Curve Cryptosystem (ECC), in particular the Menezes-Vanstone implementation [1].

Elliptic curve based cryptosystems have the useful properties of being asymmetric, non-commutative, secure with shorter key lengths, and easily implementable. One disadvantage of ECCs is that they use key pairs. Key pairs would normally double the size of the encrypted image, but the Menezes-Vanstone cryptosystem exploits this property, using it for pixel-masking [1].

The watermark embedding method used was Cox's algorithm [6]. This method uses the idea of spread spectrum communications to hide a watermark within a cover work. Essentially, a cover work is spread, in this case via the discrete cosine transform (DCT), and the watermark is distributed throughout this spread. Finally the reverse of the spreading transform is applied to the watermarked data. Cox's algorithm was chosen because DCT is used in the compression of JPEGs, and for its elegant simplicity, aiding ease of implementation.

3.1   Algorithm

Given that A and B possess the particulars of the process as outlined in Table 1, the algorithm is as follows in Table 2.

Table 1. Setup information

Watermarking and encryption setup.
A has
(a) a message, M, $m \times n$ image matrix, values in $[0, 255]$, arranged into pairs, (M_1, M_2),
(b) a watermark vector, W, of N random doubles $(N \ll m \times n)$,
(c) the watermarking strength, α, and
(e) a secret key, $0 < k_A < \#\mathcal{E}$ (where $\#\mathcal{E}$ is the number of points in $\mathcal{E}$, see [15]).
B has
(a) a large prime number, p,
(b) an elliptic curve, $\mathcal{E}$,
(c) a point, P, on $\mathcal{E}$,
(d) a secret key, $k_B < \#\mathcal{E}$, and
(e) another point, $Q = [k_B]P$ (which reads as k_B multiples of P, i.e. $\overbrace{P + P + P + \ldots + P}^{k_B \text{ times}}$.)
— Public info: $K_e = (P, Q, \mathcal{E}, p)$
— Private info: $K_d = (k_B)$

3.2   Implementation and Attacks

Figure 3(a) is the original image and Figure 3(b) is the image after encryption. As can be seen, encryption has altered the image considerably. Image 3(d) shows that despite the watermarking stage between the encryption and decryption stages, the image is still recoverable. This result supports the use of the staining

Table 2. Detailed step-by-step guide to implementing the protocol

Algorithm steps.
1. A encrypts the image using B's public key set, K_e, by computing
(a) $y_0 = [k_A]P$,
(b) $(c_1, c_2) = [k_A]Q$,
(c) $y_1 = c1 \cdot m_1 \pmod p$, and
(d) $y_2 = c2 \cdot m_2 \pmod p$.
2. A obtains the encrypted watermarked image by
(a) applying direct cosine transform (DCT) to the encrypted image, $\underline{En}(I)(= (y_1, y_2))$,
(b) selecting N largest values, except for DC component,
(c) altering by $\underline{En}(I)'_i = \underline{En}(I)_i(1 + \alpha w_i)$, and
(d) applying inverse DCT to $\underline{En}(I)'$ which produces $\underline{Wm}(\underline{En}(I))(= (y'_1, y'_2))$.
3. A sends y_0 and $\underline{Wm}(\underline{En}(I))$ to B.
4. B decrypts, using private key set, K_d, by computing
(a) $(c'_1, c'_2) = [k_B]y_0$,
(b) $m'_1 = (c1')^{-1} \cdot y'_1 \pmod p$, and
(c) $m'_2 = (c2')^{-1} \cdot y'_2 \pmod p$,
to obtain the cover work, with distorted watermark, decrypted image, $\underline{De}(\underline{Wm}(\underline{En}(I)))$.

protocol, since such a process should theoretically render the image irretrievable, given the exacting nature of cryptograms.

For the comparison 3(e), we used the similarity measure described in Cox's paper [6]:

$$\text{sim}(X, X') = \frac{X' \cdot X}{\sqrt{X' \cdot X'}}$$

against a test set of 100 different watermarked images. Here X' is the images from the test set and X is the image we are testing for a match. The spike shown in Figure 3(e) indicates a match to the watermark at index 27, which is the correct result.

To test the robustness of our system to disruption, we began attacking it. The results are displayed in Figure 4 and Figure 5. When deciding on the extent of attacks, we assumed that an attacker will only be willing to distort the image to the point that the resulting image can still be easily viewed. With this in mind, the attacks chosen were:

- forcing pixel values to unsigned 8-bit integers,
- JPEG conversion, to image quality 10%,
- cropping an amount (50 out of 256 pixels) from the edges, replacing the cropped areas with the same areas from the original image,
- downsampling by 2, via decreasing to half size then enlarging to full size,
- adding Gaussian noise, with zero mean and standard variance 0.01, and
- applying a second watermark, at index 28.

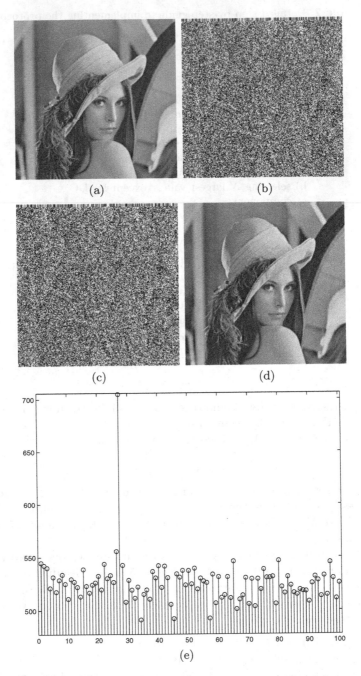

Fig. 3. a) Original cover work "Lena", courtesy of the Signal and Image Processing Institute at the University of Southern California, b) encrypted cover work, c) watermarked, d) decrypted, and e) similarity between the final image and 100 watermarked images, with our watermarked image expected at 27

We have also tested the algorithm on the Baboon image with similar results. Bearing in mind that we applied no pre- or post-processing to any of the images, and that the watermark should theoretically render the data indecryptable, the watermark comes through better than expected, standing out above the clearly random line.

4   Discussion of Problems

As we explored the feasibility of the staining protocol, we encountered several issues that must be addressed. Not the least among these was the incompatibility of the majority of cryptosystems with watermarking methods.

4.1   The Exacting Nature of Cryptograms

Our initial approach was to regard the cryptographic and watermarking stages as separate components. We sought to find cryptographic algorithms that can survive the distortion caused by the watermark, since watermarks are more malleable than cryptosystems. However, it became clear quite rapidly that such a distinction will not be feasible, considering that the two stages are intertwined.

Though watermarking and cryptography share a common history and sometimes a common basis as well [16], they are remarkably different in how each can be manipulated. The difference is primarily in how errors are handled. Watermarks are formed with the understanding that they *will* be altered, by attacks as well as normal image processing operations, and are hence built to withstand errors. Cryptograms are created to be *fragile*, and are hence destroyed on attack.

Another issue is key length. The longer the key length, the more likely the watermark will be destroyed. Further, the likelihood that decryption will be unsuccessful increases with the key length. Compared to RSA [14] and ElGamal [10], elliptic curve cryptosystems use much smaller keys and this was a primary reason for choosing this system.

We are aware of critical practical implementation issues such as the encryption process causing a significant processing bottleneck and we can consider implementation to be a key area of future research.

4.2   Cryptosystem and Watermark Requirements

From our analysis, we note several additional requirements on the choice of cryptosystem. The cryptosystem needs to be asymmetric, to prevent A from easily reversing the encryption from the data given by B. Also, the cryptosystem needs to be non-commutative with the chosen watermarking methods, so the crypto-process will be assured of distorting the watermark.

The method of identifying the stain would depend on the watermark embedding method. The embedding method itself already has several well established requirements [2,8,18] which need to met. These are:

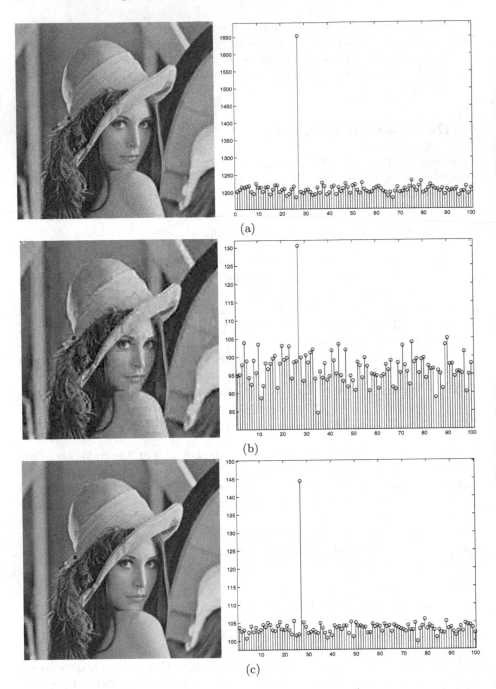

Fig. 4. Decrypted image and similarity measure versus 100 different watermarked images after a) forcing values to 8-bits, b) JPEG conversion to 10% quality, and c) cropping by 50 (out of 256) pixels from the edges, replacing cropped with pixels from unwatermarked image

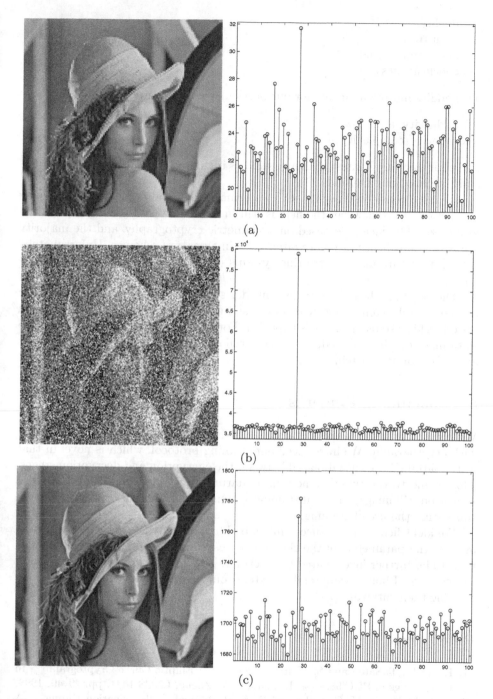

Fig. 5. Decrypted image and similarity measure versus 100 different watermarked images after a) scaling by half, then rescaling back to full size, b) adding Gaussian noise of mean zero and variance 0.01, and c) watermarking twice

- fidelity,
- robustness,
- detectability, and
- conclusiveness.

Two additional requirements for our particular methods are:

- additivity, and
- capacity/complexity.

It is clear that our greatest challenge still lies in finding compatible cryptosystems and watermarking methods.

We have considered asymmetric watermarks as an alternative to public-key encryption [9,11], however the field is still in its infancy and is currently limited in its uses. The ideas are based on asymmetric cryptography, and the majority are fragile and hence are more often used in signature schemes. Unfortunately, though there are many interesting systems [5,12], none currently suit our purposes.

The results, which vary in magnitude, show that the detection method is not completely compatible with our system as we no longer follow the usual watermarking steps as in Cox's paper [6]. For now, it is sufficient to see that the watermark can be detected, but a more reliable method of detection is another area of ongoing research.

5   Concluding Remarks

We have identified a weakness in current methods of combining watermarking with cryptography. We introduced our staining protocol, which is novel in that watermarking is not usual placed between the encryption and decryption stages. This is due to the typically non-linear nature of cryptosystems. We have also shown, on still images, that our staining system can survive basic attacks, thereby supporting the use of staining.

We identified that the successful embedding of the watermark seems dependent on the parameters of the chosen cryptosystem. These parameters will also need to be further investigated to determine how best to achieve the maximum success rate. Finally, we intend to extend our algorithm to video and see how staining then survives.

References

1. K. Araki, T. Satoh and S. Miura, "Overview of Elliptic Curve Cryptography", In Proceedings of PKC'98, eds. H. Imai and Y. Zheng, LNCS 1431, pp. 29–49, 1998.
2. R. J. Anderson, M. G. Kuhn and F. A. P. Petitcolas, "Information Hiding — A Survey", Proceedings of the IEEE, vol. 87, no. 7, pp. 1062–1078, Jul. 1999.
3. R. W. Butler, "Movie industry battles film piracy on many fronts", KansasCity.com: The Kansas City Star, Jun. 2003.

4. S. Byers *et al*, "Analysis of Security Vulnerabilities in the Movie Production and Distribution Process", Proceedings of 2003 ACM Workshop on Digital Rights Management (DRM 2003), Oct. 2003.

5. H. Choi, K. Lee and T. Kim, "Transformed-Key Asymmetric Watermarking System", IEEE Signal Processing Letters, vol. 11, no. 2, pp. 251–254, Feb. 2004.

6. I. J. Cox *et al*, "Secure Spread Spectrum Watermarking for Multimedia", IEEE Transaction on Image Processing, vol. 6, no. 12, pp. 1673-1687, 1997.

7. K. Dean, "Court Hears DVD Copying Dispute", http://www.wired.com/, May 15, 2003.

8. E. J. Delp, and C. I. Podilchuk and R. B. Wolfgang, "Perceptual Watermarks for Digital Images and Video", Proceedings of the IEEE, vol. 87, no. 7, pp. 1108–1126, Jul. 1999.

9. J. J. Eggers, J. K. Su and B. Girod, "Asymmetric Watermarking Schemes", Sicherheit in Netzen und Medienstr omen: Tagungsband des GI Workshops "Sicherheit in Mediendaten", Berlin, Germany, Sep. 2000.

10. T. El Gamal, "A public key cryptosystem and a signature scheme based on discrete logarithms", IEEE Transactions on Information Theory, vol. 31, no. 4, pp. 469–472, Jul. 1985.

11. G. Hachez and J.–J.Quisquater, "Which directions for asymmetric watermarking?", Proceedings of the 11th European Signal Processing Conference (EUSIPCO 2002), vol. 1, pp. 283–286, Sep. 2002.

12. G. Kazakevičiūtė *et al*,"Tamper-Proof Image Watermarking, Based on Existing Public Key Infrastructure", INFORMATICA, vol. 16, no. 1, p.p. 75–92, 2005.

13. A. J. Menezes, P. C. van Oorschot and S. A. Vanstone, "Handbook of Applied Cryptography", CRC Press, Oct. 1996, ISBN 0-8493-8523-7 (online at http://www.cacr.math.uwaterloo.ca/hac/).

14. R. L. Rivest, A. Shamir and L. Adleman, "A method of obtaining digital signatures and public-key cryptosystems", Communications of the ACM, vol. 21, no. 2, pp. 120–126, Feb. 1978.

15. R. Schoof, "Counting points on elliptic curves over finite fields", Journal de Théorie des Nombres de Bourdeaux 7, pp. 219–254, 1995.

16. J. Yang *et al*,"Elliptic curve cryptographic watermark technique", In Proc. of SPIE: MIPPR'03, eds. H. Lu and T. Zhang, vol. 5286, pp. 155–158, Beijing, China, Oct. 2003.

17. P. K. Yu, "How The Motion Picture And Recording Industries Are Losing The Copyright War By Fighting Misdirected Battles", FindLaw's Writ: Legal Commentary, Aug. 2002.

18. Y. Zhou, "Copyright Protection of Compressed Video Using DCT-based Watermarking Technology", Telecommunications Software and Multimedia Laboratory: Seminar on Network Security, 2000.

ViWiD : Visible Watermarking Based Defense Against Phishing

Mercan Topkara, Ashish Kamra, Mikhail J. Atallah, and Cristina Nita-Rotaru

Center for Education and Research in Information Assurance,
Computer Sciences Department, Purdue University,
West Lafayette, Indiana, 47907
{mkarahan, akamra, mja, crisn}@cs.purdue.edu

Abstract. In this paper, we present a watermarking based approach, and its implementation, for mitigating phishing attacks - a form of web based identity theft. ViWiD is an integrity check mechanism based on visible watermarking of logo images. ViWiD performs all of the computation on the company's web server and it does not require installation of any tool or storage of any data, such as keys or history logs, on the user's machine. The watermark message is designed to be unique for every user and carries a shared secret between the company and the user in order to thwart the "one size fits all" attacks. The main challenge in visible watermarking of logo images is to maintain the aesthetics of the watermarked logo to avoid damage to its marketing purpose yet be able to insert a robust and readable watermark into it. Logo images have large uniform areas and very few objects in them, which is a challenge for robust visible watermarking. We tested our scheme with two different visible watermarking techniques on various randomly selected logo images.

1 Introduction

Our society has increasingly become a digital society where many critical applications and services are provided on-line. Examples of such applications are financial services, retail services, on-line news channels and digital libraries. This paradigm shift has had a beneficial effect on business and education by providing faster and easier access to services and information. Unfortunately, it has also exposed these services to malicious attacks that are more difficult to detect and defend against. One of the major security concerns in cyberspace, having impact on individuals as well as businesses and organizations, is identity theft. According to a recent Congressional Statement of the FBI Deputy Assistant Director [1], on-line identity theft represents a significant percentage of the total number of crimes committed in cyberspace.

Phishing is a form of on-line identity theft in which attackers send fraudulent e-mails and use fake Web sites that spoof a legitimate business in order to lure unsuspecting customers into sharing personal and financial data such as social security numbers, bank account numbers, passwords, etc. The incidence

M. Barni et al. (Eds.): IWDW 2005, LNCS 3710, pp. 470–483, 2005.

of phishing attacks has increased significantly over the last couple of years. By the end of December 2004, Symantec Brightmail AntiSpam antifraud filters were blocking an average of 33 million phishing attempts per week, up from an average of 9 million per week in July 2004 [2]. Acknowledging that phishing is a significant threat to e-commerce, over 600 organizations formed the Anti-Phishing Working Group [3] focused on eliminating identity theft due to phishing.

Due to the rapid growth in the impact and number of phishing attacks, there is a considerable research effort going on both in academy and industry for developing robust and easy to use defense systems. Most of the currently available defense systems against phishing either limit the access of the user or display warning messages when they detect suspicious activities. Examples of such systems include e-mail spam filtering or browser plug-ins specially designed for monitoring user's transactions, e.g. SpoofGuard [4], Netcraft [5] or Ebay [6] toolbar. Another approach focuses directly on mitigating man-in-the-middle phishing attacks through a multi-factor authentication scheme [7]. We will briefly review these existing approaches in Section 2.2.

1.1 Our Approach

In this paper, we propose a defense system, ViWiD, that mitigates phishing attacks through an integrity check mechanism built on visible watermarking techniques. This mechanism is based on asking the user to check the validity of the visible watermark message on the logo images of the web pages. We propose two types of watermark messages: The first type is the time only watermark when the company's web site embeds only the current date and time of the user's time zone into the logo image. Recall that IP address can be used to determine the time zone of the user machine. An example of this type of watermarked logo can be seen in Figure 2[1](a). The second type of watermark message includes a secret shared between the user and the company together with the time stamp, as shown in Figure 2(b). The logo images with this shared secret watermark message can be displayed either after the user logs in, or through the usage of cookies. Since this watermarked logo displays a secret shared only between the user and the genuine company, the appearance of such information on the logo is enough for the user to confirm the genuineness of the web site.

The integrity checking system is designed to include a shared secret between the company and the user in order to prevent the phisher from performing the current "one-size-fits-all" attack. This means that even if the phisher is successful in removing the watermark, he can not insert back the expected watermark without knowing the shared secret between the company and the user.

The reasons for following this particular approach are as follows. First, phishing is primarily a social engineering attack which involves the active participation of the users to succeed. Thus, the approach towards mitigating such attacks must also include the co-operation of the users to some extent. Indeed even today, the

---

[1] There is a quality loss in the displayed images through out the paper due to the conversion from Graphics Interchange Format (GIF) to Post Script (PS) format.

company web sites advise the users to follow well-known safety measures such as checking the padlock at the bottom of the screen and the 'https' sign in the URL, both of which signify a SSL connection. But, most of the victims of phishing attacks today are naive users who are not tech savvy enough to check the certificates or security sign. Also, the presence of a SSL connection by itself does not confirm the true identity of the web site. Any site, even a spoofed site, can establish a SSL connection. Communicating to naive users the true identity of the web site is a challenging problem. Hence, we propose the use of a shared secret which the user chooses himself when he registers with the original site. This shared secret can be easily recalled and recognized by the user. Using this secret, the company authenticates itself to the user. In the remaining of this paper, we will refer to this secret as a *mnemonic*.

Second, we chose *the web site logo* as a carrier for the watermark message, since the user always expects to see a logo on a web page. Besides this, the phisher always has to re-use the web site logo when he imitates the pages of the original web site. Since the original logos are always watermarked in our approach, it is not trivial for the phisher to remove them and insert his own watermarks. Even if the phisher is able to remove the watermark, he will not be able to insert the mnemonic for each user. More details about the proposed framework are presented in Section 3.

The rest of the paper is structured as follows. Next section provides a brief introduction to the anatomy of phishing attacks, state-of-the-art defense systems against phishing and summarizes the visible watermarking technique we use. We introduce our experimental set up and results in Section 4 and discuss possible attack models in Section 5. We conclude in Section 6.

2   Background

2.1   Phishing Attack Overview

In a typical phishing attack, a person receives an email apparently sent by an organization that the person interacted with before, and with which he has possibly built a trust relationship (e.g., his bank or a major retail on-line store). The email usually projects a sense of urgency, and asks the client to click on a link that, instead of linking to the real web page of the organization, will link to a fake web page that is subsequently used to collect personal and financial information. There are two victims in phishing attacks: the customer being tricked into giving away personal information and thus allowing the attacker to steal its the identity, and the company that the phisher is posing as, which will suffer both financial loss and reputation damage due to the attack.

Unauthenticated E-mail. The major mechanism to start the attack is using forged e-mails. The phisher can forge e-mails by faking the source information displayed on the e-mail programs. Moreover, phishers can forge the content of the e-mail by getting a template of the style of legitimate e-mails when they subscribe to the company. The attack has a great impact because e-mail is the main communication channel for the online services. The subscribers or customers are expected to follow their transactions and receive confirmations via e-mails.

User Actions. Phishing requires human interaction as like many of other online attacks do. However, unlike other attacks (worms or viruses spreading via e-mail) where one click is enough to trigger the attack, phishing requires active participation of the user at several steps, including providing personal information.

Deceptive View. The core of the phishing attack lies in the ability of the phisher to create a web page looking very similar to a web page of the legitimate organizations by simply copying the logos, and using a style and structure similar to those on the legitimate page. In other words, the information displayed on web pages is not tied to its creator or owner in a way that removing that tie, will deteriorate the data beyond repair. In addition, many browsers are modifiable on the client side, allowing a phisher to remove buttons, not to display certain information, or to mislead the user by playing with the graphics.

A major challenge in addressing phishing attacks lies in designing mechanisms that are able to tie the data displayed on a web page (or related with a web page) to its legitimate owner. This is a difficult task because of the nature of the information displayed, its heterogeneous nature, and the dynamic characteristic of web pages.

2.2   Previous Approaches to Prevent Web-Based Identity Theft

Secure Email. Many forms of phishing attacks can be prevented by the use of secure email tools such as Privacy Enhanced Mail (PEM), Secure Multipurpose Internet Mail Extension (S/MIME) and Pretty Good Privacy (PGP). However, to this date, secure email is not widely used over the Internet, because of scalability, trust, and difficulty to deploy it. A good discussion of certificate based security is provided in [8] by Ellison and Schneier.

Client-Side Defense. One direction in addressing the phishing attack was to provide the client with more accurate information about the web sites that he accesses. Various tools empowering clients with more information have been designed to mitigate phishing attacks. One such tool is SpoofGuard [4] which computes a spoof index and warns the user if the index exceeds a safety level selected by the user. The computation of the index uses domain name, url, link and image checks to evaluate the likelihood that a particular page is a spoof attack. One component of SpoofGuard maintains a database of hash of logo images and corresponding domain names. Later on a web page when the hash of the logo image matches a hash in the database, the current url is compared with the expected domain name, if these do not match the user is warned.

Netcraft, [5] also has released an anti-phishing toolbar that provides information about the web sites that are visited by a client such as the country hosting the sites and enforces the display of browser navigational controls (toolbar and address bar) in all windows.

Herzberg and Gbara [9] proposed establishing, within the browser window, a trusted credentials area (TCA). It is the browser that protects the TCA by preventing its occlusion. The scheme has its costs (it requires logo certification, logo certificate authorities, etc), but tolerates more naive users.

Cryptography-Based Defense. TriCipher, Inc. very recently introduced TriCipher Armored Credential System (TACS) against man-in-the-middle phishing attacks [7]. TACS works when the SSL client authentication is turned on. This means that the SSL protocol will have three steps: authenticate the web server to the client browser, set up encrypted communications and authenticate the end user to the web server. Common usage of SSL consists only of the first two steps. TACS uses two different types of credentials. The first one is called *double armored* credentials, and requires the users to install the TriCipher ID protection tool on their machine. The tool automatically pops up when the user goes to a page that is protected by SSL and encrypts (signs) the password using a key stored in the Trusted Platform Module or Windows® Key Store. Then the TACS appliance at the web server side authenticates the user. The second type of credentials is called *triple armored* credentials which uses, besides the user password and the key stored on the user's machine, a smart card or a USB memory stick to store a key or a biometric. The user's password is signed both with the key on the user's machine and another key stored elsewhere. The *triple armored* credential system raises the bar for the phisher because even if he is able to steal the key on the user's machine, he also has to steal the key stored on an outside system.

Shared Secret Schemes. More recently two new authentication schemes, similar in nature to our system, have been brought to our attention. PassMark Security, Inc.'s [10] *2-Way Authentication Tool* helps the users identify known servers. In this scheme, the user provides the server with a shared secret, an image or a text phrase, in addition to his regular password. The server presents the user with this image, and the user is asked to recognize it before entering his password and authenticating himself to the server. Passmark images are randomly assigned to users from a pool of over 50,000 images and later the users can change their Passmarks, like they change their passwords, by selecting new images from the pool or by uploading an image of their choice.

In a very recent paper, Dhamija and Tygar proposed using Dynamic Security Skins [11] as a defense against phishing. Their system is based on having a *Trusted Window* in the browser and using the Secure Remote Password Protocol (SRP) [12] for authentication. Spoofing of trusted window is prevented by providing an image which is a shared-secret between the user and his browser. This window is dedicated to username and password entry. SRP is a *verifier-based protocol*. SRP provides the functionality for the server and user to authenticate each other over an un-trusted network by independently generating a session key based on a verifier. User sends the verifier to the server only once when he is registering. In Dynamic Security Skins, this verifier is used by the browser and the server to generate *a visual hash* that is displayed in the background of the trusted window and in the server's web site. To authenticate the server, the user needs to visually compare the two images to check if they match.

2.3   Limitations of Previous Approaches

Even though the client-side defense tools raise the bar for the attackers, they do not provide a complete solution. Many checks and enforcements used by the client-based defense tools can be fooled by attackers having a reasonable understanding of web site construction [4]. For example, the image check system of SpoofGuard can be fooled by a mosaic attack where the attacker partitions the logo image into pieces, but displays them in appropriate order so that the user thinks that he is looking at a legitimate logo.

Moreover, any "client side only" defense mechanism will suffer from false positives. Too many warnings will interfere with the user's browsing experience and the user will simply turn off the protection mechanism in such cases.

In addition to the above limitations, the "client side only" schemes leave all of the defensive actions and computational costs up to the user's machine, even though the companies have larger computing power at their disposal and can do more to mitigate the risks. Moreover it is the companies who create the content (logo, style etc) that the attackers seek to imitate and/or misuse. Therefore, we believe that companies can play a larger role in the overall defense strategy to mitigate phishing attacks.

On the other hand, cryptography based tools require the user to download a tool on every machine he uses to access his online accounts, and/or the user is required to carry another medium e.g. a smart card or USB memory stick with him when he wishes to access his accounts. One other limitation for TACS [7] is that it is designed to work only for man-in-the-middle phishing attacks. When the phisher directs the users to his web page which might have a SSL connection but without the client authentication module turned on, the TriCipher ID protection tool will not pop up and sign the password.

The shared secret schemes introduced in Section 2.2 are similar to our approach in the sense that they focus on how a legitimate server can authenticate itself to the user. However, our approach and these two approaches diverge on the generation and presentation of the shared-secret. The main drawback of Pass-Mark approach is that the shared secret is not bound to a particular location on the original web page. This makes the scheme less user-friendly as across different service providers, the users will have to look at different places to find their shared secret on the web page. On the other side, Dynamic Security Skins [11] scheme suffers from asking the users to dedicate part of their browser window to the Trusted Window. Besides, this scheme trusts the client's browser on vital security processes such as storing the verifier and generating the visual hash.

Overall, a complete solution for defense against phishing, must address all three causes that allow a phishing attack to be possible: unauthenticated e-mail, user actions and deceptive view. Thus, a complete solution should include mechanisms that can analyze what the user sees, analyze the e-mail and web page content, and provide integrity checks for these components. In addition, such a system should be easy to use and deploy.

2.4   Visible Watermarking Overview

Visible watermarking is the insertion of a visible pattern or image into a cover image [13]. A useful visible watermarking technique should meet the following requirements: preserving the perceptibility of the cover image, providing reasonable visibility of the watermark pattern and robustness [14]. Huang and Wu summarize the insertion of a visible pattern into the cover image as:

$$I' = K_1 \cdot I + K_2 \cdot W \tag{1}$$

$$D(E_I(I'), E_I(I)) < Threshold_I \tag{2}$$

$$D(E_W(I'), E_W(I)) < Threshold_W \tag{3}$$

In Equation 1, I represents the cover image, W represents the watermark image and I' represents the watermarked image. Equation 2 represents the boundary on the distortion of the perceptibility of the cover image, while Equation 3 represents the boundary on the distortion of the visibility of the watermark patterns. D is a distance function measuring the perceptible difference of its two entries. E_I is a image feature extraction function for the cover and watermarked images. E_W is a separate image feature extraction function for the watermark pattern. $Threshold_I$ and $Threshold_W$ represent the largest allowable distortion on perceptibility of the cover image and on the visibility of the watermark pattern respectively.

In ViWiD, we use visible watermarking in order to provide the users with visibly watermarked logo images and the visible watermark pattern is generated dynamically depending on a shared secret between the user and the company.

3   Proposed Approach

The content of the e-mail and the spoofed page are the means through which the "social engineering" aspect of phishing is carried out. The phisher tricks the user into submitting sensitive information by using the content and the style stolen from the legitimate company. A good defense mechanism must require an integrity check method that "travels with the content" when it is used or misused. One way to achieve this is digital watermarking. Our approach watermarks the content on the legitimate web page in a way that provides an integrity check. We use the logo images as the watermark carriers, based on the observed fact that nearly all phishing attacks re-use the logo images.

3.1   Design Goals and Motivation

The user can be tricked into a phishing attack, only if the phishing e-mail is imitating a company with which the user has previously established a trust relation. All companies, targeted by phishing attacks, have large numbers of users

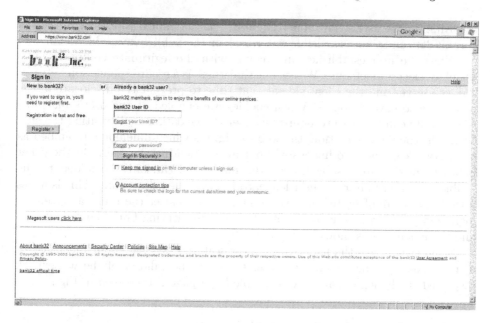

Fig. 1. A generic login page with a watermarked logo image, scaled to half of its original size for space requirements

using their online services. Many of the users use several varieties of browsers and more than one computer to access their account online. A key-based watermark detection system requires the keys for detection and extraction to be distributed to all the users. We avoid the key distribution problem by using a visible watermark, with a human involved in the detection process. This way we also give the user an active role in the defense against a social engineering attack.

We seek to thwart the "one size fits all" attacks by designing the visible watermark message such that it is unique and varies with time. ViWiD embeds a local time stamp which is updated periodically and a mnemonic selected by the user while the online account established. The rationale for using the time stamps is that phishing sites are usually up for 6 to 7 days [3], and unless the phishers are able to remove the watermark, their stolen logo cannot display a fresh time to all the intended victims. Also, this system should never ask for the user's mnemonic after the online account is established in order to avoid the possibility of revealing the mnemonic even if the user mistakenly enters his login and password to a spoofed site.

3.2 Framework Description

On the publicly available web pages, the logo images display the date and time of the day as a visible watermark. An example is shown in Figure 2 (a). In these logo images, date and time are periodically updated to show the current time according to the user's time zone. The user will be trained to expect to see the current date and time as a visible watermark on the publicly available web pages.

When the user establishes an account with the legitimate company, he is asked to select a mnemonic. We assume that there is a secure connection between the web server and the client side at that time to prevent the disclosure of the mnemonic to eavesdroppers. When cookies are enabled at the user's machine, the web site can use it to recognize the user the next time he is visiting the site. Using the cookie information, the web site knows which mnemonic to embed as a watermark in the logo images without authenticating the user. On the other hand, if cookies are disabled, then the mnemonic can only be added to the visible watermark after the user logs into the established account. This is a less satisfactory form of protection, as the alarm comes after the user has given his login and password. An example of a logo image carrying both the time stamp and the mnemonic is shown in Figure 2 (b).

In order to make the user expect these watermarks, the companies need to display messages that remind the user to verify the validity of the watermark displayed on the logo images. An example login page can be seen in Figure 1.

4   Experimental Set Up and Results

We collected logo images from randomly selected web pages of 60 Fortune 500 companies and the Center for Education and Research in Information Assurance and Security (CERIAS). All of these logo images were colored Graphics Interchange Format (GIF) images. GIF is the preferred format for displaying logos on web pages because GIF images are 8-bit palette based images, hence their sizes are small. In our experiments, we tested the effectiveness of several visible watermarking algorithms on 61 logo images. The size of these logo images ranges from (18x18) to (760x50).

Even though there is a vast amount of literature on invisible image watermarking techniques, there have been relatively fewer visible image watermarking schemes developed to date [14]. We tested several different visible watermarking techniques on our logo images database. Visibly watermarking color logo images brings many challenges compared to watermarking gray scale images or JPEG images. The main challenge is to maintain the aesthetics of the watermarked logo so as to not to damage its marketing purpose yet be able to insert a robust and readable watermark into it. Moreover, visible watermarking on the logo images is rather less robust because these logo images have large uniform areas and very few objects in them. Besides these the time and memory requirements of the watermarking operation should be very low in order for the web server to be able to dynamically update the time stamp on the logo images frequently. We used the following two techniques in order to verify the applicability. In all these tests, we used a watermark image that is the same size as the cover image.

- $ImageMagick^{TM}$'s embedded watermarking module [15].
  $ImageMagick^{TM}$ is a free software suite for the creation, modification and

(a)   (b)

Fig. 2. Logo images watermarked with $ImageMagick^{TM}$: (a) time only watermark (b) watermark with both time and mnemonic, in this image the mnemonic is *Kakkajee*

display of bitmap images. $ImageMagick^{TM}$ version 6.2.0 watermarking scheme updates brightness component of HSB color space of every pixel in the cover image using the following equations to embed the watermark:

$$B'_{i,j} = B_{i,j} + \frac{(p \cdot offset^w_{i,j})}{midpoint} \qquad (4)$$

where $B'_{i,j}$ is the brightness of the watermarked image pixels, and $B_{i,j}$ is the brightness of the cover image pixels.

$$offset^w_{i,j} = I^w_{i,j} - midpoint \qquad (5)$$

where $I^w_{i,j}$ is the intensity of the watermark image pixels.

$$midpoint = \frac{maxRGB}{2} \qquad (6)$$

$maxRGB$ is the maximum value of a quantum, where a quantum is one of the red, green, or blue elements of a pixel in the RGB color space. In our experiments, $ImageMagick^{TM}$ was compiled with 16 bits in a quantum, thus giving $maxRGB$ equal to 65x535.

p is a user selected parameter for the percentage brightness of the watermark pixel. An example of this embedding with $p = 0.3$ can be seen in Figure 2.

Hue and saturation of the cover image are not affected in the watermark embedding process. The value of the p parameter controls the visibility of the watermark. Figure 3 shows and example of the watermark embedding where the same watermark is embedded with varying p.

In order to preserve the aesthetics of the cover logo image, we used RGB (midpoint, midpoint, midpoint) as the background color in our watermark images. This is because, with these RGB values, the corresponding $offset^w$ values, in Equation 5, become 0.

We have observed that the background color, the text geometry on the watermark image and parameter p have to be adjusted according to the cover image properties in order to reach an acceptable level of watermarked image quality. Figure 4 shows examples of (a) a light and (b) a dark background logo images watermarked. In both Figure 4 (a) and (b) background of watermark

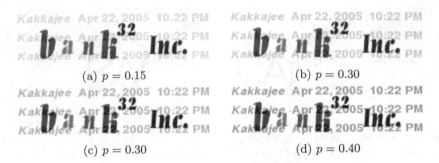

(a) $p = 0.15$ (b) $p = 0.30$

(c) $p = 0.30$ (d) $p = 0.40$

Fig. 3. Logo images watermarked with $ImageMagick^{TM}$ using various p values

(a)   (b)

Fig. 4. Logo images watermarked with $ImageMagick^{TM}$ parameter $p = 0.40$ (a) a white background and (b) a dark background

image is RGB (midpoint, midpoint, midpoint) and $p = 0.40$. The color of the text of watermark image is black in Figure 4 (a), and white in Figure 4 (b).

- **Mohanty et al.'s approach [16]** In their visible watermarking scheme, the modification of the gray values of the host image is based on its local as well as global statistics.

$$I'_n = \alpha_n \cdot I_n + \beta_n \cdot I_n^w \tag{7}$$

where I'_n is the intensity of the n_{th} block of the watermarked image. I_n and I_n^w are the corresponding intensity values of the cover and watermark images respectively. α_n and β_n are the scaling and embedding factors depending on the mean and the variance of each block, and the image mean gray value. In [16], it is stated that for color images the watermark should be put in the Y component (luminance). However, when this approach is applied on logo images with white background, even a small change in the luminosity of the background will disturb the aesthetics of the logo image. An example of this phenomenon can be seen in Figure 5 (a). On the other hand, logo images with dark background gave better results, see Figure 5 (b) for an example. However, we observed that the K component of the $CMYK$ colormap can also be used to insert the watermark into logo images. This modified approach gave us better results on logo images with white background, see Figure 6.

We are not able to provide samples from the watermarked version of the logo images we collected from Fortune 500 companies' web pages due to copyright

Fig. 5. Logo images watermarked with Mohanty et al.'s watermarking algorithm (a) a white background and (b) a dark background

$$\mathbf{bank}^{32}\ \mathbf{Inc.} \qquad \mathbf{bank}^{32}\ \mathbf{Inc.}$$

(a)   (b)

Fig. 6. Logo images watermarked with modified version of Mohanty et al.'s watermarking algorithm (a) Time only watermarked logo image (b) Watermarked logo image with Time and Mnemonic

issues. In addition, there is a quality loss in the displayed images through out the paper due to the conversion from GIF to Post Script (PS) format. In order to provide GIF versions of the watermarked logo images and a controlled access to these logo images, we have created a demo page which can be reached at http://projects.cerias.purdue.edu/viwid/.

5   Security Analysis and Discussion

A phisher can try to break the above system through the following three attacks. First attack is to insert a valid watermark message after removing the existing watermark from the logo image. The second attack is to recreate the logo image from scratch and later insert a valid watermark message. The third attack is to perform a man-in-the-middle attack. We explain below why these attacks are not easy for an attacker to carry out.

Success of the first attack depends on the robustness of the underlying visible watermarking algorithm and on the success of the phisher at generating the valid watermark messages for the targeted users.

Huang and Wu , in [14], show successful attacks on well known visible watermarking systems [16,17] with the help of human intervention. Huang and Wu's system requires the shapes of the watermark patterns to be marked manually. Results in [14] show that the image inpainting techniques are very effective in removing simple watermark patterns composed of thin lines or symbols. For more sophisticated watermark patterns such as thick lines or bold faced and multi-textured text, Huang and Wu propose an improved scheme where thick watermarked areas are classified into edges and flat areas. Later flat watermarked areas are recovered by refilling them with unaltered flat neighbours. Edged watermarked areas are recovered by approximated prediction based on adaptation information of nearby pixels.

However, in ViWiD, even if the attacker is able to remove the watermark successfully from the watermarked image, he can not insert a completely valid watermark message. The valid watermark message consists of the date and local time of the day for the user's time zone, and the user's mnemonic. The mnemonic is unique for every user and the attacker does not have access to any user's mnemonic. If he can have such access, his attack ceases to be a "one-size-fits-all", and thus we have succeeded in increasing the attacker's cost.

The second attack, which requires recreating the logo image from scratch, can also be thwarted by the fact that the attacker is unable to generate the valid watermark message for every user.

The man-in-the-middle attack is one of the most successful ways of gaining control of customer information [18]. However, besides directing the user to his machine through social engineering, it is difficult for the phisher to be successful in this attack. He has to either manipulate the DNS or proxy data on the user's machine, or locate the attacking machine on the real company's web server's network segment or on the route to the real company's web server. Even if the phisher performs a man-in-the-middle attack in order to bring a fresh logo every time a user requests the phisher's web page, the web site would only provide the logo specifically watermarked for the time zone that is assigned to the attacker's IP address. In such a case the attacker would need to have available as many man-in-the-middle's as the number of time zones he wants to attack.

6   Concluding Remarks

We have presented a defense system, ViWiD, that mitigates phishing attacks through integrity checking of web site logos using visible watermarking techniques. The valid watermark message consists of the date and local time of the day for the user's time zone, and the user's mnemonic. The watermark message is designed to be unique for every user and carries a shared secret between the company and the user in order to thwart the "one size fits all" attacks.

Unlike the other systems proposed for preventing phishing attacks, ViWiD performs all of the computation on the company's web server and does not require installation of any tool or storage of any data, such as keys or history logs, on the user's machine. ViWiD also involves the user in the integrity checking process, which makes it harder for the phisher to engineer an attack, since the integrity checking mechanism is not fully automated.

One of the pre-requisites of the proposed scheme is that it requires the users to be trained to expect a valid message to be displayed on the logo images when they perform sensitive transactions. Users are also provided the opportunity to adjust the parameters of the watermark and logo image according to their reading needs and appeal. For example, a user might select a larger font size for the embedded watermark message, or he can as well select a larger logo image.

As part of future work, we plan to perform a large scale user study for validating the effectiveness of our approach. In addition to that, the robustness of the watermarking techniques can be improved by using high quality logo images in JPEG format or by spreading the message over all images in a web page.

Acknowledgments

The authors would like to thank Chris Baker, Umut Topkara, Eugene Lin, Prathima Rao, Ardalan Kangarlou-Haghigh and Saraju Mohanty for their helpful comments.

References

1. S. M. Martinez, "Identity theft and cyber crime," September 2004. Federal Bureau of Investigation, http://www.fbi.gov/congress/congress.htm.
2. "Symantec internet security threat report highlights rise in threats to confidential information," http://www.symantec.com/press/2005/n050321.html.
3. "The Anti-Phishing working group," http://www.antiphishing.org.
4. N. Chou, R. Ledesma, Y. Teraguchi, and J. C. Mitchell, "Client-side defense against web-based identity theft," Proceedings of the Network and Distributed System Security Symposium, 2004.
5. "Netcraft," http://www.netcraft.com.
6. "ebay: buyer tools: toolbar," http://pages.ebay.com/ebay_toolbar/.
7. "Preventing man in the middle phishing attacks with multi-factor authentication," http://www.tricipher.com/solutions/phishing.html.
8. C. Ellison and B. Schneier, "Inside risks: Risks of PKI: secure email," Communications of the ACM, vol. 43, no. 1, p. 160, 2000.
9. A. Herzberg and A. Gbara, "Trustbar: Protecting (even nave) web users from spoofing and phishing attacks," Cryptology ePrint Archive, Report 2004/155, 2004.
10. P. Security, "Protecting your customers from phishing attacks - an introduction to passmarks," http://www.passmarksecurity.com/.
11. R. Dhamija and J. Tygar, "The battle against phishing: Dynamic security skins," Symposium on Usable Provacy and Security (SOUPS), July, 2005.
12. T. Wu., "The secure remote password protocol," In Internet Society Network and Distributed Systems Security Symposium (NDSS), Mar 1998, pp. 97–111.
13. N. Memon and P. W. Wong, "Protecting digital media content," Commun. ACM, vol. 41, no. 7, pp. 35–43, 1998.
14. C.-H. Huang and J.-L. Wu, "Attacking visible watermarking schemes," IEEE Transactions on Multimedia, vol. 6, no. 1, February, 2004.
15. "Imagemagick studio llc," http://www.imagemagick.org.
16. S. P. Mohanty, K. R. Ramakrishnan, and M. Kankanhalli, "A dual watermarking technique for images," MULTIMEDIA '99: Proceedings of the seventh ACM international conference on Multimedia (Part 2), 1999, ACM Press, pp. 49–51.
17. G. W. Braudaway, K. A. Magerlein, and F. C. Mintzer, "Protecting Publicly Available Images with a Visible Image Watermark," Proceedings of the SPIE International Conference on Electronic Imaging, vol. 2659, February 1-2, 1996, San Jose, CA.
18. G. Ollman, "The phishing guide," http://www.ngssoftware.com/papers/NISR-WP-Phishing.pdf.

Author Index

Lecture Notes in Computer Science

For information about Vols. 1–3577

please contact your bookseller or Springer

Vol. 3629: J.L. Fiadeiro, N. Harman, M. Roggenbach, J. Rutten (Eds.), Algebra and Coalgebra in Computer Science. XI, 457 pages. 2005.

Vol. 3628: T. Gschwind, U. Aßmann, O. Nierstrasz (Eds.), Software Composition. X, 199 pages. 2005.

Vol. 3627: C. Jacob, M.L. Pilat, P.J. Bentley, J. Timmis (Eds.), Artificial Immune Systems. XII, 500 pages. 2005.

Vol. 3626: B. Ganter, G. Stumme, R. Wille (Eds.), Formal Concept Analysis. X, 349 pages. 2005. (Subseries LNAI).

Vol. 3625: S. Kramer, B. Pfahringer (Eds.), Inductive Logic Programming. XIII, 427 pages. 2005. (Subseries LNAI).

Vol. 3624: C. Chekuri, K. Jansen, J.D.P. Rolim, L. Trevisan (Eds.), Approximation, Randomization and Combinatorial Optimization. XI, 495 pages. 2005.

Vol. 3623: M. Liśkiewicz, R. Reischuk (Eds.), Fundamentals of Computation Theory. XV, 576 pages. 2005.

Vol. 3621: V. Shoup (Ed.), Advances in Cryptology – CRYPTO 2005. XI, 568 pages. 2005.

Vol. 3620: H. Muñoz-Avila, F. Ricci (Eds.), Case-Based Reasoning Research and Development. XV, 654 pages. 2005. (Subseries LNAI).

Vol. 3619: X. Lu, W. Zhao (Eds.), Networking and Mobile Computing. XXIV, 1299 pages. 2005.

Vol. 3618: J. Jedrzejowicz, A. Szepietowski (Eds.), Mathematical Foundations of Computer Science 2005. XVI, 814 pages. 2005.

Vol. 3617: F. Roli, S. Vitulano (Eds.), Image Analysis and Processing – ICIAP 2005. XXIV, 1219 pages. 2005.

Vol. 3615: B. Ludäscher, L. Raschid (Eds.), Data Integration in the Life Sciences. XII, 344 pages. 2005. (Subseries LNBI).

Vol. 3614: L. Wang, Y. Jin (Eds.), Fuzzy Systems and Knowledge Discovery, Part II. XLI, 1314 pages. 2005. (Subseries LNAI).

Vol. 3613: L. Wang, Y. Jin (Eds.), Fuzzy Systems and Knowledge Discovery, Part I. XLI, 1334 pages. 2005. (Subseries LNAI).

Vol. 3612: L. Wang, K. Chen, Y. S. Ong (Eds.), Advances in Natural Computation, Part III. LXI, 1326 pages. 2005.

Vol. 3611: L. Wang, K. Chen, Y. S. Ong (Eds.), Advances in Natural Computation, Part II. LXI, 1292 pages. 2005.

Vol. 3610: L. Wang, K. Chen, Y. S. Ong (Eds.), Advances in Natural Computation, Part I. LXI, 1302 pages. 2005.

Vol. 3608: F. Dehne, A. López-Ortiz, J.-R. Sack (Eds.), Algorithms and Data Structures. XIV, 446 pages. 2005.

Vol. 3607: J.-D. Zucker, L. Saitta (Eds.), Abstraction, Reformulation and Approximation. XII, 376 pages. 2005. (Subseries LNAI).

Vol. 3606: V. Malyshkin (Ed.), Parallel Computing Technologies. XII, 470 pages. 2005.

Vol. 3604: R. Martin, H. Bez, M. Sabin (Eds.), Mathematics of Surfaces XI. IX, 473 pages. 2005.

Vol. 3603: J. Hurd, T. Melham (Eds.), Theorem Proving in Higher Order Logics. IX, 409 pages. 2005.

Vol. 3602: R. Eigenmann, Z. Li, S.P. Midkiff (Eds.), Languages and Compilers for High Performance Computing. IX, 486 pages. 2005.

Vol. 3599: U. Aßmann, M. Aksit, A. Rensink (Eds.), Model Driven Architecture. X, 235 pages. 2005.

Vol. 3598: H. Murakami, H. Nakashima, H. Tokuda, M. Yasumura, Ubiquitous Computing Systems. XIII, 275 pages. 2005.

Vol. 3597: S. Shimojo, S. Ichii, T.W. Ling, K.-H. Song (Eds.), Web and Communication Technologies and Internet-Related Social Issues - HSI 2005. XIX, 368 pages. 2005.

Vol. 3596: F. Dau, M.-L. Mugnier, G. Stumme (Eds.), Conceptual Structures: Common Semantics for Sharing Knowledge. XI, 467 pages. 2005. (Subseries LNAI).

Vol. 3595: L. Wang (Ed.), Computing and Combinatorics. XVI, 995 pages. 2005.

Vol. 3594: J.C. Setubal, S. Verjovski-Almeida (Eds.), Advances in Bioinformatics and Computational Biology. XIV, 258 pages. 2005. (Subseries LNBI).

Vol. 3593: V. Mařík, R. W. Brennan, M. Pěchouček (Eds.), Holonic and Multi-Agent Systems for Manufacturing. XI, 269 pages. 2005. (Subseries LNAI).

Vol. 3592: S. Katsikas, J. Lopez, G. Pernul (Eds.), Trust, Privacy and Security in Digital Business. XII, 332 pages. 2005.

Vol. 3591: M.A. Wimmer, R. Traunmüller, Å. Grönlund, K.V. Andersen (Eds.), Electronic Government. XIII, 317 pages. 2005.

Vol. 3590: K. Bauknecht, B. Pröll, H. Werthner (Eds.), E-Commerce and Web Technologies. XIV, 380 pages. 2005.

Vol. 3589: A M. Tjoa, J. Trujillo (Eds.), Data Warehousing and Knowledge Discovery. XVI, 538 pages. 2005.

Vol. 3588: K.V. Andersen, J. Debenham, R. Wagner (Eds.), Database and Expert Systems Applications. XX, 955 pages. 2005.

Vol. 3587: P. Perner, A. Imiya (Eds.), Machine Learning and Data Mining in Pattern Recognition. XVII, 695 pages. 2005. (Subseries LNAI).

Vol. 3586: A.P. Black (Ed.), ECOOP 2005 - Object-Oriented Programming. XVII, 631 pages. 2005.

Vol. 3584: X. Li, S. Wang, Z.Y. Dong (Eds.), Advanced Data Mining and Applications. XIX, 835 pages. 2005. (Subseries LNAI).

Vol. 3583: R.W. H. Lau, Q. Li, R. Cheung, W. Liu (Eds.), Advances in Web-Based Learning – ICWL 2005. XIV, 420 pages. 2005.

Vol. 3582: J. Fitzgerald, I.J. Hayes, A. Tarlecki (Eds.), FM 2005: Formal Methods. XIV, 558 pages. 2005.

Vol. 3581: S. Miksch, J. Hunter, E. Keravnou (Eds.), Artificial Intelligence in Medicine. XVII, 547 pages. 2005. (Subseries LNAI).

Vol. 3580: L. Caires, G.F. Italiano, L. Monteiro, C. Palamidessi, M. Yung (Eds.), Automata, Languages and Programming. XXV, 1477 pages. 2005.

Vol. 3579: D. Lowe, M. Gaedke (Eds.), Web Engineering. XXII, 633 pages. 2005.

Vol. 3578: M. Gallagher, J. Hogan, F. Maire (Eds.), Intelligent Data Engineering and Automated Learning - IDEAL 2005. XVI, 599 pages. 2005.